Following Jesus

Following Jesus

Discipleship in the Gospel of Luke and Beyond

PHILLIP C. THRAILKILL

RESOURCE *Publications* · Eugene, Oregon

FOLLOWING JESUS
Discipleship in the Gospel of Luke and Beyond

Resource Publications
An Imprint of Wipf and Stock Publishers
199 W. 8th Ave., Suite 3
Eugene, OR 97401

www.wipfandstock.com

PAPERBACK ISBN: 978-1-6667-4346-3
HARDCOVER ISBN: 978-1-6667-4347-0
EBOOK ISBN: 978-1-6667-4348-7

10/12/22

Dedicated to of some of the faithful disciples
I found in each place I served.

Wake Forest University: Jim Morgan, Jan Fogleman,
Rich Montgomery, Jimmy Myers, Dr. Charles H. Talbert
Candler School of Theology: Dr. George Morris
The Fairfield Circuit: Huley and Sherrill Perry
Northeast UMC: Bill and Lois Ball
St. Mark UMC: Lora James, Susan Caulder
Duncan UMC: Jack and Janet Rockey, Dot Porter
St. Luke UMC: Leroy McCoy, Gerry Caffee
Main Street UMC: Glenn Williams, Kit Atkins, Kathy Kelly,
Howard Thomes, Michael Fisher
Cheraw First UMC: Pam Baker, Jimmy Duffy, Sammy Quick
Lee Road UMC: Gene Turner, Laurie Fite, Jimmy Gaddy
The Mission Society: Dick McClain, Frank Decker, Jim Ramsay, Al Vom Steeg
The Confessing Movement: Dr. Billy Abraham, Senator Pat Miller,
Dr. Thomas Oden, Dr. Maxie Dunnam,
At Home: Lori Thrailkill

"Follow me." These two simple words of invitation and command stand at the head of every relationship with Jesus, the Son of God, whether spoke on a Galilean lake shore, on the streets of Lusaka, or in a hospital in Chicago.

Like every child responding to the outstretched hand of a parent, Simon and Andrew, Mary and Salome, and millions of Christians through two millennia have accepted that simple invitation in faith and often with minimal understanding of the life-transforming decision they have taken.

To follow Jesus of Nazareth into his cosmic reign is simply the most challenging, the most beautiful, the most costly, the most rewarding journey we could ever choose to begin.[1]
—Bishop Ng Moon Hing

In the same way the Church exists for nothing else but to draw men into Christ, to make them little Christs. If they are not doing that, all the cathedrals, clergy, missions, sermons, even the Bible itself, are simply a waste of time. God became Man for no other purpose.[2]
—C.S. Lewis

Most books have their origin in some kind of enduring mental distraction that has grown so large and ungainly in the author's mind that only hammering it out at book length will fully exorcize the thing.[3]
—Mary Eberstadt

1. The Most Reverend Ng Moon Hing, Bishop of the Diocese of West Malaysia and Primate of the Church of South East Asia, "Forward," *Intentional Discipleship and Disciple-Making: An Anglican Guide for Christian Life and Formation*. vii.

2. C.S. Lewis, *Mere Christianity*, 199.

3. Mary Eberstadt, *How the West Really Lost God*, 3.

Contents

Introduction

THIS BOOK IS AN outgrowth of a larger project begun in September 2017. Since then I've been putting my work on the Gospel of Luke in a teachable order. The core research now stretches to 3000 pages with each of the ninety-four thought units[1] in Luke having been identified and analyzed for genre, structure, flow of thought, possible sources, and implications for his two most important questions: 1) Christology (Who is Jesus?) and 2) Discipleship (Who are his followers?), and each with a sermon appended as an example of biblical exposition. Three manuals for teaching at seminaries in Africa have resulted from a condensation of the research: Volume I: Introduction and Essays (181 pages), Volume II: Luke 1:1–12:12 (342 pages), Volume III: Luke 12:13–24:53 (in production)

As part of the first volume I decided to add several essays to supplement the other introductory materials. The first essay, *Mapping the Shape of the Text* was begin in June 2020 and finished in September the same year. It is Chapter 4 of this book and serves to orient the readers to the way texts were shaped in the ancient world for an audience used to hearing texts performed in oral discourse. My thesis is that units of text are first to be mapped according to the conventions of ancient literature, then read for content and all that follows from it: history, theology, ethics, proclamation, exhortation, Christian praxis, prayer. A second essay was titled, *Discipleship in Luke*, and I expected it to be about the same length as the first. But when I reviewed all ninety-four units of Luke and found that fully fifty-one touch directly on what it is to be a follower of Jesus, I knew it demanded more than a cursory treatment, thus this volume. I began writing in September of 2020 and finished the first draft in June 2021.

The core of the book is an analysis of Luke's fifty-one discipleship units using an eight part sequence (Chapter 5). Before this are four chapters in the form of two cautions (Chapters 1, 2), a summary of our inheritance (Chapter 3), and the material on literary method (Chapter 4). It is followed by a catalog of the fifty-one summary statements on discipleship, one from each unit (Chapter 6). This is followed by six chapters on what the biblical scholars say about discipleship in Luke (Chapter 7), what

---

1.. See Appendix 1, "Identifying Luke's Thought Units" and Appendix 2, "Synoptic Comparisons: The 51 Key Lukan Discipleship Units."

modern researchers are discovering about discipleship in our day (Chapter 8), a short chapter on the pragmatics of discipleship (Chapter 9), a re-reading of Matthew's Great Commission (Chapter 10), a case study on doctrine and discipleship using the United Methodist Doctrinal Standards as a source (Chapter 11), an evaluation of discipleship assessments (Chapter 12), a brief Afterward, and concluding appendices and bibliographies.

May this book increase your desire to follow Jesus in the midst of his peoples![2]

2.. While I draw on Wesley and the Methodists throughout, this volume is intended for a broader audience who may apply to my research their own denominational challenges.

1

A First Caution

Why Pragmatism is Always Premature

THE MOST BASIC PHILOSOPHY of the American people—and so also of Christians in America—is *pragmatism*. Pragmatism is a pop theory of knowledge that says, "If it works, it must be true," and, "If it works, it will help me succeed, achieve my potential, and fulfill my dreams." Its adoption is found in viral form among some of our more ambitious clergy who quickly adopt every new marketing ploy and leadership fad in a breathless effort to stay relevant and trendy. It's what happens when church is just another platform and when the ways and means of Jesus are no longer primary.

Pragmatism is not something we have to learn because it's the air we breathe, our default approach to life, more caught than taught, more absorbed than consciously learned. It has a place in decisions, but it cannot be first because it simply runs over and ignores every other factor but the bottom line, and the name for that is *reductionism*. It's ruthlessly efficient, but intellectually and morally sloppy, not to speak of spiritually ignorant. And, in its more extreme individual form, the only concern is, "What's in it for me?" But even in more benign forms, it stifles serious thought and spiritual discernment. The practical and the pressing and the possible is not always the true or the good or the wise.

Pragmatism—the desire for a method that produces results—is the reason so many self-help books, including the supposedly Christian ones, have some form of sequential steps in the titles: "Five Spiritual Steps to Health, Wealth, and Six-pack Abs," or "Nine Keys to Success for your Local Church." They cater to the mind that thinks, "Skip all the theory. Just give me the bottom line. We want results and want them now!" But the easy path and the quick fix are the very opposite of a slow, deep formation as an ever-fallible follower of Jesus. Are you starting to see how incompatible the two approaches are? Jesus, our risen and lively Lord, dare I say it, is not a modern American pragmatist. He offers a better way: slow, deep, sustainable, relational, dependent, and substantial.

But there is, I readily admit, a measure of truth in the pragmatic way, because in the end, life comes down to a test, and the standard is: What did you do with what you knew? Did you exercise trust in Jesus, put it to the test, and find it reliable? Jesus applied this measure as a sober warning to his followers in the story of the two houses, one built on bedrock and the other on sand, the difference being that acting on what Jesus teaches links us to him so strongly that we become solid and reliable enough to endure the trials that come in a world like ours (Luke 6:46–49).

So let's give pragmatism the nod it deserves, but it cannot be first in our consideration of anything. It is, in my view, a lesser, moderate consideration. Jesus is our focus and following him is our path, so to turn his wisdom into a technique for our benefit apart from his ongoing friendship is to seek what he did not come to offer—a life of independence from God, the very thing he came to heal.

Having a proven method to achieve results is the goal of the pragmatic way, and if it works in manufacturing or sales, why not the church as well? A flow chart of Inputs, Through-puts, and Outputs? It's all the same, isn't it? Well . . . Rather than learning the pastoral trade itself with all its complexities and nuances, we want *the tricks of the trade*, or *the hacks* as they are now called.[1]

But people are not things to be run through processes, and the church is not our little self-enhancement project. It belongs to another, One who lived and died and rose and reigns to create for himself a people, a new tribe: the people who love and follow Jesus as their doorway into the life of the Triune God. And of his life, his traveling academy, his message, and his method, we have four complementary treatments to explore, a little library of Jesus' comings and goings as vindicated in a singular resurrection.

We agree that Jesus was supremely effective at doing his Father's will with the Spirit's enablement in a tough neighborhood. The early church read the life of Jesus through a tri-personal lens and later a fully articulated Trinitarian prism. Beginning with the annunciation to Mary (1:26–38) and Jesus' baptism (3:21–22), Luke makes clusters of references to God/Father, Jesus/Son, and the Holy Spirit in deep cooperation.[2]

My read is that Jesus, the incarnate Son, obeyed the Father's will and was illumined and empowered by the immediacy of the Holy Spirit in moment by moment divine revelation. In other words, he was a dependent disciple, an exemplar and model

1. A treatment of ministry I often return to is Oden, *Pastoral Theology: Essentials of Ministry*. He sits me down for a seminar with the church fathers/mothers and the best pastors across the ages. It sobers me up!

2. See Appendix 3: "The Raw Materials of the Holy Trinity: Tri-Personal References in Luke's Gospel."

for those who followed. Jesus had integrity as one whole person in what he offered. He did not speak or act independently, as he happily affirmed in John 5:19:

> "Jesus said to them, 'Truly, truly, I say to you, the Son can do nothing of his own accord, but only what he sees the Father doing; for whatever he does, that the Son does likewise.'"

His intuition was immediate and accurate.[3] So might we not learn from his methods, which are—as we like to say now—*life-on-life*?[4] And if we continue his work of making disciples, the basic questions are the essential ones (Who? What? Why?), not the pragmatic ones (When? Where? How?). Jesus stands in opposition to some of our most cherished and unexamined cultural assumptions.

Those of us Protestants with the world *method* hidden in our names are perhaps the most vulnerable to the distortions of the pragmatic way because we think practicality a virtue. Our founder, John Wesley, found himself as the leader of a spiritual awakening and so he fashioned—through necessity coupled with trial and error—systems and methods to nourish and channel the revival, the more prominent of which were well trained lay-preachers, society and class meetings, robust teaching on discipleship, Christian growth in love, and a hymnody that let the faith be sung in order to be understood.[5] It was apostolic Christianity refitted to mid-18th century England, and it caught fire as it offered the spiritually hungry a reliable way to follow Jesus together.

Think of John Wesley and his network as a para-church movement that could afford to specialize on conversion and growth in holy living because so much was already in place when Wesley began his work as an evangelist and renewalist. There was a national church integrated with the monarchy and parliament, a standard English Bible, the sacraments, the Creeds, and the Book of Common Prayer as a tool of daily devotion.

The Thirty-Nine Articles gave doctrinal content and boundaries. Systems were in place for clerical training and ordination. The parish system was organized to serve and support outlets across the land. Christian universities and politicians were at least nominally committed to the doctrines of the Trinity and the Incarnation. A robust public rebuttal of deism was already in place and championed by intellectual apologists like Bishop Butler. The kingdom and government—while fully Anglican—made space for religious freedom and some experimentation around the edges of the established national church.[6]

3. For a scholarly defense of these ideas and their implications for a Spirit-filled discipleship, see Issler, "Jesus' Example: Prototype of the Dependent, Spirit-filled Life," 189–225.

4. A little classic that bears re-reading is Coleman, *The Master Plan of Discipleship*.

5. For an introduction to the man and his methods, see Vickers, *Wesley: A Guide for the Perplexed* and Sanders, *Wesley on the Christian Life*. On the recovery of the Class Meeting as a discipleship model, see Watson, *The Class Meeting*.

6. For an appreciative treatment of all the Christian infrastructure that was already in place when

Never underestimate what was already in place when Wesley went public after 1738. In a sense often ignored, he had the luxury of evangelism in an already-prepared nation. He was afforded the privilege of working out a systematic understanding of the doctrines of grace and yoking it to a system of accountable discipleship because all the big pieces of the faith were already in place and waiting for a fresh expression. The gathered kindling awaited a fresh spark and a wind to fan the flames. The house was already built, and Wesley went out to invite the riff-raff into the storehouse of its treasures.

The Methodist experiment worked well enough in England, but—when transferred to America—blazed even more brightly so that the 19th can rightly be called *The Methodist Century*. We basically over-ran the nation because of the side effects of the kind of people we produced. Consider the assessment of Dr. Kevin Watson:

> "From 1776 to 1850 American Methodists grew like a weed. In 1776, Methodists accounted for 2.5 percent of religious adherents in the colonies, the second smallest of the major denominations of the time. By 1850, the Methodists comprised 34.2 percent of religious adherents in the United States, which was 14 percent more than the next group."[7]

But when something works this well for decades and does so much good on so many fronts, the temptation is to forget the primary agency of divine providence, to minimize the church's classic faith and doctrines, and to shift attention to the methods and practices as if the life was in them and not in the trust in God they supported and expressed. The name I give this failing is *The Methodist Sin*. Other denominations will have to name and claim their own peculiar forms of treason, but this is surely ours.

Whenever we Methodists lose momentum and fall into the doldrums, as happens with churches birthed out of the heat of spiritual awakenings, the call is not to turn to God in repentance and prayer with a fresh attention to Scripture and our doctrines as means of grace but to dicker with our structures and methods under the illusion that, "If we can only get the structure and supervision right, the thing will come alive again and thrive."[8]

So experts are gathered, committees formed, surveys taken, reports issued, and suggestions made to fix the machinery of the system. But it never works because it cannot. It is a fundamentally flawed, false approach. The institution that was created to point to the Triune God as the source of life and hope keeps pointing back to itself! But the church was not our creation, and we cannot fix it. It's not a project for the high-minded and well-meaning. We have now been reduced to a lumbering

---

Wesley launched out and on which he built his disciple-making renewal movement, see Abraham, *Wesley for Armchair Theologians* and his *Methodism: A Very Short Introduction*, Chapter 2, "Supporting Background Stimuli," 17–27, Chapter 8, "The Decline of Methodism," 107–22.

7. Watson, *Class Meeting*, Kindle: 21–22.

8. The echo of many a Methodist lament.

bureaucracy laced with heavy doses of useless nostalgia for "our great history and all our contributions."

It's amazing we keep doing this kind of thing in spite of such meager results. Having been through wave after wave of such grand ecclesial schemes for self-repair, I wonder what's beneath such a persistent pattern of self-deception, and I fear the answer.

Is it not that we have acted as if the church belonged to us and not to God? It's become our project, our responsibility, our institution, our guilty burden, our platform and microphone for this or that righteous cause, our laboratory for continual human improvement in the service of a vague cultural sense of progress, and if only we can get the method right and the people lined up, then it can be what we want. This is a fundamental lie and so deeply embedded in our common life that it has become a cancer eating away at what remains of a lively and trusting faith in Jesus Christ.

The call from leaders to pastors in my forty years of serving (1977–2017) was always a patronizing form of "do better" and "do more" and "try this new thing" and "attend this seminar" and "read this book" and "make sure to pay your apportionments" and "come to the meetings." It was soul-numbing and discouraging in the extreme. I do not remember leaving a district meeting with any fresh wind of the Holy Spirit fluttering and filling my sails. Jesus Christ had become for us a decoration on our causes, not the one under whose risen rule we were to live and love one another as we engaged in mission.

So I went to the meetings, paid my dues, kept my union card punched, served on boards and committees, set up a serious program of study and writing, did what I could locally, taught various studies, worked in prisons, prayed for healing with the sick, worked in the shadow church, embraced world mission, and generally found spiritual and intellectual life elsewhere.[9] Ours was an advanced form of religious pragmatism gone to seed with the sub-text from on high always being a new form of "If you would only, then . . ."

I resented the constant pressure and career threats, but I did not understand the spiritual and intellectual disease from whence they came and in which we were all caught. We had turned the church into our project and all but forgotten the Jesus who died and rose to give it birth and who sustained it through his Holy Spirit and all the varied means of grace in our canonical heritage.[10]

So if you are looking for a case study of a people who forgot the faith and its purposes and wandered off to their own demise, it's us![11] We Methodists are the poster

9. Most notably *The Mission Society for United Methodists* (now *TMS Global*) where I served on the board for thirteen years and four as Board Chair. There I received a superior education in global mission which fuels me to this day. I found myself around a table with the likes of Maxie Dunnam, George Hunter, Billy Abraham, Darrell Whiteman, and Thomas Oden. Quite an education it was!

10. To regain my bearings on the full scope of God's provision for his people across time, I often return to the collection of essays in Abraham, *Canonical Theism*.

11. For a chronicle of our amnesia and wandering, see Heidinger, *The Rise of Theological Liberalism*

children for what a bad philosophy can do to a once-vibrant Christian movement. What once worked to build disciples of Jesus Christ no longer works, and hasn't for a very long time. We idolized our methods and forgot the Master. We have lived off the accumulated piety and institutional resources of earlier generations of the faithful and are now running on fumes and slouching towards schism.

The church is not a machine to be tinkered with; it's the body of Christ, his beloved bride, a living thing, God's own creation. So there is no technique, no formula, no whiz-bang pastor, no marketing savvy, and no four-step plan to fix our malaise. God is not manipulated into action by human techniques. The names for this approach are *magic and sorcery*, the notion that we can gain leverage on God or the gods by the right formulas, sacrifices, or techniques. It seems that the further we move away from the center of the classic Christian faith, the closer we come to the embrace, not of atheism, but of a renewed pantheism, paganism, and polytheism.[12] The old powers are having a renaissance in our midst.

Might it be that God has folded the divine arms and said to the angels, "I'm going to back up and see if they notice the absence of the presence? The Methodists appear to think they can run the church on human wisdom without me. It will be painful to watch, and even worse for them."[13]

In my reflections on our painful, pitiful situation and my complicity in it, I've read several articles on the philosophy of pragmatism and on a classic series of six questions which may be applied to any circumstance to aid in information gathering and problem solving.[14] We know them as "The Five W's and one How," and they are typically cast as a series of one-word questions: *Who? What? Where? When? Why? and How?*

Building on a long discussion begun in Aristotle's *Nichomachean Ethics*, Thomas Aquinas summed up the basic elements of any circumstance in a pithy summary:

> For in acts we must note of *who* did it, by what aid or instrument he did it (*with*), *what* he did, *where* he did it, *why* he did it, *how* and *when* he did it.[15]

And *The Decline of American Methodism*. Parallel treatments on other denominations are emerging as the great post-mortem on the mainline churches begins in earnest. On our mother, The Episcopal Church, see Murchison, *Mortal Follies: Episcopalians and the Crisis of Mainline Christianity*, and more recently Virtue, *The Seduction of the Episcopal Church*. On our grandmother, The Church of England, see the wickedly accurate pathology report of Brown and Woodhead, *That Was the Church That Was*. We've all caved into the culture and its obsessions with the ever-expressive self and its sexual preferences, becoming its smiling chaplains and guilty defenders. We have lost our capacity to be "for the world" by standing "over against it" as an annoying alternative. What was is crumbling around us, and what's next?

12. For a prescient read from a quarter-century ago, see Braaten and Jenson, *Either/Or: The Gospel of Neopaganism.*

13. The classic text is Romans 1:18–32 with its triple refrain of "God gave them up."

14. en.wikipedia.org/wiki/Five_Ws.

15. *Summa Theologica: Great Books of the Western World*: 19.

And while the order of the four internal elements often changes, the list is textually stable with *Who*? most often heading the list and *How*? ending it, with some variety within the frames. It was left to Thomas Wilson to make it memorable in 16th century verse when he wrote:

> Who, what, and where, by what helpe, and by whose:
> Why, how, and when, doe many things disclose.[16]

But it was Rudyard Kipling who made the list (and its limits!) most memorable with his analogy to six honest servants and his rearrangement of the six to establish a rhyme:

> "I keep six honest serving-men
>   (They taught me all I knew);
> There names are What and Why and When
>   And How and Where and Who.
> I send them over land and sea,
>   I send them east and west;
> But after they have worked for me,
>   I give them all a rest."[17]

This pithy list of six queries has a track record in journalism, the Catholic confessional, criminal investigations, business management, biblical exegesis, and all manner of problem solving and project planning. It's useful as a means of organizing the basics of any situation, and it's frankly hooked my curiosity as I consider why pragmatic questions can never be primary.

The classic list of " Five W's and an H" can be logically divided into two groups of three. The first group is Who? What? and Why? The second is When? Where? and How? The second trio are pragmatic questions concerning calendars, venues, and methods. They concern action and execution, in other words, *getting something done with efficiency*, which is the heart and soul of pragmatism. It's all about achieving something, of making progress, of more and better and faster, and in the process justifying ourselves as *go-getters*, or more recently *pro-actives*. Yes, and when this method reigns in the churches because of success elsewhere, something precious is lost and dies of neglect. And we all know it.

So where does that leave the first group of three? Do they also fall into a natural grouping? Yes, though of a different type. I think of them as *Primary* instead of *Secondary*, *Essential* instead of *Derivative*, *Substantial* instead of *Contingent*.

Before you can answer the When? Where? and How? operational questions, you need answers to the Who? What? and Why? substantial questions. The substance of a matter precedes action upon it. To know what's important precedes doing something

---

16. *The Arte of Rhetoric*, Book 1.
17. "I Keep Six Honest Serving Men," allpoetry.com/I-Keep-Six-Honest-Serving-Men,

about it. Diagnosis before Prescription, to use a medical analogy. It's a properly basic distinction, and you either see it and get it, or you don't.

As I've read the emerging and increasing wave of literature on Christian discipleship, I've noted, as expected, how infected it is with the virus of pragmatism, of a nearly manic drive towards a proven method that if properly implemented will produce mature followers of Jesus Christ. There are those who protest,[18] but their minority report is minimized. It's another version of the old Methodist lie, "If we just get the form and machinery right, it will work again." And frankly, there's little to distinguish this strategy from the mythic search for the right magic formula to make all things well. And it will not work.

It's against just this kind of thinking that this book, *Following Jesus: Discipleship in the Gospel of Luke and Beyond* is directed. As Luke goes, discipleship is a secondary, derivative issue, the first being the answer to the essential three: *Who* is this Jesus of which Luke speaks? *What* does he offer? And *Why* does he matter? In dealing with his followers, the same primary questions must be asked: *Who* is a disciple? *What* do they learn and become in his company? And *Why* do they matter? Only at the end of this work will the pragmatic issues be touched on, and then only lightly and likely to no one's satisfaction. It is not my intent to frustrate readers but to raise an alternative thesis, to help us put Essentials back in first place. The alternative idea is this:

> If we majored in the essentials of *Who* and *What* and *Why*,
> almost any *How* could work,
> with the *When* and *Where* left to local discretion.
> Or, in its most optimistic form, "Right *Who,* almost any *How.*"

If we are clear on who is the Jesus that we follow, we can afford to be flexible on methodology and local adaptations. First the Triune God, then a consideration of all this means for where and how we live into this wonderful divine revelation.

What if the person and work of Jesus Christ again became our new fascination, that he regained our full devotion and allegiance because he is supremely trustworthy?

What if the answer to the *Who* question is "Jesus of Nazareth, the Father who sent him, and the Spirit who accompanied him: the Triune God whose story is Scripture."

What if the answer to the *What* question is "Because we who are headed towards death, bound in sin, tormented with evil, and who cannot save ourselves, need him to rescue and rehabilitate us in the fullest sense."[19]

18. See Scazzero, *Emotionally Healthy Discipleship* for a minority report. He's onto something worth examining, the conviction that most of our discipleship methods are shallow.

19. If you find this assertion overly gloomy, read Article VII of the United Methodist Articles of Religion, "Of Original or Birth Sin." Nothing is more counter-cultural than this statement of the depth of sin and basic depravity of every human being:

> "Original sin standeth not in the following of Adam (as the Pelagians do vainly talk), but is the corruption of the nature of every man (and woman), that naturally is engendered of the offspring of Adam, whereby man (and woman) is/are very far gone from

What if the answer to the *Why* question is "That they might relearn to love this God with all that they are and others as themselves until the kingdom of God comes in fullness." With these in place, almost any *How* will work as long at it never forgets the *Who*: Jesus, the *What*: following, and the *Why*: divine and human love spread abroad.

My aim is that this volume, except at the end, be devoted to the Essential Questions, the Who? and the What? and the Why? of Jesus Christ and of following him together as students, apprentices, witnesses, and mimics.

I have long drunk from the poisoned well of pragmatism. I need a break, a fresh hope, something more life-giving than the mindless religious activism it so gladly promotes. So if you seek a quick fix and a verified formula to mass produce saints, please stop reading now. I am your sworn enemy. But, if you hunger for more, read on!

---

original righteousness, and of his own nature inclined to evil, and that continually" (*The Book of Discipline* 2016, 67).

It's not just what we do but who we are and what we all become that's the issue. Pop-psychology and can-do pragmatism both take a big hit here!

2

A Second Caution

On the Overuse of Transformation Language

THE LANGUAGE OF TRANSFORMATION and change is not absent from the New Testament, and while it is represented by only a few texts and three Greek verbs, that does not mean it's an unimportant idea in the unfolding of divine revelation towards the kingdom of God. Those texts are:

1. "Do not be conformed to this world,
   but *be transformed* (Gk. *metamorpheo* [passive]) by the renewal of your mind,
   that you may prove what is the will of God,
   what is good and acceptable and perfect" (Rom. 12:1–2).

The text falls into two couplets. In the first, the outward pressures of the world—classically enumerated as the powers of sin, death, and evil—are countered by God's renewal of our minds so that we see and think differently. And why is that? As the second couplet happily announces, it is so that we, in the midst of a world that is not changed, may see and do God's will, which is always in line with God's character which is good, pleasing, and mature. What is radically changed is the way we now think about everything. That the verb *be transformed* is in the passive voice indicates divine action. We are the active receivers of the gifts of another, so don't fight the new mind God gives. Instead welcome it, and let it rewire the way you see everything.

2. "And we all, with unveiled face,
   beholding the glory of the Lord,
   are *being changed* (Gk. *metamorpheo* [passive]) into his likeness
   from one degree of glory to another;
   for this comes from the Lord

who is the Spirit" (2 Cor. 3:18).

The analogy Paul uses is from Ex. 34:29–30:

> "When Moses came down from Mount Sinai, with the two tables of the testimony in his hands as he came down from the mountain, Moses did not know that the skin of his face shone because he had been talking with God. And when Aaron and all the people of Israel saw Moses, behold, the skin of his face shone, and they were afraid to come near him."

But we, says Paul, are invited to gaze upon the glory of the Lord Jesus and to let that sight do its work in us as we are "being changed into his likeness from one degree of glory to another." Then comes a statement of who is the agent of this restoration, "for this comes from the Lord who is the Spirit." Moses put on a veil to shield the people, but we are unveiled to see our Savior and be changed by his Holy Spirit. That this is a process is clear in the phrase "from one degree of glory to another." Jesus is the agent of our change over time. It's not self-help, not self-transformation; it is change by exposure to him. When we look at and to him, something changes in us!

These two texts from Romans and Second Corinthians speak of a process of change that happens now. God works to give us new minds that see everything from God's perspective for the sake of faithful action. As we focus on Jesus and refuse to look away from his light, something amazing is happening: we are being made into new people fitted for service now and glory later. The passive voice of the verbs is a strong indicator that it is not what we do for or in ourselves through the application of some spiritual technology or psychological tool that makes the difference. It is what God offers and we enter by trust that makes the difference. We let it happen because we cannot make it happen. We remain forever dependent.

3. "But our commonwealth is in heaven,
and from it we await a Savior, the Lord Jesus Christ,
who *will change* (Gk. *metaschematixo* = change the form of 'x')
our lowly body to be like his glorious body,
by the power which enables him even to subject all things to himself" (Phil. 3:20–21).

Here the focus shifts from Jesus' present effects on us to our participation in the reception of resurrection bodies like his own at the end of the age, meaning the arrival of Jesus, the kingdom of his Father, and the transformation of the whole cosmos, us included! It's not something we can do, but only him. We gladly participate, but the power to effect real and permanent change in our bodily existence now, or in the world to come, is not ours.

4. "Lo! I tell you a mystery.
We shall not all sleep, but we shall all *be changed* (Gk. *allasso*, [passive]),
in a moment, in the twinkling of an eye, at the last trumpet.
For the trumpet will sound,
and the dead will be raised imperishable,

and we shall *be changed* (Gk. *allasso*, [passive])" (1 Cor. 15:51–52).

This is the same event as Philippians 3:20–21 but with the use of another Greek verb (*alasso*) for variety. Those believers who've died and those still alive, will, at the instantaneous inbreaking of God's rule, be reclothed in marvelous new frames fit for life in the old world made new. We participate in the gift, but we do not cause it. The self has not the power to be changed except God initiate it and enable our assent and cooperation. Whatever good comes from self-help is common grace, but the change Jesus offers his followers of gradual change now and sudden change at the end is not a human possibility.

5. "And, Thou, Lord, didst found the earth in the beginning,
and the heavens are the work of thy hands;
they will perish, but thou remainest;
they will all grow old like a garment,
like a mantle thou wilt roll them up,
and they will *be changed* (Gk. *allasso*, [passive]).
But thou art the same,
and thy years will never end" (Heb. 1:10–12).

In a hymn of praise to Jesus the Son, the author makes sure to draw the whole of creation into the scene with a text from Psalm 102:25–27. And what the author envisions, using the humble image of a change of clothes, is that creation as it now is will be rolled up, not to be discarded but to be remade, "and they will be changed."

The raw materials of the old are recast in the new heavens and new earth, so that Jesus' resurrection is not only the template for our futures but the refitting of all creation. Again the verb is in the passive voice (*be changed*) indicating divine action. We may be good stewards of the earth, but cannot save the planet. But God can and will because God's character has never changed, "But thou art the same, and thy years will never end."

For all the changes by degree that we may enter now, the change that comes only at the end is total. In that moment we are in a new realm beyond the reaches of sin, death, and evil, which are themselves done away with as the enemies of God are vanquished. The changes we long for, and find hints and glimmers of from time to time, will be ours forever and only deepen because the God in whose Triune circle we will live is inexhaustible. Degrees now, total later. Struggles now, fulfillment later. Pains now, ecstasy later. Ignorance now, illumination later. Awkward now, natural then. Bumbling now, graceful then. Compromised now, integrity then.

This brief reflection on five key texts on the transformation God promises brings me to my concern and caution. As part of a generalized *hyping-up* of rhetoric in the media in order to grab attention, Christian speakers and authors have followed suit so as not to be left behind. But not everything is *stunning* or *amazing* or *earth-shattering*, or *life-changing* or *trending* or *revolutionary* or *disruptive* or even *transformative*. It's just not.

Much is mundane and unremarkable, ordinary and slow, hard and boring, tedious and full of duty and routine, until in a rare moment of review and looking back you see that your inner world has made a noticeable shift and your character changed in the direction of holy love. You are now different than before, and you thank the source who's been present as the hidden one all the time, displacing your vices with his virtues and your sins with his savvy alternatives. Not yet transformed, but your movement is in the right direction, and this uneven process is what we name *sanctification*. It's what God continues to do in us after we begin to trust and follow Jesus as his apprentices. My own Wesleyan tradition has highlighted this process, and one of our most concise doctrinal summaries is titled *Of Sanctification*:

> "Sanctification is that renewal of our fallen nature by the Holy Ghost, received through faith in Jesus Christ, whose blood of atonement cleanseth from all sin; whereby we are not only delivered from the guilt of sin, but are washed from its pollution, saved from its power, and are enabled, through grace, to love God with all our hearts and to walk in his holy commandments blameless."[1]

We want to change. We need to change. We hurt for change and imagine how good the new freedoms would feel. We are ashamed by what we do and don't do, mocked often by our own best intentions and how quickly they vaporize like the last diet or exercise program. This is why the words *transform* and *transformative* are overused and thus over-promised. They express a deep longing, and so we go hunting for the Jesus version of quick-fix. After an initial burst of enthusiasm and fresh resolution, we soon enough stall and stumble, but the longing does not go away.

As an example of our bind, two of our best resources, the Lifeway (Southern Baptist) research project on *Transformational Discipleship*[2] and the new book by Peter Scazzero, *Emotionally Healthy Discipleship: Moving from Shallow Christianity to Deep Transformation*, both use the same codeword with Scazzero going one better, not just *transformation* but something better—*deep transformation*. Maybe others will soon be touting *total, deep transformation*, or perhaps *mega-transformation*, but this is only to poke a little fun at those whose work I admire.

Both use the same *transformation* codeword, and for the same reason, which is to stand out from others who promise less than the supposed best, and with the very best of motives. They are eager to move beyond the shallow, low-expectation following of Jesus that characterizes so many of our church folk, a situation often termed *the crisis of discipleship*, and even here note the use of alarmist rhetoric—*crisis*. I understand their frustration; it's mine as well. So being a bit of a smart aleck, I ask, "Why a crisis of discipleship if such amazing, deep transformation is this close at hand?"

These are excellent resources, but we must be very careful in the over-use of the rhetoric of transformation. It promises more than we can deliver, and it verges on

---

1. *Book of Discipline 2016*, 72.
2. www.lifeway.com/en/product-family/transformational-discipleship.

promising more than God is willing to deliver in the present. Slow and incremental and degree-by-degree? Yes. Occasional breakthroughs? Yes. And what amazing gifts these are. But transformation—if the plain sense of the world retains its meaning? Then No, and not until the end and the new beginning of all things as heaven comes down to kiss the earth.

Sin and death and evil still roam the land stalking every soul and will until the end. Everyone is under constant pressure, fallible and frail. These are the ones God loves, the ones Jesus' shepherds and encourages, not just the transformed Christian superstars because, while many may follow such with awe, there are none, just inflated images and puffed-up personas.

So what's wrong here? Answer: we have over-promised in the short range and under-promised for the long haul. And here we must use some technical language. The kingdom of God that stood at the center of Jesus' program is both *here-and-now* and *then-and-there*. The classic formulation of the tension is that the kingdom of God in Jesus is both *already* and *not yet*.[3] To use a food analogy, it's appetizers now, full feast only later. Or a marital one: a kiss now, the full embrace later. We live in the conflicted overlap of the world as it is and the world as it is to be. Real tension, real conflict, real life with us, real change in us, and the transformation of everything only at the end when Jesus says, "I'm back!"

The triune kingdom of the Father in the Son and the Spirit is near enough to make a difference as it applies the pressures of God's holy love to a rebellious and out-of-sorts world, but it has not yet engulfed and transformed the whole of creation and done away with our enemies, and that is the tension in which we live. How much can be expected now, and what must wait? On this the churches and their best thinkers differ.

Pentecostals around the world agree that cessassionist[4] Presbyterians expect far too little and miss out on many of the Spirit's best gifts, whereas the same Presbyterians write off their high-voltage distant cousins as credulous (too easy to believe), flaky, and foolish for reading the Gospels and Acts as if they were last Sunday's paper and today's to-do list.

---

3. Several of our best formulations of this tension between what's normally available from God now and what is reserved for the end are written by Vineyard pastors and theologians, many of whom are quite knowledgeable, both academically and experientially, about miracles, signs and wonders, and the more dramatic of the Spirit's gifts. I have found help from Nathan and Kim, *Both-And: Living The Christ-Centered Life In An Either-Or-World*, 175–201, from Hopping, *The Here And Not Yet*, and from Venter, *Doing Healing*, Chapter 4, "Understanding the Kingdom of God," 66–82. For a brief treatment by a New Testament scholar, see Bauckham, *Jesus: A Very Short Introduction*, Chapter 4, "Enacting the kingdom of God," 35–56, and Chapter 5, "Teaching the kingdom of God," 57–83.

4. Cessassionists believe, to put it crudely that "God used to be in the miracle business but quit when we got the Bible." God ceases miracles, thus cessassionism, and that is now how things are. For the argument against this position, see Deere, *Why I Am Still Surprised*, 72–105, and Keener, *Miracles Today*, 14–15.

So to use some additional technical terms, our Pentecostal hypotheticals would say of the sons and daughters of Calvin, "They have an *under-realized* eschatology," meaning that too little of the kingdom's future goodies are available in the present. And the *Presbies* would retort with the opposite charge with equal conviction:

> "And you, our unstable, excitable cousins have an *over-realized* eschatology, meaning that you claim as common in the present things for which you have no evidence but your over-heated piety and standardized testimonies, neither of which bear up well under critical inquiry and the demand for credible evidence."

All the other churches range somewhere on the gradation between these two extremes. Too-much-for-the-now and too-little-for-the-now mark the ends of the spectrum, with the rest of us perhaps wanting more and dreaming of it, but not quite sure if we have a right to expect it from God in the here and now. We hear of miracles elsewhere, but not so much in our neighborhood. But didn't Jesus . . . .

So it is with the over-use of *transformation* rhetoric. How much can we expect now, and what only later? Transformation is an ultimate term, implying a great change to something much better. Not just slightly improved or greatly improved, but *transformed*!

If interviewed, I think both Scazzero and the Baptist researchers would fess up that the titles bear the influences of the marketing and sales departments. It's driven by the hope that such promises will motivate more casual believers to get off dead center and start growing again because this is the ugly truth of American churches of all brands and styles. Promise them *transformation* and they might do something besides yawn, "Haven't we already done that program?"

In every church there are persons of deep piety, real generosity, mature love, the wisdom that comes where Scripture meets life, and a kind of infectious joy about small things that makes you want to be around them. The old writers called it *conspicuous sanctity.* Their candles are lit, and their song is one they learned long ago at Bible School, "Give me oil in my lamp, keep me burning. Keep me burning till the break of day!" Some of their names are found on the cover of this manual. But just down the pew or on the inactive rolls are old friends who are small and sour and shriveled, for whom the most basic truths of the faith seem never to have penetrated very far. But isn't our promise of *transformation*, when read through cultural lenses of self-help and quick-fix, just a pious lie? I think so.

So let's go light on the *transformation* language, first because in the slender New Testament usage it's typically in the passive voice, which indicates not my actions but the actions of another upon me along the way of discipleship towards the end of all things, and only then will the promise of transformation be completed.

And secondly, because once you join the inflated rhetoric school of marketing and promotions, there's nowhere to stop. You have to keep on lying and looking for the next clever term to cover over the modest and uneven gains we see at ground level.

And thirdly, because Jesus was patient with his faulty followers for three years, losing only the one who wanted to speed up the process for more tangible results. They were not that impressive when they started and not that impressive when their friend was suffering, and this was after a full-on exposure for up to three years.

Fourth, and finally, the most subtle sleight-of-hand is here at work. Transformation has become a term on our side of the scale. It's about our advancement, our spirituality, our status, our image with others, our inside track with Jesus, our becoming our best self now. But isn't that the very opposite of the real deal? How subtle and strategic is the Enemy of our Souls, to turn the best to the worst. So go light on transformation language; better yet, save it for the future!

A classic case of the running together of biblical realism with utopian understandings of transformation was the creation of a new mission statement for the United Methodist Church at the General Conference of 2008. The statement now reads, "The mission of the church is to make disciples of Jesus Christ *for the transformation of the world*."[5] The italicized phrase was added in 2008 to a statement first approved in 2000 that read, simply enough, "The mission of the church is to make disciples of Jesus Christ."

When the Council of Bishops met in the fall of 2004, they asked themselves, "To what end do we make disciples of Jesus Christ? Is making disciples an end in itself, or does God have a purpose for which He redeems us, recovers us and makes us whole?"[6] The bishops had a nagging sense the statement was incomplete, and so four years later the phrase *for the transformation of the world* was added and overwhelmingly supported by the delegates at General Conference. I count it as a mistake, but a highly revealing one because here the modern ideology of progress was grafted onto a biblical imperative to reproduce apprentices of Jesus. How subtle are the corruptions of alien ideas.

Jesus mandated a multi-generational disciple-making mission accompanied by his presence and culminating in *the end of the present evil age* (Galatians 1:4) when he returns to reign. The end of making disciples is to live in creative obedience to Jesus Christ in the present. Anything beyond this is up to him, and those who follow him know he is more than capable. So why does this grand mission of the largest possible scope need a further, and arguably extraneous purpose, "for the transformation of the world?"

Why? Because our United Methodist bishops are modern utopian dreamers with a progressive doctrine that human beings are on a long course of progress and advancement towards a perfected world this side of the kingdom of God. And so their

5. The United Methodist Book of Discipline 2016, 93.
6. House, "United Methodist Mission Statement Revised."

job is to point the way and lead the way until our efforts finally cross the bridge into a new world where God awaits our arrival with a grand welcome, "What a good job you've done!"

But I see little evidence of their much-touted notions of progress. Oh, I see changes, and many of them good and great, but I also see an equally countervailing reality at work so that for each advance there is a retreat, a retrenchment, a new form of an old evil. Because despite all our tinkering with the surface of things, sin and death and evil and unbelief and the one who delights in all their pain (the Evil One) still rules the earth in spite of their being principled pockets of resistance across the lands. Genocides continue. Thugs bully democracies into submission. Wealth piles up in well-protected silos. Women and children remain particularly vulnerable. Slavery as human trafficking makes a big comeback. And the only way the bankrupt idea of progress can be maintained is by ignoring the contrary evidence and piling up the transformation promises that are soon to be realized.

The really big and anti-human issues of sin and death and evil are not something we can do something about, primarily because we are all embedded and controlled by them. Ameliorate some of their worst effects? Occasionally, and for a while in our near neighborhood. But these powers remain ensconced and ever-creative in their ability to blunt and undermine and twist the very best of human resistance. They have been named and challenged by Jesus Christ; their doom has been pronounced, but the final penalty has not yet been executed. And so it will be until the reappearing of Jesus Christ to reclaim all that is and establish the kingdom of the Father and the Son and the Holy Spirit across the cosmos.

So what's the problem? The added statement "for the transformation of the world" leaves us with the impression, and perhaps this was the intent, that the metamorphosis of the world is something we humans bring about within time and history and not something that comes only as God's gift at the arrival of the kingdom of God upon the earth at the end of the age. This error is easily joined to modern notions of human progress and the over-confidence of utopian thinking, the idea that the world as it now stands is perfectible by human efforts if only we can make enough disciples of this grand movement towards progress.

So to a clear biblical mandate to make disciples among all the peoples, we now have a statement that promotes a more ultimate mandate of transforming the world in our time. This is naive, simplistic, unbiblical, and overconfident. It is more motivational rhetoric than justifiable Christian thinking. We have added to the Great Commission because we simply do not trust God's people to live out their discipleship in ways that go beyond inward piety. They must be pushed and bullied towards the real agenda, which is to fix the entire planet, to enable its transformation by a good Methodist effort and four year quadrennial plan. What a futile and ultimately cruel joke to inflict on God's people. How silly! How Methodist!

This is a human centered, ideologically driven, over-realized eschatology that is naive about the deep and continuing grip of sin, evil, and death in our world and the fact that they will not be overcome or displaced by well-meaning Methodists but only by God at the end of history as we've known it.

I could have lived with a more modest version, something like, "The mission of the church is to make disciples of Jesus Christ *as we await the transformation of the world*," but the utopians among would likely have found this formulation much too passive and not nearly motivating enough to push the Methodists out of the pews and into the streets. Changes do happen, and some are enormously good, like the near-elimination of some infectious diseases and the globalization of capitalism which have raised many out of radical poverty, but as soon as one issue is addressed, another appears.

So, is the church primarily a platform for progressive social advocacy, or are we the trusting followers of a Jesus who has no trouble at all guiding his people to wherever a faithful witness and costly service are needed? We are first realistic disciples who await the coming kingdom and are leary of promised utopias. We live out radical faith in every venue and welcome whatever good comes of it. But we do not over-promise what can be done now. We do not bait people with easy promises of transformation. Our hope is bigger than what we can accomplish. But there is one at work among us at all times, and in him we hope.

3

Our Inheritance

The Two Big Questions in Luke

THE GOSPEL OF LUKE is one of four ancient biographies of Jesus that open the New Testament and serve as the foundation for all that follows.[1] In the conscious ordering of the canon, we are first invited to spend time with the church's four complementary portraits of Jesus before moving on to the mission and expansion of the church (Acts), its struggles and opportunities (the Epistles: Pauline and General), and the climactic ending of history (the Apocalypse). Thus, a story that begins in Jesus and his first followers ends in the new heavens and new earth of the Kingdom of God[2] and the healing of all creation from the triple curses of sin, death, and evil, with the Old Testament as prequel and prologue.

This is the most basic story line of the New Testament and of the church's two part canon as a whole.[3] The Jesus who is God the Son displays the kingdom of his Father and the Holy Spirit in his person (who he is) and work (his words and deeds), part of which is to call and shape *disciples/followers*[4] to continue his witness and deeds

1. For an introduction, see Bird, *The Gospel of the Lord*, Chapter 6, "Why Four Gospels?" 299–320. A foundational article on the reliability of the gospel memories is Keener, "Assumptions in Historical-Jesus Research," 26–58.

2. For an introduction to the kingdom of God as the integrating image of Jesus' mission, see Dunn, *Jesus' Call to Discipleship*, Chapter 2, "The Call of the Kingdom," 6–31. And more recently, Perrin, *The Kingdom of God: A Biblical Theology*.

3. For the larger story see Pelican, *Whose Bible Is It*, Chapter 6, "Formation of a Second Testament," 99–118.

4. Synonyms are apprentices, adherents, understudies, proteges, trainees, *grad students!*

after his death, resurrection, and ascension. God's new movement is now afoot upon the earth and has a training department!

The tri-personal language of the four gospels with both their direct and indirect references to the Father, the Son, and the Holy Spirit serves as raw material for the development of the church's full-orbed doctrine of the Holy Trinity.[5] The canon as an official list of books to be read in worship and the Great Creeds (Apostle's and Nicene) as an official list of affirmations to be confessed—initially at baptism—grew up together as mutually influential, and both are necessary; think heart and lungs! To be orthodox is to read the church's book through the lens of the church's Trinitarian and Incarnational faith, and that is the perspective of this book and our reading of Luke.[6] We read with the church and for the world.

A larger project than this book might be *Discipleship in the Four Gospels*[7] broken into two sections: 1) Discipleship in the Synoptic Gospels, and 2) Discipleship in the Gospel of John, with a concluding synthesis and the setting of a trajectory into the rest of the New Testament. But this extended essay is more narrow in scope and deals only with discipleship in the Gospel of Luke[8] with occasional references to his second volume (Acts).

This introduction will be followed by a literary, exegetical, and practical treatment of the fifty-one key discipleship units in Luke's Gospel,[9] a summary of our

5. See Witherington and Ice, *The Shadow of the Almighty*; Coppedge, *The God Who is Triune*, Chapter 1, "The New Testament Foundations for the Trinity," 13–52; O'Collins, *The Tri-Personal God*, Chapter 2, "The History of Jesus and His Trinitarian Face," 35–49; Sanders, *The Triune God*, Chapter 6, "Trinitarian Exegesis," 155–90.

6. The essay that reshaped my thinking was Gavrilyuk, "Scripture and the *Regula Fidei*" in Abraham, *Canonical Theism*, 27–42.

7. For basic scholarly treatments on discipleship, see Green, *Dictionary of Jesus*, "Disciples," 176–92, "Discipleship," 182–88; Wilkins, *Discipleship in the Ancient World* and his *Following the Master*, "Jesus' Form of Discipleship," 98–173. In addition, Keener, *The Historical Jesus of the Gospels*, "Disciples and Teachers," 147–49, "Kingdom Discipleship," 196–213; Bosch, "The Meaning of Being a 'Disciple'"; Green and Stevens, *New Testament Spirituality*, Chapter 2, "Disciples of Jesus," 23–40; Dallas Willard, "The New Testament Picture of Discipleship," "Discipleship"; Dunn, *Jesus' Call to Discipleship*; Samra, "A Biblical View of Discipleship," 219–34; H. Weder, "Disciple, Discipleship." *Anchor Bible Dictionary*. New York: Doubleday, 1992, Vol. II, 207–10.

8. Speciality works on discipleship in Luke include Sweetland, *Our Journey with Jesus,* his "Following Jesus: discipleship in Luke-Acts," 109–23; Longnecker, "Taking Up The Cross Daily," 50–76; Green, *New Testament Theology,*" Chapter 5, "Let them 'take up the cross daily,'" 102–21; du Plessis, "Discipleship according to Luke's Gospel," 58–71; Martin, "Salvation and Discipleship," 366–80; J. Karris, "Women and Discipleship," 1–20; Bock, *A Theology of Luke*, Chapter 15, "Discipleship and Ethics in the New Community," 311–32; Hacking, *Signs and Wonders*, "Overview of Discipleship in Luke," 159–64; Wilkins, *Following the Master*, Chapter 11, "Luke: Followers on the Costly Way," 203–23; Fitzmyer, *Luke the Theologian*, "Discipleship in the Lucan Writing," 235–56, and his *Gospel According to Luke*, "Discipleship," 117–45; Talbert, "Discipleship in Luke-Acts," 62–75, also his "The Way of the Lukan Jesus," 237–49.

9. In my analysis of Luke I find ninety-four thought units grouped into six larger sections. For a listing of the units including their Inclusions (boundaries) and Internal Structures (mainly concentric), see Appendix 1: "Identifying Luke's Thought Units." From this larger pool I've selected the

findings on discipleship in Luke, a survey of what the scholars are saying, a report on what thoughtful researchers and practitioners are offering, and a trajectory for what a contemporary discipleship with a Lukan flavor might look like in its recovery. To this is added a bibliography for further study, and appendices.

Two basic questions must be answered anew in every generation because the truths that do not change are lived out in cultures that do, and the two questions are:

1. Who is Jesus? This is the Christology question.

2. What does it mean to follow him together as a group? This is the disciple question, the continuity question, and the church question all in one, as Alison Morgan epigrams, "The plural of disciple is church."[10]

With the decline and marginalization of the church in the increasingly post-Christian West, these two questions are acute. The title *Christian* has for many become threadbare and problematic because of the dark side of church history, and some suggest that being a *follower of Jesus* is much better because of its *return to basics* associations. To say, "I'm a Jesus follower," is just odd enough to invite curiosity and conversation. We still carry the complex baggage of the title *Christian*, but we do not always lead with it.

Like all good stories, Luke is read at several levels. The first and most obvious is as a layered biography of Jesus from conception to ascension with Mary as his mother, John as his prophet, the disciples as his memory bank, select Jewish and Roman leaders as his opponents, the Father and Holy Spirit as his invisible co-champions, and Luke as one of his chroniclers. In each successive thought unit[11] we learn a bit more about who Jesus is (his person) through what he says (his words), what he does (his deeds), what others say about him (his predecessors and various audiences), and what God says about him (the divine witness of the Father and the Spirit). The philosophical insight is that actions (words + deeds) reveal essence. By listening to his words

---

units that speak most directly to the issue of discipleship, of which—to my early surprise—there were fifty-one. It's a major theme in Luke.

10. Her book *Following Jesus* has the evocative sub-title "The plural of disciple is church."

11. A "thought unit" is a designation I first learned under Dr. Charles H. Talbert at Wake Forest University in the early 1970s. Parallel terms are *pericope* or *paragraph*. However, a *thought unit* may be a single paragraph or a larger composition bringing together several paragraphs around a theme. I propose for this work that a thought unit be understood as "a clearly bounded literary unit with a clearly identified internal structure." Most often it is the repetition of key words and phrases at the beginning and end of the unit that act as verbal brackets or inclusions to clue the listener to the parts within a larger discourse. In Luke the internal organization of most thought units is concentric (also known as chiasm or ring structure) in which ideas are first presented and then re-presented with variation and in reverse order with a single (1–2–3–2'–1') or double center (1–2–3 // 3'–2'–1'). A single center (1–2–1') or double center pattern (1–2 // 2'–1') can be short or expanded into longer patterns, but the arrangement is always a series of frames around a central pivot point. For a fuller treatment, see my Chapter 4, "Mapping the Shape of the Text."

and observing his deeds, we build a layered portrait and work our way towards the question: Is this Jesus trustworthy and worth following?

Not until the story ends do we have the full portrait of Jesus' person and work.[12] You must first read it all the way to the end, and then—in light of the great surprise of Jesus' resurrection—go back and read the whole again in a new light. He's alive and therefore available to seek and to know, so read the story and check out one of Jesus' diverse franchises! They typically have crosses on top and so should be easy to locate. And since Sundays are their big day, it's a good time to show up with awkward questions.

Luke's story is progressive and developmental. The more of Jesus that is revealed, the more we know about *The New Reality*[13] and the One to whom we're apprenticed. Luke is constructing a narrative Christology,[14] preserving and retelling the stories that will later be abbreviated and epitomized in the early creeds for the evangelism, catechesis, and the liturgical confession of new disciples.[15]

A second level is that of reading the diverse responses to Jesus from his family, his fans, his followers, and his foes—both human and demonic. And here we focus particularly on his friends, those who followed Jesus as the earliest band of students— both male and female. Over time they became his agents and apostles, a smaller group of whom were given the symbolic title *The Twelve* as the leaders of the new Israel.[16] Theirs is also a progressive, developmental story, and entirely dependent on the One they follow. Jesus leads, and along the way they learn to dance to his beat. That is the story line of this volume, to trace that narrative and note its turning points.

As the third gospel was read to early audiences, they would have experienced it as a whole of several strands as the characterization of the various audiences was built

---

12. *Person* and *Work* are the two basic categories for confession and theology as found in the early creeds which introduce each person of the Trinity with a statement about identity or person, e.g. "I believe in God, the Father Almighty," and then statements about the activity or work that grounds the identity, e.g "maker of heaven and earth." Thus the second person of the Trinity is introduced by an identity statement of a name and three titles, "and in Jesus Christ (1), his only Son (2), our Lord (3)," followed by a series of saving activities beginning with the relative pronoun *who*, "who was conceived by the Holy Spirit . . . who will come to judge the living and the dead." The person of the *Holy* Spirit is followed by a list of *holy* things the Spirit generates: *holy* church, communion of the *holy ones*, and by the three gifts God the Trinity bestows at the end of the age on all the faithful: forgiveness of sins (the cure for rebellion), resurrection of the body (the cure for human frailty and death), and entry into God's kingdom (the world healed, thus a comprehensive new environment).

13. *The New Reality* is my paraphrase and substitute for the well worn phrase *the kingdom of God*, which—while valid—is so overused as to guarantee misunderstanding, whereas *The New Reality* engages the imagination, invites curiosity, and speaks of something substantial, not just a future ideal.

14. Rowe, *Early Narrative Christology*.

15. Luke has had a large effect on the Creeds because of his focus on Mary in his birth narrative and that he alone of the four gospels chronicles Jesus' ascension.

16. See the missions of the twelve (9:1–6), the seventy (10:1–24), and the gathering of the one hundred and twenty (Acts 1:15) for a sense of Jesus' expanding entourage.

up.[17] All the stories are about Jesus in one way or the other, and that's fitting since it's his essential biography that Luke is collecting and editing, arranging and composing. But a second strand woven throughout the whole is the story of his followers, those he called into a special relationship as students and apprentices, his traveling companions and side kicks, his memory bank, and eventually his official Spirit-empowered witnesses.

At the most basic level, these young-adults were to be *with him* in order to become *like him*.[18] They were observers who became participants in his mission of announcing, interpreting, and demonstrating the power of divine love found in the kingdom of the Father, Son, and Holy Spirit . The *new reality* was on display at ground level in the Son who became flesh in Jesus of Nazareth. It was him they followed and to him that they became attached over time. Their allegiance was to his person and his personal agenda. They were called and equipped to become his living extensions, his sent apostles, his authorized agents, his commissioned ambassadors. They were glued to him, and only one of the twelve was lost and not recovered and restored—Judas.

This is a dangerous business with genuine casualties, and to have been called and included in the powers of the new age was no guarantee of a good ending. Evil is always observing and probing for a weak spot.[19] Testing is revelatory; it reveals what's inside us! And if we take our messes to Jesus instead of hiding in guilt and shame, we again meet his mercy, love, wisdom, acceptance, healing, and companionship. To believe that you are too far gone to be turned around is the greatest lie of our enemy and one that Judas swallowed.

Each of the ninety-four thought units in Luke have implications for discipleship since each and all are about the One we follow, and once the public ministry begins in 4:31 with the exorcism in the Capernaum synagogue, we may assume that at least some of the disciples are present in each scene, even where not explicitly mentioned.

They were immersed in Jesus' life and travels, his stories and ways of relating to people, his signs and wonders. He was center stage, and they had the best seats in the house! It was an education like no other, rigorous and loving, probing and stretching, giving them a pain in the brain and an ache in the heart, living in the deep rather than the shallow end of the pool and waking each morning—I suspect—wondering what strange things Jesus will do today to heal many and offend others. He was someone you just could not control! And here I can't help but quote the justly-famous dialog from C.S. Lewis' *The Lion, the Witch, and the Wardrobe*:

> "Aslan is a lion—the Lion, the great Lion."
> "Ooh" said Susan. "I'd thought he was a man. Is he—quite safe? I shall feel rather nervous about meeting a lion . . ."

17. On the art of oral reading to audiences in the ancient world, see Wright, *Communal Reading*.

18. On Jesus' example as the decisive model, see Sanders and Issler, *Jesus in Trinitarian Perspective*, 189–225.

19. For a fresh treatment, see Tyra, *The Dark Side of Discipleship*.

"Safe?" said Mr Beaver . . . "Who said anything about safe? 'Course he isn't safe. But he's good. He's the King, I tell you."[20]

An apt analogy for being a disciple is basic training in the Army. Being sworn in, placed under orders, and in constant training where another sets the agenda and obedience is expected. The recruit surrenders to an identity and skill formation process in which all the basics of life are under the control of another—a drill sergeant who is not your mother! What walks into the office is a recruit. What marches in review at the end of basic training is a soldier headed to their *A School* and later a first deployment. It's an immersion in new realities, new habits and skills, new friends, a *Band of Brothers* to use the title of a recent WWII saga.[21]

What comes out on the other side of such a process is the same person with a new identity. In the journey of the disciples with Rabbi Jesus, we see the effects he has on those who were his first apprentices and understudies in the new reality of God's kingdom of love and power at ground level. If love had an army, what would the training look like? Answer: like the Gospel of Luke with Jesus and his disciples, the aim of which is to create a new kind of human being as a pointer to the One they follow.

Our English word *disciple*, from the Latin noun *disciplus* (learner) and verb *dicere* (to learn), is a translation of the Greek *methetes* from the verb *manthano* (to teach) and refers to a student or pupil, and by extension an adherent or follower of a teacher (Gk. *didaskalos*).[22] It was first used by Herodotus nearly half a millenium before Jesus. And since all serious learning in the ancient world was on the apprentice model, *disciple* came to mean one who was committed to learning the ways and means, the skills, and teachings of a master, to be—so far as possible—poured into their mold as a living replica, as Jesus acknowledged, "A disciple is not above his teacher, but every one when he is fully taught will be *like his teacher*" (Luke 6:40).

Universities as we know them as a diverse faculty of experts are a medieval Christian invention and did not exist as such in the ancient world.[23] What you had, in contrast, was a teacher of philosophy accepting a number of pupils who were willing to mimic and thus appropriate the whole of their master's life and outlook: Plato and the Platonists, Epicurus and the Epicureans, Moses and the Jews. Philosophers gave birth to schools of thought, and Jewish rabbis to methods of understanding and applying Torah in their circle of students.[24]

20. www.goodreads.com/quotes/344456-aslan-is-a-lion—the-lion-the-great-lion-ooh

21. If you have an inclusive image which retains the keen sense of shared mission and bonds of loyalty as this one, I'd love to hear it. It may be that women have to mint their own to enrich the rest of us.

22. *Mathetes* is used 261 times in the New Testament. On terms and definitions, see Wilkins, *Following the Master*, 39–42; Fredrichsen, "*Disciple(s)* in the New Testament," 717–39.

23. On the modern university as a gift of the church to the world, see Dickerson, *Jesus skeptic*, 87–106.

24. The Old Testament has no parallel technical term but speaks of *talmudiim* (pupils), a term Josephus translates as *methetes*. Communities such as the "sons of the prophets" (2 Kgs) provide a rough parallel. While there were rabbis and their pupils in Jesus' day, the more developed forms derive

As an example of what such a relationship meant in the ancient world, consider the first century appeal of Seneca, not just to the teaching but also to the living voice and common intimacy of life in the disciple/teacher relationship. Note how it maps so well onto the pattern of Jesus and his followers:

> "Cleanthes could not have been the express image of Zeno, if he had merely heard his lectures; he also shared in his life, saw into his hidden purposes, and watched him to see whether he lived according to his own rules. Plato, Aristotle, and the whole throng of sages who were destined to go each his different way, derived more benefit from the character than from the words of Socrates."[25]

So the disciple/master model was not one Jesus created but one he inherited, adapted, and extended from his two overlapping cultures, Jewish and Greco-Roman. It's how philosophers and rabbis were trained and formed in their master's ways of thinking and living, acting and teaching, and a true philosopher or rabbi was one whose life embodied his teaching. The core issue was integrity, and in the Gospel of Luke we see Jesus putting his teaching into consistent action as a true philosopher. He does what he says and says what he does. He speaks about the future, and it happens. He knows and exposes the secret thoughts of people. Jesus was clearly a prophet with access to privileged information. It would have impressed an ancient audience, whether Jewish or Greek.

Jesus is a true teacher whom the God of the Jews backs with wisdom and power. He is faith-filled and faithful, worthy of being followed and imitated. Luke's biography portrays Jesus as fully worthy of allegiance. He overcomes the Evil One, and he'd rather die in agony rather than give up his mission and break trust with the Father and Spirit who sent him.

Faith is trust based on multiple lines of evidence and leads to loyalty and active obedience. In his recent book on Jesus, *The Galilean Wonderworker*, Ian Wallis—after reviewing the reckless trust that Jesus' suppliants for healing often showed—writes that "faith means radical trust in Jesus expressed through personal investment and concrete action."[26] That's it! It's what the disciples did one by one, and sometimes in pairs: Simon and Andrew, James and John. And how do I know? Because Peter and the rest are now found as traveling companions of the One who said, "Follow me!" Each of the early disciples was in some sense a convert.[27]

---

from the second century and beyond. On the basic model, see Wilkins, *Following The Master*, Chapter 4, "Discipleship in the Greco-Roman World," 51–69, and Chapter 5, "Disciples in the World of Judaism," 80–97.

25. Seneca. *Epistles 1–65*, 27–28.

26. 91.

27. See McKnight, *Turning to Jesus*, 27–48. The genius of this book is its correlation of biblical studies with contemporary conversion stories to reveal common issues and patterns.

Being a disciple or apprentice in the kingdom school of Professor Jesus was a whole-life, highly-relational process of formation and imitation.[28] It's the way advanced education was done in that world, one mind shaping others, one life molding others, lecture and lab together in a seamless process of *hear* and *see* and *do*, of modeling and imitation with lots of questions thrown in. So when the New Testament speaks of "disciples of John" (Matt 9:14), "disciples of the Pharisees" (Matt 22:16), and "disciples of Moses" (John 9:28), it required no explanation since it was so common a process. Think of how easily we speak of someone *going off to college*.

The followers of Jesus, traveling with him and learning his ways, would have been seen as *the school of Jesus* in which he was both professor and curriculum, both teacher and text. There was teaching, but it was not the mastery of a system that most counted. Instead, they were to be mastered by him and *The New Reality*. What Jesus taught and did was not severable from who he was. The man was the message and the means and the meaning and the manner of its transmission. His life rubbed up against theirs like sandpaper against the grain, and at times it rubbed them raw with frustration.

Jesus' call was unavoidably personal. "Follow me," he said to Levi at the toll station (5:27c), as if he had every right to interrupt and redirect a life. It was a call to personal allegiance, to be glued to him in a bond of love and loyalty.[29] It was also high cost and high demand involving the disruption of family loyalties, of one's work, of one's time, of one's future, of one's worldview, of one's inherited religion. It was personal, but never private. Disciples followed Jesus and lived with one another from the start with him as their common center of reference. The miracles were unforgettable, as were the stings of his many corrections and rebukes. The genre of the *Disciple Correction Story* is one of Luke's favorites and has the following four parts: 1) A provocative word or action of Jesus, 2) A misunderstanding by the disciples, 3) Further corrective teaching by Jesus, 4) Resolution.[30]

Theirs was an invitation to a dangerous new life as a Jesus follower, one that generated controversy everywhere they went. It was a surrender to uncertainty, a change of life script, and involved a great deal of trust based on whatever evidence Jesus gave. And after he changed them, he changed the world through them and the disciples they made, and so the story continues.[31] The plain fact is that much of our Western culture, for all its resistance to all things Christian, cannot be understood

---

28. On the difference between how he did it and how we do it, see Appendix 4: "Contrasting Biblical Discipleship And Modern Church (Club) Membership." It's interesting to have two people read in alternating voices from the two columns and for the cumulative impact of the contrasts to make the case. Then ask, "What happened?"

29. On allegiance, see Bates, *Salvation by Allegiance Alone*.

30. The title *Disciple Correction Story* is not one found in the literature but one I coined to summarize a common pattern. I await correction!

31. For a contemporary analysis of the complex journey of discipleship, see Whitesel, *Spiritual Waypoints*, and his less technical *Waypoint: Navigating Your Spiritual Journey*.

apart from the values and institutions the church created and bequeathed as blessings to the world.[32]

At first they were all Jews, and theirs was a shared inheritance of Jewish scripture and its interpretation, the worship institutions of the temple and synagogue, the calendar of pilgrimage and holy times, a distinctive ethnic identity, an ethical and a holiness code, and a common—though varied—religious culture. Several Jewish renewal and political groups were vying for validity: Essenes for isolation and purity, Zealots for violent political revolution, Pharisees for priestly purity among the laity, Saducees for political realism and the preservation of the Jerusalem temple. And now there was added an upstart movement around Jesus the kingdom preacher and healer emerging at the margins as a new option and corrector of them all.

Everyone in that day was asking the same question, "Who are God's true people and how can we spot them?" but each with differing answers. Then Jesus dropped into the yeasty mix with his own new angle, in effect saying, "I am the true Jew, the new location of God's presence, the temple and the text in flesh, so follow me into *the new reality*!" How abrupt. How surprising! How singular and offensive!

All these Jesus assumed as background and foreground as he initiated a reconfiguration of Judaism around himself as his words and deeds gave new meaning to old titles like *Messiah*, *Son of Man*, and *Son of David*. He, without apology, is the new Judaism in person, and again the call is to "Follow me." In his company and by the illuminations of the Holy Spirit, his adherents learn a new world view and with it new possibilities for action. Jesus is a window into God's new world, already being previewed at ground level in his words and works.

As yourself: What it would mean, even with our habitual frailties and besetting sins, to see as Jesus sees and for our love to reflect his own, including a radical openness to the immediate wisdom and gifts of the Holy Spirit? With his vision we would see every person as an image bearer, every person loved by God, every person bound by sin and open to the intrusions of evil, every person with painful memories—and some of them horrific and traumatic, every person subject to deception, every person worth dying for, every person a potential follower, every person needing Jesus and what he alone offers. What an intoxicating, counter-cultural way to see the world and to live in it, and how disturbing to what passes for polite normalcy in the churches.

And this is precisely the effect Jesus has on his followers. In his company they see and live differently, and if they don't, it's someone else they're following!

Throughout Luke's gospel there is an alternation between Christology (the emerging identity of Jesus), and the profile of discipleship (what it means to follow him together as a team, an interdependent body). Who he is and who we become

---

32. For an accounting of this history and its effects, see Dickerson, *Jesus Skeptic* and Carol and Shiflett, *Christianity on Trial*. For a sweeping historical treatment, see Holland, *Dominion*. For a catalog of seven dangerous Christian ideas that are still shaping our world, see Samples, *7 Truths That Changed the World*.

under his influence are reciprocal, and the most basic goal is to not stop following but to spiral deeper and deeper into the love and wisdom he embodies and freely offers.

According to the consensus of early church teaching, Jesus is the visible member of the Triune God, the Son of the Father, the Agent of the Holy Spirit, and thus inexhaustible.[33] Discipleship is forever. He leads us back to the Father and fills us with his Spirit. Discipleship is life within the circle of love and light that is the Holy Trinity, and it's forever. And it begins now, with a bit of curiosity moving towards trust and surrender to Jesus. And since Luke has taken such exquisite care to tell the story of the man and his friends so expertly, it deserves our close attention and best efforts. So join me!

33. See Sanders and Issler, *Jesus in Trinitarian Perspective,* Chapter 1 by Sanders, "Chalcedonian Categories for the Gospel Narrative," 1–43.

4

Mapping the Shape of the Text

An Essay on Identifying Thought Units in Luke's Gospel: Rhetoric, Chiasm, Inclusions, Links, Genre

RHETORIC WAS THE DOMINANT communications discipline of the ancient Greco-Roman world[1] (300 BC to 200 AD) and is understood as the *art of persuasion*,[2] primarily in oral discourse, and—by extension—into written texts read by trained lectors to audiences[3] where the written text is most often a substitute for the author's presence—as in Paul's letters. This was the world in which the author of the Third Gospel was intellectually shaped and rhetorically formed. Augustine Stock offers a summary:

> "From the beginning of the Empire, rhetoric prevailed over all other genre and invaded all the other fields: grammar, drama, history, and philosophy. All ancient writing was meant to be read aloud, which brought it about that the rules of oratorical discourse invaded the world of texts."[4]

1. On rhetorical education in the Greek and Latin traditions, see Stock, "Chiastic Awareness," 23–27); Bonner, *Education in Ancient Rome*; Parsons and Martin, *Ancient Rhetoric*, 1–16; Mack, *Rhetoric and the New Testament*.

2. Witherington, "Sacred Texts in an Oral Culture."

3. For a breakthrough work on texts and public reading in the ancient world, see Wright, *Communal Reading*. For an interview, see Lindgren, "Reading Together, Early Church Style." On the recovery of communal reading, see Wright's "Don't Just Read Alone." And on the new discipline of *Performance Criticism* (how the text sounds when performed before an audience), see the fifteen volumes of the Wipf & Stock monograph series, *Biblical Performance Criticism*. For additional background, see Harvey, *Listen to the Text*, Chapter 2, "Orality and Literacy in the First Century," 35–59.

4. Stock, "Chiastic Awareness," 26.

Werner Kelber confirms this assessment:

> "No one could not move ahead in the world, get a job and earn a living, without intricate knowledge of speech, of modes of argumentation, of the inducement of emotional states in hearers, of the retention of words and images in memory, and, above all, of mental compositioning and oral performance. If you wanted to embark upon a career as a politician, a civil servant, a lawyer, a writer, a physician, a philosopher, a priest, an academician, etc., you had to have a basic training in rhetoric"[5]

The purpose of this essay is to introduce preachers and teachers to several of the tools and patterns of rhetorical presentation that Luke employed as he constructed his life of Jesus, the founder of a new *Kingdom of God* movement. If Luke is a layered series of thought units[6] in a variety of clusters and larger arrangements, then understanding the *flow of thought*[7] within each thought unit and between them will—in effect—map Luke's presentation for the careful reader and thus aid in interpretation and in the re-presentation of teaching and preaching the whole of Luke's portrait.

A Word About Luke's Gospel

In a sense which distinguishes him from other revered ancient figures, the one about whom Luke writes is not merely as a noble figure of the past but is the risen Jesus, now ruling over his people and eventually ushering in the fullness of God's kingdom at the end of the age. Thus, what was read *about him* was also read *in his presence* with the intention of mediating an encounter through the Holy Spirit. Scripture understood in this way is sacramental, a means of grace and lifeline whereby the Jesus who was *then and there* becomes *here and now* to those who listen in faith and respond in trust and obedience.[8]

Thus the Gospel of Luke is an introduction to the person, words and works of the one who was then and is now *messin'* with his people according to a very particular script. From the beginning he glues men and women to himself through a call to discipleship[9] and then begins the long work of transforming the way they see him, themselves, the world, and the future. In him they have a window into a new world right in the midst of the old regime.

---

5. Powell, "Redaction Criticism," 3.

6. I define a thought unit" (other terms for which are *paragraph* or *pericope*) as the smallest unit of discourse that has two characteristics: 1) clear boundaries (verbal frames or inclusions) at the beginning and end, and 2) a definable internal structure (typically concentric).

7. Also from Talbert and now included as a heading in the commentaries of the *Paideia Commentaries on the New Testament* as *Narrative Flow*. The skillful sequencing of thought units with one another creates a story with forward movement, thus the image of *river* and *flow*.

8. Talbert, "The Bible as Spiritual Friend," 55–64.

9. Dunn, *Jesus' Call to Discipleship*.

They live with the one who knows and loves God completely and people fully, even as he is fully aware of all their sins, prejudices, petty jockeying for honor, hatreds, demons, and compromises. This is who he came to save and all he has to work with! Jesus is very impressive; they not so much. And they are us.

Every paragraph in Luke is about Jesus and his various interactions, but also—a bit more indirectly—about what it means to be his follower. When Luke, and the other three gospels as well, are embedded in the mind and imagination through repeated exposure and fresh reception, they give an internal radar to spot and track the present workings of the risen Lord through the Holy Spirit given to us.[10] It is an ancient text about a living, interactive Savior, not a dead hero. Luke is the template for following one who is now invisible but very much present and active. It's an adventure story we do together.

Knowing Luke's portrait of Jesus' deeds and words allows us to welcome interactions that match his picture and resist those that do not. He thus serves as a boundary as to what is *in* and what is *out* in terms of Christian belief, piety, and practice.

There is continuity of character and action between the Jesus of history and the risen Lord since they are the same person in two complementary human modes: 1) embodied at ground level as one of us—the divine incarnation, and 2) re-embodied after death in a prototype resurrection body in heaven—the divine vindication. His incarnation continues in a resurrection body.

The one who was among us is now over us and stands at history's end. In hearing Luke read unit by unit and thus building up a portrait of Jesus layer by layer, the early hearers were—a bit at a time—invited by the church into Jesus' new reality, the present and future kingdom of God's rule that sets life right again.

Luke's biography of Jesus, once copied beyond the original (like Mark before him which Luke used as a primary source[11]), could be transported and read to new audiences by those who were trained to analyze and orally interpret the *scriptio continuo* in which the scrolls, and later codices, were written.

Scriptio continua is a series of Greek majuscles (capital letters) written margin to margin on papyrus without spaces between the words or any punctuation, capitalization, indentions, or quotation marks. Luke's first line, while in Greek, looked something like this:

"INASMUCHASMANYHAVEUNDERTAKENTOCOMPILEANARRA-
TIVEOFTHETHINGSWHICHHAVEBEENACCOMPLISHEDAMONGUS."

Therefore, one of the tasks of a rhetorical student was to break down the text, separate the words, determine punctuation, distinguish the phrases and sentences, locate questions and quotations, form the text into lines to be scanned according to the conventions of prosody and meter. The text was essentially chewed and absorbed

---

10. On this model, see Burridge, *Four Gospels, One Jesus.*

11. On Markan priority, see Porter and Dyer, *The Synoptic Problem,* 28–35.

in great detail. The one who read Luke in a gathering would necessarily have acquired all such skills in order to sight-read the text and in the process of public performance offer an oral interpretation through changes of tone, pauses, changes of voice, and occasional interpretive comments. It is for this reason that the lector later became a minor order in the church as a necessary skill for worship. A good modern analogy for the skills of an ancient lector is that of a master pianist sight-reading and playing a score for the first time, to the amazement of all.

It was, to use a generalization, an oral culture supported by written texts and not—like ours—a text culture supported by occasional oral performances.[12] Texts were written to be heard by the ear as a living word, and so the best way to approach a Gospel is to read it aloud to a group and note how different the dynamics are from reading silently in private. Hearing a Gospel read was a primary form of evangelism. It's still good to read the primary documents out loud before people!

Literacy rates—the ability to read and write in one or more languages—in the first century are estimated at between five and twenty percent depending on the culture and sub-culture in which one resided,[13] but that does not mean unlettered audiences could not understand and appreciate the beauty and forms of public rhetoric, as Jesus himself said, "He who has ears to hear, let him hear," not, "She who is literate and has special training, let her read aloud in private."

You do not have to be a trained art historian to enjoy a gallery. Learned commentary is helpful, but it never replaces primary engagement with the thing itself. Analysis may deepen appreciation, but they are not the same thing. Primary engagement precedes secondary reflection, and so it was with the Jesus and later with the outline of his person that Luke creates.[14] We are only beginning to understand the *book culture* of the ancient world and how widespread and popular the public performance of written texts actually was.[15]

While a literate Jesus on occasion read from Old Testament texts in synagogue worship,[16] and more often quoted such texts from memory before audiences, most of his communication was in oral discourse without access to a sacred scroll. It was

---

12. See Witherington, *New Testament Rhetoric*, Chapter 1, "The Oral Cultures of the Ancient World," 1–9; also his *What's In The Word*, Chapter 1, "Oral Examination," 7–18.

13. Witherington, "Sacred Texts," 5.

14. On Luke and elite literacy, see Kuhn, *The Kingdom according to Luke*, Chapter 3, "Luke's Place in Caesar's Kingdom," 55–70.

15. Wright, *Communal Reading*.

16. See Luke 4:16–30, especially vv.16b–17, "And he stood up to read; and there was given to him the book (scroll) of the prophet Isaiah. He opened the book and found the place where it was written . . . ." Thus posture, liturgical propriety, the proper handling of scrolls, and public reading in Hebrew (and perhaps a Targum [paraphrase] in Aramaic) were among his skills. And if the Book of James is assigned to Jesus' younger brother, then the skill James demonstrates in his rhetorical forms raises questions, "Was Jesus also tri-lingual (Aramaic, Hebrew, Greek)? And did he also have the same rhetorical training as James?" My guess is Yes. Perhaps Nazareth was not as rustic and backwoods as some claim; it was only four miles from Sepphoris.

delivered to smaller (male and female disciples) and larger groups (public proclamation) inside homes or outside utilizing his skills as a wit, storyteller, close observer, poet, invoker of proverbs, prophet, debater and controversialist, healer, exorcist, rabbi, and traveling phenomena. Mark notes, "And the great throng heard him gladly."[17] The sacred scrolls were in the synagogue and temple, but at a practical level you knew only what you'd memorized and could either quote, paraphrase, or summarize, and Jesus regularly did all three.

Now when the traditions about Jesus were collected and ordered into a written biography (Gk. *bios*/ life), the authors used the rhetorical conventions that were so much a part of their world.[18] Recovering those conventions and how they aided persuasion is part of the methods of Rhetorical[19] and Narrative Criticism,[20] with the first being the foundation for the second. When we understand the forms and how the thought units are linked together in small and larger clusters, we have the basis for asking, "Why did Luke do it in this way, and what is he saying about Jesus?" Knowing the parts helps us appreciate the story.

There are two approaches to introducing students to the new rhetorical approach, one playful, the other more academic, and we now turn to the first.

Teaching Ancient Rhetoric with a Nursery Rhyme[21]

HICKORY DICKORY DOCK

> Hickory dickory dock,
> The mouse ran up the clock.
> The clock struck one,
> The mouse ran down,
> Hickory dickory dock.

Hickory Dickory Dock is an English nursery rhyme. It was first recorded as *Hickere, Dickere Dock* by Tommy Thumb in his *Pretty Song Book* collection (London, 1744). Another version was later published in *Mother Goose's Melody* (1765) and titled *Dickery Dock*. There are two tunes for the song, one sung in the UK, one in the USA.

---

17. 12:37.

18. For an outline of the process, see Powell, *Fortress Introduction To The Gospels*, Chapter 1, "From Jesus to Us," 15–56; Bird, *The Gospel of the Lord*, Chapter 1, "Introduction: From Jesus to the Gospels," 1–20. For an exhaustive treatment, see Keener, *Christobiography*.

19. Witherington, *New Testament Rhetoric*, Chapter 3, "Gospels of Persuasion: Mark and Luke," 23–43.

20. For introductions, see Powell, *What Is Narrative Criticism?* and Resseguie, *Narrative Criticism*.

21. I was first alerted to the concentric structure of this nursery rhyme by Reid, *Preaching Mark*, x.

At its origin, *Hickory Dickory Dock* was probably a counting-down song starting with a couple of sounds that imitate clock sounds, *Hickory, dickory, dock.* The words *hickory, dickory and dock* come from an old Celtic language spoken in the British Isles, and they mean *eight, nine* and *ten.* Shepherds used to count their sheep using these words even when they already spoke English. The fourth line has several other versions (textual variants): "down the mouse run," "and down he run," "and down the mouse ran."[22]

So now, as with the New Testament, we have a canonical text, a bit of history, speculation on original language and meaning, and several textual variants. The base genre is poetry, and the sub-genre a children's nursery rhyme from 18th century Britain. It was meant to be sung, so the term *lyrics* is apt. There is also a longer multi-stanza version, but for our purposes Stanza 1 of the standard text is sufficient:

1. Hickory, dickory, dock.

2. The mouse ran up the clock.

3. The clock struck one,

4. The mouse ran down,

5. Hickory, dickory, dock.

The first thing we notice is that lines 1 and 5 are identical, "Hickory, dickory, dock," thus providing a Verbal Frame or Inclusion[23] to mark the beginning and ending of the stanza. The second is that the lines two and four concern the upward and downward motions of the mouse on a clock. It is in line three at the center that we learn that the clock sounds the hour, and since the mouse is seen, it's likely one o'clock in the afternoon, not one o'clock at night, unless of course you're up late with candle in hand like Wee Willie Winkie.

Now if we indent to show how the outer frames (lines one and five are identical and that the inner frames have the same topics of *mouse, clock,* and the opposing directions of *up* and *down* (lines two and four), this leaves line three at the center as follows:

---

22. Compiled from a Google Search on *Hickory, Dickory, Dock.*

23. An Inclusion (Gk. *Inclusio*) is a literary technique that "Uses repetition to mark the beginning and end of a section, framing or bracketing an episode it contains" (Crain, *Reading The Bible*, 161). In an oral presentation an Inclusion alerts the ear of the auditor to a new paragraph or section within the larger discourse. What indentions, paragraphing, and headings do for the eye of a reader considering a modern page of text, Inclusions or Verbal Brackets do for the ear of a listener in an oral culture where clues are auditory for the ear and not graphic for the eye. On its usage in the New Testament, see Resseguie, *Narrative Criticism*, 58. On the Old Testament usage of boundary markers, see Dorsey, *The Literary Structure of the Old Testament*, Chapter 2, "Literary Units," 21–25.

Numbered for linear sequence	Numbered for concentric parallels
1. Hickory, dickory, dock,	1. Three nonsense words
2. The mouse ran up the clock.	2. mouse up
3. The clock struck one,	3. clock sounds one
4. The mouse ran down,	2' mouse down
5. Hickory, dickory, dock.	1' Three nonsense words

This literary pattern of a center (3) bracketed by frames (2//2', 1//1')[24] is known as a *Chiasm* (Greek *Chiasmus* from the Greek letter Chi/*X*, pronounced ky-AZM), other names for which are *Inverted Parallelism, Ring Structure, Concentric Composition.*[25] A Chiasm is defined as "a stylistic literary figure which consists of a series of two or more elements followed by a presentation of corresponding elements in reverse order."[26]

a b
  X
b' a'

The designation (a-b // b'-a') is read,
"Parts a and b are parallel to parts b prime and a prime."
The following models illustrate some of the possibilities in a chiastic/concentric form. The simplest form is three parts with a single center. And the pattern of a single or doubled centers can be greatly expanded:

- 4 Parts, 2 Centers

  4:2 Chiasm

  a.
     b.
     b'
  a'

- 3 Parts, 1 Center

  3:1 Chiasm

  a.

---

24. When the *prime* mark is added to a number, 1 ➜ 1', it is read as *one prime* and indicates that the two elements stand in parallel to each other as a pair. Thus, in a 6:2 pattern (six parts with a double center), parts 1–2–3 stand in reverse parallel to parts 3'-2'-1' (1–2–3 // 3'-2'-1'). The double slanted lines (//) are read "is parallel to."

25. Other less-used descriptions are *circular construction, the pedimental mode, mirror image, envelope construction, recursion, correspondence* (Gk. *epanodos*). For a survey, see Welch, *Chiasmus in Antiquity,* 9–16.

26. Bailey and Vander Broek, *Literary Forms,* 49.

      b.

a

- 6 Parts, 2 Centers

  6:2 Chiasm

  a.

     b.

        c.

        c'

     b'

  a'

- 5 Parts, 1 Center

  5:1 Chiasm

  a.

     b.

        c.

     b'

  a'

The classic form of a chiasm has two ideas presented and then re-presented in reverse order, thus four parts and a double center (with letters [a-b //b'-a'] as in the above diagram, or with numbers [1–2//2'-1']). When there are more than four elements, or an odd number of lines, as in the five lines of the nursery rhyme "Hickory, Dickory, Dock" (1–2–3–2'-1'), some scholars term it an *inverted parallel*, while others continue to use *chiasm*.[27]

The most concise description is that a chiasm involves "the use of bilateral symmetry about a central axis."[28] Another in a standard reference work is, "A Semitic poetic form, sometimes also used in prose arrangements, that juxtaposes, reverses, or contrasts words, dialogs, episodes, scenes, and events."[29] It is found in early Greek and Latin literature, in the thought and speech patterns of Semitic culture, and is widespread in the Old Testament.[30]

In such a figure a series of items leads up to the center; the ideas are then presented in reverse order with variation so that the corresponding pairs of lines echo one another from the center to the frames and from the frames to the center.[31] In

27. There is as yet no standard technical terminology, so expect variety in the literature.

28. Norman, *Samuel Butler and the Meaning of Chiasmus*, 276.

29. Crain, *Reading The Bible*: 155.

30. Mann, "Chiasm in the New Testament," 6.

31. On the modern history of the recovery of chiasm as a tool for mapping the text, see Breck, *The Shape of Biblical Language*, Chapter 2, "Rediscovering Chiastic Patterns," 15–20; Bailey, *Poet and Peasant*, 45–47; Mann, *Chiasm*: 7–13; Porter and Reed, "Philippians As A Macro-Chiasm," 213–21.

such an arrangement the focus is on the center as a pivot or turning point, and it may consist of a single part, as here (a 5:1 chiasm, 1–2–3–2'–1'), or a double (a 6:2 chiasm, 1–2–3–3'–2'–1'). The outermost frames (1//1') with their common terms, ideas, and forms mark the beginning and ending of the unit as Inclusions or Verbal Brackets.

In beginning the analysis of a longer text such as Luke, the primary work is to identify the individual thought units through their inclusions and internal structures. This gives boundaries and an internal map for each thought unit in sequence. The second task is to ask, "What are the rhetorical links between the units, and how are they arranged into larger literary and thematic groupings: Clusters, Essays, Parts.[32]

Since our nursery rhyme has five lines with a single center and two sets of frames, we refer to this as a 5:1 Chiasm with the first number (5) indicating the number of lines and the second number (1) indicating a single center or pivot. The single focus is at the center with the sound of the clock striking one in an otherwise silent setting. In lines 2//4 we have repetition with variation on the ascent and decent of the mouse, and in lines 1//5 an exact echo so we end where we began but with something new and humorous in the middle three lines. It's all very memorable, but this is what nursery rhymes are all about and why they are such a delight. So, with this as the structural analysis, let's examine each line. It makes every child a rhetorician!

The first two words, "hickory, dickory," rhyme and have three syllables, while the second and third, "dickory, dock" begin with the same letter, thus alliteration. And, after a pair of three-syllable words, the single syllable *dock* is abrupt and brings us to a quick stop. It's not *Hick-o-ry, Dick-o-ry, Dock-e-ry* but *Hick-o-ry, Dick-e-ry, Dock!* It's a nonsense line, deliberately so, and models four rhetorical tools: 1) rhyme, 2) alliteration, 3) a series of three, and 4) a climax.

It is with line two that the tale begins, "The mouse ran up the clock," with *clock* rhyming with *dock* to bind lines 1 and 2 together. Line 4 is then its mirror in the other direction, "The mouse ran down," only this time with "the clock" omitted: an ellipsis for the sake of poetic economy. So what caused the sudden reversal? It's found at the center where the great *bong* of the chime startles the poor little rodent, "The clock struck one."

What we have before us is a humorous sight giving birth to a memorable rhyme. It's also a 5:1 chiasm with inclusions in the outer set of frames and echoes in the inner frames. It offers the rhetorical techniques of rhyme, alliteration, a series of three, climactic centrality, repetition with variation, ellipsis, reversal, and surprise, all of which we will meet again as we attempt a close rhetorical reading of the Gospel of Luke. The content of Luke is singular in its religious claims, but the rhetorical and dramatic tools

---

32. On the links between thought units, see Dorsey, *The Literary Structure of the Old Testament*, "Techniques for Creating Internal Cohesion," 23, "Techniques for Linking Units," 32–33. On chain links in Luke and Acts, see Longenecker, Rhetoric at the Boundaries; also Mealand, "The Seams and Summaries," 382–502.

he employs were the common inheritance of his culture, and by studying texts from in and outside the New Testament we learn their forms and functions.

Other Modern Examples

Remember the words of John Kennedy? "Ask not what your country can do for you, but what you can do for your country."[33] What makes them memorable? Is it the dashing leader dreaming of an American Camelot? Yes. Is it the call for a return to civic responsibility? Yes. But what about the form of the words? If we diagram Kennedy's words to reveal repetitions, we find a center (d) and a series of concentric frames (c//c', b//b', a//a'), each with paired words, thus a 7:1 chiasm: seven parts in three frames with a single center:

"Ask not what your *country* a. country

    can do   b. can do

        for *you*,   c. you

        BUT

        what *you*   c' you

    can do   b' can do

for your *country*."[34] a' country

Chiasm is a sophisticated form of parallelism[35] and often used for contrast and antithesis, as here. In his couplet, President Kennedy invites a shift from *me to we* and to *us* from *I*. Chiasm is also aesthetically pleasing to the ear in the manner in which the alternating form reinforces and strengthens the content. It seduces the ear and fixes itself easily in the memory. Once you know the first half of the quote, you easily lay out the second half in reserve order.

In the oral/rhetorical culture of the ancient world, a time where texts were often committed to preservation through memory, the concentric patterning and inherent repetition of chiasm is an aid to memorization. And while concentric parallelism arose in ancient Semitic culture and was developed later in Greco-Roman oratory and literature—and thus in the New Testament as a document of the time—it has

---

33. President John F. Kennedy's Inaugural Address, January 20, 1961.

34. The layered use of indentation, bolding, underlining, italics, capitalization, and lines of relationship (my term) in parallel frames makes the inclusions (a//a'), the echoes (b//b', c//c'), and the centers (d) easier to see. The single word "But" at the center (d) indicates that a contrast follows.

35. The options for the parallelism of two lines are 1) *synonymous*: the second line rephrases the first, 2) *antithetical*: the second line opposes the first, 3) *synthetic*: the second line extends the meaning of the first with new material. In a paragraph or thought unit, three sets of two parallel lines would be diagramed as a//a', b//b', c//c'. If in an alternating step pattern they would be diagramed as a-b-c // a'-b'-c'; if in a concentric form, a-b-c //c'-b'-a' (summarized from Bailey, *Poet & Peasant*, 47–50.

continued to be used in all kinds of subsequent literature, both deliberately by design and unwittingly by reflex and imitation of cultural patterns.

Examples from *Yelland's Handbook of Literary Terms* include Alexander Pope, "A wit with dunces, and a dunce with wits," and Samuel T. Coleridge, "Flowers are lovely, and love is flowerlike."[36] Both are 4:2 chiasms (wit, dunces // dunce, wits; flowers, lovely // love, flowerlike). Once noticed, it's like buying a Volvo; you begin to see them everywhere.

While listening to country music, the chorus of a Clay Walker song caught my attention because of its overall 4:2 concentric structure and a secondary 4:2 chiasm buried in the b' component (doin', love // lovin', do):

    a. "If I could make a livin' out of lovin' you
        b.   I'd be a millionaire in a week or two
        b'1   I'd be doin'
            2   what I love
            2'   and lovin'
        1'   what I do
    a' If I could make a livin' out of lovin' you."

The frames (a//a') are identical and serve as inclusions/frames to open and close the chorus, while the two central components (b//b') offer a riff on conventional riches and the riches of love. Words beginning with *L* and their abbreviations (*living. . . lovin' . . . love . . . lovin' . . . livin' . . . lovin'*) serve as *catchwords*[37] to give a unifying *alliteration*[38] to the catchy chorus.

The reason the rhetorical technique and patterns of chiasm have endured for so long across cultures is that it simply works with some of our most basic human linguistic structures. It is aesthetic, sticky, memorable, and easily replicated. And whether ancient or modern, it has an effect on hearers long before there is any consciousness of its literary form or technical usage.[39]

Turning To The Scriptures

The primary characteristics of the concentric literary form or chiasm are three:

36. Welch, *Chiasm in Antiquity*, 9.

37. A *catch word* or *link word* is a word or phrase repeated multiple times in a thought unit to sound a theme and give cohesion to the unit.

38. *Alliteration* is the deliberate stringing together of words that begin with the same sound in a series.

39. Talbert writes, "Though most today [and then] are not thus culturally attuned to chiastic structures, yet they probably do instinctively respond to expressions of symmetry and balance—such expression somehow 'seems right'" ("Artistry and Theology," 341–66). It was the way writing was done for hearers in the ancient world; it was common and assumed.

1. balance,

2. inversion, and

3. climactic centrality.[40]

The halves and pairs can be balanced in a *complementary* way (presenting the same idea), an *antithetical* way (presenting oppositions), or in a *supplemental* way (advancing an argument to the next step).

And while there is an ornamental or stylistic flourish to the concentric form, it remains a key to meaning because of the way the form displays ideas in pairs to be read in terms of each other. Angelico di Marco has defended the conviction that form and content together:

> Chiasm is no mere artistic flourish, but rather a key to meaning because the parts elucidate each other [and] are complementary to one another . . . The architecture of a section is naturally bound up with its meaning, namely, through the correspondence of the individual parts: every element is the complement of its corresponding element; the form is closely tied to the meaning.[41]

A *complementary* New Testament example is Matthew 7:6[42] where the two central elements (b//b') deal with pigs which trample, while the two framing components (a//a') deal with wild, Mediterranean dogs which travel in packs and tear their prey:

a. "Give not what is holy to dogs	dogs
b. nor throw your pearls before swine,	swine
b' lest they trample them under their feet	swine trample
a' and turning, tear you to pieces."	dogs tear

If the 4:2 chiasm of Matt 7:6 is understood, then one action is attributed to each animal: 1) dogs tear (a//a'), and 2) swine trample (b//b'). If the chiasm is not noted, then in a conventional linear reading the same two destructive actions are attributed to each animal: 1) dogs trampling and tearing, and 2) swine trampling and tearing, which in this combination is contrary to fact. The translators of Today's English Version made allowance for this in their translation, "Do not give what is holy to dogs—they will only turn and attack you; do not throw your pearls in front of pigs—they will only trample them underfoot."[43]

Thus, at the micro level of a single aphorism, an appreciation of the concentric inversion in Matthew 7:6 yields two insights: 1) If possible, evaluate the character

---

40. The apt summary of Augustine Stock, "Chiastic Awareness," 23.

41. "Der Chiasm in der Bibel," 55–56.

42. Other Synoptic aphorisms which share the 4:2 (a-b//b'-a') pattern are Mark 10:31, Matt 20:16, Luke 13:22, 30, Mark 2:27. Matt 10:29 is a 6:2 Chiasm.

43. Mann, "Chiasm," 2.

and tastes of your hearers before you decide to offer them your best, 2) Do not be surprised at negative surprises when you preach and teach Jesus and his message.

Any unlettered Jewish peasant, not a rabbi or scribe, upon hearing these words of Jesus, would understand both the content and the form since they were common and assumed. It's the form in which many proverbs were shaped. They lived in an oral culture where their ears were trained to make such distinctions. But when a modern print-oriented Westerner reads these words, we wonder if the hogs and hounds form a pack together. Unless we understand the form and function of a simple four-part chiasm, we miss the content and perhaps dismiss the author as misguided in his understanding of animal behavior.

An example of the *antithetical* form of a simple 4:2 chiasm is Mark 2:27:

a. "The sabbath was made
  b. for man,
  b' and not man
a' for the sabbath."

The idea of sabbath as God's gift is strengthened in its impact by being stated first in the positive form (a-b) and then reversed in the negative (b'-a'). The sabbath is a gift of grace for human welfare, not a religious burden for the sake of duty.

An example of the *supplemental* form in a simple 4:2 chiasm is Matthew 4:10:

a. "You shall worship
  b. the Lord your God
  b' and him only
a' shall you serve."

Here "worship"(a) and "serve" (a') are both positives, with the second building on the first and the center providing the object of worship (b. "the Lord your God) with an intensification (b' "and him only"). Because of the form, a lot of theology is able to be packed into a small unit. The vertical element of liturgy (worship) and horizontal element of life (service) are held together in an exclusive loyalty to the one God who cares both about the love we offer him and one another.

But chiasm can be much more complex than the simple inversion of 4 parts (a-b//b'-a'). As the structure expands, the number of elements (depending on the oral and/or literary skill of the author), the abrupt repetition by which the last elements of the first half of the presentation become the first elements of the second half can draw unusual attention to the central terms, which are repeated in close proximity to one another. This leads to a third critical element in addition to balance and inversion, and that is climactic centrality.

Whether with a single (a-b-c-b'-a') or a double center (a-b-c//c'-b'-a'), a focus is established. A skillful author presents the critical idea at the core and frames it with supporting materials in a series of matching frames. At the center is an insight, a surprise, a reversal, or a shift of perspective with the layers of frames building to the center and then away from it in reverse order. The classic example of Luke's artistry is 4:16b–20 (a 13:1 chiasm: thirteen parts with a single center):

a. v.16b *the synagogue*

    b. v.16c *stood up*

        c. v.17a *given to him*

            d. v.17b *opened the scroll*

                e. v.18a *the Spirit of the Lord*

                    f. v.18b *to preach*

                        g. v.18c *sent me . . . release*

                          h. v.18d *recovery of sight to the blind*

                        g' v.18e *send forth . . . in release*

                    f' v.19a *to proclaim*

                e' v.19b *the acceptable year of the Lord*

            d' v.20a *closes the scroll*

        c' v.20b *gave it back*

    b' v.20c *sat down*

a' v.20d *the synagogue*

The same patterns are apparent in Psalm 3:6–8:

a. I do not fear the arrows of *people* who have set themselves against me round about.

    b. Arise, *O YHWH, Save* me, O my God!

        c. *May you smite*

            d. All my enemies

                e. On the *cheekbone!*

                e' The *teeth*

            d' Of the wicked

        c' *May you break!*

    b' *O YHWH, Salvation*

a' Upon your *people* is your blessing. Selah.[44]

I have placed the word *people* in bold to illustrate an abiding characteristic of concentric patterning: inclusion. In a written culture we have visual conventions that divide up written material for us: headings, titles, paragraphing, chapter and sectional titles. Not so in an oral culture which must give clues to the ear as to breaks in thought

44. *Psalms*, 3 volumes. Garden City: Doubleday, 1966.

and the beginning and end of compositions. Thus key terms, ideas, phrases, or sequences are often presented at the beginning and end of a unit to indicate its literary boundaries.[45] What we see on a page and intuitively interpret, they heard with the ear and did the same.

We moderns expect thoughts to unfold in a linear, sequential fashion without redundancy towards a conclusion at the end, not in a circular fashion which values creative redundancy with the focus at the center. Our jokes have punch lines at the end, but in the ancient world theirs were often in the middle. An end focus is not the only way to bring about emphasis. And while the end focus was used on occasion in the ancient world, the center focus was much more common, and sometimes the two are found together.

The basic contrast here is between *linearity* (one thing after another in a straight line towards a conclusion or climax) and *circularity* (building to a center and then reviewing the topics in reverse order).

In eighth grade English and in preparation for my first term paper, we were given a basic outline of acceptable formal composition, and it included the following parts in sequence:

1. A thesis statement of what we sought to illustrate or prove, followed by

2. a series of developmental paragraphs that built the case with evidences and arguments from us and others that would first be arranged on note cards for easy reference and accurate footnoting of sources, concluding with

3. a summary of the case along with any scintillating insights illumined along the way with penalties from the teacher being assessed for the flagrant sins of grammatical and punctuation errors, bad structure, unnecessary redundancy, sloppy typos, and insufficient attestation (plagiarism) which amounts to intellectual theft, a grave flaw in a culture of individual intellectual property.

It was condensed linear writing to efficiently read, one part leading to the next in a straight line with summary or rehearsal allowed only in the conclusion. The logic, though informal, was mainly syllogistic involving premises, evidences, and rational conclusions. Even when dealing with a story, this was the mold into which the analysis was to be poured.

And when trained in this manner of lean and linear style, we assume it as the norm and—unless someone teaches us another rhetoric—tend to read the Scripture through the same set of suppositions, wondering why there is so much repetition of ideas and end up placing the emphasis wrongly at the end of a passage instead of at the center(s).[46] Much can still be gained from such a misreading, but how much more

45. On Inclusion understood as the beginning and ending markers of thought units, see Dorsey, *The Literary Structure*, 21–23.

46. For an essay on the history of this transformation from orality to literacy and from performance to print, see Kelber, "Western Culture as Communications History," rice.edu/ presentat/kelberpres.

when the rhetorical practices of the author are brought to bear that we might map the text and more easily follow the flow of the author's thought according to the patterning of ancient rhetorical models.

One way to quickly grasp the difference between a narrative with a linear plot which is read as a series of episodes building to a climactic point and followed by a brief denouement or resolution and a story with a chiastic plot line using a symmetrical order on either side of a central hinge is to plot them visually:[47]

1. Linear Plot: Conclusion Near End (F), Followed By Resolution (G)

2. Chiastic Plot: Climax At Center, Followed By Repetition With Variation.

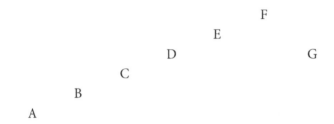

Now if No. 2 above is not read on its own terms but on the linear assumptions of No. 1, it will be misconstrued, at least in part. But when read on its own terms in light of ancient conventions, new depths are made available because we rightly construe the literary patterning and note the center and the multiple parallels between the parts.

However, at the risk of a new elitism, remember that when the Bible is read in worship over time, and in personal meditation as well, the Holy Spirit has the creativity to speak and guide the believer, whatever their literary skills or lack thereof. We aim not at a new Gnosticism of elite readers but at a fuller appreciation of the culture in which the texts were formed and preserved for us all.[48]

But how different is our modern print-oriented, linear model when compared with the world view and rhetorical conventions of the ancient world in which the New Testament is embedded. Far fewer were literate in reading and writing. Writing

47. Wilson, *Divine Symmetries*, 49–50.

48. On the authority of Scripture, see Wright, *The Last Word*. On the relationship of Scripture to a larger ecology of the means to grace God has given the church, see Gavriluk, "Scripture and the *Regula Fidei*," 27–42.

materials and scribal skills were expensive to obtain. There was no quick way to duplicate a text before the revolution of moveable type, and the trained expectations of listeners, whether formally literate or not, were very different. They had learned to listen for such patterns, and it was expected.

So whether in the synagogue with a trained reader or in the forum with a trained philosopher, they were not all reading the same manuscript but listening to the same discourse so that cues were given to the ear, not to the eye.

And while one-thing-after-another in a linear sequence is the pattern of letters forming words in a modern document, where there is creative repetition and a circling over common themes, the effect upon the ear and the intuition and—ultimately— upon understanding, is not that of a straight line but that of a spiral moving down to the center of an idea and then back up again in reverse for forward progress. Burton Mack summarizes the situation as:

> All people, whether formally trained or not, were fully schooled in the wily ways of sophists, the eloquence required at public festivals, the measured tones of the local teacher, and the heated debates where difference of opinion battled for the right to say what should be done. *To be engulfed in the culture of Hellenism means to have ears trained for the rhetoric of speech.*[49]

My thesis is simple. The way we print our Bibles inevitably leads us to misread them since the oral patterning of an ancient text is hidden in the transfer from the oral to the written mode. But then—to think of it—this issue is not much different from the Greek manuscripts written in *scriptio continua*, the critical difference in reception being that they were read publicly by lectors trained in rhetoric performing the text for audiences, most of whom could not read and write, which is not an intelligence issue but an issue of opportunity.

As a modern master pianist can sight read a score and play it well after an initial reading, so an ancient lector with a manuscript could re-present it with a high level of skill and engagement.[50] But when the texts were no longer read publicly by those trained in the same rhetorical understanding as the authors, something was lost.[51]

The material in the New Testament was created and preserved for public reading. And, with a little skill, it can be put back in a schematic form that helps us hear and not just read the material. As I often say to audiences, "I want you to see what they heard."

To print the New Testament in neat, justified columns, as we've done since Gutenberg, is a fine means to put as much readable print on a page as possible. But it

49. *Rhetoric,* 31, Italics added.

50. "According to Petronius, the person who could read such a book with such prior preparation was worthy of praise" (*Satyricon*, as found in Morrou, *Education,* 75).

51. Putting a date, or even a period, on this transition is difficult. It has to do with the loss of rhetorical training at the end of the Classical Era, and also with the addition of word spacing, punctuation, and paragraphing to biblical texts so they could be read by those with more rudimentary skills.

is to miss the immense sophistication and aesthetic beauty of the various rhetorical forms which are critical to reading and interpretation.

But, if I can put on a different set of lenses and map the text according to its own forms so that I now see what they heard, I have a much better chance of engaging the original intent of the author and of appreciating not only what they wrote but how. The content and the aesthetic style are both important.

When we read, the focus is on what comes at the end, the climax! But with biblical material, we learn to read another way, from the ends towards the center and from the center out to the circumference. It requires a change of sight and a change of mind. After fifty years of using and refining this method, I'm convinced it is a powerful tool for biblical interpretation, and especially for preaching.[52] Stated again, my thesis is:

If I can map the text,

I can follow the flow of the author's thought

and better translate their insights across time and into the present.

This is the purpose of the expository and theological preaching of God's Word.

Several New Testament Examples

One of the most impressive examples is John 1:1–18, the Prologue to his Gospel. Many of the themes found in the work are previewed in the Prologue as a kind of table of contents. What an Overture is to a symphony, John's Preface is to his Gospel.

You can easily locate the parallel sections within the prologue (1//1', 2//2') and even the concentric structures within sections (2a-b-a', 3a-b-a', 2'a-b'-a'). Everything revolves around the center (3. vv.11–13) which is John's fulcrum/focus. Note how the frames (1//1', 2//2') reinforce each other through a creative return to selected themes.

John 1:1–18

The Prologue of John's Gospel

1. vv.1–2 The Word with God in the Beginning

2. vv.3–10 The Word and All Creation

a. v.3–5 All Things Were Made Through Him: Light and Life

b. vv.6–8 John's Testimony fo the Word/Light's Primary

a' vv.9–10 World Made Through Him: Light and Life Rejected

3. v.11 The Word and His Own: Not Received

3' vv.12–13 The Word and His Own Received

2' vv.14–16 The Word and the Believing Church: Grace and Truth

52. It has been my practice during forty years to preach through books of Scripture with occasional exceptions for special series. I have refined the basic method of Rhetorical/Chiastic analysis I was taught by Dr. Charles Talbert, later modeled in his commentaries (John, 1–2 Corinthians, Matthew, Ephesians, and Colossians) and now in the *Paideia Commentary Series* by Baker Books. Each week involved the production of a "Scripture Sheet" and a sermon manuscript based on these principles. I have worked completely through all four Gospels, Acts, Romans, First Corinthians, James, the Johannine Epistles, Jude, and Revelation and find that "mapping the text" with this method applies to them all.

a. v.14 The Word Brings Grace and Truth

    b. v.15 John's Testimony to the Word's Pre-Existence and Primacy

a' vv.16–17 The Word Brings Grace and Truth

1' v.18 The Son with God and Made Known in Salvation History

So if the first section of the Prologue (1. vv.1–2) is this carefully arranged, what about its parallel at the end (1' v.18)? Might it not also receive a flourish as well?

Since John works with the ancient principle of knowledge that "like is known by like,"[53] and since Jesus is the incarnation of the *Logos* who was with God as God, he is the only adequate revealer. What vv.1–2 makes possible, v.18 makes actual, both sections working with the concept of a distinction of agents within an identity of deity.

God is self-revealing in an ultimate sense only in Jesus. The assertion of v.18a is modified by the revelation of v.18d. So, using the order of the Greek words, here is the 4:2 Chiasm of John 1:18:

a. v.18a   God no one has seen ever (at any time)!   a. Negation

   b. v.18b The only begotten God,   b. Identity

   b' v.18c the one who is in the bosom of the Father.   b' Distinction

a' v.18d   this one has made him known.   a' Affirmation

A second example is from a different type of literature, an ancient letter from Paul. Note the literary form (a chiasm), also Paul's Inclusions, his use of rhyme, and ridiculous humor:

First Corinthians 12:12–27

Understanding the Body of Christ

1. v.12 The Controlling Metaphor: Human Body (Many/One), So Christ

   2. vv.13–14 Entering the One Body by Baptism and Spirit, Diversity

      3. vv.15–21 Diversity and Mutuality in the One Body

      a. vv.15–16 Body Parts Speak: Issue of Inferiority

         b. vv.17–18 Two Absurd Questions: Loss of Diversity

         b' vv.19–20 Absurd Question Recast: Loss of the Whole

      a' v.21 Body Parts Speak: Issue of Superiority

   2' vv.22–25 Living in the Diverse Body: Honor and Care

1' vv.26–27 The Controlling Metaphor: Body, Christ, Members

Overall, this is a 5:1 Chiasm (1-2-3-2'-1') with Inclusions in the outer frames (*body, members, one, Christ* [v.12 // vv.26–27]) and Echoes in the inner frames (2. vv.13–14 Entering the body // 2' vv.22–25 Living in the body). In 3a. v.15–16 body parts speak twice, and in 3a' v.21 body parts speak once).

53. Talbert, *Reading John*, 77.

In the twin centers (b. vv.17–18 // b' vv.19–20) a double (v.17) and single question (v.19) prepare for an answer beginning with *nuni de* (v.18) // *nun de* (v.20) translated, "But as it is . . . ." Christians are to be together because of their baptism into Christ and participation in the Spirit. All matter; all need each other.

A still different type of literature is the controversy dialogs and parable of Luke 10: 25–42.

Luke 10:25–28, 29–37, 38–43
Ordering Our Loves Aright

      a. vv.25–28 Controversy Dialog 1: Command of Love for God and Neighbor
    1. v.25 Lawyer: Question 1
      2. v.26 Jesus: Question 2
      2' v.27 Lawyer: Answer 2
   1' v.27 Jesus: Answer 1

      b. vv.29–37 The Love of Neighbor
    1. v.29 Question 3
      2. vv.30–35, 36 Story + Question 4
      2' v.37a Answer 4
   1' v.27b Answer 3

      a' v.38–42 A Disciple Correction Story: The Love of God in Jesus
    1. v.38 Martha Receives Jesus: Conventional Role
      2. v.39 Mary Receives Jesus: Unconventional Role as Student
        3. v.40 Martha's Rebuke of Jesus as Uncaring
        3' v.41 Jesus' Rebuke of Martha: Major in Minors
      2' v.42 Jesus' Commendation of Mary's New Role
   1' Deliberately Left Open-Ended by Jesus, Question: Did Martha repent?

This cluster on the love of God and neighbor is composed of three thought units, each with its own boundaries and internal structures: a. 10:25–28, b. vv.29–37, a' vv.38–42. The two shorter units (a//a') surround the longer central unit (b), and all three are built around questions and answers. Together they demonstrate the layered complexity of which concentric arrangements are capable.

Unit a. 10:25–28 is a 4:2 Chiasm in which two questions are answered in reverse order. The Inclusions are the question, "what shall I do to inherit eternal life" (v.25), and the concluding command, "do this, and you will live" (v.28). Unit b. 10:29–37 also has two questions answered in reverse order, thus forming a second 4:2 Chiasm.

Unit a' 10:38–42 concludes the three subunits with another controversy dialog on the love of God in Jesus (an indirect Christology dependent on 10:25–42 being read as a three-part whole with the love of God and neighbor then unfolded in reverse order with a story on the love of neighbor and a story on the love of God in Jesus as demonstrated in Mary's devotion as a female disciple.

That Jesus left the last story open-ended is an invitation for us to make a decision where to sit and who to listen to. So we have three thought units arranged in a 3:1 Chiasm (a-b-a'). The first commands love of God and neighbor as the way to life eternal; the second shifts love into the key of compassion and costly action; the third does not use love/compassion but instead puts Mary in a position of devotion to Jesus and his teaching from which Martha seeks to dislodge her. Reading the three paragraphs together, as Luke designed it, gives us a layered narrative on what loving God in Christ looks like in action. Each of the stories has the capacity to stand on its own, but when brought together in three interrelated 4:2 Chiasms, the effect is multiplied.

Luke, Concentric Construction, Genre, and Linkages

Luke is the author of a sophisticated Greco-Roman *bios* (biography) of Jesus, Son of God, Savior, founder of a new *kingdom of God* movement offering a healed relationship with the God of Israel through himself. Luke uses multiple sources, edits, compiles, and rearranges them to present his distinctive portrait of this remarkable life. And so close was the resemblance of Luke's portrayal to the One who'd walked among them, that the early church recognized it as gift from above and incorporated it into a collection of four such biographies that form the first section of the New Testament. We enter the New Testament through a portrait gallery. The theological mystery of Jesus is too rich and deep for a single rendering, but four and no more does quite well.

When reading Luke with an analytical eye and a new set of rhetorical lenses, the first task is to read the whole as the matrix of all the parts working together. The second is to identify the parts and their arrangements. Werner Kelber has commented on the whole and the parts:

> (Each) gospel represents an intricately designed religious universe, with plot and character development, retrospective and prospective devices, linear and concentric patterning, and a continuous line of thematic cross-references and narrative interlockings. The art of interpretation consists in analyzing the complexities of the narrative construction and to comprehend individual parts in connection with the total architecture.[54]

54. Resseguie, "Redaction Criticism," 4–6.

At present I identify ninety-four thought units[55] in Luke which are grouped—in ascending size—into Clusters,[56] Essays, and Parts.[57]

Further, observe that each of the thought units, identified by their boundaries and internal structures, are not casually but carefully composed, most often using the concentric patterning of Chiasm as explored in this chapter.

The thought units are then linked together in a sequence or chain using various linking devices: Time Signatures and Sequence Cues, Travel Reports, Geographical Notices, Echoes with Parallel Units in a Larger Whole, and Repeated Transition Formulas: *Kai egeneto*: "And it happened," *Egeneto de*, "Now it happened," and others. And the test of the process of multi-layered analysis is this question: Does it make sense of the text before us as we test it anew with each unit? My answer is, "Yes, it does, and with a remarkable consistency."

One of the surprises of this work has been the number of separate thought units that share the same basic 4:2 chiastic structure (a-b // b'-a', four parts with a double center). Over a third of Luke's units share this basic pattern in which two elements are introduced and then reviewed and modified in reverse order.

So while plotting the units and their structures helps us follow the unfolding progress of Luke's presentation, there is another issue, and that is the question of genre or literary type[58] To put it simply, a parable is not a miracle story is not a call story is not a feeding narrative is not a controversy story is not a pronouncement story is not a commissioning story is not a literary preface is not an extended block of teaching. Each is distinct.

If the whole of Luke displays the markers of the ancient biography with its topics, expectations, and conventions,[59] then what of its parts? Do each of the thought units

---

55. A Thought Unit is the smallest discourse unit with Inclusions and Internal Structures. The first work, after reading the whole, is to identify the Thought units, then to place them in Clusters, Essays, and Parts as indicated by Luke's cues and clues.

56. A Cluster is several Thought units brought into a larger grouping which also has Inclusions and Internal Structures. As an example, four thought units, each a 4:2 Chiasm, might be brought together in a Cluster with a 4:2 concentric pattern). These sub-units are formed to be read together and advance a common theme, issue, or topic. For example, the three thought units of Luke 10:25–42 (analyzed above) that together unfold the meaning of the dual command to love God and neighbor with the whole self.

57. A Part is a collection of Essays to form one of the major internal divisions of Luke, of which there are three: Part 1: Luke 1:1–4:30, Part 2: Luke 4:31–9:51, Part 3: Luke 9:51–24:53.

58. The description of Jeannie Crain is a good place to begin: "*Genre.* A French term derived from the Latin *genus, generis* meaning 'type,' 'sort,' or 'kind.' It designates the literary form or type into which works are classified according to what they have in common, either in their formal structures or in their treatment of subject matter, or both. Genre can be said to form a narrative covenant between author and reader, creating a framework of norms and expectations that shapes both the composition and the reception of the text" (*Reading the Bible*, 160). On Luke's often-used genres, see Kuhn, *The Kingdom according to Luke*, Chapter 4, "The Building Blocks of Luke's Narrative," 73–102. And, more recently, Naselli, *How To Understand And Apply The New Testament*, Chapter 1, "Genre," 15–35.

59. For an introduction, see Burridge, *Four Gospels, One Jesus*, Chapter 1, "Four Gospels," 1–34.

also enact an identified, specific genre? Yes and No. Some are clearly identified by genre type in the critical literature, while others have not yet been so specified.[60]

Genre and Surface Structure overlap in the same unit, but they are not the same and need to be distinguished. Genre has to do with *what a thing is;* Surface Structure has to do with *how it is organized rhetorically.* For example, the five standard parts of a miracle story (problem, encounter, cure, proofs, reactions) may be told in several patterns. It is important to know just what we are reading (the genre question) and to discern how the story is formed and told (the structure question). It is also important to recognize that some texts may be outlined in more than one way; there may be multiple overlapping patterns to be acknowledged.

A prime example is Luke's first long sentence: Luke 1:1–4. It is normally divided into two panels or halves (a. vv.1–2, b. vv.3–4), each with three parts (1. vv.1a, 2. v.1b, 3. v.2 // 1' v.3a, 3' v.3b, 2' vv.3c-4) and ending with a reference to *logos* (v.2b) or *logoi* (v.4b). Thus there are two, three-part stanzas ending in a common reference and each containing a series of four characteristics of Luke's project, as follows:

Luke 1:1–4

Make a Good Beginning

1. 1:1–4 Luke's Literary an Rhetorical Preface to his Gospel.
a. vv.1–2 Gospel Writers and Teachers Before Luke: 3 Parts
1) v.1a Who?
    2) v.1b What?
        3) v.2 Why?
b. vv.3–4 Luke's Own Gospel Research and Writing: 3 Parts
1) v.3a Who?
    2) v,3b-f What?
        3) v.4 Why?

Another consideration is that of sources, their existence, and modification. And where clear sources are indicated, as in Luke's use of Mark, paying attention to Luke's practices of editing are high revealing since he often edits in order to add Inclusions, Echoes, and to complete the structure of a unit. Luke is a conscious author fully aware of his choices and their outcomes.

Yet an additional item is the links that are observed as one thought unit is marked out and linked with its successor. Careful observation of Luke's habits makes me aware of how careful he is in maintaining continuity in his narration through this technique. A brief observation of the opening and closing of the thought units in Luke's first essay (IA. 1:1—2:52) sets a pattern for the remainder of the Gospel.

---

60. There are several thought units in Luke where the disciples make an error in judgment or action and are then rebuked/corrected/taught by Jesus, and for these I cannot find a specific genre designation in the literature. Until corrected, I refer to them as *Disciple Correction Stories.*

Noting the Links Between Thought Units in Essay IA: Luke 1:1–2:52

Thought Unit	Opening/ Bridge	Closing/Transition
Preface, 1:1–4	"Inasmuch . . . of the word (*logos*)	"these matters/events (*logoi*)"
1A1. 1:5–25	Bridge + Time Signature: "And it happened (*Kai egeneto*) in the days of King Herod . . ." (v.5)	Time Signature: "After these days" (v.24c) Ends with Elizabeth's voice (v.25)
IA1' 1:26–38 Same genre at 1:5–25	Time Signature: "In the sixth month the angel" (v.26)	Time Signature: "This is the sixth month" (v.36b) Ends with Mary's verbal ascent (v.38)
IA2. 1:39–56	Time Signature; "In those days, Mary arose and went"(v.39) Travel report	Time Signature: "about three months and returned to her home" (v.56a) Travel report
IA3. 1:57–80	Time Signature: "Now the time came (*te de kronos*) . . . and it happened (*kai egeneto*) on the eighth day" (vv.57a, 59a)	Time Signature; "until the day of his manifestation to Israel (v.80b).
IA3'. 2:1–21	Time Signature: "Now it happened (*Egeneto de*) in those days" (v.1). "And it happened (*Kai egeneto*) while they were there" (v.6). "And it suddenly happened (*Kai exaiphnes egeneto*) (v.9a) = 3x.	Time Signature: "And at the end of eight days" (v.21)
IA3b. 2:22–39	Time Signature: "And when the days were fulfilled" (v.22). Travel report	Time Signature: "And when they had performed everything." Travel report
IA3c. 2:40–52	Growth Formula "And the child grew and became strong" (v.40)	Growth Formula "And Jesus increased in wisdom" (v.52)

If the thought units are properly distinguished, and if the overall pattern of their grouping into an Essay is valid, then the opening and closing links of the thought units to one another are an additional evidence of Luke's intentional patterns. And here, after the Prologue (1:1–4), we have a series of seven discrete thought units, the first six of which both open and close with *Time Signatures*, and the seventh of which abandons this established pattern for *Growth Reports* at the start and finish as an example of a Series + Climax.

And since all of the material in 1:1–2:52 is assigned to Luke's Special Source (L), we have here the best material for a case study of Lukan strategy and style of forming and linking thought units. His style and techniques are on full display.

So, in this work on discipleship in Luke, the goal is to identify and analyze all of Luke's thought units with a consistent method by observing and verifying:

1. Their inclusions and boundaries;

2. their internal structures, most often—but not always—concentric;

3. their respective genres;

4. their identifiable sources, if any;

5. their fit into larger wholes: Clusters, Essays, Parts.

Definitions and Descriptions of Chiasm and Inclusion

Defintions of Chiasm

1. "The use of bilateral symmetry about a central axis."[61]

2. "A Semitic poetic form, sometimes also used in prose arrangements, that juxta-poses, reverses, or contrasts words, dialogs, episodes, scenes, and events."[62]

3. "A stylistic literary figure which consists of a series of two or more elements followed by a presentation of corresponding elements in reverse order.[63]

4. "The position of members in a chiastic structure indicates points of emphasis. In respect to both form and sense, the rest of the structure pivots around the center, which may be either a single or a double unit. Thus, the exegete must attach special importance to the center of a chiastic structure."[64]

5. "Chiasmus is inverted parallelism, a passage in which the second part is inverted and balanced against the first. The two main elements of chiasmus, inversion and balance, produce a third, climactic centrality."[65]

6. "Chiasmus, then, may be best described by the expression *concentric parallelism*. The point to be stressed here is that parallel structuring can be achieved by the repetition of *themes* or *ideas* as well as by repetition of verbal expressions."[66]

61. Norman, *Samuel Butler and the Meaning of Chiasmus*, 276.

62. Crain, *Reading The Bible*, 155.

63. Bailey and Vander Broek, *Literary Forms*, 49.

64. Meiser, *Chiasm . . . Paul's Missionary Sermons*, 7.

65. Stock, "Chiastic Awareness," 23.

66. John Breck, *The Shape of Biblical Language*, 19.

7. "The basic concept, however, is that of a symmetrical structure involving an inverted order of corresponding elements."[67]

8. "a rhetorical term designating a reversal of the order of words in two otherwise parallel clauses."[68]

9. "a stylistic literary figure which consists of a series of two or more elements followed by a presentation of corresponding elements in reverse order."[69]

10. "Chiasm is the term used to describe the literary flow of a passage in which each element of the first half of the poem or story or discourse is mirrored in a similar element in the second half, inverted in order. Most often, though not always, a center element will be unparalleled, and will carry a unique statement of the most significant idea intended by the author."[70]

11. "the use of inverted parallelism of form and/or content which moves towards and away from a strategic central component."[71]

12. "chiasm may be said to be present in a passage if the text exhibits bilateral symmetry of four or more elements around a central axis, which may itself lie between two elements, or be a unique central element, the symmetry consisting of any combination of verbal, grammatical, or syntactical elements, or, indeed, of ideas and concepts in a given pattern."[72]

13. "Chiasmus is a pattern that pairs the first and last ideas in a unit and the second and third ideas (a-b // b'-a'). When a chiasm has more than four lines, the pairings continue until the ideas merge in the middle. The thought reverses at the middle back up the chain in the opposite direction."[73]

Definitions of Inclusion(s)

1. "Uses repetition to mark the beginning and ending of a section, framing or bracketing an episode it contains. The repetition can be a word or phrase, a sentence, or even two concepts, their use being that they bind parts together."[74]

2. "the use of the same word(s) to begin and end a discussion. e primary purpose of inclusion seems to have been to delimit discrete topics in an extended discussion."[75]

---

67. Harvey, *Listening To The Text*, 99.

68. Dahood, "Chiasmus," 145.

69. Man, "Value of Chiasm," 146.

70. Brouwer, "Understanding Chiasm," 99–127.

71. McCoy, "Chiasmus," 3.

72. Thomson, *Chiasmus in the Pauline Letters*, 25–26.

73. Bock, *Luke*, 89, n.49.

74. Crain, *Reading The Bible*, 38, 161.

75. Harvey, *Listening to the Text*, 102–03.

3. "Known among classical scholars as 'ring composition,' inclusion is a storyteller's technique in which what is said at the beginning of a piece is repeated at the end. The repetition forces the reader's attention back to the beginning and thus serves as a frame for the piece as a whole. More than anything else, inclusions clearly help the exegete (interpreter) to divide the Gospel into distinct parts, chapters, and paragraphs."[76]

4. "Inclusions, also known as the 'envelope effect,' are created by paralleling the first and last elements of a literary unit . . . [It] can involve the repetition or reversal of an action, by repeating or inverting key themes. It serves to complete a tradition as well as to frame it."[77]

5. "In an oral presentation an Inclusion alerts the ear that a new paragraph or section is beginning or ending. What indentions, paragraphing, and headings on a page do for the eye of a modern reader, inclusions do for the ear of a ancient auditor" (Pastor Phil Thrailkill).

6. "Inclusions act in pairs to bracket a text, usually signaling the beginning, end, or transition to another section. They are very common in orally conditioned literature."[78]

How To Locate And Map A Chiasm[79]

1. Create a copy of a New Testament book without the chapters or verses.

2. Read the book aloud, using your ears to hear the sounds of the words and their patterns.

76. Ellis, *The Genius of John*, 9–10.
77. Breck, *The Shape of Biblical Language*, 32–33.
78. Wilson, *Divine Symmetries*, 38.
79. There is a robust, ongoing, and at times acrimonious debate concerning the criteria by which one defines and identifies a chiasm or concentric structure. The smaller they are, the more agreement; the longer they are claimed to be (especially at the level of large sections, or even of books as a whole), the more disagreement. The micro are largely agreed on; the macro are much debated because of their dependence on thematic correspondence and not a clear verbal correspondence as in smaller units. There is an art and a science to the recognition and validation process with advocates at either end of the spectrum. Proposals and critiques include DeSilva, "X Marks the Spot?" 343–37. On the affirming side, see Luter and Lee, "Philippians As Chiasmus," 89–101. And on the skeptical side, Porter and Reed, "Philippians As A Macro-Chiasm," 213–31; Brower, "Understanding Chiasm," 99–127; Clark, "Criteria for Identifying Chiasm," 63–72; Go, "Understanding the Chiastic Structure of the New Testament," dx.doi.org/10.17156/BT.77.11, 317–44. Also Thomson, *Chiasmus in the Pauline Letters*, 22–34; Mc-Comiskey, *Lukan Theology in the Light of the Gospel's Literary Structure*, "Eleven Tests for Intentionality," 8–12; Harvey, *Listening to the Text*, Chapter 5, "Categories and Controls," 97–118. For a chart of criteria, see http.chiasmusresources.org/criteria-chart. Also the chart in McComiskey, *Lukan Theology*: 11. For cautions on an over-zealous and under-critical approach to the identification of concentric structures, see Thomson, *Chiasm*, 13, 22, 28–29. In my use of headings I am to summarize common elements between parallel parts, not to impose a pattern where it is not found on other grounds.

3. Take a guess as to what is the first thought unit.

4. Underline or circle repeated words and phrases. They may signal an Inclusion or at least a link-word within the unit. Use a concordance to see if the English words are Greek equivalents. Look for repetitions of words, ideas, commands, questions, places, persons.

5. Identify, if possible, the Genre and its expected components.

6. Note the use and alternation of Narrative Discourse and Direct Discourse.

7. Count any series that seems to be present. How many parts are there?

8. Note the way the verses are linked together. What are the bridge words or phrases that you observe: *and, but, and it happened that, now, then, when, for, because*?

9. Place a slash (/) after what seem to be the internal breaks in the text: a change of place or time or person or event.

10. Copy and paste the possible thought unit on a blank piece of paper and put extras spaces between the internal breaks. Play with indentions to see if you find any patterns or echoes between the pieces.

11. Look at the whole of the hypothetical unit with an eye for internal movement and parallels of any kind: questions, speakers, vocabulary, Old Testament quotes, actions, etc.

12. Read the text aloud again using what you have discovered. What do you hear now?

13. Ask the question, Is there a center? And is it one or two members? Try one, and if you notice parallel materials both before and after it, you may be onto something!

14. Reorder the text on your page with spaces between segments, increasing indentation by section, then circle or color code common words, phrases, ideas, forms of speech, themes, and actions at the beginning and end of the unit.

15. Only then consult the critical commentaries to see if the experts picked up on and arranged the clues you have noticed in your primary observations. I often find that they have not.

16. In the case of Luke, is there a Synoptic parallel? If so, note Luke's edits which can be clues as to his purpose and literary patterning. He edits with an eye to structure.

17. Be playful in your approach. Experiment with various parallel patterns until you think that you have indeed mapped what the author intended. Happy hunting![80]

---

80. For other listings of possible steps, see Chadwick, *Both Here And There*, 7–9; Ellis, *The Genius of John*, 17; Wilson, *Divine Symmetries*, 305–09.

A Brief Summary of Insights

1. Rhetoric was pervasive in the ancient world, and one of its organizing tools was the figure of Chiasm (concentric construction) for beauty, for memory, for internal organization, for the development of parallel ideas around a focus, for an appeal to the ear of the auditor who came to the event with expectations.

2. Inclusions (common words, ideas, locations, grammatical forms) are used to open and close a thought unit to give it boundaries from what came before and what follows. It is an aural clue to the listener that a paragraph starts and finishes.

3. All of Luke's thought units have an internal organization which is most often chiastic, with either a single or double center. Luke groups them into Clusters, Essays, and Parts to build up his layered portrait, a *bios* of Jesus the Savior.

4. Thought units (think photos or brief video clips) are linked in a sequence that may itself be concentric in form. The links may be time references, travel reports, geographical sites, continuations, formal cues (*And it happened that, And behold, Now/And/But.* They provide the flow across units.

5. Symmetry and centrality were valued, but also look for asymmetries which break expectations, change patterns, and introduce surprises. They too are the work of a careful composer. For example, the stories of Mary and Martha [10:38–42] and the Parable of the Prodigal Son [15:11–32]) both leave the final expected member of the chiasm open-ended, thus calling for our response. We go from being a listener to being a character in the story!

5

Key Discipleship Passages In Luke

WE ADMITTED EARLIER THAT Luke as a unified whole is the proper curriculum of discipleship and that every thought unit and paragraph reveals a new layer of the Jesus we are following. But that said, within Luke are also a series of paragraphs that focus on discipleship in a more explicit fashion, and it is these that are considered, of which we count fifty-one.

If Luke is a single rope woven of two cords, the Jesus cord in gold and the disciple cord in blue, we have an image for how the two stories are interlaced. Jesus—as the revelation of the Triune God, has come among us to create a new community, the people of God remade around himself and *the new reality*, and this is his story and theirs.

The format for the treatment of each of the fifty-one units is the same. The texts are numbered in order and followed by a summary title and a designation of genre.[1] This is followed by a quotation from a patristic commentator on the text under consideration.[2] Then come eight sections, each of which answers a question:

1. Justification: Why is this a discipleship unit?

2. Shape: What are the clues to the rhetoric and structure of the unit?

3. Content: What is the thought unit about?

4. Then: What does the unit teach about being a Jesus' follower?

5. Now: How do we bridge from then to now and from there to here?

6. Summary: Can we state what we've learned in a brief paragraph?

---

1. In some cases the unit embodies a single genre or literary type on which many scholars agree: miracle story, parable, pronouncement story/chreia. But in many others Luke has woven together several genres into a new whole. These will be labeled as a *Hybrid Genre*.

2. All quotes are from Just, *Luke: Ancient Christian Commentary*.

7. Insights: What deserves further thought and serious action?[3]

8. Disciplines: What means of grace are present: Observation + Action?

A. DISCIPLESHIP IN THE PREFACE AND BIRTH NARRATIVES (1:1–2:52)

1. Luke 1:1–4

Make a Good Beginning
Genre: An Ancient Literary Preface

Luke was by race an Antiochian and by profession a physician.

He long had been a companion of Paul

and had more than a casual acquaintance with the rest of the apostles.

He has left for us, in two inspired books,

examples of the work of healing souls

that he obtained from them.

—EUSEBIUS OF CAESAREA[4]

Justification

This formal dedicatory preface is absent in most surveys of discipleship in Luke because it does not deal with the first round of Jesus' followers: Peter, Andrew, and others. It deals rather with a longer view from the perspective of several generations of followers and thus as an indirect proof that the disciples made more disciples, some of whom began a tradition of taking the communal memories of Jesus and writing them down.[5]

In the oral culture that was the first century, all disciples retold the stories of Jesus they received from eyewitnesses. But some—a literate few, starting with Mark, began to order them in sequence and arrange them in a narrative. Think of these as *special purpose* disciples of the second and third generations who were moved by circumstances and the Holy Spirit to record the accounts that were then circulating in written and oral form and thus to fix them in new documents. Luke is just downstream from those early headwaters.

---

3. Each of these units can be used for individual or group study with 1–4 above on what the text says and 5–8 on how it's translated into the present.

4. Just, *Luke: Ancient Christian Commentary on Scripture*, 2.

5. On the reliability issues, see Roberts, *Can We Trust the Gospels?*; Williams, *Can We Trust the Gospels?*

Who knows how early this process began to occur? Scholars disagree. But the end of the process was a first manuscript of the Gospel of Mark, and then later of two Synoptic expansions of Mark in Matthew and Luke, and finally the more independent Gospel of John. With these in hand, the church said, "It is enough." These four, when read, preached, and taught in the church, shape faithful disciples and keep us in the faith. The challenge of passing on the new faith is a task of disciples, and here—in order—Luke honors others gospel writers before him, the initial eyewitnesses and preachers, his own careful work, and his initial hearer and likely patron—Theophilus, who will benefit greatly by having his convictions about Jesus strengthened.[6] This is a disciple text because following Jesus is an intergenerational process that involves the faithful transmission of the apostolic witness.

In his formal preface consisting of a single sentence in two sections (a. vv.1–2 those who came before, and b. vv.3–4 Luke's own composition), and with each section having three parts, Luke places himself among an earlier group of special purpose disciples. Note how "the word" (*logos*, v.2b) and "the matters" (*logoi*, v.4) end each section and how the four marks of the reliable sources in the first half (v.2) are matched by the four marks of careful composition in the second (v.3b). Luke creates a layering of stages as he speaks of his predecessors and their work (v.10), the quality of the tradition's history (v.2), his own calling and careful research (v.3), and the type and purpose of his biography (v.4). An outline is:

    a. vv.1–2 Gospel Writers and Preachers before Luke: 3 parts
    1. v.1a Who?
      2. v.1b What?
        3. v.2 Why?
    b. vv.3–4 Luke's own Research and Writing in this Ongoing Tradition: 3 Parts
    1. v.3a Who?
      2. v.3b What?
        3. vv.3c–4 Why?

Content

In an ancient biography it's important to make a good beginning, and that Luke does by situating himself in an ongoing tradition of writers who were attentive to the careful passing on of those traditions by eyewitnesses. His interest is historical and a preview of what is to come. The note of fulfillment, "the things that *have been* (passive voice) accomplished among us," hints at divine agency, that God is the hidden actor. The name of Jesus is not yet introduced. Everyone is a new Theophilus, and Luke is

6. On technical issues and the history of scholarship on 1:1–4, see Bauckham, *Jesus and the Eyewitnesses,* "The Preface to Luke's Gospel," 116–23; Parsons, *Luke: Storyteller,* Chapter 3, "Luke 1:1–4 and Ancient Rhetoric," 40–52.

careful in building a sense of trust about the quality of what follows. He aims at order and credibility, which is why these four verses are critical to Luke's evaluation as an ancient historian and biographer.

Hearing the fuller story with its careful attention to sequence and plausibility (*an orderly account*) will firm up and bolster Theophilus' confidence. He's already *been instructed* (v.4), and now he will be even more convinced. Luke has evangelistic, theological, pastoral, and apologetic functions all in one preface.

Then

Converts bring their history, skills, and education with them into the church, as well as all their accumulated crud and entanglements, and sorting it out is a long haul affair. With the gifts the Spirit adds and the immersion into the community of Jesus, there begins a providential process that shapes the specifics of each vocation. For Luke the physician and traveling companion of Paul, his medical and missionary labors lead him eventually to become an historian and one of the four official biographers of Jesus. His early training in rhetorical composition came to fruition later in life.

To survive across time with an array of needed resources, the church cooperated with the Holy Spirit to raise up its own academic department of foundational writers (Gospels and Acts), occasional pastoral writers (Epistles), visionary prophets (The Apocalypse) and later on Creedal composers, Liturgical and Musical composers, Apologists, Theologians, Church Historians, Catechists, and Sacred Artists or Iconographers.[7]

Remembering is a one to three generational event, but soon after must come historians and researchers, writers and editors, the use of whatever communications technology is at hand, and a commitment to both the continuity and internal consistency of the faith received as it is passed on and defended in the public square.

This too is the work of the Holy Spirit and a great means of grace for the long haul of living into the future with continuity of faith. All disciples are to follow Jesus as his apprentices and students in the ways and means of the kingdom of God, *the new reality* which we already encounter in part. But some, a minority, have an academic spin to their callings, and Luke—after a stint as a doctor and missionary apprentice—became one of those. And because of his enabled faithfulness, we have twenty-seven percent of the New Testament in his two volumes: Luke and Acts.

Now

Disciples of Jesus use their histories, gifts, training, and opportunities in his service and encourage others to do the same, just as Luke did by building on a gospel-writing

7. See Abraham, *Canonical Theism* for a collection of essays on the full ecology of the means of grace given by the Spirit to sustain the church over time.

tradition that preceded him. We, after all, are one, multi-gifted, communion centered in the risen Jesus, who does wonderful things with surrendered people. The church is always engaged in serious scholarship and writing to preserve, illumine, offer and defend the deposit of divine revelation we have received.

Luke models a serious engagement with the tradition and with the church and culture to which it is addressed. There is no room in the church for a style of faith that denies the life of the mind[8] and the responsibility to creatively preserve the faith across generations. Good storytelling is critical, and logic is our friend.

Summary

Disciples honor the gifts given to others, particularly those whose creativity and skill let them preserve and interpret the apostolic tradition to current and future audiences. Historians and poets, bards and musicians, prophets, storytellers and liturgists are all needed.

Insights

1. The faith of disciples is trust based on multiple evidences. Take some time for Apologetics and learn the typical routes through which people come to faith.

2. Ours is a faith grounded in the datable events of history, not myth and legend.

3. Luke was a researcher and skilled ancient writer, so aim at excellence in your witness.

4. Never be afraid of answering awkward questions from new converts.

5. Above all, keep retelling the story and stories of Jesus at every opportunity.

6. Find a way, as Luke did, to build a bridge to the best of your culture's traditions.

7. Note Luke's plurals (*many . . . us . . . us . . . me also*). Discipleship is not a solo project.

Disciplines

Observation: Christian study and teaching, knowing the core traditions about Jesus.
Action: Immersion in and meditation on the four gospels is primary.
Observation: Forming new disciples in the faith and building their confidence.
Action: Communicating what you know in formal and informal settings.

---

8. For defenses of loving God with intellect, see Moreland, *Love Your God, with All Your Mind*; McGrath, *The Passionate Intellect*.

2. Luke 1:5–25

How to Build a Prophet
Hybrid Genre: The Angelophany of a Saving Birth, A Call and Commission Story

I do not know what is the most important thing we should preach—
that he [John the Baptist] was wonderfully born or more wonderfully slain—
for he was born as a prophecy and murdered for truth.
By his birth he announced the coming of the Savior,
and by his death he condemned the incest of Herod.
—MAXIMUS OF TURIN[9]

Justification

Our most fundamental teaching is that the one God is a Triune communion of the Father, the Son, and the Holy Spirit. When we speak of God's *grace*, it's not just a Theistic but an ever-Triune reality: the grace of the Father through the Son as administered by the Holy Spirit. When we find righteousness and genuine piety in the Old Testament era, as here, it's the result of engagement with the Triune God, even if as yet unnamed in that fashion. This extraordinary couple qualify as faithful followers of Yahweh the Lord, as pre-Jesus disciples.

Shape

The literary genre of 1:5–25 is a hybrid of *The Angelology of a Saving Birth*, and *A Call and Commission Story*.[10] A providential pregnancy and a pious Jewish home will prepare John for a divine commission, a season of public service, the baptism of Jesus, and finally his own martyrdom by decapitation after a frontal challenge to the king over his immoral, scandalous lifestyle. The one who goes before Jesus as a prophet is, paradoxically, also his follower and disciple, a model preacher and teacher of kingdom ethics.

Inclusions which open and close the thought unit are *In the days of* (v.5) // *After these days*, (v.24), *Elizabeth* (v.5b) // *Elizabeth* (v.24), *the Lord* (v.6b) // *the Lord* (v.25), problem: *they had no child* (v.7) // resolution: *conceived . . . take away my reproach* (v.25). The first hearers were alert to auditory cues at the start and finish of thought units, and Luke supplies them.

9. Just, *Luke*, 7.

10. The basic research is that of Hubbard, "The Role of Commissioning Accounts in Acts," 187–98, as expanded in Sweetland, *Our Journey with Jesus*. This genre figures heavily in Luke's theology of discipleship since it is devoted to the phenomena of God's call and commissioning.

The structure of the thought unit is an elaborate concentric pattern with a single center containing a three stanza angelic oracle (b3. vv.14–15a, 15b–16, 17) with the third line of each stanza making a statement about the *Lord* (vv.15a, 16, 17c). At the core of the nine lines (v.15c, line 5) is a statement that John "will be filled with the Spirit from his mother's womb," indicating that John is a prophet from the start.

A new prophetic voice is to be heard thirty years hence. The following diagram demonstrates that the story has nine parts with four sets of frames around a single center:

1	a. vv.5–7 Zechariah and Elizabeth: Priestly, Righteous, Old/Barren
	b. vv.8–23 Annunciation by Gabriel, Zechariah's Doubt/Judgment
2	1. vv.8–10 Zechariah's Temple Service Begins, People Pray Outside
3	2. vv.11–12 Unidentified Angel Appears, Zechariah is Fearful
4	3. v.13 Conception Announced to Zechariah
5	4. vv.14–17 Gabriel Proclaims John's Significance
6	3' v.18 Conception Questioned by Zechariah
7	2' vv.19–20 Angel Identified, Zechariah Struck Dumb
8	1' vv.21–23 People Outside Wait and Wonder, Zechariah's Service Ends
9	a' vv.24–25 Zechariah and Elizabeth: Promise Fulfilled, Elizabeth's Response

Content

If Luke is a *post-disciple*, meaning he was not part of the first generation (which he admits in vv.1–2), then Zechariah and Elizabeth, the parents of John the Baptist, are surely *pre-disciples* who with their only son also help prepare the way for Jesus to make his entrance (v.17). Both are of priestly lineage (vv.5–7) and represent the very best of Jewish piety, as Luke notes that they were, "righteous before God, walking in all the commandments and ordinances of the Lord blameless" (v.6).

Their response to the grace of God in their Jewish tradition had, over time, produced two remarkably faithful saints. Their faithfulness is shown in their endurance as they deal with the mystery of being childless, and more particularly sonless. It is then, as Zechariah is performing a once-in-a-lifetime priestly privilege, that the angel of the Lord appears with a word of promise that Elizabeth will soon be pregnant and that the son is to be named John.

Their prayer was heard long ago, but the timing and means of its fulfillment is God's. John will be filled with the Spirit in utero and thus a prophet. His adult ministry is the preparation of a repentant nation (vv.14–17), and the "Lord" to which Gabriel makes three references (vv.15a, 16, 17c) is the Lord Jesus, and to him is applied the Greek equivalent (*Kurios*, Lord) of the Hebrew Yahweh.

However, Zechariah's trust falters as he questions the promise and comes under a judgment of silence during the whole of Elizabeth's pregnancy. Faithfulness and frailty travel together in all God's friends. The surprise pregnancy comes to pass, and the last voice we hear is that of Elizabeth marveling at what God has done (vv.24–25). Themes of divine providence, promise and fulfillment, the Spirit's empowerment, human faithfulness and frailty, liturgical worship, angels as messengers, and prayer are all present in this theologically dense unit which stands at the hinge of the old and new eras.

Then

If a disciple is one who loves and obeys God, even amidst disappointments and postponements, then surely Zechariah and Elizabeth are exemplars. And to boot, theirs is a shared, marital spirituality, and the distinct voices of each are heard in this passage. Through the arrangement of providential circumstances, Zechariah is found doing his duties which suddenly opens up into a mediated divine encounter with the highest of angels. It is in the faithful performance of our duties, in times good and times difficult, that God grants fresh visitations. The divine presence is woven into our duties and opportunities.

Disciples show up prepared and know that present orders stand till new orders come. That Zechariah stumbled in his trust should not offend us since frailty is not banished by faith. To follow is not to be protected from exposure and correction, as Luke's chronicle of the disciples' repeated failures makes clear.[11] God is faithful, and part of divine faithfulness is the exposure, correction, and restoration of his servants. As Hebrews 12:6 reminds us, "For the Lord disciplines him whom he loves, and chastises every son (and daughter) whom he receives." It is the voice of Elizabeth that ends the thought unit (vv.24–25), and it is a preview of the presence and influence of women in Luke's biography of Jesus.

Now

Disciples of Jesus look for examples of faithfulness across time, men and women who responded to the grace given before Jesus came, during his time among us, and after his resurrection and ascension. And while vivid spiritual encounters happened then and continue now, they are not our regular diet and always come as surprises. Disciples live in marriages and as celibate singles, each with its challenges. And over time, God forms and reforms us, laying down layers of virtue and habit and faithful persistence so that we may be ready when fresh opportunity arrives. And correction, when it comes as we are exposed, is never easy because it always goes to the deepest part of the person. And when we submit to its demands, a new level of fruitfulness is ahead. The pains and the promises are always with us; every follower walks with a

---

11. The *Disciple Correction Story* (my designation) is a favorite of Luke and will be highlighted throughout this book. For the first example, see Unit 8: Luke 5:27–39.

limp of some kind. And disciples, whether married or single, live with respect for and delight in one another, welcoming the gifts of gender, sexuality, and family formation under God's good limits.

To ignore or minimize or silence the voices of women cripples the body of Christ and robs the world of a richer witness of full equality and rich complementarity. Zechariah's experience takes up most of the text, but he is then silenced so that Elizabeth's praise of God ends the episode—as does Mary's in the next unit! How prominent are the voices of girls and women in our circles of discipleship? Single gender gatherings can be helpful, but what the world needs to see is the richest forms of female and male partnership under the common lordship of Jesus. We are better together, and the work is worth it!

Summary

Disciples learn that divine providence, the ordering of events to God's purpose, is an exceedingly complex arrangement involving family and their histories, divine appointments, angelic mediation, prophetic promises, human frailty and sin, long periods of waiting, and not a small bit of pain and doubt, even divine discipline. It is only in looking back that the patterns are clarified, the connections made, and God's deep goodness appreciated. Providence never has to hurry, though events may coalesce quickly when the time is right.

Insights

1. A faithful, obedient life is its own reward, no matter what happens or never happens.

2. It is in the prayerful performance of one's duties that God is most likely to show up.

3. God has not forgotten the prayers and hopes you long ago gave up on.

4. Joy and the gift of repentance are two of God's best gifts to keep us whole.

5. Even the best of God's servants have pockets of unbelief and faithlessness.

6. Angels are God's agents of revelation and protection, messengers from God.

7. God has the right to bless and discipline his servants. Loyalty is not without pain.

8. Our goal, like John, is to prepare the way and point the way to Jesus Christ.

Disciplines

Observation: Zechariah and Elizabeth lived faithfully and with pain and longing.
Action: Embrace the ordinary as opportunity; trust God with your hopes and dreams.
Observation: Zechariah was engaged, corrected, disciplined, and trained by God.

Action: Embrace God's course corrections and savor the learning.

3. Luke 1:26–38

One of a Kind

Hybrid Genre: The Angelophany of a Saving Birth, A Call and Commission Story

Wonder! God is come among humanity;

he who cannot be contained is contained in a womb;

the timeless enters time, and great mystery:

his conception is without seed,

his emptying without telling.

—JOHN THE MONK[12]

Justification

It is impossible to overestimate the influence of this thought unit on the church's theology, particularly of the incarnation and the means of God's coming through Mary's assent and the Spirit's overshadowing enablement.[13] But what is more interesting to me— at least as far as our topic of *Discipleship in Luke* is concerned—is that Mary may be both her son's first follower and the first to experience the revelation of Israel's God as a communion of three whose every act is the work of all.

Mary says Yes to the angelic news and soon enough finds herself reshaped by Jesus' growing presence within. There are explicit references here to the *Lord* (v.28b) and to *God* (vv.30b, 32c, 35e), to *Jesus* as *Son* (vv.31b, 32b, 35e), and to the *Spirit* (vv.35).

We evangelicals often speak of *accepting Jesus into our hearts*, but Mary accepted Jesus into her womb and lived with him for nine months. She accepted Gabriel's prophetic song (vv.32–33), and humbly surrendered to the divine invitation as her call, "Behold, I am the handmaid of the Lord; let it be to me according to your word." She is a Christmas disciple, a Cross disciple, a Resurrection disciple, and a Pentecost disciple. Her following is one of a kind, but it is a deep following none the less, and one with increasing appeal.[14]

---

12. Just, *Luke*, 17.

13. My church's (United Methodist) official doctrine statement on the Incarnation and all the benefits that flow from it is found in Appendices 5 and 6.

14. A Protestant reappraisal of Mary is underway. Samples include McKnight, *The Real Mary*, Collins and Walls, *Roman but Not Catholic*, Chapter 15, "Mary: Why She Matters," 28–299, Chapter 16, "Mary Again," 300–20; Evangelicals and Catholics Together, "Do Whatever He Tells You."

Shape

Like the paragraph before it, Luke 1:26–38 is a hybrid genre using elements of the *The Angelology of a Saving Birth* and a *Call and Commission Story*. Inclusions are *the sixth month* (v.26a // v.36b), *angel* (v.26b // v.38d), *God* (v.26b // v.37), *Mary* (v.27c // v.38a). Time signatures are used to open and close the thought unit.

The center or pivot of the story is v.32c, "And the Lord God will give to him the throne of his father David," as the Messiah. There is a narrative introduction (vv.26–27), a block of direct address and dialog (vv.28–38c), and Narrative Ending (v.38d). The story has seven parts with a single center and three sets of parallel frames, as follows:

1	1. vv.26–27 Introduction: Joseph and Mary, Angel Sent
	2. vv.28–35 The Annunciation by Gabriel
2	a. vv.28–29 Call + Reaction, "The Lord is with you."
3	b. vv.30–31 Future Conception Announced by Gabriel to Mary
4	c. vv.32–33 Gabriel's Canticle Proclaims Jesus' Destiny
5	b' v.34 Imminent Conception Questioned by Mary
6	a' v.35 Means, "The Holy Spirit . . . will overshadow you."
7	1' vv.36–38 Conclusion: Mary's Consent, Angel Departs

Content

This parallel scene is not in the temple as with Zechariah but is an example of village piety. Joseph and Mary are a second male/female pair following Zechariah and Elizabeth. Here a young woman of no apparent status is the recipient of angelic revelation and dialogs about obstetrics with Gabriel. The parallels with 2. 1:5–25 include Scriptural echoes, divine revelation, angelology, promise and fulfillment, emotional and intellectual responses to the unveiling, the creative activity of the Holy Spirit, and responses of trust and surrender.

The story begins with a sexually inexperienced village girl with the commonest of names, *Miriam*, who is promised to Joseph as his wife in a legal betrothal. Without warning she is graced with an appearance of Gabriel concerning the gift of a son to be named Jesus. Her informed protest (v.34) is met with a promise of divine creative action, "The Holy Spirit will come upon you." (v.35b). With this word and the sign of cousin Elizabeth's remarkable pregnancy through less spectacular means, Mary names herself as the Lord's *handmaid* and willingly surrenders to divine action, "Let it be to me according to your word." God delights in partnerships, and in Mary a faithful partner takes the risk of trust.

At the center the divine voice states that Jesus is the promised Davidic Messiah. This is the center and high point of the narrative. The synergy of grace is that God proposes and that Mary, the already graced one (v.28b), willingly offers herself as a junior partner. She signed God's dance card, "Yes, I'd love to dance to the tune and lead of your Spirit."

Then

What makes this unit singular is that it's the first interaction that God the Son has with the human being who will be the matrix of his incarnation as the human Jesus. Though Mary the virgin is her son's first follower, she—like all the rest of us sinners—needs the benefactions he alone supplies, and here Protestants, Roman Catholics, and the Orthodox all have our disagreements and party platforms. What we agree on is that to Mary is given the first revelation of the Holy Trinity as the Most High sends the Son into her unoccupied womb by the power of the Holy Spirit.

Discipleship means trust and surrender to Jesus as he opens to us the Father's purposes and the living energies of the Holy Spirit. And the first to do so are not Peter and his friends but Jesus' own adolescent mother. They will bear him to the world in their words; she carries him around in her belly. She is, as the church later confessed, the *Theotokos,* the God-bearer, and hers is a one-time mission but with implications for all Jesus' later followers. An empty womb filled and an occupied tomb evacuated are the bookends of the life of Jesus among us. It takes God to explain this life.

Now

Disciples come in both genders and all ages. God needs no permission to recruit a new agent, and Mary is a model disciple. Neither Mary's father nor her to-be Joseph are consulted ahead of time. Mary is assertive in her dialog with the highest of angels, and when her questions are answered, gives a bold *Yes.* Disciples often have questions, and with the light God gives, be it great or small, we surrender anew at each turning point.

Dealing with Jesus Christ is an ongoing adventure of invitation and embrace. There is pain and suffering ahead for Mary, the loss of an oldest Son to a strange new mission, and at the end a mother at the foot of a cross. But Mary endures and is found among other disciples on the day of Pentecost. In the mold of Mary, women are full participants in discipleship, facing the same demands and opportunities, as evidenced in the next unit (1:39–56) where Mary and Elizabeth act as prophets of the new kingdom.

Summary

Disciples see Mary as her Son's first follower, a model disciple who answered the divine call with surrender and trust in an uncertain future. Disciples sometimes experience angelic visitations and communications.

The explicit naming of the Father, the Son, and the Holy Spirit makes the whole of discipleship a Trinitarian event. Mary was drawn into a life of participation with the Triune God. Repeated surrender to divine invitations is the path we walk with Jesus and his mom!

Insights

1. God does not ask the permission of men before he speaks to daughters and wives.

2. Young people can have profound encounters with God and the angels.

3. Mary is the first Trinitarian theologian as she dialogs with an angel about the work of the Father, the Spirit, and the Son.

4. All our seeking and all our questions are not fruitful without selling out to God.

5. Mary is her son's first disciple; she welcomes him, then watches herself get reshaped.

6. Following will send us on many pilgrimages; Mary's was to fulfill an angelic sign.

Disciplines

Observation: Mary had a world view to understand special revelation.
Action: Study the variety of ways God is self-revealed in Scripture.
Observation: Mary said Yes to all God's invitations, and with humble trust.
Action: In prayer say "Yes, Lord" aloud several times and notice the change within.

4. Luke 2:1–21

What's the Big Deal?
Genre: The Angelology of a Saving Birth Fulfilled

He was a baby and a child,

so that you might be a perfect human.

He was wrapped in swaddling clothes,

so that you may be freed from the snares of death.

—AMBROSE[15]

15. Just, Luke, 38.

Justification

Along the way I've crafted a maxim, "No one disciple is sufficient, but in a band of followers, outsiders may catch a glimpse of Jesus." And this appears to be Luke's strategy in his justly famous birth story. Joseph and Mary embody obedience to Imperial decree (vv.1–5) and Jewish law (v.21). They are not rebels but peaceful and pious. The shepherds receive and act on the surprise of divine revelation in the heavens. They confirm the divine word (v.16) and depart as joyful evangelists (vv.17, 20). Mary meditates upon the mysteries in which she is embedded (v.19). Jesus is the center of focus, and in this variety of reactions and responses Luke begins to sketch the outline of a disciple.

The heavy use of the technical language of Imperial propaganda (*All the world . . . Caesar Augustus . . . the Lord . . . good news . . . is born . . . Savior . . . peace*) is a key to a deeper, more radical politics.[16] Not Caesar but Jesus is the true and good king the world needs. It's a sophisticated political cartoon, and it demonstrates how disciples are to live in a world they do not control. We do not challenge directly, but we do undermine through example and subversion, offering outsiders a new world view and a better life.

Shape

This thought unit continues *The Angelology of a Saving Birth* by recording the birth of Jesus and several responses. The unit has three parts (a. vv.1–7, b. vv.8–20, a' v.21) with several echoes in the outer frames, including a time signature: *in those days* (v.1) // *at the end of eight days* (v.21), Mary's status: *who was with child* (v.5) // *he was conceived in the womb* (v.21b), Jesus' parents' obedience to Roman decrees (vv.1–5) and Jewish Torah (v.21).

To stop the story with v.20, as we do in our Christmas Eve readings, is a literary and theological error. The thought unit clearly includes v.21, and Jesus is a circumcised Jewish male from an obedient family with a name given by Gabriel. To minimize Jesus' Jewishness is a dangerous omission. He is universal, but nothing about him is generic. He is embedded in the the history of God's chosen people, and in him it finds a new way forward.

The structure is a single center (4. vv.13–14) with four sets of balancing frames for a total of nine sections. The opening and closing paragraphs (a. vv.1–7 // a' v.21) are narrative, while the center and longer paragraph (b. vv.8–20) contains actions and speeches by angels and shepherds. The whole unfolds as follows:

16. On this issue, see Borg and Crossan, *The First Christmas*. 153–67. For samples, see Appendix 7, "Luke and Roman Imperial Theology and Propaganda."

1   a. vv.1–7 Historical Events: Sign of Birth Fulfilled (Prophecy of 1:30–31.
                 b. vv.8–20 Shepherd's Trek and Angel's Chorus
2   1. v.8 Shepherds in the Field
3   2. vv.9 Angelic Message to Shepherds
4   3. v.12 Manger Sign Given by Angel
5   4. vv.13–14 Angels Sing the Meaning of Salvation
6   3' vv.15–16 Manger Confirmed by Obedient Following
7   2' vv.17–19 Angelic Message Shared by Shepherds
8   1' v.20 Shepherds in the Field
9   a' v.21 Jewish Initiation: Sign of Naming Fulfilled (Prophecy of 1:30–31)

Reading the unit as designed by Luke focuses our attention on the center in b4. vv.13–14. It's message, as summarized by Dr. Charles Talbert, is worth repeating:

> The recovery of wholeness in human relationships, which is due to God's acts in Jesus, reflects honor to God. In other words, what is good for human beings glorifies God; what glorifies God is good for human beings. Glorifying God and recovering human wholeness are not mutually exclusive: they are an indissoluble whole. When the angels sang of the benefits of Jesus' lordship, they sang both 'glory to God' and 'peace to men'—one song, heralding a dual benefit of Messiah's birth. That is a good news of great joy.[17]

Content

Jesus' birth is set in a secular dating scheme as an implicit challenge to the ruling powers: a new ruler is now arriving! Joseph and Mary are not nationalist zealots; they obey the registration for taxation decree. Joseph's lineage is Davidic with a proper lineage for Messiahship and born where David was. Divine providence uses the decree to get Jesus to Bethlehem. An angelophany to unlikelies (shepherds) draws in a new audience through revelation and pilgrimage; Jesus is the friend of sinners.

The third shift shepherds are responsive to the good news of an angelic announcement concerning the birth of one who is for *all the people* and who bears the three titles of *Savior, Messiah,* and *Lord.* They are moved to action by the divine clue that the child will be found in an unlikely place, a feeding trough for animals, but wrapped—as with all newborns—in snug wrappings. The house is full of family, so Jesus' crib is a feeding trough on the lower level of the house. The use of the language of Imperial worship is applied to the newborn Jesus in a political cartoon that a new and unlikely ruler has made his first appearance. Upon finding the mother and child,

17. *Reading Luke,* 36.

they testify to their experience. They are now *gospelers*,[18] good *newsers*, evangelists all, which is a mark of following Jesus.

Mary's response, however, is by contrast. She wonders and ponders, muses and meditates, rolling the mysteries over in mind and heart to draw out their significance. This is another mark of faithful following: we apply all our faculties to the substance of what God is up to. Curiosity merges with wonder, and understanding with appreciation. And at the end of eight days Jesus is circumcised and inducted into the covenant of Abraham. He bleeds.

Then

Disciples live in a *thick* multi-layered world of visible and invisible agents who obey and glorify Jesus Christ. Disciples delight in the providences of God, the hidden arrangements into which we regularly stumble. And here the actors are four: the angels who bring divine revelation in oracle and song, the shepherds who become itinerant pilgrims and singing evangelists, Mary who observes and meditates, and the synagogue community to which Jesus' parents bring him to spill his first blood as he is marked out as the next Jew.

Now

It is the hidden working of divine providence that moves the holy family towards the city of David. It is an angelic intrusion that moves the shepherds from the hillside to the manger, and it is obedience to Scriptural commands that move Jesus' parents to mark him as a Jew in the initiation rite of circumcision. And it is this same web of divine action, hidden and visible, in which disciples are embedded.

While following Jesus is more than adventure, it surely is not less. If we are the agents of the risen Jesus, then why should we be surprised when we find ourselves in unusual circumstances with unusual opportunities for service and witness? And if there are no Wow! moments from time to time, it might be good to ask, "Am I still following, or have I been cleverly diverted?"

Nothing is a more sure sign of walking in the Spirit than a series of *divine appointments* and unsought opportunities. How often we stumble ourselves through little obediences into the lively will of God.

Discipleship is about glad obedience, but not autonomous initiative. It is, rather, deeply responsive to God's initiatives. In this dance God always leads, and we are attentive to cues that enable our responses. Jesus is a Jew, and his resurrection body still

---

18. On the recovery of *gospeling* and *good-newsing*, see McKnight, *The King Jesus Gospel*, Chapter 6, "The Gospel in the Gospels," 78–91.

bears the scar of that first surgery. It is the God of the Jews whose personal agent he is, and anything that is anti-Jewish is against the church's Lord.[19]

Summary

Disciples stand in wonder and awe at the Jewish Savior's manner of coming, and if—as it sometimes does—our following becomes more about our performance than the glory of his person, then we've taken the center again and must be displaced. The joy of the third-shift shepherds and the pondering of Mary are our twin modes of operation. We follow him in both action and reflection.

Insights

1. Following Jesus is personal but never private; we live with him in the public square.
2. Beneath and behind and above the chaos and cruelty of this present evil age, God is at work bending history to a good and glorious end.
3. Never compromise the *All* of Jesus; he matters ultimately for every human being.
4. When God reveals something, it's meant to stir awe and ultimately obedience.
5. Never minimize the *Jewishness* of Jesus; it is secured by Mary and his circumcision.

Disciplines

Observation: Note the theme of angelic and human joy that's interwoven.
Action: Go on a hunt for Jesus every day; he hides in order to be found.
Observation: Observing and pondering is part of Mary's discipleship.
Action: At the end of prayer, spend a few minutes daydreaming over whatever.

B. DISCIPLESHIP IN THE EARLY MINISTRIES OF JOHN AND JESUS (3:1–4:30)

5. Luke 3:1–22

The Beginning of Revival
Hybrid Genre: A Lukan Mix

Christ is born; the Spirit is his forerunner.
Christ is baptized; the Spirit bears him witness.

---

19. For biblical critiques of contemporary Christmas sentimentality, see Garland, *Luke*, "Christmas Fantasy versus the True Christmas," 128–30; Bailey, "The Manger and the Inn."

Christ is tempted; the Spirit leads him up.

Christ performs miracles; the Spirit accompanies him.

Christ ascends; the Spirit fills his place.

—GREGORY OF NAZIANZUS[20]

Justification

Luke 3:1–4:30 is an essay in four parts. The first and last units present John's preaching and rejection (3:1–22) set in parallel to Jesus' initial preaching and near murder (4:16–30). In between are a genealogy that announces that Jesus is the Son of God by lineage (3:3–38) and his testing in the wilderness where he is revealed as the faithful Son of God (4:1–15). Together with Mother Mary, John the Baptizer prepares the way for Jesus, she by giving him flesh and he by preaching repentance, ethical living, and pointing to the greater one to come. John speaks truth to wicked power, is jailed and later killed for questioning the bedroom activities of Herod, but not before he has baptized Jesus. John is then moved off stage, his work done and faithful to the end.

Like his parents, John is also a pre-disciple and the tipping point between the two eras. As a prototype of the Christian evangelist, John preaches Jesus and an ethical lifestyle of love for neighbor, including the sharing of goods.[21] Real repentance is a graced gateway to real forgiveness, meaning a healed relationship with God leading to love and service.

Shape

When taken as a whole, this thought unit is a 5:1 chiasm, with five paragraphs and a single center (1. vv.1–6, 2. vv.7–9, 3. vv.10–14, 2' vv.15–18, 1' vv.19–22). There are ten deliberate echoes in the first and last paragraphs that act as inclusions to set 3:1–22 off from what comes before and after: *Herod the tetrarch* (v.1c // v.19a), *brother* (v.1d // v.19a), *word came* (v.2b) // *voice came* (v.21e), *John* (v.2b // v.21e), *son* (v.2b / /v.21e), *baptism* (v.3b // v.21a-b), *voice* (v.4b, v.21e), *All* (vv.3a, 6 // v.19b, c, 21a), Isaiah Quotes (vv.4b–6 // v.21e), and time signatures (v.1a // v.21a). And at the center (3. vv.10–14) John the prophet becomes John the pastor as he gives answers to the single pressing question expressed by all, "What shall we do?' An outline gives us a map for the whole:

    1. vv.1–6 Herod, John's Baptism, and Scripture
    a. vv.1–2a Dating: 7 Political and Religious Leaders
    b. vv.2b–6 John's Call and Baptism, Is. 40:3–5 is Quoted
        2. vv.7–9 John's Preaching No. 1: Fruitful Repentance, Fire of Judgment

20. Just, *Luke*, 67.
21. Talbert, *Reading Luke*, 31.

3. vv.10–14 John Answers the Same Question Three Times
2' vv.15–18 John's Preaching No. 2: End-Time Savior, Fire of Judgment
1' vv.19–22 Herod, John's Arrest, Jesus' Baptism, Prayer + 3 Heavenly Portents
a. vv.10–20 Dating: Herod and John's Imprisonment
b. vv.21–22 Jesus' Baptism and Call, Is. 42:1, 44:2, 61:1 are quoted
Luke employs a blend of genres in this hybrid thought unit:

1. A list of leaders, which is a convention of Greek historiography (vv.1–2a),

2. The call of a prophet (vv.2b–6),

3. The message of a prophet (vv.7–9, 15–18),

4. A dialog of question and answer (vv.10–14),

5. The rebuke of a Jewish king (vv.19–20),

6. The confirmation of a hero's identity in a *Bios* (vv.21–22),

7. A Lukan summary (v.18),

8. A Revelatory Vision: Prayer Scene plus 3 Heavenly Portents (vv.21–22).

Content

God's work is set amidst the world as it now is (vv.1–2a) as a pyramid of power and public honor. The deep drama of history is found in the phrase, "and the Word of God came . . ." (v.2a), and this Word of divine revelation is a tipping point. God calls a prophet to fulfill that for which he has been prepared, as echoed in Scripture from Is. 40:3–5. Life at ground level is about to encounter a prophet announcing God's arrival in Jesus and calling for repentance, a radical turning toward God and God's invitation. A great division is coming: saved and lost, wheat and chaff, granary and the destruction of unquenchable fire.

A faithful church follows John as fellow evangelists and points to Jesus Christ, the final agent of God's presence in grace and judgment. Confronting corrupt power is baked into the cost of a public faith. Jesus is God's Beloved Son. The Holy Spirit's presence is necessary for participation in Jesus' ministry. Repentance involves radical integrity and generosity of all (vv.10–14), but also conventional sexual morality (vv.19–20). Jesus is the one over whom heaven is open, the one in whom the Holy Spirit is present; he is the one who is uniquely related to God as authorized Agent and Son. He is without parallel.

Then

A sword was promised by Simeon to pierce Mary's heart, and a sword severed John's head from his shoulders. Luke early on alerts us that both family pain and public pain are found on the path of Jesus. Family tries to control and corral; kings resist their sins being named in public. Like later followers, John is called and commissioned to go public with his confrontive message of fresh repentance and real heart change to prepare for the great separation as with grain and chaff. And when asked about the specifics of a turn-around, he counsels generosity and integrity: share with the poor and don't misuse your power.

But John does not stop here; instead, he points beyond himself to the mighty one, the personal agent of God's fiery judgment and final separation. John prepares the way without getting in the way. Jesus and his disciples will also preach repentance and a new life of compassion and integrity, offer specific counsel, point to the coming of the Spirit and the coming judgment, all of which are previewed in John's brief career as prophet and evangelist. Thus Mary and John are the two premier pre-disciples who prepare the way, though in different ways: private and public, family and nation.

Now

John the Baptist is a pre-disciple and a prophet of the Father who sent the Son in the power of the Holy Spirit, and he calls for a change of heart and life now in light of the coming future of God's truth-telling and separation. But then, all discipleship is oriented to the future kingdom of God that Jesus previews in the present.

Jesus and John share a world view about where creation is headed and how people will be divided into two and only two piles, one to be treasured and the other disposed of. A disciple of Jesus is one who has been turned in the right direction and begins bearing the good fruits of a new life, part of which is a special concern for the poor and vulnerable and also the social dimensions of personal integrity. Included in this new life with Jesus is a sex ethic that honors God's boundaries of fidelity in marriage and celibacy in singleness and a willingness to advocate for it in public, as John did at great cost. Our following Jesus is word and deed, lifestyle and outlook. It's not self-powered but enabled by the continuing gift of the Holy Spirit who inwardly assures us we are God's beloved sons and daughters. Nothing can separate us from this Triune, divine love, and it is the drawing power of this love in Jesus that glues us to him in allegiance. There's none like him.

Summary

Disciples face the challenges of repentance—a change of mind, heart, and hand— and from time to time return to the Jordan to listen to John the Baptist who prepared

God's people for Jesus' emergence. Disciples are courageous in addressing sin, exposing excuses, giving specific counsel, warning of judgment, and pointing to Jesus as God's ultimate agent, even if it brings scorn and danger. And what we offer others, we apply to ourselves.

Insights

1. No instant prophets. They require long preparation to be able to answer God's call.

2. The most disruptive force is a fearless prophet with a heart for God and people.

3. Inherited religion is a rich reservoir, but no substitute for a changed life of love.

4. A heart of compassion, a hand of help, and a life of integrity mark disciples.

5. Jesus is the continental divide; where we stand with him is where we stand with God.

6. Spirituality is formed at the interface of solidarity with people and openness to God.

7. A faithful sexual ethic of celibacy in singleness and fidelity in marriage is consistent with our allegiance to Jesus Christ. People are not playthings to be used and tossed. The bodies of disciples belong to Jesus and to their spouses alone.

8. The filling and empowering of the Holy Spirit is necessary for kingdom work; good intentions are not enough. Disciples are not self-propelled.

Disciplines

Observation: John turned to God in the wilderness, then call others to turn in public.
Action: Never stop turning back to God in repentance, and call others to the same.
Observation: John engaged the awakened in the particular challenges of their jobs.
Action: Learn the art of deep listening; trust the Holy Spirit for the gift of wisdom.

DISCIPLESHIP IN THE GALILEAN MINISTRY (4:31–9:51)

6. Luke 4:31–44

Glimpse of a World Set Free
Hybrid Genre: A Lukan Mix

That irreverent men do not believe, the spirits see—that he is God.

So they flee and fall down at his feet,

saying just what they uttered when he was in the body.

—ATHANASIUS[22]

22. Just, *Luke*, 85–86.

Justification

One of Luke's literary techniques is to pair two sequential units as a set of panels using the same underlying sequence. This is the arrangement of 4:31–44 // 5:1–16. Both panels share a theme, which is Jesus' kingdom ministry and power evangelism. Both have five parts and end with a retreat for prayer. Christology and discipleship are here joined.

1. Setting and teaching,

2. Miracle 1: Power over demons and over nature,

3. Miracle 2: A healing after a request,

4. Mass healings and deliverances,

5. Retreat for prayer and new mission.

Panel 1 (4:31–44) is primarily about who Jesus is and Panel 2 (5:1-16) about becoming his follower. The golden cord of Jesus is woven together with the blue cord of discipleship; they are distinguishable but inseparable. Jesus begins alone, but is not a solo operator, because as soon as practical, he makes a case and forms a community around himself. Being a follower is never only a *Jesus and me* thing; it's a *him and us and all the world* thing. Panel 2 (5:1–16) is a disciple unit in its explicit call of Peter and implicit call of three others: Andrew—Peter's brother, and the brothers James and John. But Peter also has a cameo appearance in Panel 1 (4:38–39), thus linking the two panels.

Shape

The two panels are to be read as a mutually interpretive pair on Christology and Discipleship. And while the panels are in the same order, you will also notice below a variation in the ordering of some elements: the spread of the report (4:37 // 5:15a), a Petrine tradition (4:38–39 // 5:1–11), *cities* (4:31b // 5:12). Here a chart is helpful:

Luke 4:31–44 (Panel 1: 5 Parts)	Luke 5:1–16 (Panel 2: 5 Parts)
1. vv.31–32a Setting: Synagogue teaching	1. vv.1a, 3d Setting: Lakeside teaching
"teaching" (v.31c)	"word" (logos) (v.1a)
"word" (logos) (vv.32, 36a)	"taught" (v.3d)
2. vv.31d–37 Teaching + Power	2. vv.1–11 Teaching + Power
Ministry to first individual	Ministry to first individual, "And it happened"
Jesus' command (v.35b)	Jesus' command (v.4b)
Resistance (v.34)	Resistance (v.5)
Jesus has power over demons	Jesus has power over nature, over sin/shame
"All astonished" (v.31d)	"All astonished" (v.9)

"cities" (vv.31b)

Report spreads (v.37)

3. vv.38–39 Healing After Request	3. vv.12–14 Healing After Request
Ministry to second individual	Ministry to second individual, "And it happened"
Extreme case: "*high* fever,"	Extreme case: "*full* of leprosy"
"besought"	"besought"
Jesus' command (v.39b)	Jesus' command (v.13b)
"it left"	"leprosy left"
"immediately"	"immediately"
(Petrine tradition: Family memory)	"hand"
	silence: "charged him to tell no one"
	"cities" (v.12)
4. vv.40–41 Mass Healings/Deliverances	4. v.15 Mass Healings of Infirmities
Ministry to crowds	Ministry to crowds
"healed them all"	"healed of their infirmities"
silence: "not allow them to speak"	
"hands"	
v.15a Report spreads	
5. vv.42–44 Jesus Retreats for Prayer	5. v.16 Jesus Retreats for Prayer
"departed and went to a desert place"	"withdrew to the wilderness and prayed"
"cities" (v.43)	

As before, you note where a thought unit begins and ends by an echo of terms (an inclusion). And that's true in 4:31–44 which has a series of inclusions which forms a verbal bracket around the unit: 1) A travel report: "And he went down to Capernaum" (v.31) // "he departed and went to a lonely place" (v.42b), 2) A designation: "a city" (v.31b) // "other cities" (v.33b), 3) A province: "Galilee" (v.31b) // "Judea"(v.44), 4) Sabbath instruction: "teaching them on the Sabbath" (v.31c) // "preaching in the synagogues of Judea" (v.44).

The thought unit consists of six paragraphs with a double center (as in the structure below). The ordering is designed to illustrate that Jesus' kingdom ministry of word and deed occurs in a variety of settings: the Synagogue (vv.31d–37), a home (vv.38–39), outside in a courtyard (vv. 40, 41), on mission in other cities (vv.42–44) and with differing audiences: a demonized man, a fevered woman, crowds with a variety of issues. An emphasis on Jesus' scope of operations is highlighted in the summary of v.40 with its string of inclusive references, "All . . . any . . . various . . . every one of them." Who is he? Jesus is an everywhere, everyone healer. A new movement has broken out in the villages of northern Galilee.

The thought unit includes two miracle stories: an exorcism (vv.31d–37) and a healing (vv.38–39), plus two summaries concerning healings (v.40) and exorcisms (v.41).

Luke uses the standard five-part miracle story form for the exorcism and the healing: 1) Setting: vv.31d–32 // v.38a, 2) Problem: v.33 // v.38b, 3) Healer Acts: v.35 // v.38c–39a, 4) Healing: v.35c // 39b, 5) Proof/Crowd Response: vv.36–37 // v.39b. Parallel travel and ministry reports open and close the unit: v.31a-d //vv.42–44.

An outline reveals the concentric structure with healings and mass healing at the center (3. vv. 38–39 // 3' v.40), individual and communal exorcisms using the term "rebuked" in the next outward layer from the center (2. vv.31d–37 // 2' v.41), and travel, sabbath, and mission reports in the outside frames (1. vv.31a-c // 1' vv.42–44), as follows:

> 1. vv.31a-c Travel Report: Arrival in Capernaum and Sabbath Teaching
> > 2. vv.31d–37 Exorcism in the Synagogue: 2 Titles of Jesus
> > > 3. vv.38–39 Healing at Peter's Home, Prayer
> > > 3' v.40 Mass Healings in Peter's Courtyard
> > 2' v.41 Mass Deliverances in Peter's Courtyard: 2 Titles of Jesus
> 1' vv.42–44 Travel Report: First for Prayer, Then for New Mission

It's clear Luke has shaped and intends 4:31–44 to be read and heard as a distinct unit of thought, a sort of mini-essay on what a day in the life of Jesus looked like. This is the kind of life his soon-to-be followers are invited into; this is the game Jesus plays. It's high-stakes, dangerous, and for keeps, involving both the visible and invisible worlds.

Content

Have you ever wondered, What was a typical day for Jesus? This is it! It begins in the Capernaum synagogue on the Sabbath, goes through that evening, and concludes early the next morning. And in it are compressed many of the classic elements of Jesus about-to-unfold ministry: his travel (v.31a), his teaching in the synagogue (vv.31c, 44), his extraordinary authority, his power over the demons (vv.31d–37), his growing reputation (v.37), his power over disease (vv.38–39), his healing and deliverance ministry not only with individuals but with the diverse crowds that gather after the sabbath in Peter's courtyard (vv.40–41), the use of various titles set in parallel sections (2 // 2') to highlight Jesus' complex identity (vv.34, 41a, c), his prayerful dependence on the Father in prayer (v.42), his keen sense of mission coupled with a resistance to human control (vv.43–44), and an integrating emphasis on the inbreaking of the kingdom of God through himself as its chief agent (v.43).

This is what a day was like in which *the new reality* was put on display in word and deed in a diversity of settings. Where Jesus goes, unusual things happen; life is put right again and function is restored. And remember: this was *a new thing* for him as well. To shift from *Nazareth-builder* to *Galilee-kingdom-displayer* was a steep learning curve, and there was a first time for everything! And whatever surprises and challenges meet Jesus, he responds out of the love and power of God's immediate, guiding presence through the Holy Spirit. In this deep dependence, the loving power of God goes out through him.

The operational model I've come to use to interpret Jesus' words and deeds is explicitly Trinitarian: the Father wills it, the Son obeys it, the Spirit energizes it, thus one will and divine action in three persons; what theologians label *inseparable operations*.[23]

Jesus knew what to do and what to say in each new situation because of direct revelation and inspiration. He spoke what he heard, and did what he saw. It unfolded in front of his own eyes, and those of his followers. And it happened over and over and over, as did his withdrawals for prayer which are testimony to his radical dependence on the Father and the Spirit. He is no magician who manipulates unseen powers; he's a prayerfully dependent Jewish male who is—simultaneously—God the Son at ground level, embracing the limits of human knowledge and living in trust that when he needs insight and divine energies, they are right on time! He is divine agency on the move, a paradoxical display of human limits infused with divine love and energies. He is not an independent operator.

So, having now bested the devil in the wilderness (4:1–15), and having announced his mission as the fulfiller of Isaiah's promises, and having resisted Nazareth's parochial claims and violence, Jesus launches out in his ministry of freedom and release along multiple fronts demonstrating that he is Lord over demons (vv.31d–37) and disease (vv.38–39) in a variety of settings.[24] Jesus is an *every place* and an *every person* Savior. He's not interested in demonic testimony, however accurate, because it does not come from trust.[25]

Jesus reclaims and restores the whole person to robust function. As he teaches the kingdom, the Holy Spirit turns up the lights of spiritual illumination to expose the demons people are hosting. Jesus operates in two dimensions at once, the seen and the unseen. He is powerful and merciful, but he will not be controlled by anyone but the Father. Nazareth cannot kill him nor Capernaum corral him. He is the agent of his Father's new thing and empowered by the Spirit. He lives under a compelling divine mandate: *I must preach* and *I was sent* (vv.43–44).

23. See Holmes, *The Quest for the Trinity*, 107–09, 132–33.

24. I have used Appendix 8, "A Checklist of Possible Spiritual Openings For Evil" in churches, in prison ministry, in Kazakhstan, and in three African nations as an awareness tool concerning the dangers of the occult in all its forms and of habitual sins as openings for evil. It must be used with pastoral wisdom and not without a careful reading of the Scriptural passages that ground each topic of the inventory. Confession and forgiveness are the first remedy for any involvement, but if there are associated spiritual phenomena, consult a pastor for aid. For a recent treatment of severe cases by a Christian psychiatrist, see Gallagher, *Demonic Foes*. For a comprehensive approach, Sam Storms, *Understanding Spiritual Warfare*; Bielby and Eddy, *Understanding Spiritual Warfare*.

25. On the demonic, see Appendices 11, 12.

Then

What does it mean for Jesus to be—as the titles indicate—*the Holy One of God* (v.34d), *the Son of God* (v.41), *the Messiah* (v.41c)? It means that wherever he goes, life is restored by the God of Israel so that no single title captures the fullness and richness of his identity. The earlier agenda of *release* (4:16–20) announced in Nazareth and there rejected is now being implemented in line with the ancient promises of Isaiah.

The forces of disease, demons, ignorance, and sin are pushed back and God's image-bearers are restored and invited into the expanding mission of Jesus (vv.42–44). God's presence breaks through repeatedly with immediate results. This is a present act of love and a preview of the cosmic restoration at the end of the age with the full unveiling and revealing of the same kingdom. It is, as they say, "a preview of coming events."

While some may resist the notion as demeaning, as a loss of identity and personal initiative as a willing being, I believe we may legitimately speak of the *discipleship of Jesus*, meaning his own following as moment by moment he lives in surrender and obedience to the will of the Father and the energies of the Holy Spirit. Luke's biography is his chronicle of that loving, faithful obedience in the face of constant resistance at multiple levels (demonic and human). Jesus follows the Father's will in the Spirit's guidance and energies, and we follow him wherever he goes. We observe his prayerful, humble obedience and what happens through it. It's a new way to live.

Think about it! There was a first time Jesus cast out a demon, a first time he rebuked a fever, a first time he faced a crowd where every able-bodied person brought someone who was sick or injured, a first time he had to resist the pressure to set up a *kingdom shop* in one town. It was all new behavior, not a change of character but a change of realized potential that came with the anointing of the Spirit just after his baptism.

He was now practicing his intimacy with the Father and the Spirit on a very public stage, a tight-rope walker on a high wire with no safety net. What had not happened before now occurred regularly. God cared this much for the miseries of his people, and in the presence of Jesus the most remarkable things happened to suffering people.

Now because Simon Peter's home and mother-in-law are mentioned in v.38, this is a disciple—or perhaps a pre-disciple story. Though not stated, we presume Peter's presence in the synagogue, in his home, in his courtyard, and perhaps even the next morning by those who want Jesus to set up shop in their town. All this material precedes Peter's explicit call and commission story in 5:1–11.

The plausibility of Peter's call is made more likely by prior exposure to the man from Nazareth, his marvelous words, mighty miracles, and expanding mission (unlike Mark 1:16–20 where there is no record of prior acquaintance with Peter). And here the evidence is heavily supernatural, namely multiple exorcisms and multiple healings in which the twelve and the seventy will soon share (9:1–6, 10:1–24). That was part of the case Jesus built prior to the additional miracle of the miraculous catch which hooked Peter.

Miracles as acts of divine power leading to awe may be a catalyst to faith, though not always. The *authority* of Jesus is that his words and deeds of power are backed by the God in whose Spirit he operates, and his followers are invited into a world where this was a constant experience.[26] That we minimize the effects of such constant exposure distorts our understanding of what it meant to be apprenticed to Jesus. They were to be *with him* in order to become *like him*, and he was soggy with the Holy Spirit every day!

There is an unavoidably charismatic dimension to Jesus as he obeys the Father in the powers of the Spirit to great benefit for broken, infested, diseased people. Knowing the Bible and living an ethical life are marks of discipleship and rightly valued, but also are prayer, hearing from God in the immediacy of circumstances, and the exercise of spiritual gifts under divine guidance and in a team ministry.

Could it be that our current models of disciple-making are way too skeptical and way too reticent about this prominent dimension?[27] Yes. And can we lead others into what we have not-much experienced? I doubt it. There is an empirical, experiential, experimental, and risky element in following a Jesus who does such wild and amazing things as a matter of course.[28] To follow him is to admit how little you really know and be willing to look stupid and incompetent much of the time, but that is the price of admission.

Now

The common trope of "I like your Jesus but not his followers" always has some bite because of the gap between us and him, but how could it be otherwise? We are stumbling along after the one who was perfect wisdom and love in human flesh. This is why Luke is jammed with *Disciple Correction Stories*, and every one of them is based on Jesus' closest associates getting it wrong and then getting correction. Discipleship is the very best venue for looking foolish and stupid in public. We who follow are just

---

26. Healings and exorcism stories are found in all the major sections of Luke, not just the early materials.

27. For a report from two pastors, see Bannister, *The Word & Power Church*; Hull, *Straight Talk on Spiritual Power*; and from Ruthven, *What's Wrong With Protestant Theology*, Part V, "How Protestants Messed Up Discipleship," 243–98.

28. In six recent books on disciple-making, all of which I would recommend as good on other grounds, I note a gaping absence on the gifts and power of the Holy Spirit for healing and deliverance as part of the training of new apprentices. They are: Watson and Watson, *Contagious Disciple Making*; Harrington & Patrick, *The Disciple Makers Handbook*; Allin, *Simple Discipleship*; Hull & Sobels, *The Discipleship Gospel*; Springer, *How to Follow Jesus*; English, *Deep Discipleship*.

like the rest of the sinful, broken, ignorant, dying world with one addition: we have a hope and a home in Jesus Christ.

That we fail and fall, and sometimes spectacularly and with great harm to others, should surprise no one but the naive in our own ranks and the cheap critics around us. And so when the trope is invoked, my new answer is, "If you like him as you claim, then are you his follower as well, and how can you help the rest of us be more faithful?"

The simple truth is that following Jesus is highly unpredictable, and so if comfort and safety are your highest values, you will not follow him very far. He is wild in the precise sense that he cannot be tamed but lives in the freedom of God's love for everyone he meets and everyone he calls. So if 4:31–44 is indeed *a day in the life of Jesus*, then it serves as a baseline for the rest of the story as arranged by Luke.

That this thought unit unfolds in four separate sequential spaces (synagogue, home, outdoors, the next village) indicates that Jesus invades all locations with his disturbing presence. Following him is not a segmented life of religious and non-religious compartments. He is an every-place and all-the-time agent of the kingdom, and he is disruptive of current arrangements, not in a cavalier style of destructive rebellion but by bringing a new order into play in the midst of the old regime.

Jesus is at war with all the powers that distort the human person in all their relationships: empty religiosity, demonization and colonization, disease and sickness, the sins of selfishness and all attempts to control him for personal benefit. And the blessing—the sheer and astounding goodness of his presence—is what keeps us intrigued as he cracks us open to a new ordering of life.

So expect to be confused and bewildered, expect to feel exposed and vulnerable, be prepared for lots of *I don't knows*. Learn that messy is the new normal, and get used to having your heart pierced by the pain of people and the love that flows through Jesus. He does not call us in order to make life-as-currently-defined better. He comes to give us a new life with a new center of love and allegiance, and the precise form of such a life cannot be precisely determined ahead of time because it is constituted in an ongoing fashion by his initiatives and our responses. Discipleship is a dance, a genuine chess match, a truly interactive affair. And if we say, "This far and no further," something vibrant begins to wither. To say "Yes" to Jesus is to grow in trust of the only one who is fully trustworthy.

Summary

Disciples follow a confrontive Jesus who demonstrates what *the new reality* looks like, and two of its most dramatic effects are demon expulsion and physical healing. Freedom and function matter to Jesus. We follow One who loves but will not be controlled by others and is passionate about getting *the new reality* to others. This is why he was sent.

Insights

1. Mission always has detractors; disciples follow Jesus beyond conventional wisdom.

2. In company with Jesus, we learn to operate in the visible and invisible realms.

3. Everyone is a battleground of some sort, so use spiritual authority and be gentle.

4. The Holy Spirit supplies illumination to expose pockets of darkness and infestation.

5. Jesus is not interested in demonic confessions. They hate and cannot trust him.

6. Mission in obedience to the Holy Spirit will always be full of surprises.

Disciplines

Observation: Jesus was not hesitant to engage whatever pained people.
Action: When a needs crosses your path, stop and listen and pray then and there.
Observation: Jesus snuck off for solitude, listening prayer, and debriefing with God.
Action: Daily prayer, a weekly sabbath, and occasional retreats keep us open to God.

7. Luke 5:1–16

How Jesus Operated
Hybrid Genre: Call & Commission Story + Gift Miracle + Healing + Summary

For the net is still being drawn, while Christ fills it,

and calls to conversion those who, according to the Scriptural phrase,

are in the depths of the sea,

that is to say, those who live in the surge and wave of worldly things.[29]

—CYRIL OF ALEXANDRIA

Justification

This is a disciple unit on the call of Jesus' first followers. It's two sets of brothers, and all are fishermen: Philip and likely Andrew as well, James and John (5:1–11). Their quick immersion in the kingdom ministry of Jesus and his healings, as well as the regular habits of retreat and prayer, is immediate in the three paragraphs that follow (vv.12–14a, 14b, 15–16).

29. Just, *Luke*, 88.

Shape

That 5:1–16 stands in parallel to 4:31–44 was established in the last section:

1. Setting and teaching (vv.1–3d),

2. Miracle 1: miraculous catch (vv.4–11),

3. Miracle 2: healing with request (vv.12–14),

4. Mass healings (v.15),

5. Retreat for prayer (v.16).

As for genre, it's a Lukan hybrid with vv.1–11 as a *Call and Commission Story* including a gift miracle, vv.12–14 being as a Healing Story in five standard parts,[30] and vv.15–16 being as a Lukan summary and prayer report. The standard components of the *Call and Commission Story*, perhaps Luke's favorite genre, are:[31]

Text	Intro.	Confront	Reaction	Commission	Protest	Reassurance	Conclusion
1:5–25	vv.5–10	v.11	v.12	vv.13b–17	v.18`	vv.13a, 19–20	vv.21–25
1:26–38	vv.26–27	v.28	v.29	vv.31–33, 35	v.34	vv.30, 36–37	v.38
2:8–20	v.8	v.9a-b, 13–24	v.9c	vv.11–12	x	v.10	vv.15–20
*5:1–11	vv.1–2	v.3	vv.8–10a	vv.4, 10c	v.5	v.10b	v.11
24:1–9	vv.1–3	v.4	v.5a	vv.6–7	x	v.5b	vv.8–9
24:36–53	v.36a	v.36b	vv.37, 41	vv.44–48	x	v.49	vv.50–53

The 5:1 concentric structure of the Call and Commission Story (5:1–11) is:

```
1        a. vv.1–3 Introduction: Fishermen and their Boats Claimed by Jesus
2              b. vv.4–5 Dialog 1: Jesus and Simon, Title, Resistance + Obedience
3                    c. vv.6–7 Miraculous Catch of Fish after Obedience.
4              b' vv.8–10 Dialog 2: Simon and Jesus, Title, Resistance + Obedience (v.11)
5        a' v.11 Conclusion: Fishermen Claimed by Jesus, Boats Left Behind
```

The story consists of five sub-units with a single center (a. vv.1–3, b. vv.4–5, c. vv.6–7, b' vv.8–10, a' v.11), and it is at the center (c.vv.6–7) that the gift miracle of fish is presented. On either side of this in b. vv.4–5 // b' vv.8–10 are dialogs of Jesus and Peter in which Peter shows resistance and only later obedience. The two outer frames, the Introduction (a. vv.1–3) and Conclusion (a' v.11) use "boats" and "land" as verbal echoes and inclusions.

The subsequent miracle story proper falls into two parts (5:12–14a, v.14b-c), the first having four parts and a double center as the structure indicates:

---

30. Most Gospel healing and exorcism stories share a common form in five parts: 1) Setting (5:12a), 2) Problem (12:5b), 3) Healer acts (v.13), 4) Healing (v.14a), 5) Reactions and Proofs (v.14b-c).

31. For an analysis of Luke's first call story (5:1–11), see Sweetland, *Our Journey with Jesus*, "The Call of the First Disciple," 19–25.

a. v.12a Condition: Man with Severe Leprosy

    b. v.12b Leper Speaks to Jesus in Posture and Prayer

    b' v.13 Jesus Touches and Speaks to the Leper a Prayer of Command

a' v.14a Cure: Man without Leprosy

The second part (vv.14b-c) functions as the proof of healing (component 5 of the miracle story form). The concluding Lukan summary (1' vv.15–16), short as it is, touches on three characteristics of Jesus' public works: 1) the news spread quickly (v.15a // 4:37); 2) it was a dual ministry of teaching and then demonstrating *the new reality* in healings (v.15b); and 3) Jesus' habitual response was to retreat for prayer (v.16).

Content

To this point there have been pre-disciples (Zechariah and Elizabeth, Mary, Simeon and Anna, John the Baptist), but here Jesus calls his first three followers, or is it four with Andrew assumed to have been present? It's early morning. Peter and friends are wrapping up a night of fruitless labor, and already a crowd has gathered to hear Jesus. The locale remains Capernaum, and so Jesus' brusque announcement of v.43 does not mean an immediate departure.

Now remember the miracles Peter has already witnessed at the hands of Jesus. Perhaps this is why he complies so readily to Jesus' request for a floating pulpit (vv.2–3). But then comes what Peter took as a foolish command to launch out and let down the nets for a catch (v.4). Peter's complaint is registered, as is his obedience and the reason for it, "but at your word" (v.5). What happens is a *gift miracle* of divine abundance,[32] and the sudden enormity reveals the divine identity of Jesus to Peter and pushes him to his knees in the pain of God's knowledge of him.

Jesus is not just prophet, healer, and exorcist; he mysteriously participates in deity, thus Peter's address of him as *Lord* (the Greek translation of the Hebrew divine name *Yahweh)*. Jesus speaks to his emotions with a command of assurance, "Do not be afraid," then offers him a new future as a participant in Jesus' own work, "henceforth you will be one who nets people."[33]

And while Peter is in the spotlight (a literary technique in ancient biographies[34]), James and John are also included in the event and, like Peter (and Andrew?), leave the tools of their trade on the shore "and followed him." Symbols of the old life are set aside. We moderns would love a script of Peter's discussion with his wife and what following Jesus meant for their life together, but such is not to be. What is clear is that

---

32. On the so-called *nature miracles*, three of which are found in Luke (5:1–11 [miraculous catch], 8:22–25 [stilling the storm], 9:10–17 [feeding five thousand]), see the series of philosophical and exegetical essays in Twelftree, *The Nature Miracles of Jesus.*

33. The felicitous translation of Johnson, *Luke*, 87.

34. See Licona, *Why Are There Differences In The Gospel?* 93 for a list of examples of this technique.

Jesus claims the right of disruption, to interrupt, lay claim, and redirect a life into *the new reality.*

That they did indeed go with Jesus is implicit in v.12a where we find him, and them by implication, "in one of the cities." The miracle of the healing of the man with severe leprosy is cast in the five classic parts of a miracle story:

1. Condition/Illness (v.12a),

2. Confrontation with Healer (v.12b),

3. Action and Word of the Healer (v.14),

4. Report of Healing (v.14),

5. Responses or Aftermath (v.14b, 15–16).

Like Peter, the leper addresses Jesus as *Lord,* and as leprosy was often associated with punishment for sin, it is not only the man's skin that is cleansed but his heart as well. With the certification of the local priest, he may be officially restored to community.

When the word gets out, throngs come to hear and be healed, to be taught the kingdom and have Jesus apply the energies of love to them. As before, the demands of serving the sick is followed by a retreat for communion and refilling (vv.15–16). Think of a reusable battery being drained through heavy use, then put back into the cradle for a fresh charge. Nothing is more exhausting, as I have observed in myself and others, than praying with and for the sick and afflicted. You ask for peace and burn adrenaline by the quart!

Jesus' communion and intimacy with the Father and the Spirit is a priority; it is the source out of which he works. Jesus ministers to individuals (vv.12–14), indirectly to priests (v.14c), to crowds (vv.15–16), and then isolates himself. It's his normal rhythm of intense engagement followed by strategic disengagement. His ministry is not a sprint but a three year marathon for which he's been in preparation and training his entire life in the ordinariness of Nazareth. As a human being, even one without sin, Jesus has human limits. He is voluntarily and gladly dependent on the Father and the Spirit, and it is his glory.

Then

Peter was after fish and the income they produced; it's what he knew best, but Jesus was fishing for Peter and landed his first disciple and several family and friends as well. They came in as a cluster from one occupation and location, two sets of brothers who partnered in fishing (v.9).

Social networks are influential in the spread of the faith, then and now, and for those of us addicted to Western individualism with its *sovereign I* and *solo decisions,* people movements take some getting used to. With each potential follower Jesus is building a case and presenting evidence for his being true and trustworthy. And with Peter, and likely the ones who came with him, it was signs and wonders in a series, both before (4:31–44) and after their call and surrender (5:12–16). And with the certification of divine power came the authority to make demands of Peter (vv.2–3, 5, 10–11), and each time with increasing cost Peter obeyed.

Jesus made his case, and for the first group of disciples it was now day one of a new life. They came as a cluster of friends to Jesus, who from the first was dealing with Peter as if he were already a leader. The tipping point of obedience has both a before and an after: the case being made, the tipping point of trust, the implications of the new relationship. And so Jesus began to have a community of helpers, trainees, and witnesses around him, marveling and remembering, asking questions, wondering each day what they'd gotten themselves into. It was a strange new world with their new friend as tour guide.

Now

Each disciple has a call and commissioning story to tell, and whether low or high voltage, it is your witness to the action of the risen Jesus in your life, so when nudged by the Holy Spirit, tell it and retell it. What came before, what came during, and what came afterwards, just like Peter. Meditate on the careful case Christ built to get your attention and eventually claim your loyalty. What divine appointments, answers to prayer, or tests of obedience were involved? What moved you towards him in trust? And what did you have to lay down in order to take up his invitation to enter his academy of discipleship? How disruptive of normalcy was your new faith? And how has your life been different because of his tutelage and lordship? Did any family or friends join you on the journey?

When you retell your tale, you will find your own heart leaping again at delight and wonder at what happened when he interrupted your life and set you on a new path. That Peter made a habit of such retelling, especially in light of his later betrayal, is the reason we have such personal reminisces as this and the story of the healing of his mother-in-law.

So when you feel the nudge, glance upwards in prayer, then speak. Nothing is so jolting or arresting as a good, honest testimony of how you came to be a believer who followed. It will captivate the interest of people and perhaps draw a few snide remarks and cheap shots. And if—as with the leper—you have an even more dramatic story of healing and restoration, give that as well. Never, ever be ashamed to bear a simple, personal witness and then to answer questions if they come. It's one of the ways the fire spreads from one heart to another.

Summary

Disciples respond to a call in the midst of life. Jesus builds a case that he is trustworthy, then issues a summons for costly personal allegiance and the promise of a share in his mission, "Follow me, and I will make you . . ." The case may involve signs and wonders, though not all do. Observing Jesus teach and enact *the new reality* is an amazing privilege as the crowds gather. Observing him isolate for prayer reveals his source.

Insights for Disciples

1. Luke took great care to tell the details of Simon's call to discipleship. Have you written yours out with skill?

2. How can church be more *out of doors* and *in the workplace* as here? What are we missing inside buildings?

3. Peter had seen miracles in his synagogue, his home, and now his nets. What case is Jesus building with Peter and his friends?

4. If Jesus, as Lord, is both willing and able to heal, why so little evidence today? Are you willing to be an apprentice and learner in this disputed area?

5. Being a disciple means voluntarily being around needy, desperate, and annoying people. What's your current exposure to such people?

Disciplines

Observation: Jesus built a case that a loving, creative God is active and engaged.
Action: Do not pull back from difficult situations that need divine action. Pray!
Observation: Jesus is fully able to build whatever case is needed.
Action: Learn to ask, What case does Jesus seem to be building with this person?

8. Luke 5:27–39

The Problem of Conventional Religion
Blended Genre: A Classic Call Story + Symposium and Controversy Dialogs

He has not called those who, wishing to establish their own justice,

has not been made subject to the justice of God.

He calls those who, being conscious of their weakness,

are not ashamed to confess that we have all offended in many things.

—BEDE

Justification

As a call story, and with a symposium dialog attached to it at Levi's home, this two-part thought unit clearly belongs in our list of discipleship passages.

Shape

The basic form of this thought unit is that of a provocative or critical incident (the call of Levi), leading to a discourse of Jesus, in this case two controversy dialogs with "the Pharisees and their scribes" in a double question (vv.30, 33) and double answer format (vv.31–32, 34–39). The Incident plus Response pattern is common in Luke.

First is the genre of the call story. If Peter's is a fulsome account of a *Call and Commissioning Story* (5:1–11), then Levi's is the lean, abbreviated version.[35] Of the seven possible components of the call as a summons (1. Travel, 2. Initiative, 3. Initial sight, name, and occupation, 4. Parents, 5. Dialog, 6a-b Call and Promise, 7. Cost of Obedience),[36] five are present:

1. Jesus travel (v.27a),

2. His initiative (v.27a),

3. Sight, Name, and Occupation (v.27b),

4. Call as command (v.27c),

5. Cost and Obedience (v.28).

Omitted are the references to parents (4), to a dialog (5), and to a promise attached to the call (6b). It is clear Luke understands the genre, uses it numerous times, and adapts it to his own interests, thus the bare call story is expanded by giving Levi's second response to Jesus, which is to throw a party for his friends at which Jesus defends his associations with such sinners and rogues.

A second genre is one for which I cannot find a scholarly consensus. I label it a *Disciple Correction Story* in which Jesus responds to an error of his friends or enemies, and it typically has five parts:

1. A setting (v.29),

2. An action or word of Jesus (v.29b),

3. A misunderstanding or criticism (v.30),

4. Corrective teaching or action by Jesus (vv.31–32),

---

35. See Sweetland, *Our Journey with Jesus*, "The Call of Levi," 25–28.

36. On the contrast between Jesus and the Rabbis of his day, see Dowd, *Reading Mark*, 16–18. Also Appendix 13.

5. Resolution or further teaching (vv.33–39).[37]

A third genre is the Symposium, a religious or philosophical discussion at a meal, here in two rounds (vv.29–32 and vv.33–39). The themes of "eating and drinking" (vv.30b, 33b, 39) and the commonality they imply tie the unit together. A symposium is characterized by three standard features, all of which are present in vv.29–39:

1. A common cast of characters: a host with means (Levi), a chief guest (Jesus), and other participants (tax collectors, Pharisees and their legal experts),

2. A common narrative structure including the identification of guests (v.29), the topics(s) of discussion (vv.30, 33), and discourse itself (vv.31–32, 34–39).

3. The expectation of a friendly exchange, an expectation Jesus reverses because of the hostile accusations that he is breaking with common standards of holiness (vv.30, 33).

Such meals, banquets, and symposia are Luke's favorite venue:[38]

Text	Contents
5:27–39	Jesus eats with Levi, tax collectors, and others. The Pharisees and scribes complain.
7:36–50	Jesus eats with Simon the Pharisee; a sinner woman drenches Jesus' feet with perfume, tears, and wipes them with her hair; Simon complains.
9:10–17	After the return of the twelve from a successful mission of healing and exorcism, Jesus withdraws, people follow, and healings continue. This leads to the feeding of 5,000 men.
10:38–42	The duty of hospitality is good, but paying attention to Jesus is better.
11:37–54	Jesus eats with another Pharisee, who is offended by Jesus not washing; Jesus verbally chastises his guests, other Pharisees and scribes, who react with anger.
14:1–24	Jesus eats with a third Pharisee and his guests, scribes and Pharisees; Jesus heals a man and tells a controversial parable, offending the guests.
15:1–2, 13–35	Again, Jesus is criticized for eating with *tax collectors and sinners*. Jesus defends his conduct in three stories, and the parable of the wandering son includes a grand, welcome feast to which the older brother is also invited.
19:1–10	Jesus eats with Zacchaeus, the chief tax collector; the whole town is offended.
22:4–38	Jesus eats with his disciples, who are explicitly designated as sinners during the meal.
24:13–35, 41–43	The risen Jesus breaks bread with two disciples in their home and disappears.

37. Other examples I have identified in our listing of fifty-one discipleship units in Luke are 9:12–17, 9:18–22, 9:28–36, 9:37–51 (a cluster of four Disciple Correction Stories in a larger unit), 18:15–17, 21:31–34, 22:39–46, 22:47–53, 24:1–12.

38. Expanded from Vinson, *Luke*, 151–52. For a thorough treatment, see Smith, *From Symposium to Eucharist*, Chapter 8, "The Banquet in the Gospels." 219–78.

Content

Throughout Luke's biography Jesus practices free association with all sorts. He is thus *for all* without exception. His is a holiness which cannot be compromised by association or contagion; rather, he brings with him a force of love that invites others into his circle of new life in the kingdom. Thus, when Levi gives Jesus access to his circle of collaborators and Jewish law breakers, he gladly participates. Jesus invited Levi to discipleship, and Levi in turn invites Jesus into his social network.

But this is a problem for the Pharisees and their scholars with their understanding that the call to holiness requires separation from such folk as tax collectors, and particularly from sharing a meal with them since it implies a fellowship that is not possible so long as they continue in their offensive ways.

But Jesus reclines on a couch, knows the rules of a symposium, and waits for an opening which comes in the form of an indirect question to his disciples, "Why do *you* (plural) eat and drink with tax collectors and sinners?" And Jesus, in defense of his new followers answers with a proverb about himself, "Those who are healthy have no need of a physician, but those who are sick," and on this all agree; it is a truism. But then Jesus applies it to himself in a mission statement in which the righteous are the healthy and the sinners are the sick, "I have not come to call the righteous, but sinners to repentance."

The edge, however, is the question, Who are these two groups? Is it Matthew and his friends, Matthew who followed and his friends who are apparently enjoying the presence of Jesus? Or is it the serious group who critique his free association? If to be rightly related to God means trusting Jesus, what he says and does, then tax collector outsiders are the new insiders, and old insiders the new outsiders! Jesus flips the table and leaves them with a conundrum: Who really needs to see the doctor?

Jesus calls followers as apprentices in God's new thing displayed in himself, and the cost is high. It is a major dislocation of the whole of life around a new center and an uncertain future. A sign of the kingdom—the new way of living—is eating with old outsiders, who now become new insiders so that the old outsiders complain about the new social and inclusive spiritual map Jesus draws.

For Jesus, grace and welcome precede the deep change of repentance.[39] When hostiles ask questions, Jesus patiently and skillfully responds with proverbs and analogies to reason with them about his ways and means. This too is grace in patient reasoning and instruction, but Jesus states how hard it is for people to leave old maps for new and old wine for new, as they say to one another, "The old is good." In a time of kingdom fulfillment, we feast; in a time of absence and longing for Jesus' return, we return to fasting as a discipline of longing. Jesus understands and preserves the new that he enacts. It is incompatible with the old. He warns against rejection.

---

39. For an accessible treatment of the full range of grace, see McKnight, *Embracing Grace*, Chapter 11, "Diminished by Exclusion, " 128–39, Chapter 12, "Enlivened by Embrace" 140–51.

Then

Peter is a sinful man by his own confession (5:8) and the healed leper by common conviction. Levi participates in a tax system that oppresses fellow Jews and involves constant contact with Gentiles. He is not serious about practicing his faith according to a Pharisaic reading of Torah. He is a traitor and unclean, not qualified for temple worship. But Jesus reaches across the boundaries, as earlier with Peter and the leper, to invite Levi into his new movement without taking a vote from those who are already his followers.

Whomever Jesus calls, and whoever responds, is now family. We do not get to pick our fellow disciples, and wherever the church becomes a club of only the socially similar, something essential is lost. Jesus is disruptive of all such habits; he broadens our world! He likes people I want little to do with!

Now

Wherever people are, there God may lead us, and the more dangerous or morally scandalous the places are, the greater the discernment required as to who and how and how long. Sending new believers with an addiction to gambling back into a casino is an invitation to disaster. Wisdom is needed, and it takes time—sometimes considerable time—to strengthen new disciples in new habits and reliable virtues.

In my own case I had to resign from my fraternity because some of the group's behaviors with alcohol, drugs, and females were still far too attractive for a fresh convert. I needed time in the fellowship of new Christian friends to cut some new, deeper grooves into my character. But now, while I am still cautious about my sinful nature and its capacity for deception, my associations are free, broad, and largely without fear. I exercise caution, but I sometimes say to those who inquire, "There are some places I can't be seen, but there's no place I won't go at Jesus' invitation. And by the way, I'd like you to go with me."

Summary

Disciples need to craft, like Levi, an *elevator speech* of how they came to be a Jesus' follower. People are interested in people, so carry in your head a brief outline you can adapt to any listener without sounding *canned*. And recognize that, again like Levi, you came to Christ with a mission field. It's your network of family and friends, so throw a party and come to terms with the sheer newness and freshness Jesus brings to any situation. He loves hanging out with the wrong folk, even you!

Insights

1. Don't be surprised if the Spirit sometimes leads you through people you notice.

2. Do we spend time listening to people in their work places? Jesus did!

3. A simple definition of a Christian is a *follower of Jesus*. Why complicate it?

4. How is Levi's dinner party a great example of new life evangelism?[40]

5. Jesus spoke of himself using the images of *physician* and *bridegroom*. Why these?

6. When the newness of Jesus is lost, what remains is conventional religion. Why?

Disciplines

Observation: Jesus is interested in all the difficult people you'd rather avoid.
Action: Break bread with and befriend your "unlikelies," then watch what happens.
Observation: Jesus referred to himself as a physician and bridegroom.
Action: Sign up for a residency program with Dr. Jesus the party planner!

9. Luke 6:12, 13–16, 17–19, 8:1–3

Jesus Expands his Reach
Hybrid Genre: Prayer Report, Listing of Tribes, Lukan Summary, Female Disciples

When he had appointed the holy apostles,

he performed many wonderful miracles, rebuking demons,

delivering from incurable diseases whoever drew near.

Christ did not borrow strength from some other person, but being himself God by nature, even though he had become flesh,

he healed them all, by the demonstration of power over the sick.[41]

—Cyril of Alexandria

Justification

This is one of the central discipleship units in Luke as it marks a designation within the larger band of disciples. After a night of prayer, a dozen are chosen by Jesus from the rest and are henceforth labeled *the Twelve*, a visual symbol that Jesus is renewing God's people by providing new leaders on the model of the earlier twelve tribes of

---

40. On recovering the dinner party as a Jesus place, see Springer, *How To Revive Evangelism*.

41. Just, *Luke*, 102.

Israel, each headed by a patriarch.[42] And since they are to be sent out as his official ambassadors, a second title is also added; they are *Apostles/sent ones.* They remain disciples, but now with a new symbolic function and an official commission for mission. This thought unit is dense with insights into being a follower. That women are also called as disciples is indicated in a later passage (8:1–3) with a similar—albeit shorter—listing.

Shape

There are times when explicit materials on discipleship are woven into larger structures, and such is the case here where our three paragraphs (6:12, 13–16, 17–19) are part of a larger thought unit. The unit as a whole is 6:6–19 in which two disciple paragraphs (b. 6:12, b' 6:13–19) are placed between a healing story (a. 6:6–11) and a healing summary (a' 6:12–19). There are four paragraphs with a double center (a 4:2 chiasm) as follows:

a. vv.6–11 Two Part Healing of a Man with a Paralyzed Hand

    b. v.12 Disciples 1: Prayer Before Selection (short)

    b' vv.13–16 Disciples 2: Symbolic Community of Twelve and Listing

a' vv.17–19 Crowds Come to Hear and to be Healed, A Universal, Effective Mission

Thus, Jesus' prayer and his choice of the twelve as future ambassadors is set in the midst of his ministry of kingdom preaching and the deeds of power and love.[43] This is the dynamic reality into which the twelve will soon be immersed (9:1–11), and after them the body of seventy disciples as a whole (10:1–24).

Then

Thus far the disciples have been following, observing, and listening as Jesus interacts with a leper, with crowds who desire teaching and healing, with the scribes and Pharisees who protest his claims to forgive and his working and healing on the sabbath, with a tax collector Levi and his friends. His audiences are diverse. And they have the best seats in the house to observe *the new reality* coming to expression in Jesus, God's rule and loving power at ground level teaching the truth and setting life right again since the same love that expels demons also heals bodies, forgives sinners, and calls followers.

42. On the twelve, see Bock, *Who Is Jesus?* Chapter 3, "The Choosing of the Twelve," by Scot McKnight, 39–47; Hacking, *Signs and Wonders*, Chapter 15, "Luke and the Twelve" (6:12–16), 173–80; Sweetland, *Our Journey*, "The Choosing of the Twelve," 28–31.

43. On the recovery of healing ministry in the church, see Venter, *Doing Healing: how to minister god's kingdom in the power of the spirit*, 2009.

But with 6:12–19 we come to a tipping point. Brief references to Jesus' prayer (4:42, 5:16) become an all-nighter (6:12) as he, in the face of rising opposition (6:11), leans deeply into the Father for fresh wisdom. It is now time to add two other designations to *Disciples. Twelve* will be chosen from his entourage to symbolize and visualize the full restoration of Israel, and in addition they will be installed as *Apostles,* as those sent out as his personal agents, which is just around the corner (9:1–11).

It's time for a promotion into Jesus' ministry as participants, the one he earlier promised Peter, "henceforth, you will be catching men (and women) alive" (5:10c). They've watched him fish and heard him teach the kingdom; soon it will be their turn to do both at a distance from him. Thus, discipleship is being *with him* as a learner in order to become *like him* in mission together. They never quit being disciples, but to it two further specifications are added: they are a 1) symbolic and 2) missional identity. Early the next morning Jesus gathers the larger group (likely the seventy of 10:1–2 in addition to the Twelve here chosen), elects twelve from the number, and formally labels them *Apostles* (the ones *sent out*).

There follows a list of twelve Jewish males in three groups of four. Its current form as post-resurrection is indicated by Simon after his restoration being the head of the list and Judas Iscariot the traitor at the end. We begin with two sets of brothers (the ones called in 5:1–11) and end with four whose tag lines distinguish them from others with the same common names (vv.14e–15b), with the four in the center having no tag lines (vv.15c–16), thus there is also a logical and a mnemonic arrangement to the listing. They now have a new cohesive identity bestowed upon them by Jesus.

The concluding scene (vv.17–19) is deliberately cast in a concentric pattern with four sections and a double center. A double center on hearing and healing (b//b') is set between the outer frames (a//a') with their common references to *all* and the *crowd.*

> a. v.17a   Action/Movement, "And he (Jesus) came down to a level place"
> v.17b-e   Participant List, "great *crowd* of disciples, great multitudes of people
> Geographic List, "*all* Judea and Jerusalem (Jews),
> and the seacoast of Tyre and Sidon (Gentiles)"
> b. v.17f Reason 1: came to hear (learn the kingdom)
> b' v.17g–18 Reason 2: came to be healed, cured of spirits (see the kingdom)
> a' v.19a   Action/Movement, "And *all* the *crowd* sought to touch him"
> v.19b   Reason, "for power came forth from him and healed them all"

In addition to this literary ordering as a review and summary of all that's come before, there is a concentric ordering in a. v.17a-e. Think of a series of circles within a larger circle. At the center are Jesus and the twelve, "And he came down with them." The next circle is "a great crowd of the disciples," and beyond them a third circle "a great multitude of the people," understood as Jews since they are "from all Judea and

Jerusalem." The outermost ring is a clear reference to non-Jews, to the Gentiles, "and the seacoast of Tyre and Sidon."

Here is Luke's earliest version of the Great Commission, and all the groups in proper array. *Hearing* the kingdom message and experiencing the *healing power of divine love* originate in Jesus. They then pass through his apostolic agents to his own people the Jews and then beyond to the outsiders who make up the rest of the world. Thus the world mission is not just added at the end of the Jesus story but presented early on with Gentiles already participating. This Jesus thing and *the new reality* is aimed at the whole world and all its peoples.

I have chosen to deal with 8:1–3 out of narrative order because of the cues Luke gives that 8:1–3 is to be read in parallel to 6:12, 13–16, 17–19. It is a summary passage, mentions travel (v.1a), notes the kingdom of God in word and deed (v.1b), and is clear that—as in 6:17a—the twelve are *with him*. It then adds this loaded note, "and also some women who had been healed of evil spirits and infirmities" (8:2a).[44]

Like the list of men, the shorter list of women is also likely post-resurrection in its ordering since "Mary and Joanna" appear in the same ordering later in 24:10 as among the first witnesses to the resurrection message. They were, in one of my favorite quips, "the epistles to the apostles!" So Luke's trajectory is towards women disciples having equal dignity and ministry in the church. They cannot be among the symbol of "the twelve" since the dozen patriarchs were all men. But they have their own list in the same basic form of name-plus-tag-line, follow Jesus because of the new freedoms he restored, keep the show on the road with their giving, and will eventually be the last at the cross and the first at the tomb. Three are named, but there are also "*many others who provided for them out of their means.*"

That the women are disciples is demonstrated by the disciple activities they demonstrate:[45]

1. Follow and serve, 8:1–3, 23:49, Mark 15:41, Matt 27:5–56

2. Witness Jesus' death, 23:49, Mark 15:40, Matt 27:55, John 19:24–27

3. Saw where Jesus was buried, 23:55, Mark 15:47, Matt 27:61

4. Return to find tomb empty, 23:56–24:12, Matt 16:1–8, Matt 28:1–8, John 20:1–2, 11–13

5. Commissioned, 24:7–8, Mark 16:7, Matt 21:7, John 20:2

6. Report/ Testify, 24:10–11, John 20:2, 18

44. For a fresh and challenging read, see Dorothy A. Lee, *Ministry of Women in the New Testament*, 2021.

45. Fredricksen, "*Disciple(s)* in the New Testament: Background usage, characteristics and historicity," 725–26.

One of the features of Jesus' recasting of the inherited model of discipleship is his inclusion of women as peers.[46] It is not fully egalitarian and could not be in that culture, but he sets a trajectory that moves in that direction, and the evidence for such is clearly preserved in Luke's highlighting of women in the birth narratives, in the public ministry, and in the passion and resurrection stories. Disciples live together in a messy community of equals. We are better together, and the church has an uneven track record of grasping this call.[47]

One of the proofs that Jesus was not a magician using secret knowledge to manipulate spiritual powers is Luke's regular report of his prayers which signal dependence on the God of Israel. He seeks divine guidance in extended prayer, then acts on it. His movement is not private but public and invokes one of the deep symbols of Jewish history, the twelve tribes and their patriarchs. In him and his followers, the dream of Israel restored is coming to pass.

Something big is happening, and so to be a disciple—as with the twelve and the women— is to be caught up in something much bigger than ourselves, something mysterious and intensely meaningful. It's the call of a lifetime, to follow the one God sent to give hope and help to all the world, one who welcomes us into his company and then sends us on mission across the street and around the world, daring to see each person through the eyes of his love and his hopes for them. We go and look and listen and pray and love and look for clues of where the Holy Spirit is already at work and prayerfully join in.

Now

Just who are we following? Just who is Jesus the Jew? He is the restorer and Messiah of his people, a Savior for all the Gentiles to whom Abraham and his offspring were to be a blessing. In Jesus and the Holy Spirit who filled him, Yahweh the Lord opened the divine heart to the world, and we beheld the Holy Trinity. By choosing twelve from the larger pool of disciples and giving them an unmistakable new identity for his Jewish audience, Jesus was making a public statement about himself and them: they are the tribal heads of the new people of God, and he has the power to appoint them!

As disciples we are forever dependent on the witness of the apostles; they were the memory bank of all that Jesus said and did—a mutually corrective community of eyewitnesses guaranteeing integrity, and in following him we have to go through them. Immersing ourselves in the four gospels is to immerse ourselves in the apostolic witness to Jesus. What an impressive scene it is for them to come down the mountain together to face the rest of the disciples, the multitude of Jews, and the Gentiles drawing near.

46. For a defense of women's ordination see Wright, *Surprised by Scripture*, 64–82.

47. On women and Jesus, see Talbert, *Luke*, 93–96; Willard, *Renewing the Christian Mind*, 421–23. Hyun, *The Quest for Gender Equity in Leadership*, 96–108. Also see Appendix 9 .

Our mission as followers is to stay close to the apostolic memories and to bear our witness to Jesus and the rule of the Triune God he brings near. And as we follow Jesus together and dance to the beat of the Holy Spirit, we will find people healed and set free. Churches that welcome and celebrate men and women as full peers in the new reality will model a new way of living together with mutual and rich appreciation, and this is something the world around us needs to see.

Ours is a *post* world: post-apostolic, post-Christendom, post-Enlightenment, post-modern, even post-truth. But we are not post-miracle or post-healing or post-conversion because with our commission goes the promise of power from the Holy Spirit—Jesus' alter-ego. So Luke hammers away at the unity of true words and power-ful deeds in the presentation of the new reality of the kingdom of the Father in the life of the Son who is in our midst and calling followers. Disciples have more than meth-od, more than texts and programs and goals; we have a risen Jesus and an indwelling Spirit who serves as a communication link between the visible and invisible worlds.

So count on the Scripture to be illumined and the presence to go before you. Count on divine appointments to unfold and for resources to arrive as needed. Count on the Spirit's nudges to alert you to the presence of further giftings, and pray with and for the sick and tormented, knowing that you have nothing to give them, but the Risen Jesus much. Live in dependence and availability. Every encounter is full of hidden opportunities, and kindness is the key that opens most doors.

Summary

Disciples observe that Jesus is faithful to us in his prayers and that his choice of us was no mistake. He hears from the Father and places us in service as his personal representatives with portfolio, thus his ambassadors, his apostles. With him we face a needy, broken world together, trusting the Holy Spirit to bring whatever gifts and energies are needed. With Jesus, though not as often with the church, women are full partners as Jesus' apprentices and understudies.

Insights

1. One of the disciplines that sustained Jesus was isolation, solitude, and listening prayer.

2. The ones who head and end the list of twelve have much in common as deniers.

3. Jesus' mission to the world was embedded in his ministry early on.

4. Learning to teach the faith and to pray with the sick and tormented are basic skills.

5. Every follower has a testimony; live in such away that they will share it with you.

6. Men and women follow the same Jesus; the gifts of all must be welcomed.

Disciplines

Observation: Before major decisions, Jesus isolated himself to listen and receive.

Action: Once a month spend a half day with an open heart and an open Bible.[48]

Observation: Men and women are called across the street and around the world.

Action: Aim at a dual footprint of prayer and service: near and far, local and global.

10. Luke 6:20–26

The Charter of Discipleship 1: Finding You Place, Now and Later

Hybrid Genre: A Rhetorical Exhortation of Blessings and Corresponding Woes

If you propose a choice between these two things, which is better, to laugh or to cry?

Is there anyone who wouldn't prefer to laugh?

Because repentance involves a beneficial sorrow,

the Lord presented tears as a requirement and laughter as the resulting benefit.[49]

—AUGUSTINE

Justification

If 4:16–21 is Jesus' *Magna Carta* of kingdom ministry (and it is!), then the three thoughts units of 6:20–26, 27–38, 39–40 are his *Constitution of Discipleship*.[50] Both are constitutive of Jesus and his labors, laying down the basic imprint. The apprentices have been with him for a season and watched him deal with individuals and crowds. They've seen his practice of retreats and prayer. Twelve have now been selected as renewers of all Israel, and the world mission through Jews to Gentiles is forecast. Crowds have been healed and set free, and now the chief Rabbi, having created a highly receptive audience through his grand procession and display of loving power, launches into an extended discourse for disciples (6:20a).

The implication is that the twelve and the larger pool of disciples are his primary audience. The Jews and Gentiles who are not yet followers have already greatly ben-efitted from him and are now listeners and potential followers. Luke's *Sermon on the Plain* is an open, public declaration of Jesus' upside-down kingdom and a compressed outline of what is offered to and asked of his male and female apprentices. The new regime is for all. Jesus alone makes people whole in love.

48. For a starter, read the Navigator article, "How to Spend Extended Time in Prayer," www.navi-gators.org/resource/spend-extended-time-prayer.

49. Just, *Luke*, 105.

50. A great monograph is Topel, *Children of a Compassionate God: A Theological Exegesis of Luke 6:20–49*, and on this unit see 55–96, 97–126.

Shape

The technical name for a blessing is *macarism* from the Greek for blessed (*macarios*), the opposite of which is a *woe* (Gk. *Ouai*).[51] From his position of sharing God's future knowledge, Jesus announces ultimate winners and losers in a series of four Congratulations and four parallel Condolences. The form of all eight assertions is the same in four parts: 1) Pronouncement, 2) Audience, 3) Reason, 4) Promise, as in v.20b which sets the form, *Blessed are/ you poor/ for/ yours is the kingdom of heaven.* In the Woes the promises are negative and final.

The blessings and woes are structured into two panels of four each (vv.20b–23, 24–26) arranged in opposing pairs: poor-hungry-weeping-true prophets // rich-full-laughing-false prophets. The contrast is between two types of people seen from four angles: kingdom insiders and kingdom outsiders, now in part and later in full.

Another structuring principle is the use of tense and time. The first and last pairs in each panel use the present and past tenses; the middle pairs use the word *now* and the future tense. Luke's fourth beatitude (vv.22–23) falls into two parts, each with four statements: v.22, *hate/exclude/revile/cast out* // v.23, two joy commands plus two reasons using *for/* Greek *gar*. The fourth Woe in the second panel (v.26) is stated more briefly, "Woe to you, when all men speak well of you, *gar/for* so their fathers did to the false prophets." Flattery is a danger signal that you are playing to the wrong audience. Luke takes great care in his rhetorical ordering of the tradition. It is true and memorable as well.

Content

In the four Congratulations (*Blessed are . . .*) to the disciples (6:20b–23) and the four Condolences (*But woe to . . .*) to the non-followers (6:24-26), Jesus stands at the last judgment and tells who is blessed in the present and who is not and what trajectory is now theirs. There are only two ways, says Jesus: his way, and the other way. These are not eight different kinds of people but two types of people each described in four parallel ways. Note how the two panels of four members are coordinated in parallel: *poor/ rich, hunger now/full now, weep now/laugh now, men hate you/men speak well of you.*

The good life (vv.24–26) as defined by riches, gluttony, laughter, and public honors tell us much about first century aspirations, and every century since! Self-sufficiency, the satisfaction of appetites, amusing entertainments, and the envy of others is their reward. But they are on the wrong side of God. It is *now,* but has no future and will be revealed as fraudulent when the kingdom comes and they find that the judge is the same Jesus they neither listened to nor followed.

On the other hand, Jesus' disciples—having left their livings—are now dependent on others for the basics, and with that comes the vulnerabilities of hunger (unable to

---

51. On both, see Pennington, *The Sermon on the Mount and Human Flourishing*, 41–68.

guarantee their next meal), sorrow (Peter's grief at his sin), and persecution for their association with Jesus. But, with what's ahead for them—the fullness of the kingdom, they are joyous in the midst of trials and find themselves among the faithful prophets (v.23).

There are also false prophets who bless the current obsessions of the non-disciples and their *winner* status. But at the end, it is disciples who will receive divine approval since they followed and non-disciples who will receive divine rejection because they rejected Jesus the Son and the humbler life of service he offered. If I'm going with the flow of the culture, its current values and obsessions, then I'm probably in the wrong column. If life is centered in the exaltation of the self and its appetites, and if life has not been recentered in Jesus, I'm already on the wrong path. So wake up!

Then

To follow is to be identified with a person as a pupil, and the person for Christians is Jesus. To accompany him where he leads is to share his life and lifestyle, to eat what he eats and sleep where he sleeps, and this is the catalog of the four blessings of vv.20b–23. But where does it end? In the fullness of God's kingdom with some of its previews in the present. To share his life, his love, his wisdom, is worth an occasional aching stomach and sorrow over your own sin and the world's rejection of the one you love and admire. It helps us understand the Hebrew prophets and both their criticism and love of their own people.

Now

Four diagnostic questions, each of which matches one of the marks of faithful followers in vv.20b–23, are:

1. Do I neglect the poor and arrange my life so as to avoid them?

2. Do I practice the discipline of fasting and support feeding ministries?

3. Am I moved to sorrow over my own sins and the agonies of our world?

4. Do I speak well and often of Jesus Christ, or am I a silent follower?

The lure of the seven deadly sins and all their combinations are before us every day.[52] The four symptoms of Greed, Gluttony, Frivolity, and Image-management/Pride are highlighted in vv.24–26 and were later in the tradition expanded to eight and then reduced to seven. But the most severe symptom is to join the crowd who resists God's warnings as an intergenerational habit, "for so their fathers did to the false prophets."

52. On this ancient Christian monastic list of deadly vices and the virtues they corrupt, see DeYoung, *Glittering Vices*; Hunter, *Our Favorite Sins*. For a classic reading of virtues and vices in the moral life, see Kreeft, *Back to Virtue*.

To pamper and cater is not true prophecy when God's people are entrenched in behaviors which lead to death. True prophecy, spoken in love, also comes with stinging indictments and warnings. If it's a bit too smooth and fits a bit too snugly with cultural obsessions, it's not from above.

A great way to be gripped by a disturbing text is to imagine its opposite, and that is what Brian Wilkerson does in his mirror image of Jesus' words. He writes, "Suppose we were to come up with a set of Beatitudes for the 21st Century:

Blessed are the rich and famous,

   because they can always get a seat at the best restaurants.

Blessed are the good-looking,

   for they shall be on the cover of People magazine.

Blessed are those who party,

   for they know how to have fun.

Blessed are those who take first place in the division,

   for they shall have momentum going into the play-offs.

Blessed are the movers and shakers,

   for they shall make a name for themselves.

Blessed are those who demand their rights,

   for they shall not be overlooked.

Blessed are the healthy and fit,

   because they don't mind being seen in a bathing suit.

Blessed are those who make it to the top,

   because they get to look down on everyone else."[53]

Taken together, this satire is too close for comfort as regards our current culture. As I've warned myself and others before, "If you go with the flow of our culture, if it's habits become your own, it will carry you far away from God and from all that is deeply good."

Summary

Disciples understand how high the stakes are because at the end there's only the Blessing or Cursing of God. Disciples are not self-sufficient (poor), often lack (hunger), share the pain of the world (grief), and are rejected because of friendship with Jesus (hated). We live cross-grained to a world that values riches, gluttony, the mockery of others, and public honor, none of which will enter *the new reality* of which we already have a preview. Following Jesus is the highest privilege because we drink from the joy cup even now.

53. "The Heartbreak Gospel," www.preachingtoday.com.

Insights

1. Jesus healed the sick and tormented and only then laid out the costs of apprenticeship. Mercy first! It gains a great hearing!

2. To follow Jesus is to be God-dependent, ravenous for justice, broken-hearted, and often misunderstood.

3. There is a joy in Jesus, and sometimes even a raucous hilarity found nowhere else.

4. Regular previews and sightings of God's kingdom keep us encouraged.

5. Jesus is the ultimate divider; to live forever without his goodness is horrific.

Disciplines

Observation: Jesus teaches everyone that life is the highest stakes game of all.
Action: Go walk through a cemetery knowing that everyone is saved or damned.
Observation: Following Jesus sets you contrary to much of what your world values.
Action: Arrange your life to include nursing homes, soup kitchens, laundromats.

11. Luke 6:27–38

The Charter of Discipleship 2: Living Like God
Hybrid Genre: Proverbs, Rhetorical Questions, Focal Instances, Rhetorical Fantasia

The practice of mercy is twofold:
when vengeance is sacrificed and when compassion is shown.
The Lord included both of these in his brief sentence,
"Forgive, and you shall be forgiven; give and it will be given to you."[54]
—AUGUSTINE

Justification

Since this thought unit is one of three that together form Luke's *Sermon on the Plain* as a Charter of Discipleship, all three should be included in our consideration.

Shape

The second section of Luke's Discipleship Sermon has three paragraphs (1. vv.27–31, 2. vv.32–36, 1' vv.37–38) held together by three commands to *love* (vv.27b, 35a), *do*

54. Just, *Luke*, 110.

good (vv.27c, 33a, 35b, 38b), and *give/lend* (vv.30a, 34a, 35c, 38a). Each paragraph has three parts.

There is also *rhetoric of 4* in the first paragraph (four commands [vv.27–28] + four examples [vv.29–30]) and in the third (four commands [vv.37–38a] + four markers [v38b]).

The central paragraph has a *rhetoric of three* (three rhetorical questions [vv.32–34] three commands and rewards for obedience [v.35]). Each of the sub-units ends with a memorable moral maxim as a pithy summary of the paragraph (vv.31, 36, 38c). An outline is helpful:

1. vv.27–31 Undermining the Pyramid of Reciprocity 1.
a. vv.27–28 Four Commands Which Challenge the Rules of Reciprocity
    b. vv.29–30 Four Examples of Creative Response (Focal Instances)
        c. v.31 Moral Maxim, Summary: The Golden Rule
    2. vv.32–36 Undermining the Pyramid of Reciprocity 2.
    a. vv.32–36 Three Rhetorical Questions & Commands: Love, Do Good, Lend
        b. v.36 Three Commands and Rewards of Obedience
        c. v.36 Moral Maxim, Summary: The Mercy Rule
1' vv.37–38 Undermining the Pyramid of Reciprocity 3.
a. vv.37–38a Four Commands and Outcomes for Disciples
    b. v.38a Four Markers of Divine Generosity
        c. v.38b Moral Maxim, Summary: The Reciprocity Rule

This tight rhetorical arrangement makes the extended thought unit (vv.27–38) all the more memorable in an oral culture where memorization and recitation were the norm for disciples and pupils of a master. The maxims are a hook on which to hang big ideas.

Content

Think of these three paragraphs as a cohesive teaching on counter-cultural living out of the rich resources of the kingdom of God. We are to startle the world into listening to our message because God's love fuels us, God's goodness is constant, and God's resources enable radical generosity. We who are followers—reflecting the reality of Jesus—are to model a new way of living in the midst of an old world. And when we follow our Rabbi, we undermine the tit-for-tat, this-for-that mentality that structures our current world. We become an outlet for *the new reality* in the midst of the old. We are startling and refreshing and surprising in our unlikely responses, just as Jesus was, opening up all sorts of new possibilities where others only see dead ends.

And with every one of these difficult commands—starting with loving the enemy, and all of which go against the grain of self-protective human nature—comes the promise of the ability to fulfill them, meaning that what Jesus commands, he enables. He lives this way in front of his disciples as *the new possibility,* and it is now on the agenda for them to mimic him with others, as he now instructs them. These challenges of Jesus are not just another law, something heroic done to win God's favor or to show ourselves more noble than others. No, they are new possibilities because disciples are learning to see the world through Jesus' eyes and to respond out of his pure confidence in the Father and the Spirit.

In a world of strict reciprocity, we are not to reciprocate or retaliate but offer the very opposite of what people have been trained to expect (the four commands of vv.27–28 and the two focal instances of vv.29–30). To insults and coercion, to requests and confiscations, we respond with vulnerability and generosity. After all, the God we serve owns it all and is more than able to provide for whatever we need to continue the mission. And, with the maxim of v.31 that we should offer others what we wish for ourselves, we upend the scarcity mentality and zero-sum thinking. "So," says Jesus, "how do we act in order to make new friends of old enemies?" "By living as I do," he said, "out of the immediacy of God's presence and provision."

This second paragraph of the three (6:32–36) is an unmasking of the nature of conventional living according to the ancient map of reciprocity. Jesus' new reality means he is solidly against the calculations of tit-for-tat in which we give only to those who can give back to us and which turns every relationship into a calculation of personal benefit in which people are strictly means to ends. It's a rigid social map with no place for love or grace and new possibilities, all of which Jesus embodies.

So if I love only those who first love me, do good only to those who do good to me, aid only those who are pre-qualified to do good in return, then I'm living just like all the people around me because this is how the ancient world of interchange and expectation is structured. No grace in that, no need for God in that, no fresh resources in that. It's how sinners, those who ignore God, survive socially and economically in Jesus' world, by fitting into the systems of reciprocity and learning its calculated moves and counter-moves. So is that slavery or freedom?

We are, rather, to upend standard expectations by seeking the good of enemies, by doing good not just some of the time and to all that we meet, by being generous with no expectation of a return on investment, except perhaps in new friendships and people who ask, "Why did you do that? It's crazy!" "Yes it is," you reply, "but it makes perfect sense if I'm a child of God and want to display the family likeness." Then the dictum that summarizes the deep intent of vv.32–36, "Be merciful, even as your Father is merciful" (v.36). In other words, says Jesus, look for chances to be kind and merciful and surprise people with a reflection of God's own character in your open heart and open hand.

Paragraph three (1' vv.37–38) represents a shift from what to do (love, do good, give) to what not to do. We are to surrender condemning judgments and leave them to the competent God (v.37a-b).[55] We are to release grudges through forgiveness and resources through generosity since our Father has plenty of both (vv.37c–38a). And the motive is named in v.38c, "For the measure you give will be measured back to you by God." What I need from God is what I offer others, and in this new way of living I am changed. And if I don't, then the world's grip on my mind and heart grows tighter, and I more fearful and resentful.

The four imperatives of vv.37–38a fall into two parts, two behaviors to stop (judging, condemning) and two to start (offering forgiveness, giving aid). We are in no position to judge anyone in an ultimate sense since only God is competent at this level. This is not about giving up biblical moral discrimination. It is, rather, about avoiding taking a seat on God's throne and issuing verdicts on the worth of people. Only the One who knows the heart and is qualified, and that's not any of us! We are all bidden not to harbor grudges but to release people, and in addition to not holding them to a strict accounting to be generous towards them since this is how the God of forgiveness and generosity behaves. We imitate God.

It is important to register another level of motivation for such radical actions as these. The passive voice of "*be* judged . . . *be* condemned . . . *be* forgiven . . . *be* given to you" are divine passives implying divine actions. If I judge, condemn, harbor revenge, and live stingily, then the maxim of v.38c teaches that this is how God will treat me at the end. Could it be I am shaping the terms of my own judgment? Yes, and the four markers of divine generosity in v.38b, "good measure, pressed down, shaken together, running over" work for both forms of divine response. Life is a serious moral venture. Disciples aspire to share God's merciful character but also to avoid harsh judgment at the end. It's push and pull!

Then

Following Jesus as a disciple/apprentice/understudy sets one on a new path, and that way is often crosswise to the way the world currently operates, so it's full of opportunities for tension, misunderstanding, hostility, even persecution. The honesty of Jesus is that, after a time of calling disciples and giving them an initial immersion in the new reality—the kingdom of God and its surprising operations, he pauses for a lecture on just what it means to be his follower. It's about *counting the cost* ahead of time.

In line with the ethical model of Jewish *two-ways* teaching—as typified in Psalm 1, a sharp contrast is drawn between *this way* and *that way*, the good way that leads to blessedness versus the other way that has another ending, thus the Congratulations and Condolences of Jesus' blessing and woes. There really are only two destinies, and our loyalties now are predictive of one or the other at the end. And if life is centered in the self and its demands above all, then I am now in column two (vv.24–26), and

55. On the necessary art of making moral evaluations without arrogance, see Cooper, *Making Judgments*.

while to others I appear to have made it, the Lord has the opposite opinion, not *Woe is me!* but *Woe is you!* I am worshiping the wrong local deities, and in the end they will not rescue me, and I will arrive before God with nothing and no one to commend me.

But if, in following Jesus, we find ourselves living near the edge, hungry and aching for a world not yet here, seeing what makes us weep in ourselves and others, being shoved out of our old circles of association and slandered because of Jesus, then finding utter delight that his friendship sets you in line with the world that is already coming. Disciples often live out-of-joint with the values, practices, world views and mindsets of the world around them, so don't be surprised! And while we do not seek to make things harder than they have to be, such tensions are an indicator we're still walking in his footsteps.

Many have lamented that our English word *love* is so over-used it's threadbare, akin to a *like* on Facebook, but what other word is there to carry the weight of putting the deep welfare of others at the center of my actions? So I vote we keep the word but then tell stories in which Jesus is the original lover and his followers the imperfect copies. Passion and appreciation and regard and action and longing and goodness and mercy and truth and delight and honesty and suffering and challenge are all components of what love Jesus-style means, and in 6:27–38a love is defined by *doing good* and *doing good* by *giving*.

Jesus gives us radical new possibilities for response, and if we never learn to draw on them, how are we different than non-followers? We aren't! We are living out of a relationship that gives us options the world knows little about, so we come across as odd, as non-conventional, as crazy, as impractical when we break the cycles of reciprocity by giving others what they did not expect: loving actions to enemies, doing good to no-goods, giving as a gift with no obligations.

We do not parade around issuing moral citations. We stop such habits and develop new habits of giving our pain to God in order to release others and releasing our goods in order to make room for God's riches. Discipleship is a new way to think and a new way to live, not because we are such good folk but because this relationship with Jesus is always welling up with divine possibilities at just the right time. There is much *un-learning* and much *de-toxing* in being a follower of the strangest of all men, Jesus of Nazareth.

Now

One thing Jesus has is perfect timing, and here it's on perfect display. His own statement of first principles is laid out in his home synagogue (4:16–30), and on that charter he operates for a season (4:31–39). He defines himself, his mission, and then goes to work facing down evil, freeing captives and forming up a group of trainees. But then, at just the right time, he has a long talk about why it matters (6:20–26), how disciples have to unlearn and relearn all they know (6:27–38), and how the standards are a level of love and goodness they see only in him.

It's a costly trek to follow this man. He looks just like everyone else, but what comes out in his looks and his words and his touch is *the new reality* at ground level. So every now and then a season of self-examination is in order, and it's not you being an overly-humble fake critic of yourself. It's much more like a yearly physical where the doctor examines you, does the tests, and tells you the truth in private. And the physician in this case is one who loves you and wants more for you than you want for yourself.

Jesus has plans for you to become like him in all the ways that matter so his *new reality* can flow through you and others as well. Still, it's you. Still under construction. Still dependent and needy. Still capable of disasters, but solidly in *the Jesus camp* and trusting him more than you trust yourself. This is the faith that leads to increasing faithfulness. Not faith in me or faith in faith but trust in his utter reliability to deal with me in love.

Summary

Discipleship is the privilege of a new kind of life, one that in increments becomes more like Jesus and *the new reality* of the kingdom of God he embodies. Three marks of this life are love—even for enemies, doing good— again, even to enemies, and radical generosity towards all. All of this is sourced and enabled by *the new reality*. We live the new ethics of Jesus, abandon the role of ultimate judges, and relish the riches of God's mercy. Such a life will generate many questions from observers.

Insights

1. The demands of Jesus are enabled by him through us; we are not self-propelled.

2. When we respond not in kind but out of God's abundance, we open up new possibilities for all.

3. In following Jesus as apprentices, we are drawn ever deeper into a new world that will one day be the only one there is.

4. If following Jesus is not stretching my comfort zones, something vital is missing.

5. Disciples do give up honest evaluations, but they are de-linked from condemnation.

6. The greatest delight of a follower is getting to get to show a family likeness with the Holy Trinity.

Disciplines

Observation: Taking the initiative to love, do good, and give is Jesus' public profile.
Action: For a day and with each person pray, "Lord, show me what love means now."
Observation: Jesus lived dependently and freely out of God's lavish generosity.
Action: Save a hundred dollars and pray, "Lord, show me how to give this away."

12. Luke 6:39–49

The Charter of Discipleship 3: How A Follower of Jesus is Repaired
Genre: Diatribe and Paranesis (Moral Exhortation and Teaching)

The good tree is the Holy Spirit. The bad tree is the devil and his underlings.
The person who has the Holy Spirit manifests the fruits of the Spirit,
which the apostle describes when he says,
"The fruit of the Spirit is love, joy, peace, patience,
kindness, goodness, faith, gentleness, self-control.
The one who has the opposing power
brings forth briars and thistles, the passions of dishonor.[56]
—Origen

Justification

This is the third and final thought unit of Luke's fifth essay (6:20–49), normally labeled Jesus' *Sermon on the Plain*. It is included in our treatment of discipleship passages because the whole of the essay lays out the resources, conditions, and expectations of being a Jesus' follower. It is the largest single block of teaching in Luke.

Shape

The thought unit falls into three paragraphs in a 3:1 chiasm:
    1. vv.39–42 A Disciple Leads Through Apprenticeship and Self-Examination,
      2. vv.43–45 A Disciple Bears Good Fruit from the Heart,
    1' vv.46–49 A Disciple Builds to Endure.
Each paragraph addresses a common defect in the life of disciples: defective sight and defective judgment (1. vv.39–42), defective fruit and defective speech (2. vv.43–45), defective hearing and defective behavior (vv.46–49). Part of Jesus' training regimen is to warn his apprentices where disaster lies and how they can be prepared to survive and thrive in a hostile and deceptive environment.

56. 197 Just, *Luke*, 112.

Paragraph 1. vv.39–42 contains two sets of double questions (a. v.39, a' vv.41–42a) alternating with answers (b. v.40, b' v.42b). Paragraph 1' vv.46–49 opens with a single question (v.46) followed by a double answer, first positive (vv.47–48), then negative (v.49). The central paragraph of the 3:1 chiasm, 2. vv.43–46, does not use questions but instead offers three natural observations about trees and their fruits (vv.43–44) as an analogy for three observations about human beings and their speech (v.45).

Everyone has a center, a heart, and as with trees the quality of the root determines the quality of the fruit. Thus, being precedes and determines both act (v.43) and speech (v.45c). Who and what we are will show! In addition, two examples of *Absurdity plus Disaster*: a blind leading the blind (v.39) and a man building his house on sand (v.49), frame the passage, as do the parallel words *fall* (v.39c) and *fell* (v.49d). Luke has taken great care and displays his rhetorical skill in the construction of this block of teaching.

Content

In the third section (6:39–49) of Jesus' extended teaching, the issues are internal to the movement, having to do with the signs of maturity and fruitfulness in his followers, as well as the lack thereof! To be as fully taught as our teacher is to have a new way of seeing ourselves and others. We learn to see through Jesus' eyes, and we notice that what we see in others that is objectionable is most often in the self as well. So the first question is not, "What's wrong with you?" but "What is it in me that needs correction from Jesus before I ask his permission to speak to you?" You have to trust someone greatly to let them remove a speck from your eye, no matter how large it is, and Jesus—with jest—said some are log size!

So what are the effects of following Jesus? Am I a fig or a bramble—again a vivid image? Has his goodness made me good? Has his friendship rearranged the way I think and feel and speak and act? If my words were recorded for a week, have they produced good in others? We are living in the midst of the most radically transforming relationship ever with God the Son as our daily tour guide to *the new reality*, and if he's not rubbing off on me, there's a disconnect.

But the clearest diagnostic is that I love and admire him enough to actually practice what he preaches, and that means digging down to bedrock and then being rebuilt as a life that can endure whatever comes. I actually have to do something whenever he speaks, however difficult. It's not just note-taking for a test later on; it's a present choice. So what must I do? And what must I stop? And what must I confess? And to whom? And what risk must I take to prove him true? And if you ask, he will tell you. You can follow Jesus and still end up a wreck. Why? Because you did not act. You treated him as if his was just another opinion to be considered. You can also end up a fortified castle because for you the bricks of obedience were put in place one at a time, and that gives staying and sticking power. It is in proving him right and true one issue at a time that we ourselves are constructed.

It was a custom of Jesus to ask and answer his own questions, sometimes a double question as in v.39. No, they can't lead. And Yes, all will take a tumble. This is Jesus' indirect, critical comment on the Jewish leaders of his day who opposed him. The indirection continues in the answer of v.40 where Jesus refers to himself as "his teacher." In his company disciples receive the sight that is insight, and every day the disciples were with a Master who stunned them with his insight into people, their needs, and agendas. It was by observation and the aid of the Spirit that he knew the hearts and thoughts of people with such accuracy. And if we learn to see as he sees, then our leadership will not destroy people. This is then applied to intra-disciple relations where we see the flaws of others more easily than our own. As in vv.39–40 a double question (vv.41–42a) precedes an answer (v.42b). We are to aid one another with blind spots, but only after careful self-scrutiny from Jesus, the only one who sees us clearly and wholly with no naivete about our moral flaws. We are much more likely to approach a fellow disciple with humility and gentleness after we have prayed, "Show me, O Lord, how you see me." Only when we see others in love are we prepared to be their spiritual physician and offer aid.

That we reproduce what we are is the observation that underlies the comparisons of the second paragraph. The three natural observations of vv.44–45 covers the same truth from three perspectives for the sake of emphasis. Repetition with variation enables memory and rich reflection. The character of a person precedes and determines their actions; so with useless and useful fruit trees.

So do not be surprised with what people say or do, because it reveals something deep about them. So, in addition to the three natural observations are now added three human observations in v.45. Again, we produce what we are. Our essence becomes our actions. Our words and deeds reveal out hearts; the inner becomes outer. Examine people closely, especially religious leaders, to see what they produce in their words and deeds and in their followers. In the presence of Jesus as his pupils, the one who gives us his sight (vv.39–42) can, over time, impart his good heart to us so that we have new motivations and lives that nourish others as good fruit (vv.43–45). Remember, our goal as disciples is to be with him in order to become like him, something he does in us and then through us. Everyone is being shaped by someone, and for apprentices it's Jesus.

Jesus did not avoid confrontations, and his honesty is bracing. So he turned from analogies to direct confrontation, "Now why do you call me *Lord, Lord,* and do not do what I tell you" (v.46)? Why a correct confession followed by an obedience gap? Answer: because we have much hearing and little doing, and only in the doing is the hearing translated into character and the endurance to stand trials. In the three-part sequence of v.47, "Every one who *comes to me* (initial discipleship) and *hears my words* (ongoing exposure) and *does them* (risky practices), we observe the process of how our character is changed.

Come-hear-do is a single dynamic, and is most often derailed and rendered impotent and ineffective by a lack of action. Easier to come and listen, as in church on Sunday, and never to go through the struggle of testing it out. But when pressures come, the infrastructure is not present and we fold and fail and say stupid things like, "It worked for others, but not for me." And that is because you did not work out in life what he worked in by companionship and teaching.

Then and Now

Much of what usually falls under this heading has already been covered in the above analysis. So here I offer a series of questions for the self-examination of disciples, what spiritual directors have termed *an examination of conscience*. So take time with one or more, read them aloud, then ask, "Lord Jesus, as your follower, show me the truth about my discipleship, and I will obey with your help. Amen."

Defective Sight (vv. 39–42)

1. Whom have I led astray by my example, particularly those younger than me?

2. Where have I been a fan and admirer of yours instead of a serious student?

3. What do I object to in others that I refuse to address in myself?

4. Am I willing and do I desire that you expose all that is false in me?

Defective Fruit (vv. 43–45)

1. What is the fruit of my life? In my work, my relationships, my children?

2. Am I the kind of person that feels safe and good to others?

3. Am I willing to surrender to Jesus all the crud and garbage that fouls my heart?

4. If someone was to record me for a week, what would we both learn?

Defective Hearing (v. 49)

1. Am I willing to honestly name all the reasons I'd rather not obey Jesus?

2. Where have I, in recent memory, crumbled when I needed to be strong?

3. What about my life or thinking is shallow, trivial, shoddy, or careless?

4. How could I learn and practice the spiritual workout of *come-hear-do*?

Summary

Disciples learn that nothing is more consistently demanding than cycling through the process of *come-hear-do* with Jesus. It re-programs our every impulse and idea, every habit, attitude, and all that we allow out of our mouths. This process, or the lack thereof, determines what kind of person we become, a person of depth and substance who stands or a shallow person who crumbles at challenge or hardship. We are being remade in his company, and it requires surrender, trust, correction, perseverance and many failures.

Insights

1. A disciple is a learner, and Jesus will deal with every hidden part of our lives.

2. We all need correction, but it's best received when the corrector has been corrected.

3. The center of the self, its loves and imaginations, comes out in deeds and words. The heart is seen and heard every day in our speech.

4. If I confess Jesus as *Lord*, it carries with it the idea that he knows more than me and is to be obeyed, not just admired.

5. That followers tumble into pits or collapse under pressure should surprise none of us. Jesus predicted it of all who short-circuit the *come-hear-do* cycle.

Disciplines

Observation: The great gift of Jesus is to aid us in seeing as he sees.
Action: When I see a fault in another, quickly ask, "Lord, is this in me as well?"
Observation: Our words and deeds are the true revelation of the inner self, the heart.
Action: It is in hearing Jesus' truths and turning them to deeds that I am changed.

13. Luke 8:1–21

The Seeds that Win
Hybrid Genre: Summary, Parable, Private Teaching, Allegory, Pronouncement Story

When you come out of the church,
do not begin to be distracted toward empty and useless matters,
lest the devil come and find you occupied with them . . .
The devil removes the memory of these words of catechetical lecture from your heart,
and you find yourselves empty and deprived of beneficial teaching.[57]
—Symeon the New Theologian

57. Just, *Luke*, 133.

Justification

Were we to select a large paragraph from Luke in which are concentrated so many of his major themes, it would be this one. And why? Because it gives us the minority report:

- that women were disciples and traveled around with Jesus and the boys;
- that Jesus saw the world as a war zone and spoke of precious seed that was *trodden* and *devoured, withered* and *choked,* all of which are verbs of violence;
- that once the disciples crossed the threshold of initial obedience it opened up— through Jesus—into the mystery of *the new reality* of God's rule and all its surprises;
- that every hearing of God's word is a dynamic process that reveals who people are;
- that one day all will be made clear;
- that we must act now on what we hear;
- that Jesus is creating a band of brothers and sisters whose bond is beyond the glue of inherited DNA;
- and, that the coming harvest is colossal and cosmic and will include a final separation and sifting.

The key to participation is not first action, which comes later, but hearing and listening, absorbing and digesting the mysteries in Jesus' stories as words from God. If we pay attention to him, the Holy Spirit will illumine us to see clearly enough to act in trust. This thought unit is a gem on what being a faithful apprentice means.

Shape

Luke 8:1–21 is a thought unit, meaning it has clear boundaries fore and aft plus a clear internal structure. It is shaped as a 5:1 chiasm:

 a. vv.1–3 Hearing and Doing the Kingdom: Jesus' New Family
  b. vv.4–8 Parable of the Sower and Seed (4–8a), Call to Hear (v.8b)
   c. vv.9–10 Privileges of Discipleship: Kingdom and Word
  b' vv.12–18 Allegory of the Soils (vv.11–12), Call to Hear (vv.16–18)
 a' vv.19–21 Hearing and Doing the Word: Jesus' New Family

There is a cluster of terms in a. vv.1–3 with parallels at the end (a' vv.19–21), and echoes of the same the center (c.vv.9–10): *preaching and proclaiming . . . the kingdom of God . . . the twelve . . . some women* in vv.1–3; *his disciples . . . the kingdom of God . . . hearing . . . word of God* at the center in vv.9–10; and *his mother and his brothers . . . hear . . . word of God . . . do it* at the end in vv.19–21. So the frames and the center echo the same themes.

On either side of the center are the framing stories of *The Parable of the Seed* (b. vv.4–8a) and *The Allegory of the Soils* (b' vv.12–18) which mutually influence each other.[58] So, we have three sections on discipleship at the start (vv.1–3), at the center (vv.9–10), and at the end (vv.19–21) plus two parallel stories—a parable and an allegory— about why it's so hard to get a harvest of wheat or people!

Content

This new community Jesus is forming lives in a rough neighborhood and works against great odds, visible and invisible. The group is inclusive of women and exceeds the natural family in demands which go beyond the obligations of kinship to obedience to Jesus. It's all about hope and perseverance, and in observing Jesus closely in all settings, he models what he teaches. He keeps calling, keeps sowing, keeps lifting up the vision of the harvest, keeps revealing *the new reality* to his friends, keeps diagnosing the crowds, keeps issuing warnings, and holds his followers to himself through the bonds of affection and imitation. The new reality is making its way in a tough, demanding neighborhood of many foes.

It was life together, travel together, listen together, obey together, and then do it again the next day, all the while being set up for the cross and resurrection, the deepest and most cruel disappointment and the most joyous recovery. Jesus was leading them day by day into the beating heart of God and the deepest drama of history. What a privilege and peril and opportunity for these few. Luke 8:1–21 is all about being a follower of Jesus.

Then

These people, these first men and women who hoisted their sails into Jesus' breezes to be blown about with him, spent all their time together, and in that sense it was *all about relationships.*"[59] In between the scenes Luke so carefully arranges there was much time spent in walking and talking together, hoping the next town had food and enough room for all to sleep inside that night. It was a laboratory of human relations,

58. For a reading of the parable and allegory by scholars, see Snodgrass, *Stories with Intent*, 145–177; Hultgren, *The Parables of Jesus*, 181–201.

59. In our culture of Western individualism, personal independence, social isolation and the pathology of loneliness, it's hard to imagine the fruitfulness of such a deep immersion in community, and yet we must find ways to push back against the forces of atomization that make it hard to love one another in the details of life. We have all but lost a sense of spiritual family. For an alternative, see Hellerman, *When the Church Was a Family*, which he structures around four New Testament values: 1) We share our stuff with one another, 2) We share our hearts with one another, 3) We stay, embrace the pain, and grow up with one another, 4) Family is about more than me, the wife, and the kids. It takes time and patient investment.

and most of the conflicts and daily stress never made it into the gospels, with a few exceptions of course.

Several of the women, it appears, had dramatic stories to tell about how Jesus had freed them from occupying spirits and illnesses. Telling their stories gave hope to other high and low born sisters. The fact that it was the funds of the highly placed females that kept the entire entourage on the road is a fascinating tidbit on the practicalities of such a long venture. Did they have budget meetings and pledge campaigns?

They were now *insiders*, and in trusting Jesus enough to respond to his call and follow him, they got to see and know what outsiders did not. They heard his words and perhaps the touch of his powerful love, but the inside operations and the bigger picture were not theirs unless they too became committed to him as more than consumers of his merciful administrations. Jesus showed kindness to many who never formally became his followers. He sent them home whole and free, knowing in their bones that the God of their fathers loved them as his children. The stories they remembered and told about him remained in circulation well towards the end of the first century. They were the common background against which the gospels made sense when read. "Oh Yes," a hearer might add, "let me tell you what my grandfather told me about when Jesus came to town."

Being a follower is an exercise in honesty as we live in the reflection of the One who was, according to John, the light of the world. The world as currently arranged and ruled by an evil squatter is actively opposed to *the new reality*, and when the holy prince showed up, the opposition kicked into full assault mode. Stop him, slander him, mock him, threaten him, discourage him, seduce one of his closest friends, challenge him with the cruelest tortures, then string him up naked in public and mock him till the end. But he will have his harvest with himself as its first fruits.

And so when the Evil One reaches in to steal the seed where it lands, and when he weakens folk to the point they can't stand much temptation and crumple, and when he distracts some with too much stuff, God still has a prepared people, the honest and the good and the patient (relatively speaking!), who are ready for a chance to respond. They are the receptive ones, and while we write-off no one, we look for the people whom the Holy Spirit is opening and readying for a seed of new life in Jesus.

Now

That our world and every person is a battleground is demonstrated by the casualties that are all around us and never ending. Behind appearances a constant battle is underway, a terrorism of disinformation, lies, allurements and outright assaults. Our fallen condition and the presence of evil as orchestrated by the Evil One makes sure that pain is ever-present. And everyone is involved in this struggle all the time because, while there are respites, there is no *rear area* in this fight. When one engagement ends, another soon begins, and this is why *martial* language will always be part of the church's liturgy, hymnody, and prayers. Recent attempts to gut the conflict and war imagery as if this would suddenly make the world more peaceful is ultimately an attack on Scripture and Jesus' view of the world. We live in two dimensions at once, and naivete is no virtue in either realm.

Jesus modeled an open appreciative relationship with women that went beyond his culture's norms. They were called as apprentices and followed him with others, gave of their resources, and told their stories. He was a man, but different than others. Vital, yet under perfect self-control. No lust with him or leering. No double agenda. No woman was ever an object or disposable, but always a person to be respected and trained in *the new reality*. And as his followers, this is a growing edge for many of us, especially in our porn saturated culture. Full, equal, different, complementary, and when both genders are in the room, better is the discernment of Jesus' living voice in the church. Why leave out half our brain?

There is a bracing realism about Jesus, precisely because of who he is and how clearly he sees, thus his analysis in *The Allegory of the Soils* about all the forces that block reception of *the new reality* in its verbal form, "the Word." Thus every time the Book is open and a disciple speaks, all sorts of short and longer-term dynamics are operative: the devil is scavenging, the shallow are exposed as rootless, the easily distracted do not persevere.

But then, there are people who by their previous responses to God's grace have developed the elemental virtues of honesty, a good heart, and patience and in whose lives a harvest is found. They are the lights on the stand and show others the way until the greater light is seen and all secrets laid bare. Then come the rewards and judgments of v.18, "For to him who has (the fourth example of v.15), and from him who has not (the three examples of vv.12–14), even what he has will be taken away (passive voice, *by God*).

Whenever the Book is opened, destinies are at stake, and so disciples take every opportunity to pray for the light and help of the Holy Spirit. There is always more going on than you see. You were once a beginning hearer yourself, so be both clear and kind in your presentation.

If our natural family is our factory, then other disciples are our future, a new family, and in the meanwhile the two clusters of loyalty overlap in challenging ways. We honor father and mother as able, as the fourth of ten commandments requires, even if they now or never share our faith. We honor but no longer obey as when we were children. And when the great division comes, and it will, it cuts right through families without regard for our bonds.

The preservation of the natural family or tribe in the life to come is a Mormon, not a Christian teaching. It underestimates the discontinuity between this life and the life to come and fails to reckon with the new forms of intra-personal communion resurrection bodies provide. "Mother and brother," and thus "father and sister" continue as metaphors, but the criteria for inclusion in Jesus new circle is hearing and obeying God's communications, "the word of God."

Summary

Disciples learn to follow in a new set of partnerships with Jesus, with one another, with high and lower status women disciples. The twelve are a potent symbol of the new Israel and the partnership of women a potent challenge.

The seed Jesus spreads has violent forces arrayed against it, thus it is trodden down, withers, is choked, and still yields superabundantly. Disciples are realistic and tough-minded, but also persistent and hopeful. Jesus has made them insiders to *the new reality*. They are his new family who hear the Word, enact it, and receive more revelation, part of which is to understand all the differing kinds of people who listen to their preaching.

Insights

1. Jesus changed the rules for the relationship of men and women in his culture.

2. The first task of discipleship is to stay in relationship no matter what, to be *with him*.

3. Never dismiss the forces that *devour, wither, and choke*. It's a tough neighborhood.

4. To follow Jesus is to have our cognitive senses healed and opened to divine insights.

5. Disciples listen at more than one level: with the ears and with the heart, expecting divine insight and obeying them.

6. If you pay attention to how people respond to the Word about Jesus, you will see the same responses Luke did. Culture has changed; human nature surely has not.

7. If you pay attention to the long-term, you will see the vices made people sick.

8. Jesus has restored the flame; we flicker in his hand as an offer to others. So shine!

9. Disciples live into the light, knowing that one day there will be no more secrets.

10. Hearing is a lifestyle, as is obeying; they are the oscillating cycle of spirituality.

11. There is no passive discipleship; when we stop hearing and obeying, a subtraction process sets in, and we begin to shrink.

Disciplines

Observation: Jesus enacted *the new reality* and formed a community around himself.

Action: Put your local church and its vitality near the center of your concerns.

Observation: Jesus was acutely aware of all the forces arrayed against him.

Action: Put aside your spiritual naivete and enter the fray for the lives of people.

14. Luke 8:22–26

Layer One of Demonic Resistance

Genre: An Epiphanic Rescue Miracle (saved from danger by a deity)

We are sailing on a voyage, not from one land to another but from earth to heaven.

Let us prepare our power of reasoning as a pilot able to conduct us on high,

and let us gather a crew obedient to it.[60]

—Chrysostom

Justification

Following Jesus is akin to military training. Our leader has every right to put us in dangerous situations that we might learn how faithful he is. So it is with the stories of the storm on the lake and the Gerasene man, both of which involve demonic resistance. This unit is included in our list because it makes clear the link between who Jesus is (Christology) and those who follow him into the dangers of mission beyond the borders (Discipleology!).

Shape

This shorter thought unit is carefully constructed. It opens with a command of Jesus and the disciples' obedient response (a. v.22); it closes with a mocking question of Jesus and the disciples' questioning response (a' v.25). In the next inward layers, Jesus sleeps and the storm arises (b. v.23), and Jesus wakes and the storm is silenced (b' v.24c-f). At the center the disciples take action and offer a desperate prayer (c.v.24a-b). The outline is:

a. v.22 Setting: Jesus' Speech + Disciples' Response

b. v.23 Jesus Sleeps, Storm Arises

c. v.24a-b Disciples' Actions and Prayer

b' v.24c-f Jesus Wakes, Storm Rebuked

a' vv.25–26 Conclusion: Jesus' Speech + Two Responses of Disciples

The technical name for this story is an *Epiphanic Rescue Miracle* (unveiling of a deity to rescue),[61] and like most miracle stories has five expected parts:

60. Just, *Luke*, 137.

61. On rescue miracles, see Theissen, *The Miracle Stories of the Early Christian Tradition*, 99–103.

1. Setting (v.22),

2. Problem (v.23),

3. Action of leader (v.24c–d),

4. Results (v.24e–f),

5. Responses (vv.25–26).

There is, interestingly enough, a series of commonalities between the stilling of the storm (8:22–25) and the two-part stilling of the demoniac (8:26–33, 34–39), indicating that both are demonic confrontations.[62] A chart demonstrates the commonalities:

Likenesses Between The Two Stories: How They Illumine One Another[63]
(* = My Additions to the Literature)

Item	Luke 8:22–25	Luke 8:26–33, 34–39
Travel report on the lake	v.22	v.26
Dramatic details of the calamity	vv.23–24a	vv.27, 29b–30, 32–33
Jesus commands chaotic forces	vv.24b, 25c	v.29a
Serenity that results	v.24c	v.35
Responses of fear noted	v.25b	vv.35c, 37b
Question Of Identity/Answer*	v.25c (Question)	v.28b (Answer)
Use of two questions*	vv.25a, c	vv.28b, 30a
Exorcistic language*	v.24b "rebuked the wind"	v.29a, "commanded the unclean spirit"

Content

Jesus' invitation, "Let us go across to *the other side of the lake*" (the Gentile, pagan territory of the Decapolis) is a veiled command, and if they obey they leave holy ground for unholy. On a lake where a few of the twelve were professional fishermen, a sudden storm threatens to swamp them and calls forth a desperate prayer, "Master, Master, we are perishing!" And when Jesus takes action, it's the strangest thing they've ever seen. He awakes from sleep, stands up, and speaks to the wind the same way he'd earlier spoken to demons and diseases and with the same effect of immediate transformation, "Now he awoke and rebuked the wind and the raging waves; and they ceased, and there was a great calm."

Jesus has power over all enemy tactics, and he mocks their lack of lack of trust, "Where is your faith?" This is something new, and in awe they ask each other, "Who then is this that he commands even wind and water, and they obey him?" He has

---

And on their historicity, Keener, "The Historicity of the Nature Miracles," 41–65.

62. See Appendix 12 on the demonic from a psychiatrist.

63. Modified from Green, *Luke*, 331. * = added by author.

power to rescue, but does not always use it. Whether or not we are rescued, our trust is in him alone. Jesus discerned a spiritual reality behind a natural phenomena. How odd to us. How natural to him. He sees with a depth we do not.

Then

Here the ante is upped a bit to severe physical danger. This is, as we say, their first *foreign mission*, and if here as well, then Jesus has authority not just on Jewish but also pagan turf. He's an *everywhere* and *anyone* Savior, and his trajectory is through Jews to others. Jesus crosses cultural, religious, and political boundaries with the good news of God's *new reality*, the kingdom of God with him as its point man.

Disciples will always be entering new situations for which there is no adequate preparation but only the resources of trust and experience. Over time we develop a track record with our Lord and his other followers, and so—when surprised or under pressure— we ask, "What are you doing, Jesus, and how can we join in?" Then we wait, and while we wait, we love and listen. Over time we become not just a trained follower but a prepared one, one enabled to enter new, strange, even dangerous situations and there to wait faithfully for further instructions. Jesus was the master of every situation precisely because of his trust in the Father and the Spirit. Our lives are in his hands, and he is our strongest friend and best teacher. He is developing you to be an agent of his kingdom and to live your life as an outlet of his brand of love and wisdom.

Now

Life in the kingdom with Jesus in the lead is nothing less than an adventure. Every day the disciples were observing him doing what they'd never seen before, and yet otherwise he appeared so normal, so much like them, only with him there was no habit of internal rebellion against God but only glad cooperation with the Father and the Spirit. Same hardware as them, but running a software never before seen, a Jew who shares in the life of God in ways that startle, stun, and stupify. They must have been asking constantly, "What's he going to do now?"

In his presence they were learning a new way to see themselves and the world around them, including all its precious image bearers. In other words, Jesus was fully human and yet without our impulse to rebellion. He was sinless, pure, centered, content in God, and with his passions and impulses not prone to misuse. Tempted? Yes. Defeated? Never.

But there was a dark force that was always present, just around the edges and always looking for an opportunity to intrude. Jesus had enemies in the invisible world, and if they couldn't kill him in the wilderness or in his home village, maybe they could drown him before he built a bridge to the Gentiles.

So never underestimate your spiritual enemy, the devil and his demons who are the hidden *x factor* in any situation. They are the ultimate *opportunists*, looking for openings, weak spots, and blind spots to distort and compromise. Walking with Jesus is thus a safe and a dangerous way to live because you've gone up on the Enemy's hit list. You are now at the front lines of what God is doing, and that is where the clashes most often occur, as in the two stories before us.

Our leader has every right to put us in uncomfortable circumstances to teach us trust and to challenge our every ugly, hidden prejudice about the kinds of people we are to stay away from. We are being remade, so why be surprised when we are stretched and overwhelmed? Following Jesus with others is life's finest education and training. Observing his dealings with extreme cases is a laboratory in the power of divine love to heal and restore.

Summary

Disciples follow a Jesus who refuses to remain inside our comfort zones. His heart is for the world beyond our prejudices. He pushes us into frightening encounters, there to learn desperate prayers and to find him more than adequate. The one we follow is Lord over demons, diseases, death, and the whole of nature.

Insights

1. Jesus regularly crossed boundaries to spread the kingdom. Count on having your prejudices revealed and dismantled!

2. Following Jesus may on occasion put you in physical danger. It's a good time to pray for protection!

3. Part of following is having our weak trust—and sometimes our no trust—exposed to the light in embarrassing ways.

4. All our lives we will be asking and exploring the question, "Who then is this?" Jesus always has more!

Disciplines

Observation: Following Jesus guarantees new places and stranger people!
Action: Take opportunities to go on mission in other cultures to learn trust.
Observation: Jesus discerned that behind this storm was a hostile, demonic power.
Action: When you meet stiff resistance, ask, "Jesus, where is this coming from?"

15. Luke 8:26–39

Layer Two of Demonic Resistance
Genre: An Expanded Miracle/Exorcism Story

In great misery and nakedness, he wandered among the graves . . .
Here was a proof of the cruelty of the demons and a plain demonstration of their impurity.
Whoever they possess and subject to their power,
at once they make him an example of great misery,
deprived of every blessing, destitute of all sobriety, and entirely deprived of reason.[64]
—CYRIL OF ALEXANDRIA

Justification

This is clearly disciple material as it continues the previous unit (8:22–25) and shows the disciples drawn into Jesus' mission to Gentile territory in a preview of Luke's second volume—Acts. In the language of mission, it's a classic power encounter.

Shape

What makes this next unit interesting is that it falls into two paragraphs (a. vv.26–33, b. vv.34–39), each with its own inclusions and internal ordering.[65] The first opens with the problem of a man with demons (a. vv.26–27) and closes with the solution of the man without the demons (a' v.33). The next set of internal frames shows the demons resisting Jesus with an emphasis on their power (b. vv.28–29) and the demons begging Jesus as they face his superior power (b' vv.31–32). At the center is Jesus' question and the spirit's answer (c. v.30). Note that all five of the standard components of a miracle story are present:

1. Setting (v.26),

2. Problem (v.27),

3. Encounter with healer (vv.28–32),

4. Healing (v.33a),

5. Responses and Proofs (v.33b).

But it is the fifth component (Responses and Proofs) that is greatly expanded in the second paragraph (b. vv.34–39). The outline of the first paragraph is:

---

64. Just, *Luke*, 139.
65. The two marks of a thought unit.

a. vv.26–27 Problem: Man with Demons
   b. vv.28–29 Demons Resist Jesus: Their Power is Emphasized, *commanded*
      c. v.30 Jesus Extracts the Demon's Name
   b' vv.31–32 Demons Beg Jesus: Their Defeat is Emphasized, *commanded*
a' v.33 Solution: Man Without the Demons

The travel of the herdsmen back into the city (a. v.34) and the travel of the former demoniac back into the city (a' v.39c-d) frame the second paragraph, as do the *echo words city* (v.34b // v.39c) and *told it* (v.34b) // *proclaiming* (v.39c-d). In the center are two parallel scenes (b. vv.35–36 // b' vv.37–39a) that treat the crowd first (vv.35, 37) and then the man (vv.36, 38–39b). Fear is noted in both scenes (v.35d // v.37b).

The people are hostile and beg Jesus to leave, which he does. The man, however, wants to go with Jesus back to Jewish soil as a disciple, and he is not allowed to do so but instead is directed to a ministry of local testimony (vv.38–39a). As everywhere, Jesus receives mixed reviews. He casts demons out of the man, and the city folk cast him out of their territory, so who still has the problem? The second paragraph is a 4:2 Chiasm:

a. v.34 Herdsmen Tell It in City and Country
   b. vv.35–36 Part 1: Jesus, People (2 groups), Disciple, Fear
   b' vv.37–38a Part 2: Jesus, People (1 group), Missionary, Fear
a' vv.38b-d Man Proclaims It in the City

Content

Here we cross the Sea of Galilee into unclean Gentile territory with its pig farms and reach a new mission field where we are presented with the pitiful scene of a fully infested man. He is Exhibit A for the devil's agenda of dehumanization and degradation. It's the most severe of cases.[66]

Again, as on Jewish turf, Jesus is an effective exorcist, and when it's over and the town's people gathered, we find the man freed and seated at Jesus' feet as a learner and disciple. Think about what this meant for the disciples. They may be secretly wondering, "Is he now one of us?" And the answer is both Yes and No. Yes, one of us; but No, not our Jewish entourage on our side of the lake.

But that he wishes it were so is clear in v.38a, "Now the man from whom the demons had gone begged that he might be *with him* (a euphemism for following as a disciple). And to his desire Jesus says No and instead commissions him as a local apostle, "Return to your home, and declare how much God has done for you." And

---

66. For a fresh treatment of extreme cases by a noted Roman Catholic professor of psychiatry, see Gallagher, *Demonic Foes*. It's interesting that Dr. Gallagher identifies occult involvement as a common entry point into demonization, and with him I agree.

this he does, only with a fresh Christological insight, "And he went away, proclaiming throughout the whole city *how much Jesus had done for him*" (v.39c-d). The future world mission to the Gentiles is thus embedded in Jesus's own ministry. It is not an afterthought or add-on, but intrinsic from the beginning, though its full development is strategically delayed.

Then

Jesus, as the lead agent of *the new reality*, leads his followers directly into the face of full blown spiritual warfare, first in the storm, then in the demonized gentile. Someone does not want Jesus and his friends on their turf freeing prisoners. And there Jesus finds and frees a new witness, whom he formally commissions. Personal testimony, especially such a credible and dramatic *before and after* story as this one, raises hopes for which only Jesus is the answer. "Let me tell you what he's done for me" is always a good lead line.

But what about the man's desire to be a full-time follower as with the others who came with Jesus across the lake. Can he not be the new man? Yes, but not using the present model. He is to be something new, a commissioned witness who, like John before him, prepares the way for a future mission. His love for and desire to be *with* the one who gave him new life is endearing, but at this point impossible to implement. So he must obey as well, and does. It's no longer life on my terms but on Jesus' orders, and he is faithful in traveling and telling his story. He fulfills the standard of 8:21 as a new member of the family of Jesus; he hears and does the word of God.

Now

The issue of demonization, how the human self can be penetrated—and at some level come under the influence (minor to major) of a demonic spirit—is controversial, as is its treatment.[67] In forty years as a pastor I've dealt with several cases in the low to mid range of the spectrum. Most arose through experimentation with the occult, though several others were born into families that had occult ties, and some others seem to have been compromised due to trauma, particularly sexual abuse. The analogy I find most helpful is the human cell with its semi-permeable membrane. It has boundaries, as does the self, but may also be punctured and taken hostage by a virus or other microbial.

My policy has been to take a history, ask about medical or mental health diagnoses and medication, review their spiritual history, and inquire about besetting sins,

67. For the insights of scholars, Twelftree, *Jesus the Miracle Worker*, 156–57, 281–92. Also his *In the Name of Jesus*, 25–56; Bock, *Who is Jesus?* 79–92; Kay and Parry, *Exorcism and Deliverance*, 153–78; Tyra, *The Dark Side of Discipleship*. For a seasoned introduction to healing and deliverance by a Vineyard practitioner, see Venter, *Doing Healing*.

obsessions, or any unusual spiritual phenomena. Where referrals seem indicated, I make them, whether for medical or unaddressed mental health issues. One man came to me hearing voices and claiming he was possessed. I was skeptical for many reasons, and when he saw a psychiatrist and was properly treated with medication, the voices stopped. His issue was medical, not strictly spiritual. It sometimes takes several sessions to gain an accurate profile, and if you build trust, you'll hear some great stories.

At some point—often after a first conversation—I give two assignments. The first is to read one of the four gospels with two simple questions in mind: If the Jesus I read about is alive and loves me, is he trustworthy? And should I turn to him for help?

I also ask them to read and respond to The Occult Inventory Sheet[68] being careful to first read the Scriptural materials attached to each category. My intent is to force them to face what Scripture says about these forbidden practices, their dangers, and their consequences. There is no innocent experimentation; all of it is dangerous.

If they carry out the assignments, it's an encouraging sign. If not, I probe their resistance and find out what the difficulties are. You may be surprised at what you hear. One woman who'd been exposed to seances in Hong Kong said that when she tried to read her Bible, the words went blurry and moved around, and she was as sane and reality oriented as I was! My inward prayer was, "OK, Lord, I get it!"

At some point it's necessary to ask several pointed questions: Have you been baptized? Have you made a basic commitment to Jesus Christ, and do you intend to be his faithful follower? Do you want to be rid of your tormentors, or have they become your *special friends*? Are you willing to rid yourself of any paraphernalia associated with the occult or false religions? Are you willing to separate yourself from those who engage in such practices. If there is hesitance about any of these—as there sometimes is—we punch the pause button. Some return for our next appointment; others do not.

You can always tell when they are ready to confront their intruders. Their hope has shifted towards Jesus Christ, and you can sense it. Where possible, and this is always recommended, I have another mature Christian present for the prayers, and if the person is a female, to have my companion be female as well. It's just smart and protects everyone.

We begin with a simple prayer for Jesus to rule over us and the Holy Spirit to be present. I then guide the person through a prayer of the confession of sin, including all the breeches of sin they agree to and any that arise during the prayer. Using the inventory of Step 4 of Alcoholics Anonymous can sometimes be helpful if the history is long.

I require them to name the wrong action by the biblical name and not a polite euphemism, name it as sin, make a decision to renounce and not return to it, and at the end I announce forgiveness in Jesus' name, using supporting Scripture (1 John 1:9) and the church's Trinitarian form of absolution, "Almighty God have mercy upon you, forgive you all your sins through our Lord Jesus Christ, strengthen you in all

68. Appendix 8.

goodness, and by the power of the Holy Spirit keep you in eternal life."[69] The issue of where to make amends where possible— and where prudent—is saved till later.

Then, having taken back lost ground, I move to either a renewal or a first taking of the church's baptismal vows after some brief teaching on what it means to say No to sin and evil and Yes to Jesus Christ and his church. We then recite the Creed together. We then lay hands upon their head, after gaining permission, and with gentle authority but no theatrics, command any spirits to quietly go in Jesus' name. And if there is resistance within the person, we pause and have another conversation. One man, who'd had several knuckles sacrificed in rituals, looked up in fear, "They're screaming at me, 'Get out of here!'"

The process, while somewhat confrontive, is very respectful and full of love and kindness. This general model, which is found in many of the more reputable treatments of the issues, is generally effective. The client has been welcomed, listened to, respected, taught, evaluated fairly and made a full and informed participant. At the end there is often an immense sense of relief and a common consent that *something just happened.*

It is critical, where at all possible, to follow up with the person to strengthen their newly found faith in Jesus, including participation in a local church. They are casualties in a much larger war, and the spiritual equivalent of rehab services is critical.

The above outline—though compressed—is something of an ideal, and not all meetings can be so carefully scripted. The most critical elements are the confession of sin and forgiveness, being as specific as possible, the clear and total renunciation of all occult practices, a clear confession of Jesus Christ as Lord, and the prayer of authority.

You never know when or where God will bring this stuff before you, and it's not always possible to have the luxury of several appointments and interviews. People are complex, multi-faceted, with their own histories of sin and evil, of abusing and being abused, and they are loved by God and need your highest respect. Never aim at a deliverance ministry. Aim only at a full gospel ministry, of which this kind of encounter is a small but important part. I once heard a wise practitioner say, "Jesus and his friends did not go looking for trouble, but when trouble found them, they knew what to do!" Do you?

Summary

Disciples live on a battlefield of multi-level conflict with invisible foes and with the peoples they've influenced through idolatry and sorcery. At Jesus' behest we are to go to them, to face resistance at every step, and to announce and demonstrate the kingdom in the light and powers of the Spirit. It will lead to division and rejection by some; it always does. Jesus comes to defeat the Evil One and all his forms of bondage, in us and all he loves.

69. *The U.M. Hymnal*, No. 390.

Insights

1. The self is permeable to the Holy Spirit and unholy spirits; both make a difference.

2. Spiritual warfare and power encounters are to be expected. We live on a battlefield.

3. Jesus did not require a confession of sin before the deliverance. Be gentle with precious people, but not with demons.

4. Jesus went to free the demoniac, get the community's attention, risk their rejection, and leave a witness. It was a great success.

5. Living out the new life and bragging on Jesus is the best form of pre-evangelism. A changed life and a new love are hard to deny.

6. The Gentile man went from demoniac to disciple, and then from disciple to missionary in very short order. Release people quickly!

Disciplines

Observation: Jesus enacted the kingdom, and when hostiles emerged dealt with them.
Action: Since people are complex, keep demonization in your catalog of possibilities.
Observation: Jesus left a living example of the new reality among a resistant people.
Action: Find ways to tell your Jesus story honestly, faithfully, in long and short forms.

16. Luke 8:40–56

When You're Hot, You're Hot!
Hybrid Genre: Two Healing Stories Interlaced

If the woman once cured had withdrawn from him in secret,
our Lord would have deprived her of a crown of victory.
It was fitting that the faith that shined out brightly in hidden agony was publicly crowned. He wove an elegant crown for her, because he said to her, "Go in peace."[70]
—Ephraem the Syrian

Justification

It was not until the fifty-one units had been written that I again reviewed all ninety-four of Luke's video vignettes, and—to my surprise—found one I'd overlooked, a double miracle taken over from Mark 5:21–43 and preserving its form of one story inserted into another. It's a verbal sandwich in which the story of Jairus' daughter

70. Just, *Luke*, 145.

begins (1. 8:40–42a), is interrupted by the story of the woman with the hemorrhage (2. 8:42b–48), then concludes at Jairus' home with the girl's resuscitation (1' 8:49–56).

What makes this a disciple passage is not so much that the disciples are presumed to be with Jesus in his return from the Decapolis, "Now when Jesus returned . . ." (v.40a), but that three of the twelve are singled out to go with him into the home, "And when he came to the house, he permitted no one to enter with him *except Peter and John and James*, and the father and mother of the child" (v.51).[71] This demonstrates the oft-noted insight pattern that within the twelve was an *inner three*.[72]

Shape

The genre of the two stories is the common miracle story in five parts:

1. Setting	vv.40, 49a	v.42b
2. Problem	v.42a	v.43
3. Engagement with healer	v.41	v.44a
4. Healing and Proof(s)	v.55a, b-d	v.44b
5. Reactions	v.56	vv.45–48

What is also interesting is how many parallels there are between the two stories:

Common Element	Jairus and daughter (vv.40–42a,49–56)	Woman with bleeding (vv.42b–48)
Status	High status male, approaches directly, helpless daughter	Low status female: assertive, low honor, indirect coming
Falling before Jesus	v.41	v. 47
Daughter	v.42	vv. 48–49
Twelve years (from/for?)	v.42	v. 43
Desperate circumstances	v.42, v.49	v. 43
Immediacy of healing	v.55	v. 44, 47
Touching	v.53	vv. 44, 45, 46, 47
Ritual Impurity	vv.53–54 (Corpse)	v.43 (Flow of blood)
Faith/Saved-Healed	v.50	v.48
All	v.40	v.47
House	v.41b	v.51a

Note that when the middle story is withdrawn, the two seams of the Jairus story fold neatly back together, "because he had an only daughter, about twelve years of age, and she was dying . . . a man from the ruler's house came and said . . ." The linking phrases that bridge in and out of the central story are v.42b, "Now as he went," and

71. 5:10 (the call story) and 9:28 (the transfiguration) also highlight the same three.

72. For a review, see Bruce, *Peter, Stephen, James & John*.

v.49a, "While he was still speaking." The two were already together in Mark, likely because this is how it happened and was retold using the proper genre. This way, each story interprets the other to demonstrate Jesus' authority over both disease and death. No unclean condition stumps him, and his powerful holiness of love and mercy is for all, the high born and the low.

The surface structure is a 3:1 Chiasm with three parts and a single center:

1. vv.40–41 Jairus Part 1,
    2. vv.42b–48 Woman with hemorrhage,
1' vv.49–56 Jairus Part 2.

Inclusions are *house* (v.41b // v.51a), *ruler* (v.41a // v.49a), *daughter* (v.42a // v.49b). The middle story, 2. vv.42b–48, is a 5:1 Chiasm:

a. vv.42b–43 Problem: Woman with a Flow of Blood
    b. v.44 Woman *Behind* Jesus: Came/Touched/Immediately Healed
        c. vv.45–46 Dialog and Misunderstanding
    b' v.47 Woman *Before* Jesus: Came/Touched Healed
a' v.48 Solution: Jesus Confirms Healing, Blesses Her

Content

Jesus is a true incarnation, the obedient Son of the Father, filled with the Spirit, wisdom, power, and love for the healing of people, and finally of all the creation in which they are embedded. Where he goes, life is restored to full function as God's incoming kingdom displaces the false, interlocking kingdoms of sin, evil, and death. His popularity among the crowds is high because of his deeds and words as he returns from a campaign among the Gentiles in the Decapolis (vv.40–42).

As soon as he and his team land back on the eastern shore, crowds await him. Among them is a high-status synagogue leader, Jairus, whose only daughter is dying, and Jesus agrees to go with Jairus to her. But he is soon interrupted by a chronically bleeding woman who sneaks up behind for a touch that immediately communicates healing. Jesus reveals that he felt power leave him; he is fully aware of physical phenomena that happen as the Spirit moves through him.

Yet he did not know who touched him. Some items he knows; others he must inquire about, thus his question. Jesus operates both by immediate divine revelation and also through questions and observation. He then waits patiently as the woman prostrates herself and gives her witness of long illness and immediate healing. Jesus is available, attentive, patient, and both affirms her as family and gives her a public blessing, "Daughter, your faith has made you well. Go in peace!" There's no rushing with Jesus; he stays with an opportunity as long as necessary. No need to hurry. Meanwhile, a frantic Jairus is silent.

Because of Jesus' delay with a non-crisis divine appointment, Jairus' daughter dies, and since death is final, there's no more need for the Rabbi, thus the messenger's advice to "not trouble the Teacher any more" (v.49b).

But Jesus, with a sure word from God, calls for extreme faith from Jairus, "Do not fear, only believe, and she shall be well (saved)." Jairus has just seen the woman's cure, but this is death. But Jesus is not discouraged by the report; he continues the trek and goes into Jairus' home with an inner circle of three disciples and the girl's parents.

The form of the story contrasts Jesus' confidence and the mourners' mocking disbelief at the center (c. vv.52–53). But at his touch and with his command, "Child, arise," her breath is recalled and she immediately sits up, an indication of strength. Jesus' command for her to receive food means she's not a ghost but fully restored. Her parents' marvel, and Jesus asks them to keep quiet about the event. He is God's agent who gives life and pushes back death's awful power. His faith and faithfulness persevere! Imagine the joy of handing a daughter back to her father and mother.

Then

Announcing *the new reality* and with it *the new opportunity* for healing and exorcism, Jesus moves across the landscape in the power of the Holy Spirit, and everywhere he goes the extraordinary happens. There is with Jesus and so in Luke a density of miracle reports and miracle summaries unparalleled in the ancient world. And not just isolated individual accounts but a steady flow of the same patterns of healings, exorcism, and occasional resuscitations from the dead. The impression Luke leaves is that such events were a daily occurrence, and that they were acknowledged to be so by others, and not all of them friendlies: insiders (John the Baptist [7:18–35]), outsiders (e.g. Herod [9:7–9], Jewish observers [11:15, 13:14]).[73]

Twice in the next two chapters, first 9:1–11 with the twelve, and secondly in 10:1–24 with the seventy, we see the authority of Jesus officially transferred to followers so that each group finds itself empowered to do as Jesus had done: 1) preach *the new reality* and then 2) demonstrate its benefits in healings and exorcisms. He has now replicated himself in others. Could this be a dimension of disciple-making that we have ignored? If a disciple is one who is *with him* in order to become *like him*, why are healing and exorcism not in the core curriculum?

As we review the joining of these two powerful demonstrations of kingdom love from the Father, through the Son, and energized by the Spirit, we must come to terms with the constancy and immediacy of Jesus being a follower. He is guided and directed, first to go to the home of Jairus, then to be interrupted by a woman who snuck up and touched him in faith, then to ignore the report of the girl's death, then continue to Jairus' home, then to take the inner three with him to observe, then speak to her a command given him from above, then and observe the spectacular effects as

73. For an accessible summary, see Strauss, *Introducing Jesus*, 116–29.

she is restored. Moment by moment and thought by thought and action to action he is led and obeys. He goes where the Father leads, speaks what he hears, does what he sees. It's total and complete availability; Jesus lived a radically dependent life, tempted to step out of rhythm, but never doing it. And the sheer delight of this partnership is to recreate the life of a suffering woman and present a daughter back to her dad and mom. All in all, a good day's work.

Now

Yes, it is our call to follow. Yes, it is our duty. But even more, what a privilege and a delight to be a modern day follower of Jesus of Nazareth. To live in his company—though in a different mode than our first forebears—and to learn his ways through listening and learning, risk and reward, service and suffering, repentance and rebuke, friendship and following. As I often say, it was the finest education ever offered, to be constantly in the presence of one fully able to teach you everything you need to know and to know yourself being deeply changed in the process. Weaknesses revealed, blind spots on full display, prejudices made public, unlearning much of what you thought to be true, and seeing what you believed to be—if not impossible—then extremely rare. And all because he crossed their paths with an invitation and a promise.

Let us admit that we suffer from low expectations for what it might mean to follow Jesus today.[74] A mostly good life, a ticket to the next, a God who listens to our confused prayers, a local church full of mostly-nice people, church softball, a men's club, a place for baptism, marriages, and death, a pastor to call when pain hits or illness intrudes. You know what I mean, and all of it good, but far short of the drama and high-stakes adventure afforded the women and men who first say *Yes* to the stranger with the penetrating eyes.

Could it be that one of the side-effects of making discipleship safe is that we've made it boring and a chore? I think so, and that means that *discipleship recovered* will have to embrace much more risk and face the needs around us much more directly and in ways that demonstrate dependence on the Holy Spirit from start to finish. Not methods, not strategies, but living dependence on the third person of the Holy Trinity and a willingness to look stupid in public! How to listen for the nudge and the guidance, how to welcome and use the gifts and energies of the Spirit, how to wait on God before we speak or act. These are the disciplines of dependence and divine-human cooperation and synergy. So who will sign up to learn to dance with God? To keep time with the beat and melody God plays?

---

74. For a tonic, see Moreland, *A Simple Guide to Experience Miracles.*

Summary

Disciples learn that every day is a learning opportunity. Whatever our situation is, we keep dialing our awareness onto the Jesus channel with questions like, What are you doing here, Lord? Where are love and service needed? Who do I need to pay attention to? Who are you sending me? What prayers should I offer? What should I say? Then take a first action, expecting more light as you walk in obedience to impressions that are loving, true, sometimes risky, and always kind.

So it was with the first followers; watching Jesus operate under the Father's will and with the Spirit's empowerment was like nothing they'd ever seen. He did it all the time and then launched them into the same spiritual dynamic.

Insights

1. Following Jesus puts you in the people business. Interruptions are often opportunities. Discern!

2. Desperate people will look to you for what can only come from God. Refer them in love!

3. People have histories and problems they are ashamed and embarrassed to reveal. Build trust!

4. Superstition is not to be rejected; it is to be instructed and the hope redirected to Jesus. Look deeper!

5. To be near Jesus is to be near love and power fused together in a perfect union. Expect both!

6. The healing of the sick through non-medical means remains a common sign of God's kingdom. Pray!

Disciplines

Observation: Jesus was about the business of healing and restoring the human person.
Action: Learn the art of *ministry prayer* and learn to pray wherever you are.[75]
Observation: Jesus was ever-alert to the opportunities that came in interruptions.
Action: Practice paying real attention to the people who come your way.

---

75. For a report from a long-term Vineyard pastor on *ministry prayer*, see Turrigiano, *I'm No Superman*.

17. Luke 9:1–11

Doing the Impossible with the Invisible
Genre: A Modified Commissioning Account

The grace bestowed upon the holy apostles is worthy of all admiration.

But the bountifulness of the Giver surpasses all . . .

He gives them, as I said, his own glory.

By the might and efficacy of the Holy Spirit, burning them as if they were on fire,

they make the devil come forth

with groans and weeping from those whom he possessed.[76]

—CYRIL OF ALEXANDRIA

Justification

This is one of several hinge passages in Luke, a turning point, and it fulfills the earlier installation of the twelve as Jesus' *apostles/ambassadors*.[77] They have the new title, and here they are invited as participants into Jesus's public kingdom operations. He heals and delivers in divine power (the Holy Spirit's presence and gifts, 6:17–19), and now they are sent in to do the same. And since there is no mention of going out in pairs (as later in 10:1–24), we presume they went as a whole since they are named as "the twelve" (v.1a).

And while the full immersion in the wind and fire of the Spirit is reserved for Pentecost, the best way, perhaps, to understand the current mission is as a temporary endowment, an experimental commission, a trial run of sorts in which they get a taste of doing what Jesus did each day. They watched him for a season. Now they go out with his promises to see what happens. And it works! Disciples are offered a share in the ministry of Jesus.

Shape

The literary structure of the thought unit is in three parts, a sending (a. vv.1–6) and return (a' vv.10–11) in the frames, and at the center a report from inside Herod's palace about how the mission was spreading the fame of Jesus (b. vv.7–9). Inclusions in a//a' are: *the twelve* (v.1a) // *the Apostles* (v.10a), *sent* (v.2) // *return* (v.10a), *kingdom of God . . . heal* (v.2) // *kingdom of God . . . heal* (v.11c-d), *receive* (v.5a) // *received-welcomed* (v.11b). The Herod episode (b. vv.7–9) is inserted between the sending (a. vv.1–6)

76. Just, *Luke*, 147–48.

77. See Sweetland, *Our Journey with Jesus*, 31–33.

and return (a. vv.10–11) to give *narrative time* for the mission, where Herod reviews options for Jesus' identity. The outline of the unit is:

> a. vv.1–6 Jesus Sends Out The Twelve With His Own Authority
> 1. vv.1–2 Commissioning and Sending
> 2. v.3 Mission Speech 1
> 2' vv.4–5 Mission Speech 2
> 1' v.6 Obedience In Departure and Mission
> b. vv.7–9 Herod Raises A Theological Question
> a' vv.10–12 Return of the Twelve and Display of Jesus' Healings

The genre, apart from the insertion, is a modified Commissioning Account (vv.1–6, 10–11) with six of the seven elements present:

1. Introduction (v.1a),

2. Confrontation (v.1b-c),

3. Reaction/Obedience (v.6),

4. Commission (vv.3–5),

5. Protest (absent),

6. Reassurance (absent), [Inserted Herod account]

7. Conclusion (vv.6, 10).[78]

A second genre, *A Confrontation with a King* (vv.7–9), is sandwiched between the sending and return of the twelve.

To announce the kingdom (v.2) and then demonstrate its benefits (v.1c) is a deeply political act that challenges current arrangements (vv.7–9). Note the three times that preaching the kingdom and demonstrating it in healing are highlighted (vv.2, 6, 11c-d). Some new prophet and his friends are now doing for people what only God can do, and if God is operative at ground level, then all power arrangements are now under review, so Herod seeks an audience with an emerging rival (v.9c).

Content

Thus far the Spirit-filled Jesus is the sole outlet of *the new reality* and its power to set life right. But after a period of calling and training (6:19–8:56), the Twelve are commissioned and authorized to be his field agents and extensions.[79] No longer observers,

78. Modified from Hubbard, "The Role of Commissioning Accounts in Acts," 187–91.

79. See Hacking, Signs and Wonders, 181–88. On how Jesus' words and deeds interpret one another, see Bock, *Jesus the God-Man*, 98–121. For a narrative treatment of Luke 9:1–11, see Witherington, *The Gospel: A True Story Of Jesus*, 150–56. On a world view that makes sense of Jesus' teachings, healings, and exorcisms, see Wright, *Simply Jesus*, 119–30, 131–50. For a recent appropriation for the

they are now participants, albeit in a limited way, in the same reality. Before no power, now his power. Jesus gives them a mission-specific anointing or filling of the Holy Spirit so there is continuity between his ministry and theirs. This has clear implications for our understanding of the church, as evidenced in Acts.

The paradox is between his gift of an invisible resource and the stripping away of all external supports. With his empowerment goes radical vulnerability. So none of the normal accessories of foot travel (v.3), and their mission—as an extension of his own—is high stakes. To refuse them is to refuse him, and by extension his Father. Their obedience (v.6) is a success report for both Jesus and them. He has transferred authority, and they have enacted it at a distance. Imagine the excitement of the de-briefing that followed the multi-day experiment. His authority goes with them and operates at a distance. Thus the later apostolic mission in Acts is grounded and modeled in the ministry of the risen Jesus, just as here with the pre-Easter Jesus.

The Herod interlude (vv.7–9) alerts us that news of Jesus and his band of agents spreads quickly to high places (8:3). It leaves us with the possibility of state violence against Jesus, just as for John the Baptist. Jesus is here cast as a miracle worker like Elijah and clearly a prophet. If God is visiting his people, then it's a clear threat to Herod Antipas' governance. Multiple reports leave this dangerous man both perplexed and anxious. He wants to examine Jesus! That the return from mission occasions a retreat is Jesus' compassion on his friends. That he is then interrupted by the crowds and responds so graciously is also a lesson for the Twelve. Access to the kingdom and its resources is the mission of Jesus.

It is interesting that the successful mission, however long it lasted, generated several responses. Herod heard of the commotion, surveyed opinion, and wondered aloud if he might have to do with the new prophet what he did with the old, but for now it was enough to send emissaries and seek an interview, "And he sought to see him." When the new reality lands, everyone can feel the rumblings.

A second response is that Jesus receives them back for a de-briefing where "they told him what they had done." He prepares, commissions, equips, waits behind, receives back, and now lets them tell their stories. What happens before and after a mission is as important as what happens during it. His strategic withdrawal with them to Bethsaida is likely modeled on his own regular isolations for prayer and refilling. They are not just to be used but cared for. Adrenalin is useful, but you can't live on it for long. But because of his, and now their reputations as healers, fresh crowds arrive, and what does Jesus do? What he always did, and they're watching him is a new lesson in dealing with unbidden opportunities, "and he welcomed them and spoke to them of the kingdom of God, and cured those who had need of healing" (v.11). This is his ministry; this is what love looks like; this is *the new reality*.

---

church, see Venter, *Doing Healing*, 157–72, 173–86.

Then

There are some thresholds that, when crossed, you can never go back again because your identity is changed, and the effects are with you forever. Examples are wedding vows— if honored, military vows—if kept, becoming a parent—if faithful, and being a participant in the powers of the kingdom of God. To this point the disciples were fellow travelers, observers, and admirers as they watched Jesus preach and heal, but at this point they are invited to cross over into the same experience and to learn it is indeed transferable to ordinary folk. And once it happened through them, they were hooked at a new level. God was healing and freeing fellow Jews through them as a display of *the new reality* Jesus introduced. God was re-visiting his people and setting life right again by restoring function and spiritual freedom.

Now

As a pastor I have prayed for healing with droves of people, and only on occasion have I been able to see something happen, either in the moment of prayer or afterwards. We listen, we love, we pray, we invoke the Holy Spirit, and wait upon the various gifts. We avoid making promises only God can keep. We encourage the use of medical means. We refuse to allow our fears to keep us from loving and praying for those in pain and with trauma. And then we receive a surprise from above and find courage to continue looking weak and helpless because we cannot of our own make anything happen, and we don't know much to begin with.

But the history of the church is littered with stories of startling healings and dramatic deliverances. We live in a world where God upholds creation and welcomes interaction, sometimes with surprising results. And when visited by the signs and wonders of the kingdom, they are meant to increase the fame of Jesus and to make his love visible.   The Jesus movement that continues in his church is a truth and healing movement, and in spite of the skepticism that is so much of our current climate— and some of it, I might say, well deserved—discipleship without a commitment to prayer for healing in full awareness of the gifts and person of the Holy Spirit is simply defective by omission. Our world is so constituted as to make it *user-friendly* to divine action, and it has not changed.

Because healings are relatively rare, and because we have so many other means where modern medicine thrives, it's easy for the church to marginalize and eventually dismiss such supernatural possibilities and to focus on the things we can predict and control, which are among the highest values of our late-modern culture. We want things to work, to work quickly, to be turned into a method and technology we can predict. But God is not like this, and were God to allow such manipulation, we would be back into a world of magic, which is one of the alternatives a robust biblical conception of God delivers us from.

Healing is about creative dependence and vulnerability, both to the person in need and to the guidance of the Holy Spirit without whom nothing happens. But as we learn to *dance with the Holy Spirit,* we will be regularly surprised at the mercies which come. And when they come, we must take the time, as Jesus did, to savor the stories and excitement of seeing God at work. Nothing builds confidence in God like fresh testimonies from people you already trust.

Summary

Disciples are *with* Jesus in order to become *like* him. This involves sharing his *new reality* mission, including announcing the kingdom, healing the sick, freeing the demonized, facing local rejection, and popping up on the political radar. It is a grand experiment in trust because he is not with them. They are sent together, stripped of normal supports, and must trust the Holy Spirit to provide what's needed. The idea of a discipleship without such training is foreign to Jesus. After a time of observation, they are thrust into participation and return with amazing field reports. They have moved from lecture to laboratory.

Insights for Disciples

1. Though the ministry is his, Jesus freely shares with his friends. Do we want it?

2. In a culture of control, predictability, and self-sufficiency, Jesus has the right to strip us down for a lean mission. Does this scare you?

3. Jesus was not politically correct about what it meant to spurn him though his agents. He issued clear warnings of God's judgment.

4. God's kingdom in Jesus is a threat to all other forms of governance. Herod was right to be concerned about *the new reality* showing up on his doorstep.

5. Take time to retreat and debrief. Savor and celebrate, learn and re-calibrate together.

6. Jesus was interruptible! Are you? Human need, wherever encountered, was an occasion to welcome, instruct, and heal.

Disciplines

Observation: The empowerment of the Spirit is not for entertainment but ministry!
Action: Take the risk of praying with people wherever you are. Listen to the Spirit!
Observation: Jesus alternated ministry with crowds with time apart from them.
Action: Use your calendar as a planning tool, and stay open to divine appointments.

18. Luke 9:12–17

A Feast in the Wilderness
Hybrid Genre: A Feeding Miracle, A Disciple Correction Story

God has broken five loaves and two fishes and fed five thousand.
With these foods that satisfy to the fullest their hunger.
Then twice six baskets are filled with the fragments that are left over:
Such is the bounty dispensed from the heavenly table forever."[80]
—PRUDENTIUS

Justification

We all recognize teachable moments when learning is enriched and made relevant by the press of circumstances. And so it was regularly with the disciples. They were always operating at the edge of their understanding. The literary form that most clearly captures the teachable moment is what I label *A Disciple Correction Story*. They are a regular feature of Luke's layered biography and typically contain five parts, as here:

1. Setting and problem (vv.12, 13c-d)

2. Jesus speaks (vv.13a-b)

3. The disciples misunderstand (vv.13c–14a)

4. Jesus corrects them with fresh teaching, (vv.16–17a)

5. A solution is offered, perhaps with additional teaching (v.17b)

The disciples bump up against the limits of their understanding; Jesus then opens up a new possibility. They learn he is adequate for any situation, and that what he commands he enables. They are his pupils, and this unit clearly belongs in our catalog.

Shape

This unit of thought has three paragraphs (a. vv.12–14, b. v.16, a' v.17) and each is shorter than the one before it. Inclusions which frame the unit are *the Twelve* (v.12b) // *twelve* (v.17b), *all* (v.13c) //*all* (v.17b). The genre is a hybrid of a Miracle Story, in this case a nature miracle of provision, and a Disciple Correction Story. At the center are five actions enacted by the host at most Jewish meals (v.16), but here by Jesus with extraordinary effect. This is the template of his actions at their last meal together and later in the church's Eucharist. The outline is:

80. Just, *Luke*, 152–53.

a. vv.12–15 Problem: Too Little Food

b. v.16 Jesus' Blessing Prayer, Five-Fold Action:
taking, looked up, blessed, broke, gave

a' v.17 Solution: More Than Enough Food

Content

The distinction often drawn between *nature miracles* (the great catch of fish, stilling the storm, multiplying food) and the more-numerous *healing and exorcism miracles* is a false distinction since people and their disorders are also part of nature.[81] And Jesus, it appears, is as comfortable with one as the other. God's power and authority works through him whatever the challenge or medium of expression. Creation is user-friendly to God.

And here the issue is hungry crowds (v.11) who've stayed to near sunset with no food or lodging. Who provides the hospitality: food and lodging? Well, Jesus provides for the first, and presumably sends them home to sleep for the night.

The dialog of vv.12–14 is instructive because the disciples have just returned from a healing mission and then seen Jesus do more of the same (vv.10–11). It's been an amazing display of kingdom power reordering life. Jesus does storms and demons and disease, but what about hunger?

But when he commands the twelve to feed the people, all they have are excuses. He then steps in, organizes the mob, uses disciples as waiters, and acts like a family host at a Jewish meal. The miracle itself is not narrated, only its after-effects. All are fed with leftovers, twelve baskets— one for each table waiter! What's it mean?

The setting and problem is found in vv.12–14. It's late, time to eat, and the twelve come to Jesus with a consensus proposal: the people are to be sent away for lodging and provisions while it's still light enough to travel. The speech of Jesus is brief and confrontive, an impossibility, "You yourselves give them something to eat" (v.13). The disciples' misunderstanding is made clear in v.13c-d where their thinking is limited by the scarce resources at hand, "We have no more than five loaves and two fish—unless we are to go and buy food for all these people," the colossal number being saved to the end as a punch line of another impossibility, "For there were about five thousand men." Jesus has commanded them to do what does not make sense. He has created a teachable moment about the more-than-human resources at his disposal.

Jesus' fresh teaching is found in his command of vv.14b–15 and his prayerful actions of v.16 in five verbs: *taking . . . looked up . . . blessed . . . broke . . . gave*. The fifth and final component, the solution, is given in v.17, "And all ate and were satisfied. And they took up what was left over, baskets of broken pieces, twelve." The needs of the

---

81. On the history of the interpretation of the nature miracles, see Twelftree, *The Nature Miracles of Jesus*, 3–40. Also Keener, *Miracles*, 579–99.

crowd and their own needs are more than met by a miracle of supernatural provision. It was a teachable moment that became a memorable event.

The disciples have just seen Jesus heal and exorcize through them at a distance (9:1–11). Now they learn that Jesus is not only a physician but quite a caterer as well. People need healing and deliverance; people also need food and an experience of God's radical generosity. Jesus shook their world on a daily basis as he set up situations that required divine action. Bit by bit they are being exposed to a new world in the midst of the old. This is the school of Jesus they were immersed in for around three years.

Then

In any good novel the characters are developed by layering as each new scene opens up a bit of who they are and what they are about. It all started with following Jesus in the simplest form possible: where he went, they went. And when he entered a village, they listened as he spoke and observed how he behaved. And then, when the Holy Spirit indicated, he spoke to conditions, touched the ill and tormented with great effect. How utterly astounding that must have been the first time it happened. So if we take every paragraph of Luke as an incident in the curriculum of discipleship, we see how demanding was Jesus' program of formation and how revolutionary the learning format.

With 8:22–25 and the units immediately after it there is a new intensity of exposure. First the storm on the sea and their rescue (8:22–25), then the confrontation with a bizarre Gentile demonic in two scenes (8:26–33, 34–39), then the intercalated stories of Jairus' daughter and the woman with the hemorrhage (8:40–56), then the miraculous mission of the twelve (9:1–11), and now the feeding of the five thousand (9:12–17), followed by the confession of Peter (9:18–22), a unit on the cost of discipleship (9:23–27), the transfiguration of Jesus on the mountain (9:28–36), and a unit featuring two exorcism stories (9:37–43a, 49), the second passion prediction (vv.43b–45, 50–51), and a teaching on the place of children (9:46–48). It is positively dizzying in its raw exposure to the power of the new reality Jesus embodies and shares with them.

Their old world is now brimming with new possibilities. Is there anything he can't do? Only one. He will not disobey and break the fellowship he has with the Father and the Spirit, and he'd rather die than betray his mission. He is our rabbi, our leader, our friend, the reason we are together, and he is utterly faithful to the Lord God of Israel. And in his company we are exposed to the light and love of our Maker. It's a good way to live.

Now

So why follow Jesus with all the dislocations it entails? Why take the risk of learning his way of living? Some of my reflections are:

"We follow him because of who he is;
we follow him because he hooked us;
we follow him because he's like no one else;
we follow him because of his clarity of vision;
we follow him because of his promises;
we follow him because he speaks truth in love and never deceives;
we follow him because the love and presence of the Father is palpably present;
we follow him because his interest in us exceeds anything we've know from family or friends, spouses or wise men;
we follow him because he restores people to sanity and health;
we follow him because he let us in on his mission to spread *the new reality*;
we follow him because he called our name and issued an invitation, 'Follow me;'
we follow him because there is so much joy and life swirling around him;
we follow him because he might just be the preview of a whole new world;
we follow him because he surrendered to crucifixion and received resurrection;
we follow him because he lit us on fire with the energies of the Holy Spirit;
we follow him because any other pursuit is a waste of time and energy."

Remember, when following Jesus together we are not in control. We can quit and leave, abandon his call, but what situations we face in the curriculum are designed by another. The very purpose of discipleship, of being Jesus' follower and apprentice in *the new reality*, is to be driven deeper and deeper into who he is and what his vision is for the healing of world. And the more he reveals—and there is always more to him—the deeper our dependence, our awe, our gratitude, our worship. We spiral into his depths.

Summary

Disciples find themselves in circumstances where no amount of human cleverness or resourcing are adequate. We feel overwhelmed and undone. This is part of *the new reality* curriculum, and the best response is to pause, dial down anxiety, and ask, "What do you want to do, Lord Jesus, and how can we join you?" Then wait and listen. Operating out of invisible resources in impossible situations is what he did every day, and the reports are that he was quite adept at it. Keep your eyes wide open and pray!

Insights

1. Get used to being in impossible positions. Looking foolish is the norm!

2. Jesus does demons and diseases through the twelve, but what about bread and fish? It was a new frontier, and we always remain learners.

3. Obedience to Jesus often goes against common sense. He lives in and moves out of *the new reality*, and it's hard for Western, Individualist, Achievers!

4. As we follow him and serve, our needs are met. One basket reserved for each waiter!

Disciplines

Observation: Jesus regularly places his friends in difficult, impossible situations.
Action: Get used to facing needs and problems that no human resource can address.
Observation: Jesus arranged for there to be one basket of leftovers for each apostle.
Action: To live on the scraps of Jesus is a feast indeed; servants are not forgotten.

19. Luke 9:18–22

A Public Poll and Peter's Confession
Genre: A Disciple Correction Story, A Passion Prediction

He took away the sin of the world,

opened the gates above to the dwellers on earth, and united earth to heaven.

These things proved him to be, as I said, in truth God.

He commanded them, therefore, to guard the mystery by a seasonable silence,

until the whole plan of the dispensation should arrive at a suitable conclusion.[82]

—CYRIL OF JERUSALEM

Justification

This is another of the hinge passages in Luke's biography of Jesus and his apprentices. It catches up what's come before and gives new clarity to what's ahead. This is clearly both a Christology and a discipleship text where the golden chord of Jesus and the blue cord of his followers are woven tightly together.

Shape

The structure of this unit is revealed in the pattern of two questions of Jesus (vv. 18b, 20), each followed by an answer, first of the disciples as a group (v.19), then of Peter alone (v.20). Three inadequate answers (John the Baptist . . . Elijah . . . one of the prophets (v.19b-d) give way to a more correct answer from Peter (*God's Messiah,* v.20c). Then from Jesus himself comes the true answer that he is not understood properly without a deep entry into voluntary suffering, death, and a vindicating resurrection

82. Just, *Luke*: 155.

as the Son of man.[83] So the progress is from the three prophetic options (v.19) to the single Messianic option (v.20c), then to a surprising redefinition of messiahship as the suffering and rising Son of man. Thus Jesus fills old titles with new and surprising content.

This leaves us with the two outside frames (a. v.18a // a' vv.18–22) and the question of their relationship to each other, and here there are no verbal inclusions. But note that in 1. v.18 the order is Jesus at prayer and then the disciples, but in 1' vv.21–22 it is the disciples who are first, then Jesus. The initial order has been reversed: Jesus . . . disciples // disciples . . . Jesus forming a concentric or chiastic pattern. So where did the detailed passion prediction of v.22b-e come from? Verse 18a gives the answer, "It was received in prayer."

It is in regular prayer that Jesus discerns his path and what it means. Prayer is the setting for fresh revelation for the next phase of obedience and for surrender to whatever it means. And with these insights secured, the structural outline of this unit is:

1. v.18a Introduction: Jesus at Prayer

    2. vv.18b–19 First Question and Answer: Public Opinion

    2' v.20 Second Question and Answer: Peter's Confession

1' vv.21–22 Conclusion: The Outcome of Jesus' Prayer is Insight

As with the previous unit (9:12–17, feeding five thousand), the form of 9:18–22 is a *Disciple Correction Story* only this time with two rounds of dialog in vv.18b–19, 20:

1. Setting	v.18a
2. Jesus speaks 1	v.18b
3. Disciples report misunderstanding	v.19
2' Jesus Speaks 2	v.20a-b
3' Peter misunderstands	v.20c
4. Jesus chastens them	v.21
5. Further teaching	v.22

Content

The setting is the paradox that Jesus "was praying alone" and that "the disciples were with him" (v.18a). The implication is that they were near enough to observe his prayer and perhaps praying themselves. What emerged from Jesus' prayer were two questions about his identity addressed to his followers. First, "Who do the crowds say that I am?" followed by three prophetic options all of which are misunderstandings, and secondly to his disciples "But/Now, who do you say that I am?" followed by Peter's climactic confession based on what he has observed thus far, "The Messiah of God."

---

83. For a summary of research on Peter's confession, see Bock, *Who is Jesus?* 93–102. On Luke's resurrection stories, see Thrailkill, *Resurrection*.

His answer is not wrong based on current evidences of Jesus' extraordinary powers, just inadequate as to the kind of Messiah Jesus is to be, one who suffers. This is clearly both a Christology and a discipleship text.

The surprise of the thought unit is that Jesus does not praise Peter for his insight but commands Peter and the others in the strongest terms not to tell this to anyone, however correct it might be, and also how easily misunderstood in a political fashion. Instead, he is a new kind of Messiah, one who carries out the will of his Father that he suffer, be rejected, be killed, and on the third day be raised.

Jesus redefines what it means to be "The Messiah of God" with nearly unthinkable content. Peter is partly right, but there is much more to Jesus than his kingdom preaching, healings, and exorcisms (acts of spiritual power). His identification with us goes much deeper than the temporary relief of healing. He actually takes upon himself the suffering and sins of the world, and this he does as an innocent man, a perfect human being, one who never sinned in action and never rebelled inwardly against God in any way.

Yes, we humans in our rebellion are vulnerable to disasters, damage, disease, and demons, but beyond that lies the fearsomeness of death and the righteous verdict of God's judgment. But in his own body Jesus defeats death in resurrection and seals God's forgiveness for all who place their trust in him.

Then

The statement that identity determines discipleship is a truism that needs to be repeated often because of our natural— and sinful—tendency to remake Jesus in our image and preferences. Immersing ourselves in the four gospels and practicing active obedience with others is the only way to stay de-toxed from all the partial and false portraits that cater to our whims and fantasies. And if the disciples had to go through regular correction, then so do we, and here is a classic case.

There is always more of Jesus to discover precisely because he is God the Son enfleshed, and God cannot be exhausted. The more we know about him, the clearer it is what it means to follow. When this faith and this walk become boring, jaded, irrelevant, passe, predictable, conventional, and religious in the artificial sense, it means we've missed something because the Lord has not changed; we have drifted. Not that times of aridity are not normal, only that when Jesus is gradually displaced from the center of our affections and focus, drift sets in as with any human relationship, and the first awareness of the shift in interest is a call to self-examination and a fresh grace-aided turn back towards the center. The United Methodist teaching on repentance after conversion is clear and very encouraging:

Article XII: Of Sin After Justification

"Not every sin willingly committed after justification is the sin against the Holy Ghost, and unpardonable. Wherefore, the grant of repentance is not to be denied to such as fall into sin after justification. After we have received the Holy Ghost, we may depart from grace given, and fall into sin, *and, by the grace of God, rise again and amend our lives* (ital. ad.). And therefore they are to be condemned who say they can no more sin as long as they live here; or deny the place of forgiveness to such as truly repent" (*The Book of Discipline 2016:* 68).

Thus far Peter and others have been trekking around after an utterly victorious Jesus. He defeats the three big *D's*: disease, demons, death. He strides across the countryside in unbroken victory, with perhaps a little rearguard sniping from his opponents. But it will soon enough be interrupted by a big collision in Jerusalem, and it will mean the very worst of suffering and shame for him, ending in death, but restarting in a solo resurrection, whatever that might mean.

But to follow Jesus in the light is not a part but the whole of his story. It is to relish the power of his love shown in signs and wonders and then to draw the link between that form of divine love and form demonstrated in his voluntary suffering and cruel death because both are from the same source. The miracles deal with how vulnerable we all are, and the climactic events deal with the truth that we are all sinners headed for death. No part of the human condition is omitted from the cure Jesus' embodies and freely offers. It is salvation, the full restoration of the human person, along every axis: our relationship with God, with creation, with others, and with ourselves. It is being made whole again through the divine gift of right relationships, starting with God. Jesus heals our relationship with God.

Now

How many times have I sung and given fresh assent to a verse of the hymn "Come Thou Fount of Every Blessing":

> O to grace how great a debtor
> daily I'm constrained to be!
> Let thy goodness, like a fetter,
> bind my *wandering* heart to thee.
> Prone to *wander*, Lord, I feel it,
> prone to leave the God I love;
> here's my heart, O take and seal it,
> seal it for thy courts above.

The double use of "bind my wandering heart to thee" and "Prone to wander" in close proximity make wandering a habit of the heart and something quite below conscious control. It's no longer something I choose to do; that would be *departure*, not *wandering*. It's just where I find myself over and over through distraction or allurement or just plain old boredom. And my awareness of it is the first sign of grace to turn again and turn back, with every return as an act of faith and obedience.

Jesus includes the prophetic categories of the crowds, but he is more. He also embraces Messianic confession of Simon Peter, but he is more. He is the suffering Son of man who embraces suffering and death while awaiting a glorious resurrection and the reconstitution of his movement. He has what it takes to win our wandering hearts back to his Father. He wins our trust by being utterly trustworthy. At the end of this ancient biography of Jesus, Luke has a question for all this hearers, "Is Jesus trustworthy or not?"

Summary

Disciples are students always learning from two major sources, the Gospel portraits of Jesus and what they know of him through the living interaction of religious experience, with the first as the standard for the second. The constant question is, "But who do you (plural) say that I am?" to which our answers are always less than he is. Any theology of discipleship that has no place for suffering is inadequate. Obedience is costly. Disciples remain open to correction.

Insights for Disciples

1. Followers should expect a deepening development of their appreciation of Jesus' identity. Always more!

2. Popular evaluations of who Jesus is will always be less than the church teaches. Start there and build bridges to new audiences.

3. Jesus' prayer is the setting for religious experience and fresh divine revelation. Set up a listening post!

4. The mission of Jesus is not complete until he fully engages the very worst the world of religion and politics have to offer in his torture and death. He is a true radical.

Disciplines

Observation: In prayer Jesus discerned his suffering, death, and resurrection.
Action: Showing up often at *the listening post* is a declaration of dependence.
Observation: Jesus was teaching them who he was every day, including pop quizzes!
Action: Learn to ask people, "Who is Jesus to you?" and then follow the trail.

20. Luke 9:23–27

The Cost and Promise of Following
Genre: A Teaching Discourse of Jesus on Discipleship[84]

For we must deny ourselves and take up the cross of Christ and thus follow him.
Now self-denial involves the entire forgetfulness of the past and surrender of one's will—
a surrender which is very difficult, not to say quite impossible,
to achieve while living in the promiscuity customary in the world.[85]
—JEROME

Justification

From time to time Luke pauses to give us a mini-discourse on discipleship, and this is one of those occasions.[86] The language of "come after me" is what it means to follow Jesus from the perspective of the pupil. Jesus commands "Follow me," and the fledgling pupils get in line and begin walking behind him.

After a first enlistment in the Army, a soldier may choose to *re-up*, to sign a new contract for service. The underlying challenge is, "Are you still with us?" And that is the purpose of this little block of teaching. Jesus lays out the cost, the challenges, the warnings, and the hopes, then asks—in effect, "Are you still with me?" That it begins with "all" (v.23a) and ends with "some" (v.27b) is an indicator of a sifting, a reduction, a winnowing.

Shape

The first passion prediction of 9:22 is followed in the next thought unit by a series of five discipleship sayings in a concentric pattern with a single center (1-2-3-2'-1'). The outer frames (1. v.23 // 1' v.27) contain the verbal cue, "And he was saying" // "But I tell you truly" and the contrasting elements of "all" versus "some." The next inward layers (2. v.24 // 2' v.26) open with identical invitations, "For whoever," and the parallel expressions "for my sake" and "of me and my words."

The central element or hinge (3. v.25) is a probing question, "For what does it profit a man if he gain the whole world and forfeits himself?" The presentation begins with the qualifications of entry into the way of Jesus (v.23) and is then followed by three supportive reasons beginning with "For/*gar*" (vv.24, 25, 26) and concluding

---

84. Other samples of this genre (a teaching discourse on discipleship) are 6:20–49, 8:1–21. From time to time Jesus pauses to deliver an extended treatment of the same topic. Thus far I cannot find a technical term for this genre.

85. Just, *Luke*, 156.

86. Another short example is 9:57–62; longer examples are 6:20–49, 8:1–21, 12:35–48.

with a solemn promise, "But I tell you truly" (v.27). In terms of sheer density, this is a discipleship passage *par excellence*. An outline is:

    1. v.23 Introduction: Call to Discipleship and Self-Denial for all Candidates
       2. v.24 Whoever: On Losing and Saving Life (A Paradox)
          3. v.25 What? This World and the Coming New World
      2' v.26 Whoever: On Being Ashamed of Jesus and Facing Judgment
    1' v.27 Conclusion: Promise of Seeing the Kingdom (as a glorious preview)

Content

After Jesus discerns that his path of power will soon become the way of suffering and vindication (v.21), he applies it to his followers. Their job description is now rewritten, and the way is reopened to *all* (v.23a). This is a shift Jesus discerns in prayer (v.18a); a new and difficult path is before him, and so for them as well. The one carrying a cross is separated from the demands of this world. It is not just *stuff* and *other relationships* that are denied but the *self itself* and all its incessant demands. The struggle to be defined by God and no other attachments never ceases.[87] To lose myself in this loyalty is to be found and is the sanest calculation. Being bold about this loyalty is the path to life, then (v.26) and now (v.27).

This gem of a unit is a rhetorically sophisticated brief catechism on disciple-ship, structured so as to fix itself in the memory and with a probing question at the center awaiting an answer. And the only answer is "Nothing at all." To enjoy the world requires a world and a self, but what if the self is lost or forfeited in a frenzy to gain the world apart from its Maker and his Agent—Jesus. What if a false and foolish quest makes a false, foolish, futile, and empty quester? The financial metaphors Jesus in-vokes—*profit, gain, loses or forfeits*— are all about the calculations of risk and reward, so go figure and make a decision!

There is a logic and sequence in the five correlated sayings. First comes the en-trance saying to all persons in which the parallel phrases "come after me" (v.23b) and "follow me" (v.23e) indicate discipleship, while the cost is found in the two central ideas of denying the self (v.23c) and taking up the cross daily (v.23d).

To us it sound religious, but to them it spoke of a death sentence applied to oneself each day. I must drop my agenda, all I've invested in it, and join Jesus in his agenda, and every day we die a bit. Jesus keeps us in the world but sets us against its deepest loyalties and means. It's cross-grained living, swimming against the tide, contrary to what most count as common sense. It's both the deepest dislocation and most profound homecoming, and only Jesus' presence makes it durable.

We are living in two worlds at the same time, and the clash between them, both inwardly and outwardly, is constant. No wonder his first followers so often acted in a

---

87. See Talbert, "The Way of the Lukan Jesus," 237–49.

goofy fashion and needed so much correction. Every day Jesus did naturally what was impossible for them.

The second saying (v.24) makes explicit what was implicit in the first. The ways of the old self must be deconstructed, unraveled, unlearned, and let go of in the presence of Jesus and under the pressure of his love and truth. Living with him this closely means there's no place to hide, none of what we moderns think of as privacy. Discipleship is voluntary vulnerability to Jesus in a traveling community of goofballs. The old way of seeking to fulfill the self is a dead end, but to lose one's life in Jesus and *the new reality* is to find a new world for the self to thrive in. The self is perpetually hungry, and it matters where and from whom we are fed.

The central question (v.25) has already been dealt with above, but that it is a question cues us to Jesus' method of *challenge + freedom*. Questions clear spaces for answers, and Jesus lives with whatever is our reply.

The fourth saying (v.26) echoes the second (v.24) with its initial *Whoever*, and makes it clear that the *for my sake* of v.24 means *me and my words*. The Jesus who stands before them, he is the issue: his person, his words, his deeds. Discipleship is not a course to be completed. It is, rather, an ongoing relationship of love and obedience to the one who will, in the end, be the standard of ultimate judgment. He it is who as *the Son of man* returns at history's end to sort everything and everyone out. To be aligned with him through trust as demonstrated in following is to be prepared for that day. He is the climax of all history and towards him it bends.

The fifth saying (v.27) is a promise that not all but *some* who are present will not die before *they see the kingdom of God,* not however in its final form which remains future but in a preview of Jesus' glory (9:28–36) and later as the risen Lord (the appearances of Luke 24). To follow Jesus with others is a Yes to him and a No to yourself and its schemes. But paradoxically, a life of new fulfillment is made available, now and later. Preview now, fullness later. Hints now, substance later. Appetizer now, banquet later. Trust now, sight later. Conflict now, bliss later.

Then

Jesus never made it easy to join his roving kingdom band, but he kept opening the possibility to any who'd listen, thus, "And he was saying *to all . . .* " (v.23a). And this is one of the tasks to the church, to enter the public square with a demanding new possibility and an unparalleled opportunity to be enrolled in the *Jesus' school of life re-education.* And we are to cast the offer in the same ultimate and risky terms Jesus offered.

You may gain all you've ever dreamed of, but what if the process of acquisition makes you less than human? In the end Jesus saves the self in an ultimate fashion (forgiveness + resurrection body + new community in a new world). He ushers us ultimately into a full enjoyment of the new world, his kingdom of life and love apart from fouling effects of sin, death, and evil. It's what we were made for, and in Jesus we have a foretaste and forecast of just that kind of world. And the trajectory is set now. What will I pursue, the world apart from God, or the one God sent to give us a preview of the world to come?

Now

We have mistakenly thought in recent years that to grow the church requires softening the demands, rounding the edges, making Jesus more user-friendly to lifestyle consumers.[88] And that, we now see, is why people stay away in droves. Jesus will not be added to any other agenda, and he rules by substitution. He demands to be central, to set the terms, to shape the path and what is learned along the way. He claims to be the lord and judge of history and every life, the only one the Father and all the holy angels will back when the time comes.

To stand with him is to stand against the world as currently constituted. And if you are ashamed of him in any way because you still seek approval from the current order, then you are shaping the terms of your own judgment which he will repay in kind, "of him will the Son of man be ashamed when he comes . . . ." Life is high stakes, and Jesus offers himself as the path to a life beyond the best of imagination. There is no discount Jesus, no bargain gospel, no half-measures, no easier way. Life is at stake, and a church that goes fuzzy and soft and easy and pliable and indulgent and lazy is a dangerous place, because it always has to say, "Now what Jesus really meant was . . . ."

Summary

Disciples begin with a big dose of naivete about Jesus and his calling, but how could it be otherwise? But along the way are check-points and off-ramps, times when the cost and terms are clarified, and we either re-up or take a different path. It's about trust in and allegiance to Jesus with all his titles, all his mystery, and all his terrifying promises.

Insights

1. Discipleship is a counter-cultural way of living. It is not the American dream with Jesus sitting atop it with a snappy slogan for instant inspiration.

2. To follow Jesus and risk your all on his being right is a protest against the way the world is currently run.

---

88. For help with discipleship in the church, see Hull, *The Complete Book of Discipleship* and his *Conversion & Discipleship*. Also notable are Gallaty, *Rediscovering Discipleship*; Hirsch, *Untamed*; Ogden, *Discipleship Essentials*; Wilson, *The Imperfect Disciple*.

3. Since Jesus uses five different metaphors (execution, battlefield, marketplace, courtroom, new world) for the same call, it's as big and comprehensive as all of life.

4. Under the guidance of the Holy Spirit, Jesus and his agenda are always to be advocated, no matter where, and no matter who's listening.

Disciplines

Observation: Jesus never lowered the demands for being his follower.
Action: Stop at least once a week and read this text out loud for a course correction.
Observation: Where we stand with Jesus now is where we stand with God at the end.
Action: Learn to laugh at commercial for luxuries and use Jesus' name out loud often.

21. Luke 9:28–36

Whom to Listen To
Hybrid Genre: An Epiphany, Lukan Prayer Scene, Disciple Correction Story

He was bright as lightning on the mountain,

and became more luminous than the sun,

initiating us into the mystery of the future.[89]
—GREGORY OF NAZIANZUS

Justification

This story is included in our catalog of disciple passages not because it is a spectacular epiphany, a shining forth of divine glory, but because it is a Disciple Correction Story in which the rebuke and teaching is not from Jesus but from the Father who speaks as at Jesus' earlier baptism.

It is a key disciple passage because it clarifies the identity of the one we follow. God the Father declares the identity of the Incarnate Son as the one to pay attention to, to the one who is greater that either Moses or Elijah, both of whom had unusual transitions to the world above as God buried Moses and Elijah was carried aloft in a fiery chariot. Jesus own *exodus* will be by resurrection, followed days later by his ascension.[90]

89. Just, *Luke*, 161.
90. On the transfiguration, see Wright, *Simply Jesus*, 131–50.

Shape

The five expected parts of a Disciple Correction Story are all here:

1. Setting (v.28)
2. Event (vv.29–31)
3. Misunderstanding (vv.32–33)
4. Correction (vv.34–35)
5. Outcome (v.36)

Interestingly, this is the first of five consecutive Disciple Correction Stories with the Transfiguration as a stand-alone, while the next four (vv. 37–43a, 43b–45, 46–48, 49–50/51) constitute a separate thought unit. The inner three—Peter, James, John—have now experienced more revelation than the rest, but down the mountain at ground level there is much more error to be surfaced and corrected.

The story opens and closes with a time signature: *about eight days* (v.28a) // *in those days* (v.36c) as an echo to cue hearers to the boundaries. The concentric format continues with two parallel manifestations of glory (2. v.29 Jesus is Transfigured // 2' vv.34–35 The Father's verbal affirmation), and inside these frames with an appearance of Moses and Elijah (3. vv.30–31) and their disappearance (3' v.33). This leaves the single center as 4. v.32 which reveals the sleep and awakening to glory of Peter, James, and John. The pattern may be outlined as follows:

1. v.28 Introduction: Jesus on the Mountain in Prayer
    2. v.29 1st Manifestation of Epiphany: Light, Jesus Transfigured
        3. vv.30–31 Appearance of Moses and Elijah
            4. v.32 Center: Awakening of the Disciples, Faithless
        3' v.33 Disappearance of Moses and Elijah
    2' vv.34–35 2nd Manifestation of Epiphany: Voice, Jesus Affirmed
1' v.36 Conclusion: Jesus Alone, Awe-filled Silence

Then

At this point a differentiation is made among the twelve, a distinction hinted at in the prominence of Peter's call story (5:1–11) and his heading the listing of the twelve (6:14–16). Peter, followed by James and John, now appear as an inner circle of leaders in training, and to them is given the vision of a glorified Jesus and of Moses and Elijah with Jesus preparing him for his upcoming *exodos*. They go with Jesus to a high place to pray, and it is in the middle of Jesus' prayer that the heavenly world intrudes on the earthly.

The three disciples are sleeping and wake into this amazing scene. When the glory and the heroes withdraw (v.33a), the spontaneous response of Peter is to make the site a memorial of the three, which is understandable since Moses and Elijah were such towering figures in Judaism. But Jesus is in a category all by himself, and so there is a second epiphany as a cloud appeared and covered them, out of which came the divine voice in three scriptural echoes, "This is my Son (Ps. 2:7), my Chosen (Is. 42:1); listen to him (Dt. 18:15)!" There is no equal billing; Jesus has a status with God shared with no other. For all their history with God as premier prophets, Moses and Elijah are at our level, not his.

Jesus has every right to call whom the Father chooses and every right to offer special experiences and extra-special corrections to those few to whom he will entrust the leadership of his new community. So within the larger group of the disciples, there is a second call of twelve, and within the twelve an implicit special call of three. How Jesus deals with others is none of our business; it's part of trusting him and dealing with our ambitions. The challenge is love and faithfulness, not competition, as he will soon make explicit (vv.46–48).

Disciples may be given extraordinary experience of revelation, and whatever their ecstasies and mysteries, the purpose of such sights and sounds is to clarify the unique status of Jesus. They are explicitly Christological. Thus, when the second theophany recedes, "Jesus was found alone" (v.36a), and they "kept silence and told no one in those days anything of what they had seen." It wasn't for publication yet, and it did not give them bragging rights. In fact, it reduced all three to reverent, reticent silence. It was a call to insight, devotion, and worship.

Now

We are always living in and interacting with two realms that overlap and interlock always, and sometimes in surprising ways, as here. With divine revelation as the decisive theological category, what we know of God comes from God to us through various channels or means, among them creation itself, informed human conscience, the story of Israel, the person of Jesus, and the gifts and illuminations of the Holy Spirit. And they may show up on the receiver's side in intuitions, in dreams, in visions, in auditions, in unbidden circumstances, in prayer, in altered states of consciousness, in divine rescues, in the forceful illumination of Scripture, in open doors and providential ordering of our path, and each is divinely fitted to the person and the circumstances and the divine intent.

We live at all times in the mundane ordinary at the edge of holy mystery. And if our faculties are opened by the Holy Spirit, we enter a parallel reality, not far away but just beyond sight. And this is what happened on Jesus' mountain of prayer as the three were included for a short time in Jesus' kingdom reality, and then a second time by the visible presence and voice of the Lord whose words echoed Scripture, thus the One who first inspired the sacred writings now uses the texts and echoes them as a sign of continuity. Why should it surprise us when God speaks Bible!

So as we follow Jesus, we do not seek the extraordinary because there is plenty to keep us occupied with the ordinary, but if and when it comes, we welcome and test the content with what is already known of God in the tradition: Holy Scripture, Holy Creeds, Holy Persons. God is thrilling and awesome and numinous and overwhelming, but God does not self-reveal for our entertainment or to beg for anything. And with every fresh insight comes the challenge of obedience and faithful courage. It was not to the crowds but to three who were already obedient that the new light came.

Jesus moves the disciples and the twelve and the three along rather rapidly through daily exposure to his unveiling of *the new reality* and in special experiences, as here. He is shaping them at a pace which must have left them dizzy and undone. So much, and so soon. And then, one fine spring Friday, it all crashed and burned. But then . . . . This Jesus has every right to mess with our hearts, scramble our ideas of what's possible and real, call us beyond ourselves, and leave us broken and humbled for a season. To follow is to belong to another, and we are his—forever.

Summary

Disciples live with Jesus at the boundary of two worlds, and sometimes the invisible world intrudes into the visible with effects, something seen (visual) and something heard (auditory). Such events clarify Jesus' deep identity with Scriptural echoes and confirm our continuing frailty and lack of comprehension as his followers. They are not merit badges for display or comparison. But once insight is given, we never think of Jesus in quite the same way. In him and in his ordinariness, the very presence and glory of God is concealed.

Insights

1. We are asleep to Jesus, just like the three. Expect to be rudely awakened regularly!

2. Believers sometimes say stupid things. Do not be surprised or offended when you do!

3. Jesus is not on par with other religious or intellectual leaders. He's a category of one.

4. Jesus is more than a single title or category. It takes multiple angles to see his depth.

5. There is a glory in Jesus that is always just below the surface of the Gospels. Watch for it to shine forth!

Disciplines

Observation: God's veils the glory of Jesus to most, but to three as a preview.
Action: That God the Son is hidden in the flesh of Jesus stirs awe in his friends.
Observation: God is utterly committed to the vindication of only One: Jesus the Son.
Action: Observing and listening to Jesus is the central habit of his followers.

22. Luke 9:37–50, 51

Failures of the Followers
Genre: Four Disciple Correction Stories

This lesson proves that he delivered us from the power of unclean spirits.
The manner of his approach was not free from fault,
because he shouted loudly against the company of the holy apostles,
saying that they could not rebuke Satan.
It would have been more fitting for him to honor Jesus
when asking his aid and imploring grace.[91]
—CYRIL OF ALEXANDRIA

Justification

The next four paragraphs (9:37–43a, 43b–45, 46–48, 49–51) are all about the mis-understandings and failure of Jesus' disciples, his insiders. The first and last concern exorcism, while the second and third reveal a lack of comprehension of the coming passion of the Son of man and of the inversion of values Jesus upholds. The four form a cohesive thought unit and each begins with the same Greek particle (*Now/de*). The concentric form of the unit as a 4:2 chiasm (1–2//2'-1') is Luke's way of cuing us to read them together as a whole.

It's not a complimentary portrait since Jesus' closest friends and confidants come across as dunces, but that is an encouragement to the rest of us who tend to view them as professional spiritual athletes, with all but one making it into the Christian Hall of Fame.

Shape

There is a density of echoes and repetitions in the first (1. vv.37–43a) and last (1' vv.49–50,51) paragraphs to mark the boundaries of the thought unit, and they are:

---

91. 232 Just, *Luke*, 162.

1. a time signature (v. 37 *on the next day* // v.51 *when the days drew near*),

2. direct address (v.38b *Teacher* // v.49a *Master*),

3. demonic expulsion (v.40 *cast it out* // v.49a *casting it out*),

4. a sequencer (v.37 *Now it happened* // v.51 *Now it happened*),

5. a travel report (v.37 *when he had come down from the mountain* // v.51b *he set his face to go to Jerusalem*).

In the two central components inside these frames the disciples misunderstand the passion (2. vv.43b–45) and misunderstand worth and greatness (2' vv.46–48). The word *all* is used three times to indicate universality (vv.43a, 43b, 48d). With these insights in place, the outline of the unit is as follows:

1. vv.37–43 The Disciples Fail at Exorcism After Earlier Success

   2. vv.43b–45 The Disciples Misunderstand the Passion

   2' vv.46–48 The Disciples Misunderstand Worth and Greatness

1' vv.49–50, 51 The Disciples Misunderstand Cooperation and Competition

The literary genre that makes the most sense of these scenes is *A Disciple Correction Story* with its five standard components. A chart is helpful to demonstrate the consistency of the form:

	Introduction, Setting	Jesus' Word/Deed	Disciples Fail, Misunderstand	Correction	Outcome
9:37–43a	v.37	vv.38–39 (delegated)	v.40 (reported)	v.41 (shamed)	vv.42–43a
9:43b–45	v.43b	v.44	v.45	X	X
9:46–48	v.46	v.47	v.46	v.48a-c	v.48d
9:49–50, 51	v.49	X (vv.37–43a)	v.49	v.50	v.51

When four similar stories are clustered together in a cohesive thought unit, it is not necessary to follow the full form in each instance. It may be modified and shortened, with some elements inferred rather than stated as a matter of good rhetorical style which leaves room for the listener to fill in the gaps.

Content

While Jesus and the three insiders are on the mountain of revelation and shrouded in glory, hell has broken loose down below, and in spite of their earlier success (9:1–11), the nine who remain at ground level fail at the exorcism of a father's tormented son. Disciples soon learn that past success is no guarantee of future success, and that actions independent of Jesus and his anointing are futile.

That Jesus rebukes them publicly is grounded in his leaving them behind to take care of business, and together they fail, a problem he quickly remedies and which ends in awe and worship, "Now all were astonished at the majesty of God" (available in his Agent Jesus).[92]

In the second paragraph (2. vv.43b–45) Jesus moves deftly from revealing the majesty of God to revealing his upcoming suffering, and the response of the disciples, including *the three* now, is quite complex. They didn't get it; it was concealed and so not perceived, and they were too afraid to ask for clarification. How could the one who just exercised the very authority of God contemplate such an impossible idea? But Jesus always tells the truth, and this one does not compute. Some things must happen before they are understood.

In the third sub-unit (2' vv.46–48) we see just how petty and competitive for honor the disciples were, but then we know that this was in their culture the most coveted of aspirations, to have the top place of honor in whatever hierarchy you were embedded within. Jesus countered their world view by taking one from the lowest ranks of honor, a child, and standing beside him as an example of what he was about to say.

It is when we listen to and receive those at the bottom of the the status ladder that we do business with Jesus, the Father who sent him, and the Spirit who keeps the lights on. To follow this Jesus who came down to us is to be downwardly mobile and find delight in all the people and places others so want to avoid as lowering one-self and thus forfeiting honor and status. Jesus sees the world upside down from his friends and tells them he's watching them all the time, "for he who is least among you is the one who is great."

In the last paragraph (1' vv.49–50, 51) the issue is competition, not within a group as in vv.46–48 but between groups, in this case with outsiders who also invoke the fame of Jesus' name. Jesus is generous with his friends, but he resists their wish to be an exclusive franchise. Freedom and ministry are wherever you find the fruits, and so long as Jesus is honored, then welcome outsiders as co-belligerents.

Evil is not just found in the demonized but among the followers of Jesus who—in their unthinking assent to the culture's obsessions—step over one another to ascend the ladder of honor by ignoring the ones who cannot contribute to their honorable names: children. The price of following this man is to be constantly befuddled and embarrassed, as he uses every single occasion to rewire assumptions. Yet it's all worth it, because in him love is remaking them into something spectacular and doing it a day at a time. He's opening their eyes to the way he sees the world in depth and its people with mercy and understanding.

---

92. On healings and exorcisms in a cross-cultural context, see Oyemoni, "The Challenges Of The Concept Of Medicine And Healings In The Gospel Of Luke For The Church In Africa," 113–27; Roschke, "Healing in Luke, Madagascar, and Elsewhere," 460–71; Kay & Perry, *Exorcism & Deliverance: Multi-Disciplinary Studies.*

Then

Because this thought unit is a deliberate clustering of four discipleship stories using the same genre, it deserves special attention because all four stories revolve around a single idea, and that is the failure, denseness, obtuseness, and pettiness of Jesus' closest followers. And if them, how much more us!

Ignorance and failure are normal for disciples, and these are things we instinctively avoid, but here they are paraded in pubic and preserved for posterity. Even after extended time with Jesus, and even after beginning to share in the powers of the new reality to heal and deliver, they remain incompetent, dull, self-focused, and highly brand conscious, "We alone are the true followers of Jesus."

This is an insight into how broken and out of touch we are with the Jesus we continue to seek. It's also a glimpse into how slow and prone to reversals the process of change is, even with the best teacher ever.

Discipleship is not quick-fix or instant anything; it's slow progress with abundant failures and setbacks, but in the middle of the mess stands Jesus, and he never tires of us, our foibles and our sins, our treacheries and our stumbles since he sees in us more than we see in ourselves or each other. Patience is his watchword and persistence his method, doing for and with them what they will mimic with others when he is ruling them from above rather than face to face. In this unit the failures of Jesus' followers are four:

1. A failure to remain dependent on the Holy Spirit when faced with evil. They are, in Jesus' diagnostic terms, "faithless and perverse," though just earlier they were quite successful (9:1–11). It doesn't carry over automatically!

2. They rebel inwardly and go stupid when Jesus speaks of being surrendered into the hands of those who hate him. Their theology of glory is onward and upward.

3. They continue to play out the culture's script of jockeying for public honor using each other as stepping stones; but to Jesus no one is a means, only an end.

4. They defend their group's access to Jesus as the only option. And the truth is they are powerless apart from him. They cannot fathom a suffering Savior. They are using *the Jesus thing* for their own advancement and want to manage his kingdom franchise as its dedicated brokers.

There's nothing like following Jesus to reveal the very worst that's in you. It is not about looking good but about staying in the light no matter how much it makes you cringe. You'd rather hear a hard word from him than the ignorant praise of the crowds.

Now

In the Mediterranean world of Jesus' day it was an *honor-and-shame* culture that was rigidly and hierarchically ordered, and to obtain and hold honor was the name of the game. Assert your superiority, accumulate honor for your family name, look up the ladder of status for new opportunities to gain praise from your superiors "from whom all blessings flow."

Now some of this is still with us, but ours is not so much an *honor-and-shame* culture but a *winner-and-loser* culture, just as vicious but along a different set of axes. And this is one of the reasons we have such an obsession with sports and with the beautiful and the rich and the powerful, all of which are winners at the apex of one of our four highest goods: money, beauty, power, and fame. How we love the fulfillment of human potential and the inflation of the self in all its glory. *Diva* and *Divinity* are not so far apart!

Learning is hard enough, but even more difficult is un-learning. And so much of Jesus' teaching and actions are about un-learning. Breaking old habits is hard, especially when they are taken as normal in your culture so that alternatives are rarely considered.

But then along comes Jesus to your boat or tax office with an offer, a new possibility:

- to know the Triune God,
- to un-learn all that is false,
- to re-learn all that is good and true and beautiful,
- to become a new kind of man or woman,
- to recover the freshness and fullness of who you were created to be,
- to be with him in order to become like him,
- to become with others an agent of *the new reality*.
- How intoxicating is that?
- How attractive and fearful?
- How uncertain and unpredictable?
- How cross-grained?
- How utterly engaging?
- Some said Yes then; some say Yes now.
- Are you among them?
- If not, why not?
- Do you have a better idea?
- Do you realize how high the stakes are?

Summary

Disciples get used to the idea of getting it wrong and of having their worst moments placed in public view. So if image management is dear to you, life with Jesus will make you miserable. It's not that we're worse than others but that we follow the one perfect man who ever lived. How can we not fall short and feel stupid? But we can place our trust in the reliability of his call over our abilities. It's not about performance. It's about him and his ability to make us into a new kind of human who loves God fully and people faithfully.

Insights

1. If you are allergic to failure, shame, and embarrassment, do not follow Jesus.

2. That the disciples worst moments were preserved means there's nowhere to hide.

3. Only one hero in this story, and it's not any of us. At our best we reflect him into the world.

4. Ministry in the power of the Spirit is often hit and miss, and we don't often know why.

5. Followership that does not face the reality of suffering is deficient for living.

6. The Presence is everywhere to be discovered, most often down the ladder of status.

7. If Jesus sends us the unlikelies and misfits, we need to acknowledge their Sender.

8. Jesus is not a franchise we need to protect. He's bigger and badder than any of us.

Disciplines

Observation: If we are to be deeply aligned with Jesus, it is through much correction.
Action: Never be surprised how much your fallen human nature resists your Lord.
Observation: Among the tormented, ignorant, children, and outsiders we find him.
Action: Social climbing, in all its subtle forms, puts us farther from Jesus.

DISCIPLESHIP ON THE JOURNEY TO JERUSALEM (9:51–19:28)

23. Luke 9:51–56

Jesus is Patient for Now
Genre: Another Disciple Correction Story!

For their benefit he rebuked the disciples
and gently restrained the sharpness of their wrath,

not permitting them to grumble violently against those who sinned.

He rather persuaded them to be patient

and to cherish a mind that is unmovable by anything like this.[93]

—CYRIL OF ALEXANDRIA

Justification

To the five sequential Disciple Corretion Stories before us in 9:28–36 and 9:37–50/51 we now add a sixth (9:51–56) on the issue of Jesus' honor and dishonor among the Samaritans. That Luke has clustered so many similar stories together—at least as far ad genre is concerned—is a cue this is a major theme: the sheer difficulty of inducting his followers into *the new reality*. We underestimate the sheer challenge of the worldview and lifestyle revolution Jesus brings. Much is said of *the victorious Christian life* but very little of the *stumbling and fumbling Christian life* that Luke consistently highlights.

Shape

The long journey to Jerusalem (9:51–19:28 [44]) is a discipleship classic. Jesus' life is soon to end, and downloading the content of divine revelation to his friends in a variety of settings is an urgent task, but one taken care of at the pace of walking and talking, thus a *paced urgency*. As before, the five parts of the Disciple Correction Story are present:

1. Setting (v.51)

2. Action/Commission of Jesus (v.52)

3. Misunderstanding of disciples (v.54)

4. Jesus' Correction (v.55a + textual variant v.55b-c?)

5. Resolution/Outcome (v.56)

The surface structure of the unit is a 4:2 concentric pattern having four parts and a double center (1. vv.51–52, 2. v.53 // 2' vv.54–55, 1' v.56). The words *a village* (v.52) // *another village* (v.56) frame the unit as well as travel references *who went* (v.52b) // *they went* (v.56) to mark it out from what comes before and after. The unit has a clear beginning and ending plus an internal structure; it's clearly a discrete unit of thought in an ongoing chain of short videos. And in between the frames are two negative reactions, the first from the Samaritans (2. v.53), the second from the disciples (2' vv.54–55). The outline is:

    1. vv.51–52 Travel to Samaritan Village, Preparation for Ascension in Jerusalem

---

93. Just, *Luke*, 167.

2. v.53 Response 1 (Negative): Jesus Not Received Because of Jerusalem

2' vv.54–55 Response 2 (Negative): Disciples Defend His Honor, Rebuked

1' v.56 Travel Report: Another Samaritan Village

It is instructive to note that 9:51–56 has many parallels to the earlier rejection in Nazareth (4:16–30). Jesus is rejected before his Galilean ministry, and here Jesus is rejected at the start of his trek to Jerusalem where his earlier rejections will come to a climax. Luke strategically places the stories to reinforce the theme of Jesus' rejection, first by village and clan in Nazareth, then by the outcast Samaritans, and finally by the leaders of his own people as aided by the Imperial administration. That these two thought units are so much alike is not an accident but a deliberate clue from Luke as to where and how this will all end.

Item	4:16–30	9:51–56
Arrival	v.16a (Nazareth)	vv.51–52 (Samaritan village)
Theme of fulfillment	v.21, "Today this Scripture has been fulfilled"	v.51b, "when the days were fulfilled for him to be taken up"
Location	v.23c, "in your own country"	v.52, "village of the Samaritans"
Authorization, Sent	v.18, "sent me to proclaim release to the captives . . . to send forth the oppressed in relief . . ."	v.52, "And he sent messengers ahead of him . . ."
The Lord	v.18a, "The Spirit of the Lord is upon me"	v.54b, "Lord, do you want us . . ."
Rejection	v.24c, "no prophet is acceptable in his own country:"	v.53, "but the people would not receive him . . ."
Elijah/Elisha Comparison	vv.25–27 (1 Kgs. 17:1–24, 2 Kgs. 5:1–19)	v.51a (2 Kgs. 2:11), v.54 (2 Kgs. 1:10–12)
Rebuke	vv.23–24 (to synagogue)	v.54 (to disciples)
Jesus' Departure	v.30, "But passing through the midst of them, he went away."	v.56, "And they went on to another village."

Content

The thought unit begins with a solemn introduction that announces the climactic event of Jesus being taken up (in resurrection + ascension), and so with resolute determination he turns and begins a long march towards Jerusalem. In so doing he avoids the Trans-Jordan route around Samaria and heads straight south through Samaria, sending an advance party to prepare for his arrival in one of the villages. And just as the Galilean ministry began with a rejection (4:16–30), so the Jerusalem journey also begins with a rejection, "but the people would not receive him, because his face was set towards Jerusalem" (v.53).

Because of the long and bloody history of antipathy between Jews and Samaritans and between Mount Zion and Mount Gerazim, they are not prepared to welcome him as a guest and to host Jesus and his considerable entourage. Whatever Jesus' reputation as a crosser-of-boundaries, he remains *other*, not one of them. So if the response of James and John shortly after the experience of the Transfiguration seems overly harsh, "Lord, do you want us to bid 'fire come down from heaven' and consume them," it's precisely because the one honored by the Lord atop the Mount of Transfiguration has now been publicly spurned and dishonored by the leaders of a Samaritan village. Just who do they think they are!

This is an insult that requires a response from those who are concerned for the public honor of their rabbi and his *new reality* movement. James and John presume that the Lord God who honored Jesus would now honor their call for a holocaust of fire from above to destroy them all.

But they are more concerned for Jesus' honor than he is. And so instead of approval for the divine murder of this village, Jesus turns and issues a sharp rebuke, and here Jesus uses the same word he used earlier with demons, "But he turned and *rebuked* them." Now whether v.55b-c is a gloss or original, it is a logical expansion of v.55a. For him to say, "You do not know what spirit you are of," is an indirect way of saying they are *under the influence* of Satan. To this is contrasted his own sense of mission, "For the Son of man is not come to destroy lives, but to save them."

Their honor through their association with Jesus is what's at stake, not his, so be careful of hiding your own agenda behind the Lord. The resolution of the slight is that Jesus moves on to another village, and perhaps this one was more receptive, "And they went on to another village" (v.56). Where there is receptivity, Jesus moves in with his kingdom words and kingdom deeds. But where resistance rears its ugly head, he respects their freedom and moves on. No vengeance allowed. Jesus does not level our ethnic scores.

Then

Tribal, ethnic, and religious hatreds run long and deep, particularly in Jesus' corner of the world. And when combined with issues of honor and shame, it does not take much of a spark of offense to cause a violent conflagration to settle a score. But to follow Jesus is not to be in charge of his reputation or public status. For Jesus, that validation is surrendered to the Father and the Spirit who demonstrate their commitment later in his resurrection and appearances.

We who follow Jesus as apprentices and who rightly worship him may be hurt, even angry, when his name is misused and his cause maligned. We may also grieve that in not welcoming him people miss his many benefits. But, unlike some zealots, we do not invoke jihad or go on a crusade to defend our friend. Jesus expects rejection along the way, and he is headed into the teeth of the greatest rejection of all with exquisite poise.

His biggest issue is not a resistant Samaritan village but two insiders—James and John— who still do not *get it* even after so much exposure. How long is the process of coming to share the way Jesus sees the world and its peoples! Later on in Acts 8 there is a great revival in Samaria, so don't raise such a ruckus over one slight. Disciples have to be very careful about the dark side of allegiance and its capacity for exploitation by evil. So when I think that my enemies are also God's enemies, it's time for a course correction.

Now

A tribal god may need my defending, but Jews and Christians prefer to engage in witness and apologetics, a conflict of visions and ideas, rather than fisticuffs and violence, though we have not always been able to keep our own best standards, especially at the volatile boundaries of ethnic and political conflicts.

I find it interesting that the traveling Jesus movement had grown to the point that an advance team was now required to arrange reception and hospitality, as if to say, "We are on the way through your town, and do we have the official welcome of village elders?" It was both a necessity and a courtesy, the intent being to bring *the new reality* Jesus embodied to bear on the village. But when we receive a clear No to our witness, it must be respected.

Not all harvests ripen at the same time, and the goal is to work with the ready and the responsive, not to wrap up lots of energy with the resistant. We count the Yes's and leave the No's to idle a bit while looking for fresh approaches and preparations of the Holy Spirit. Receptive people and communities are all around us, and with a little sociology, a bit of psychology, a dose of the love that is willing to listen, and a sensitivity to the nudges of the Holy Spirit, it's surprising what can be uncovered right where we are.

Summary

Disciples are a preview team for Jesus; people meet us before they meet him, and it can get ugly on both sides. Stress and rejection resurface old prejudices, and every cross-cultural meeting is a grand opportunity for tribal conflict. And while Jesus hoped for a reception in Samaria—which is why he sent them, he was never surprised by rejection and just moved on. Handle resistance gently and wait for a fresh opening of receptivity.

Insights

1. To follow Jesus means he knows where he's going, even if the path wanders a bit!

2. Do not be surprised when Jesus sends you to people and groups you'd rather avoid.

3. Everyone exists on an axis of receptivity and resistance, and Jesus dealt with both extremes and everyone in between.

4. The gospel and the powers thereof are never to be used to settle old grudges.

5. Mission will reveal every dark, ugly corner of your heart. Ask James and John!

Disciplines

Observation: Jesus is very likely to march us into the middle of people who hate us.
Action: Never quit following him, because there's simply no better way to live.
Observation: Fire in his eyes and an edge in his voice is a cue we've crossed a line.
Action: Thank Jesus out loud several times a day for not firing you from his team!

24. Luke 9:57–62

Disrupted Attachments
Genre: Three Call Stories in Abbreviated Form

A person who wishes to become the Lord's disciple
must repudiate a human obligation, however honorable it may appear,
if it slows us ever so slightly in giving the wholehearted obedience we owe to God.[94]
—BASIL THE GREAT

Justification

This unit is devoted to the topic of discipleship in an explicit manner.

Shape

The three brief paragraphs (1. vv.57–58, 2. vv.59–60, 1' vv.61–62) that compose this thought unit are tightly edited. All three contain the word *follow* and include a title for Jesus (*the son of Man* [v.58b], *Lord* [vv.59b, 61b]). The second and third invoke *the kingdom of God* (vv.60b, 62b). In the first and third an applicant comes with the

---

94. 235 Just, *Luke*, 169.

promise, "I will follow you." but in the central paragraph it is Jesus who gives the call to "Follow me."[95]

Thus disciples may come from attraction or from Jesus' personal word of invitation, and in all cases the warnings and demands are significant. An inclusion or verbal bracket is the use of "follow *me*" in the first and third paragraphs and "follow *you*" in the second. The unit may be outlined:

1. vv.57–58 To Follow = Lose Security: Dependence on Others

    2. vv.59–30 To Follow = First Things First: Jesus Over Family

1' vv.61–62 To Follow = Not Look Behind: Jesus Over Courtesies

In each the call of Jesus demands priority and disrupts other common loyalties: to the comfort of the self, to family duties, to cultural practices. The genre of each paragraph is the same; they are all in the form of a Call Story, and since the three are treated together in an edited series, some of the seven possible parts are omitted to avoid undue repetition.

Here a chart will indicate Luke's adaptation of the Call Story genre.[96]

	9:57–58	9:59–60	9:61–62	5:27–28 (Levi)
Type	Attraction	Summons	Attraction	Summons
1. Travel	v.57a	Assumes v.57a	Assumes v.57a	v.37a
2. Initiative	Someone	Jesus	Another	Jesus
3. Sees, Name Given	x	x	x	v.37b
4. Parents	x	v.59b	v.61b (implied)	x
5. Dialog	x	vv.59b–60	vv.61–62	x
6. Call/Promise	x	v.59a	x	v.37c
7. Cost: Obey/Disobey	v.58	v.60	vv.62	v.28

Content

To break with one's former life for the disruption of following Jesus is costly, and it is not an additional loyalty set alongside the others.[97] It is the central loyalty around which the others are now reorganized and revalued in light of the pressing presence of *the new reality* Jesus embodied and offers. So when a potential disciple makes a grand promise, "I will follow you wherever you go," Jesus' reply may be paraphrased, "Are you sure? The foxes and birds have dens and nests, but me and my mob may sleep under the stars tonight. How much discomfort can you manage?"

95. See Sweetland, *Our Journey with Jesus*, 33–35.

96. Adapted, Dowd, *Reading Mark*, 16–18.

97. On the issue of conversion, see the topical bibliography on discipleship under "Making a Good Beginning: Conversion."

And when, in the second scene, Jesus offers an invitation, "Follow me," he meets with an excuse that made sense to every Torah observant Jesus, and particularly sons, "Lord, let me first go and bury my father. Let me free myself of this duty, and then I'm free to follow." But Jesus was blunt in his reply and deliberately offensive by saying that the spiritually dead should be left to bury the physically dead and that the call is to follow *now*, not *later*. Do you not honor God by responding immediately to the call of his Agent when it crosses your path? And are there others, not so called, to fulfill the duties surrounding death?

The third scene is a softer variant of the second and again regards the central place of the family as an identity source in Jewish piety. As some still say, "Family is everything," when it is not. Family is a dear idol with many ties that bind, and Jesus calls for an immediate change of heart because of the extraordinary opportunity he offers. To plow a straight row means looking ahead, not back. "You need my approval," he said, "not that of your family, dear as they are. I have a right to leave them thinking badly of you."

Then

What kind of man is this Jesus, one who disrupts so many of life's basic attachments? Well, he welcomes the direct address *Lord,* a name for the God of the Jews. And he speaks of himself without embarrassment as *the Son of man,* an exalted title Daniel 7 concerning the one whom God vindicates. Following him is likely to be physically uncomfortable at times, but it is the price of his companionship, to go where he does and share his lot in life. It's a shift of loyalty to him which removes the excuses of filial piety as currently practiced. It is a demanding following, not a cushy cruise, and those with whom you have lived and worked may not speak well of you. Can you handle this for the sake of being at the cutting edge of God's *new thing*?

To follow Jesus as a daily apprentice is disruptive of all other loyalties, even religious ones. It is physically challenging and disruptive of assumed family loyalties, i.e. that you will stay close to us and always do the right things. To follow is to give up predictable comforts, perhaps even the most basic of a roof over your head at night. It is to move from the roots, place, and belonging you have always known for a new, mobile family of those who hear the word of God from Jesus and do it in one village after the next.

It's a new, risky life of trust and obedience, and with it comes a ring-side seat on the operations of the kingdom of God in and through Jesus. It is the greatest thing that ever happened, and he is making a place for you, but there are high costs in saying Yes.

Now

It goes by at least two names, and neither are compliments: *cheap grace* and *discount discipleship*.[98] To make cheap what Jesus made dear, to lower the high bar he set, to make him one loyalty among others instead of the living center of all attachments: these are the common distortions of discipleship, and our current conspiracy of shop-keeper pastors and consumer-minded laity is the reason we are weak and increasingly despised. We are not different enough to offer a living alternative.

When this walk and this way of life are renewed and reinvigorated, one of the factors is the call to costly commitment and genuine sacrifice. To empty our hands in order to receive what Jesus is giving. And if it does not make us different in our capacity to speak the truth in love and love the neighbor and live with integrity and rejoice in all that is good and reject all that is not good for people, then why do we continue? Is it nostalgia for the golden days when our pews were full and all the decent people were with us? It is force of habit? Or is it just the best we can do in these days when God seems to have left us high and dry, living off the spiritual and moral capital of our ancestors as the balance of assets declines toward bankruptcy?

So what is our response? The most faithful response may be the simplest. Not more seminars on church growth or the latest management and communication techniques because ours in not a strategy or method problem. Our issues are much more basic. They have to do with seeking and knowing the Triune God, of honesty and repentance, of reading the Bible together, praying to God and listening to one another, learning the practical art of loving the next person we meet—whoever they are, and of taking risks to obey the promptings of the Holy Spirit. And such gatherings of small platoons of hopeful saints in living rooms, public spaces, and church social halls is very low cost.

The cost is time and an admission that church as we practice it no longer works very well, but that perhaps God is not yet through with us, just waiting for our pain and longing to get keen enough for a return to basics. Jesus first, the Bible as our map, the Holy Spirit as our energizer, the neighborhood as our mission field, the Creeds as our list of most-basic convictions, the Lord's Supper as the promise of the presence, and a willingness to seek and listen to God together. And maybe, just maybe, when the kindling is piled high, and the time is right, we may receive what we most need, which is a restoration of the felt presence of the Living God hovering near and about to descend in flame to reclaim his people again. Is your home open for such?

Summary

Disciples come to Jesus by two paths, either attraction or summons, but the call for all is to leave an old life and its loyalties in order to follow him as an apprentice, to be

---

98. See Hull & Cook, *The Cost of Cheap Grace.*

with him with others in order to become like him like others. Jesus comes with friends already attached, so we get him and them. Some are heroic and need warning. Others have a *family first* commitment that needs confrontation. Others want approval before such a decision and need warning. All who come to Jesus face major challenges. It's never easy.

Insights

1. Discipleship is enacted at the boundaries of discomfort and uncertainty with a wandering Jesus.

2. Loyalty and obedience to Jesus disrupt and supercede every other human claim. He reorders life with himself at the center.

3. It is the call of Jesus and not the support of one's family that defines discipleship. It is an intensely focused life with a clear center and purpose.

Disciplines

Observation: Jesus claims the right to reorder all loyalties and hopes around himself.
Action: Listen to the excuses you offer for not following, then tear them down.
Observation: Following Jesus is a calculated risk of trust based on his character.
Action: Whenever you start a *Plan B* list, ask, "When did my trust start to crumble?"

25. Luke 10:1–24

Everyone Gets to Play[99]
Genre: A Modified Commissioning Account + An Apocritic Chreia!

The proof that the Son knows the Father
perfectly rests on the fact that he is 'the one who is from God.'
The Son has clear knowledge of the Father, because he is from God.
An inferior essence would not be able to have clear knowledge of a superior essence, even if the difference between them were slight.[100]
—CHRYSOSTOM

---

99. The title is borrowed from Wimber, *Everyone Gets To Play*.
100. Just, *Luke*, 76.

Justification

The sending of the seventy (two) is parallel to the earlier sending of the twelve (9:1–11).[101] It's another short-term mission of preaching the kingdom of God and demonstrating its loving effects in healings and exorcisms, only now with a much larger group of two-person teams outside the twelve. It's the next stage in Jesus' training of followers in trust and in the powers of *the new reality*. They've watched him, and now they are delegated a share in his *new reality* work. This is discipleship, being an agent of Jesus' kingdom.

Shape

This thought unit is one of the longest and most involved in Luke. That it is indeed a single unit is indicated by the sending (vv.1–2) and return (v.17–24) of the seventy-two and a number of repeated terms of inclusion in 1. vv.1–2 // 1' vv.17–24: "these things" // "all things, "Lord//Lord," "seventy-two // "seventy-two," "pray . . . the Lord" // "thank . . . the Lord" to form a verbal bracket.

It is, by my account, an 8:2 concentric pattern (1-2-3-4//4'-3'-2'-1') with the central components (4. vv.8–9 // 4' vv.10–11) offering the two results from the kingdom's having come near in Jesus: 1) if received, then blessing (vv.8–9); 2) if rejected, then cursing (vv.10–11). The stakes are high, now and later, immediate and ultimate. An outline helps us visualize the parts and how they relate to one another in pairs:

    1. vv.1–2 Seventy (two) Appointed and Sent Out, Prayer for Laborers
      2. vv.3–4 Three Instructions for Mission: Action, Danger, Dependence
        3. vv.5–7 Peace (2x)/ Salvation Announced and Received as a Sign
          4. vv.8–9 Example 1 (+), Kingdom of God is Near, Blessing
          4' vv.10–11 Example 2(-), Kingdom of God is Near: Cursing
        3' vv.12–15 Woes (2x) Announced on Those Who Did Not Turn
      2' v.16 Three Instructions for Mission: Agents and Senders
    1' vv.17–24 Seventy (two) Return: Jesus' Prayer and Blessing

The genre is a Modified Commissioning Account that roughly parallels the sending of the twelve in 9:1–11, and its components are:

1. Introduction + Time (v.1a)

2. Confrontation (v.1b–2)

<hr>

101. On the sendings, see Hacking, *Signs and Wonders*, 89–205. On the relationship of Jesus' healing commission to the larger culture and its models, see Bazanna, "Early Christian Missionaries as Physicians," 232–51. On Jesus as the Lord of the mission see Rowe, *Early Narrative Christology*, 133–42. On Jesus' vision of Satan's fall and the disciples' ministry of exorcism, see Garrett, *The Demise of the Devil*, 50–55; also See Sweetland, *Our Journey with Jesus*, "The Mission of the Seventy," 35–38.

3. Reaction/Obedience (implied in return)

4. The Formal Commission (vv.3–15)

5. Prayer (v.2c, 21b)

6. Protest (implied, v.3b)

7. Reassurance (v.16)

8. Conclusion (vv.17–24)

The Conclusion, 1' vv.17–24, is united in a specific genre. It is an elaborated *Apocritic Chreia*, [102] a technical phrase for the expansion and elaboration of a key saying, as follows:

Components:	Luke 10:17–24
Setting	v.17a Successful return of disciples
Verbal Chreia	v.18 Memorable saying of Jesus
Elaborations On The Chreia:	
Brief Praise	v.17b, Jesus is *Lord* . . . in your name
Anecdote	x
Rationale	v.19, "Behold, I have given you authority . . ."
Contrast	v.20, "Do not rejoice in this . . . but rejoice . . ."
Comparison	x
Example (of why they should rejoice)	v.21a, "In the same hour he rejoiced in the Holy Spirit and said"
Citation Of Authority	v.22a, "All things have been delivered to me by my Father."
Conclusion	vv.23–24 "Blessing of the disciples" above *the greats of Israel*.

Since 9:1 Jesus, it appears, has been in the *sending mode*, extending his words and his works through authorized disciples. The Father sent him; now he sends and empowers them. A table demonstrates the common patterns of the three sendings:

---

102. Parson, *Luke*, 175–78.

Item	9:1–6	9:51–56	10:1–24
Introduction	x	v.51	x
Time	x	v.51	v.1
Appointed/ Commissioned	vv.1–2	v.52	v.1
Title/Number	*the Twelve* (v.1a)	*messengers* (v.52)	*seventy-two* (v.1a)
Sending	*sent them out* (v.2)	*sent messengers* (v.52a)	*I send you out* (v.3b)
Departure	v.6	v.52b	x
Jesus' Face	x	v.51c	v.1b
Places	*house* (v.4a), *town* (v.5c), *villages* (v.6a), *city* (v.10c)	*a village* (v.52b), *another village* (v.56)	*town and place* (v.1c), *house* (vv.5a, 7 = 3x), *town* (vv.8a, 10a, 12b)
Kingdom of God	vv. 2, 11c	x	vv.9a, 11b
Heal	vv.1c, 2a, 6b, 11d	x (opposite, harm)	v.8c
Exorcize	v.1c	x (themselves!)	v.17
Mission Speech(gear)	v.3	x	vv.3–4
Mission Speech (receptivity issue)	vv.4–5 (-/+)	v.53 (-)	vv.5–15(-/+)
Judgment	v.5	v.54 (negated by Jesus)	vv.11, 12–15
Interlude Report	vv.7–9	x	x
Return And Report	v.10	v.54	v.17
Titles	*the Twelve* (v.1a), *Apostles* (v.10a)	*messengers/angeloi* (v.52a), *disciples* (v.54a)	*seventy-two others* (v.1), *disciples* (v.23a)
Bethsaida	v.10c	x	v.13b

Content

It is clear in Luke that *the twelve* are a symbolic community chosen by Jesus to be sent out as apostles, and that within the twelve are *the three* (Peter, James, John) who are with Jesus at certain times that the remaining nine are not. It does not surprise us, then, when he sends the twelve out as a body with his blessing and empowerment to do what he did. First he announced the change (6:13), then implemented it (9:1–11).

But there was no such status change for the rest of his entourage who were not among the sacred dozen. But here seventy-two *others* are sent out in pairs in essentially the same mission, only here they cover much more territory, as Jesus said, "The harvest is plentiful, but the laborers are few," and what they pray for is what they become! More laborers! They are sent into kingdom ministry but not called *apostles*. But, as with *the twelve* (the tribes of Israel), *seventy-two* is also a symbolic number, generally taken to be the number of Gentile nations, thus all the people of the earth who are not Jews.

The mission is, symbolically speaking, first to Israel by the twelve and then to the Gentile nations by the seventy-two. The missions to Jews and Gentiles are both embedded in the ministry of a Jesus who delights to extend the kingdom, its benefits and accountability, through others. Thus, to be a disciple/follower/apprentice/understudy of Jesus is to risk getting caught up in his radical words and deeds. They are all authorized, likely through a temporary corporate group gifting of the Holy Spirit, to preach and heal and deliver. And as they go, *the stuff happens!*[103]

So the question is, Should we expect disciples today to participate in the same powers of the kingdom? My answer is Yes, but to answer in the affirmative is not so simple as it appears. Luke's presentation of following Jesus is an organic whole of trust and obedience in community, and a part of that whole is to enter the spiritual dynamics that accompany *the new reality,* what we might term *the person and giftings of the Holy Spirit.* We are following Jesus, and this is part of his holy work of love. He loves, heals, and frees.

The world is so constituted by the God who both creates and upholds what is created that the world is open and permeable to divine agency. The God who is holy and transcendent is not distant but near, and sometimes with astounding effects opening up new possibilities. Healing is mercy made visible, love made palpable, and life enhanced and extended. This is the deep impulse carried by all who care for the sick and tormented, including the entire medical system.[104]

Following Jesus is not possible apart from the drawing, sustaining, probing, illumining, protection and empowerment of the same Holy Spirit that engulfed Jesus after his baptism and energized and made effective his every obedience to the Father. How easily we who lived under the hangover of *Cessationism*[105] reduce our following to Bible knowledge and moral rectitude. Is it any wonder we too often appear as Pharisees instead of those who've been immersed in Jesus' vision and practices?

That v.1 has a deliberate echo of 9:51–52 invites us to go back two units and see what wonderful things the Samaritans missed by their resistance to the Lord's approach. Resistance has terrible consequences in unhealed adults and children and in persons who remain in demonic bondage. They missed the felt presence of the love of the Holy Trinity enveloping their village as happened earlier in Capernaum (4:31–44). They were Nazareth and not Capernaum, the resistant instead of the receptive. The

103. For a vulnerable and humorous account of *doin' the stuff* again, see Wimber, *John Wimber,* 159–209.

104. On the modern hospital and the medicine that supports it as a Christian invention, see Dickerson, *Jesus Skeptic,* 107–25.

105. On a popular level, *Cessationism* means that Jesus used to *do the stuff* with and through his first followers, but then it all stopped because we got the Bible. I think it was a bad deal! On ceasing with Cessationism, see Deere, *Why I Am Still Surprised,* 72–105, 160–67, 168–77.

leaders no doubt felt justified, but the people suffered and were confirmed in their anti-Jewish prejudices.

So contrast this tragedy with the unfolding layers of 10:1–24. Jesus turns to his non-apostle disciples and appoints seventy-two to go in pairs to the locations to which he is soon to come, and even with that number of agents, he calls them in v.2 to pray for more because just beyond even their reach the harvest is ripening. And as with the earlier mission, the watchwords are *vulnerability* and *urgency,* think sheep among wolves for the terror of it!

None of the equipment of self-sufficiency go with them—not purse, bag, extra sandals, but instead a sense of mission and urgency that renders normal courtesies and greetings an encumbrance, "and salute no one on the road."

Jesus' instructions about approach and contact are specific including the initial words of greeting and what sort of person might welcome them. If rejected, no fire is to be called down, just move on until you find a receptive host, "a son of peace."

And, however humble the home and how great your results, there you are to stay; no upgrades allowed! Eat their food; sleep on their floors, and release the presence of *the new reality* with the scripted words so that all are on the same page in all thirty-six different locations, "The kingdom of God has come near you." Then cooperate with the Holy Spirit in healing the sick and evicting demons. But if, as with the Samaritans, an entire town resists your approach, enact a symbolic judgment that marks them as unclean outsiders and highlight what they've missed, "that the kingdom of God has come near." One village becomes a new Capernaum, and the one just down the road a new Nazareth, and on the last day it will not be a happy event but a funeral dirge of enacted Woes.

The kingdom of God swings on the hinges of welcome and hospitality, and its goal is to explain and demonstrate *the new reality* so that ordinary village folk can heartily and gladly return to the God of their Fathers. First healing love, then a fresh return through repentance. And to fully authorize his mission teams, Jesus makes the linkage clear, "To receive you is to welcome me and the One who sent me, but also the reverse; to reject you is to reject the Sent and the Sender." This is the authority of full agency.

What joy upon their return! It worked! But *it* was not an *it* but the presence and giftings of the Spirit, just as with Jesus. The demons had listened and vacated their human premises. Jesus saw it all at a distance in a spectacular vision, Satan falling like a bolt out of the blue, his local kingdom vanquished, and not a one of his emissaries damaged (v.19). His only caution was for them not to get so caught up in the victories of warfare but to remember the source from whence it springs, their secure relationship to the Father (v.20).

What then happens in Jesus' exultation (vv.21–24) is a feast of divine revelation. His dynamic is concealed from the ones who are already full of learning (v.21a-b) but opened like a treasure to those who don't know much but who know and obey Jesus (v.21c-d). And who is he? He is the Son of the Father and the agent of divine revelation. Jesus is the Yahweh franchise, so that only the Sent One gets to reveal the Sender. He lets disciples in on his relationship with the Father and the Holy Spirit. They are invited to taste the love and life that dances among the three persons of the one true God. It is, as Jesus announced in vv.23–24, the greatest show on earth and the event that changes everything.

And this, friends, is the arena and the reality Jesus opens to his followers for the sake of the world. Our world is responsive to the touch of its Maker. And for decades afterwards there were the living witnesses who told the same story, "Let me tell you what happened the day two smiling friends of Jesus showed up on Main Street."

Then

What we label *supernatural* and call *miraculous* was never far from the disciples as day after day they traveled about with Jesus. They lived in the ordinary world they'd always known but also in *the new reality* that never abandoned their Rabbi. It was the borderlands of the possible, and Jesus' clear understanding is that his work is transferrable as vindicated by the gifts and energies of the Holy Spirit, even at a distance.

The clear implication of the sending is that Jesus did not accompany them, so his physical presence or proximity is not required for their work, but his official sending is. They have already obeyed by following, and now they obey again, so their trust and obedience are part of the dynamic, and—to put it crudely— *it worked*. This was a formative experience they'd never had before, and here it happened to thirty-six teams of two simultaneously. Their calling card was the news that "The kingdom of God has come near to you," and the effects were exorcisms and healings en masse. They had become the extension of their Rabbi, his voice and his hands and his loving, healing powers. He was working through them at a distance, in this case horizontal, but later vertical and from above after his resurrection and ascension. The analogy is imperfect but remains valid.[106]

Now

Now how to cooperate with the risen Jesus and dance in public with the Holy Spirit are not much discussed in our circles any longer.[107] Our teachers are not much experienced in this arena and cannot pass on what they do not know, and so they reproduce after their kind. Better to study church history and doctrine and leadership and management and Biblical languages, and I am for all of these. But to what end? To run a denominational franchise? To have a clerical career? To inherit a platform for

---

106. See Talbert, "Discipleship in Luke-Acts," 62–75.

107. For a remarkable sampling of such from the Journals of John Wesley, see Jennings, *The Supernatural Occurrences Of John Wesley.*

social change? But this kind of risky, experimental and experiential training in the supernatural in and through the Spirit was standard curriculum for the disciples, so why do we omit it so casually? Because it is not merely a human activity but requires God's presence for validation. If nothing happens, it can't be faked.

So in addition to academic and historical learning, we need the modeling of those with track records in this style of ministry, and the sad truth is that we currently have to go outside of our churches and schools to find it. But my testimony is that once you pray a risky and vulnerable prayer and God answers with something in the life of the other person, you will be hooked and *know-in-your-knower* the joy of having the one you claim to follow actually work through you for the good of another. The *new reality* actually showed up and made a difference. And according to Jesus' own testimony, it's not for the sophisticated and the learned, but for those with a child-like trust in the goodness of God and the faith that *something just might happen.* God is not against the learned, but God's favorite currency is trust that takes risks.

So at a minimum, disciples must spend time with people in distress and not hide from them, and we must learn from mentors how to pray with and for the ill and tormented. But if looking good and having high success are near the top of your values, you will not have the perseverance needed to see much fruit.[108]

It was Jesus' great and ecstatic joy to hear the field reports of his followers when they returned because here in this wild experiment the Father was being revealed in the Son through the Holy Spirit. The *new reality* is meant to express itself in us as well.

Summary

Disciples are agents and ambassadors, living extensions of Jesus and *the new reality.* Under his authority we go in small teams, pray for more helpers, live vulnerably and simply, announce and enact *the new reality,* deal with opposition, representing the rabbi who sent us and the Lord who sent him, bring back reports from the field, and keep listening to Jesus' abundant encouragements. It's an adventure to share life with this crazy Jew.

Insights

1. You were called and enlisted to be deployed. You should not be surprised when sent.

2. The recruiting for helpers is prayer. Beseech God's HR department for help!

3. Lambs amidst wolves is a disturbing image. Jesus fixed it in their imaginations.

---

108. For a clear statement on prayer and healing, see "VIII. Healing Services And Prayers, Introduction," *The United Methodist Book of Worship,* 613–14. On *dancing with the Holy Spirit,*" see Storms, *Understanding Spiritual Gifts.*

4. God has divine appointments ahead, and you walk into them bearing *Peace*.

5. Basic provisions—signs, wonders, and a simple message—are our equipment.

6. Be prepared to meet resistance and find ways to make the consequences clear.

7. The mission is always high stakes. Some villages and towns say a corporate No.

8. Watching people freed from illness and evil is exhilarating. Having a future with God is better.

9. The mission is finally Trinitarian, and the relations of the divine persons in the dynamics of the mission are an endless fascination.

10. Jesus is the cosmic tipping point; the Son comes to us from inside the divine life.

Disciplines

Observation: Jesus trained and quickly deployed his agents to extend his work.
Action: Ask, "Where can one find such training today?" Send me an answer.
Observation: Jesus is in the divine revelation business, but only to the receptive.
Action: Remind yourself daily, "What a privilege it is to be attached to Jesus!"

26. Luke 10:25–28

Ordering Our Loves
Genre: A Controversy Dialog

What is the greatest and first commandment of the law?
He said to him, 'You shall love the Lord your God, and your neighbor as yourself.'
All this teaching is held high through two commandments,
as though by two wings, that is, through the love of God and of humanity.[109]
—EPHRAEM THE SYRIAN

Justification

I find it interesting that a long thought unit on the mission and power of the kingdom of God through the disciples (10:1–24) is followed by a brief controversy and dialog on what is most important: the love of God and the love of neighbor that is meant to flow from it.[110] Nothing is more basic to being a disciple than love on these two axes. If there is a thought unit that begs constant reflection, it's this one.

109. Just, *Luke*, 178.
110. On the dual love command, see McKnight, *The Jesus Creed*; Ortberg, *Love Beyond Reason*. Wesley, *Sermon 139*.

Shape

While in our treatment of disciple passages 10:25–29, 29–37, and 30–42 are approached as if they are separate units, that's not the whole story. They are actually part of a larger clustering of stories around the double command of love for God and neighbor, as the following list demonstrates:

1. A possible inclusion for the whole is the parallel between *inheritance* (v.25b) and *portion* (v.42a) which are sometimes taken as synonyms (Ps. 15:5 LXX).

2. The Jewish form of exposition is a dialog and disputation about texts (vv.25–28) followed by two stories (*haggadah*) which deal with the texts in reverse order: vv.29–37 with the love of neighbor and vv.38–42 with the love of Jesus as Lord. This forms a 4:2 concentric pattern of themes as follows:

   a. Dt. 6:5 The love of God with the whole self.

   b. Lev. 19:18 The love of the neighbor as the self.

   b' Story 1: Parable of The Good Samaritan on the love of neighbor.

   a' Story 2: The love of Jesus as the love of the Lord with the whole self.

3. The first two units (1. vv.25–28, 2. vv.29–37) are of the same genre, a *Controversy Dialog* as follows:

a. Scribe's Motive And Question	v.25	v.29
b. Jesus Counter-Question	v.26	vv.30–36
c. Lawyers's Answer	v.27	v.37a
d. Jesus' Command (Do)	v.28	v.37b

4. The genre of the third unit (3. vv.38–42) is a *Disciple Correction Story* with the five expected components:

   a. Setting (v.38a-b)

   b. Positive Example 1 (v.38c)
      Positive Example 2 (v.39)

   c. Charge Evidencing Misunderstanding (v.40)

   d. Correction Of Example 1 (v.41)
      Commendation Of Example 2 (v.42)

   e. Open-Ended Conclusion

5. Verbal and formal links between the three units are:

   a. *do* (vv.25b, 28c, 37a, 37b)

   b. *neighbor* (vv.27g, 29b, 36)

   c. Synonyms: *love* (vv.27b), *compassion* (v.33c), *mercy* (v.37a)

   d. Questions (vv.25b, 26, 29, 36, 40)

   e. *Lord* (vv.27b, 39b, 40c, 41a)

   f. Commendation (vv.28b, 42)

   g. Direct Address (vv.25b, 40c, 41b)

    h. *life/live* (vv.25b, 28c)

6. Each unit contains character introductions to distinguish them:

v.25a	Jewish Legal Expert, Jesus
vv.30–35	Traveler, Robbers, Priest, Levite, Samaritan
vv.38–42	Martha, Mary

Our conclusion is that Luke 10:25–42 is intended to be read as a literary whole on what is most basic: the love of God and neighbor, including Jesus as divine and ourselves as his devoted friends.

So back to 10:25–28. The unit is composed of four parts and consists of a scholar's question (v.25) and a counter-question of Jesus (v.26), which are then answered in reverse order by the scholar (v.27) and then by Jesus (v.28), thus four parts and a double center (a-b//b'-a').

In the frames (a. v.25 // a' v.29) we find an emphasis on action ("what shall I do" // "do this") and on the desired outcome ("inherit eternal life" // "live"). At the center Jesus asks two questions about Torah (b. v.26) and in turn receives two citations (b' v.27), Dt. 6:5 and Lev. 19:18. An outline is:

    a. v.25 Lawyer: Question 1

      b. v.26 Jesus: Question 2

      b' v.27 Lawyer Answers Question 2

    a' v.28 Jesus Answers Question 1 + A Command to Action

Content

That the inquirer already knew what was required and so put Jesus to the test is clear, but Jesus reversed the inquiry with his own question to test the man's skill with Torah and then congratulated him as a teacher might a junior pupil with both praise, "You have answered rightly," and a challenge, "do this continually, and you will live." To live totally along both axes is already a taste of life in the kingdom and the surest way to prepare for it.

Our Torah scholar is left flat-footed but now with more respect for Jesus the debater. But what does it mean to love God with all one's capacities and the neighbor with the same regard we give ourselves? The only adequate answer is that in the person and work of Jesus that we see what it looks like to live in robust love all the time. It cannot be done apart from him, and so the unanswered question is, Did this scholar become a follower in order to fulfill his own question? We don't know. It's left open-ended, just as with us.

Do we really want to be consumed by the love of God and for it to change the way we see and regard and serve and love the next person we meet, and the one after that, and the one after that until the flow of love to us from God and from us back to

God becomes a fountain of life for all who meet us. Was it not that way with Jesus? So think of the most consistently loving person you've ever known up close, and then ask, "How did they get this way?" Then ask them.

Then

The only one who ever loved God totally and others utterly faithfully was Jesus. And if this is who he is, then it's who he has come to make us to be. Jesus is the dean of God's University of Love and shows us what it's like to have a seamless life. Love comes. Love goes and embraces. Love teaches and reasons. Love heals and restores. Love sticks. Love takes the heat. And Love suffers for the sake of others, and Love trusts all outcomes to God, including the vindication of resurrection.

We learn this Love in the company of Professor Jesus, in his lectures and in his lab. And his students are called *disciples*. We follow a Lord who welcomes our questions, but who always manages to take every trick and win every argument. How could it be otherwise? He is wisdom personified and love in dialog with whoever stands before him. Beyond his knowledge of the Jewish Bible, another call was waiting for the Jewish scholar, and that was to follow Jesus and to know the love of the One to whom Scripture owes its origins.

Now

Love for God is not a concern for God's welfare, though it may contain a concern for God's reputation at ground level. But love for God includes awe, fascination, devotion, holy respect, dependence, a delight in the creation and all its capacities, plus worship and obedience. To love the Father, Son, and Spirit in all their perfect operations is a communion of perfect love we will never exhaust. And this love is rightly ordered as first, but then close behind is the love of neighbor with all of the same attention and regard with which we love and provide for ourselves.

So what is a follower of Jesus? One who, in community with other apprentices, is growing in the desire and ability to love God fully and others faithfully. This is what a prepared person is, one who in all circumstances knows that vertical and horizontal love are the most powerful and reliable forces in any situation. Not fear, not prejudice, not habit, not indifference, not status or beauty or knowledge, but love for God and love from God for whoever stands in front of you next. Disciples are learning to keep the faucet on and never turn it off. Because of the faithfulness of Jesus' friendship and love for us, we fling our hearts wide open to divine love and put our bodies on the line. We are being changed into a new kind of person, one who through Jesus is wise in the ways of divine love.

Summary

Disciples are always called back to basics, and nothing is more basic than love in two dimensions—for God and people, and on two axes—vertical and then horizontal. To love God with all we are and others as we love ourselves is not only our call; it was Jesus' daily practice. It's what he did, and into it we are invited as newbies, fumblers, goofballs, and wanna-bes. Something inside keeps whispering, "This is life. For this you were made." Robert Palmer was right, "Might as well say you're addicted to love."

Insights

1. Jesus is the master teacher; bringing him our hard questions is a high compliment.

2. Jesus will push you back to Scripture for insight. He inspired and shaped it.

3. To love God with the whole self makes us an outlet for whoever crosses our path.

4. Eternal life is not earned; it's a gift now and an appetizer for what's ahead.

5. Rightly ordered love includes God, the self, and the next person. It's true wisdom.

6. Love not acted upon is short-circuited and frustrated. It's meant to become a habit.

7. In some situations we debate Scripture and in others tell disturbing stories. Jesus did both, as must we.

Disciplines

Observation: Jesus taught that following is about the love of God and others.
    Action: Say, "I love you," to God when you wake; seek to channel that love all day.
    Observation: There is no question too tough or too tangled for Jesus to unravel.
    Action: Write down your five most pressing questions and present them in prayer.

27. Luke 10:29–37, 38–42

What Love Looks Like
Genre 1: A Controversy Dialog
Genre 2: A Disciple Correction Story

We are all neighbors, all people of one family, for we have one Father.
—JEROME

Justification

Jesus has declared that the love of God with the whole of the self and the neighbor as oneself is what eternal life consists of; it's the most basic summary of what God desires, and in the person and work of Jesus we see a living example of the two loves in daily practice. And since he is the one we follow, this is a preeminent discipleship passage.

Any spiritual practice that does not end with increased love of God and an increased overflow for the next person in front of me is alien to Jesus Christ and is to be culled. In the company of Jesus the created self is fulfilled in three-dimensional love: in God, in me in relation to God, and my neighbor in relationship to me and God.

Shape

While the previous unit is on loving God and neighbor as the gateway to life in the kingdom now and later (10:25–28), the following two units, the Parable of the Good Samaritan on the costly love of neighbor (10:29–37) and the the superior love of Mary for Jesus (10:38–42), are stories that illumine the love of neighbor and Jesus as God's human face. And since they are so closely related as examples of the double love command, we deal with them together. The genre of literary type of the first is a Controversy Dialog, a debate over the meaning of a text in four parts with a double center as follows:

a. v.29 Question of Lawyer to Jesus for Clarification
　b. vv.30–36 Counter-Question by Jesus, Halakah (story) on Halakah (text)
　b' vv.37a Lawyer Answers Jesus' Counter-Question
a' v.37b Jesus Answers Lawyer's Initial Question

The second is a Disciple Correction Story involving two sisters, Martha and Mary:

1. Setting (v.38a-b)

2. Example 1 (Martha, v. 38c),Example 2 (Mary, v.39)

3. A Charge Showing Misunderstanding (v.40)

4. Correction of Example 1 (v.41)

5. Commendation of Example 2 (v.42)

Note that the surface structure of the story is open-ended for audience response and is arranged in a concentric format as follows:

a. v.38 Martha Receives Jesus: Conventional Female Role
　b. v.39 Mary Receives Jesus: Unconventional Role as a Disciple
　　c. v.40 Martha's Rebuke of Jesus as Unaware/Uncaring
　　c' v.41 Jesus' Rebuke of Martha as Majoring in Minors

b' Jesus' Commendation of Mary's New Role
[a' Left Open-Ended as an Invitation to Hearers: What was Martha's Response?]

Content

Having been bested in round one of the debate with Jesus, the Jewish scholar picks up a term of the debate and asks, "Who is my neighbor?" which implies that some are non-neighbors and therefore not to be loved, say a Gentile or an apostate Jew. The question is about boundaries, who's in and who's out. But Jesus responded to the request with an elaborate seven stanza story in which two Jewish clergy avoid the call to love a man who was mugged while the most unlikely character, and the one the lawyer was least likely to identify with, saved the day at considerable personal cost—a loving Samaritan. Then a question, "Who was the neighbor here?" Answer: the outsider who showed mercy. So Jesus concludes with the same command as before, "You, go and do likewise." Love God, love the neighbor without boundaries, even Samaritans.

The next story jumps over considerable terrain and lands us near Jerusalem in the village of Bethany, the home of two sisters whose brother is Lazarus, and they are of different dispositions on what's to happen when Jesus shows up as a guest with friends. Martha needs help in the kitchen but Mary sits at his feet in the posture of a disciple, devouring his words which are food for her soul.

Mary's priority is devoted to Jesus and his teaching, while Martha is devoted to her hospitality for him and is full of both anxiety and anger, a toxic brew. So Martha seeks to leverage her sister by having Jesus triangled into their tension, but he refuses to do Martha's bidding and instead takes Mary's side, "For Mary has chosen the good portion, and it shall not be taken from her," which in effect says, "No, I will not."

In other words, what she is doing is preferable to Martha's harried, hurried, scattered ways. In loving Jesus Mary loves God with all she is. So the question is, What happens next? This is one of Luke's open-ended stories, and it invites us to consider Martha's options. I imagine two possible outcomes:
"And Martha left her impressive meal for the visiting evangelist
and came and sat at the Lord's feet
and there fed on his teaching with her devoted sister Mary
whose contemplative spirituality she now deeply appreciated!"
Or,
"And Martha went off into the kitchen sulking,
angry at her lazy sister Mary
and this impractical Jesus who probably never cooked a meal in his whole life.
She stuffed herself on a quart of Breyer's and a whole carafe of red wine
till she was fat and happy."

Then

Good teaching, teaching that goes to the heart, is pithy and memorable, invokes both the generality of principles and the specificity of examples, and both are necessary. And here the yoked biblical commands to love God and neighbor (10:25–28) each receive an example in reverse order and end with the Christological insight—left implicit in the story—that to love and listen to Jesus is the same as loving God with the whole self.

Working for Jesus is to be an outworking of love for him.[111] But how common it is to separate the work from the person and to be "busy with many things." When duty replaces devotion something's lost, and when devotion does not lead to zeal about duties, there's been a short circuit. The centrality of Jesus is first, and it is to him that we are to return when delight and fascination evaporate under the pressures of service.

Worship and prayer and study are central, and when service flows from these, we are not so easily depleted in anger, blaming, and exhaustion.

Now

Nothing is more radical than the ability to state what is most basic in ways which command assent so that people intuitively see and feel the truth pressing in upon them. That Jesus led a Jewish scholar to state the double love command with such simplicity and clarity is a tribute to his ability not only to teach the truth but to draw it out of others in debate.

To love God with the whole self and the next person with the same regard I give myself, is already to live in a new world right in the middle of the old. But it must be done, be acted out, be translated from conviction into action, and that means risk and cost (Good Samaritan), including the risk of public embarrassment and correction (Martha). So if it does not increase the capacity to love vertically and horizontally and for the two to inform each other, it's not Jesus-style discipleship but something less.

How often I have been set back on my heels by some saint who loved God and people more than I did, but who did not have my level of knowledge or study. They had simply marinated in Jesus and the gospels for such a long time that whatever they faced, love came out. Scholars calls it *conspicuous sanctity*, and it is clear to everyone but the person themself because for them it's *normal*, just who they have become.

And that is what the world needs to see and feel. So whatever spiritual disciplines or acts of mercy or justice we embrace, if they do not keep us alert to the dual commands and how they express one another to change our character, it's time for a re-evaluation. We follow Jesus to become like him, and in him the perfect love of the Father and of all people was seen and felt and admired and emulated. And in the end

---

111. On how discipleship works best when *working for Jesus* comes out of *being with Jesus*, see Scazerro, *Emotionally Healthy Discipleship*, 37–60.

this love cost him the life that was given back to him in resurrection. Love is risky, and it is our path.

Summary

Disciples are interruptible! We avoid avoidance and engage engagement. It's not a crusade but acts of costly compassion and passionate mercy that startle the world into paying attention to the One we follow. And when we see such anywhere and from anyone and from whatever faith or lack thereof, we are seeing the hidden Jesus at work and should ask, "What urged you to do this? Do you know his name?"

And in such engagement there's always the danger that our attention shifts to us and our duties and away from his truth and beauty. Disciples are constantly being turned back to Jesus as the deep source of our actions.

Insights

10:29–37

1. Jesus was a poet and story-teller. The Good Samaritan is genius. Jesus is smart!

2. Jesus makes us vulnerable to the next person. Am I too important to interrupt?

3. Love is where you find it, and with a new set of lenses, it's everywhere.

4. Love, Jesus' style, is compassion leading to active mercy. It pays the cost.

10:38–42

1. Doing good things with anxiety and anger is a clue something's wrong!

2. It is easy as disciples to replace first things (devotion) with secondary things (service).

3. In the circle of disciples, men and women sit and stand together on equal footing.

4. Don't expect Jesus to fight my battles. Sometimes he defends others against me!

5. When our cups are at least half full, it's easier for others to draw a refreshing drink.

6. Jesus is always waiting for our active, free, trusting response to the love of his personal corrections. You may bristle, but to soften makes correction effective.

Disciplines

Observation: For Jesus, every encounter is an opportunity to love with power.
Action: Make your default setting a move towards human pain and suffering.
Observation: In the midst of many options, Jesus deserves my utmost attention.
Action: Glance at him often, and meditate upon him often in the Gospels.

28. Luke 11:1–13

Beginning to Pray
Genres: The Lord's Prayer, A Parable, A Poetic Exhortation to Persistence

Divine wisdom arranged the order of this prayer with exquisite choice.
After the matters that pertain to heaven—
that is, after the name of God, the will of God, and the kingdom of God—
it should make a place for a petition for our earthly needs too![112]
—TERTULLIAN

Justification

The praying Jesus is a major theme of Luke, and here Jesus invites his curious friends into a prayer that carries their Rabbi's vision, priorities, and hopes.[113] It's all about—as we saw before—of being *with him* as a follower in order to become *like him* as a living extension. In this unit Jesus teaches his apprentices how we pray to the Father and welcome the gift and gifts of the Spirit.[114] It's a Trinitarian communion into which we're being drawn.

Shape

Because of the prominence of the prayer Jesus gave his disciples to express their relationship with him before the Father, it's easy to miss that it's embedded in a larger thought unit of four paragraphs: 1. vv.1–4, 2. vv.5–7 // 2' v.8, 1' vv.9–13 which form a 4:2 chiasm. The words *Father, holy, bread, everyone, temptation* found in 1. vv.1–4 are echoed as inclusion in 1' vv.9–13: *everyone, father, bread, evil, holy*. So it is Luke's intent that the Lord's Prayer not be read alone but with a centrally placed parable in question and answer form (2. vv.5–7, 2' v.8) and finally with a concluding poetic exhortation (1' vv.9–13). It may be outlined as:

1. vv.1–4 The Model and Pattern of Prayer to the Father
    2. vv.5–7 Parable of Friend at Midnight: Question
    2' v.8 Parable of Friend at Midnight: Answer
1' vv.9–13 Poem on the Father's Gifts: How Much More!

---

112. Just, *Luke*, 187–88.

113. For a survey, see Marshall, "Jesus: Example and Teacher of Prayer," 113–31. And from a Roman Catholic theologian, O'Collins, *The Lord's Prayer*.

114. Wright, "The Lord's Prayer as a Paradigm," 132–54. On the history of the prayer, see Stevenson, *The Lord's Prayer*. A good introduction is Hill, *The Lord's Prayer*.

The intent of the whole unit is to build confidence in the One who is addressed as "Father/*Abba*."[115] This God will defend the divine name and bring the kingdom, and in the meantime sustain servants with bread for hunger, forgiveness for sins, and protection in temptation. And if it is unimaginable for a friend to deny his neighbor bread when the reputation of the entire village is at stake, how much more can we expect God's responsiveness? So if you ask and seek and knock, there is One listening who will respond with only good gifts, nothing fiendish (vv.11–12), the greatest of which is the Holy Spirit as a permanent, empowering and guiding companion.

This is a tri-personal passage (Jesus, Father, Spirit) and thus raw material for later Trinitarian reflection. Prayer Jesus' style is a Trinitarian event as we obey the Son, speak to the Father, and welcome the aid and energies of the Spirit. In prayer we enter the divine circle of life.

Then

Prayer is both communion and communication, an ongoing dialog with the Lord's Prayer as the basic script, not only in its personal address to God but in its topics, in their order and progression. The disciples' question was for a prayer that summed up their mission and is a reminder that Jesus was not the only one with followers, "as John taught his disciples." And that John, now deceased, still had followers who had not come over to Jesus, is a warning that the followers of the last move of God may miss the current one out of devotion to their courageous master.

The Jesus who had called a few followers into his life now welcomes them into his prayer in a brief format that falls into two stanzas of three lines each: an address followed by two *thou* petitions and three *we* petitions plus as qualification, "as we forgive everyone who is indebted to us."

Christian prayer, prayer in the key of Jesus, is first about being brought back into a healed relationship with the one who sent him, the Father whom they are to address with the simplicity of a child, "Pappa/ Dear Father." Is this really who God is? Jesus thinks so and invites them into his form of prayer.

The next two petitions are for God to do what only God can do, which is stick up for his holy name and all that it means and to unleash his rule and dominion over an unruly world. And the one means the other, so the parallelism between the first two petitions is roughly synonymous. Paraphrased, it's something like, "Reveal yourself. Show the world who you are and fix things."

We stand in the present and ask for the end of life as we have known it. Our horizon is the end of our world and its complete reconstruction by the Father who is Sovereign. Prayer is a restored relationship in which the things that are dear to God the Father become pressing to us. In this prayer we are invited to look down on the world and re-imagine what it's going to look like when God finally answers.

115. For a popular treatment by a Christian psychologist, see Crabb, *The Pappa Prayer*.

But until that culmination, we need help and sustenance in three areas, all of which are properly basic. We need food and all that goes with it for nurture and community, something to eat and someone to eat with. We need divine aid for a free flow of forgiveness to us and through us. We remain a band of sinners in close quarters. And we need divine protection from being overwhelmed by fiery trials and the deception of evil.

Our most basic three needs as we follow Jesus are physical, communal, and spiritual, and in all three realms we are to offer fearless petitions and then observe how God responds. It's lean living and passionate pursuit. Disciples learn from Jesus the melody line for prayer, then play it with all the variations of life, in major and minor keys, and in the native tunes of every culture. The thoroughly Jewish quality of Jesus' prayer is illustrated in a chart of comparisons on the Lord's Prayer and Jewish Parallels:[116]

Lord's Prayer	Jewish Parallels
Father	Is. 63:16, 64:7, 1 Chron. 29:10, Tobit 13:4, Sirach 51:10
holy be your name	"May his great name be extolled and hallowed in the world which he has created according to his will" (*Qaddish* [How early?]).
your kingdom come	"May he cause his kingdom to rule in your lifetime and in your days and in the lifetime of all the House of Israel" (*Qaddish*).
Give us each day our daily bread	"Provide me only with the food I need" (Prov. 30:8).
and forgive us our sins, *for we forgive everyone* *who is indebted to us*	"Forgive us, our Father, for we have sinned, for we have transgressed" (*Amidah* 6). "Forgive your neighbor the wrong he has done, and then your sins will be pardoned when you pray" (Sir. 2:2).
and lead us not into temptation (fiery trial)	"Bring me not into the power of sin, or into the power of guilt, or into the power of temptation (b. Ber 60a)."

Now

On the basis of divine revelation in Jesus, what God shows us of the divine life at ground level, disciples learn what it means to speak to God and bring the whole of life into the ongoing conversation that is prayer. We ask God for divine action to set it all right and for interim supplies to sustain us. Famine would kill us, so bread. The bitterness of sin would divide us, so forgiveness. And evil in all its shifting forms would crush us, so protection. "We are yours. Sustain us in this holy work of following the Lord Jesus at all times and in all places."

Those who pray admit their fragility and band together to offer this prayer which is in the third person (*us . . . us . . . we . . . us . . .*), thus the prayer of a community of disciples who are following Jesus as a band of brothers and sisters.

---

116. Extracted from Fitzmeyer, *The Gospel According to Luke, X-XIV*, 900.

The supplemental materials that follow the prayer, a *How Much More* parable of question and answer (2. vv.5–7, 2' v.8) and a three stanza Poetic Exhortation (1' vv.9–11) are both confidence builders from Jesus not to quit praying.

Keep praying this prayer (ask, seek, knock) and all that it stirs in you in all its associations across the whole of life and in all your circumstances.[117] Expect God to reply and sustain you. James Bryan Smith pairs the lines of the Disciples' Prayer with characteristics of a God worth trusting:

Father	God is near, a trusted parent
hallowed be thy name	God is pure, not tainted with mixed motives
thy kingdom come	God is powerful, not impotent
daily bread each	God provides and gives us strength
forgiveness to, through me	God pardons and enables us to do the same
lead us not into temptation	God protects and turns all for our good[118]

Summary

Disciples learn to pray from Jesus who gives them a model as an outline. He is the one who knows the Father and honors the sacred identity, who opens the kingdom to the world, who supplies his followers for physical strength, relational healing (forgiveness), and protection from evil and the Evil One. The disciples' prayer is thus an outline of how Jesus loves the Father and the ones the Father's given him. It's who he is.

Insights

1. At its center, being a follower involves Jesus drawing us into his circle of communion and communication with the Father and the Spirit.

2. Jesus' ministry of word and deed was grounded in his prayerful dependence.

3. Return to the simplicity of the Lord's Prayer and let the Spirit breathe it through you.

4. Prayer can be taught, just as Jesus did. When teaching others, always start here.

5. That God is eager to hear us is a new idea to many who assume he's just too busy.

6. Jesus teaches that the Father is to be sought and pursued in prayer. It stretches and deepens our desires. Prayer expands our capacity for prayer.

7. God is not a tyrant with all power and no benevolence. No tricks, no cruelty, no deceptions, only good gifts.

8. Prayer is vulnerable and honest and gritty. Weave your life into this prayer.

117. For a rich study, see Ayo, *The Lord's Prayer.*
118. *The Good and Beautiful God,* 55–73, with the correlations slightly edited.

9. This is the prayer of a community yearning for the great liberation of God's rule.

10. Pray the prayer slowly. Pause between petitions for God to stir heart and mind.

Disciplines

Observation: The one who knows the Father best gives us a map for prayer.
Action: Pray many other prayers, but always pray this one first and last.
Observation: The prayers of Jesus, though agonizing, are erected on the deepest trust.
Action: Make the whole of life, all your desires for good, the raw materials of prayer.

29. Luke 12:1–12

Life is on the Line
Genre: Four Prophetic Warnings and Encouragements

The Preserver of the universe
extends his aid to things so worthless and descends to the smallest animals.
How can he forget those who love him,
especially when he takes so great care of them.[119]
—CYRIL OF ALEXANDRIA

Justification

This is counted as a disciple unit because it's addressed to them in v.1a, "he Jesus began to say to *his disciples*," and with a fresh direct address in v.4a, "Now I tell you, *my friends*," and in v.8a, "Now I tell *you*." Disciples are the audience for the whole unit.

Shape

A warning is issued in the form of prophetic speech. By divine revelation coupled with sharp observation, Jesus knows the dangers ahead and alerts his companions as to what's at stake and how to behave, as if to say, "These things are coming, and I am preparing you to face them with courage and an assurance of the Father's unfailing care."

Inclusions for the thought unit are Jewish leaders (*Pharisees*, v.1d // *synagogues and the rulers and the authorities*, v.11a) and the verbal cue *to say* (v.1c // vv.11b, 12).

The five paragraphs are arranged as a 5:1 concentric pattern, having five parts with a single center (3. vv.6–7b) which uses a question (v.6a) and answer (vv.6b-7) to affirm their great worth to God. In 2. vv.4–5 and 2' vv.8–10 the emphatic "I tell you,"

---

119. Just, *Luke*, 204.

is used concerning whom to fear and whom to confess. The two sub-units (2//2') also contain a clear threat of judgment: *cast into hell* (v.5b) // *denied before the angels of God* (v.9). With these cues understood, the thought unit should be read and interpreted as a whole:

1. vv.1–3 The Speech of Disciples is Heard and Judged
    2. vv.4–5 Whom to Fear (*I tell you, cast into hell*)
        3. vv.6–7 Assurance of the Father's Care, Question + Answer
    2' vv.8–10 Whom to Confess (*I tell you, denied/not be forgiven*)
  1' vv.11–12 The Speech of Disciples is Aided by the Holy Spirit

Content

We may take 12:1–12 as a private teaching to the disciples.[120] The crowds are now so massive and impatient to get to Jesus that they "trod upon one another." He's a rock star, an icon of healing, a spigot for divine love, and it is precisely when facing this highly pressured situation that "he began to say to his disciples *first*," not meaning them first and then the pressing crowds, but that the first thing he said to them were the anti-Pharisaic warnings of vv.2d–3.

Hypocrisy is when I teach more than I live, but if that is true of everyone but Jesus, then what is his concern when he invokes the Pharisees as a negative model? The teaching of v.2 is about transparency, that what we hide from one another is already known to God and will, at the end—if not now—*be known* and *be revealed* (a reverential passive = *by God*). The parallel teaching of v.3 applies this principle to the activity of our speech which is never private to God, again with the passive voice indicated divine action (*shall be heard . . . shall be proclaimed*). Have the Pharisees forgotten that God sees and knows all?

We are to be careful in our living and especially careful with our words because, at the right time, God is the teller of all secrets, so privacy is no privacy at all. So when the crowds are eager and desperate and we have something to give them, do not put up a false front of any kind and do not think of money or any other benefit. It is in being real with God and clear with people that the blessings come through you but not from you. Yet people, because God is invisible, will often look to you and exalt you, a great temptation.

In the second warning (2. vv.4–5) Jesus addresses fear, that nearly paralyzing sense that I am in danger and that self-protection is my top concern. This is the fight-or-flight we are so familiar with, including the physiological chemistry of adrenalin and steroids. But Jesus addresses this supreme fear head on in a bracing manner, "They may be able to kill you, but then what more is there they can do?" And the answer is "Nothing!" though that may not be particularly consoling!

---

120. For some of the scholarly insights incorporated into my treatment, see Sweetland, "Discipleship and Persecution." 61–80; Wuellner, "The rhetorical structure of Luke 12," 280–310.

This kind of fearless self-abandonment in the midst of a threat is possible only if there is one higher who has the highest of our respect, and therefore of reverent fear, the only one who has the right and power to kill and condemn, and that is God. "Fear God," says Jesus, "and let that put all other fears in proper order."

We, as Jesus' followers, stand before an audience of one, and if properly understood, it frees us to live without crippling fear when the threat is real. So fearless but not reckless, and confident but not cocky, and bold without brass and bravado: these are our stances in the present world because, in the end, we belong to Jesus and he is responsible for us in life and in death and in life beyond death. We make our witness and wait to see what happens.

At the center of the warnings is a deep counter-affirmation (3. vv.6b–7). The God who tracks the sparrows with a Creator's care not only knows the number of the hairs atop our heads but values us above all others. When hardship comes, we wonder, Where is God? Do we not much matter to God? And while understandable, they are not true. So when tempted to give up the faith, find a bird to observe and say to yourself, "If God delights in this little one, how much more in me." Faith as trust in God's character will carry us over a raging sea of fear and doubt. God has every possible capacity to prove that our trust is rightly placed, and if alert, you will learn to spot the encouragements coming your way.

It is in 2' vv.8–10 that the intensity of the warnings increase, and the "Now I tell you" (v.8a) echoes the "Now, I tell you" of v.4a. It is a solemn introduction, second only to the oft-used, "Amen/Truly, I say to you." The issue is the great coming division, and whether one is acknowledged or denied by the Son of man (Jesus in his role as eschatological judge) depends on whether he was confessed or denied during life.

This is the tipping point and continental divide of the cosmos, either allegiance and loyalty to Jesus or it's denial to avoid the consequences of being associated with him, and that standard is announced by Jesus to his disciples long ahead of time. And if this denial persists, in spite of the reminders of the Holy Spirit, then what hope remains for repentance? None at all. This is the intent of v.10. To speak ill of Jesus when under fear or threat is forgivable, as with Simon Peter's triple denial. But to spurn and reject the internal and providential work of the Holy Spirit is to cut myself off from the possibility of ever turning around since I have willfully gone deaf to God. In the United Methodist Articles of Religion, this hopeful statement is found, and I have used it to encourage many:

> Article XII, Of Sin After Justification:
> "Not every sin willingly committed after justification is the sin against the Holy Ghost, and unpardonable. Wherefore, the grant of repentance is not to be denied to such as fall into sin after justification. After we have received the Holy Ghost, we may depart from grace given, and fall into sin, and, by the grace of God, rise again and amend our lives. And therefore they are to be

condemned who say they can no more sin as long as they live here; or deny the place of forgiveness to such as truly repent."[121]

Just as there was encouraging teaching at the center (3. vv.6–7b) on our high worth as individuals, so at the end in 1' vv.11–12 there is the encouragement of the promise of divine presence as an antidote to fear. So, when fearful about what to say before authorities who have power to harm, dial up your awareness of the Helper who is already present and able to speak through you in the moment.

If your intent is to honor Christ more than preserve yourself (v.8), then speak what comes to mind when questioned, trusting God all the while. Your heart may be beating out of your chest with dread, but the Holy Spirit will not leave you without enlightenment or words of true witness. God's promises can be proven under pressure.

Then

It is because God cares for what's of little value to us (sparrows), and knows what we do not (the number of our hairs) that Jesus—as God's unique Agent and Son—is enabled with accurate insight into his opponents' cardinal sin (hypocrisy) and to what will happen at the end.

On that day there is no place to hide as all is revealed (vv.2–3); on that day some will be assigned to Gehenna as God carries out the garbage (v.5). Those who confessed Jesus will be claimed before the cosmic audience; those who consistently denied him will be denied and remain in their sins. In the end it's really *all about him*. After all, he equates himself with the *Son of man*, and speaks without apology of *acknowledging* or *denying me*. He is God's salvation in flesh and word and deed. God is fully able to sustain any who trust him through the dangers of persecution. They belong to Jesus and to the one who sent him.

There is no privacy with God, not even in our thoughts, or the impulses and desires that arise from the depths of the heart. *Omniscience*, a classic attribute of the Triune God, is the Creator's exhaustive knowledge of all possibilities, including all of ours. We are fully known. All of my lies and deceptions are exposed in the presence of Jesus Christ, and that had to be one of the more unnerving aspects of being in his physical presence as his followers were. Who knew when the X-ray vision was going to be switched on by the Holy Spirit and he would "read your thoughts"? All deeds and words are subject to the divine gaze, and it is only by first lying to ourselves about this that we permit ourselves to act and speak in certain ways.

To live under the divine gaze is the intent of the warning Jesus gives to his friends in vv.2–3. This awareness and its constant refreshment is the work of the Holy Spirit and a cure for much mischief and foolishness, as well as a source of honesty and courage.

---

121. *The Book of Discipline 2016*, 68.

I am known. I am loved. My future is secure, and my present is a challenging time of confessing Jesus and not surrendering to fear. The aid and strength of the Spirit is never far away. I am immensely valuable to God (3. vv.6b–7). I am vulnerable to fears of all sorts —being hurt, being excluded, being slandered, being marginalized, but with the assurances of forgiveness and the strengthening of the Spirit, I will be kept faithful. These were Jesus' warnings and encouragements to his friends, and they extend to us today.

Now

The world is full of casualties, and the simplest reason is that we are living on a battlefield littered with the wounded and dying, whether it be the current plague of Covid-19 or the waves of betrayal and non-discipleship Christianity that plague the church. You are not paranoid if the threats are real, and they are, so what is needed is what soldiers call *situational awareness,* the trained habit of keeping your eyes and ears and intuitions on alert status. We live in the light, not the shadows, and the Holy Spirit is fully competent to alert us to hidden threats and devious strategies of the enemy and his pesky underlings.

We do not walk around at all times on *high alert*; we were not designed for such and our adrenal responses would soon be exhausted. What we cultivate is a *relaxed awareness*, a trusting in God's ability to sustain, protect, speak, arrange, and alert me to opportunities and threats in the visible and invisible worlds.

We live amidst continuous possibilities. Such is the weight of the gift of freedom, and to follow Jesus is essentially a *responsive life.* And so when I practice the discipline of relaxed awareness in non-crisis times, then when the pressure rises and the stakes increase, I'm prepared, not to face things on my own as an autonomous self, but to live in the same trust as in non-crisis times. Call it *spiritual poise*, call it *Holy Ghost savvy*, call it *relaxed obedience*, call it *active following*, call it *just-in-time-divine-delivery*. The descriptors are many but the experience is both singular and repeatable, meaning that each is distinct as fits the occasion, and they come one after another. As my clever brother once quipped in a reversal of *deja vu,* "This is *vuja de:* I ain't never been here before!"

This is the practical meaning of being *filled and refilled* with the Holy Spirit for love and obedience in each new, unpredictable event. It is possible to develop a track record with the Holy Spirit, so that when surprises come, the response is not the paralysis of fear but an upward glance of faith and expectation coupled with a simple prayer, "Lord Jesus, I am yours, and I await the light of your Spirit." Then listen and engage because this is precisely the course Jesus recommends in vv.11–12.

So whether the new thing is high or low stakes, the discipline is the same. It can be something as normal as a surprise phone call or as loaded as a legal deposition. And it is by trial and error, by success and failure, by coming into the light, and by post-incident reflection with God and our fellow-disciples that we come to trust ourselves and our futures to this marvelously creative Triune God.

We become, over time and with many failures, *a prepared person*, not meaning one who has all the answers and all the moves ahead of time, but one who because of a history of faithful reliance on the Triune God, has invisible resources that open up dead ends into new possibilities that bring praise to the name of the one under whose banner we march. For the God who blew the end out of Jesus' grave, there are no dead ends. We are warned and equipped and encouraged by Jesus in the same speech, and if we can be both realists about our world and about God's promises, we become delightfully dangerous and seriously subversive, a bit more like our Master.

Summary

Disciples know that following is more than external conformity to a new culture or set of norms. Rules are not the center but a relationship with Jesus Christ that goes to the center of the soul, to the self's control room, there to shine his light on all secrets and all fears, all issues of worth and value, all concerns about this life and the one to come. Disciples are accompanied on the inward and outward journeys by the Holy Spirit who is our tutor in the ways of Jesus Christ and who is fully able to communicate with us all.

Insights

1. The gap between the heart and the appearance has an ugly name, *hypocrisy*, which is when image management rules a life.

2. Living in a community that speaks the truth in love is God's best medicine for the widening gaps in our life.

3. In the end there are no secrets; all our life is lived in the view of the other world, angels and all.

4. Fear can make you into a coward, even a traitor. So fear God, know your value to God, and risk being bold.

5. In moments of extreme pressure, remind yourself, "Hell, all they can do is kill me!"

6. God values what we discount and knows what we do not. We are of great value.

7. At the end God tosses the garbage into Gehenna. Treasured or trashed are the only two destinies.

8. Pay attention to your desires, your thoughts, your words, and your fears. They are a map of the deeper self.

9. Do not spurn or reject the steady illuminations of the Spirit. You do not want to live in the dark when the pressure is high.

Disciplines

Observation: Jesus teaches that every thought, emotion, and desire is known.
Action: A disciple is transparent, truthful, valued, bold in witness, open to the Spirit.
Observation: For Jesus, each is precious, damaged, and in need of divine aid.
Action: Learn to discern beyond appearances where a person is hungry for God.

30. Luke 12:13–21, 22–31, 32–34

When Enough is Not
Genre: An Elaborated Saying/Chreia on the Topics of Greed and Anxiety

He uselessly accumulates wealth when he does not know how he will use it . . . .
The things that we cannot take away with us are not ours either.
Only virtue is a companion of the dead"[122]
—Ambrose

Justification

The designation of this three-part thought unit as disciple material is a bit more subtle. The initial audience for the rebuke (v.14), ethical warning (v.15), parable (vv.16–20) and application (v.21) is not a disciple but "one of the multitude" (v.13a), in this case an aggrieved petitioner asking Jesus for a legal ruling on inheritance from the Torah. But, in the paragraph that follows (2. vv.22–31), Jesus turns immediately and speaks "to his disciples" (v.22a) an extended teaching on anxiety, which implies they were present as observers in 1. vv.13–21. They overhear, and are now addressed, and since 12:13–34 is to be read as a whole, it may be counted as primary disciple material.

Shape

The large Lukan thought unit 12:13–34 falls into three parts:
    1. vv.13–21 Question and Parable of the Rich Fool
      2. vv.22–31 Jesus Speaks to Anxiety Over the Basics
    1' vv.32–34 Radical Trust, Generosity, and God's Kingdom
    The word *possessions* (v.15b // v.33a) serves as a verbal inclusion for the whole, as do *treasures* (v.21 // v.33) and the use of direct address (*Teacher, O Man* [vv.13, 34] //

122. Just, *Luke*, 208.

Little Flock [v.32a]). Thus Luke intended 12:13–34 to be read as a three part whole on the relationship of disciples to the vice of greed and the place of necessities.

There are two additional features of this thought unit that deserve special mention, and the first is the genre or literary type. In the technical language of ancient rhetoric, Luke 12:13–34 is an *Elaborated Chreia*, meaning that a key saying (a *chreia* [v.15], what scholars used to call a *pronouncement*) has been expanded into a full argument on the topic of greed, which was among the standard topic of ancient philosophy and ethics.[123] This common genre has been received by Luke and used as a model for Jesus' portrayal as a wise philosopher discoursing on a common vice and its accompanying symptom of anxiety. The form has eight standard parts, all of which are present in this extended thought unit:

1. Note of praise/encomium for the speaker — v.13
2. Chreia or pronouncement — vv.14, 15a–b
3. Rational/Explanation of chreia — v.15c
4. Statement of the opposite or contrary — vv.16–20, 21
5. Statement from analogy (social order/nature) — vv.24, 25–26, 27–28
6. Statement from example (usually historical) — vv.27b–28, 30b–32
7. Statement by an authority — vv.28, 30b–32
8. Closing exhortation with rationale — vv. 32, 33–34

A second prominent feature, often unnoticed, is the sheer density of echoes and cross-references from Scripture, other Jewish literature of the period, and Greco-Roman philosophical sources on the same topics of greed and anxiety:[124]

v.14b, "Who made me a judge or divider over you?"	Ex. 2:14
v.20, "But God said to him, 'Fool'"	Ps. 13:1
v.24, "Consider the ravens"	Ps. 147:9, Job 38:41
vv.27–28, "wild flowers . . . grass"	Is. 40:6–8
v.32, "Little flock"	Ezek. 34:11–24, Ps. 78:52–55
v.19c, "Eat, drink, celebrate"	Ecc. 2:24, 3:13, 22, 5:18
vv.16–20	Sirach 11:18–19,
	1 Enoch 97:8–10,
	Seneca, *Ep. mor.* 17:5
vv.33–34	Sir. 29:11–13, 14
v.34	Epictetus *Dia.* 2.22.19

123. On this comparison, with its implication for Luke's level of rhetorical training, see Parsons, *Luke*, 203–08. The underlying research is that of Stegman, "Reading Luke 12:13–34 as an Elaboration of a Chreia," 328–52.

124. These examples are extracted from Parsons, *Luke*, 203–08.

The complex adaptation of a known genre, the concentric surface structure, and the wide-ranging echoes other literatures all give evidence of Luke's care and skill in the organization of his materials about Jesus. Luke was intelligent, savvy, and faithful as a special purpose intellectual disciple, an early example of the church's *brain trust*.

Content

The inquiry of v.13 is for Jesus to issue a Torah ruling for a man's brother to divide their father's legacy according to the law, and the supplicant saying in effect, "I only want what's lawfully mine." But behind the legal request is the lie that *more money means more life* and indicates an underlying covetousness, to which Jesus responds sharply in v.15.

There follows the tale of the foolish farmer who in a windfall year thought only of himself and his pleasures as if his soul was not on loan. He is both a practical atheist and a hedonist. And because nothing is shared, it all goes to others at his sudden death and judgment (v.20).

To think only of money and to wrap all one's vital energies in its pursuit, in this case a legally-valid inheritance, is to make a fundamental error and believe the deadly lie that more beyond the basics is an unqualified good. True wealth is to join Jesus "to gather riches for God," an alternative metaphor to the earlier "fishing for people." And his promises are for his followers, not non-followers, as wisdom for living.

We all have bodies that need care and the provision, two of which Jesus highlights as food and clothing (vv.22–23, 29). But our emotions also quickly come to bear in our fears, worries, and anxieties. We may have enough for today, but what about tomorrow and the day after that? And Yes we agree with Jesus, life is more than physical necessities, but it cannot be less if we are to live. What Jesus commands his followers is to live with him and learn that they can live without anxiety as his companions.

So look at the ravens, all very busy hopping around pecking away for seeds, but no worries. God meets their needs and even more so yours since you bear the image. Gaze on the transient flowers and their fashionable natural beauty. So if God can do such for the lesser, then why not for you as well?

At the center are two questions: 1) If you can't make yourself grow, then why worry about the really big stuff (vv.25–26?), 2) Can you trust the one who sent Jesus to call you into *the new reality?* So take your fears as a call to walk in trust, and don't act or think or worry like the pagans who have too many gods to please instead of the one who created and provides it all.

Seek *the new reality,* the active rule of God in every moment, and then all you need to continue the work will show up on time. Under the kingship of our Father is all you need and more. In fact, when you turn stuff into coins to meet the needs of others, you demonstrate the trust that will also sustain you in receiving from God. If you live by trust and generosity in *the new reality,* then your account in the next world will be filled as you count Jesus, his Father, and his Spirit as your most precious asset. Jesus is teaching his disciples a new way to live in the same world as others yet with an invisible partner.

Then and Now

Is it possible to live an open-hearted, open-handed life that honors the genuine and good limits of the body and makes room for others? "Yes," says Jesus the master builder as he enters an itinerant, dependent life for three years or so, "Watch me do it and learn." He was used to providing for himself, family, and others through his own labor as a craftsman. But now he is radically dependent on the one who sent him, the Father, and on the one who was his companion, director, and alter-ego, the Holy Spirit, and on the horizontal level on ordinary people for the gifts of food, clothing, and shelter.

All his students, if they stick long enough, must learn the lessons of vulnerability, trust, provision through others, gratitude, and day by day trust in the Triune God whose servants we are. And in a culture like ours that prizes predictability and self-sufficiency, this can prove extremely difficult.

So with the man who wanted to use Jesus as a club to beat his brother into legal submission. His trust is in what's rightly coming to him rather than in God; he's in danger of becoming like the rich, independent farmer whom Jesus mocked because he was a fool, a truly senseless man (16:1–31).

We live, as some say, in an *age of anxiety,* in a culture bearing a constant level of fear and uncertainty that saps vitality and builds mistrust instead of the currency of social capital between people. In some sense our emotions are a truer indicator than the casual answer "Fine" we give when someone asks, "How are you?" We are not fine but fragmented, not focused but scattered and distracted. The old certainties are eroding, and where to find new ones, who knows? But Jesus Christ is the Prince of Peace, the Provider and the Provision itself, and in his resurrection life he is universally available to everyone at every moment.

The deepest cure for what ails us is to answer Jesus' call and enroll as a follower, an apprentice, a student. His availability is the antidote to fear and his faithfulness the balm that calms chronic anxiety. Everything tastes better with him at the table, and the whole of our embodied, creaturely life is rendered sacramental for that reason. We are to seek for the very thing the Father is most ready to give, which is *the new reality* of the rule and reign of the Triune God and all that comes with it, which is the whole of creation as our home and all its riches as our inheritance, as he promised, "and all these things shall be yours as well." So enter into this friendship head first and heart first. Surrender to him and take your place with his other pupils in a new family. Invite him to infuse you with himself, to see as he sees and act as he acts. It's the path to a new life.

Summary

Disciples are wary of the desire for always more, first because it's so prevalent and secondly because their security lies elsewhere. We have an alternative accounting system, and it's titled *Gathering Riches for God*, and that means investing everything Jesus gives us into people. And when we feel worry and anxiety, we go birding or stare at a flower and its gratuitous beauty.[125] And with our equanimity restored until the next time fear pays a visit, we pay fresh and full attention to *the new reality* and all its resources which are never far away. We live with an open heart to God and an open hand to other members of our *little flock* and to the poor and love-starved around us.

Insights

1. Jesus issued a teaching on a common topic of Greco-Roman morals: *greed*.

2. What is it about our desires, that they are so easily taken hostage by addiction?

3. Why did the rich farmer not discuss his bounty with his wife, children, neighbors, rabbi, the Lord? Was his isolation as deadly as his avarice?

4. How is chronic anxiety about security a form of unbelief?

5. God delights to open the kingdom and its resources. Have you learned to give?

6. What your heart and imagination turn to in moments of leisure is a clue to your treasure and its location. What is it?

7. With the diagnosis of greed, Dr. Jesus also gives the cure, which is time immersed in nature and the disciplines of voluntary simplicity.

Disciplines

Observation: Jesus lived in the new reality without worry and invites us to join him.
Action: Write down your top three worries, then go bird and flower watching.
Observation: If there is no generous Father, then fear and greed makes perfect sense.
Action: Hire a simplicity consultant to audit you, then monitor de-accumulation.[126]

31. Luke 12:35–40, 41–48

The Glory and the Gore
Genre: Two Parables of Readiness as Eschatological Warnings

---

125. For a recent report on immersion in nature, see Robbins, "Ecopsychology: How Immersion in Nature Benefits Your Health." Positive effects were noted after only two hours.

126. A good place to start is Foster, *Freedom of Simplicity*.

"What is the mark of a Christian?

It is to watch daily and hourly and to stand prepared

in that state of total responsiveness pleasing to God,

knowing that the Lord will come at an hour he does not expect."[127]

(BASIL THE GREAT)

Justification

The imagery of the two coordinated parables is the familiar pairs of *Master/slave* (1. vv.35–40) and *Master/steward* (2. vv.41–48b). These are metaphors for Jesus authoritative relationship with his followers. They are under him in authority, and to them is delegated the care of his household: the church. That Peter follows the first story with a question means he is likely speaking for them all rather than just himself, "Is it for *us* (twelve + disciples) or for *all* (the crowds)?" That Jesus answers with a story of care for a household is transparent to the church in the post-resurrection setting. This solidifies the unit as disciple material since followers often become church leaders.

Shape

The two paragraphs of the thought unit have much in common and may be considered twins as a chart demonstrates:

	1. vv.35–40	2. vv.41–48
Master/Lord	vv.36, 37b	vv.41, 42a, b, 43, 45, 46, 47
slave/servant	vv.37a, 38c	vv.42, 43, 45a, b, 46, 47
Blessed	vv.37a, 38c	v.43
Truly, I say to you	v.37d	v.44
hour	vv.39, 40	v.46
comes	vv.36a, b, 37c, 38, 39, 40	vv.43, 46
Chiasm	vv.35–40 (7:1 Chiasm)	vv.41–48 (Question + 4:2 Chiasm)

The issue in 1. vv.35–40 is the call to readiness and vigilance because we have no timetable for the Son of man's appearance, and the issue in 2. vv.41–48 has to do with interim faithfulness, how leaders behave while they wait. Disciples are alert to the Lord's nearness and diligent in caring for his people. The Lord Jesus is always near and ever-observant.

The first thought unit is framed with imperatives on readiness (a. v.35 // a' v.40). Inside the frames are two analogies, the first a wedding image (b. v.36), the second a robbery image (b' v.39). At the center (c. vv.37–38) is a double blessing on diligent

---

127. Just, *Luke*, 215.

servants and the extravagant promise that the Master will reverse the normal roles and serve them to honor their faithfulness. A keen awareness of Jesus Christ, his nearness and dearness, puts disciples on a high state of readiness with a willingness to interdict dangerous intruders (v.39). An outline is:

1. v.35 Command to Readiness For All
2. v.36 Analogy 1: Wedding Image: Positive Expectation
3. vv.37–38 Promise: Blessing On Alert Servants
2' v.39 Analogy 2: Thief Image: Negative Expectation
1' v.40 Command To Readiness For All

The second paragraph is structured around a question of Peter (v.41) followed by a counter-question and answer of Jesus (vv.42–48). Peter's question about the intended audience of vv.35–40 makes it clear that Jesus is addressing Peter's *us* (disciples who are also leaders) and not his *all* (followers who are not leaders). An outline is:

1. vv.41–42 Introduction And Question: Who Is Entrusted?
2. vv.43–44 Faithful Servants Rewarded (Short)
2' vv.45–48c Unfaithful Servant Punished (Long)
1' v.48d-e Double Proverb Of Judgment On What Is Entrusted

Content

In the extended analogy, the Master is soon to be absent and entrusts the care of his household servants to a steward, a household manager, one of whose jobs is to feed them the proper amount at the proper time. If the steward is faithful, commendation follows, and they will be rewarded with a larger trust. But if the absence is misused to exploit the servants (v.45a) and engage in self-indulgence (v.45b), the penalty is death by dismemberment, "and will cut him in two," and a permanent separation, "and put him with the unfaithful" (v.46).

Pastoral treason is a capital crime. But here there are three levels of punishment. The overt are punished in an ultimate fashion (v.46), the knowledgeable but lazy receive a severe beating (v.47), and the ignorant but culpable a lighter whipping (v.48).

Leaders care for, lead, and serve persons who belong to Jesus Christ. To neglect this sacred trust for any reason may be deadly, but always painful when the Lord appears. The principle that underlies both paragraphs is stated at the end: to have been entrusted by Jesus with his people is as great a responsibility as there is, and the standards are high (v.48d-e). And if it operates on a human level with leaders, how much more with under-shepherds of Christ?[128]

---

128. The classic volume on pastoral calling and work remains Oden, *Pastoral Theology: Essentials of Ministry*; also his companion volume, *Becoming A Minister*. A helpful text is Willimon, *Pastor: The Theology and Practice of Ordained Ministry*.

Then

All that Jesus does is with a view to his coming absence (9:51) and to what shall become of his kingdom movement, his people, his church. Who will lead and teach and serve them and keep them in *the new reality*? Answer: his disciples who became twelve apostles, and some of whom become, in Luke's terms, "faithful and wise stewards" over the Master's household. And remember that in the ancient world the household/ Gk. *oikos* was the basic unit of social organization, an extended family including servants and clients.[129]

Three of the cardinal virtues Jesus highlights for pastors/ leaders are:

1. an awareness of his nearness (vv.35–36),

2. a willingness to name and repulse invaders (v.39),

3. a loving diligence in serving the saints (vv.43–44).

It is not our bride but his that we attend to, his house and not ours that thieves wish to plunder, his brothers and sisters who are too often treated shabbily. The church is often weak because of its leaders, and their accountability, their rewards and judgements, are matters to which the Lord promises personal attention, either by honoring their service at a banquet or inflicting much pain on them, and on some severance and banishment. Disciples who continue with Jesus will become disciple-makers and find themselves, whether officially or not, functioning as stewards in Jesus' household. And so the teaching of Jesus on awareness, courage, and diligence applies not just to the ordained but to all his followers.

Now

Following Jesus is a purposeful life in which we are formed and shaped by his life and into his priorities, and he loves and cares about people. His first followers have had the finest training possible, living daily for three years with a man from Nazareth they have only just begun to understand. So following him means entering the same daily human mess he joyfully embraced. Needy people, curious people, sick and tormented people, young and old people, prostitutes and swindlers, the pious and the profane, the eager and the suspicious. And if he took time with such, a fact to which Luke amply testifies, then his followers, and particularly their pastoral leaders, must do the same.

Jesus engaged deeply and then retreated strategically, but he never spent all day in a study. Every day was rough and tumble, teaching precisely what the Spirit indicated and counting on the same Holy Spirit when healing and deliverance were needed. Jesus lived a fully cooperative life with the Father and the Spirit. So wherever

---

129. On the early church as family, see Hellerman, *When the Church Was a Family*, 182–204.

we find ourselves, that is our posting and the place to which we've been sent. And it is there that we count on the Spirit to be at work.

Across forty years of pastoral ministry the most sobering meeting each year was the Clergy Session that opened Annual Conference because here vows were taken and accountability administered for those who had been brought up on charges, tried in church courts, and removed. And when, eventually, some of the removed were my seminary classmates and colleagues, it was sobering. "Could that be me?" I asked with a gulp. And the internal answer was always, "Yes, unless you stay aware, courageous, prayerful, humble, and diligent."

A discipline that came out of this yearly meeting was that I carried in my notebook a copy of my conference and ordination vows for regular review. And when tired or bored or frustrated or lazy or tempted to quit, I'd pull them out and read them aloud. The effect was always sobering and bracing, sometimes followed by tears and always by a prayer for renewed love and fresh energies. The notion of Jesus hacking me in pieces with a broadsword or lacerating my back with a whip before the angels supplied an extra level of motivation! "This is very serious business," and it is, and at the end only joy for the faithful.

Summary

Disciples have a stance of readiness and alertness to the One who lives just beyond sight. This does not mean we cannot rest and unplug from time to time, but that even here we do not lose our awareness of Jesus' nearness and our accountability. He wants his people well-tended, not used or abused. Servant leadership in the community of Jesus is a serious matter, and a death sentence is possible for any who fleece the flock and live as scoundrels. With God the judgment always fits the crime, and rewards are hidden within faithfulness. Never forget the one who is near and observant to all who bear his name.

Insights

1. Does the risen Jesus, his nearness and his call, have my full attention?

2. In a day of endless distractions, what does it mean to be ever-alert to Jesus Christ?

3. If Jesus said the hour of his return is *unexpected*, why so much foolish speculation?

4. That the risen Jesus delights to serve his faithful people is evident as he girds himself and has them sit for the meal.

5. The call is not to *get ready* but to *stay ready* in the daylight and in the dark. Am I?

6. Leadership, lay or clergy, is a privilege with real responsibilities and high accountability.

7. Aim at wisdom and faithfulness; you will grow in the knowledge of Jesus Christ.

8. If you know and indulge, it's death. If you know and neglect, it's pain. And if you don't know, why not?

9. Before God and people, those who've been given much, of them much is expected!

10. At judgment, the truth is public; for some it means great pain, for others great joy.

Disciplines

Observation: If the risen Jesus is totally alive and ever-near, why not pay attention?
Action: Sin as amnesia is chronic among all, so call Jesus to mind at every reminder.
Observation: Jesus says to corrupt the church through neglect or treason is damnable.
Action: Treat the church as if she were the bride of your best friend because it is.

32. Luke 14:25–35

The Cost of Following—and of Not
Genre: A Discourse on the Cost of Vocation (// Epictetus *Diatribes*)

In times past, when heresies prevailed,
many chose death through martyrdom and various tortures.
Now, when we through the grace of Christ live in a time of profound and perfect peace,
we learn for sure that cross and death consist
in nothing else than the complete putting to death of self-will.[130]
—SIMEON THE NEW THEOLOGIAN

Justification

There are two previous thought units that lay out the explicit costs of discipleship, 9:23–27 and 9:57–62, to which we now add 14:25–35 as a third of this type.[131] From time to time in his travels Jesus pauses to address the multitudes and his friends about what it means to be more than a member of the mob. He is clear on the initial and on-going cost of being his follower and apprentice: one who with others and by constant exposure is taking on the teaching, priorities, and worldview of a master.

They are to mimic Rabbi Jesus who embodies his Father's kingdom in the power of the Holy Spirit. Jesus called followers to himself, "Follow *me*," then immersed them in the multivalent conflict between the kingdom of God and the ruling powers of this world, visible and invisible. Jesus was the engine; they were the rail cars who hooked

---

130. Just, *Luke*, 241.

131. On his historicity of Jesus' call to discipleship, see Keener, *The Historical Jesus*, 196–255.

their future to his, and he pulled them all over the place making whistle-stops in village after village.

Shape

The literary shape of 14:25–35 is an alternating 4:2 stairstep pattern in which 1. vv.25–27 // 1' v.33 teach the cost of following and invoke a clear boundary, "cannot be my disciple" (vv.26f, 27c, 33c), while 2. vv.28–32 // 2' vv.34–35 offer pointed examples for clarification. The organization of the unit was for repetition with variation and as an aid to memorization, a key task of disciples as the *communal memory bank* of Jesus. The passage may be outlined as follows:

> 1. vv.25–27 The Cost of Discipleship: Family and Self as a Blockage
>> 2. vv.28–32 Two Examples of Counting the Cost Beforehand
> 1' v.33 The Cost of Discipleship: All One Has as a Blockage
>> 2' vv.34–35 Single Example of Counting the Cost Beforehand

Content

The word *disciple* is used 269 times in the New Testament, the word *Christian* only thrice.[132] There were no universities in that day; one learned in a formal apprenticeship with a master, much as one studies plumbing or carpentry today. Jesus learned the building trade from Joseph, the skills of the kingdom from his heavenly Father and the Spirit. The twelve, who stood at the core of Jesus' renewal project, stumbled along after him, and the costs were high. They were together a little platoon that was profoundly for the world by standing over its current organization and culture in God's name.

That this thought unit is aimed at casual followers/*the multitudes* is made clear from the series of open-ended invitations, "If anyone . . . Whoever . . . Which of you . . . Or what king . . . whoever of you . . . he who has ears." Jesus calls people from the multitudes to step up to being a follower and student, but he never makes it easy. To count the cost you have first to know the cost, and that means putting loyalty to Jesus above the bonds of family (v.26a-e), above one's own life (v.26f), and all entanglements and possessions (v.33). Discipleship is disruptive of all other people and plans that strive for centrality as idols. Jesus must become the new center around which the whole of life is reorganized. He rules not by addition but by replacement, and such is painful. He is not added to our personal pantheon but arrives to bring them crashing down for his central loyalty.

That Jesus glanced at the crowds, then "turned and said to them," indicates his obedience to the Spirit's lead that *now is the time for this tough teaching*. It's an

---

132. For a technical article, see Timothy A. Fredrichsen "'Disciple(s)' in the New Testament: Background, usage, characteristics, historicity," *Salesianum* 65 (2003), 717-739.

in-your-face moment, a public challenge to their tag-along mentality. Now since the inter-generational family lay at the core of Jewish religious and social identity, to displace them—as Jesus had done at Nazareth (4:16–30) and repeated later in public (8:20–21)—was taboo.

But Jesus then raised the price another notch with his "yes, and even his own life," and then became graphic and horrifying in his, "Whoever does not bear his own cross and come after me, cannot be my disciple." Bam, Bam, Bam! Family, self, the most shameful death: this was the cost. Not casual association for the show and the benefits; that's not following. It's something much harder and more demanding.[133]

To Jesus' credit, he did not just leave them with a bald confrontation. He followed it in 2. vv.28–32 with two culturally-relevant examples, both of what have to do with facing the costs and counting the costs. The first is a construction project never finished because money ran out, the second a defeated army because of overwhelming opposition, both of which are occasions for being publicly shamed and losing whatever honor one had accumulated. To be so ridiculed was a horrible fate in a shame-and-honor culture. Jesus said:

> Do the math, because either way your life is at risk. Not to follow me is a risk
> to miss the kingdom, and to follow me is a risk because it disrupts the whole
> script of life. You are no longer normal. You no longer fit in. You become weird
> in the same way that I am strange.

So which do you want? And even if you follow, there's another risk. And that's losing your character as salty people. The cost of following are then followed by threats peculiar to disciples. This new life, and you along with it, can become as insipid and worthless and tasteless and no count as something that looks like salt but is not. What is more worthless and worthy of scorn than the naked shell of building, a defeated army led by a foolhardy king, or fake salt? So, he ended, "He who has ears to hear, let him hear." And my guess is that the crowds were smaller by sunset.

Then

Here we face some of Jesus' most difficult, offensive teaching. In order to be rightly attached to him, all other loyalties are relativized and their claims to primacy dissolved. Now scholars tell us that *to hate* is typical Middle Eastern hyperbole for *to love less*, and I agree, but it's still about radical displacement.

The ties that bind must be dissolved, including my attachment to my own life, my future, and my reputation, and all that I have that is linked to my sense of identity and security. If any of these are put before Jesus, or even alongside him as an equal, I cannot be his apprentice in the kingdom of God.

---

133. For a rereading of Jesus' demand for the modern church, see Hull and Cook, *The Cost of Cheap Grace*.

The following chart demonstrates the paradox of discipleship in Luke.[134] It's both giving and receiving. All are called to utter allegiance. Jesus determines our places, our particular service, our challenges, and the challenges open into opportunities.

Disciples Give	Disciples Receive
Forsake Family (14:26)	Bring family into the fellowship (Acts. 16:33 1 Cor. 7:12, Col. 3:18–21)
Bear one's own cross (14:27)	Bear the burdens of others (Gal. 6:2)
Forsake all things (14:33, 18:29)	Receive all things (Luke 12:22–32, 14:1, 18:30)
Give all things to others (Luke 10:38, 22:10–12, Matt 25:36–37)	Put in charge of Master's possessions (Luke 12:44)
Come to the Lord and serve him (Luke 14:26)	The Lord comes and serves his disciples (12:36–37)

Now

About the closest I can come to an analogy for the radical shift of focus discipleship to Jesus entails is Marine boot camp.[135] Your head is shaved, a number given, civilian clothes put aside, and a new identity both bestowed in a vow and proven in rigorous training predicated on the fact you know nothing and are issued everything. And if not issued, then you don't need it. When you sleep and eat are regulated by another, and obedience is the currency that counts. An old identity is dissolved and new identity erected over its rubble. And on graduation day, you are hardly to be recognized. Thirty pounds lighter, all spit and polish, ramrod straight, full of new manners and habits—a Marine!

I've seen the results, and it is amazing to behold as a punk kid in twelve weeks becomes a gentleman and a soldier, courteous, honorable, a United States Marine bearing the permanent stamp of *Semper Fidelis*—always faithful—and willing to give his life to protect others. As outsiders often comment with a faint wisp of envy at the achievement and the bonds forged in that unique crucible, "Once a Marine, always a Marine!" This is the power of high expectations and exhaustive training for a larger cause.

134. Extracted from Edwards, *Luke*, 429.

135. On the challenges of contemporary discipleship see one or more of the following: Willard, *The Great Omission; Renewing the Christian Mind;* Hull, *Conversion & Discipleship, The Complete Book of Discipleship;* Hull & Sobels, *The Discipleship Gospel;* Allin, *Simple Discipleship;* McKnight and Miller, *Following King Jesus;* Vanhoozer, *Hearers and Doers;* Williams, *Start Here: Kingdom Essentials for Christians;* Breen, *Building a Discipling Culture;* Watson, *The Class Meeting, The Band Meeting;* Gallaty, *Rediscovering Discipleship;* Hirsch and Hirsh, *Untamed;* Ogden, *Discipleship Essentials;* Jared C. Wilson, *The Imperfect Disciple.*

So if Parris Island knows how to make Marines, then does Jesus know how to make a different kind of man or woman, a disciple who has been trained in the ways, means, and operations of the kingdom of God?

Yes, but the church has all but forgotten this art. All grace instead of grace-fueled effort, all grace and no demand, all love and no expectation. And if our clergy are not first disciples but only learned instead of trained and well-formed, is this not why our fellowships are so weak and flaccid?

That even the children of John Wesley have lost their discipline and their doctrines, their core beliefs and their disciplined behaviors demonstrate just how corrosive and persuasive is the culture around us with its flexible convictions and easy accommodations.

So in addition to the recovery and defense of classic Christian faith, there must be a disciplined recovery of the ways and means, the cost and convictions of classic Christian discipleship, and if it does not offend the comfortable and frighten the domesticated, then it's not yet what is required. So let the Methodists revive the Class Meeting and begin to pray together for a fresh jolt of love and grace and disciples.[136] What if a flame sprang up from these ashes?

The most offensive aspect of this faith is Jesus himself, especially his demand to be the living center of one's allegiance, loyalty, focus, and affections. He kept using the pronouns *me* and *mine*, "Follow *me* . . . cannot be *my* disciple . . . " The Father has made the Son the means and test of salvation. The Holy Spirit has illumined the Son with light and is pointing everyone in his direction. Is he not already the flaming center?

We follow a risen person, one whose relevant history is chronicled in four approved biographies, and if as you read with an open mind you also pray, "Show yourself to me," something will soon happen so that you hear his footsteps behind you and the echo of his voice in your conscience. You are being pursued and given multiple evidences that are worthy of your trust.

It is all leading towards a confrontation only he determines and to a decision only you can make, "Follow me, and I will make you . . . " And if your reply is *Yes* after counting the costs, then he decides what you keep and what you leave behind, whom you serve with and where you go, how you suffer and for how long, and your placement in his long conflict with the world as it now is. You are now apprenticed in love to one who has the final verdict on the whole of your life. This is the big risk and the great adventure!

The text *A Covenant Prayer in the Wesleyan Tradition* sums up the multiple levels of surrender that mark the path of disciples:

> I am no longer my own, but thine.
> Put me to what thou wilt, rank me with whom thou wilt.

136. Our best new resources are Watson, *The Class Meeting, The Band Meeting.*

Put me to doing, put me to suffering.
Let me be employed by thee or laid aside for thee,
exalted for thee or brought low for thee.
Let me be full, let me be empty.
Let me have all things, let me have nothing.
I freely and heartily yield all things
to thy pleasure and disposal.
And now, O Glorious and blessed God,
Father, Son, and Holy Spirit,
thou art mine, and I am thine. So be it.
And the covenant which I have made on earth,
let it be ratified in heaven. Amen.[137]

If, as Bill Hull often says, "The gospel you preach determines the disciples you make,"[138] then why have we set the bar so low for being a Christian, a church member, a disciple? Is it not the consumer mindset that "everyone likes a deal"? Is it not that Jesus is just not taken seriously? I think so, but look what it yields? Non-disciple disciples with a supposed pre-punched ticket for heaven and a free pass for whatever they find appealing. Not a pretty picture, is it?

Summary

Disciples regularly go through reality checks. The old life, its rhythms and comforts, loyalties and habits, keep displacing Jesus. We lose focus, and clarity is forfeited. Our primary loyalty is him and *the new reality*, and all other good things—be they family, safety, all the supports of life—remain secondary.

If restored to primacy, we have, in effect, resigned our commissions and lapsed back into *the great multitude*. It's a different life, as distinct as the taste of salt, so the question is: How badly do you want it? Salt stings!

Insights for Disciples

1. Jesus never discounts his call; it's always at a premium price because it's worth it.

2. To find a new center in Jesus is disruptive of the way life's been organized.

3. We come *to Jesus* in order *to come after* him, to be where he is, doing what he does.

4. Do not be surprised when some who matter to you do not like what *the new reality* is doing to you.

5. Jesus refuses to be a religious decoration; he demands to be the ruling center.

137. *U.M. Hymnal*, No 607.

138. See Hull and Sobels, *The Discipleship Gospel*, 17–26.

6. To start well, we have first to counts the costs; but to end well, we must be undiluted and savory all the way.

7. Some of the costs may be alienation from family, public shame, fear, falling short, internal conflicts, a daily martyrdom.

Disciplines

Observation: Jesus taught that life's greatest opportunity is not cheaply acquired.
Action: Learn to spot, mock, and reject all schemes that sell Jesus at a discount.[139]
Observation: An urgent Jesus rushed none to decision without counting the costs.
Action: Find a few honest zealots to help keep you on the narrow way to life.

33. Luke 16:1–8, 9–13

Money and the Life of Following
Genre 1: The Fable of the Sly Manager and the Cornered Master
Genre 2: Three Epilogues on the Single Fable

Those of us who possess earthly wealth

open our hearts to those who are in need . . . .

Let us do this so that we may receive what is our own,

that holy and admirable beauty that God forms in people's souls,

making them like himself, according to what we originally were.[140]

—Cyril of Alexandria

Justification

This two-part thought unit is addressed directly to the disciples in v.1, "And Jesus said to his disciples," and the audience reaffirmed in v.9, "To you I say." That the audience is shifted to the Pharisees in v.14, "The Pharisees, who were lovers of money, heard all this and scoffed at him," further indicates that it is to his disciples that Jesus speaks in 16:1–8 (a parable) and in 16:9–13 (three epilogues or applications of the parable).[141]

---

139. See Hull and Cook, *The Cost of Cheap Grace*.

140. Just, *Luke*, 256.

141. Exegetical treatments include Bailey, *Poet and Peasant*, 86–118; Klyne Snodgrass, *Stories with Intent*, 401–19; Hultgren, *The Parables of Jesus*, 146–56.

Shape

The two paragraphs are linked by a series of catchwords for unity:

doing/make	vv.3,4	vv.8, 9
theme/scheme	v.4	v.9
unrighteous/*adikia*	v.8,	vv.9c, 11
steward/stewardship	vv.1b, 2b, 3a, 4b	v.8a
mammon		vv.9, 11, 13
master/Lord	vv.3, 5, 8	v.13

A basic outline for the two paragraphs is:

1. 16:1–8 The Parable of the Shrewd Manager, A 6:2 Chiasm
a. v.1 Rich Man and Steward: Bad Report and Poor Manager
   b. v.2 Problem: Crisis of Accountability
      c. v.3 Question to Himself: Facing His Limits
      c' v.4 Answer to Himself: An Idea for a New Future
   b' vv.5–7 Solution: Quick Action to Make New Friends, Master's Honor
a' v.8 Rich Man and Steward: Good Report and Clever Manager
2. 16:9–13 Three Epilogues on Mammon and the New Life with God
a. v.9 Mammon (Money), Angels, and God (Shorter)
   b. vv.10–12 Mammon and True Riches (Longer: Double Lines)
a' v.13 Mammon and God, Use of Money Reveals Ultimate Loyalty

Content

The attitude towards and use of money as an indicator of discipleship is a theme that runs throughout Luke and Acts, and here in 16:1–8, 9–13 it's brought to a focus. It begins with a rather odd—and to us controversial—story about an estate manager caught in waste and then later commended for his cleverness to save his own hide.

As the tale begins, a household/estate manager is ratted out to his employer for profligate spending, not necessarily dishonest but wasteful. Now in the gap of time between the charges and the interview he asks himself a question (v.3) and comes up with a plan to secure his future after his dismissal (v.4).

Since he has access to financial records, he goes to each of his master's creditors, and in an act of largesse they naturally attribute to the Master through his authorized agent, their bills—if paid immediately—receive drastic discounts, the first fifty percent, the second twenty percent.

Since these creditors will now praise their Master in public, his honor is increased in the community, so that if he comes back later with the story of his agent's fraud and demands full payment, his honor becomes a long-remembered dishonor. So when the time for accountability comes, the Master commends the spendthrift steward because he acted so shrewdly to increase his Master's reputation and to secure his own future with others.

The story is left open-ended as to whether or not he was let go. Conclusion 1 (v.8a) is part of the story, with Conclusion 2 (v.8b-c) being Jesus' comment about how much wiser *worldlings* are at using money to secure their futures than *the son of light in their own generation*. And if they do it for this world alone, what about the next?

So why this story and Jesus' enigmatic commentary? It's not that we should misuse the resources of another who trusts us, or lie to gain credit for ourselves. It's that there are ways to use money that both increase God's honor and indicate our commitment to and investment in the world to come.

Money is a tool that reveals where security lies, and its use either reveals and negates all that we claim about God and the coming kingdom. So make sure all your financial dealings increase the fame and reputation of the God you claim to know. We have balance sheets for the present, and do we have accounting for the life which is after this life? Do we live in light of that not-as-pressing reality?

It would be a mistake to reduce the three appended epilogues to bare morals or common sense lessons or general principles. They are, rather, three insights into the whole, each with multiple resonances for reflection and insight. How do we demonstrate kingdom reality as *the sons and daughters of light* who live amidst often clever *worldlings*?

If the indirect *they* of v.9e refers to angels and the *eternal tents* to dwellings in the world to come, then making friends of them means using money in a way that reflects their understanding of what matters since they are the agents of God and active in the final judgments. When you give secretly out of love, the angels make a mental note. So who am I trying to cooperate with? And who am I in league with? Who knows my secrets? And who will be my friends at my dying breath when worldly wealth is proved impotent? It is the secretly generous who sing with faith, "Swing low, sweet chariot, comin' for to carry me home, a band of angels comin' after me, comin' for to carry me home."

The second epilogue begins with a positive and negative statement of a proverb about money and character (v.10a-b), *faithful* and *unfaithful*. It then shifts the register from money in this world to truth in the next, assuming that the currency of the coming kingdom is not legal tender but *the truth about God*. And the mode of accumulation also differs between the realms, since money is normally *earned* while truth— by contrast—is entrusted by God. A third contrast is that money is always someone else's before it passes through our hands, but with God there is a measure of truth just for us, "*the what is your own*" (to use the awkward grammar of the original) that none can take from you.

All we take to the next world is the love and character and truth we have received and developed in this one, and with God there is no limit except our own to how much of each we can have. So to the question, What is my net worth? there are two accounting systems, one for money, the other for character. Which do I care the most about?

Then the third epilogue, and here the issue of loyalty dominates. What do I love and am drawn towards, and what do I despise and am repelled from? What is the polarity of my person? What pulls me towards and what pushes me away? Jesus makes it clear that *mammon* (wealth in this fallen world) is a presently alluring but finally impotent deity. Stuff is not God, though it is a form of power that impresses nearly everyone.

It is an issue of first commandment faithfulness which Jesus states in an uncompromising manner, "You cannot serve God and mammon," because one will always be first and the other second. In the end we become like what we worship, love, and find security in, and it is not hard for God to know the difference.

Then

Money is sweat and perhaps smarts congealed into currency. It's hard to operate without it, then and now. And because it enables much and promises more of everything, it is a serious rival to be one of our household deities, those powers—surely less than One, True and Living God—to whom we make ground level offerings in our advanced, modern forms of syncretism. And when empowered by the lies like *the more you own the more you are* or *all you need is more* or *if only I had more I could be happy*, its ability to grip and control the human imagination is fearsome.

So Jesus told a memorable tale about a profligate manager who used his master's money to secure his future. And if we are to be that resourceful, then we must recognize that our checkbooks, and especially our giving to people and causes near to God's heart, are a vital sign as much as our pulse and blood pressure.

Generosity is a sign of trust in God's provision, not just in my ability to accumulate and guard. Disciples learn to work and manage their money under God's eyes, have a regular plan for giving, and are open to God *squeezing them* when other needs come their way. It's life with an open heart and an open hand in partnership with the Triune God. We invest in *the new reality*, learn faithfulness in things great and small, refuse to be defined by hedonism, and ask God to reveal where mammon may be claiming undue loyalty.

Now

So why did Jesus bear down on the issue of mammon and wealth with his closest associates? Because the love of it is so common, and it is a danger to the rich and the poor, though in different ways. To the rich hoarding and hiding wealth are common, lest new friends and borrowers harass me or steal what's mine. To live in a bubble of prosperity removes one from the raw and pressing needs of many for whom the basics would be luxury. It's why nurses and teachers often make the best disciples; every day they are interfacing with needs that are hard to meet and multi-layered.

So if you find yourself avoiding *that kind of people*, then that is precisely where God is calling you to engage, and it can begin as simply as tutoring a child in a public school, giving a few hours a week at the local food bank, or volunteering at your local church with the *walk-ins* who always have the same question, "Does your church help with . . . ?

Learn not just to give but to build friendships, share faith, and pray with the needy. Share food and rent money and medicine and Jesus. Risk becoming involved outside your comfort zone. Let God break your heart and raise hard questions about your giving and your loving and your advocacy.

Over the years some really good folk have come to me with a lament that goes something like this, "Pastor Phil, I used to feel close to God but now I feel far. What's wrong?" So I listen as they fill in the details. They are reading the Bible, praying, serving in the church, giving time and money, not violating their conscience, but all the color has gone gray.

So somewhere along my pastoral path I learned to ask, "Whom do you know who is poor or lonely or hurting or hungry or depressed or addicted or ill or isolated or incarcerated, or without sufficient food, housing, clothing, and transportation?" And when they give me the blank look or a list of the charities they support with checks from a safe distance, I ask, "How did this happen to you? How did you end up being cut off from the human pain Jesus came to engage?" This is perhaps the cleverest of all Satan's ploys, that if he cannot lure us into serious sin, then the next best thing is to insulate us in a bubble of comfort that grows thicker and thicker till we can no longer hear the cry of the needy and the wail of the world's pain. At some point I nod and say:

> I've seen this before, not only in others but in myself, and the cure is not difficult though it will be hard. You must ask God to punch a hole in your well-maintained bubble and let in some of the world's agony, and if you do, then God is going to break your heart. And that will be the beginning of a cure. You feel far from God because God is where the pain is, and when you go there it will make you hungry and desperate for God. Prayer and Scripture will begin to mean something vital again. Start loving outside your comfort zone, and then you will start living in partnership again with the God whose presence you once enjoyed. At times it is not any issue of *more* of anything (Bible reading, prayer, giving) but a *new thing*, not more Christian information but Christian love in action.

Summary

Disciples use all their resources to advance *the new reality* and to increase the reputation of the One who embodies it—the Jesus we follow. This takes insight, cleverness, and decisive action. Carrying out kingdom assignments puts us in line with the angels who are our invisible friends, now and at our death. Being faithful in small matters prepares us for a much larger scope, now and in the coming new world. Worshiping God and using money is wise, whereas the reverse—worshiping money and trying to use God—is death.

Insights

1. That Jesus told a trickster story about a clever scoundrel means he knew the appeal of it. Do we?
2. Prudence is wisdom plus urgency plus action; both Jesus and the Master praised it.
3. Many are the clever in this world, but where are the opportunists in our ranks?
4. If we show the family likeness in our generosity, heaven is an afterthought.
5. Faithfulness, the ability to be worthy of trust, opens us to God's riches, now and later.
6. What matters most is who we love most; it is on display before the world and God!

Disciplines

Observation: Jesus told scandalous stories because everyone loves a clever rogue.
Action: Never miss an opportunity disguised as a crisis. Pray and act boldly.
Observation: Jesus trains stewards who are good with money and kingdom riches.
Action: Invest your little with God and it will keep you from false worship.

34. Luke 17:1–10

Discipleship Up Close
Genre: An Intensive Discipleship Teaching (No. 4)

A mustard seed looks small.
Nothing is less noteworthy to the sight, but nothing is stronger to the taste.
What does that signify
but the very great fervor and inner strength of faith in the church?[142]
—Augustine

142. Just, *Luke*, 267.

Justification

This thought unit is included in our catalog because it is clearly addressed to the *disciples/apostles/servants* (vv.1a, 5a, 10). Like 9:23–27, 9:37–50, and 14:25–35, it is one of Jesus *periodic pauses* for instruction and clarification on being his follower and a servant leader in the new community he's creating. Jesus calls them as his understudies and then, along the way and as needed, offers a refresher course. He's an *on-time teacher* who does not download everything at once but fits it to the audience and the occasion.

Shape

The outline is a 3:1 Chiasm with 1. vv.1–4 and 1' vv.7–10 each having two parts::
   1. vv.1–4 The Sin Issue in the Community of Jesus
   a. vv.1–2 Inevitable Temptation and the Care of the Little One's
   b. vv.3–4 Confronting Sin and the Habit of Forgiveness
       2. vv.5–6 The Faith Issue: A Little Rightly Placed is Enough
   1' vv.7–10 The Issue of Duty and Commendation
   a. vv.7–9 Three Rhetorical Questions and Answers: No/Yes/No
   b. v.10 Application to Disciples: Don't Look for Praise for Duties

The sequence of the unit is in three paragraphs (1. vv.1–4, 2. vv.5–6, 1' vv.7–10). The first and third (1//1') have two parts (a, b) and the second only one. The first and last are speeches of Jesus, while the second is a dialog consisting of an exclamation from the apostles (v.5) plus Jesus' response (v.6). There are three uses of *sin* in 1. vv.1–4 and three uses of *servant* in 1' vv.7–10, but no pattern of three at the center in 2. vv.5–6.

The phrase *in the sea* is a link between the first two paragraphs (v.2a // v.6c). The longer units are in the frames (1//1') and the shorter in the center (2). Each paragraph contains a designation or title for the audience: *disciples*/pupils (v.1a), *apostles*/ambassadors (v.5a), and *unworthy servants*/slaves (v.10) as a shocking end note!

Content[143]

The first paragraph has two parts (a. vv.1–2, b. vv.3–4) both of which have to do with sin in the family-like community of Jesus' followers. "These little ones" is a euphemism for weaker, more vulnerable members of the community of whatever age. While the nature of the current fallen world is that opportunities to sin are everywhere and always, to be the agent who trips up another brings judgment, "but woe to him *by whom* they come" (v.1c), the horror of which is seen in the millstone image (v.2). Better to

---

143. For exegetical treatments, see Parsons, *Luke*, 251–54; Levine and Witherington, *The Gospel of Luke*, 464–68; Hendricks, *The Third Gospel*, 248–61; Carroll, *Luke*, 339–42.

be crushed in the depths than crush the trust of *a little one*. To corrupt one for whom Christ died is to become an agent of the Evil One, and to do his work is damnable.

If vv.1–2 works off the polarity of *the strong* and *the weak*, then vv.3–4 uses the more mutual image of *brothers* (and sisters) who work against the creeping corrosion of sin in the community. All are accountable, all subject to correction, and—if there is repentance— repeated and immediate forgiveness. It's communal spiritual hygiene in a world-wide toxic environment where stumbles, traps, and snares are inevitable. Disciples nourish and protect the weak even as they hold themselves highly accountable in love. This is the medicine of love and realism that keeps a community healthy. Being loved this way is serious.

That such practices are hard to maintain is indicated by the *apostles'* unified request for more faith (v.5), literally "Add faith to us." Jesus' reply in v.6 is a mild rebuke in that the issue is not *more faith* but the use of the *little faith* they already have. The hyperbole contrasts the proverbially small mustard seed with the proverbially deep roots of the black mulberry. If placed in God, small faith is quite enough because it is rightly placed in the one for whom power is never an issue. Obey, be faithful, stay faithful, and watch God work to change the landscape and root up deep issues. Faith must make a beginning in obedience.

The third paragraph has two parts. In a. vv.7–9 is a parable in three carefully structured questions, the first (1. v.7) and last (1' v.9) of which expect a *No* answer, and the middle (2. v.8) a *Yes* answer. Then, in b. v.10 the analogy is unambiguously applied, not to masters as in "Will any one of you who have a servant . . . ?

That Jesus readily uses *master/slave* language does not imply his approval of the institution; rather, he employs a widely understood social structure as an apt analogy for his followers' voluntary relationship to himself. The setting is a small farmer with one slave who does outside and inside chores. No one expects him to eat first or to be thanked because he did what was commanded since such is the nature of the relationship. And when we do our duties, Jesus is not in our debt.[144] All rewards are intrinsic. To serve him is the highest office.

Then

If we formulate the issue each paragraph addresses, it looks like this:

    1. vv.1–4 Sin

    Question: What are disciples to do?

    Answer: Be realistic about sin, influence others for good, guard the vulnerable.

---

144. On the Protestant rejection of *works of supererogation* and the merit system of medieval Catholic theology, see the U.M. *Articles of Religion XI*: "Of Works of Supererogation" (*BOD 2016*: 68) which quotes Luke 7:10. For a theological treatment of this Article which John Wesley brought over without change from the Anglican Thirty-nine Articles, see Bray, *The Faith We Confess*, 82–84; Rogers, *Essential Truths For Christians*, 299–305.

2. vv.5–6 Faith

Question: Are we able to do it?

Answer: Yes, if the little trust we already have is rightly placed.

1' vv.7–10 Service

Question: Do we understand the term of our following of Jesus?

Answer: Obedience to Jesus does not earn merit, but is our normal duty as slaves.

Now

The community of Jesus lives in a world of multiple threats on hostile ground, so stumblings, sins, missteps, heresies, and moral failures are inevitable and to be expected as much as casualties on a battlefield. What is not inevitable is that the more mature members of the community should lead *the little one's* astray. It is a sin deserving the most severe punishment. Leaders must protect and not exploit the vulnerable and easily led.

Keeping the community healthy also involves mutual correction and forgiveness since our sin is not only against God but one another. We are to watch out for the weak and not let the bumps and bruises of close community leave us bitter and separated. The remedy is loving confrontation, hopefully resolved in repentance and full forgiveness. It is this practice, often ignored in our day of individualism and autonomy, that either keeps us unified or tears us apart. And whereas it is understandable that the apostles were daunted by this level of love and mutual care, the answer is not additional faith but actionable faith. When they act and speak together as Jesus taught, big things happen. His people stay healthy.

Finally, we should not expect special praise for doing our duties of leading and serving the community of Jesus. Following him and sharing his care for his people is our reward. In the end, we owe him, not he us.

Summary

Disciples are not naive about the insidious power of sin, in themselves and their colleagues. All are accountable and called to account, but those who deliberately corrupt others—and particularly the vulnerable—are judged ahead of time. It is strenuous work to be an agent of correction and mercy and to humbly receive what you offer others, but what a safe people to live among! No one is allowed to stumble alone. Pastors are not police, but their care of Jesus' people includes confrontation, confession, forgiveness, and healing discipline. It's a duty that must be done, but it earns us no points. Obeying Jesus is enough of a privilege.

Insights

1. That Jesus regularly pauses for instruction in following and leading is instructive.

2. Jesus' friends are to pay special attention to young and vulnerable believers.

3. A holy and happy life in service of Jesus Christ will not lead many astray.

4. Nothing is more healing than a fellowship that loves enough to correct and forgive.

5. When we think we need more faith in order to obey, we are postponing what we already need to do.

6. Jesus bought us, owns us, has authority to dictate our duties and expect joyful obedience.

7. The deepest rewards of following the Lord are all intrinsic, part of the thing itself, not an add-on or bonus.

8. Duty, the idea that I am bound to do what I ought to do, is not neglected by Jesus.

Disciplines

Observation: The spiritual hygiene Jesus provides includes confronting sin.
Action: Ask, "Why are we so hesitant to name what is killing a brother or sister?"
Observation: For Jesus, the greatness of faith is not in itself but where it is placed.
Action: Start using the little bit of faith you have, then watch God stretch you and it!

35. Luke 17:20–37

Question About the End
Genre: An Eschatological Discourse of the Prophet Jesus

At the end time of the world,
he will not descend from heaven obscurely or secretly,
but with godlike glory
and as dwelling in the light which no one can approach.[145]
—CYRIL OF ALEXANDRIA

---

145. Just, *Luke*, 271.

Justification

This is a four part unit arranged as a 4:2 Chiasm (1. vv.20–25, 2. vv.26–30 // 2' vv.31—35, 1' v.37). It opens with a question from the Pharisees about "when the kingdom of God was coming" (v.20a) and a brief answer by Jesus (vv.21b -22). The remainder of Jesus' discourse (vv.22–37) is directed "to the disciples" (v.22), and that qualifies its inclusion in our list of discipleship passages.

Shape

The thought unit is framed by the questions of *When?* (v.20) and *Where?* (v.37), each of which receives an answer from Jesus (vv.20b–21, 37b). In between are two parallel paragraphs (2. vv.26–30 // 2' vv.31–35), the first of which invokes two biblical examples of sudden judgment in the "days of Noah" (vv.26–27) and in the "days of Lot" (vv.28–30), and the second of which invokes two contemporary images of division for people at work in the fields (v.31) and asleep at home (vv.34–45). It is not a time to cling to the old life (v.33) as Lot's wife did in her fatal glance back towards Sodom (v.32). A sudden division is coming, and the teaching of Jesus is the only warning we are given. The outline highlights the four paragraphs with a double center and their answers to the four "W" questions: *When?* (1. vv.20–25), *How?* (vv.26–30), *Who?* (vv.31–35), *Where?* (v.37):

> 1. vv.20–25 The *When* Question Asked and Answered: Without Signs
>> 2. vv.26–30 The *How* Question Answered:
>> Two Genesis Examples
>> 2' vv.31–35 The *Who* Question Answered:
>> Two Examples of Sudden Division
> 1' v.37 The *Where* Question Asked and Answered: Everywhere

Because this unit is a literary hybrid, listing its various genres is helpful:

Question and Answer	vv.20–21, 37
Prophecy	vv.22–25, 26–30, 31–35
Biblical Examples	vv.26–27, 28–30
Discipleship Proverb	v.33
Cryptic Saying/Chreia	v37b

Content

We've heard much from popular teachers, prophets, and prognosticators that we are living in *the last days* and should stay alert for *the signs of the times* using their charts and broadcasts as our guide to readiness. Among some segments it functions as a sort of secret knowledge denied to the less enlightened. It's elitist in all the bad ways and none of the good. A fresh reading of Luke gives us fresh antibodies against such end-time viruses.[146]

When 17:20–37 is read as a whole, it's intent is clear. The kingdom of God, *the new reality,* is already in our midst, and when it emerges full force there will be no preliminary signs, and all such reports are to be resisted (v.23). It will arrive as suddenly as a bolt of lightning as the Son of man appears in an instant, and then it's all over (vv.24–25).

And this is how God operates in continuity of character, as in the Genesis examples of Noah and the flood and Lot and the destruction of Sodom (2a. vv.26–27, 2b. vv.28–30). Life was going on as normal, "They ate, they drank, they married, they were given in marriage" (v.27a). "They ate, they drank, they bought, they sold, they planted, they built (v.28b)." And then suddenly, "the flood came and destroyed them all" (v.27c)," and "fire and sulphur rained from heaven and destroyed them all" (v.29b).

And so will it be, as quick as lightning, as sudden and devastating as the flood and the flames. The two male examples of v.31, one man keeping watch and the other working the fields, and the two female examples of vv.34–35, two sisters in bed and two women milling, means that the division is for all and in all settings at once.

It is only those who have followed Jesus as preferable to gaining their lives by current standards who will survive the vision, and in a flash the world as we have known it is ended and all judgments executed.[147]

And so the question is, Are you ready for such a sudden end, whenever it comes and wherever it reaches? So when will it come? Answer: Suddenly! And where? Answer: Everywhere all at once. It will interrupt the closest of family relations, reach all males and females. For those who are not alert to the availability of the new reality and live life in deliberate ignorance, it means destruction as everything they've known and depended on is suddenly undone and remade by the advent of the risen Jesus as the Son of man.

All else is foolishness, so do not listen to the false prophets and those who claim to have discovered secrets in the Bible not available to others. The time to get ready is Now! Disciples remain alert to the hints of the *new reality* in our midst in order to cooperate and further its agendas even now behind enemy lines. They have made a decision that what is found in Jesus is of more worth and value than all of the world's schemes for making life work to our advantage, and in the loss they have found a new treasure, and one day a whole new world.

If the elements of 17:20–37 are taken out of their literary order and placed in a chronological order, it helps us grasp the larger time line:

146. On the error of so called rapture theology and it's appeal in the United States, see Rossing, *The Rapture Exposed*; Hill, *In God's Time*, 130–69, 199–209; Efird, *End-Times*, 17–37, 38–52; Koester, *Revelation and the End of All Things*, 19–25; Witherington, *Revelation and The End Times*, 76–82; Brown and Keener, *Not Afraid of the Antichrist*; Howard-Brook and Gwyther, *Unveiling Empire*, 3–19. For a recent historical treatment, see Akenson, *Exporting the Rapture*.

147. For a summary of teaching on the end, see Oden, *Classic Christianity*, 767–856.

The Big Story and Time Line of Luke 17:20–37

Chronological Ordering	Corresponding Reference In 17:20–37
1. Jesus' Ministry	"the days of the Son of man" (vv. 22, 26)
2. Dead/Risen/Ascended	"But first he must suffer many things and be rejected by this generation" (v.25b)
3. Interim Period	"The days are coming when you will desire" (v.22b)
4. Son of Man's Revelation	"so will the Son of man be in his day" (v.24b) "so it will be on the day when the Son of man is revealed" (v.30)
5. Judgment	"and destroyed them all" (vv.27c, 29b), "will lose it" (v.33b), "left" (vv.34b, 35b)
6. New Age/World	"when the kingdom of God was coming" (vv.20a, 21b), "where the body is, there the eagles will be gathered together" (v.37a).

Then

It is significant that Jesus and his Pharisaic questioners had something in common, and that is the conviction that the rule of Yahweh, the Lord God, was ultimate, was future in its fullness, and would change Israel forever. So they asked him, "When?" to which he gave a two part answer, which we may summarize as *now hidden* (v.21b) *and later revealed all at once* (vv.22–25). We follow Jesus with an eye to the end while we follow its hints and opportunities in the present (v.21b).

To seculars who believe it all ends in a cold whimper of entropy, and to Eastern mystics who see life as a repeated circle, the disciple says:

> Yes, history as we have known it as the history of sin and death and evil has an end, but that end is also a new opening into *the new reality*, and both history and its climax are a time line. There are hints of truth in your philosophies and world views, but when you pass them through the *Jesus lens* you see how partial they are. The one who spoke of the end experienced it after his death in a glorious bodily resurrection that confirmed his every word as a word from God, so he is to be listened to before and beyond all others.

So what do disciples do? We study the words of Jesus on the end with all the tools available; we stand with the church's great hope and minimalist teaching in the Great Creeds that there is an end and that Jesus is bringing down an everlasting kingdom with him upon his sudden arrival. Therefore, we resist all detailed timetables and specific schedules as none of our business and a positive threat to our mission. We delight in all the great and small previews of the *new reality* we find in our midst; we look at every person as needing love in the present and the truth of the two futures now available to them.

Further, we do not live with the illusion that all our family will end up on the right side of history; we know that only God has the wisdom to make right judgments about the destiny of individuals and are happy to leave it there. And, as the Nicene Creeds ends in hope, we confess, "We look for the resurrection of the dead and the life of the world to come." Until then, we do all our feasting and marrying, our commerce and construction projects in light of what's ahead, knowing that all that was good from this life will go with us into the next.

But for those who habitually resisted the overtures that came from God in all the good things of life, and even in moments of extraordinary illumination, there is no future and no hope. The final measure of a human being, one unable to erase the indelible image in the self, though it may be defaced in great variety, is a question: Did I recognize and respond to the one who created me and who nudged me all my days to turn around and face the love that made me? And if not, why not? The grace of the Triune God is towards every person every day with a single call, "Return to me for life."

Now

Rescue is what God does for us; God saves us for himself and the new heaven and earth, which is the old earth and heavens recast in the form of Jesus' resurrection applied to the entire cosmos, meaning continuity of identity and discontinuity of form.

But that is not the same as the *escapism* that characterizes so much of American piety with its embrace of *rapture theology,* which I capsulize as *the go-up before the blow-up* or perhaps *the lift off before the meltdown.*[148]

In other words, since we are a special and chosen nation, God loves American Christians, and any who wish to join us, too much for us to pass through the great suffering, and so we get a free pass, an elevator to heaven and grand stand seats on the unfolding spectacle of suffering below.

That this erroneous reading of Scripture has found such purchase and popularity in our recent history says much about our inflated self image and sense of entitlement, even from God. It is our grand illusion, and so whatever may come, say the plague of Covid-19 or worse, we are not spared or protected or insulated in ways superior to others. Just as vulnerable, just as fragile, just as mortal.

Faithful disciples may love land and nation, but must do so critically, not buying into national myths, common idolatries, and indulgent speculations. We are not the last, best hope of humankind, and the turning point of history was not July fourth but Good Friday. And when the kingdom of the Holy Trinity arrives, it will not be with a long chain of prior warnings beyond what all Christians have always observed.

No two minute warning will be sounded, but an abrupt arrival it will be, between blinks and with complete glory and utter devastation in its wake. And with it the great

148. For a recent critique, Brown and Keener, *Not Afraid of the Antichrist.* For a digest of classic teaching on last things, see Ward, *What the Bible Really Teaches,* 156–84.

and final separation to vindicate Jesus before the whole creation and preserve all the image bearers who responded to his graces with trust and hope. This is what we anticipate when we confess in the Apostles' Creed, "from thence he shall come to judge the living and the dead," to which the the Nicene Creeds adds, "and his kingdom will have no end." The future is not a democracy of voters but a kingdom of followers and worshipers. We are headed towards new theocracy.

Summary

Disciples live in the interim between the *already* of Jesus and the *not yet* of the coming kingdom, and so it's always been. Our stance is to *stay ready* not *get ready*. When Jesus shows up, it will be all at once and everywhere at the same time. Life goes on and then suddenly stops as the great division is enacted. The *When* is suddenly, the *How* is disastrously, the *Who* is everyone, and the *Where* is everywhere. Don't be distracted. Love God with all your capacities now and your neighbor as yourself now.

Insights

1. Time is linear; the world as it is has an expiration date; only God knows when.

2. If you have a heart to see, the signs of the coming new reality are already among us.

3. If we allow the pressures and demands of normal living to consume us and exhaust our attention, we will forget God and miss out.

4. The division that is ahead will slice all the way down into the most intimate of family relationships.

5. If I lose my life in and for Jesus and his mission now, then the kingdom will be all I longed for and more!

Disciplines

Observation: History as we've known it will end between blinks in a flash of light.
Action: The only way to get ready is to stay ready, so keep your eyes on the prize!
Observation: Jesus warned that there will be prognosticators who deceive the naive.
Action: Resist all attempts to control the church with secret, elite knowledge.

36. Luke 18:1–8

Do Not Quit Praying
Blended Genre: A Parable on Prayer Plus Exhortations to Pray

The present parable assures us God will bend his ear

to those who offer him their prayers,

not carelessly or negligently but with earnestness and constancy.[149]

—CYRIL OF ALEXANDRIA

Justification

This unit is included with 17:20–37 as a disciple unit because it continues the previous audience with an introductory bridge phrase, "And he told *them* a parable, to the effect that they ought always to pray and not lose heart" (18:1). Jesus here speaks to disciples.[150]

Shape

This four-paragraph thought unit is a 4:2 chiasm bounded by two exhortations to faithfulness, the first a Lukan summary (1. v.1) and the second a question of Jesus (1' v.8b). In between are a parable of the widow's vindication (2. vv.2–5) and an explicit application to the disciples in the form of a double question (2' v.6–7b, c) and answer (v.8). The Greek word translated *vindicate* (*edikeso*) is used repeatedly in the parable and its application (vv.3c, 5b, 7a, 8). God will do the right and righteous and good and faithful thing, not because we nag him as the widow does the judge but because we are his beloved, his chosen, the ones who have trusted him in constant prayer, the ones straining towards the appearance of the Son of man. A Father listens to his children; how much more this God!

Since seeing the literary structure gives us a kind of map for reading the text and understanding its parts, I offer the following:

    1. v.1 Introduction: An Exhortation to Persistence in Prayer

       2. vv.2–5 Parable: The Unrighteous Judge and the Persistent Widow

       2' vv.6–8 The Parable Translated: God and the Vindication of the Elect

    1' v.8a Conclusion: An Exhortation To Faith as a Question

Content

It is easy to misread the parable as an exhortation to nag a reluctant God into answering. But the logic of the parable is the reverse of this common misreading because if even a wicked judge can be cajoled to give a right verdict to a persistent and powerless wisdom, *how much more* can we expect a right response from the God whose

---

149. Just, *Luke*, 276.

150. For analysis, see Through Peasant Eyes, 127–41; Snodgrass, *Stories With Intent*, 449–62; Hultgren, *The Parables Of Jesus*, 252–62.

character is polar opposite to the judge. God is not corrupt, not bribable, not indebted to any but receptive to all who cry out. "And so," says Jesus, "Shall not this God do right for his children?" the answer to which is a resounding *Yes*.

Even more, God is patient with those, who like the wicked judge, sin through the misuse of power against the poor, but that patience has an end if there is no repentance, and that end is the sudden coming of the Son of man, who when he arrives will delight in the prayers offered and show how they were woven into the larger purposes of divine providence. God uses our prayers in the moment by moment shaping of history.

Then

Luke is *the prayer gospel*, and in it we have the prayer of Jesus after his baptism, his regular withdrawals for prayer, the prayer he gave his disciples, this parable and exhortation on prayer, and his prayer in Gethsemane.[151]

We intuitively know human relationships are kept alive through contact and communication, and that analogy fits our relationship with God the Father, who through Jesus reveals the divine love at ground level and by his Spirit who sets up a communications link within. When life is all its complexity is not sustained and illumined by an ongoing conversation with the Father, through the Son, and in the Spirit, something is amiss. Jesus lived in and out of this communion, and to follow him means an end to isolated, independent living, and unaided striving. Disciples follow, and in the following we learn the utter availability of a God with ears to hear and hands to act.

Now

"Our Father, who art in heaven . . ." And if that's all you can say, you've already made a good beginning in imitating Jesus, which is your primary job as one of his apprentices and agents. Prayer is primary research and a laboratory of learning.[152] It is personal, vulnerable, longing, and at its best highly and deliberately transparent about our fears and desires. It is life laid out before the God who already knows, yet welcomes our partial understanding of our own circumstances.

Prayer is a place to get clear, to ponder, to discuss, to listen, to reflect, to form intentions and wait upon the subtle movements and illuminations of the Holy Spirit. It can be long or short, working with a written or memorized script, a spontaneous outpouring, in the vernacular or in tongues, in shouts or silence, in tears or joy or boredom or annoyance, eloquent or not so, and still God hears and welcomes your

151. For a listing of prayer passage in Luke, see Just, "The Gospel of Luke and the Acts of the Apostles," 13–14.

152. On prayer see Harrington, *Jesus and Prayer*; Koenig, *Recovering New Testament Prayer*; Foster, *Prayer*.

reaching up in faith, even if it's little and riddled with doubt. And then one day, when it's all made clear, you'll see that every prayer, small and large, petty and important, was heard and woven into the goodness of the divine purpose with results you could not comprehend until the end. You will nod and say, "Yes, Jesus was right when he told us not to quit. Just look at what he did with my fumbles and mumbles!"

So how do disciples survive and thrive in the interim till the kingdom comes in a flash? Through the honest and intimacy with God that is prayer. Keep praying because God keeps listening and weaving divine responses into the unfolding equation. Keep praying because you need God's constant resourcing. "Keep praying because I (Jesus) said so. Turn every situation and every challenge and every new opening into an upward glance and heartfelt plea, then keep your eyes open for my responses."

Prayer is our communication link from field operations to the operations' control center. Followers of Jesus have the Father's ear and the Spirit's hand nearby, so look to prayer first and not last, as a steering wheel and not a spare tire in case of emergencies.

What is prayer? It is the practice of a life-long conversation with the one and living God, who comes with a human face in Jesus, and whose holy and energizing Spirit is near us always. In a world of injustice, pain, and evil, prayer includes tears, lament, complaint, petition, thanksgiving, anger, and yearning to a God who hears, acts, and will act.

It is Luke who especially highlights the prayers and prayer practices of Jesus, as well as his regular teachings on the matter. Jesus lives in conscious dependence on the Father and the Spirit for all he is and does. Prayer is the practice of radical dependence on the faithfulness of God, a relationship that—from our side—is stressed when we are put under pressure from circumstances and also from God's lack of immediate relief. This is the school of fortitude and persistence that develops the deeper realms of trust. As the spiritual moans, "Keep your eyes on the prize, hold on."

Just as the kingdom has preliminary signs of a coming fulfillment, so with prayer. God is the ruler of history as a whole and of our lives within that larger frame. The kingdom is coming. Jesus will be vindicated, and we will share in the benefits.

To pray is to stay in the relationship and to refuse to abandon it, and here the pushy widow is our unforgettable model. But, to limit the reaches of allegory, God is not the unjust judge, and we are not the pushy widow. The argument of Luke is a double negative comparison and a *how much more* argument. If her with him, then how much more us before our Father?

Summary

Disciples keep the prayer line open and operating, especially when courage fades and fatigue creeps in. "Just don't quit!" is Jesus' exhortation. God is listening, hears your words, knows your feelings, delights in your trust, and will act. The question for discussion is not God's faithfulness but ours.

Insights

1. Prayer is an invitation, an art, a discipline, a listening post, a launching pad.

2. Jesus engaged the lives and imaginations of his hearers with outrageous stories.

3. At the moment after our demise, or when the final curtain falls on the last performance, there is Jesus.

4. The kingdom is the place where justice—making things right, kisses love—making things warm.

5. Jesus lived what he taught; his prayer to remove the cup was denied. Instead, he was raised bodily from the dead.

6. When the kingdom arrives suddenly, there is no longer the chance to repent, thus God's patience with the wicked in the here and now only.

Disciplines

Observation: Prayer is an open-ended dialog with God with nothing off limits.
Action: Never quit turning to God in tears, in laughter, in confusion, in petition.
Observation: When we practice the trust of faith, the fruit is faithfulness.
Action: Aim at steadiness in all things, paying attention to the details of service.

37. Luke 18:15–17

Only Children Get a Ticket
Genre: A Disciple Correction Story

Unconscious of spite and fraud,
we must live in a simple and innocent manner,
practicing gentleness and a priceless humility
and readily avoiding wrath and spitefulness.
These qualities are found in those who are still babies.[153]
—CYRIL OF ALEXANDRIA

Justification

As a *Disciple Correction Story*, this is obviously a disciple passage.

153. Just, *Luke*, 281.

Shape

This unit is one of an ongoing series of *Disciple Correction Stories* and displays the expectations of the genre in a simple form:

1. Setting and

2. Incident (v.15a)

3. Misunderstanding of disciples (v.15b)

4. New Teaching and Correction by Jesus (v.16)

5. Resolution, in this case a generalized principle for all (v.17)

Catchwords that unify the presentation are *infants/children/child* (vv.15a, 16b, 17b) and *the kingdom of God* (vv.16c, 17b). Note that two actions (v.15a-b) are followed by two speeches of Jesus (vv.16, 17). The assumption of such stories is that the disciples' world view and social habits are out of sync with Jesus' new reality. Part of his induction of his friends into the new world is repeated, sharp, and immediate correction. It stings to follow Jesus!

The text has four parts (a, b // b', a') with a double center (a 4:2 chiasm). Two actions (vv.15a, b) are followed by two speeches of Jesus (vv.16, 17). The concentric pattern is:

    a. v.15a Action 1: Infants Welcomed and Blessed by Jesus

      b. v.15b Action 2: Disciples Rebuke the Parents

      b' v.16 Speech 1: Jesus Corrects the Disciples, Double Command + Reason

    a' v.17 Speech 2: Children as the Model for Receiving the Kingdom[154]

Content

In a world of only primitive medical care, where infant and child mortality was high,[155] and where Jesus had a growing reputation as a healer and conveyer of God's blessing, it's understandable why parents sought his touch upon their little ones, and on this occasion there were many, "And they were bringing even infants to him, that he might touch them." Natural affection for their children is what drives them to him and not others, and where such natural affection is lacking, children are all the more vulnerable.

What is interesting is the response of the disciples to the pressure of the parents, "Now when the disciples saw it, they *rebuked them* (a strong term used earlier in Jesus' exorcisms) repeatedly."

---

154. For exegetical and cultural insights, see Carroll, "What Then Will This Child Become? 177–94; Allen, *For Theirs Is the Kingdom*, 75–122; Francis, "Children and Childhood in the New Testament," 65–85; McKnight, *It Takes a Church to Baptize*, 63–86.

155. Our best estimates are that thirty percent died in childhood and that sixty percent did not make it to adulthood.

The disciples see themselves as intermediaries, as gatekeeper to Jesus' presence, and since children had low status in ancient culture, he had more important things to do. It was a worldview and cultural practice that both the disciples and the parents lived in and assumed when dealing with important people of high status who were considered to be patrons, and that is surely who Jesus had become by this time. If there were others of higher social status than the children in the crowd, then let them come first.

It's how the world worked, but not in *the new reality* Jesus represents where those of low status are called to the center and honored by time and attention, while those of higher status stand and watch with some confusion, "What is this strange man doing? Doesn't he know who I am?" And it was, as we say, a *teachable moment*, but then so was every engagement with Jesus.

In contrast to the blunt language of the disciples to the parents, Jesus calls his associates to himself and issues two commands to reverse their practice, "Let the children come to me and stop putting roadblocks in their way. I am open access not controlled access, and you are not my handlers and brokers," then a supporting reason, "for to such as these belongs the kingdom of God."

These children have as much need of *the new reality* as the rest of the world. And to cap it off, and with a solemn introduction, "Truly, I say to you," Jesus make the dependence and vulnerability and trust of children the standard for the entry of anyone into *the new reality*. It's not about status but about need and trust.

Then

Neither status nor power nor learning nor piety nor supposed moral achievement nor anything that commends us gives us entry into *the new reality* of the kingdom of the Father that Jesus displays in the Spirit's power. What commends us is the indelible divine image impressed upon our person and our need for mercy and forgiveness. We have immense worth, a grave and systemic moral disease, an appetite for evil, habits that corrode character, and cannot cure ourselves. We are utterly dependent on God for what we most need— healed relationship with our Maker, and here infants are a better example than adults since their powerlessness is obvious, which is precisely why Jesus contradicts social customs so completely in this focal instance. It is not just the children that are in focus, but every person present that day, and especially the ones in training with Jesus. We all come to God weak and needy.

It was not their supposed innocence that commended the children to Jesus, a romantic notion we moderns inherited from Rousseau.[156] Jesus was not naive about the fallen condition of any who came to him or were handed to him, even the smallest. He

---

156. On the modern notion that the self arrives natural and innocent as *a noble savage* with a *tabula rasa* (a blank slate) and is only then corrupted and oppressed by a distorted culture and society, see Trueman, *The Rise and Triumph of the Modern Self*, 105–28.

was the only one without sin, and while little ones are not yet objectively guilty of transgression, they have the disease and will soon enough evince all the common symptoms.

It is a good thing that the church's non-modern teaching on the universality and power of sin's infection is included in our United Methodist Articles of Religion, Article VI: Of Original or Birth Sin:

> Original sin standeth not in the following of Adam (as the Pelagians do vainly talk), but it is the corruption of the nature of every man, that naturally is engendered of the offspring of Adam, whereby man is very far gone from original righteousness, and of his own nature inclined to evil, and that continually.[157]

So how does a child receive a gift? Most often with surprise, delight, and wonder. And not by a self-administered moral calculus that they deserve it. To enter the new reality at any age or stage is a gift of and from God's Triune person. The One who made us and knows us best offers us a healed relationship, a new life from the inside out that will carry us into the new heavens and the new earth at the end of the age.

Luke's story of the pre-natal interactions of John and Jesus with the Holy Spirit and with one another (1:39–56) indicates that the Triune God has full access to all human beings across the whole of natural life—from conception to natural death—and into the two stages yet to come: 1) heaven after death for the faithful, and 2) at the end of the age the kingdom's descent to transform the cosmos, including the re-clothing of the saved in resurrection bodies like that of Jesus.

Following Jesus as his disciples always has, not a childish, but a child-like quality, a freshness and wonder that marvels in God's wisdom and goodness. It is grace enabled and trust activated, so what will we do with the gift of Jesus Christ and all the gifts that come with him? Is it too good to be true, or are we so jaded that mistrust seems preferable?

Now

Every culture has its status hierarchies, and every church has an intuitive sense for *our kind of people*. The problem with both systems—and particularly the church—is that it leaves large numbers at the bottom, and so what Jesus does in this unit is give primary attention to the least powerful ones of all, infants and small children. Jesus' friends thought it was not worthy of his time to invest in such, but he surprised them again with his example and corrections.

So in a world that pressures aspirants to be upwardly mobile and to advance their cause by associating with those above them on one of the scales of status, the gravity of Jesus is to be downwardly mobile, to associate with those who cannot enhance our resume, not in the old sense of fashionable *slumming* but with the expectation of meeting Jesus there and being graced by the lives of those invisible people for whom

157. *Discipline 2016*, 67.

the Lord has special care. For many it happens on their first mission trip, the purpose of which is not to bring aid or build something—though these are necessary—but to have your heart broken and your priorities turned upside down, to be de-toxed from the cultural calculations of *winners and losers*.

Yes, Jesus died for *my kind of people*, since he came for all. But also for every other grouping of *our kind of people*, whatever their location on the social map. So to change the way you observe the world, let the Lord take you to some of the places you avoid, and others you've never seen, that you may walk away in tears, touched by the new friends and the new problems you never considered.

Summary

Disciples have their blind spots and prejudices regularly exposed by Jesus, and the pain, no doubt, fixes it deep in the memory. In a culture where time with children enhanced no one's honor or status, Jesus took time for the smallest and blessed them with his touch. There is no age or intellectual requirement to enter *the new reality*, and since trust is the currency of the kingdom, children are the models for us all.

Insights

1. When we're too important or too distracted to pay attention to the neglected, we've already missed Jesus.

2. The most important, impressive, accomplished people you meet come to Jesus in utter dependence, just like everyone else.

3. When the church, like the disciples, gets in the way of people coming to Jesus, we need correction!

4. Jesus is fully able to relate to people along the whole development spectrum, from womb to tomb.

Disciplines

Observation: Jesus was a magnet for parents and their little ones.
Action: Find a way to stay connected to children, especially if you don't have any.
Observation: The *new reality* is accessible to every human being; Jesus made it so.
Action: Pray with and for children, the vulnerable, the elderly, the broken.

38. Luke 18:18–30

One Who Said *No,* Those Who Said *Yes*

Genre: An Expanded Rejected Call Story

It is one thing not to wish to hoard up what one does not have.
It is another thing to scatter what has been accumulated.
The former is like refusing food; the latter, like cutting off a limb.[158]
—AUGUSTINE

Justification

That this unit is a *Rejected Call Story* qualifies it as a disciple passage.

Shape

Two references to *follow me* (v.22e) // *followed you* (v.28b) frame the unit, and Peter who is already a disciple speaks in v.28. A second inclusion is *eternal life* (v.18b // v.30), with its synonym *the kingdom of God* (vv.24b, 25b, 29b) as a stitch word.[159] While the unit consists formally of a Rejected Call Story (vv.18–25) and Jesus' further commentary on the same in answer to a question (vv.24–30), it is a single literary unit formed as a 7:1 concentric pattern: seven parts with three sets of frames [a//a', b//b', c//c'] with a single center (d):

    a. vv.18–20 Then and Now: Eternal Life
        b. vv.21–22 Call To Leave All and Follow Jesus
            c. vv.23–25 Impossibility Offered
                d. v.26 Central Question: Who Can Be Saved?
            c' v.27 Impossibility Answered
        b' v.28 Those Who Have Already Left All and Followed Jesus
    a' vv.29–30 Now and Then: Eternal Life

Several comparisons help us understand the function of Luke 18:18–30 within Luke's unfolding story of Jesus the founder and the disciples as his apprentices. The first is that the previous unit (18:15–17) and this one are in some sense a pair:

Links Between Luke 18:15–17, 18–30: A Mutually Interpretive Pair (Short + Long)

---

158. Just, *Luke*, 284.
159. See Sweetland, *Our Journey with Jesus*, 39–41.

The Ends of the Spectrum of Status and Honor: From an Infant to a Rich Man

Item	18:15–17 (The Standard)	18:18–30 (-/+ Examples)
children	*infants, children, child* (vv.15, 16, 17)	*children* (v.29)
kingdom of God	*kingdom of God* (2x, vv.16–17)	*kingdom of God* (3x, vv.24–25, 29)
End, Truly I say to you	*Truly, I say to you* (v.17a)	*Truly, I say to you* (v.29)
Warning	*shall not enter it* (v.17b)	*How hard it is . . .to enter* (v.24)
Issue of entry	*Children do*	*Rich man does not*
Disciples	*when the disciples saw it* (v.15b)	*Peter said, "Lo, we."* (v.28)

Secondly, that Luke 18:18–30 has another twin in Luke 10:25–42, both having the same eight components, including the identical question, "Teacher, what shall I do to inherit eternal life" (18:18 // 10:25a)?[160]

Item	Luke 10:25–42	Luke 18:18–30
Questioner	Legal expert/lawyer	A certain rich man
Hostile Motive	v.25a, "to put Jesus to the test"	No motive mentioned.
Direct Address, and Question	v.25a, "Teacher, what shall I do to inherit eternal life?'	v.18, "Good Teacher, what shall I do to inherit eternal life?"
Counter-Question	v.26, "What stands written in the law? How do you read?'	v.19, "Why do you call me good?"
Reference to Commandments	v.26, "What stands in the law? How do you read?"	v.20, "You know the commandments . . ."
Love God and Neighbor	v.27, "You shall love the Lord your God. . . . And your neighbor as yourself."	v.22 "Sell all . . . and distribute it to the poor (neighbor), and come follow me (God).
Jesus' Response	v.28, "You have answered well; do this and you will live."	v.22, "One thing you still lack . . ."
Parabolic Image	vv.29–37 Parable of Good Samaritan	v.25 Camel and Needle's Eye

The literary form of *A Call Rejected*, like *A Call Accepted* (5:1–11, 27–28), is found in the Greco-Roman philosophical tradition and comes in two basic forms:

1. the summons and response model in which the teacher takes the initiative, and

2. the attraction model where a would-be pupil takes the initiative of approach, and the story before us is the second variety.[161] Two examples of unsuccessful calls from the philosophical tradition are:

Example 1 (*Lives Of The Eminent Philosophers*, 6.36)

1. "Someone wanted to study philosophy under him (attracted to Diogenes the Cynic)

---

160. Adapted from Neale, *Luke*, 175–76.

161. See Dowd, *Mark*, 106.

2. Diogenes gave him a fish to carry (challenge to obedience)

3. and commanded him to follow him (call to follow),

4. But the man threw it away out of shame and departed (failure of obedience)

5. Sometime later Diogenes met him and laughed and said,

   "Our friendship was broken by a first" (failure by a trivial thing).

Example 2[162]

1. "The Cynic Diogenes castigated Alexander the Great for concupiscence in this regard (summons):

2. "If you wish to become good and upright, throw aside the rag (i.e. crown) you have on your head (challenge to obedience)

3. and come to me (call to follow),

4. But you certainly cannot (failure of obedience)

5. for you are held fast by the thighs of Hephaestion" (failure by a trivial thing)

Five Parts Of A Failed Call Story	Luke 18:18–30	Diogenes Laertius, Lives 6.36
1. Person makes request, attraction to a teacher	v.18a	No. 1 above
2. Teacher gives difficult assignment, defies convention as an obedience test	vv.19–20, v.22a-d	No. 2 above
3. Command to follow (enroll as an apprentice)	v.22e	No. 3 above
4. Person departs with negative emotional response.	v.23	No. 4 above
5. Further teaching on the costs/rewards of discipleship.	vv.24–30	No. 5 above

Content

The narrative order is not hard to follow. A man of status asks Jesus the ultimate question, which, when paraphrased, "How shall I be found to be among God's people when the end comes?" To this Jesus responds, first with a challenge in the form of a question, "Why do you call me good?" an answer, "No one is good but One: God," and then with a sample from the second table of the decalogue (v.20). The man's answer is that he has kept these five his whole life, and we have no reason to doubt his evaluation.

But then Jesus the prophet, who knows the man's heart by the Spirit's gift of knowledge, names the man's idol and calls for a great reversal, "One thing you still lack. Sell all you have, and distribute it to the poor, and you will have treasure in heaven; and come, follow me." His former confidence now turns to visible grief. Jesus then makes a penetrating commentary with him as Exhibit A, "How hard it will be

162.. Edwards, *Mark*, 314, n. 37).

for those who have riches to enter the kingdom of God," followed by a proverb of impossibility featuring a large camel and a needle's eye. We do not know how the man responded; it's left open ended, but it likely was negative. His security and overly-confident religious image meant too much.

The Gospels are clear that Jesus did not get all that he asked for. In this case a rich man rejected his call, and Judas—who at first accepted—later opted out under Satan's inducements and his own motives.

Jesus' invitation to a new life now and later does not undermine freedom and self-determination or remove the lures of sin and evil, self and social pressures. It's an invitation to a rigorous process of exposure and transformation, not a religious quick fix, and it requires both risk/faith and perseverance/fidelity, both of which are enabled since grace and promise always precede and undergird obedience and continuance. Jesus upholds the human freedom to say No and cling to other more-immediate options. Grace postponed is grace rejected, at least for the moment, and is not without consequences. A hardened heart is much less responsive to the divine knock.

It is in v.26 that we find that Jesus' conversation with the rich man was not in private, and that is because the disciples immediately ask the same basic question as v.18b, "Then who can be saved?" to which Jesus responds that is it not a human possibility but only with God from the beginning to the end, "What is impossible with men is possible with God." Salvation— the long process of being remade by God—is God's work, and God's desire is willing human participants, which is why God upholds such freedom, even if with each rejection the human person is in some way hardened and diminished.

Then Peter, as spokesman no doubt, reminds Jesus that they have obeyed, "Lo, we have left our own things and followed you." And Jesus responds with a most-solemn reminder that he too is keeping his promises, both now, "Truly, I say to you, there is not man who has left wife or brothers or parents or children, for the sake of the *the new reality,* who will not receive more in this time," and later, "and in the age to come, eternal life" (vv.29–30). So to the initial question, "Good Teacher, what shall I do to inherit eternal life?" the answer is, "Follow Jesus, not letting anything or anyone be more important than him." And that is something God is in from start to finish.

Then

What an incredibly rich passage. Well formed and skillfully told about ultimate matters. *Eternal life* is not, as in the popular imagination, merely life that goes on forever—though that is a part. It is, more literally, *new age life,* meaning a new quality of human life apart from sin, death, and evil in the age to come, so not just quantity unlimited to quality unimagined. And it is a corporate future for the faithful who honor the commands and follow Jesus. All other loyalties—status, wealth, family, religion—are relativized by this central one. Will I follow the one God sent, the one who is God at ground level? Or do I have better options?

Status and money are major obstacles and often very respectable ones, and at the other extreme are the lures of transgressive vice: infidelity, disregard for life, theft, deception, neglect of parents and family. But these leave the person locked up in a small circle of the self and its unruly passions. They do not open up into anything larger and good in the deepest sense of love and appreciation, of wonder and service. But Jesus stretches and dredges and enlarges the self and draws it into his own world, which is good beyond imagination with a taste now to keep us attached to him. A church that makes this trivial is a criminal enterprise.

Now

An idol, a false god, is anything—how apparently innocent or not so—that competes with Jesus Christ for the center of life. We all have them, and they stay in the fight all our days making promises they cannot keep. Our heart, said John Calvin, is an idol factory, meaning that it keeps on producing new and improved models. So do not be surprised that from time to time, and it is never convenient, the Holy Spirit walks through our inner and outer life conducting an idol inventory and pointing out our fresh collection of household gods.[163] I cringe, I argue, I defend, I resent, I bargain, I accuse, but if I am to continue as a disciple, then each must be deposed and destroyed. House-cleaning if the image is a home, weeding if the metaphor is a garden, demolition if the picture is a temple. Part of the love of God is to challenge other loves and to keep challenging us to monitor their right ordering. Not that it is wrong to love other good things—a wife, a child, all the wonders of creation and all its common pleasures—just not to let any of them usurp the center because that is the control center of the human person, the heart where dwell our deepest desires.

As a mortal creature, one who will die and who daily faces the fact of sin and evil, within and without, I still have limited freedom as part of my being stamped in the divine image and supported by prevenient grace. The image is marred, even defaced, but not eliminated. I am bounded and hemmed in by all sorts of constraints and limits, but never in such a way that my inward intentions and outward actions have no force or consequence, and this fundamental experience we name *freedom* or *free will* or *personal responsibility*.

And while God approaches and graces and cajoles and warns and lures and invites and chastens and allows pain and disappointments to flourish, God does not coerce or overpower or bully because this is what God is after, love returned, and so no means that are incompatible with love are deployed. The God who with a Creator's knowledge can envision all futures in which we respond and all alternatives in which we do not. The future really is open because that is what the dignity of freedom entails.

163. For an analysis, see Wright, *Here Are Your Gods.*

It's this way or that with my vote carrying full weight. God counters and counters again and never quits, but also never coerces.

If I persevere in resistance and rejection, then what hope is there if I wish to live in this world or the next apart from the divine presence. And the answer is, "None at all." The observation that Jesus issued honest invitations, as with *a certain ruler*, and accepted his rejection is an affirmation of the above convictions. The gate of the will as the citadel of the self is opened from the inside, and when the one who made us, who knows us best and loves us most, comes knocking, it's good to take a risk and turn the latch. All will be changed, but all will be so much more. You will be made whole and hopeful along the way to eternal life and the serious joys of a resurrection body like that of the risen Jesus.

As a spiritual discipline and a check against the accumulation of idols, consider an *examination of conscience* using either the Ten Commandments or The Blessings and Cursings of Luke 6:20–26. Hang them as a plumb line in your soul and ask the Holy Spirit to lead you in an inventory. It can be quite enlightening.[164]

Summary

Disciples are not surprised when anyone refuses Jesus' invitation because they know that freedom is always part of the equation. Grace woos; it does not compel or coerce because Jesus is after trust, not merely compliance. Being a Jesus-follower is not a capstone to an otherwise impressive moral resume. It demands surrender and will expose whatever internal blockages are near and dear, in this case wealth and all it affords, which for many was taken as a sign of divine favor, but not with Jesus. And to those who leave one life for another, the promises are enormous, something only God can guarantee.

Insights

1. How does it change your reading to know that the rich ruler was present for the incident with the children?

2. Jesus not only answered the questions of seekers, he questioned their basic assumptions as well.

3. Religious conformity rarely exposes the deep idols we cherish. That requires personal revelation.

4. It is the good things in life that most often compete for a radical attachment of Jesus at the center of loyalty.

---

164. The following are helpful for thinking through the issues of discipleship to Jesus, the law, and financial stewardship: Hellerman, "Wealth and Sacrifice in Early Christianity;" Fuller, "The Decalogue in the New Testament;" Witherington, *Jesus and Money*, 153–64; Bailey, *Through Peasant Eyes*, 157–70.

5. The coming new reality, already in our midst, has multiple dimensions: kingdom, eternal life, saved.

Disciplines

Observation: In the presence of Jesus all our internal resistance is exposed.
Action: Ask, "What guarantees and comforts stand between me and obedience?"
Observation: Jesus invites men and women to follow him into riches untold.
Action: Do a cost/benefit analysis: what have I lost and gained with Jesus Christ?

39. Luke 18:31–34

Jesus Again Announces His Mysterious Future
Genre: A Prophetic Oracle of Jesus

To prepare the disciples' minds,

the Savior of all tells them that he will suffer the passion on the cross

and death in the flesh as soon as he has gone up to Jerusalem.

He added that he would also rise wiping out the pain

and obliterating the shame of the passion by the greatness of the miracle.[165]
—Cyril of Alexandria

Justification

That this is a disciple passage is clear from the opening line, "Now taking the Twelve
aside, he said to them," (v.31a). Some instruction is for this group only, and this is one
of those times.

Shape

Our brief paragraph falls into two sections (a. vv.31–33, b. vv.34), each with three
parts that are not in parallel. In the first section, Jesus pulls them aside (1. v.31a),
announces that a prophecy is coming (2. v.31b-c), then gives the details in three lines
of downward movement (3. vv.32a–33a) and one of utter vindication (v.33b). This is
followed in the second section by three lines in synonymous parallelism for repeated
effect (1. vv.34a, 2. v.34b, 3. v.34c), and these three lines together are the disciples'
response to Jesus' unsettling announcement of his future.

165. Just, *Luke*, 286.

They do not get it three times in a row! They cannot get it and will not for the time being. It's beyond them, but they will soon enough observe it, and it will change them forever, because now all the scattered pieces will come together by the actions of a divine hand, and they will understand there was no other way and no easier way and no more transparent way to accomplish the divine mission of opening the heart of God in a world of sin, evil, and death than the voluntary self-giving of Jesus over to death. An outline is:

    a. vv.31–33 Jesus the Prophet's Fourth Passion Prediction (Most Detailed Yet)

        1. v.31a Cue to Direct Discourse

            2. v.31b-c Oracle of Prophetic Fulfillment in Jerusalem

                3. vv.32–33 Reason/*gar*, Four Predictions, Seven Future Verbs

    b. v.34 The Denseness of the Disciples in Active/Passive Voice, 3 *Kai*

        1. v.34a And They Understand Nothing

            2. v.34b And The Saying Was Hidden

                3. v.34c And They Do Not Grasp What Was Said

Luke has taken great care in the composition of v.34. Three synonymous lines, and each line in three parts:

    1) A link word (Gk. *Kai*/*And*),

    2) a reference back to Jesus' prophetic word:
    none of these things . . . this saying . . . what was said,

    3) a statement of incomprehension:
    did they understand . . . was hidden from them . . . they did not grasp.

The first and last of the three (vv.34a, c) are in the active voice indicating personal agency: *none of these things did they understand . . . they did not grasp what was said.* But the middle member (v.34b) is in passive voice indicating divine action: *this saying was hidden from them* (by God). And in the third line there is a reverse. In the first two the order is a reference to prophecy + reaction (vv.34a, b), but in the third it is reversed to a reaction + reference to prophecy which gives an end stress to *what was said.* In the end they don't get it because God has not yet revealed it.

Content

Each of the events Jesus forecasts is observable and has happened to others in the same city since crucifixion was common, but not until all comes to pass with Jesus will they put the pieces together as the light dawns. What happens here was common, but this one to whom it happens in this case is uncommon, one of a kind, unique in his person and work, his identity and mission. He is God the Son in flesh.

Jesus' words are dark, mysterious, threatening, and utterly necessary. Jesus has integrity, and his promises come true. He is utterly reliable, and even when horrifying, his words are true. It appears for a moment that others (*the Gentiles*) have seized control, but Jesus' prophetic word ahead of events to his inside circle demonstrates that the deeper story is that the divine will remains and will over-rule the worst that human beings can accomplish, be they Jewish or Pagan.

After all, what do we do through our institutions? We ignore Jesus, and when he will not be ignored, we torture and kill him in the cruelest manner possible as a warning to all others who will not go along with current arrangements. This is who we are and what we are capable of through the institutions of government and faith. This is the sneering face of sin and evil in our corporate life. We would rather run temple and crown on our terms and for our benefit than surrender life to Jesus and his right to rule. And that is precisely what his resurrection means. He is utterly vindicated by the highest authority, and his is both the rule that is coming and the one that's already been let loose in the world.

Then

The first disciples have ringside seats—to use a boxing analogy— on the person and events that change history forever. And we understand boxing, its rule and regulations, because they are common enough. But we do not understand all that Jesus is doing because there is nothing common about him; he is one of a kind, unrepeatable, God the Son as Jesus and about to take on the resistance, anger, hatred, rebellion and evil of the whole world and be raised triumphant over it.

As for his closest companions, his pupils, his ambassadors in *the new reality,* there is much mystery and darkness, confusion and incomprehension on the part of the disciples, and never more so than in his Passion Predictions, of which this is the fourth (9:22, 44–45, 17:22, 18:32–34).

As a prophet, Jesus at times knows the secrets of people by divine revelation. He also knows his own end by the same source, and here—for a fourth time—announces it to *the twelve.* But it is so different than the future they imagined, so contrary to all hopes and dreams, it is incomprehensible, beyond understanding, shrouded in the depth of divine purpose until revealed in Jerusalem. Messiahs don't die at the hands of enemies. They rule. But this one does, and it is his ultimate qualification.

Jesus' faith and trust is that he would rather die than be disobedient to the Father. He is marching into the camp of his murderers with eyes wide open. He is about to expose the worst that is in us, the very core of sin and evil, of our rebellion against God and our appetite for all that is perverse and cruel. Jesus voluntarily takes all this history into himself in order to expose it to the light.

This is the combination of church and state that conspire together to murder the only innocent man who ever lived, the one whose word and touch brings life. This is how the world responds when God shows up in person and looks you in the eye, "We must get rid of him." His *new reality* is the undermining of all we know and love. He is God's threat to all current arrangements.

Now

Walking with Jesus, the one who is the light, does not mean that all occurs in the clear light of day. To be joined to him in surrender and trust means we walk through shadows and into the dark with him, and here a pious couplet holds true, "I do not know what the future holds, but I know who holds the future."

The details are hidden because the future is unfolding precisely as we participate in it, and the world has not yet changed, but we have as we walk this maze. Learning that Jesus is trustworthy in the midst of events we'd all rather avoid is part of the path, as we observe in the turning-point text before us. Verse 34 is not a common memory verse, but I recommend it. There is much to know and learn in the school of Jesus which is in session all the time and never ends, even as we sleep and dream and wake again to a new day of lecture and lab, observations and experiments in *the new reality*.

But because of who he is, we are ever participating in divine mysteries and larger issues we cannot yet grasp. And is that OK? If not, and if you prefer a more predictable and secure route, less messy and more to your liking and temperament, try it and see where it leads.

But beware. The general observation is that such a choice will over time make you smaller and more constricted, cramped in your comforts and bigoted in your criticisms, less able to love and with less light to understand both yourself and the world around you. In other words, you will shrink and wither and become much less interesting.

Jesus is God's definition of love available and life abundant, and the price of faith is risky trust in him. Sorry, but there's just no other way to receive what he promises. This is what it looks like. You enroll as his newest disciple and then go through all the same stuff as his first recruits, only this time customized to you and your surroundings two thousand years further down the time line. And here a justly famous quote from C.S. Lewis' *The Four Loves* is worthy reading, and reading aloud!

> To love at all is to be vulnerable. Love anything and your heart will be wrung and possibly broken. If you want to make sure of keeping it intact you must give it to no one, not even an animal. Wrap it carefully round with hobbies and little luxuries; avoid all entanglements. Lock it up safe in the casket or coffin of your selfishness. But in that casket, safe, dark, motionless, airless, it will change. It will not be broken; it will become unbreakable, impenetrable, irredeemable. To love is to be vulnerable.[166]

God has become vulnerable to us in Jesus Christ. He is human, warm, available, supple and breakable, full of surprises, a great friend, and supremely worthy opponent. He is the one through whom light and love and delight shine most clearly, the one who never flinches to show us the painful and ugly truth about ourselves and the battleground we currently inhabit. In his words he calls us to the truth, and in

---

166. www.goodreads.com/quotes/3058-to-love-at-all-is-to-be-vulnerable-love-anything.

his deeds of forgiveness and healing puts the broken pieces of life back together as a preview of *the new reality.*

What about Jesus is not worthy of your trust? And be assured that he will give you a new script for life, a better one, with more drama and challenge and love than you would have ever invented for yourself. The crucified and risen Jesus is alive and available, bringing his influences upon you every day to make his case and issue you an offer, "Follow me, and I will make you . . ." High drama, real suffering, a deepened life of growing in love, and a glorious outcome. This is what it is to be a follower.

Summary

Disciples live amidst mysteries and purposes that are beyond understanding, which is what it means to be restored to a healed relationship with the Father and the Son and the Holy Spirit. We see—but not well, and know—but only a little. It's when we look back that we see and grasp more deeply. All God's work comes to focus in Jesus and especially in his self-surrender to suffering, humiliation, and death with a trust in resurrection. That he announced it, and that it happened as he said, is one more reason to trust him as trustworthy.

Insights

1. To follow is to grow in trust that we are not alone and are indeed being led.
2. The bodily resurrection of Jesus was God's "Yes" to trump the world's brutal "No."
3. There is much we cannot understand because it's not time yet, and we are so dense.

Disciplines

Observation: Being his disciples is an immense privilege. We are led into his light.
Action: Once a week sing the hymn, "On Christ the Solid Rock I Stand."
Observation: There is always much we do not yet understand, so keep trusting.
Action: Learn the grace of regularly admitting, "I don't know yet." It's freedom.

40. Luke 19:11–28

Waiting on Another World
Genre: A Parable of the King's Return

When you hear the Word,
if you act according to those words that you hear and live according to these words,
then you are preparing interest for the Lord.

Each of you can make ten talents out of five.[167]

—ORIGEN

Justification

The *they* of 19:11 is the disciples, and the parable is about their accountability for what Jesus has entrusted to them. It's a teaching for disciples who are about to become leaders in the earliest church, a privilege for which there is high accountability.

Shape

A parable is a comparison of one whole to another in a story that opens up into another reality, often with a surprise or twist; the operations of *the new reality* Jesus proclaimed and enacted. An allegory, however, is a story in which all of the parts have an exterior reference, and the meaning is unlocked when the key is rightly understood in the form of a *this means that* correspondence. The real story is not the surface narrative but the deeper allegorical correspondence. And while allegories and parables are distinguishable genres, there is sometimes overlap, meaning parables can contain allegorical elements and allegories contain parabolic imagery and comparisons.

Thus the thought unit, 19:1–28, is a complex amalgam where Jesus speaks in an indirect manner about events in which he is the key actor, a strategy easily understood since he told it when "he was near to Jerusalem" (v.11b) and political speculation was intense, "because they supposed that the kingdom of God was to appear immediately" (v.11c). It's hard to imagine a more pressurized scene than this one.

For him to say in the barest terms, "I am God's king, and if you do not come under my rule, I will cut you to pieces," would be to invite an immediate crackdown, and so he spoke indirectly of three potential audiences: one composed of faithful followers, one of unfaithful followers, and a third of those who want nothing to do with him or his rule—and all under a common designator: *servant/s* (vv.13a, 15b, 17, 22b).

The story has three parts: 1. v.11, 2. vv.12–27, 1' v.28, thus two short frames (1//1') and a long parable/allegory at the center (vv. 2–17). The frames are marked by inclusions indicating the beginning, "he proceeded to tell a parable" (v.11a) and ending, "And when he had said this" (v.28) of the central story, which falls into two three-part stanzas:

    a. v.12 His Departure and Promised Return

        b. v.13 Stewardship Among His Servants During the Absence

            c. v.14 Resistance to His Reign Among Non-Servants

            "We do not want this man to reign over us."

    a' v.15a His Return with Kingdom Credentials

---

167. Just, *Luke*, 294.

b' vv.15b–27 Accountability, Degrees of Reward & Punishment
c' v.27 Dealing with the Rebellious
"who do not want me to reign over them"

Now the commentators note that this story of Jesus is not without historical and literary precedents, and they are three:

1. The rhetorical/moral *topos* of an evil tyrant;

2. the Common Jewish lore of a servant(s) left in trust during a Master's absence in which the servants' character is revealed (Luke 12:36–46, 19:11–27, Mark 13:34, Matt 25:14–30);

3. a Cultural Type Scene from recent Jewish history having three parts: a. a Jewish royal embassy to Rome for legitimation, b. with vocal opposition, and c. concluding with a slaughter of enemies. Note also how v.14 echoes Gen. 38:7 and v.27 echoes 1 Sam. 15:33, both found only in Luke who highlights the deliberate rejection of "this man's rule *over us*."

What Jesus has done is draw on a rich tradition of the complex relationships of masters and servants in that culture to address his central role as the agent of God's ultimate judgment and to squelch speculation that the arrival of God's kingdom with all its complements is just around the corner. There is an interim between the nobleman's departure and return, and this is a time that reveals character or the lack thereof of those to whom the household is entrusted.

Content

It seems that the nearer Jesus came to Jerusalem, the more intense was the expectation of God's rule coming in power, the same rule Jesus has been exercising over the enemies of disease, demons, and death. If he can defeat our personal enemies, why not our political ones as well? National fantasies were running high and hot, so Jesus crafted a complex story to reframe the timing of events, that the kingdom comes only after an indeterminate interim in which all are tested.

The plot is simple. A nobleman goes away to receive a promotion to king from an Imperial authority and in the interim distributes his wealth evenly, ten minas per servant, with the same command to all, "Trade with these till I come." He expects a return on investment. Then comes the contrary report that the citizens— and not the servants—resist his receiving kingly power and say so quite openly (v.14b), in effect treason. So two dramas are in play, the investing of the servants and the hostility of the citizens; the nobleman has two initial audiences.

Then, upon his return, "having received the kingdom" (v.15a), the accountability of the servants is first and the order is from the most profitable to the least. The first servant multiplies the capital ten times and receives the rulership of ten cities, an incredible promotion, and with it a commendation, "Well done, good servant!" Likewise the second with a five fold return and a like proportion of cities. But the drama comes with the third who slanders the character of his Master and reports that the single mina was buried in fear.

The master counters that if he was as the servant reported— a dishonest, rapacious man, then why not at a minimum give it to the bankers for whatever interest they pay? Not only stupid, this servant is wicked, and so no reward. He's missed out on the gift of trust, which is a great treasure on its own.

The trustworthy keep on receiving, while the slackers lose it all (v.26), because that is the internal logic of *the new reality*. But it is the rebellious who receive a violent death sentence, "bring them here and slay them before me" (v.27b). The long story ends on a gory note of finality. Being a servant in this household is the gift of a great opportunity.

One way to miss out is to misread the character of the Lord and reveal oneself as a reluctant and mentally-divided disciple: weak, fearful and unstable (vv.20–26). And so it will be with some pastors and church leaders on the last day. But far worse to have persisted in rebellion against the only one worthy of ruling the new world, Jesus Christ. Jesus has enemies, then and now, and while they are allowed to persist in their treachery, one day they will be in pieces, dismembered (v.27).

Judgment is assured, and it's not only between the church and the rejecters but within God's people, as Peter noted, "For the time has come for judgment to begin with the household of God; and if it begins with us, what will be the end of those who do not obey the gospel of God" (1 Peter 4:17)? To reject Jesus as God's mirror is to reject the ontology and reality of God's rule, and since it will be universal, there's no place left for me. In the end God takes out the trash.

Then

For those on the inside of discipleship, the two-part story of absence and arrival is not cloudy but transparent. It makes sense because the outline of the same story is the one we retell in the Apostles' and Nicene Creeds of Jesus' current absence and coming return. That we repeat it so often dulls us to the glory and terror of the affirmations.

The Lord is about to leave his household to his apostles and expects them to respond with effort and increase. But in the end some will be found faithful and others not. To be shamed is their punishment, but not death, which is reserved for those who hated and resisted *the-nobleman-become-king*, which is a word picture for Jesus.

Jesus is now absent from us, at least the way he was before in his physical presence. His resurrection, ascension, and session—his being seated at the Father's right hand a co-regent—are indicators of his vindication and installation as Son of God, Messiah, and Son of man with full powers of commendation and condemnation. He will always have those who hate and fear, resent and resist them, then and now and at the end.

Such are doomed, having no place in the world to come, so God gives them what their lives cried out for, which is to be removed from the rule of Jesus, and that means that there is no place for them to go but separation and death. To live in the last days is to live between Jesus' resurrection and his return. It's history's last chapter, and how long it continues does not change the basic structure of the affirmation.

To be a disciple is not risk-free nor a free pass. It requires the best you have to offer every day until your end or the end. And such efforts and exertions are not earning or works. They are what trust and love mean in a world where the stakes are always high. And when we partner with the Lord in any venture as his cooperative friends and approved agents, the risks and rewards are both high. Some have more gifts than others, this being the meaning of one hundred and fifty percent returns of the first two servants. A twelve ounce glass and a six ounce glass can both be filled to overflowing, and happy about it!

Whatever capacity your faithfulness brings from a lifetime of service, you will be filled by love, and the possible gradations of God's intimate knowledge of all of his servants is endless, so customization is no problem.

But for those who did not take the risks that faith calls for and lived with a distorted image of the Lord Jesus, how little will be their capacity, how minuscule their grasp of the energies of grace, how restricted their joy when the Lord reviews their life and works and fills them up. A thimble and tank can both be filled, and if you asked them their status, the replies are the same, "We are full."

What a shame to be preserved but to have changed so little in the process. Loved by God but nearly useless, a foolish but saved servant. But such is the mercy of God towards those with even a shrunken faith and little obedience.

Now

It's been said so well by Charles Wesley that it needs only to be sung to remind us of the magnetic glories and awful realities of the great truth-telling that's ahead. The hymn is *A Charge to Keep I Have*, with the key verse behind its composition being Leviticus 8:36, "Keep the charge of the Lord, that ye die not" (KJV):

A Charge to Keep I Have
Text: Charles Wesley, 1707–1788
Music: Lowell Mason, 1792–1872, Tune: BOYLSTON, Meter: SM

1. A charge to keep I have,
   a God to glorify,
   a never-dying soul to save,
   and fit it for the sky.
2. To serve the present age,

my calling to fulfill;
O may it all my powers engage
to do my Master's will!

3. Arm me with jealous care,
as in thy sight to live,
and oh, thy servant, Lord,
prepare a strict account to give!

4. Help me to watch and pray,
and on thyself rely,
assured, if I my trust betray,
I shall forever die.[168]

With the privileges of discipleship, of being a Jesus' follower in the company of others, accountability goes up. It means we choose to live under his rule in *the new reality* and for him to be our Boss/Leader/Rabbi/Lord/Teacher/Protector/Corrector/ Friend. It means we accept the assignments he offers and the risks they entail. It means continuing engagement and continuing trust based on his proven character and faithfulness, not retreating, letting fear dominate, or making excuses for inaction.

Our Lord wants and enables a return on investment through us, and that means disciple-making in every venture. We grow in our trusting dependence on him at every turn, and in the process we ourselves are changed.

Summary

Disciples live in light of the end but prepare for the long haul. Our daily goal is to live gladly under the benevolent rule of Jesus Christ, to be faithful to the trust he's put in us and fruitful in the labor he's assigned. To use a market metaphor, he's looking for a *return on investment*, which means holy living (loving God) and disciple making (loving people). Stakes are high and risks necessary; it's a genuine drama. Gains of tenfold and fivefold are possible for those who turn trust into action. But woe to one who slanders his patron's character and lives in fear as a failed follower. Why live such a shrunken, shriveled life?

Insights

1. The God of holy love comes to us in Jesus, always offering opportunities for trust, for risk, for accountability.

2. If Jesus has been raised and vindicated, he's the world's ultimate ruler.

---

168. *The United Methodist Hymnal,* 413.

3. If I am a believer in order to be a follower, what does it mean for Jesus to *reign over me* as Friend and Judge?

4. Faithfulness in small things develops character to be faithful over larger matters.

5. The loving honesty of God cuts through his own people as well as the world.

6. The miracle of compounding interest is a banking issue and a kingdom dynamic.

7. If I trust that Jesus trusts me, then I can take prayerful risks with his gifts.

Disciplines

Observation: The pressing issue is not when he returns but what I've been doing.
Action: When you pray "Thy kingdom come," add, "I welcome your rule over me."
Observation: Jesus is an investment banker who expects you to trade for returns.
Action: No day on this trading floor is wasted, a day to pray and love, love and act.

DISCIPLESHIP DURING JESUS' FINAL DAYS IN JERUSALEM (19:28–24:56)

41. Luke 19:28–48

The Tragedy of Missing God
Genre: The Celebratory Welcome of a Dignitary's Arrival (Gk. *Parousia*)

"Untie the donkey and bring it to me."
He began with a manger and finished with a donkey,
in Bethlehem with a manger, in Jerusalem with a donkey.[169]
—EPHRAEM THE SYRIAN

Justification

This thought unit is included because of its mention of *the disciples* (vv.29b, 37b).

Shape

The outline of the passage is a 4:2 chiasm (four parts with a double center):
    1. vv.28–36 Prophetic Action 1: Entering as a Peaceful King
       2. vv.37–40 Rejoicing and Peace: The Stone's Cry Out
       2' vv.41–44 Lament and Peace: The Stone's Torn Down
    1' vv.45–48 Prophetic Action 2: Entering the Temple, Halt the Whole System

169. 10 Just, *Luke*, 297.

This unit is framed by two public prophetic actions of Jesus: 1. vv.28–36 his entering Jerusalem as a peaceful king // 1' vv.45–48 his entering the temple to temporarily halt its operations. At the double center are two paragraphs of rejoicing by the crowds (2. vv.37–40) and lament by Jesus (2' vv.41–44), each of which uses the images of *peace* (v.38b // v.41b) a*nd stones* (v.40b // v.44b).

The progress of Jesus' arrival is marked by three sequential uses of *drawing near* (vv.29a, 37a, 41) which climax in his arrival at the temple, "And he entered the temple" (v.45). Luke has taken care in the composition of this thought unit. The disciples are viewing the actions and words of Jesus as he enacts two public dramas to draw attention to himself and the meanings of *the new reality* as it clashes with, mocks, and exposes the old.

The genre Luke employs is *The Advent of a Pagan King*"[170] and has five of the seven expected parts (brackets [ ] indicate omissions):

1. Status and credentials made clear: "Son of David" in 18:35–43 is assumed here. There is a royal requisition (v.31c), an unridden colt (Zech 9:9, 1 Sam. 6:9), a formal mounting which "set Jesus upon it" (1 Kings 1:33), and the acclamations of disciples (v.38). All are part of the establishment of royal prerogatives.

2. Approach of the dignity in procession, "drew near . . . drawing near . . .drew near . . . entered" (vv.29a, 37a, 41a).

[3.] Met outside city by dignitaries with grand rhetoric. Not present.

4. Escorted into the city by citizens/army with symbols, here in garments, but no palms (symbol of nationalism). Escorted by a "multitude of disciples" (v.37b).

[5.] Speeches of welcome are absent. Note its opposite, the sharp criticism of Pharisees (v.39).

6. Conclusions at the temple, a nationalist stronghold (v.45ff), but with none of the expected sacrifices or blessing of the city, both of which varied from the expectation of the genre mold. Thus Jesus is working from an inherited cultural script and adding his own modifications, many of which have deliberate scriptural echoes.

7. If welcome is lacking or not fitting, a royal figure my take violent actions to defend his status. Jesus instead prophesies the fall of the temple and temporarily stops its operations as an enacted prophetic protest.

This is also a thought unit with an unusual density of Old Testament cross-references and echoes.[171] Luke is advancing his case that God's plans, as echoed in Scripture, are fulfilled and and rightly interpreted.

---

170. On the genre, see Kinman, "Jesus' Royal Entry into Jerusalem," 223–60. On the entry and its meaning, see Wright, *Jesus and the Victory of God*, 414–21.

171. See Appendix 12 "Scriptural Echoes in Luke 19:28–48."

Content

One of the prominent themes of Luke is that Jesus is a prophet who sees what others do not and proves trustworthy. So with the introductory story of vv.28–36 where two commands (vv.30, 31b) are followed by two parallel acts of obedience in reverse order (vv.33, 35) with a statement of verification at the center, "Now those who were sent went away and found it as he has told them" (v.32). For the two who were sent, and who later returned with a testimony, it was another confirmation Jesus is a true prophet, and if confirmed here, then his difficult words in vv. 41–44, 45–46 will also prove true, even if forty years hence.

In the second paragraph (2. vv.37–40) we discover that Jesus has many followers, as demonstrated in "the multitude of the disciples" (v.37b). Beyond the symbolic community of twelve, there were many others, and here they shout Psalm 118:26 because of his mighty deeds. And when the Pharisees call for Jesus, in the strongest language, to *rebuke* his followers, he responded in the language of Habakkuk 2:11 that if he squelches their praise, the stone's will fill the gap. This Jesus will not be controlled or managed. Praise is due him.

There follows in 2' vv.41–44 a prophetic oracle of judgment on the city because they have rejected him and the peace he offers for radical resistance against Rome, who will soon enough lay siege and destroy the city. The path of Jesus was hidden from their eyes (v.41b) and so they missed the opportunity of his visitation (v.44c). Other nationalistic hopes had blinded them.

The thought unit concludes with an even more confrontive prophet action in the temple, where Jesus exposes the misuse of the temple as a place for robbers/bandits/Jewish freedom fighters to take sanctuary instead of a place of seeking God in prayer. His deliberate echoes of Isa 56:7 and Jer 7:9–11, 15 highlight the theme of fulfillment. His actions halt temple operations for a short time and make his message central to all. Their politics is going to destroy the city and its temple, but the leaders of the people, "the chief priests and the scribes and the principle men of the city," would rather kill Jesus than change their dreams (v.47b). But there was an alternative audience of "the people" who welcome his teaching and shielded him from hostile action (v.48).[172]

Then

Jesus is a joy to some and a pain to others; indeed he is the continental divide of the cosmos, and where we stand with him determines our status with the one who sent him. And here we see Jesus at his public and provocative best, riding a colt instead of a war horse as a symbol of his new rule, receiving Messianic praise in the process,

---

172. On the Jewish war, 66–70 AD, see Witherington, *New Testament History,* 333–69. For Josephus' description of the war's horrific end, see Bock and Herrick, *Jesus in Context,* 149.

claiming to know the horrible fate of Jerusalem, and exposing a political takeover of God's house of prayer.

This is the man we are following who embodies God's alternative for every arena of human life. And he goes into Jerusalem acting like a king, commandeering a mount, receiving accolades, and for a moment at least reclaiming the heart of the faith—the temple as his place of teaching *the new reality*. And his disciples, meaning both his core group and the larger circle, observed it all. He was up to something big!

So we are following a Jesus who is as comfortable with street theater as with private instructions and who takes on the biggest institutions of the culture when they veer towards destruction. He sees and knows what we do not, not just from human insight, but by the revelations of the Holy Spirit. He knows what is true and makes it known, therefore the stories about him and the reports of his own speeches are dear to his followers. It is in obeying him within the boundaries of his character and purposes as laid out in the gospels that we discover that he is still telling the truth and calling us to confirm it in risky faith.

So listen and obey. Take your hunches and leadings seriously, check them against the wisdom of your friends if necessary, and begin to take the risks of obedience. It's the only way to build a track record with the same one who guided and empowered Jesus, the Holy Spirit. It's the only way to become a truly dangerous disciple.

Now

If Jesus is indeed alive in his resurrection from the dead, then he is present and universally available to all who seek and follow him. And he, through his alter-ego the Holy Spirit, is active in the life of every human being, offering new life to any who turn and face him in curiosity and wonder. He is not far away, just beyond sight, unless by his own choice he is revealed in a vision, a dream, a voice, a Scripture highlighted, a holy hunch, or in the face and need and voice of another person. His dialects and means are many, but it is always the same one we read about in the four biographies, and one of the main reasons to immerse yourself in them is to gain a profile for the one you will be dealing with all your days.

We serve a living and active Lord, not a dead hero or noble example from the past, but one unutterably alive and ever-near, knowing all about us in every moment and sending us more aid than we can calculate, bending our interests in his direction and aiming to capture us with a love that opens us to *the new reality*, the immediacy of the single kingdom of the Father and the Son and the Holy Spirit.

So Jesus' argument with us and the necessary institutions we shape to order our world (government, religion) is a lover's quarrel and one we must lose. We sit lightly in them and do not expect from them what can only come from God and among God's people. And so when our political preferences are no longer popular, or when our religious institutions crumble, or when disaster comes near, or when we refuse to join the latest version of the utopian dream, we are left with the awareness that *The Near One* is still there, still calling us to follow and obey and discover again his faithful loyalty together.

To be driven to worship and prayer and silence and waiting is a good thing. And when you read, as in this text, about all that the disciples saw and did and wondered about in Jesus' company, you see how little this ride with Jesus is under our control. It's a life of surrender and self-abandonment to another, to the faithful Lord, and our job is to stay with it and hang on. So the next time you hear someone shouting with delight or screaming with terror on a roller coaster, say, "Looks like the disciples to me!" Jesus is good, not safe; following him is messy and unpredictable. Get used to it!

Summary

Disciples are mainly in the business of carrying out assignments, of discovering over and over that Jesus is faithful: he sees what we do not and knows what we do not. And in this new life there are ecstatic moments of celebrating King Jesus and also sad, sobering moments when we see the costs of rejecting him and *the new reality* he brings. He is the dwelling place of God in flesh, and so the temple and its accouterments are now redundant.

Insights for Disciples

1. What Jesus most wants is our obedient trust, especially when things don't make sense.

2. Jesus took the cultural script of *The Welcome of a King* and rewrote it as a deliberate challenge.

3. Jesus requisitioned property as if he were a king, accepted praise as a King. Is he? Of what kind?

4. An indirect argument for Jesus' deity is that he accepted praise as if it was his due.

5. As Prophet, Jesus often knew events before they happened: the colt, Jerusalem's judgment.

6. Am I a follower of the Jesus who comes in peace to make peace?

7. Where do I weep and lament over the resistance of God's people, including myself?

8. To miss God's opportunity is not to stay the same; it is to lose capacity, grow deaf, blind, and stupid.

9. All faiths are subject to internal corruption, and Jesus calls for prayer and attention to his teaching.

Disciplines

Observation: Jesus the prophet and seer has access to information we do not.
Action: Every act of obedience is a declaration that Jesus is trustworthy.
Observation: Jesus accepted divine praise and is the divine dwelling, not the temple.
Action: The worship of Jesus as God the Son is our duty and our delight.

42. Luke 20:45–47, 21:1–4

A Negative and Positive Example Concerning Piety and Money
Genre: Two Pronouncement Stories About Money Joined as a Pair

The "widow" in the Gospel put two coins into the "treasury,"
and this surpassed all the gifts of the rich.
No mercy is worthless before God. No compassion is fruitless.
He has given different resources to human beings,
but he does not ask different affections.[173]
—LEO THE GREAT

Justification

The next two thought units are a doublet on the topic of *disciples and money,* first the negative example of the Scribes—their showmanship and greed (20:45–47), then the positive example of the widow and her sacrificial two copper coins (21:1–4). The use of money is for Luke an indicator of spiritual health or spiritual disease.

Shape

Here we have two Pronouncement Stories or Chreia[174] which consist of a narrative setting (20: 45–47, 21:1–3) and a sharp saying or punch line (20:47b, 21:4). Jesus claims to know the mind of God at the end and who will receive what measure of judgment (v.47b). He also has a new accounting system which measures true value, not just excess (21:4). The universal intent of the two brief paragraphs is signaled by four uses of *all* in such short sequence (20:45, 21:3c, 4a, 4b). The link word *widow/s* also ties the two units together (20:47b, 21:2, 3c). Following Jesus opens your eyes to the faithful and unfaithful use of influence and money, especially as it concerns your own life.[175]

173. Just, *Luke*, 317.

174. The Greek *Chreia* (from the Greek *chreiodes,* "useful") is "a brief reminiscence referring to some person in a pithy form for the purpose of edification. It takes the form of an anecdote that reports either a saying, an edifying action, or both" (rhetoric.byu.edu/Pedagogy/ Progymnasmata/Chreia).

175. On the sharp nature of ancient rhetoric, see Johnson, "The New Testament's Anti-Jewish

The structure of the first unit is a 4:2 chiasm:

a. vv.45–46a Warning to Disciples Regarding Scribes

    b. v.46b No. 1, Show of Outward Piety and Status, "the ones who"

    b' v.47a No. 2, Ruthless Corruption and Fraudulent Prayer, "the ones who"

a' v.47b Reason for Warning: Greater Condemnation by God

The outline of the second unit is a 3:1 chiasm:

a. vv.1–2 The Rich and a Widow Giving at the Temple

    b. v.3 Jesus' Pronouncement on the Scene

a' v. 4 Reason/*For*, Evaluation of the Gifts of the Rich and the Widow

Content

The double public audience of 20:45 includes *all the people* and *the disciples,* and here Jesus issues a public warning about what he considered a dangerous and corrupted body of opinion within Judaism, what we would consider to be influencers: the Scribes who were the legal and interpretive scholars in league with the Pharisees. Jesus told all his listeners to be wary of them. *Be aware! Beware the Scribes.*

Then, as the first of his evidences, he chronicled four behaviors that they *liked* and loved: 1) distinctive clothing, 2) special public greetings, 3) seats of honor at worship, and 4) the prime seats at feasts. Nothing wrong with any of these in the right place and on certain occasions, but to love them and feed on them and seek them and need them as religious leaders is to play the honor game in the extreme.

The Scribes sought honor and apparently were quite successful at finding it. But these are the same ones who in the second list (v.47a) use their legal skills to evict powerless widows while making long, pretentious, showy, empty prayers as a coverup. It's all about them and their supposed closeness to God because of their much learning, but they are vicious and greedy opportunists who have no heart for one of the groups God cares most about: widows who need legal and personal protection. "Don't copy them," said Jesus, "or you may become just like them, using our Jewish faith to forget the God of compassion and justice."

Then came a verdict from the only one qualified to give it, "They will receive (passive voice) the great condemnation." You do not at the end want to be found among those who love neither God nor neighbor, but who love public praise and money and use the faith as a ruse to gain both. "These are dangerous people," said Jesus, "thoroughly corrupted and not worth following."

The second unit could not be more of a contrast. That it occurred just as Jesus looked up, I count as a divine appointment. He was close enough to see and perhaps hear the two lepta (small brass coins) ring off the walls of the brass, trumpet-shaped receptacles. He knew the sound, and it was perhaps the dress of the woman that identified her socially as *a poor widow,* a woman invisible to most but not to God or the Son.

Slander," 419–41.

And his prophetic comment on her gift was this, "Truly, I tell you (a most solemn introduction), this poor widow has put in more than all of them," meaning the rich of v.1.

Jesus here invokes a new accounting system, not how much is the gift but how much is left to the giver once the gift is made. They gave overflow/extra/out of surplus, but she made perhaps her last offering as a radical act of faith in God. What happened to her after that is not known. Thus using the symbols of faith to cover a greedy heart is evil, as is making a show of gifts because you're playing to the wrong audience. It's the self-idolatry of the worship of one's own public image, but God knows the heart.

Then

Physicians check vital signs, and with disciples there are also vital signs. One of the most basic is how we think of money, wealth, the things they secure, and the power they bring. Jesus worked the building trades in wood and stone. Peter and his three friends were protein producers, fishermen. Matthew was part of the revenue department, and we do not know the work of the other eight. But whatever it was, they all left their old life for a new one on the road with Jesus.

Did they have savings? We aren't told. Family support? We don't know. We know that the gifts of some elevated women kept them all on the road (8:1–3). It was all about receiving what they needed when they needed it to keep them on the road with Jesus putting *the new reality* on display. Money is fuel for missions.

It was a long and adventuresome walk of trust that tested them all, and in the end only one failed *the walk of trust*, and that was Judas. And sometimes, as with the mission of the twelve and later the seventy, they were deliberately stripped of all supplies and by that made all the more vulnerable in order to learn God's provision and protection. But it was only a more intense experience of what they faced every day, so each having a basket of leftovers after the feeding of the five thousand was a reminder from God that their needs, and perhaps the needs of the families they left behind, were not forgotten but remembered in a memorable way. As if God said, "Even waiters eat well at my table."

It was in this ongoing context that Jesus issued a public condemnation of the Scribes and public commendation of the generous widow. Using religious office for self-promotion and self-enrichment at the expense of others is a moral evil that God will address. Giving in secret is never in secret since God sees and knows the faith of the giver. Money is a tool with which to demonstrate the love of God and neighbor, preferably in secret. And if not, it may weigh you down to hell itself.

Now

The formal—and often ignored—doctrinal statements of the various denominations are *means of grace*, meaning that when read and understood, kept and obeyed, they are one of the tools God uses to hold us together in the faith. They are bracing and good for us in their encapsulation of what's important, and in their lean expression leave the specific application to Christian wisdom and the light of the Holy Spirit. Such is the United Methodist teaching as found in our *Confession of Faith, Article XV: The Christian and Property:*

> We believe God is the owner of all things and that the individual holding of property is lawful and is a sacred trust under God. Private property is to be used for the manifestation of Christian love and liberality, and to support the Church's mission in the world. All forms of property, whether private, corporate or public, are to be held in solemn trust and used responsibly for human good under the sovereignty of God. (*Discipline 2016*, 76)[176]

A second statement is found in our *Articles of Religion, Article XXIV: Of Christian Men's Goods,* and here we find a special emphasis on the poor:

> The riches and goods of Christians are not common as touching the right, title, possession of the same, as some do falsely boast. Notwithstanding, every man ought, of such things as he possesseth, liberally to give alms to the poor, according to his ability. (*Discipline 2016*: 71)

Since pastors, especially the ones with advanced degrees and community status, are most prone to sins like those of the Scribes, self-monitoring is critical. As is making sure that in your pastoral rounds you do not play to elites but set aside time to visit and learn to appreciate the special challenges and faith of widows, single parents, fatherless or motherless children, those with addictions and disabilities, those confined at home or in nursing homes, the chronically ill, the mentally ill, the imprisoned, the lonely and forgotten, any who for any reason are easily overlooked. You will be surprised how it will sharpen and enrich your prayers and how alert it will make you to the pretensions that so easily creep into our hearts.

It is amazing at times how a few dollars, when mixed with kindness and prayer, make such a big difference, especially if kept secret. As an experimental discipline I recommend that disciples set aside some extra money each month after their tithe is paid, what I call *God money*, and be open to giving it away whenever a need arises. Keep it in a special pocket in your wallet or purse. You will hear the Holy Spirit whisper, "Now," and if you are obedient you will take—if only for a moment—a step into the vestibule of God's holy, happy kingdom. I know this because it happens to me on a regular basis.

---

176. For an analysis of this Article, see Burroughs (unorthodoxy.wordpress.com/2015/06/ 28/ the-christian-and-property).

Summary

Disciples understand the power of money to express love as they trust God for their physical needs and their need for deep affirmation. Hiding other agendas, most prominently status-seeking and greed, under the cover of religion and piety is a common sin.

Insights

1. Jesus sees us, each in our depths, and sends us personal warnings and cautions.

2. Jesus mocked the piety and ruthlessness of the Scribes to warn his own followers.

3. Never underestimate the power of bad and good examples to shape character.

4. There is nothing more dangerous or more damnable than church leaders *on the make*.

5. To have your conscience pricked by the Spirit is a call to immediate self-examination.

6. The best gift is to see ourselves and others through Jesus' eyes of holy love.

7. Never miss the small and the ignored and the despised things; they are windows.

8. The two best things God sends us are chances to repent and opportunities to love.

Disciplines

Observation: Jesus saw deeply into the ordinary and drew out what God sees.
Action: Practice paying attention to the mundane and pray, "Give light, Lord Jesus."
Observation: Jesus pricked and deflated the pretensions and ethics of the clergy.
Action: Walk with Jesus, avoid display, guard the vulnerable, pray lean prayers.

43. Luke 21:5–38

Get Smart! Get Ready! Stay Alert!
Genre: An Apocalyptic, End-of-Time Discourse of Jesus the Prophet

Death comes either to the soul or the body.
The soul cannot die, and yet it can die.
It cannot die, because its consciousness is never lost.
It can die, if it loses God.[177]
—AUGUSTINE

177. Just, *Luke*, 321.

Justification

The previous unit, 20:45—21:4, was expressly addressed to followers, "And in the hearing of all the people *he said to his disciples*" (20:45). Sometimes Luke continues an audience as earlier named, and that is the case in this lengthy end-time discourse. It is clear the disciples are the primary audience for the following reasons:

1. The "some spoke" of v.5a is a continuation of 20:45, "he said to the disciples;"

2. the direct address "Teacher" is invoked (v.7a);

3. the prophesied governmental persecutions of vv.12–15 and from family in vv.16–19 indicate that the targets are Jesus' followers; it is, as he said, "for my name's sake" (vv.12b, 17);

4. the "redemption" that is "drawing near" is for Jesus' followers, those who confess him;

5. the dual call to "take heed to yourselves" (v.34a) and to "watch at all times" (v.36a) are for those looking for Jesus return as the Son of man (vv.34–36), thus disciples.

Shape

This is one the longest thought units in Luke's biography, and it is elegant in its literary organization with a double center (d//d') and three sets of internal parallel frames (c//c', b//b', a/a'). This extended concentric pattern (an 8:2 chasm) is seen in the following arrangement:

a. vv.5–6 Jesus' Teaching on the Temple's Destruction, *temple/days* as frame
    b. vv.7–9 The Warning of False Messiahs
        c. vv.10–11 Standard Apocalyptic Signs: 3 Realms
            d. vv.12–19 The Inevitability of Persecution, God's Help
            d' vv.20–24 The Terrible Fate of Jerusalem, Call to Flee
        c' vv.25–26 Standard Apocalyptic Signs: 3 Realms
    b' vv.27–36 The Coming of the True Messiah
a' vv.37–38 Jesus' Public Teaching in the Temple, *day/temple* as frame

The genre of the whole is *An End-Time Discourse of Jesus the Prophet*, but within this long composition the following cluster of sub-genres are used in its composition:

- Observation and prophetic oracle (vv.5–6),

- Questions and Answers including prophetic oracles (vv.7–9),

- Catalog of apocalyptic signs (vv.10–11, 25–26),

- Prophetic Warnings (vv.12–19),

- Prophetic Counsel (vv.20–22),

- Woe + Reasons (vv.23–24),

- A Son of Man prophecy (vv.27–28),

- Parable and Nimshal/Interpretation (vv.29–31),

- Prophetic Guarantee (vv.32–33),

- Ethical Counsel (vv.34–35),

- Command and Reason (v.36),

- Narrative Summary (v.37–38).

The Thought Unit begins (a. vv.5–6) and ends (a' vv.37–38) in the present with the central core (vv.7–36) dealing with the future. Inclusions are by verbal repetition: *temple/days* in a. vv.5–6, and *day/temple* in a' vv.37–38. Who can possibly say, after reviewing the work of Luke, that he had no training as a rhetorical writer?

Content

The unit begins with a comment of praise by some for the temple's magnificence, and it draws from Jesus a blunt prediction of its utter destruction (vv.5–6). There then follow two related questions from the same groups, a *When* question (v.7a) and *What sign* question (v.7b), which Jesus answers in reverse order. To the *What sign* question he says, in effect, "There are no signs, so don't believe the false prophets and do not read to much into political events, say wars and insurrections, because they are a normal part of sinful history." To the *When* question he gives an even more enigmatic answer, saying in effect, "False prophets and political turmoil continues, but the end is not yet, so don't confuse the one with the other."

The conclusion is that there are no last-minute signs just before the end, and the only time signature is *not yet*. There then follows in vv.10–11 a catalog of standard Jewish apocalyptic images in three two-line couplets covering the three realms that make up the world as it now is: the political realm (v.10), the earthly realm (v.11a-b), and the heavenly realm (v.11c-d). And this list is the standard fare of history outside the kingdom of God. Normal life in an embattled creation.

If there is a sign, it is that Roman government and Jewish leaders find the followers of the one they crucified just as troublesome as Jesus himself, the results being seasons of persecution in which the Holy Spirit will inspire them in the moment how to witness and not concede to apostasy. Alongside official pressure there will be family pressures, even to the point of murder, but God will take believers through this awful experience and to heaven if needed where they will await the resurrection of the dead at the end of the age. "They can kill but not ultimately harm you since you are mine, and your future is mine!"

Parallel to the coming social pressures brought by Rome for non-conformity are synagogue leaders concerned about Jewish apostasy and family leaders upset by disloyalty (vv.12–19). Pressure on disciples is from all sides all at once; they live in a pressure cooker. Military pressure will be brought against Jerusalem in a great siege (vv.20–24), and here the counsel is to flee as soon as possible. The three two-line couplets of vv.23–24 use standard Jewish apocalyptic imagery, as does the subsequent paragraph, c' vv.25–26.

Even the fall of Jerusalem to Rome in 70AD, awful as it was, is still not the climactic event, just the next chapter in the ongoing agonies of a fallen world where the process of "Nation will rise against nation and kingdom against kingdom" (v.10) has never ceased. And though it is Jerusalem and hits near home for disciples, it's just more of the same. Christians were not to join the rebels on their suicide mission but flee the city and carry the message with them. When times are brutal, it may seem like the world is nearing its end, but it is not. Our world perhaps, the world as we have known it, but not *The World*.

That Jesus spoke of Jerusalem's destruction, and that it came to pass four decades later, was another witness that Jesus is a true prophet who saw that if Jewish and temple officials continued their politics of rebellion, their city and temple would come to an awful end. They counted on God to swoop down to rescue them, but God did not, and the carnage was awful. They missed the Prince of Peace who absorbed violence and were later crushed by the Roman ideology of Peace through Violence. They traded his nail-pierced hand for the closed fist of Vespasian. They wanted now what would only come later, at the true end.

It is in b' vv.27–36 that we preview the end, "And they will see the coming/arrival of the Son of Man, coming in a cloud with power and great glory" (v.27). The agonies of history continue to this moment, this sudden, universal unveiling. And just as the greening of fig leaves is sign summer has drawn near and is upon us, the cosmic sign of the Son of man is evidence the long-promised kingdom is now upon us. This is the terminal generation that witnesses the grand transformation as "heaven and earth" pass away to yield a new cosmos where all that Jesus has spoken becomes real and undeniable.

And so the real questions are not When? and What signs? but how I am to live in the present so that when the end intrudes, I welcome it. The real questions are Faith (what are my convictions) and Ethics (how is my behavior counter-cultural), which is the clear intent of vv.34–35 with its short list of conforming vices (dissipations, drunkenness, everyday concerns). That the return is abrupt, sudden, surprising, and everywhere all at once is asserted in vv.34c–35 in a double promise, "and that day will come upon you suddenly like a snare/trip, for it will come upon all who dwell on the face of the whole earth."

So the goal is not get ready but to stay ready, to—as one of the anthems of the Civil Rights Movement reminds us, "Keep your eyes on the prize, move on!" Therefore, the appropriate response is not speculation and prognostication but preparation, as v.36 intones, "But watch at all times, praying that you may have strength to escape all these things that will take place, and to stand before the Son of man."

To be ever-alert, ever-prayerful, and to live with life's ultimate appointment in mind, is what it means to be a follower of Jesus. And the next day we find Jesus again doing what he came to do, teaching and modeling *the new reality* to all who will listen.[178]

Then

The crucified Jesus is vindicated in two stages. First in his bodily resurrection plus appearances and later in his sudden and public reappearance as cosmic Lord, often labeled his *first* and *second* comings. These events are grounded in an understanding of creation and of time that has a beginning in God's creation and will end at the Son of man's return to usher in the grand transformation of the kingdom of God come down to earth, what we are calling *the new reality* and of which we have a preview in Jesus.

Now the issue Luke addresses in 21:5–38 is the interim in which the church lives and does its work. The Lord has not left his followers without clear guidance, but it does not satisfy many who want more details, more specificity, and so there's always been a market for false prophets to deceive the naive who crave secret knowledge. But the church in its Creeds has a strong affirmation of the ultimacy and finality of Jesus Christ, "and he shall come again to judge the living and the dead, and his kingdom shall have no end" (Nicene Creed), but nothing more specific, because we are not given such in the record of revelation, and the Creeds are—by their nature—conserving and conservative texts.

Disciples take their questions to Jesus and live with his answers, trusting he is able to sustain us in all circumstances, however cramped or cruel. So to When Jesus answers when it will not be. It will not be when false prophets say, "I am he," or, "The time is at hand," and it will not be with the next report of war. And to the question What sign? he gives no answer at all. Disciples live amidst the unending agonies of history which will continue until God says, "That's enough." But when the pain comes near and our world comes apart, we feel as if *the whole world* is disintegrating, which it is not. It is, as Jesus reminds us, in hard times, and particularly in pressures and persecutions, "This is a time for you to bear testimony" even as I speak to you in the moment (vv.14–15).

We use whatever platform we are given to point to Jesus Christ, and even if it costs our lives, we belong fully to God. We are not to seek martyrdom, but if it comes, God will preserve us. And while there are times to witness, there also times to leave a sinking ship in order to preserve our lives and the message we carry, so we retreat and look for new opportunities. And at a day and time known only to God, it will suddenly end in a blast of glory as the veil between visible and invisible worlds is forever

---

178. On the theology of this thought unit, see Gonzalez, *Luke*, 236–43; Jeffrey, *Luke*, 242–54.

ruptured, never to be replaced. Everywhere and all at once it will all be over, God's sudden end of history as we've known it.

Till then, disciples are on constant alert and monitor one another so they are not molded into the world's obsessions with pleasure and escape and power and comfort. The world is programmed to lure us into amnesia, into forgetting God, into *going with the flow*. We are a different kind of people, skeptic about speculations, and living every day in light of *that day*. The U.M. Confession of Faith, Article XX is titled "The Judgment and the Future State," and with brevity it states the the ultimacy of Jesus in terms of both *the now*— our life in a broken creation, and *the then*—life anew in the kingdom of God, with the link between them being "the righteous judgment of Jesus Christ":

> We believe all men/women stand under the righteous judgment of Jesus Christ, both now and in the last day. We believe in the resurrection of the dead; the righteous to life eternal and the wicked to endless condemnation[179]

Now

When there is a troublesome social trend, a thoughtful response is to ask two questions: 1) What is it? and 2) Why are so many getting on board? And for that the work of competent social scientists is very helpful. "It was," as they say, "an idea whose time has come." Buy why? And why now? And why so many? And so it is in America with the theology of dispensationalism and its teaching of the rapture or removal of the church before the worst of the end-time troubles that shapes the imaginations of many about the days in which we live. But not only is this teaching not found in Scripture, it was not created until early in the 19th century in Britain, where it has never since had much traction.[180]

But here in America with our conceits of manifest destiny, a city set on a hill, and of being a singular experiment, many cannot imagine God letting our churches go through such terrible sufferings, and so we find ourselves a free pass, an escape and lift-off just before the heat is turned up to full strength. God must offer his people an escape, and that's us!

The land of the free and the home of the brave are now those who take the last train to safety and the final flight to salvation above. But the protection God offers his people is not an easy escapism and privileged exit but the ability to bear witness and endure, all the while living with a different hope (v.36) and a different set of loyalties and practices than the surrounding culture (vv.34–35), and it is this tension that commends our witness.

179. *Discipline 2016*, 76.

180. For a helpful video, see Witherington, "Where Did Rapture Theology Come From?" youtube. com/watch?v=d_cVXdr8mVs.

When all that is stable crumbles, when our maps of reality are redrawn, when the symbols are recast, and when horror and loss are near at hand, how do disciples think and act and pray and witness and continue to live in hope? For a starter, we do not follow those in our own tribe who claim to have timetables and details plotted out, because church history is littered with their false promises and gullible followers. We do not follow the curiosities of believers who want to be *in the know with insider knowledge*. It's none of our business and we can't know.

Our business is not to get caught up in the hype (vv.7–9), to maintain a long-term view or history's repeated agonies (vv.10–11), to face the pressures and develop the virtues of trust and endurance (vv.16–19), and to not be identified with any politics that claims to force God's hand. Day in and day out, in pleasant times, unpleasant times, and in all the ordinariness between the times, we keep walking together in the same direction, following Jesus Christ with others, living in and by *the new reality*, increasing in the love of God and neighbor, and placing our hopes in nothing in this world.

Summary

Disciples do not waste time or effort with the time lines of the end-timers. We, rather, choose to live faithfully in hope whatever happens between now and the kingdom's public arrival. The signs of which Jesus speaks, including political turmoil, natural disasters, and religious persecution, are not cues that the end is near. They are the normal stuff of history in a broken cosmos in rebellion against its Maker and have never changed. Only with the sudden appearance of the Son of man in glory is the end here, and this is everywhere all at once with no warning except the words of Jesus in the gospels.

Insights

1. Pressures on disciples are internal from false prophets and external from followers of other faiths, including the secular faiths of those claiming no faith.

2. Jesus is the final dwelling place of God, and all other temples are doomed.

3. When people are under pressure, some follow any leader, however misled.

4. The agonies of history and its episodic convulsions are normal in the present, evil age.

5. When under pressure, disciples look for occasions to give a bold, true witness.

6. Courage, patience, fellowship, the touch of the Spirit, and hope sustain us in trials.

7. Horrors are everywhere and all the time; our world is not a safe neighborhood.

8. The end, at Jesus' coming, will be sudden as the old physics gives way to the new.

9. To stay alert, resist distractions, and not be consumed by vice are some of the benefits of living prayer in a community of disciples.

10. What the world is horrified to behold, the vindication of a Jesus they ignored, will be our parade.

Disciplines

Observation: Jesus warned us about overheated, false prophets within the ranks.
Action: Refuse to be carried along by any frantic speculations about the end.
Observation: Jesus knows that human history is always unfair, brutal, and deadly.
Action: Develop a sturdy realism about this world and perpetual focus on Jesus.

44. Luke 22:1–38

Eating On A Battlefield
Genre: The Farewell Testament of a Hero

Satan is crafty in working evil.
Whenever he gains possession of anyone's soul,
he does not attack him by means of a general vice.
He rather searches for that particular passion that has power over him
and by its means makes him his prey.[181]
—CYRIL OF ALEXANDRIA

Justification

Shape

Jesus eats a farewell meal with the twelve. This thought unit, like its predecessor 21:5–38, is one of the longer thought units in Luke's biography of Jesus. The words *death, Satan, Peter,* must/Gk. *dei* (indicating divine purpose), and *behold/idou* which are found in the first paragraph (1. vv.1–3) are also found in the last paragraph (1' vv.31–38), thus serving as inclusions or verbal brackets for an oral performance of the text.

The genre Luke uses is the well-attested *Farewell Testament* in which, as death looms near, a leader gathers followers for a meal and differing kinds of speeches to prepare them for the future. The seven expected components of the genre are present:

1. Death is near (v.2a),

2. Friends gather for a meal (vv.8–9),

181. Just, Luke, 327.

3. Farewell speeches (vv.15–23),

4. Memorial (v.19b),

5. Exhortation (vv.24–27),

6. Their future (vv.28–30),

7. Predictions (vv.31–34, 35–38).

Readers would have understood the general expectations and how Jesus filled them with new content. This is one of the premier or first rank of disciple passages because here Jesus begins to initiate a transfer anticipating his soon-to-be absence. It's a major turning point.[182]

The thought unit has five parts with a single center (1. vv.1–13, 2. vv.14–23, 3. vv.24–27, 2' vv.28–30, 1' vv.31–36). The concentric outline (a 5:1 Chiasm) is as follows:

1. vv.1–13 Judas' Treachery and Jesus' Passover Prediction

  2. vv.14–23 Jesus' Teaching at Table, Two Kingdom Sayings

    3. vv.24–27 Servant Leadership in Jesus' Community

  2' vv.28–30 Jesus' Teaching at Table, Two Kingdom Sayings

1' vv.31–38 Peter's Betrayal and Jesus' Provision

Content

Passover was the yearly Jewish memorial of the Exodus from Egypt under Moses, the founding event of the nation. And it's getting close, says Luke in v.1. He then clues us to the multiple levels of resistance arrayed against Jesus, visible and invisible: the chief priests and scholars who wanted him dead because of his zealous followers and also Satan who had been welcomed inside Judas' very person and now enables him to deliver up Jesus for a price. A second time signature (v.7) introduces the image of the Passover lamb. Jesus is the object of a dedicated conspiracy of the temple hierarchy with Satan serving to turn one of Jesus' symbolic twelve. Luke's worldview allows for multiple, simultaneous causation.

The second paragraph (1b. vv.8–13) is a *miracle of provision* with several parallels to the earlier provision of a mount/colt in 19:28–36. And while the provision differs, both enhance Jesus' reputation as a true prophet who sees what they do not and knows what they do not.

The story begins with a command of Jesus to "Go and prepare the Passover," and when Peter and John reply with a question, "Where will you have us prepare it?" he gives a detailed list of coming events (vv.10–12). The story concludes as expected; they go and find everything just as he predicted, and as commanded, "they prepared the

---

182. For scholarship on the Testamentary tradition and the Eucharist, see Leon-Dufour, *Sharing the Eucharistic Bread*, 230—47, where clear parallels are drawn between Luke 22:1–38 and the *Testaments of the XII Patriarchs*; Kurz, "Luke 22:14–38 and Greco-Roman and Biblical Farewell Addresses;" Kodell, *The Eucharist in the New Testament*, 105–17; Witherington, *John's Wisdom*, 232–34.

Passover" (v.13). Though hostile forces, human and demonic, are looming, Jesus the prophet is the true shaper of events and no mere victim.

In the third paragraph (2. vv.14–23) we find Jesus and the twelve reclining around a table in a sacred symposium, and his initial speech consists of two parallel kingdom sayings (vv.15–16, 17–18). This is his last Passover, and he will not eat of the ceremonial meal until fulfilled for him in *the new reality* of the kingdom, and note that it is an *I* and not a *We* statement. Something is about to happen to him in which they are not included. It is another prophecy. Same with the cup. They will drink of it as every year before, but he will not "until the kingdom of God comes," meaning the end of history altogether. He will not eat the Passover because he is the new Passover, the newer testament, as he makes clear in a second set of two sayings, in this case symbolic substitutions as a memorial. The bread is his body, the cup his blood, and body and blood constitute the whole person broken and poured out in the "new covenant" *for you*," meaning *for your benefit*. They are about to be inducted, through the whole of who Jesus is, into *the new reality*.

And whereas this paragraph began with Jesus and the apostles at table (v.14), so it concludes with a focus on Jesus and the betrayer at the same table (vv.21–23). In the moment of the greatest intimacy, there evil resides and is named and enfolded into the divine plan.

It is God's will that Jesus, the mysterious Son of man, be crucified by his enemies, and Judas—under pressure of the Evil One—proves to be the weak link. And while his treachery is used, it is not predetermined, but rather his free choice is then enfolded into the events that will land Jesus on the cross. And while free, Judas is fully accountable for resisting the grace Jesus offered, "But woe to the man by whom he is betrayed."

And since it is not clear to any but Jesus who it is, they question one another's integrity, perhaps their own as well. My read is that Judas was no less culpable than Peter since the failure of both was prophesied by Jesus. Peter was restored because he did not act as judge, jury, and executioner in his own life but wept and was restored. The bigger lie Judas believed was that his action put him beyond forgiveness and restoration, which was not humility but pride in the extreme. Had he waited and not acted as God in his own life, might not he have been restored as well?

The fourth paragraph (3. vv.24–27) is another of the Disciple Correction Stories we noted earlier. An incident of misunderstanding (v.24) about the all important cultural value of honor leads to an observation about top-down leadership (v.25), then a negation of that model in v.26. This is followed by a second reversal in which the common sense answer is that the one who is served is greater than the one who serves the lesser (v.27a), but Jesus takes the servant role, so if you want to follow him you must jettison the old model and risk being misunderstood every day. The modern idea of *servant leadership* is in debt to Jesus and his bottom-up approach. It's what he is shaping his friends to be.

In Luke's concentric pattern, the fifth paragraph (2' vv.28–30) is set in parallel to the second (2. vv.14–23) and like it contains two references to *the kingdom of God* (vv.29, 30a), as well as a common references to *table* (vv.14b, 21 // 30a) and *covenant* (v.20b) // *assign/covenant* (v.29). That they have continued with him to this point and thus shown a measure of enduring trust marks them out as apprentices, and with all the benefits now, there are even greater one's later. They will have a share in *the new reality* with two benefits receiving a highlight: 1) the intimacy and honor of a shared table with him (v.30a), and 2) a share in Jesus' kingly rule. Their relationship, however soon it is to be fractured, will endure and yield rewards.

The final section (1' vv.31–38), like the first (1. vv.1–13) has two paragraphs (1'a. vv.31–34, 1'b vv.35–38), and whereas Judas and Satan were featured in vv.1–7, so Peter and the Evil One are featured in vv.31–34. The disciples are under frontal demonic assault, and whereas Jesus succeeded in the wilderness, both crumple under pressure and one dies by suicide. Luke is realistic about our brutal foe and gives him ontological and not just mythical status. Satan is a genuine personal character in the narrative, not a human person but a fallen angelic one. He's requested to run Peter through a sifting process to see what's left, and this request has been granted. But Peter will survive and be the better leader for it. God tests us with a view to our success, whereas Satan tempts us with a view to our failure and despair.

When tests are permitted, it's not so we will fail—as did Judas; it is that we may learn deeper dependence and a distrust in all pride and bravado, as Peter immediately evidences in his boast (v.33). We have no doubt that Jesus' word about the three-fold denial will come to pass, and that is the sifting of Peter, his false self-image as a brave man from his true worth to Jesus as a humbled leader, fully aware of his frailty and cowardice. So the genre of the Disciple Correction Story, though normally addressed to the group, may also be individualized as here.

The seventh and final paragraph of the thought unit (1'b. vv.35–38) is a review of the earlier mission (9:1–11) and what they learned through it. Jesus asks what he and they already know, that they lacked nothing they needed on the mission. *But now* is a new situation, and regular provisions and protections are restored, thus teaching us the mission of the twelve was a training opportunity with unusual restrictions in order to force them into radical trust of the faithful God. A new mission is just ahead, but before it comes Jesus—in the language of Isaiah 53:12—is going to be numbered and counted among the transgressors, the innocent among the guilty in his final and deepest identification as he fulfills and completes the deepest thread of Scripture, a God who loves his world and his people enough to personally take their pain and sin into the divine life and exhaust its power.

Then

Luke has included so much in this thought unit and done it with such literary sophistication that it's hard to reduce it to something teachable. Perhaps best just to read it aloud and ask current followers to identify what most clearly challenges them. But also, since there is so much here that echoes other themes earlier presented, I will take each of the seven paragraphs and offer a summary statement:

1. Disciples live always on a visible and invisible field of conflict, and we should never be surprised by the powers that can be brought against us as we expose *the alien reality* in our following of Jesus. The sinful human being, and that is all of us, are easily corrupted and may give themselves over to evil at a deep level to become its pawns. We must stay ever-alert and allow the larger community to hold up a mirror to the vulnerabilities they see.

2. Jesus the prophet regularly set up trust experiments that could only be verified by obedience, and this is what it means to walk by faith until faith becomes sight. His words are true, and he is still speaking.

3. Holy Communion is the place where the Jesus who was *then and there* becomes *here and now* to feed us with himself.

4. Disciples follow Jesus in turning the world upside down with a leadership that takes delight in serving because we are secured in God.

5. Hanging with Jesus opens up into good and beautiful things beyond imagining, some now, the rest later. He is not embarrassed to speak of the grand outcomes of fidelity and perseverance.

6. Near to Jesus is where the heat is, and when the skillful pressure of the Evil One is applied, the very worst in your character will become public, and if you stay in the relationship, Jesus will restore you.

7. Jesus is teaching in a thousand ways that he is good, wise, sufficient, trustworthy, and that he alone fulfills all that God has been doing in Israel since the start. We are to be unashamedly dependent on Jesus and the Holy Spirit who accompanied him.

Now

Being a disciple is not a program, not a regimented plan of personal development, not a quick fix, not esoteric, or for special people only. It is a willingness to walk in a new direction with Jesus and to learn to trust and obey him in all circumstances in the company of other followers. It's not a solo trip, not based on intelligence or knowledge or any of the things our world aspires to. It's not a talent show or the company of the best and brightest. It's a face to face and life to life relationship in which he initiates and we respond, he leads and we follow, he forges ahead and we try to keep up, he models and we mimic, he exposes and we learn, he teaches and we take notes, he speaks the truth and we are jolted, he supplies and we are grateful, he heals and we watch, he delivers and we are startled, he lives in love for every next person he meets and we wonder how he does it, he does not avoid the pitiful nor shrink from powerful, whereas we often do both.

Jesus is like no one else, and his emotions are a pure reflection of his inner state. He has integrity in that his outside matches his inside with no dissonance. And he has touched something in us so deeply that we never want to be separated from who he is and what he does. He is magnetic to us and repulsive to those of opposite polarity.

This Jesus has called us, equipped us as his ambassadors in the finest classroom and laboratory experience ever designed, and it happens all day long every day and wherever we are because he is with us. You'd almost think the world was his personal property. We belong to him. He called us, trained us, befuddled us, rebuked us, gave us a share in the ministry, abandoned us one Friday, and left us dumbstruck two days later with his resurrection and all its implications.

We are part of something big, something very big, and you are welcome to walk with us a while and see if he starts a fire in your heart and brain as well. All your questions and all your doubts and all your fears and all your sins and all your hopes and dreams and dalliances with the demonic are grist for his mill, and in his presence—should you choose not to reject him when he makes himself known in order to gain your attention—you will find a depth of life and love and liberty the world knows nothing about. He made you, and now he wants you back. You have already been paid for and it's time to come home.

Summary

Disciples live in both the visible and invisible worlds and find that Jesus is skilled in both. Every encounter with him is raw material for our being shaped as his followers. He has all the love we need and all the time it takes to turn us into his agents. Remaining as a guest at his table and learning the art of serving others is where you want to be. Testing is sure to arrive; it exposes our weaknesses and hopefully increases our dependence on Christ.

Insights

1. No one is immune from the habits of sin and lures of evil. If Judas and Peter, then us!

2. Nurturing an internal spirit of independence sets us up for a big fall and a poor end.

3. Ever notice that when you plan to do wrong, opportunities start coming your way?

4. Am I aware of all the layers of opposition Jesus faced and overcame?

5. Jesus provides what is needed at just the right time. Will I trust him with that?

6. The end of this faith is not heaven above, but the whole cosmos healed and soggy with love and delight in *the new reality* of the kingdom of the Holy Trinity.

7. Charles Wesley wrote, "Come sinners to the gospel feast; let every soul be Jesus' guest"

8. The sacraments are means of grace, places to be touched, not a magical protection.[183]

9. Whatever authority apprentices of Jesus have, it is exercised in service.

10. The coming kingdom is better than any dream; it's where all the riches of love are on full display.

Disciplines

Observation: The Evil One, the great opportunist, is ever alert to our weaknesses.
Action: Clinging to Jesus and resisting the enemy's lures is our only defense.
Observation: Sacraments are where trust in Jesus is most clearly dramatized.
Action: Never minimize the table where Jesus offers himself to us every time.

45. Luke 22:39–46

The Only Hero
Hybrid Genre: The Unjust Murder of an Innocent Man: A Martyr,[184]
A Disciple Correction Story

Although he was God clearly revealed, he did not disown what was human.

He is hungry and exhausted, weary and thirsty;

he fears and flees and is troubled when he prays . . .

He asked to be excused from the suffering of the cup,

yet he was present in the world for this very reason.[185]

—HIPPOLYTUS

183. On the United Methodist recovery of the centrality of the table, see Felton, *This Holy Mystery*; Edwards, *Living into the Mystery*; Vickers, *A Wesleyan Theology of the Eucharist*; Witherington, *Making a Meal of It*.

184. On Jesus and martyrdom, see Karris, "Luke 23:47 and the Lucan View of the Death of Jesus," 68–70; Beck, "*Imitatio Christi* and the Lucan Passion Narrative," 28–47; Talbert, *Reading Luke*, 239–45.

185. Just, *Luke*, 343–44.

Justification

This story is included in our catalog because the audience is Jesus and the disciples in a time of crisis and prayer in which he looks to them for support and they fail him.

Shape

The sub-genre is a *Disciple Correction Story* in five parts:

1. Setting (v.39),
2. Initial Teaching (v.40) and Example of Jesus (vv.41–44),
3. Failure of Disciples (v.45),
4. Rebuke of Jesus in a Question (v.46a),
5. Further Teaching (v.46b).

The unit is framed by Jesus' call to pray in order not to succumb, "Pray that you may not enter into temptation/fiery trial" (1. v.40b // 1' v.46). At the center (3. vv.43–44) is an angelic appearance scene, and on either side in 2. vv.41–42 // 2' vv.45–46 the kneeling and rising of Jesus and his prayer contrasted to their sleep. The 5:1 concentric pattern is:

 1. v.39 Prayer and Temptation: Command of Jesus
  2. vv.41–42 Jesus' Response to Crisis: Prayer and Surrender
   3. vv.43–44 Angelic Visitation and Prayer of Agony
  2' vv.45–46a Disciples' Response to Crisis: Sorrow/Sleep
 1' v.46b Prayer and Temptation: Command of Jesus

Content

At regular intervals Jesus withdraws for prayer (3:21, 5:16, 6:1–2, 9:18, 28, 11:1), and here a crisis looms. He goes to his customary place to camp on the Mount of Olives (an indirect argument for his regular attendance at Passover) and gives his disciples a command to pray and the reason for it, that they need the strengthening from God that will help them endure without crumbling. They are to seek God together while he steps away from them to pray alone. In prayer Jesus addresses his *Abba/Father* in radical vulnerability and trust, asking to avoid the cup of suffering if possible, but then making his surrender to God's plan primary. His prayer is an address plus petition and complete surrender. That he is then strengthened by an angel in order to suffer faithfully is the answer to his prayer. And might this have been repeated with the disciples had they not failed and slept? Who knows?

The suffering deepens in Jesus' agony of contemplation, and his labors in prayer drench him in sweat. With strength from above, he prays even more earnestly. And when his prayer is ended and the angel withdraws, he rises to find his friends *sleeping for grief*, whatever that may mean. He asks, "Why do you sleep?" And the answers are probably as varied as the man: "I'm tired," "I'm scared," "This is just too much, " "Too much wine at Passover." Jesus' final command, a repeat of the first, is the same, "The only way to stay faithful in the midst of what's arriving is the strength God gives in prayer, so do it now because you're already falling apart" (paraphrased).

Then

The crumbling of the disciples, culminating in Judas' treachery, Peter's denial, and the flight of the rest begins here in Gethsemane with a neglect of Jesus' call to prayer. In contrast with him they are weak, fickle, unsteady, unaware, self-focused, disappointments with no leader in their ranks; in other words, just like us.

This is the human material Jesus has to work with, the likes of us. Yet— to give them credit—these are the one's who've made sacrifices and gone with him wherever for three years, so they are the best of the worst, and if not noble then at least worthy of our compassion, knowing we all might fare far worse than sleep under the same pressures.

Discipleship is never about looking good, being thought competent or professional, though we all desire it. Jesus will always look better than us, and the reason we fail so often is that the model is simply so high, a man who lives in perfect unity with the Father and perfect cooperation with the Spirit who empowers him, and perfect love for everyone he meets. He is fully human but without sin, rebellion, or deception. He is perfect and complete, a reminder of who we were meant to be before the great treachery came to be.

So when some critics, using rhetorical skill, complain about how little his followers, then and now, resemble their Master, the best thing to do is agree quickly, lift up his perfections and ask them, "How are you doing in the comparison with Jesus?" And anyway, it's about his reputation, not ours; his glory, not ours; his vindication, not ours; his work of salvation, not ours.

The one's closest to Jesus needed what every other sinner needs, a Savior who suffers and bleeds and dies for them as the only innocent, pure, holy, love-filled one who ever lived, and none of us qualify for the job. The Triune God through the willing agency of the Son, is doing for us what we cannot do for ourselves. A living model, a dying substitute, a self-offering of one who is not less than God. This is what it takes, and for rest of their lives the eleven who continued after Judas' death, when asked, would reply:

> Yes, I was one of them and I was there. While he prayed and sweated, I was dead asleep; and when they strung him up, I was at a safe distance. And that's not all, let me tell you how often I failed him when we were on the road

together. But he never let my shame consume me. His corrections were the wounds of love, and in his company I've never felt more alive. And if I have to look bad every day as the cost of being his follower, it's worth it because there is no one like this man, my dear friend Jesus.

Now

In a world of image management, Jesus prefers the real you. In a world where success and winning are everything, Jesus knows what losers the highest flyers really are. In a world where weaknesses of character and flaws of understanding are hidden out of shame and the fear of being rejected, Jesus has no illusions about what we bring to the table.

All our secrets are available, all our weaknesses, all our habitual and occasional sins, all our petty envies and private fantasies, all are laid bare before the one with whom we have to do. And we are safe with him as he changes us a bit at a time according to his own designs. What we think petty, he may think great, and what is a big sin to us may appear minuscule to him.

We are not in charge of the relationship, which means that our spirituality, whatever that shape-shifting word means, is not under our control as our next self-improvement project.[186] But is there a desire to change, to be a different kind of person, then his is the school you apply to. He will accept and enroll you and set you to the serious tasks he is about in our world. There's no lack of meaning with Jesus, no lack of wisdom, no pecking order, no pulling rank, but a love tough enough not to let you go, just as with the Twelve who first walked this path. Discipleship is a long walk with Jesus, through this life and into the one to come, *the new reality* of God's kingdom.

Summary

Disciples discover how weak and faulty we are in Jesus' presence. There are no illusions with him; he accepts us where we are, and loves us too much to leave us there. And when the pressure is turned up and you're about to crumble, humble your heart in prayer.

Insights

1. Could it be that the weakness and vice of my life is abetted through neglect of prayer?

2. Jesus' keen sense of trust and destiny was kept sharp in honest prayers of surrender.

---

186. For a challenging read from a Vineyard pastor, see Ken Wilson, *Jesus Brand Spirituality*. It could just have easily been titled *Jesus Brand Discipleship*!

3. Leaning deeply into God through prayer is the best way to receive new strength.

4. No human being, not even those closest to Jesus, could stand the pressures he faced.

Disciplines

Observation: Jesus regularly issues warnings and remedies to his friends.
Action: Ask often, "Am I alert to the *early warning system* of Jesus and his Spirit?"
Observation: Jesus' desires were clearly expressed and yielded to trust and surrender.
Action: In the midst of much we cannot control, trust is the strongest option.

46. Luke 22:47–53

The Hour and Power of Darkness
Genre: A Disciple Correction Story

They inflicted death on the righteous One,
and he healed the wounds of his persecutors.[187]
—AMBROSE

Justification

This story is included because of its explicit reference to "the twelve," to Judas' earlier listing among them (6:16b), and to the wrong action of a disciple in taking up the sword. The parts of a Disciple Correction Story are all here:

1. Setting (v.47a),
2. Teaching of Jesus (vv.47b–48),
3. Misunderstanding/Action (v.50),
4. Further teaching + action of Jesus (v.51),
5. Resolution (vv.52–53).[/NL 1–5]

Shape

The story is a 4:2 chiasm with four parts and a double center (a. vv.47–48, b. v.49 // b' vv.50–51, a' vv.52–53). The initial statement "there came a crowd" is specified at the end as "the chief priests and officers of the temple and elders, who had come out against him" as an inclusion. At the center (b//b') are Violence Offered (v.49) and Violence Rejected (vv.50–51). Three questions (vv.48b, 49b, 52b) tie the whole together:

187. Just, *Luke*, 347.

a. vv.47–48 Jesus Addresses Judas as a Betrayer: Question
  b. v.49 Violence is Offered in Word and Deed
  b′ vv.50–51 Violence is Rejected in Word and Deed
a′ vv.52–53 Jesus Addresses the Temple Leaders as Darkness: Question

Content

Judas' treachery—what it means for Satan to *enter him* (22:3)—is clear as he leads the opposition, perverts the kiss of friendship, and is called to account. Jesus reaches out with a question, but Judas does not flinch or offer a reply to his old friend. He is hardened in apostasy, impervious to the grace of repentance, and it will not end well. Perhaps he is counting on some heavenly display of Jesus to rescue himself and bring in the kingdom of God, but it is not to be. Jesus will suffer and die, his only defense being his life and words and deeds. Judas has embraced the darkness, and the disciples remain in the shadows.

But Jesus stands in the center of God's will and does not need their defense. One draws and strikes before the question of v.49b is answered, and—in a bit of poor swordsmanship—severs the right ear from behind, a cowardly move on a slave. Jesus stops the heroics, embraces providence, and in his last healing restores the man (v.51b).

The one who taught his followers to love their enemies (6:27–36) acts it out in true philosophy; the teaching and action of Jesus are a seamless whole. The earlier question to Judas (v.48b) is paralleled in a question to his entourage (v.52b), and both expect a self-convicting *Yes* answer. Yes, Judas betrays with a kiss; and Yes, they did not confront Jesus in public and in the light of day for a proper debate, in effect labeling themselves as cowards.

That their actions are at night and away from the crowds demonstrates what Jesus now names, "But this is your hour and the power of darkness." God does not cause but uses the evil that men freely will to bring about divine purposes, one of which is that Jesus be a willing, innocent victim of sin, hatred, and evil. The light calls forth and displays the darkness as cowardly, vicious, and false.

Then

At some point disciples learn the truth about themselves, and it's not complimentary. Judas welcomed darkness after three years of walking in the light; Peter cannot keep his grand promises of heroism and thrice denies the one who filled his boat with fish; the rest run and flee; one of the twelve lashes out with a sword in sheer foolishness, perhaps hoping for status as an honored martyr. Under pressure from the Evil One, from the internal pressures of an heroic self-image, and from the pressures of self-preservation, all crumble and leave Jesus alone. But that should not surprise us because we are no different.

Now

We, however, cave with much less pressure. We go silent and absent as the cost of witness goes up. We often think that we have a better way for Jesus to fulfill our plans. And so we cave and fold and crumple and retreat and deny and adopt the world's methods instead of our Master's dignity, confidence, and probing questions. To be a follower is painful and humiliating as the one who calls us takes us far out beyond our resources, there to face what we have done and have not done. In his company pretense evaporates, pride melts away, and we face not just the power of darkness without but its access within.

It's embarrassing, in a world of image management, to be so utterly exposed as false and failing. Not very manly for men, and perhaps not very loyal for women. And we fight it so, until its exposure can no longer be hidden, and we face what others already know, that we are not very good followers. Instead, we are mock-disciples building a resume, religious frauds looking for a way out, wanna-bes, empty-suits, and at the bottom broken men and women with yawning needs and wounds, character flaws and thoughts—and perhaps habits—too dark to admit. And if Jesus does not re-grace us at such moments, we are goners.

So one friend of Jesus took his life in a final act of self-rule, and eleven were more than restored because in their deserved shame they did not make the mistake of being their own judge, jury, and executioner, as did Judas. And what Jesus offered to the demonized and diseased he would soon offer them, but first the truth had to be revealed, and part of what makes this new faith credible are the ugly stories preserved about its founders. And if he could do this with them, then maybe there's room for me among his followers?

Summary

Disciples get used to exposure and a loss of naivete about themselves and others. It's part of Jesus' curriculum that the very worst in us is brought to light, that we are sinners still and vulnerable to evil. We must receive what he offers others, or we are lost. We don't save him, but he saves us.

Insights

1. What happened to and through Judas is not beyond comprehension; though a disciple like others, he became a willing agent of evil.

2. Jesus neither needs nor requires our protection; it is our devotion and trust he seeks.

3. There are times, as Jesus said, when the very worst has its moment of temporary ascendency, and we rightly wonder, Where is God?

4. Jesus loved his friends and enemies to the very end, healing a severed ear and giving the mob of temple officials a true diagnosis as cowardly clergy.

5. Jesus knows every crack in my facade, every hole in my armor, every lie I hold dear, and he has plans to deal with every one of them to fit me for his service.

Disciplines

Observation: Jesus warns that apostasy is an option for all looking for a better deal.
Action: Tremble at your capacity for treason and learn humble dependence.
Observation: Jesus desires our loyalty but does not need our defense.
Action: Make a reverent and humble witness to Jesus at every opportunity.

47. Luke 22:54–65

Peter's Failure
Genre: Prophecy Fulfilled, A Disciple Failure Story

If you perhaps fall into some sin,
because he is a witness to your secrets,
he looks at you so that you may recall and confess your error.[188]
—AMBROSE

Justification

The story of Peter's denials, and of Jesus' prophecy of the same, is a disciple story.

Shape

The parallel stories of the failures of Judas and Peter, and of Jesus' prophecy about them being fulfilled, are recounted in 22:27–54, 54–65. This is another example of Luke's theme of Jesus as a true prophet, one whose words God inspires and upholds.

The thought unit is bounded at the beginning and end by the actions of the guards "who seized and led him away" (a. v.54a) and "who were holding Jesus, mocked and beat him" (a' v.63). The next inward layers are the entry of Peter into the courtyard (b. v.55) and his exit to weep (b' vv.60b–62). This leaves the center as c. vv.50–60a where three denials in increasing strength are recorded (1. vv.56–57, 2. v.58, 1' vv.59–60), the

188. Just, *Luke*, 349.

first and third using the denial *I do not know*, while the central denial differs, "Man, I am not" (v.58). Thus the central—and focal—denial is a rejection not only of Jesus but also of the other disciples since the charge was, "You are also *from among them*" (v.58). Satan isolates the sinner. The 5:1 concentric outline is:

    a. v.54 Actions of the Guards: *seize, lead him away*
        b. v.55 Peter Enters the Courtyard
            c. Three Direct Charges and Three Denials
        1. vv.56–57 *with him*
            2. v.58 *one of them*
        1' vv.59–60 *with him*
        b' vv.60b–62 Peter Exits the Courtyard to Weep
    a' vv.63–65 Actions of the Guards: *mock, beat*

The larger theme of Jesus the true prophet is highlighted in a cluster of fulfillments:

		Foretold	Fulfilled
1.	Jesus is betrayed	22:21	22:47–53
2.	Jesus is denied	22:34	22:54–62
3.	Jesus is reckoned with lawless	22:37	22:52
4.	Jesus to be beaten and mocked	18:32	22:63
5	Peter denies Jesus thrice	22:34a	22:56–60a

Content

Once the structure of the thought unit is clear, the flow of the narrative is straightforward. Jesus is seized and taken to the high priest's courtyard. Peter follows at a distance, but then enters the courtyard and takes a seat beside the fire with the others. We assume he is alone, but it could be Luke's focal technique highlighting him alone with a spotlight. In the firelight a female slave names Peter as a co-conspirator, "This man was with him," and Peter, with the direct address *Woman*, lies about his relationship, "I do not know him," perhaps with the best of motives, in order to stay close enough to Jesus to not leave him alone, a bit of spy craft!

The second and central denial is not of Jesus but of his colleagues, and the charge is, "You are also from *among them*." And his reply, again with direct address is a lie, "*Man*, I am not." An hour later there is a stronger form of the first, "Certainly this man was also with him, for he is a Galilean," and this time Peter's plea is ignorance, "*Man*, I do not know what you are saying." It was the only way Peter could stay within eyesight of Jesus, but at the third charge Jesus looked straight at him. Peter knew the gig was up and all his schemes of heroism exposed. And he left and "wept bitterly." This was the sifting that was predicted, the irony being that while multiple predictions are being fulfilled, Jesus is mocked and beaten as a prophet who cannot see anything. They don't know who he is.

So maybe Peter was not a coward, as is often thought, but a man tripped up by his own clever schemes to prove Jesus wrong, a pride-filled fool who was taken down several notches.[189]

Then

Jesus original call to Peter back in 5:10 was, "Do not be afraid, henceforth you will be catching men alive." But here was a twist in that Jesus has now caught Peter in three lies involving both Jesus and his companions. In an effort to be near and perhaps a hero, he's become distanced from them all and exposed as a fraud. We can easily understand his motive, and if he was alone in his following at a distance, then it took a measure of courage to walk into the high priest's very courtyard. Peters' fatal flaw, his misjudgment and pride was to believe himself a better man than Jesus said he was; in effect, "Jesus is wrong about me. I'm not that kind of man." But he was, though it was through a different route than he thought. To follow Jesus is to have our dearest illusions exposed and mocked.

Now

To follow Jesus is a sifting process of wheat from chaff, the useful from the useless. And whether administered with delight by the Evil One for shame, pain, and the sheer delight of human humiliation, or through less vicious means, it's part of the Jesus school of training.[190] All we are is grist for the mill, and it never ends, as a secondary sifting of Peter is told in Acts 10 having to do with the inclusion of Gentiles.

Jesus is not an addition to an already-stellar resume. He is one who tells us the truth and rebuilds us in an ever-greater dependence upon himself, and that was Peter, wasn't it? A strong man humbled, a brave man chastened, a clever man fooled, a proud man looking into a mirror with tears and shame. This was the one Jesus forgave and restored and installed as his Chief Shepherd.

So if you aspire to leadership in the company of Jesus, you will be sifted and sifted and sifted again in a lifelong process of separation, examination, purification, and restoration. This is part of the cost of discipleship, and its purpose is to increase our trust in Jesus and our dependence upon him, the one who knows us better than we know ourselves. And so when his words sting and expose and embarrass, we runs towards them, not away. To be near him is to be near the fire, as was Peter in the flickering firelight.

---

189. On Peter and his denials, see Senior, *The Passion of Jesus*, 83–98.

190. For Anglican and United Methodist teaching on sin after baptism, see Bray, *The Faith We Confess*, 88–90; Rogers, *Essential Truths For Christians*, 315–30.

Summary

Disciples are regularly exposed and humbled because Jesus reveals what's in them. It's love and truth at work, bringing us more into alignment with the one we follow. Peter's denials did not move him out of the range of forgiveness or restoration.

Insights

1. Jesus knows every crack in my facade, every hole in my armor, every lie I hold dear.

2. Peter the pastor lived every new day forgiven for his sins of pride and denial.

3. We have the failure stories of Judas and Peter, and one day we will know the failures stories of the remaining ten that are not recorded, and they ours as well.

4. There's only one hero in this movement, and it's not any of us.

5. It is the character qualifications that are most important in this work, not the academic; the latter can be accumulated without much change in the former.

Disciplines

Observation: The one who calls us into his company knows all our weak spots.
Action: Beware of anything and anyone that weakens your loyalty to Jesus.
Observation: Peter's greatest qualification was not his promises but his deep grief.
Action: Where it is unfashionable or dangerous to speak of Jesus, do so!

48. Luke 23:26–56

A New Cast of Followers
Genre: The Death and Martyrdom of a Hero, A Righteous Man

When he was hanging on the cross,
he was looking around at the people raving against him,
putting up with their insults and praying for his enemies.
While they were killing him, the doctor was curing the sick with his blood.
He said, "Father, forgive them, for they do not know what they are doing."[191]
—AUGUSTINE

191. Just, *Luke*, 262.

Justification

This is also one of Luke's longer thought units. It's included in the core list of disciple passages precisely because the disciples are absent, their last appearance being a weeping Peter in 22:62. Jesus has, as earlier prophesied in his fourth passion prediction, now been delivered to the Gentles who have begun their ugly work, "and he will be mocked and shamefully treated and spit upon; they will scourge him and kill him" (13:32b–33a).

The disciples are not to be found, except perhaps in the oblique summary of v.49, "Now all *his acquaintances* and the women who had followed him from Galilee stood at a distance and saw these things." But here a new pattern emerges. In place of the twelve, new persons are drafted into Jesus' company, each exemplifying a mark of discipleship:

1. Simon of Cyrene is impressed to carry the cross (23:26 // 9:23 of disciples);

2. one of the unnamed criminals crucified with him makes a last minute prayer, "Jesus remember me when you come into your kingdom" and is given a promise, "Today, I say to you, today you will be with me in Paradise" (vv.42b-43 // the ask and receive of 11:9–13),

3. the confession of the centurion and head of the death squad, "Certainly, this man was innocent/righteous"(echoing Pilate's verdict in 22:4, 13d, 22a);

4. the emergence of Joseph of Arimathea who asks of Pilate the body and carries out a quick burial (vv.50–53);

5. the prominence of the women "who had come with him from Galilee" is highlighted (vv.49, 55).

Jesus will have his followers, and in them we see a reprise of earlier themes that suffering is part of following, that Jesus is the recipient of prayer and makes ultimate promises, that he is innocent and righteous, that he calls the rich as well as the poor, that women have an honored place in his company. This is a discipleship passage.

Shape

What is also notable about this thought is the large number of quotes and allusions to the Old Testament, picking up the theme that in Jesus the deep purposes of God, as scattered across the Jewish scriptures, come together in a focus on the person and work of Jesus. Those I have been able to identify are:

vv.27–29	Mal. 1:8–9, Is. 49:19–21,
v.30	Hos. 10:8,
v.32	Ps. 23:16,
v.34a	Is. 53:12,

v.34b	Ps 22:18,
vv.35–38	Ps.22:7, 69:21, Wis. 2:17–18,
v.46	Ps. 31:5,
v.47	Is. 53:11,
v.49	Ps. 38:11,
v.52	Dt. 21:22–23,
v.56b	Ex. 20:10.

In terms of the literary patterning we've come to expect, note how the unit begins with the introduction of a new character—Simon of Cyrene, the language of discipleship in his carrying the cross *behind Jesus*, and in the phrase, "And there *followed* him a multitude and the people, beating of their breasts (vv.26b, 27). Also note how it closes with a second new character—Joseph of Arimathea, the language of discipleship associated with the women, "Now the women who had come with him from Galilee *followed*" (v.55), and the multitude beating their breasts (v.48). These are three deliberate inclusions so that hearers, as the story is read, can mark off the large divisions. Think of the scenes of a play.

There are four paragraphs or sub-sections in the unit, and they are arranged in a 4:2 concentric pattern (four parts with a double center: a-b//b'-a') as follows:

a. vv.26–31 New Disciple and Women on the Way to the Cross

   b. vv.32–34 Three Responses: Criminals, Jesus, Soldiers

   b' vv.39–47 Three Responses: Thieves, Jesus, Soldier

a' vv.48–56 New Disciple and Women on the Way Home from the Cross

Content

Jesus is worthy of followers, and he will have them, one way or another. Simon of North Africa is impressed into modeling what Jesus earlier taught (9:23). As they go to the cross, large crowds follow in public mourning, and Jesus speaks an oracle of doom at the destruction that is coming to the city, to the "daughters of Jerusalem and their children."

That he is to be "reckoned with the lawless," his own words, is fulfilled in vv.32–33 with his new companions, all of them now on crosses, his royal court flanking him. And here Jesus prays for their forgiveness because their deeds are ignorant. He thus continues his ministry even in this extreme circumstance. His clothes are gambled away; he is mocked as the one who saved others and cannot save himself. And this he does, as the titulus (placard) reads, "the king of the Jews." He cannot save himself and us too, so he chooses us—his enemies.

There then follows the sight of one of the criminals pleading for rescue from the Messiah (v.39) and the other confessing Jesus' innocence (v.42). His prayer is not for rescue from death but through it with hope for a new life (v.42), a request Jesus grants with a promise of companionship in Paradise (v.43). Even here he is saving people.

And then, after three hours of apocalyptic darkness and judgment upon the temple (vv.44–45), he surrenders his life with a prayer and takes a last breath. Jesus is now dead, as he prophesied (9:22, 9:44–45, 17:25, 18:32–33).

And in partnership with the Father, he is the actor, not just a victim. The centurion, at Jesus' death, agrees with the second criminal that Jesus was guiltless, "Certainly, this man was righteous" (v.47b). When it's over, the multitude and women return home, enacting the rituals of mourning. The note of v.49 is easily passed over, "Now all his acquaintances and the women who followed him from Galilee stood at a distance and saw these things" (v.49), but it serves as eyewitness testimony to his death, and then in v.55 to his burial. He was dead, and they all knew where the body was.

The introduction of an additional *passion disciple* is saved to the end, and he answers the question: Will Jesus be buried, and by whom since most of the crucified rotted in place as food for birds and insects? And to boot, Joseph of Arimathea is a Jewish leader of status, with four of his marks of status in vv.50–51 and four of his actions in vv.52–53. The unit ends with the faithful women keeping the Sabbath and preparing the spices and ointments which had been neglected in the rushed burial, thus continuing the service of 8:1–3.

Then

This is God's will, that Jesus freely offer himself as an innocent to the worst that his own faith and the ruling powers of the Empire can give him. It is an extreme engagement to fully expose both the tenacious love of the Triune God and the gnarled matrix of sin and evil, ignorance and cruelty that is the world as it now is. Here we learn the truth about God and ourselves. This is how far God goes to engage us and all our institutions with love.

The death of Jesus is not an accident of history but the purpose of God woven into the decisions of the powers and the people who lined up against the One God sent. And on the way to death, Jesus is the same Agent and Son he's been all along. He speaks true prophesies; he evangelizes a criminal and the leaders of his death squad; he forgives and prays to his Father, and along the way the Father provides for his needs as the weight of his cross is borne by another and his burial is funded by a faithful Sanhedrin outsider.

His necessary suffering has an end, and his communion in glory is restored. What is not removed is the attempt to shame him and the ability to torture and kill him. Jesus is innocent and sinless and loving and trusting in Providence to the end and beyond. He is worthy to be followed.

Now

In the above analysis and retelling of the story-line, it's clear that all kinds of people from all sorts of backgrounds and in all sorts of circumstances come under the magnetic attraction of Jesus. It is a preview at his dying of the mission he soon bequeaths to his followers. But in our probing of the grand theme of discipleship, it's a subtle temptation to so focus on the following and the followers that we— at least for a moment— eclipse the one followed. Discipleship involves us deeply, but it's not about us.

We are the imitators, not the model; the effect, not the cause; the shadows, not the figure; the beneficiaries, not the patron; pupils and apprentices, not the teacher. Jesus has no trouble finding followers, the only questions being, Will we be among them? Will we continue faithful? And if not, will we trust him for restoration? So if we turn the spotlight back to center stage, we find him doing what he's always done with amazing consistency, even in his public, naked, mocked dying:

- The one true prophet who makes promises for God along the way.

- The one who welcomes women as followers along with men.

- The one who welcomes strangers, Gentiles, and Jews into his company.

- The one who localizes the presence of God so that the temple is now evacuated.

- The one who announces God's forgiveness and asks his Father to forgive his killers.

- The one who loves his enemies to the end.

- The one with true titles: Messiah, Chosen One, Righteous One, King of Israel.

- The one whose followers remain Torah-observant Jews.

- The one who saves all who turn to him by not saving himself but remaining obedient.

Summary

Potential disciples are always being drawn toward the mysterious, magnetic person of Jesus Christ because of his potent innocence, his blend of truth-speaking and love-showing. It's what drew us into his entourage. And if we keep our eyes open, the Holy Spirit will alert us to the curious and receptive who need our witness as a step towards trusting him.

Insights

1. Jesus calls followers as he chooses, each as unique as a fingerprint. No clone's.

2. Simon was drafted, the thief at the last moment, the centurion as Jesus died, and Joseph volunteered. So don't pour all into the same mold.

3. The utter integrity of Jesus is in continuing his work to his final breath.

4. To the daughters of Jerusalem Jesus gave a chilling, horrific, true prophecy. Warning people is part of what love does.

5. Jesus' deep identification with the least, the last, the lost, the losers, and the lofty is observable in his dying, his death, and the after-effects.

6. Human ignorance and the cruelty it breeds is something Jesus forgives.

7. Do not be surprised when you meet people who scorn, mock, hate and revile Jesus Christ. It's nothing new because he remains the greatest threat to life as it now is.

8. God finds ways to raise up witnesses to the truth about who Jesus is. Be one of them.

9. All disciples will eventually let go of this life, and Jesus' prayer is a good one.

10. The testimony of eyewitnesses is highly valued in court, and God arranged for Jesus to have plenty of it. Faith is not blind belief; it is, rather, trust based on multiple evidences.

Disciplines

Observation: Jesus never quits calling disciples, and the Father keeps sending them.
Action: Go not just for the likely but for the unlikely ones; they need Jesus too.
Observation: Sin and evil blind our sight, so that we do wrong thinking it right.
Action: Carry a cross in your pocket for a month; finger it as you pray for enemies.

49. Luke 24:1–12

Too Good Not to be True
Hybrid Genre: An Angelophany and Disciple Correction Story

Angels also brought the joyful tidings of the nativity to the shepherds in Bethlehem.
Now they tell of his resurrection.
Heaven yields its service to proclaim him,
and the hosts of the spirits which are above attend the Son of God,
even though he is in the flesh.[192]
—AUGUSTINE

192. Just, *Luke*, 375.

Justification

This is clearly a disciple passage, though not of the twelve but of the faithful women who become the first preachers of Jesus' resurrection, with some of the facts—empty tomb and linens—confirmed by Peter, only with no angelic appearance or communique as with the women.

Here we see the entwining of *Christology* (who Jesus is) and *Discipleology* (who disciples are [my neologism!]). The gold cord of Jesus and the blue cord of the disciples are woven together throughout Luke, and each implies the other.

Shape

The thought unit begins with a time signature, "now on 'day one of the sabbaths,'" at early dawn" (v.1). Inclusions include the trip to and from the tomb (v.1b // v.9a) and the parallel inspections inside the tomb from the women (vv.2–3) and Peter (v.12), thus two witnesses as required by Jewish rules of evidence (Deut 17:16ff.). In between the frames are two angelic rebukes in parallel, the first an angelic question and answer (vv.4–6a), the second an angelic reminder of Jesus true prophecy concerning himself (vv.6b-7). This gives us a 4:2 concentric pattern (1–2//2'-1') with two frames and a double center:

    1. vv.1–3 Women Journey to the Tomb to Complete the Burial Rites, Evidences
      2. vv.4–6a Rebuke 1: Angels Ask and Answer a Question
      2' vv.6b–7 Rebuke 2: Angels Issue a Reminder of Jesus' Prophecy
    1' vv.8–12 Women Journey from the Tomb, Peter's Arrival, Evidences

The literary type of this unit is a hybrid of a *Disciple Correction Story*, in this case of the women who misread the events and are corrected, and an *Angelophany* with five of the six expected parts present:

    1. Setting (vv.1–3)
    2. Reaction (v.4a)
    3. Appearance (v.4b)
    4. Responses of fear and humility (v.5a)
    5. Angelic oracle(s):
      a. Rebuke 1 (vv.5b–6a),
      b. Rebuke 2 (vv.6b–7c).

Missing is the expected command not to fear after the appearance in v.4b.

Content

The last thought unit ended with the Sabbath observance of faithful women disciples who had plans to complete the tasks of a decent burial when the Sabbath ended, including the application of spices and unguents to keep down the odors of decomposition during the week of mourning that was to follow at the site.

Jesus was really dead and soon enough would smell badly, and after that soon become unrecognizable. In a year or so his bone's, now vacant of flesh, would be gathered and placed in an ossuary box of stone, for such was the Jewish custom in Jerusalem at the time.

And while two of Jesus' four passion predictions—the first (9:22) and last (18:32–33), as well as the angels' review of the same (24:6b–7)—include prophesies of resurrection on the third day, there was no intellectual category to make sense of this since resurrection happened to the Jewish faithful at the end of the age, not to one individual in the middle of time.

So while Jesus issued predictions, the manner and time remained a surprise, needing the correction of angels and his confirming resurrection appearances to begin to understand his personal vindication.

The following chart compares four passion predictions given before Jesus death (looking forward) and four after his resurrection (looking back). It's a major theme in Luke that Jesus is the true prophet whose words are inspired and backed by divine confirmations.

Eight Passion Sayings In Luke
Four Prior To Crucifixion, Four Afterward in Chronological Order[193]

Four Before	Four After
9:22, ""The Son of man *must* suffer many things, and be rejected by the elders and chief priests and scribes, and be killed,/ *and on the third day be raised."*	24:7, "that the Son of man *must* be delivered into the hands of sinful men, and be crucified,/ *and on the third day rise."*
9:44, "Let these words sink into your ears; for the Son of man is to be delivered into the hands of men."	24:27, "And beginning with Moses and all the prophets, he interpreted to them in all the scriptures the things concerning himself."
17:25, "But first he *must* suffer many things and be rejected by this generation."	24:44, "Then he said to them, 'These are my words which I spoke to you, while I was still with you, that everything written about me in the law of Moses and the prophets and the psalms *must* be fulfilled."'

---

193. Extracted from Edwards, *The Gospel According to Luke,* 711.

18:32–33, "For he will be delivered to the Gentiles, and will be mocked and shamefully treated and spit upon; [33] they will scourge him and kill him,/ *and on the third day he will rise.*"	24:46, "and said to them, 'Thus it is written, that the Christ should suffer/ *and on the third day rise from the dead,* and that repentance and forgiveness of sins should be preached in his name to all nations beginning from Jerusalem. You are witnesses of these things.'"

Once the surface structure is mapped and the genre identified, the flow of the narrative makes sense as themes are introduced and then echoed, thus repetition with variation as in most of Luke's thought units.

As noted, Luke begins with a post-Sabbath time signature (v.1a) as the women go to the tomb with spices near daylight. Their first surprise is to find the stone rolled back (v.2), the most natural explanation for which would be grave-robbing for valuables or the use of corpses in magical practices. This is then complicated by a second surprise, discovered in an inspection of the tomb, that Jesus' body is no longer present. Luke's understatement is that "they were perplexed about this" (v.4a).

It was then that two angels appeared beside them in the apparel of light, and with fear at having the other world intrude, they bow down in humility, there to receive a mild rebuke, "Why are you seeking the living among the dead? He is not here, but has been raised" (vv.5c–6a). This is followed in vv.6b–7 by a second correction, a reminder of what they'd heard Jesus say "while he was still in Galilee" (a witness that the women were full participants) with an emphasis on "and on the third day rise again" (v.7c). The intent is this, "He said it. Did you not believe him?" Women disciples are also corrected.

The angels have their desired effect as interpreters of divine revelation, "And they remembered his words" (v.8) and with great energy returned and told the eleven and others over and over what happened at the tomb. But as yet there is no confirming appearance of Jesus, so the report is easily dismissed, "and these words seemed to them an idle tale, and they would not believe them" (v.11a).

But to his credit, and apparently alone, Peter repeats the dawn journey and inspection of the women to find it as they said, only now with an important additional detail noted, "he saw the linen cloths by themselves" (v.12). But there was no angelophany for Peter, "and he went home wondering/marveling at what had happened" (v.12d).

Divine revelation is disorienting and baffling. Intrusions of other world destabilize expectations and open new ones with dazzling possibilities. The following chart compares Luke's accounts with the other gospels and highlights the multiple lines of evidence:

Observations On The Resurrection Accounts[194]

A. Primary Elements Shared With The Other Gospels.

Item	Luke	Others
1. Early visit by women early Sunday morning	24:1	Matt 28:1, Mark 16:2, John 20:1
2. Names of the women, Mary Magdalene first	24:10	Matt 28:1, Mark 16:1, John 20:1
3. The stone rolled away from the tomb entrance	24:2	Matt 28:2, Mark 16:4, John 20:1
4. Appearance of angels in radiant clothing	24:4	Matt 28:2–3, Mark 16:5, John 20:12
5. Empty tomb itself	24:3, 6	Matt 28:6, Mark 16:6, John 20:6

B. Secondary Details And Their Sources.

Item	Luke	Others
1. Doubt/fear of the women	24:5	Matt 28:8, Mark 16:5, 8
2. Angelic declaration, "He is not here; he is risen."	24:6	Matt 28:6, Mark 16:6
3. Departure of the women to tell the men	24:9	Matt 28:9, John 20:2
4. Association of Peter with the empty tomb	24:12	Mark 16:7, John 20:2

C. Unique Lukan Materials.

Item	Citation
1. Inclusion of a Passion Prediction	24:7
2. Women as credible witnesses v. unbelief of apostles	24:8–11

Then

Disciples live in a complex, layered creation with interactions between the visible and invisible worlds. We are not the only sentient creatures. Angels are another order of being, and their ranks are divided between the faithful and the unfaithful. The good angels serve as divine messengers of a mild rebuke and of communicate what happened to Jesus and his body. The resurrection is angel-preached before it is experienced in multiple appearances.

As before and throughout, Luke highlights the women as faithful disciples and witnesses.[195] They receive the first preaching of resurrection. They are first with a resurrection appearance. Peter recounts a new piece of evidence—the abandoned linens, but there is no angelic appearance to him. He confirms the physical facts of

---

194. Extracted from Edwards, *The Gospel According to Luke*, 707.

195. For a recent article, see Bock, "A Note on the Women as Witnesses," 257–62.

the women's report. Jesus is not dead but fully alive with continuity of identity and discontinuity of form.

That Jesus was integral to divine providence is evident in his multiple passion predictions. The two pieces of evidence added to the summary of vv.6b–7 are the means of death as crucifixion and that the men who did him in were *sinful. Killed* is used in 9:44 and 18:32–33, but only in 24:7b is the means made clear—*crucified.* And only in v.7a is the true status of the leadership (Jewish and Roman) named; they are those who oppose God, thus *sinful.*

And while the empty tomb and abandoned linens are evidential, they make no sense until God gives an interpretive word through messenger. Coming to see *the new reality* is a process that includes perplexity and marveling. God has acted decisively in Jesus and upon him, and the revelation of just how is not shown all at once but in layers.

Now

The Jesus movement will continue, only in a new form ruled by the risen Lord and empowered by the Holy Spirit, and here we are at the transition point, the very hinge on which the door of history swings.

This is the one we follow, the crucified and risen Jesus, leaving a trail of evidences to female and male disciples, teasing them along until his shows himself again. The angels are always near, just beyond sight and waiting for a message to deliver. The risen Jesus is alive and thus available, guiding us through his Spirit and Word in the great adventure of loving God and people. Sometimes he even teases us and dribbles out his evidences to keep us on the trail. Several times I would swear I've heard him laughing at me. It's a great encouragement; he is, after all, about abundant, over-flowing, joyful life in the circle of the Triune God, and heaven, I am told, rings with belly laughter. Discipleship is finally a grand comedy that ends well, and of this Jesus' resurrection—which puts him out of the reach of human cruelty—is the preview.

We are the beneficiaries of enormous research into the event and meanings of Jesus' singular bodily resurrection from the dead.[196] The idea of discipleship in the church makes no sense at all unless Jesus is both alive and available for interaction with his followers now. We are following him, not just a model or an ideal or a myth but a real figure of history and one who—unlike all the others—is totally and completely alive because of God's vindication of him, a vindication to be validated before all at the end.

Being his apprentice today is grounded in and warranted by his resurrection from the dead. Every follower needs to speak from experience, "This is what Jesus has done for me," but also in the public sphere on the evidence for a raised, living, and available Jesus. The following chart is illustrative of the good case that can be built for what we claim:

196. For an important statement on the plausibility of Jesus' bodily resurrection, see Wright, *Surprised by Scripture*, 41–63.

The Consensus of Critical Historians: Ten Facts To Consider

1. Jesus died due to the rigors of crucifixion and was buried.

2. His disciples despaired because his death challenged their hopes.

3. The tomb in which Jesus was buried was discovered empty on Sunday.

4. The disciples had real experiences they believed were appearances of Jesus.

5. The disciples were transformed, even willing to die, for the truth of the events they witnessed. People do not typically die for what they know is untrue.

6. This gospel message was the center of preaching in the early church.

7. The message was soon proclaimed in Jerusalem. The authorities made no attempts to produce the body which would have ended it all.

8. The Christian church was firmly established by these disciples with great risk.

9. The primary day of worship became Sunday, the day Jesus was reported to have risen, and not the Jewish Sabbath. Something happened to cause this major shift.

10. James, Jesus' previously skeptical brother, was converted when he believed he saw the resurrected Jesus. Paul, a leader in the persecution of the church, was also converted by a real experience which he believed to be the risen Jesus.[197]

Summary

Disciples follow a Jesus who is full of surprises. That he is now beyond human cruelty and freed from the limits of space and time in the new physics of resurrection means he is near to and applying his call to every person all at once! And if you ask him, he will put you in their path as one of his witnesses.

Insights for Disciples

1. Women have a key role and especially in the events of Jesus' cross and resurrection.

2. Jesus treated women as full disciples, and so should we at all levels of the church.

3. The rolled stone, the empty tomb, and the absent body were public evidence something had happened.

4. Becoming familiar with the historical evidence for Jesus' resurrection strengthens your witness, especially to the unreflective skeptic.

---

197. This list is from www3.telus.net/trbrooks/garyhabermas. For a video, see rezproject.com/evidence-for-the-resurrection-gary-habermas. This material is thoroughly covered and critiqued in Beck and Licona, *Raised on the Third Day*, 1–14.

5. Your body and the bodies of others are designed for the glorious re-embodiment of Resurrection. Honor them now to love God and others.

6. Divine revelation concerning Jesus' new status came first in angelic preaching, then in multiple appearances, then in a Spirit-empowered world mission.

7. Part of God's vindication of Jesus was that his prophetic words were fulfilled.

8. Accepting Jesus' new status requires a layering of evidence, and not all at the same time or place.[198] Coming to a new paradigm is never simple or easy.

9. That Jesus exposed the unbelief of his male followers through his female disciples is a warning to all not to despise the witness of anyone.

Disciplines

Observation: Divine revelation is necessary; it's the only way to know certain things.
Action: Remember that if God needs to speak to you, there are multiple means!
Observation: The evidences were arranged with women as the first participants.
Action: If you want to hear God, do not ignore the voices and witness of women.

50. Luke 24:13–35[199]

Hearts on Fire
Genre: An Appearance and Commissioning Story, A Recognition Scene

Good then is love, having wings of burning fire,

that flies through the breasts and hearts of the saints

and consumes whatever is material and earthly,

but tests whatever is pure and with its fire makes better whatever it has touched.

This fire the Lord Jesus sent upon the earth.[200]

—Ambrose

---

198. See Witte, "A Manifold Resurrection,," 62–65, where he offers fives meeting points with the risen Jesus: 1) a calling by name (Mary Magdalene), 2) a delivery of peace (the ten disciples), 3) a sacramental vision (Emmaus disciples), 4) a physical encounter (Thomas), 5) a miracle and conversation (Peter). This is a fruitful line of thinking on variety in the appearances.

199. Helpful articles on Emmaus are Dinkler, "Building Character on the Road to Emmaus," 687–706; James Maxey, "The road to Emmaus," 112–23; Kuhn, "The Emmaus story," 17–39; Plevnik, "The Eyewitnesses of the Risen Jesus," 90–103.

200. Just, *Luke*, 382–83.

Justification

This, the second of Luke's resurrection units, brings before us two new disciples, Cleopas and this traveling companion (likely his wife). Jesus, ever the teacher, leads them through a review of recent events in light of Scripture and then pulls back the veil to reveal himself at the table and then disappear. Their witness to "the eleven" and others, and well as the witness of the eleven to them is that "The Lord has risen indeed and has appeared to Simon" (24:34), seals this as among Luke's most important discipleship passages. The resurrection is verified by multiple, independent witnesses. This is why the tomb is empty.

Shape

If we speak of *Lukan Classics*, then Jesus' Birth Story (2:1–21), the Parable of the Good Samaritan (10:29–37), the Parable of the Prodigal Son (15:11–32), and the Emmaus Story (24:13–35) are each on the list, and all are found only in Luke. The Emmaus Story is a masterful retelling of the first two appearances that Luke records. Just as the previous episode (24:1–12) began with the women and ended with Peter covering the same ground back and forth to the tomb, this thought unit begins with two disciples outside the circle of the twelve who have an appearance and ends with a report of Peter having received a visit as well, "The Lord has risen indeed, and has appeared to Simon" (v.34).

These two *end references* to Peter in successive units hint at the restoration prophesied in 22:32b, ". . . and when you have turned again, strengthen your brethren." The testimonies of those outside the twelve (the women of 24:10, Cleopas and his companion of 24:18) are validated by Peter's reports, thus an implicit apostolic verification and quality control. There is an unusual density of repetition and echoes at the beginning (1. vv.13–16) and ending (1' vv30–35) of the thought unit forming the outside set of frames. The seven inclusions are:

1. Appearance to two disciples (vv.15–16) // Appearance to Peter (v.34),

2. *talking* (v.14) // *talked* (v.32b),

3. *Jerusalem* (v.13//v.33),

4. *the things that had happened* (v.14) // *what had happened* (v.35a),

5. *Jesus himself drew near* (v.15b) // *he vanished out of their sight* (v.31b),

6. *their eyes were kept from recognizing him* (v.16) //

   their eyes were opened and they recognized him (v.31),

7. *And it happened that/* Gk. *kai egeneto* (v.15a // v.30).

The story has seven paragraphs with a single center and three sets of parallel frames:

    1. vv.13–16 Journey from Jerusalem to Emmaus, Non-Recognition
        2. v.17 Jesus Takes the Initiative: They Stand Still, Look Sad
            3. vv.18–21 Their Human Perspective on Jesus' Fate
                4. vv.22–24 Empty Tomb and Resurrection Message
            3' vv.25–27 Jesus' Divine Perspective on his Fate
        2' vv.28–29 They Take the Initiative: Jesus Goes in and Stays
    1' vv.30–35 Recognition, Journey Back to Jerusalem, Appearance to Peter

Note also the parallels between the several sets of parallel frames:

1. In 2. v.17 Jesus takes the initiative; and in 2.' vv.28–29 the travelers take the lead.

2. In 3. vv.18–21 we find the human perspective on Jesus' fate; in 3' vv.25–27 we find Jesus's view of the same events, using much of the same vocabulary.

3. At the center, 4. vv.22–24, we find a review of the previous unit (24:12) with an emphasis on the double witnesses (vv.22–23a // v.24) to the empty tomb, as recognized by Jewish law. And at the center of the center (23b) we find the angelic revelation that the tomb is empty because Jesus is alive again.

4. The living Jesus is hidden at the start of the story (v.16), vanishes at the end after his self-revelation (vv.30–31), and is preached at the center by angels (v.23b-c) who give the meaning of the double report of the empty tomb (vv.22–23a, 24), "he was alive." Thus, the two frames and the single center agree: Jesus is alive and re-embodied in a new form of physicality with amazing new powers; his old body has been transformed by God. He has been bodily resurrected.

Content

The dynamics of the story emerge in the first paragraph as two followers are headed home to reconstruct an old life when the risen Jesus—cloaked and in a hidden form—joins them. The risen Jesus must be revealed. He is not just seen; eyes must be opened. This allows the space for conversation without the two travelers being overwhelmed. He asks about their discussion (v.17a). Their response (v.17b) and answer (vv.18–21) lay out the story of Jesus as a grand hope of Israel and a great disappointment. Here they speak not just for themselves but also for the whole body of Jesus' apprentices.

A door of hope is left open in the stories of the finding of the empty tomb and a vision of angels *who said he was alive*. But such are not sufficient to keep them in Jerusalem. There is as yet no confirming appearance.

Now the response of the stranger to their reading of events begins with a double rebuke, "O foolish ones, and slow to believe" (v.25), then a question of divine necessity, "Was it not necessary that the Christ should suffer these things and so enter his glory" (v.26b)?" Finally Jesus offers a reading of Moses and the prophets to provide a fresh grounding for his question.

But still he is hidden, reasoning with them but not pulling back the curtain. And for disciples it raises the issue of how often we may miss his approach, but it is for the purpose of sinking them into a new reading of old traditions and waiting until a eucharistic moment to reveal himself. Thus the risen Jesus is met on the road of disappointment, in the Book of truth, in the home of hospitality, and at the table of fellowship.

That they invite him in for the night (vv.28–29) says something about them that demonstrates the effect he's already had on them. And at their table, he does the oddest thing. He, rather than being a guest, assumes the role of the head of the house and enacts the normal rituals of the Jewish table: taking, blessing, breaking, giving (v.30).

And in that moment there are two divine actions, their eyes are opened (passive voice = *by God*) and he disappears. This cancels their earlier reading of his history (vv.19b–21), in favor of the veracity of the angels' message (vv.22–24) and Jesus' confirming word (vv.25–27). Their reactions are two: they recognize the effect he had on them while still hidden (v.32), and they hurry back to Jerusalem to tell what happened and to receive the parallel report of an appearance of the risen Jesus to Simon.

Stuff is happening everywhere! Jesus is popping into and out of visibility in several places to confirm his new status.[201] He is, in fact, the preview of a new world.

Then

There are so many angles of vision here, it's hard to know where to begin. The most direct, however, is the new understanding of Jesus that his singular resurrection demands. It's unique, has happened only once, not at the end of time, but within it as a preview.

And its physics are *the new physics* of the kingdom of God and of the new heavens and earth that are promised. It's *a new world* with continuity of identity for Jesus with the present realm but in a newly embodied form without all the former limits. Thus Jesus is able to appear and disappear (vv.15b) and to be cloaked unless revealed (v.16a, 31).

To see into his new world is not for the unaided eye but only when God unveils our sight to see into the new world and its surprising interactions with the present order. During his earthly life all could see Jesus with the unaided eye, but as the risen one it's a two way operation: he is revealed, and our eyes are opened, and both are divine actions. It's much more selective.

---

201. For literary parallels of appearing and disappearing deities in Greco-Roman literature, see Johnson, *Luke*, 398; Culpepper, *Luke*, 475–76. The other world, however conceived, is highly interactive with this one.

That the risen Jesus is hidden and not immediately overwhelming says something important about the one we follow. He does not fix our problems immediately but is patient with our sadness, anger, disappointment, confusion, and errors about him. He does not too quickly banish the shadow side of life with his light. He is with us, as with Cleopas and likely his wife, but he is not a quick fix. He walks along and lets them talk. But he knows the truth about himself, and soon enough issues a complex correction to their reading of his life (vv.25–27) to which they have no reaction but to invite their interesting new friend in for the evening. But he is able, according to divine timing, to show himself and in that shock of recognition change the way everything is seen, to turn their sadness and dashed hopes into an exuberant witness.

The two had trudged home in disappointment and hurried back full of hope that *the Jesus thing* was not all over. And, to their surprise, they were not the only ones to have had such a surprise meeting. Peter had gotten back to the ten before they had, and his testimony is reported by others as, "The Lord has risen indeed, and has appeared to Simon," who— being present as one of *the eleven*, could verify with details.

Followers are often confused, disappointed, and bewildered at events which seem at odds with our view of the world. Why should this surprise us since we are deeply woven into the world as it is in spite of the special resources that come with our trust in the Father who sent the Son and the Spirit? The emotional words of the story, that they *looked sad . . . had hoped . . .* and that their hearts *burned* adds color and empathy to the story since these are common experiences.

Jesus makes a comprehensive claim on the whole human person; he reasons with them, sets their hearts on fire, opens their perceptions, and sends them on a mission. The whole of our person is responsive to his presence, and none of it is to be downgraded or despised. Dr. Chuck Hunter of Asbury Seminary once said to me:

> Phil, we used to think that people were rational creatures who occasionally had emotions, but now we know that they are emotional creatures who occasionally have rational thoughts. The Enlightenment of the eighteenth century greatly over-rated abstract rationality.[202]

It is interesting the layering of evidences and witnesses in Jesus' favor that Luke includes. First, his extraordinary life as a prophet whom God backed with power (v.19) but whom Jewish leaders delivered to Pilate (v.21) for crucifixion. Then the empty tomb and angelic message of new life. Then the verification by Peter, though without the angelic interpretation. Then the risen-but-concealed Jesus accompanies Cleopas and his wife along the road and to their home where he shows himself and vanishes. And, in the interim, there is a solo appearance to Simon, which he shares with the eleven and others, so that to them the story of Cleopas and his wife is an independent confirmation. Multiple, reinforcing lines of evidence are coming together to form a

---

202. For an exploration and defense of these proposals, see Hunter, *The Apostolic Congregation*, 37–69, particularly the subheading, "Crash Course in Human Emotion Theory," 46–48.

new conviction: that God has indeed acted to vindicate Jesus and coordinate a series of appearances to ground the conviction in multiple witnesses.[203] His movement is not ending but about to take a new form, as he had predicted.

Now

People follow the philosophies, world views, and religions of many ancient figures, and the difference with Jesus and his movement is that he's not a dead leader but personally alive in the kingdom of God with a resurrection body. This means that in addition to his words and deeds preserved in four gospels, we have an interactive presence. He can be known and followed still.

It's not just that he lives on in the influence of his teaching like other greats; he is, in fact, more alive than any of us, since our life runs out, but his never does. Jesus has been personally vindicated by the Father and the Spirit in a mighty act of resurrection. The world said No on Friday, and God said Yes on Sunday, "This is the one who came from above, and his person and work as shown in his words and deeds is divine revelation from start to finish. His resurrection is my ultimate seal of approval. Listen to him. Follow him."

So when we issue the call to follow Jesus as his pupils and apprentices, we should look for and expect divine verifications in the lives of the listeners, but these—being divine actions—are not under our control or even our prediction. It is the risen Jesus himself in partnership with the Holy Spirit who makes the case. We are not selling a religious package but pointing to a mysterious and marvelous person who will be visiting them soon and who's been at work long before we ever showed up.

In the end only Jesus can make his own case and make it stick. We read his stories and tell our histories; we speak of who he is and what he's done; we teach what he teaches and what the church teaches about him; we praise his benefits and all his excellencies; we answer questions. Then we pray and wait for him to do what only he can do, which is to alert a lost person to his presence, that what they have heard about him is true, and that they are being personally addressed. If he is already building a case with every person that crosses our path because they matter to him, then we can be both timely and relaxed in our witness, sometimes urgent but never believing the lie, "If it's going to be, then it's up to me!"

In following we learn, and in learning we grow wiser, and in wisdom is the patience and persistence to be among Jesus *cooperative friends*, partnering with him and others to make the case that he is worthy of everyone's trust and loyalty, that it is the best life now and later.

---

203. On the truth and ramifications of Jesus' resurrection, see Wright, *The Resurrection of the Son of God*, 435–40; *Simply Jesus*, 167–90; *Surprised by Scripture*, 41–63; Evans and Wright, *Jesus The Final Days*, 75–108; Wright, *Surprised By Hope*, 53–78.

This is how disciples are involved in the calling and forming of other followers. Jesus places us in all sorts of circumstances, that his light—refracted through us and reflecting from us—may draw their attention and curiosity, "What is it about you? You're different in a good way. What is it?" and our answer with a smile is, "It's not a *What* but a *Who.*"

Summary

Disciples are players in a great game of *Hide-and-Seek.* Jesus in now hidden and giving evidences for which only he is the answer. That is true if you are a long time follower or a new beginner. Only on day three did the appearances begin, and in at least two of them (Luke 24:13–35, John 20:1–18) he's at first hidden, then revealed. He's everywhere, always near, just beyond sight, the hidden factor in every moment, and so disciples often pray, "Open my eyes, Lord, inward and outward, that I may see and follow."

Insights

1. Had there been no resurrection and validating appearances, then no Christian faith.

2. In reading the gospels, we learn the character of the One who messes with us.

3. The risen Jesus is ever-near and ever-aware, and when he warms hearts and opens eyes, all changes. We find ourselves in the midst of more meaning than we know.

4. He is to be met on the road, in conversation, in grief and loss, at a family table, in his Book, in the testimonies of others, and in the hidden doors we open. There is no escape for those who call themselves his followers; he is always out ahead of us.

5. What if I prayed each morning, "Open my eyes and alert my heart to your hidden presence that I may join you in your work at every turn."

Disciplines

Observation: The appearance stories of the risen Jesus show us a new world.
Action: What if the risen Jesus was recognized as the hidden one in all our dealings?
Observation: The Bible, the sacraments, the witnesses all point to a real presence.
Action: What if every day begun with, "I'll be looking for your presence, O Lord."

51. Luke 24:36–53

The Verification of a New Beginning
Genres: Appearance and Commission Scene, Recognition Scene

The resurrection of the Lord was truly the resurrection of a real body,
because no other person was raised than he who had been crucified and died.
He did all this so that we might acknowledge that the properties
of the divine and human nature remain in him without causing a division.[204]
—LEO THE GREAT

Justification

As we noted earlier, Luke's Gospel is constructed to encourage our reading on two levels, first as the story of the founder–Jesus Christ, and secondly as a layered narrative of his core followers, with the story of his foes and non-following fans in the periphery.[205] Our controlling image has been a rope of two cords, the golden cord of Jesus interwoven with the blue cord of his followers. But if the image is expanded with the addition of two smaller strands, then his fans are in light blue and his foes, Jewish and Roman, in red.

This concluding thought unit demonstrates the unity of the founder and the followers and how tightly they are interwoven. This unit has a Janus-like quality as it looks back at the ministry of Jesus as the fulfillment of Scripture (vv.44–46) and ahead to the renewed mission to the nations in the power of the promised Holy Spirit (vv.47–48, 49) as portrayed in Acts.[206]

Shape

As a 4:2 concentric pattern, this thought unit falls into four paragraphs with a double center (1. vv.36–42, 2. vv.44–45 // 2' vv.46–48, 1' vv.49–53). There are several echoes/inclusions in the first and last sub-units:

1. *Jesus stood among them* (v.36b) // *he withdrew from them* (v.51b),

2. *Peace be with you* (v.36b) // *blessed them* (v.50b),

3. emotions: *startled and terrified . . . joy* (vv.37, 41a) // *with great joy* (v.52),

---

204. Just, *Luke*, 386.

205. I have found that the four-fold sequence of *founder*, *followers* (disciples), *fans* (crowds), and *foes* (Jewish kings, varied religious leaders, Pilate and Rome) keeps these audiences in mind as I analyze Luke's regular characterizations. It also has some rhetorical purchase as people place themselves in one of the pools as a *follower*, a *fan*, or a *foe*.

206. See Sweetland, *Our Journey with Jesus*, 41–43.

4. *hands* (vv.39, 40 // v.50b) marking the boundaries.

These framing units first deal with Jesus' appearances and the response of the disciples, including instruction on the nature of the new body (1. vv.36–37, 38–40, 41–42) and at the end with Jesus' ascension and the response of the disciples, including the promise of the Holy Spirit and their temple worship (1' vv. 49, 50–51, 52–53). The formal commission of Jesus is found in the two central sub-units (2. vv.44–45 // 2' vv.46–48, each with four parts:

1. A cue to speech (v.44a // v.46a),

2. A reminder of his words (v.44b) and Scripture (v.46b),

3. A purpose statement beginning with "that" (v.44c //vv.46c, 47a),

4. A commissioning through the illumination of Scripture (v.47b) and as official witnesses beginning in Jerusalem (v.47b).

The 4:2 concentric outline is as follows:

   1. vv.36–42 Appearance and Responses: Nature of the Resurrection Body

      2. vv.44–45 The Scriptural Witness to Jesus Required Illumination

      2' vv.46–48 The Message and Mission Requires Authoritative Witness

   1' vv.49–53 Ascension and Response: Blessing and Worship

The genre or literary type is an *Appearance and Commissioning Story* (very common in Luke) with its seven expected components:

1. Introduction (v.36a),

2a. Confrontation (v.36b),

3. Reaction(s) (vv.37, 41),

2b. Rebuke (v.38),

4. Commission (vv.44–48),

5. Protest (absent),

6. Reassurance (v.49),

7. Conclusion (vv.50–53).

To this form we note that Luke has added several significant expansions:

Expands the Confrontation with Verifications of Jesus' Identity and Physicality	vv.38–40 (Identity: hands and feet wounds)
	vv.41–43 (Human, ghosts do not eat)
Expands Confrontation with a Mild Rebuke	v.38b (Question, "Why are you frightened . . . ?")
Expands the Commission with	vv.44–45 Jesus is the fulfillment of Scripture
Pre-Commission Teaching	vv.46–48 Jesus life and benefits extended in mission
Expanded Reassurances	v.36b (Peace), v.39b ("It is I myself")
	v.49b (Gift of the Holy Spirit, v.50 (Blessing)

So, having mapped the structure and identified the genre, Luke's purposes are clarified in a story that culminates his biography of Jesus and bridges to Volume 2: Acts.

Content

There's no way for Jesus to step into visibility without nearly scaring the recipients to death! He's not there, and then he is—between blinks. His greeting indicates intent, "Peace be with you!" but they interpret his sudden presence in the categories of their culture as an apparition, a spectre, "and thought they were seeing a spirit" (24:37). We process primary sensory data through available models, and the resurrection of a single man in the middle of history–rather than at its end—is not in the computer.

The emotional language of their reaction to his sudden coming is notable:

"startled and terrified" (v.37a),

"Why are you frightened, and why do doubts arise in your heart" (v.38b)?

"in their joy they were disbelieving and wondering" (v.41a),

"and returned to Jerusalem with great joy" (v.52).

Something new has occurred, and everything is changed. Their life with him was not over, as everyone thought on Friday, and his resurrection casts a new light back on the whole of their time together. God backed him during the ministry, and God vindicated him after death. Jesus is the personal locus and focus divine revelation.

The correction Jesus offered throughout the story continues is his question of v.38b, "Why are you frightened, and why do doubts arise in your hearts?" His answer (vv.39–40) is to demonstrate that he's not a spirit or ghost of some sort but a re-embodied man, in effect:

> Hey, it's really me, tangible, touchable, real flesh and body, only now with new powers, raised, resurrected, beyond death, and the wounds in my hand and feet are the credentials of the cross. I have continuity of identity. What I prophesied has happened.

In the next two verses the same dynamic is at work in three parts:

1. v.41a   their continuing reaction,
2. v.41b   his question,
3. v.42   his answer.

And here the proof is that he eats a piece of fish, and since ghosts don't eat, he's not one of them. So the three parts of 1. vv.36–42 are a demonstration of *the new physics* in his sudden appearance and the embodied nature of his new frame, including the wounds left open as proofs of identity (cf. John 20:19–31 with Thomas). This is what the fullness of salvation looks and feels like. Jesus is the prototype of the transformed future of his followers.

Then comes the commissioning in two parts (2. vv.44–45 // 2' vv.46–48), each with four parts as noted above. Jesus is the deepest fulfillment possible of God's will in history and in one person; he is God the Son on display at ground level.

Note the unembarrassed personal focus in the phrases "my words" and "about me." That he "opened their minds to understand the scriptures" is a paraphrase of v.44. The Jewish canon is recentered in Jesus, and in him all the strands are woven together.

But to have a book you now understand is not enough for the mission. With it goes a creedal-like summary of the person and work of Jesus which echoes 1 Cor 15:3–5 and eventually became the second article of the great Creeds, "that the Messiah is to suffer and to rise from the dead on the third day," so that his benefits may be offered to all peoples, "and that repentance and forgiveness of sins (two major themes in Luke) is to be proclaimed in his name to all nations (the story of Acts)" (v.47). It starts right where they are by telling what they know, "Beginning from Jerusalem, you are witnesses of these things' (v.47b).

But still there is more. This is a proto-Trinitarian, tri-personal passage (*Jesus* [v.36b], *Holy Spirit* [v.49 implied], *Father* [v.49a]). So, to a canon re-visioned and a summary for preaching is added the empowering presence of the Holy Spirit as the fulfillment of the Father's promise (v.49). The one who filled and accompanied Jesus will soon fill and go with them as well, and for this they are to wait. Their first act of obedience is not to get busy but to wait together as a community, and what a rich conversation it must have been, a long review and consolidation before the sending out. Then came his departure, the end of a series of resurrection appearances, the length of which—forty days—we do not find out until Acts 1:1–17. They go to Bethany; he blesses them, and with his hands still in the gesture, he's gone, as before in v.31b at Emmaus.

It's not a lift-off as in the cartoon but an event (his disappearance) and its meaning, "and was being carried up into heaven," indicating divine action.[207] Jesus is now with the Father and invisible to us. His ascension, session, current reign, and coming rule are of a single piece, and as he guides us from above by his Spirit, so we go in mission.[208] And the final scene is worship at his feet, joy in Jerusalem, and worship in the temple. A new world has dawned, and the world needs to know.

Then

At the ending of older movies the film would finish, then the words *Then End* written in flowing script appeared on the screen. But that's not Luke, because his film is in two parts: a prequel and sequel, Luke on the founder and Acts on the followers. So the end

---

207. On the ascension and its meanings, see Orr, *Exalted Above the Heavens*; Farrow, *Ascension Theology*; Dawson, *Jesus Ascended*; Bird, *Evangelical Theology*, 449–59; *What Christians Ought to Believe*, 161–78; Toon, *The Ascension of our Lord*; Oden, *The Word of Life*, 502–26; Johnson, *The Creed*, 176–215.

208. On the mission, see Arias and Johnson, The Great Commission, "The Great Commission in Luke," 56–77, "The Lucan Model for Mission," 116–21; Tennent, *Invitation to World Missions*.

of Luke is more an intermission before the new reels are loaded. And what Luke has done is masterful because there is no more important transition than from Jesus to his church and the issues of continuity that accompany it. One way to organize our reflections is around four questions.

1. What is the resurrection of Jesus?

It's not spiritual, meaning less than bodily, but a full re-embodiment of the historical person in a new form with marvelous new properties, thus not the mere resuscitation of a corpse that will die again but the taking up of Jesus broken corpse into a new reality of life in the kingdom of God with a frame fit for new operations in a new realm on the other side of sin, evil, and death.

It's really him in all his particularities, including the wounds as historical credentials. He's tangible and touchable, solid, but he comes and goes from the invisible world to the visible and then back again, as if stepping in and out of a portal we can't see. It was a bodily resurrection leaving the negative evidences of a tomb vacated and linens abandoned. And when they saw him, all their mental furniture was rearranged and all their ideas of what was possible reconfigured. It's likely one of the reasons he gave them a ten day waiting period to sort it out together as they asked, "Did you see what I saw?" This the creeds capture in the sequel of "crucified under Pontius Pilate, dead, and buried . . . On the third day he rose from the dead, ascended into heaven, and sitteth at the Father's right hand" and then of our own resurrection at the end, "I believe . . . in the resurrection of the body." First him, then ours.

2. What is Jesus' relationship to his people and their Book?

The bluntest answer, and the one most offensive to current sensitivities is, "They are all, most deeply, about Jesus, one of your own and the very embodiment of our own persecutions." Whoa! And when among them, he was clear, "that everything written about me in the law of Moses, the prophets, and psalms, must be fulfilled." That's not ego but the awareness of how central he is to the divine purpose for which God formed himself a people. And from him comes a second testament beginning with four official biographies and joined in one Bible by the church which preserves and extends the story of Israel's God. And one day, as I was pondering a way to say it simply, I said to myself, "The God of Israel opened the divine heart, and we beheld the Holy Trinity." And I thought, "That's it!" That is the essence of our witness to our honored Jewish forebears.

And so we live together with our Jewish cousins in tension, love, and mutual correction. We should have been their best friends across history, and that colossal failure is a cancer on the face of the church. And while the brevity of the Creeds is a necessary limitation, its first lines evoke the first lines of the Jewish and Christian Scriptures, "I believe in God the Father Almighty, maker of heaven and earth." The usage of the Jewish names *Jesus* and *Mary* are also evocative, as are the title *Messiah* and *Lord*, and the notion of a general resurrection at the end of the age, as found in the Creed's final, climactic line, is also thoroughly Jewish, so even here there is more continuity than is often acknowledged.

3. What is the salvation Jesus brings and How?

Jesus' primary mission, the one from which all other benefits flow, is that he offers a healed and restored relationship with the God who is, as he reveals, a single living communion of Father, Son, and Holy Spirit. The One God of the Jews is a tri-personal communion of love and unified action. Our rebellion and treason, destructive attitudes and actions (sin) have put a cloud between us and God, one we cannot remove. We are independents who die, but in Jesus we get to come home and know God again, and that means the offer of forgiveness (grace), its willing acceptance (trust), and a wholehearted turning to face God and turn away from all that interferes with that primary relationship (repentance and the path of obedience toward the happiness that is holiness).

In this healed, open relationship are all the resources we need to love God and learn to love our neighbor and thus fulfill the law. Jesus is the embodiment of that offer and the one through whom it is enacted in his entire life as it comes to a focal point in his willing surrender to death and a confirming resurrection. This what sin is, that when God comes among us as a wise, innocent, truthful, loving, healing man, we torture him to death to get rid of the One he represents. His cross is deicide, and his resurrection demonstrates the absurdity of thinking God can be so easily dispatched. He will have himself a people, and he will have his world back. Jesus does not change the heart of God so much as he demonstrates God willingness to do whatever is necessary to bring home all who will. This is the intention of the lean summary of vv.46b–47, "Thus it is written, that the Messiah is to suffer and to rise from the dead on the third day, and that repentance and forgiveness of sins is to be proclaimed in his name to all nations." The world needs his message and him, and they are inseparable.

4. How are Jesus followers to enter this great work?

The response Luke offers is twofold. First, they will soon be flooded and filled with the same Holy Spirit as Jesus was at his baptism. Ministry begins in empowerment. This we may speak of as their *activation*. All that they have learned and seen in his presence, the deposit of divine revelation, will be made continually alive by *The Great Reminder* and with it the gifts of the Spirit that are required in the moment, whether healing or prophecy or wisdom or boldness or insight. The Spirit is their logistics partner specializing in *just-on-time* deliveries. They are being sent in a fully Trinitarian mission, as we note the language of v.49a, "And behold, I (Jesus) am sending upon you what my Father promised. Stay in the city until you have been clothed with power from on high (the Holy Spirit)."

Though the technical Trinitarian language is crafted and refined later on, the names, companionship, and power are now fully available. God is reaching the world through them. Secondly, that the risen Jesus will now lead and rule them from a new location, thus his Ascension back to the realm/dimension from which he came. Think of it as an invisible control room for visible operations down below. Thus, they are ruled by the same Jesus they walked with, and they are activated and resourced by the same Holy Spirit with whom he lived in such intimate cooperation.

Now

Is it possible that the same life of following is available to us? Yes, even though none of us get three years face-to-face with Jesus, we are offered a lifetime of learning and following ruled by the same Lord and with the same Spirit stirring us within and pushing us out in love and service.

It is an unending walk, a daily challenge, a perpetual adventure of obedience and discovery, as near as the next person we meet and as far as God flings us. At our death it's heaven above for a joyful interim, and then, at the end of the age, a re-embodied life in the new creation with real work to do, and all lived inside the the circle of love that is the Father and the Son and the Holy Spirit. The love we taste now and the forgiveness that gives us fresh freedom every time it is received, is utterly reliable.

Yes, there is boredom and stress, set-backs, genuine tragedies and losses, even periods of doubt and bewilderment, when prayers don't enliven and praise is duty. But this is not abnormal; it's a function of our human frailty, the fallen world in which we live, and the incessant pressures of the Evil One. And it can be made worse by isolation. Reading the saints can be helpful, as are tending to even little acts of kindness and love the Lord brings before us in the humblest of people. And with that an openness to receive such ourselves because we too are now "poor in spirit."

Faithful waiting, as the Lord demanded in v.49a, is a hard disciple, and if we can remain faithful in such and not fall into resignation or self-indulgence, when the time is right, new opportunities will open, and we will find that we have already been prepared in our wilderness in ways we did not imagine.

We are not forgotten, as I once heard from an old soldier, "Remember, Phil, present orders are standing orders till new orders come." Jesus is alive and near. When you prayerfully read the Book, he will speak.

There are people near you who need to see him in the way you live and love. The Holy Spirit is always whispering and aiding whatever you are called to do. He determines the place of your current deployment, and you should pray for open eyes to see his work and join him there. This is joy.

Summary

Disciples live in a tough neighborhood under the rule of the risen Jesus and the close supervision of the Holy Spirit. We develop convictions about the historicity of the bodily resurrection and all that it entails for our view of God's world. We read

Scripture to learn God's ways and study all the customs of the people to find entry points for the good news.

Insights

1. While there are no more resurrection appearances, his presence is often felt.

2. The other world has the potential of intruding at any time and place.

3. Challenges and rebukes, gentle or not, are expected as Jesus continues to teach us.

4. If a single human has been raised, then everyone was made for that kind of glory.

5. In fresh religious experience, fear, doubt, disbelief and wondering, are common.

6. We read the four gospels in order to be able to spot the One who deals with us.

7. The trajectory of the mission is from Jerusalem to everywhere else.

8. That we live under Jesus' blessing is not a temporary event but a permanent status.

9. The high privilege of faith is for Jesus to heal my broken relationship with God.

10. Mission is sustained in the joyful, communal worship of the living and Triune God.

Disciplines

Observation: All God's purposes and providences have been recentered in Jesus.
Action: When anyone trusts Jesus, they find themselves in Trinitarian fellowship.
Observation: The Scriptures and the Spirit are written and living avenues of life.
Action: Be immersed in the treasures of the Bible, and let your sails find the wind.

6

A Summary of Luke's Teaching on Following Jesus

1. LUKE 1:1-4

Make a Good Beginning

Disciples honor the gifts given to others, particularly those whose creativity and skill lets them preserve and interpret the apostolic tradition faithfully to current and future audiences. Historians and poets, bards and musicians, prophets, storytellers and liturgists are all needed.

2. LUKE 1:5-25

How to Build a Prophet

Disciples learn that divine providence, the ordering of events to God's purpose, is an exceedingly complex arrangement involving family and their histories, divine appointments, angelic mediation, prophetic promises, human frailty and sin, long periods of waiting, and not a small bit of pain and doubt, even divine discipline. It is only in looking back that the patterns are clarified, the connections made, and God's deep goodness appreciated. Providence never has to hurry, though events may coalesce quickly when the time is right.

3. LUKE 1:26-38

One of a Kind

Disciples see Mary as her Son's first follower, a model disciple who answered the divine call with surrender and trust in an uncertain future. Disciples may experience angelic visitations and communications. The explicit naming of the Father, the Son, and the Holy Spirit in the annunciation makes the whole of discipleship a Trinitarian event. Mary was drawn into the life and purposes of the Triune God, as are all disciples.

4. LUKE 2:1-21

What's the Big Deal?

Disciples stand in wonder and awe at the Jewish Savior's manner of coming. And if—as it sometimes does—our following becomes more about our performance than the glory of his person, then we've taken the center again and must be displaced. The joy of the third-shift shepherds and the pondering of Mary are our twin modes of operation. Jesus was a Jew, and that is never to be minimized or forgotten. We follow him in both action and reflection.

5. LUKE 3:1-22

The Beginning of Revival

Disciples face the challenges of repentance (i.e. a change of mind, heart, and hand) and from time to time return to the Jordan to listen to John the Baptist who prepared God's people for Jesus' emergence. Disciples are courageous in addressing sin, exposing excuses, giving specific counsel, warning of judgment, and pointing to Jesus as God's ultimate agent, even if it brings scorn and danger. And what we offer others, we apply to ourselves.

6. LUKE 4:31-44

Glimpse of a World Set Free

Disciples follow a confrontive Jesus who demonstrates what *the new reality* looks like at ground level, and two of its most dramatic effects are demon expulsion and physical healing; freedom and function matter to Jesus. We follow One who loves but will not be controlled by others and is passionate about getting *the new reality* out to others. This is why he was sent and why he sends us as well.

7. LUKE 5:1-16

How Jesus Operated

Disciples respond to a call in the midst of life. Jesus builds a case that he is trustworthy, then issues a summons for costly personal allegiance and the promise of a share in his mission, "Follow me, and I will make you . . ." The case may involve signs and wonders, though not all do. Observing Jesus teach and enact *the new reality* is an amazing privilege as the crowds gather. Observing him isolate for prayer reveals his source.

8. LUKE 5:27-39

The Problem of Conventional Religion

Disciples need to craft, like Levi, an *elevator speech* of how they came to be a Jesus follower. People are interested in people, so carry in your head a brief outline you can adapt to any listener. And recognize that, again like Levi, you came to Christ with a mission field, your network of family and friends. So throw a party and come to terms with the sheer newness and freshness Jesus brings to any situation. He loves hanging out with the wrong folk!

9. LUKE 6:12, 13-16, 17-19, 8:1-3

Jesus Expands his Reach

Disciples observe that Jesus is faithful to us in his prayers and that his choice of us was no mistake. He hears from the Father and places us in service as his personal representatives *with portfolio*, thus his ambassadors, his apostles. With him we face a needy, broken world together, trusting the Holy Spirit to bring whatever gifts and energies are needed. With Jesus, though not as often with the church, women are full partners as apprentices and understudies.

10. LUKE 6:20-26

The Charter of Discipleship 1: Finding You Place, Now and Later

Disciples understand how high the stakes are because at the end there's only the Blessing or Cursing of God. Disciples are not self-sufficient (poor), often lack (hunger), share the pain of the world (grief), and are rejected because of friendship with Jesus (hated). We live cross-grained to a world that values riches, gluttony, the mockery of others, and public honor, none of which will enter *the new reality* of which we already have a preview. Following Jesus is the highest privilege because we drink from the joy cup even now.

11. LUKE 6:27–38

Living Like God

Discipleship is the privilege of a new kind of life, one that in increments becomes more like Jesus and *the new reality* of the kingdom of God he embodies. Three marks of this life are love—even for enemies, doing good–again, even to enemies, and radical generosity towards all. All of this is sourced and enabled by *the new reality*. We live the new ethics of Jesus, abandon the role of ultimate judges, and relish the riches of God's mercy. Such a life will generate many questions from observers.

12. LUKE 6:39–49

How A Follower of Jesus is Repaired

Disciples learn that nothing is more consistently demanding than cycling through the process of *come-hear-do* with Jesus. It re-programs our every impulse and idea, every habit, attitude, and all that we allow out of our mouths. This process, or the lack thereof, determines what kind of person we become, a person of depth and substance who stands or a shallow person who crumbles at challenge or hardship. We are being remade in his company, and it requires surrender, trust, correction, perseverance, and many failures.

13. LUKE 8:1–21

The Seed that Wins

Disciples learn to follow in a new set of partnerships with Jesus, with one another, with high and lower status women disciples. The twelve are a potent symbol of the new Israel and the partnership of women a potent challenge. The seed Jesus spreads has violent forces arrayed against it, thus it is trodden down, withers, is choked, and still yields superabundantly. Disciples are realistic and tough-minded, but also persistent and hopeful. Jesus has made them insiders to *the new reality*. They are his new family who hear the Word, enact it, and receive additional revelation, part of which is to understand all the differing kinds of people who listen to their preaching.

14. LUKE 8:22–25

Layer One of Demonic Resistance

Disciples follow a Jesus who refuses to remain inside our comfort zones. His heart is for the world beyond our prejudices. He pushes us into frightening encounters, there to learn desperate prayers and to find him more than adequate. The one we follow is Lord over demons, diseases, death, and the whole of nature.

15. LUKE 8:26-39

Layer Two of Demonic Resistance

Disciples live on a battlefield of multi-level conflict with invisible foes and with the peoples they've influenced through idolatry and sorcery. At Jesus' behest we are to go to them, to face resistance at every step, and to announce and demonstrate the kingdom in the light and powers of the Spirit. It will lead to division and rejection by some; it always does. Jesus comes to defeat the Evil One and all his forms of bondage, in us and all he loves.

16. LUKE 8:40-56

When You're Hot, You're Hot!

Disciples learn that every day is a learning opportunity. Whatever our situation is, we keep dialing our awareness onto the Jesus channel with questions like, What are you doing here, Lord? Where are love and service needed? Whom do I need to pay attention to? Who are you sending me? What prayers should I offer? What should I say? Then take a first action, expecting more light as you walk in obedience to impressions that are loving, true, sometimes risky, and always kind. So it was with the first followers; watching Jesus operate under the Father's will and with the Spirit's empowerment was like nothing they'd ever seen. He did it all the time as a model, and then launched them into the same spiritual dynamic.

17. LUKE 9:1-11

Doing the Impossible with the Invisible

Disciples are *with* Jesus in order to become *like* him. This involves sharing his *new reality* mission, including announcing the kingdom, healing the sick, freeing the demonized, facing local rejection, and popping up on the political radar. It's a grand experiment in trust because he is not with them. They are sent together, stripped of normal supports, and must trust the Holy Spirit to provide what's needed. The idea of discipleship without such training is foreign to Jesus. After a time of observation, they are thrust into participation and return with amazing field reports. They have moved from lecture to laboratory.

18. LUKE 9:12-17

A Feast in the Wilderness

Disciples find themselves in circumstances where no amount of human cleverness or resourcing are adequate. We feel overwhelmed and undone. This is part of *the new reality* curriculum, and the best response is to pause, dial down anxiety, and ask,

"What do you want to do, Lord Jesus, and how can we join you?" Then wait and listen. Operating out of invisible resources in impossible situations is what he did every day, and the reports are that he was quite adept at it. Keep your eyes wide open and pray!

19. LUKE 9:18–22

A Public Poll and Peter's Confession

Disciples are students always learning from two major sources: the Gospel portraits of Jesus and what they know of him through interaction, with the first as the standard for the second. The constant question is, "But who do you (plural) say that I am?" to which our answers are always less than he is. Any theology of discipleship that has no place for suffering is inadequate. Obedience is costly. Disciples remain open to correction

20. LUKE 9:23–27

The Cost and Promise of Following

Disciples begin with a big dose of naivete about Jesus and his calling, but how could it be otherwise? But along the way are check-points and off ramps, where the cost and terms are clarified, and we either re-up or take a different path. It's about trust in and allegiance to Jesus with all his titles, all his mystery, and all his terrifying promises.

21. LUKE 9:28–36

Whom to Listen To

Disciples live with Jesus at the boundary of two worlds, and sometimes the invisible world intrudes into the visible with effects, something seen (visual) and something heard (auditory). Such events clarify Jesus' deep identity with Scriptural echoes and confirm our continuing frailty and lack of comprehension as his followers. They are not merit badges for display or comparison. But once insight is given, we never think of Jesus in quite the same way. In him and in his ordinariness, the very presence and glory of God is concealed.

22. LUKE 9:37–50, 51

Failures of the Followers

Disciples get used to the idea of getting it wrong and of having their worst moments placed in public view. So if image management is dear to you, life with Jesus will make you miserable. It's not that we're worse than others but that we follow the one perfect man who ever lived! How can we not fall short and feel stupid? But we can place our trust in the reliability of his call over our abilities. It's not about performance. It's about him and his ability to make us into a new kind of human who loves God fully and people faithfully.

23. LUKE 9:51–56

Jesus is Patient for Now

Disciples are a preview team for Jesus; people meet us before they meet him, and it can get ugly on both sides. Stress and rejection resurface old prejudices, and every cross-cultural meeting is a grand opportunity for tribal conflict. And while Jesus hoped for a reception in Samaria, he was never surprised by rejection and just moved on. Handle resistance gently and wait for a fresh opening of receptivity.

24. LUKE 9:57–62

Disrupted Attachments

Disciples come to Jesus by two paths, either attraction or summons, but the call for all is to leave an old life and its loyalties in order to follow him as an apprentice, to be with him with others in order to become like him. Jesus comes with friends already attached, so we get him and them. Some are heroic and need warning. Others have a *family first* commitment that need confrontation. Others want approval before such a decision and need warning. All who come to Jesus face major challenges. It's never easy.

25. LUKE 10:1–24

Everyone Gets to Play

Disciples are agents and ambassadors, living extensions of Jesus and *the new reality*. Under his authority we go in small teams, pray for more helpers, live vulnerably and simply, announce and enact *the new reality*, deal with opposition, represent the One who sent us and the One who sent him, bring back reports from the field, and keep listening to Jesus' abundant encouragements. It is an adventure to share life with this Jew.

26. LUKE 10:25–28

Ordering Our Loves

Disciples are always called back to basics, and nothing is more basic than love in two dimensions—for God and people, and on two axes—vertical and then horizontal. To love God with all we are and others as we love ourselves is not only our call; it was Jesus' daily practice. It's what he did, and into it we are invited as newbies, fumblers, goofballs, and wanna-bes. Something inside keeps whispering, "This is life. For this you were made." Robert Palmer was right, "Might as well say you're addicted to love."

27. LUKE 10:29–37, 38–42

What Love Looks Like

Disciples are interruptible! We avoid avoidance and engage engagement. It's not a crusade but acts of costly compassion and passionate mercy that startle the world into paying attention to the One we follow. And when we see such anywhere and from anyone and from whatever faith or lack thereof, we are seeing the hidden Jesus at work and should ask, "What urged you to do this? Do you know his name?" And in such engagement there's always the danger that our attention shifts to us and our duties and away from his truth and beauty. Disciples are constantly being turned back to Jesus as the deep source of our actions.

28. LUKE 11:1–13

Beginning to Pray

Disciples learn to pray from Jesus who gives them a model as an outline. He is the one who knows the Father and honors his sacred identity, who opens the kingdom to the world, who supplies his followers for physical strength (bread), relational healing (forgiveness), and protection from evil and the Evil One. The disciples' prayer is thus an outline of how Jesus loves the Father and the one's the Father's given him. It's who he is.

29. LUKE 12:1–12

Life is on the Line

Disciples know that following is more than external conformity to a new culture or set of norms. Rules are not the center but a relationship with Jesus Christ that goes to the center of the soul, to the self's control room, there to shine his light on all secrets and all fears, all issues of worth and value, all concerns about this life and the one to come. Disciples are accompanied on the inward and outward journeys by the Holy Spirit who is our tutor in the ways of Jesus Christ and who is fully able to communicate with us all.

30. LUKE 12:13–31, 22–31, 32–34

When Enough is Not

Disciples are wary of the desire for always more, first because it's so prevalent and secondly because their security lies elsewhere. We have an alternative accounting system, and it's titled "Gathering Riches for God," and that means investing everything Jesus gives us into people. And when we feel worry and anxiety, we go birding or stare at a flower and its gratuitous beauty. And with our equanimity restored until the next time fear pays a visit, we pay fresh and full attention to *the new reality* and all its resources which are never far away. We live with an open heart to God and an open hand to other members of our *little flock* and to the poor and love-starved around us.

31. LUKE 12:35–40, 41–48

The Glory and the Gore

Disciples have a stance of readiness and alertness to the One who lives just beyond our sight. This does not mean we cannot rest and unplug from time to time, but that even here we do no lose our awareness of Jesus' nearness and our accountability. He wants his people well tended, not used or abused. Servant leadership in the community of Jesus is a serious matter, and a death sentence is possible for any who fleece the flock and live as scoundrels. With God the judgment always fits the crime, and the rewards it the faithfulness. Never forget the One who is near and observant to all who bear his name.

32. LUKE 14:25–35

The Cost of Following, and of Not

Disciples regularly go through reality checks. The old life, its rhythms and comforts, loyalties and habits, keep displacing Jesus. We lose our focus, and clarity is forfeited. Our primary loyalty is to him and *the new reality*, and all other good things, be they family, safety, all the supports of life, remain decidedly secondary. If restored to primacy, we have, in effect, resigned our commissions and lapsed back into *the great multitude*. It's a different life, as distinct as the taste of salt, so the question is, How badly do you want it?

33. LUKE 16:1–8, 9–13

Avoiding a Seductive Deity

Disciples use all their resources to advance *the new reality* and to increase the reputation of the One who embodies it— the Jesus we follow. This takes insight, cleverness, and decisive action. Carrying out kingdom assignments put us in line with the angels who are our invisible friends, now and at our death. Being faithful in small matters prepares us for a much larger scope, now and in the coming new world. Worshiping God and using money is wise, whereas the reverse—worshiping money and trying to use God—is death.

34. LUKE 17:1–10

Discipleship Up Close

Disciples are not naive about the insidious power of sin, in themselves and their colleagues. All are accountable and called to account, but those who deliberately corrupt others—and particularly the vulnerable—are judged ahead of time. It is strenuous work to be an agent of correction and mercy and to humbly receive what you offer others, but what a safe people to live among! No one is allowed to stumble alone. Pastors are not police, but their care of Jesus' people includes confession, forgiveness, and healing discipline. It is a duty that must be done, but it earns us no points. Obeying Jesus is enough of a privilege.

35. LUKE 17:20–37

Question About the End

Disciples live in the interim between the *already* of Jesus and the *not yet* of the coming kingdom, and so it's always been. Our stance is to *stay ready* not *get ready*. When Jesus shows up, it will be all at once and without a two-minute warning. Life goes on and then suddenly stops as the great division is enacted. The *When* is suddenly, the *How* is disastrously, the *Who* is everyone, and the *Where* is everywhere. Don't be distracted.

36. LUKE 18:1–8

Do Not Quit Praying

Disciples keep the prayer line open and operating, especially when courage fades and fatigue creeps in. "Just don't quit!" is Jesus' exhortation. God is listening, hears your words, knows your feelings, delights in your trust, and will act. The question for discussion is not God's faithfulness but ours.

37. LUKE 18:15–17

Only Children Get a Ticket

Disciples have their blind spots and prejudices regularly exposed by Jesus, and the pain fixes it deep in the memory. In a culture where time with children enhanced no one's honor or status, Jesus took time for the smallest and blessed them with his touch. There is no age or intellectual or moral requirement to enter *the new reality*, and since trust is the currency of the kingdom, children are the models for us all.

38. LUKE 18:18–30

One Who Said No and Those Who Said Yes

Disciples are not surprised when anyone refuses Jesus' invitation because they know that freedom is always part of the equation. Grace woos; it does not compel or coerce because Jesus is after trust, not merely compliance. Being a Jesus follower is not a capstone to an otherwise impressive moral resume. It demands surrender and will expose whatever internal blockages are near and dear, in this case wealth and all it affords, which for many was taken as a sign of divine favor, but not with Jesus. And to those who leave one life for another, the promises are enormous, something only God can guarantee.

39. LUKE 18:31–34

Jesus Again Announces His Mysterious Future

Disciples live amidst mysteries and purposes that are beyond understanding, which is what it means to be restored to a healed relationship with the Father and the Son and the Holy Spirit. We see—but not well, and know—but only a little. It's when we look back that we see and grasp more deeply. All God's work comes to focus in Jesus and especially in his self-surrender to suffering, humiliation, and death with a trust in resurrection. That he announced it and that it happened as he said, is one more reason to find him trustworthy.

40. LUKE 19:11–28

Waiting on Another World

Disciples live in light of the end but prepare for the long haul. Our daily goal is to gladly live under the benevolent rule of Jesus Christ, to be faithful to the trust he's put in us and fruitful in the labor he's assigned. To use a market metaphor, he's looking for a *return on investment,* which means holy living (loving God) and disciple making (loving people). Stakes are high and risks necessary; it's a genuine drama. Gains of tenfold and fivefold are possible for those who turn trust into action. But woe to one who slanders his patron's character and lives in fear as a failed follower. Why live such a shrunken, shriveled life?

41. LUKE 19:28–48

The Tragedy of Missing God

Disciples are mainly in the business of carrying out assignments, of discovering over and over that Jesus is faithful. He sees what we do not and knows what we do not. And in this new life there are ecstatic moments of celebrating King Jesus and sad, sobering moments when we see the costs of rejecting him and *the new reality* he brings. He is the dwelling place of God in flesh, and so the temple and its accouterments are now redundant.

42. LUKE 20:45–47, 21:1–4

A Negative and Positive Example Concerning Piety and Money

Disciples understand the power of money to express love as they trust God for their physical needs and their need for deep affirmation. Hiding other agendas, most prominently status-seeking and greed, under the cover of religion and piety is a common sin.

43. LUKE 21:5–38

Get Smart! Get Ready! Stay Alert!

Disciples do not waste time or effort with the time lines of the end-timers. We, rather, choose to live faithfully in hope whatever happens between now and the kingdom's public arrival. The signs of which Jesus speaks, including political turmoil, natural disasters, and religious persecution, are not cues that the end is near; they are the normal stuff of history in a broken cosmos in rebellion against its Maker. Only with the sudden appearance of the Son of man in glory is the end here, and it is everywhere all at once.

44. LUKE 22:1–38

Eating on a Battlefield

Disciples live in both the visible and invisible worlds and find that Jesus is skilled in both. Every encounter with him is raw material for our being shaped as his followers. He has all the love we need and all the time it takes to turn us into his agents. Remaining as a guest at his table and learning the art of serving others is where you want to be. Testing is sure to arrive; it exposes our weaknesses and hopefully increases our dependence on Christ.

45. LUKE 22:39–46

The Only Hero

Disciples discover how weak and faulty we are in Jesus' presence. There are no illusions with him; he accepts us where we are, and loves too much to leave us there. And when the pressure is turned up and you're about to crumble, humble your heart in prayer.

46. LUKE 22:47-53

The Hour and Power of Darkness

Disciples get used to exposure and a loss of naivete about themselves and others. It's part of Jesus' curriculum that the very worst in us is brought to light, that we are sinners still and vulnerable to evil. We must receive what he offer others, or we are lost. We don't save him, but he saves us.

47. LUKE 22:54-65

Peter's Failure

Disciples are regularly exposed and humbled because Jesus reveals what's in them. It's love and truth at work, bringing us more into alignment with the One we follow. Peter's denials did not move him out of the range of forgiveness or restoration.

48. LUKE 23:26-56

A New Cast of Followers

Potential disciples are always being drawn toward the mysterious, magnetic person of Jesus Christ because of his potent innocence, his blend of truth-speaking and love-showing. It's what drew us into his entourage. And if we keep our eyes open, the Holy Spirit will alert us to the curious and receptive who need our witness as a step towards trusting him.

49. LUKE 24:1-12

Too Good Not to be True

Disciples follow a Jesus who is full of surprises. That he is now beyond human cruelty and freed from the limits of space and time in the new physics of resurrection means that he is near to and applying his call to every person all at once! And if you ask him, he will put you in their path as one of his witnesses.

50. LUKE 24:13-35

Hearts on Fire

Disciples are players in a great game of *Hide-and-Seek*. Jesus in now hidden and giving evidence for which only he is the answer. That is true if you are a long time follower or a new beginner. Only on day three did the appearances begin, and in at least two of them (Luke 24:13–35, John 20:1–18) he's at first hidden, then revealed. He is everywhere, always near, just beyond sight, the hidden factor in every moment, and so disciples often pray, "Open my eyes, Lord, inward and outward," that I may follow.

51. LUKE 24:36-53

The Verification of a New Beginning

Disciples live in a tough neighborhood under the rule of the risen Jesus and the close supervision of the Holy Spirit. We develop deep convictions about the historicity of the bodily resurrection and all that it entails for our view of God's world. We read Scripture to learn God's ways and all the customs of the people to find entry points for the good news.

7

What Biblical Scholars Are Saying about Discipleship in Luke

ONE OF THE UNACKNOWLEDGED and underused resources of the church is our *brain trust*, our cadre of scholars and theologians who've given their lives to research and writing. In an age of pragmatism—as ours surely is, it's easy to ignore those who work on the Who? What? Why? questions (the essentials), instead of the When? Where? How? questions (the methods and practices). In our rush to copy a proven method that will work and deliver results if only we do it properly—a manufacturing model of people and the church, often termed *programs*—we ignore the primary and essential questions, and these are the ones our scholars are best at helping with.

Yes, their work is often technical and dense, requiring the ability to follow a sustained logical argument as evidence is marshaled. It is, as a friend said, *a pain in the brain*. But if we're always asking prematurely, "But how does this apply to me or my church?" we give away our impatience, our unwillingness to seek anything but a *quick fix*, and when it comes to following Jesus together there is none. Slow is the mode.[1]

We are fortunate that with the renaissance in the study of Luke and Acts there has come in recent decades a series of scholarly articles and chapters in books on *Discipleship in Luke*. The format used to present each of these articles or chapters is the same. The citation will be listed and followed by an analysis of the author's method and insights with commentary interwoven.

The typical pattern is for a scholar to begin with a limitation of their topic, offer a theory of Synoptic origins, then move through Luke looking for repeated themes that bear on discipleship and stopping occasionally for more in-depth treatments of key passages, and at the end draw together a summary of insights.

---

1. Scazerro, *Emotionally Healthy Discipleship*, 37–86.

After working though the literature we should be able to observe a consensus emerging around Luke's understanding of what it meant for his hearers to be followers of Jesus together with others. Getting clear on the Who, What, Why questions will ground us in something solid and substantial. It will also serve as a dialog partner for my treatment of the same issues in Luke's fifty-one thought units on discipleship.

Since the initial chapter by Richard Longnecker is a fine piece and ends with a useful summary of ten lessons on discipleship from Luke, his will receive the more thorough treatment, with subsequent scholars noted where they differ or offer new insights. Some overlap and repetition is inevitable since the topic is a narrow one.

If this book has value and contributes to the conversation about discipleship, church-renewal, and mission, it may be because of its method of first identifying Luke's ninety-four thought units and then discovering how many of them touch on the theme of being a follower under development by Jesus. Christology (who Jesus is) and Discipleship (our apprenticeship to him) are reciprocal; they are distinguished and yet go together like two strands of a rope. So what are New Testament scholars saying about Luke's vision of being a Jesus follower? Let's find out!

1. Richard Longnecker, editor. "Introduction," and "Taking Up the Cross Daily: Discipleship in Luke-Acts." In *Patterns of Discipleship in the New Testament*. Grand Rapids: Eerdmans, 1996, 1–7, 50–76.

In a survey of titles and designations, Longnecker notes that *those of the Way* was likely the first self-designation of Christians (Acts 9:2, 19:9, 23, 22:4, 24:14, 22), with *Christians* (*those of the household of Christ* or *Christ followers*) a title first applied to them by others in Syrian Antioch (Acts 11:26, 26:28, 1 Peter 4:16).

Prior to these, the most common name for followers in the Gospels was the Greek *mathetes*, literally *pupil* or *learner*, most often translated as *disciple*.[2] This term was less common in earlier Jewish literature but widespread in Greek and Roman philosophical texts for one who became a follower of a particular teacher (Gk. *didaskalos*), whether then-living or deceased. Such a relationship involved learning, imitation, and often great personal loyalty and veneration. The Hebrew equivalent was *talmid*, and its presence in the Talmud, though formulated in the second century and beyond, reflects earlier understandings. The earliest tractate (chapter) of rabbinic lore in the Mishnah begins with this paragraph:

> Moses received the Law from Sinai and committed it to Joshua, and Joshua to the Elders, and the Elders to the Prophets; and the Prophets committed it to the men of the Great Synagogue. They said three things: "Be deliberate in judgment, *raise up many disciples [talmidim]*; and make a fence around the Law" (*Pirke Aboth* 1:1, italics added).

2. The word "disciple" appears 261 times in the New Testament Gospels and Acts. It's range of meanings centers around being a pupil or learner of a great teacher. See Foster, "Discipleship in the New Testament," www.sbl-site.org/assets/pdfs/tbv2i7_fosterdiscipleship.pdf Also Fredrichsen, "*Disciple(s)* in the New Testament," 717–39.

To follow (Gk. *akolouthein*) is a parallel term and indicates that learning in that world often meant walking and talking. Where the teacher went, you went. Thus, in the Septuagint,[3] Elisha is presented as one who is to "follow after" the prophet Elijah. Thus being a disciple or follower were paralleled terms whether the master was a philosopher or a Jewish sage. In Luke *mathetes/disciple* is used thirty-four times for Jesus' followers, and elsewhere in the gospels for followers of John the Baptist, the Pharisees, and Moses. "To follow" or "those who follow" is found in Luke 5:11, 27, 28, 7:9, 9:11. Jesus did not invent the terminology or the method of *learning-by-apprenticeship*; rather, he inherited and adopted it to his own purposes. It's how advanced learning and character formation were done in his world. Being molded in the ideas and virtues of another was the goal.

The conundrum is that *mathetes/disciple*, common in the Gospels and Acts and with a single addition reference in Revelation 9:14, is absent from the rest of the New Testament. And while the call to imitation and learning remains pervasive in both the Gospels and Epistles, it appears that the earlier terminology was limited to the earliest of Jesus' followers. The intent of a life transformed by Jesus' person and work remains since the goal is to become like Christ (Rom 8:29, 1 Cor 15:49, 2 Cor 3:18, Eph 4:13–15, Col 3:9–10, 1 John 3:2) but the terminology shifts from *methetes/disciple* to a range of terms related to the verb *mimeomai*: "to use as a model, imitate, emulate, follow," thus the English *mimesis* and *mimetic*.[4] Continuity and variation accompany one another in the New Testament terminology on discipleship, and to make too much of this variation is a mistake.

Longnecker observes that Luke's is the most sustained treatment of discipleship in the Four Gospels, not least because of his second volume—Acts—which demonstrates how the life of the Savior continues in the work of Peter and Paul, thus the theme of continuity between founder and followers, as he notes, "what was basic in Jesus' ministry has been and should continue to be the pattern for all of the church's life and ministry."[5]

Since Luke's use of Mark as a source is a settled issue, some of Luke's priorities are revealed in what he includes from Mark, what he omits, and what he adds from other sources.[6] And, whether Q is an independent source,[7] or whether Luke was working from

3. The Greek translation of the Old Testament (2nd century B.C.), indicated by the Roman numeral for "seventy/LXX" is a reference to the pious story that seventy translators, all working independently, came up with the same translation.

4. Samra, "A Biblical View of Discipleship," 313–23.

5. 53–54. On these correspondences as clues to Luke's theology of continuity between Jesus and his followers, see Talbert, *Literary Patterns*, 23–88; O'Toole, "Parallels between Jesus and his disciples in Luke-Acts," 195–212; Edwards, "Parallels and Patterns Between Luke and Acts," 485–501.

6. On Mark's presentation of discipleship as the basis for much of Luke's portrait, see Garland, *A Theology of Mark's Gospel*, 388–454; Stock, *Call to Discipleship*; Sweetland, *Our Journey with Jesus*.

7. Q, from the German *Quelle*/Source, is a hypothetical document or oral collection of Jesus' teachings without a narrative framework that serves to explain the numerous correspondences between Matthew and Luke, presuming they did not know each other. That standard model assumes that Luke uses three sources: Mark, Q, L (his own materials).

Matthew as well as Mark (the Farrar hypothesis), we see his hand there as well. Luke honors his sources, shapes, and adds to them his own touch (an observation made from his editing of Mark over which we have some critical controls). Luke is a creative, literary theologian working within an established tradition by filling it out and extending it.

Longnecker notes that Luke's portrayal omits some of Mark's more negative characterizations of the twelve and includes a larger circle of followers as disciples, not just *the twelve*. It's not a whitewash, but in light of their later work in Acts, is shifted away from their being total failures. Jesus will succeed in making them enough like himself for the mission to continue, as in 6:40, "Disciples are not above their teachers, but all those who are fully trained will be like their teachers."

It is in the material just after the birth narratives (3:1–22 [John's ministry + Jesus baptism], 3:23–38 [Jesus' genealogy], 4:1–15 [Jesus' wilderness ordeals], and 4:16–30 [Jesus' sermon and rejection at Nazareth]) that Luke gives us several of his most basic themes of discipleship as modeled by John and Jesus:

1. Preaching the Word of God;

2. The universality of God's grace towards Jew and Gentile;

3. The necessary accompaniment of the Holy Spirit;

4. The facts of ongoing resistance and the possibility of suffering, both from Satan and humans;

5. The fulfillment of prophetic promises, most often from Isaiah;

6. A focus on the poor and suffering with warnings for the rich and powerful.

That the disciples are soon to be *apostles* (authorized ambassadors of Jesus, 6:13–19) means they share all these dynamics from the beginning, first as observers, then as participants. Luke's six uses of *apostle* in his Gospel (whereas only once by Mark) and his thirty uses in Acts make it clear that the disciples are in training as personal agents of Jesus. He has from the start created a community and a training model around himself and his mission.

Whatever your answer to the Synoptic Problem (the literary relationship between Matthew, Mark, and Luke), about a sixth of Luke's sayings materials are not found in Mark but echoed in a second theoretical source, Matthew.[8] I agree with Longnecker that three of Luke's most important discipleship paragraphs have parallels in Matthew, though they have been—as expected—edited and reshaped:

The Beatitudes	Luke 6:20b–26	Matthew 5:3–12
Conditions of Following	Luke 9:57–62	Matthew 8:18–22
Cost of Discipleship	Luke 14:25–35	Matthew 10:37–38

---

8. I am increasingly leaning towards the Farrar hypothesis that Luke had both Mark and Matthew as written sources and that Q is a convenient scholarly invention. This dispenses with hypothetical Q. On the debate, see Porter and Dyer, *The Synoptic Problem*, 47–66.

In these three units Jesus is clear both about the conditions and cost of following. The worthy way is difficult, with Jesus' demanding to be the central loyalty around which all others are reorganized, and here family obligations take a step down from conventional Jewish practice. Following means an unsettled, insecure life by normal estimations. Disciples live light, do not give up, and trust their patron for necessities. But all this is more than made up for by the call to "proclaim the kingdom of God" and see its startling effects as life is set right again.

The core idea of following Jesus is everywhere in Luke as they are on the road together from village to village and then especially during the long trek south to Jerusalem in what's come to be called "The Travel Narrative" (9:51–19:27).[9] This block of material sheds light on echoes from Mark and Matthew and is dominated by stories only found in Luke (often designated *L* for Luke's unique sources). It is a discipleship classic with much of the teaching coming from fifteen or sixteen parables. At this point Longnecker gives us a listing of the parables by topic to demonstrate how closely they fit and strengthen earlier discipleship themes in Luke,[10]

1.	Loving and Helping Others	The Good Samaritan	10:5–37
2.	Prayer	The Persistent Friend	11:5–13
		The Persistent Widow	18:1–8
3.	Possession and True Riches	The Rich Fool	12:13–34
		Rich Man & Lazarus	16:19–31
4.	Service to God	Failing Fig Tree	13:1–9
		Proper Attitude	17:7–10
		The Ten Pounds	19:11–27
5.	Responding to God	The Great Supper	14:15–24
		Rich Man & Lazarus	16:19–31
6.	God's Love for the Lost	Lost Sheep	15:1–7
		Lost Coin	15:8–10
		Lost Sons	15:11–32
7.	Humility	Pharisee & Tax Collector	18:9–14
		Parable of Banquet	14:7–14
8.	Shrewdness in Affairs	Shrewd Manager	16:1–12

That these parables and images can be so easily grouped by the topics and virtues of discipleship demonstrate Luke's cohesive presentation across his narrative. Disciples learn to be challenged by Jesus the storyteller, to remember and reflect upon the meanings of his stories. It's why they were preserved and organized as demonstrated.

---

9. There are, upon observation, three *Travel Narratives* in Luke, the first in the birth and early ministry stories (1:1–4:30), the second around Northern Galilee (4:31–9:50), the third to Jerusalem (9:51–19:27). The second and third are signaled by a travel report: "And he went down to Capernaum" (4:31) and "But when the days drew near, he set his face to go to Jerusalem" (9:51). Following Mark, Luke presents Jesus' ministry with a single trip to Jerusalem for Passover, not the three found in John.

10. 66–67.

It is made clear in Luke's passion account, building on what came before, that Jesus is the model of the way, the exemplar and pattern of life with God in *the new reality* which embraces suffering and service. His unconditional obedience is the path for his followers. Two *cross sayings* highlight this theme, the first being 9:23 where Luke adds the adverb *daily* to his source (Mark 8:34), "Those who come after me must deny themselves and take up their cross *daily* and follow me." Thus Jesus sets the pattern. The second is 14:27, with a parallel in Matt 10:38, "Those who do not carry their cross and follow me cannot be my disciples," with Simon of Cyrene as a vivid historical example (23:26) of one who bears the burden *behind him* (9:23). Jesus marks the path for the followers as pioneer and exemplar. He would rather suffer than break his fellowship with, trust in, and obedience to the Father.

In addition, in the Last Supper Jesus is highlighted as the model servant when he says, "Who is greater, the one who is at table or the one who serves? But I am among you as one who serves" (22:27e). He also sets a pattern in prayer under pressure in Gethsemane (22:39–46), in evangelism (23:43), forgiveness (23:34), and self-surrender (23:46) from the cross.

As he moves towards the end of his essay, Longnecker writes:

> Luke's major interest in the writing of his two volumes seems to have been the everyday matter of Christian discipleship—that is, in setting out for his readers the self-consciousness that one should have and the manner in which one should live as a follower of Christ.[11]

The gift of Longnecker's treatment is not only his deft analysis but that he summarizes his findings in a list of ten characteristics of Lucan disciples of Jesus:

1. Discipleship is based on what Christ has effected for the redemption of humanity.

2. Discipleship must always be rooted in and shaped by the apostolic tradition.

3. Discipleship needs always to be dependent on God and submissive to his will, hence the importance of prayer.

4. Discipleship must always recognize the presence and power of the Holy Spirit.

5. Discipleship is to be involved in prophetic proclamation, with that proclamation focused on the work of Jesus.

6. Discipleship is to cherish, both in thought and in action, the understanding of God's grace and the gospel as being universal.

7. Discipleship is to be committed to a lifestyle that allows no allegiance to take the place of allegiance to Jesus.

8. Discipleship is to be concerned for the poor, the imprisoned, the blind, and the oppressed.

11. 74.

9. Discipleship is to follow the example of Jesus and the apostles, particularly Paul, in matters of service, prayer, and cross-bearing.

10. Discipleship is to be a life of development in both one's faith and one's practice.[12]

As we review the work of other scholars, we will make additions to Longnecker's list.

2. Joel B. Green. "'Let them take up the cross daily': the way of discipleship." In *The Theology of the Gospel of Luke: New Testament Theology*. Cambridge: Cambridge University Press, 1995, 102–21.

Green begins his essay with the claim that it's not until Volume II: Acts that the disciples move to the fore and that in Luke they are more passive and regarded primarily as the recipients of Jesus' training prior to their commissioning (22:28–30, 24:47). That Jesus is the featured character of Luke is undeniable, but that they are passive is an over-statement. They are, as a group, the second most important characters in Luke and serve as both an extension of Jesus' person and the primary audience of his teaching and miracles. They are not present in the birth narratives but after that are pervasive.

Green highlights the theme of *the way* (Gk. *hodos*) as a journey with Jesus, a road trip introduced by John the Baptist who "prepares the way" (1:76, 3:4–5, 7:27) for the coming one who will eventually, in the words of Zechariah, "guide our feet into the way of peace" (1:79). Luke's frequent travel reports continue to highlight the theme that following Jesus means being on the road with him as a fellow-traveler, especially as featured in the Galilean tour (4:31–9:50), the long trek to Jerusalem (9:51–19:25), and in the concluding Emmaus episode (24:13–35) with its frequent use of *road/hodos*.

So where does the journey on the way with Jesus begin? Often with a call and commissioning story (5:1–11, 27–28), but not everyone who receives Jesus' aid is invited into the traveling band of followers (7:1–11, 36–50, 8:43–48). Initiative remains with Jesus who goes and seeks, calls and crosses conventional boundaries to call a *sinner* (5:8), a *tax collector* (5:27), and *women* (8:1–3) as followers. The disciples are often characterized simply as those who are "with him" (6:17, 8:1, 22, 9:10, 22:11, 14, 39). They also receive instruction along with the crowds (6:17, 20, 7:1). But when the early ministry in Galilee (4:31–9:50) shifts to the long journey south to Jerusalem (9:51–19:27), the focus on the disciples and their being taught by Jesus intensifies.

As Green moves through an overview of Luke's unfolding story, he highlights themes having to do with discipleship under a series of major and minor headings. This is the same type of survey process that led Longnecker to his catalog of ten discipleship statements. The comments in parentheses are my own. Green's outline is:

Beginning the Journey

    The Initiative of Jesus (God's gracious outreach to sinners is primary.)

    Faith (Putting one's trust in Jesus, the worthy and true one, is faith.)

    Repentance (A change of mind and direction to turn towards God.)

12. 75.

Following Jesus (Life with Jesus on the road and in *the new reality.*)

Involvement in Mission (Becoming a trained, authorized agent of Jesus.)

Prayer and Praise

The *new reality* in Jesus is the cause of praise.

The one Jesus addressed as *Father* is eager to hear from and respond to us.

The Economy of the Kingdom

A poor man called *Jesus'* (Jesus issues warnings, depends on God and others.)

Wealth and power (Money is a tool. You cannot serve God and money.)

Egalitarian Community

Status-seeking (All are called to follow and to welcome the lowliest.)

The new community and the Roman world (Jesus undermines patronage.)

It is expected that scholars, while reviewing the same texts, will highlight different elements and bring them to the fore. With this in mind, we extend Longnecker's list of ten with two additional items gleaned from Green's essay:

11. Discipleship means we live together in an egalitarian community of men and women marked by joy, praise, and trusting prayer to the Father, even as we continue our mission with Jesus in a world of sin, death, and evil.

12. Discipleship means we live by God's abundance with an open heart and hand to the needs of others. Our gifts do not go with the obligation to reciprocate.

3. Ralph P. Martin. "Salvation and Discipleship in Luke's Gospel." *Interpretation*, 30 (1976) 366–80.

Martin sets the issue of discipleship against the largest of all, the issue of *salvation* (God's comprehensive restoration of persons and creation as previewed in Jesus), which he takes as the center of Luke's message.[13] This is evidenced in the birth narrative where God is Savior (1:47) and the promise made of the forerunner that he will bring "the knowledge of salvation" in the Messiah's offer of forgiveness (1:69, 71, 77). Jesus' birth is the advent of a "Savior" (2:11). Simeon then sings of "salvation" (2:30). John the Baptizer speaks of a "salvation that shall come to all people" (3:6). Four times we hear the commendation of Jesus, "your faith has saved you" (7:50, 8:48, 17:19, 18:42). And if we try to *save* our own lives by our own means instead of losing them in and for Jesus, we are tragically misguided (9:24). Then there is the question, "Are the one's being *saved* few?" (13:23). In 19:9–10 we hear that "salvation" has come to the house of a repentant Zacchaeus. God's salvation made available in Jesus is the center of Luke's concern.

Luke highlights that Jesus fulfills the hopes of full salvation, now and later, for Jews and Gentiles. His person and work make it possible, and his resurrection and ascension demonstrate that he is still about the same work, now through his agents empowered by the Spirit. Submission to Jesus as Lord and Messiah is the entry point

13. See Powell, "Salvation in Luke-Acts," 5–10.

to the full benefits of a restored relationship with the Father who sent the Son and the Spirit who filled him and now fills those who put their trust in him.[14]

The central proclamation of Jesus is that the new reality of God's kingly rule is not just future but near enough to already have major effects in the present, and so each act of forgiveness, each act of healing and exorcism, and each call answered is a window into a full restoration that remains ahead.[15] Salvation is previewed in the person and works of Jesus who crosses all sorts of boundaries to welcome people into the new family of those who follow him as they hear and keep the Word of God (8:19–21). This is the One we are following as disciples, and the future is his!

Martin speaks of the rigorism of the Christian life as disciples, and here he highlights the classic cost-of-discipleship texts of 9:57–62 and 14:25–35. No excuses are adequate for procrastination, and Jesus must be the new center of loyalty. To deny the self its incessant demands and to daily take up a cross behind Jesus is the deep meaning of turning to him in repentance. We follow in his steps on the way to salvation when the kingdom finally comes in fullness.

So if, on the basis of Martin's analysis, we were to consider an addition to the list, it might be:

13. Discipleship is a costly walk with Jesus in which we die to old agendas and find a new center of loyalty and life in him. The signs of love and life he displays give us hope for the salvation of ourselves and the whole world.

4. Isaac Du Plessis., "Discipleship according to Luke's Gospel." *R & T*, Volume 2:1 (1995) 58–71.

Du Plessis begins by restating the obvious, that Jesus begins alone but as soon as he launches out (4:31–44) begins to call followers and build a community of memory and training around himself with the dramatic call of Peter as a first example (5:1–11). The abundance of the catch draws a confession of sin from the stunned Peter, to which Jesus' reply is not, "You are forgiven," but an antidote to dread, "Do not fear," and the call to a new vocation, "Henceforth you will be netting people." Followers are disciples in training for leadership. Jesus' training model unfolds unit by unit and is full of displays of divine power over demons, disease, death, and even fish, storms, and bread![16] Luke is generally positive toward such events since, as with Peter, they can be catalysts to faith.[17]

If Jesus defines his agenda in 4:16–30, then a parallel sermon for the outlines of being a follower is his *Sermon on the Plain* (6:20–49). It is Jesus' counter-cultural

---

14. The following of Jesus is and has always been a Trinitarian event, though it has not been emphasized in the literature. It is our relationship with the Father, Son, and Holy Spirit that is healed and restored. Grace is Triune grace; healing is Triune healing; Jesus is God the Son in flesh at ground level, guided by the Father, empowered and illumined by the Spirit.

15. For a recent introduction to Jesus and the kingdom of God, see Perrin, *The Kingdom of God*.

16. On the peculiar offense of the nature miracles to modern sensibilities, see the collected essays edited by Twelftree, *The Nature Miracles of Jesus*.

17. See Talbert, *Reading Luke*, 271–76.

charter for the revolutionary new way of living he inaugurates, a way that does not avoid suffering, as he often reminds them in the travel narrative (9:51, 13:22, 17:11, 19:11, 28).

As with other treatments, De Plessis joins in highlighting 9:57–62 as a normative cost-of-discipleship passage. We surrender securities and the control of family to enroll in Jesus' traveling academy of the kingdom. But with that come privileges as well, like being an insider to kingdom operations (8:4), to hear and see what's going on. It's also the privilege of being under close observation by Jesus and of being regularly—and sometimes painfully—corrected. That Jesus had a passion for outsiders, welcomed low-status children, and invited women on an equal basis as disciples set him apart from other rabbis. The kingdom in Jesus is open to all who wish to participate. No one is excluded by definition. The Samaritan episode is a good example of Jesus' patience towards outsiders (9:51–56).

Du Plessis puts emphasis on the first (9:1–11) and second (10:1–24) rounds of mission that Jesus arranges for his core and extended followers. It's a training experiment in which they are first stripped of all common supports and then launched out to discover that the powers of the kingdom (a temporary anointing of the Holy Spirit?) accompany them. Disciples share in Jesus' continuing ministry in the power and powers of the Spirit. What they learned earlier was then officially extended in their final commissioning by the risen Jesus (24:44–52). Prominent earlier themes (preaching, forgiveness, the inclusion of the nations, the powers of the Spirit) are here tied together at the end, and with the formal commissioning we are invited to review the entire story a second time from the beginning to see how the big issues were first introduced. Luke was not haphazard but strategic, and at the end all the pieces come together as a bridge to Volume II: Acts.

Now if, after reviewing Du Plessis, we find he adds something to Longnecker and Green's contributions, it might be:

14. Discipleship means followers are not surprised when they meet hostility because of the One they represent. The Holy Spirit who enables supernatural mission also enables faithful witness under pressure, even martyrdom.

5. Michael Wilkins. *Following the Master: A Biblical Theology of Discipleship.* Grand Rapids: Zondervan, 1992), 203–23.

Wilkins, whose doctoral work on discipleship in the Gospel of Matthew and the ancient world is the academic foundation for much of current discipleship thinking,[18] begins with an arresting statement that "an attachment to Jesus radicalizes every aspect of a person's life."[19] This is discipleship, being a learner, a follower, an apprentice, a mimic, one who over time is imprinted with the life of another.

---

18. *Discipleship in the Ancient World and Matthew's Gospel.*

19. "Luke, Followers of the Costly Way," 204.

One of the helpful features of Wilkin's approach is to early on highlight six places where Luke differs in his presentation of discipleship from his two Synoptic companions, Mark and Matthew:

1. Mark 1:16–20 and Matthew 4:18–22 present a parallel incident in which Jesus, on the shores of Sea of Galilee, calls Peter and Andrew, then James and John with apparently no prior contact. He intrudes and calls; they leave their nets and follow. Jesus has authority!

But Luke 5:1–11 presents a much more elaborate call story for Peter using his favorite genre, *The Call and Commission Story*. It includes the miracle of the great catch, a confession of sin from Peter, and is preceded in Luke's narrative logic by several encounters with Peter, all involving spiritual power:

   a. the Capernaum exorcism with Peter presumed present (4:31–37),

   b. the healing of Peter's mother in law (4:38–39), and

   c. the mass healings and exorcisms in Peter's courtyard (4:40–41).

A case is built that Jesus heals and frees in God's power before the focal instance of Peter's call involving even more power. In Luke's vision of discipleship, miracles can be a catalyst to faith.

2. Matthew and Mark speak of the *twelve* and not of a larger body of followers.

In Luke 6:13–17 it is clear that "the twelve" were chosen from a larger body of disciples. A grouping of more than the twelve is also found in John 6:60–65. And, in recounting the entry to Jerusalem Luke notes, as the other two do not, that "a large crowd of disciples" were participants (19:37).

3. Mark 6:6b–13 and Matthew 10:1–14 recount a sending of the twelve on a kingdom mission.

Only Luke 10:1–24 adds an additional sending of the the seventy (two). Luke thus offers a larger picture of the disciples and the parallel training they receive to that of the official twelve.

4. Matthew and Mark have no explicit inclusion of females as disciples.

Luke 8:1–3 has a preaching and healing tour through Galilee that includes named women who support the traveling ministry in a short list in many ways parallel to the earlier listing of the twelve (6:13–16).

5. Mark and Matthew present a blunt portrait of Peter's denials.

Luke 22:31–34 gives a more nuanced portrait. Peter's denial arises from permission given to the Evil One to sift him, but Jesus prays for his restoration and a ministry to strengthen others when it's over.

6. Mark 14:50 and Matthew 26:56 include the notice that the disciples left Jesus and fled at the Gethsemane scene.

Luke does not include the flight saying, but in 22:34 notes that "all those knowing him" observed from a distance along with the women, presumably including some male disciples. That they fled in the garden, as Mark notes, and later returned to observe from a distance, as Luke records, are not incompatible historically. *Fled and hid* is not the same as *Fled and returned*.

As we have in the comments above on 6:17–19, Wilkins also uses the image of concentric circles to organize a visual picture Jesus followers. He is the center, with the first circle being the first four called: Peter and Andrew, James and John. The next circle is the symbolic community of the twelve pointing to the renewal of Israel and as Jesus' immediate co-laborers. Then the seventy (two), a larger group of followers including the women of 8:1–3. Then an even larger circle of committed followers, and finally the masses and crowds who were his beneficiaries and whose status is left open and uncertain.

In terms of the challenges of entering the way of a disciple and the ongoing costs, Wilkins highlights the *narrow door* of Luke 13:33–34, "Make every effort to enter through *the narrow door*, because many, I tell you, will try to enter and will not be able to." The entry leads in Luke to *the way*, a new pattern of life with Jesus on the road. And this companionship with Jesus is costly in terms of competing loyalties (9:57–62, 18:24–30). Disciples are to love God with all they are and the neighbor as themselves (10:25–37). Family is not first, nor is comfort, and neither is life itself (14:25–35). If you do not count the cost and plan to finish, save the costs early on.

Jesus had a high regard for marriage, but the call to follow must be more central than even this. But it is the citadel of the self, our very life and all its bundle of desires and passions, that must be surrendered (9:23–26). Jesus' new family are those who hear and obey the Word of God (8:19–21). Complete dedication is the norm, "In the same way, any of you who does not give up everything he has cannot be my disciple" (14:33).

There is a before and after with Jesus, and the stripping that precedes the missions of 9:1–11 and 10:1–24 is emblematic of discipleship as a whole. We follow the one who lives in utter dependence on the Father's will and the Spirit's energies, and his followers are equally dependent on him as their leader and model. Jesus models a life of trust and risk in his discipleship to the Father and the Spirit. His price of entry and continuance in his circle is never lowered, and the rich man is allowed to walk away (18:22–25). Wilkins is clear, "The cost of discipleship is one's life."[20] All of who you are, and all of who you're not, is put at Jesus' disposal.

Near the end of this chapter Wilkins pulls his observations into a complex definition of discipleship:

> The life of a disciple may be summed up in Luke's perspective as a person
> who has given his or her allegiance to Jesus as Savior,
> who has been ushered into the way of walking with Jesus as Master,
> and who is being transformed into the likeness of the Master

20. 218.

through obedience to his Word.[21]

In conclusion, Wilkins wraps up his insights in a quote where C.S. Lewis crafts a speech for Jesus on what discipleship means:

> "Make no mistake," He says, "if you let me, I will make you perfect. The moment you put yourself in My hands, that is what you are in for. Nothing less, or other, than that. You have free will, and if you choose, you can push Me away. But if you do not push Me away, understand that I am going to see this job through. Whatever suffering it may cost you in your earthly life, whatever inconceivable purification it may cost you after death, whatever it costs Me, I will never rest, nor let you rest, until you are literally perfect–until my Father can say without reservation that He is well pleased with you, as He said He was well pleased with me. This I can do and will do. But I will not do anything less."[22]

If Wilkins was invited to add yet another mark of discipleship, it might be:

15. Discipleship to Jesus is relational, communal, and probing. Nothing in your lives will go unexamined as he puts himself at the center. In the process you will be changed by divine love and bear his truth to others.

6. Keith J. Hacking. *Signs And Wonders Then And Now*. Nottingham: Apollos, 2006. Chapter 13, "Overview of Discipleship in Luke," 159–64.

Hacking notes, as others, that Luke's view of discipleship, while it retains an eschatology of arrival, is a perspective for the long haul of history as presented in the Gospel and illustrated in Acts which ends with Paul teaching and preaching the kingdom in Rome. The end is sure, but until then what does it mean to be a Jesus follower? Luke has an answer.

An example of Luke's vision of following is his treatment of The Beatitudes (Luke 6:20–25 // Matt 5:3–13). Matthew's eight are reduced to four and paired with four contrasting Woes to present clear choices. Matthew's presentation highlights spiritual virtues, but Luke's is a stark contrast between Congratulations and Condolences.[23] Hunger and poverty are not spiritualized in Luke's profile. Persecution as exclusion and being slandered as evil is highlighted. It's all a very *now* affair (6:21a, b, 25a, b) with Jesus as the embodiment and model of the new life into which they are invited. As Talbert notes, Jesus is the supreme paradigm for Luke as both the originator and example of a way of life that disciples must emulate.[24]

Several of Luke's nuances are noted by Hacking and confirm the judgments of other scholars. There are crowds of disciples beyond the twelve, including women

---

21. 220. While this definition has much to commend it, I'm still searching for one as clear as this that includes references to the Father, the Spirit, and the communal *we* dimension. Discipleship is a Trinitarian following with others across time and not a solo with Jesus only.

22. *Mere Christianity*, 158.

23. On the literary form of a paired genre of Blessings and Woes, see Talbert, *Reading Luke*, 71–79.

24. "Discipleship in Luke-Acts," 74.

who prove exceedingly loyal, and private instruction is played down in favor of a more public and less insider approach, as in Mark. Being a follower is more available in Luke (6:17).

As others have noted, John the Baptist (3:1–6) early on in the story models two characteristics of discipleship: 1) a proclamation of the message of God, and 2) the universality of the good news, both of which first Jesus (4:31–44) and then the disciples will reenact (9:1–11, 10:1–24, Book of Acts). There is also the overarching theme of *the way*— also spoken of as *following*—both as a metaphor for Jesus' way of life and an actual trekking with him. Hacking quotes Fitzmeyer:

> for Luke, Christian discipleship is portrayed not only as the acceptance of the master's teaching but as the identification of oneself with the master's way of life and destiny in an intimate, personal following of him.[25]

Jesus' teaching on the dangers and right uses of wealth and possessions runs throughout Luke and shapes his understanding of what following means. Disciples leave their former lives and livelihoods for an on-the-road dependency on Jesus where they see him give freely of kingdom riches and receive the hospitality that comes his way. His parables, teachings, and encounters are full of texts and sub-texts on money as an idol which pushes God to the margins. Jesus' students learn to live out of a kingdom abundance with open hands and open hearts. God provides what keeps him and them in the mission. Hacking might summarize his insights as:

16. Discipleship is a deep attachment to the person of Jesus, a risk of all you are for a chance to be his friend and mentee. The God who made it all and saved his people from Egypt has crossed our path in this most unusual man, and when we begin to obey him, we begin to see as he sees. It's a new world.

7a. Darrell L. Bock, *Theology of Luke and Acts: Biblical Theology of the New Testament* Grand Rapids: Zondervan, 2012. Chapter 13, "Discipleship and Ethics in the New Community," 311–32.

Chapter 13 is Bock's major treatment of our topic, but in his earlier "Narrative Survey of Luke" are four texts that present major discipleship topics.[26] We will review these before moving on to the fuller treatment of his "Discipleship and Ethics in the New Community."

1. 5:1–6:16 Gathering of Disciples and Controversies

From the start disciples are given the promise they will "fish for people," a great metaphor since the first four followers are professionals at fishing. That Peter utters an agonizing confession of sin amidst flopping fish is a clue the four are not chosen for their prior perfections! The forgiveness and healing of the paralytic is a case study in *the new reality* which heals our relationship with God and restores function. The call of Levi the tax man and Jesus' statement that he has "come to call sinners to repentance"

---

25. Hacking, *Signs and Wonders*, 163.

26. 70, 73, 74.

means no one is disqualified by their history if they turn and follow. That Jesus heals on the Sabbath redefines it as a day of liberation in line with the great Exodus from Egypt. Jesus is love and mercy walking around looking for a needy person. Jesus previews the message, the power, the love and wisdom into which his new friends and students are being invited. It's show and tell of a very high order!

2. 10:25–11:13 Discipleship: Looking to One's Neighbor, Jesus, and God

The debate with the legal scholar highlights texts on the love of God and neighbor and how they are joined (10:25–28). The elaborate parable of the good Samaritan (10:29–37) then showcases the active love of an unlikely neighbor, while the story of distracted Martha and enraptured Mary (10:38–42) teaches that devotion given to Jesus is transparent to loving God. The Lord's Prayer and the parables and poem that follow (11:1–13) again join God's glory and human needs, so the oscillation between the vertical and horizontal is constant in the kingdom teaching of Jesus. And for disciples, then and now, it's a stretch in both directions, i.e. to see Jesus as transparent to the Father and to love all others out of the overflow, even the enemy. We are learning to live as Jesus lives, and that he thinks it's possible with the likes of us demonstrates his own faith!

3. 12:1–48 Discipleship: Trusting God

This section is dense with teaching for disciples. Since nothing is hidden, live in the light now (vv.1–3). Only the God who can destroy the entire self, body and soul, is to be feared (vv.4–5). Since God knows all the details, you must be very important (vv.6–7b). It really matters that you claim Jesus Christ in public and not tell the Holy Spirit to take a hike (vv.8–10). And, in a pinch, the Spirit will aid in your defense (vv.11–12). Riches, especially one's unearned, will expose every flaw in your character (vv.13–21), as will anxiety and worry, so learn to trust the goodness, be about his business, and all will be well (vv.22–34). Staying alert and faithful to your duties to care for God's people is the only way to meet the end prepared (vv.35–48. Jesus offers substantive teaching for the inner and outer life; he is comprehensive in the preparation of his followers. It was the best education ever assembled.

4. 14:25–35 Discipleship in the Face of Rejection: Basic Elements

From time to time Jesus offers a reality check for his followers, and this is one of the most direct and uncompromising. As loves are ranked, Jesus must be first, not family, not even one's own life. Following is a cross-bearing privilege, the deepest meaning of being found in the company of this Jesus. Not to count the costs and to be found wanting later on is the greatest dishonor. The old life and all its accouterments are laid aside for the sake of being with him wherever he's headed. Life has a new center, and all other loyalties are demoted and reorganized around who and what is now central: Jesus and *the new reality*. The distinctness of this new life, its tang and sting, must be preserved, or it's worse than useless.

With a review of Luke in place, and with the four clusters above laying out the privileges and costs of being a follower, Bock goes on to give a full chapter to

FOLLOWING JESUS

"Discipleship and Ethics in the New Community," in other words: What are the effects of being in the committed company of Jesus?

The word *disciple* (Gk. *methetes*) is used thirty-seven times in Luke, and its most basic meaning is *learner* or *pupil*. In the Book of Acts the repeated term *believer* is its functional equivalent for those beyond the first generation of followers. Later they are called *Christians* by outsiders (Acts. 11:26, 26:28), and the last designation is *the Way*, since they point the way to God and salvation. Several texts in Acts refer to the church as *saints*," Gk. *hagios/set apart ones* who belong to the God of Jesus.

In contrast to common Jewish practice, Jesus did not call his disciples to fast since his presence was more like wedding festivities than a time of repentance or mourning. He was God's new thing in their midst, and so customs must change, even the sacred Sabbath which now allows for missions travel (6:1–5) and healing without apology (6:6–11). Jesus chooses and calls twelve followers (6:12–19), and they—in their travels—observe his miracles and marinate in his teaching. He shows God's power over demons, disease, disordered nature, even death, but will coerce none who will not follow him, though his warnings are severe and clear. He upholds our capacity to reject him.

Where the Nazarene is, there is *the new reality* of the kingdom of God. He asks what outsiders and insiders think of him, and Peter come the closest with his insight of Messiah (9:18–20), though that is soon enough to be refined in a series of passion predictions of increasing detail (9:21–22). They fail and demonstrate prejudice (9:51–56), but Jesus corrects them and keeps them at his side. They may betray and deny, but they are not disposable. They live with him the life of wanderers, dependent on the kindness and welcome of those whom they serve, and failures are aplenty, especially in villages where kingdom signs abound and yet the people do not repent (10:13–15), even in Peter's home town of Capernaum, which was also Jesus' base of operation in the Galilee ministry. He warns against the hypocrisy and duplicity of religious leaders (Scribes and Pharisees) as they jockey for honor and wealth, revealing their corrupt hearts.

The cost of being in Jesus' graduate program of loving God and neighbors is high and must be counted and not discounted, but the privilege of being with him outweigh all other issues. All resources are put at the disposal of the mission as they learn trust and dependence. It all comes to an end as he is killed as predicted, but after a pause of several days, he returns to them more alive than before in a new type of embodiment, still fully human but with marvelous new powers. Out of the crushing experience of rejection and death, Jesus is bodily raised, and they are revived in their following. It's a whole new beginning, and on Pentecost they will be filled to the brim with the indwelling Holy Spirit.

Ethics is the *ethos* (culture) and *praxis* (habits) of a religious community as grounded in their beliefs about who God is and what kind of life is a faithful response to Jesus. Bock's method here is to list eleven topics or themes that find prominent expression in Luke and Acts, each with an explanatory paragraph. We will list the topics and a single sentence summary with each:

1. Total Commitment:

   Discipleship is not part-time but an all-in venture of growth.

2. Love for God & Neighbor:

   Devotion, Prayer, and Praise overflow in good for others.

3. Prayer:

   The Father/*Abba* of Jesus delights to hear us and draws us into his purposes.

4. Persevere in Suffering:

   The world as it is cannot bear Jesus or those who imitate him.

5. Watchfulness, Patience, and Boldness:

   Jesus gives the inner strengths to be faithful.

6. Faith and Dependence:

   Jesus enables us to trust him as we rest in his care.

7. Joy and Praise:

   Excitement about God's deeds regularly burst into song and witness.

8. Testimony and Witness:

   What we see Jesus do and how he changed us is our witness.

9. Wealth and Possessions:

   The poor are not neglected but loved with all we have.

10. Hindrances to Discipleship:

    Worldly pressures make the cost of following high.

11. Commitment to the Lost:

    Jesus pushes us out to all who don't know him.[27]

The disciples lived within the Roman Empire with its strict, vertical organization and patronage system in which all that was good devolved down from the Emperor.[28] And within it the church lived out its counter-cultural faith that Jesus was God's love and mercy wrapped up in one person at ground level.

Jesus has his own manner of influence, and when lived out faithfully and confidently, it indirectly undermines and de-legitimizes the world's power systems, prejudices, lies and cruelties. Ours is a Trinitarian monotheism that challenges all atheisms and polytheisms with a Living God who is a communion of holy love for all people and the whole of creation, promising a kingdom renewal for all who honor and follow Jesus in the energies of his Spirit. Christians do not hide but slowly penetrate and leaven every legitimate realm of endeavor wherever they go. It's the *sneaky* revolution.

Bock has done such a thorough job that it's difficult to limit his insights into a single additional theme, but we will try none the less:

17. Discipleship involves the highest rewards and most daunting demands, and many are tempted not to say an outright No but to dilute it into something more

---

27. 323–21.

28. Pinter, "The Gospel of Luke and the Roman Empire," Chapter 4, 101–15,

manageable. But a free and loving Jesus exposes all frauds, all substitutes, and reissues his call, "Follow me, and I will make you . . . ."

7b. Darrell L. Bock. *Jesus the God-Man: The Unity and Diversity of the Gospel Portrayals*. Grand Rapids: Baker, 2016. Chapter 6, "Jesus' Community of the New Era: The Calling of Those Who Respond," 123–48.

While the issue remains much discussed, it is clear that Jesus from the start was forming a new kind of community around himself as God's special agent (Son) for the renewal of God's people (symbolized by the twelve). Rather than students choosing him— as was the norm in rabbinic training—Jesus takes the initiative and calls people to himself. The record is that some said No and walked away, and at least one, the Gerasene demoniac, was refused and given a local mission instead (8:37–39).

In the sociological sense, Jesus is a *charismatic* leader whose force of person and relationship with God draws people around him. And when the healings and exorcism are included, it helps explain why his fame and infamy spread so quicky to create curiosity and worry in high places. And while not yet an institution in the full sense, his movement had leaders-in-training, a distinct body of teaching and lifestyle, a go-to-others traveling ministry of preaching and miracles, a symbolic use of twelve as a clue to identity, a characteristic prayer, public acts of confrontation and witness, and at the end a symbolic meal concerning the leader's gift of himself to his followers. It was clearly a church in formation.

To repeat the last sentence: it was an institution in the making, and with Jesus' formal commissioning of his core followers after the resurrection (24:36–53), the incipient structure was solidified into a distinct community within Judaism and yet directed outwards towards the whole world. Jesus started a kingdom movement with formal markers of identity and practice, and these continue among his followers.

Jesus was a surprising catalyst to call God's people back to their first love through repentance and trust in God's ambassador, himself! This is the insight that makes sense of nearly everything else, especially Jesus' unique sense of authority and mission.

Around the edges some Gentiles began to show interest in Jesus, and were welcomed to do so. He is the trustworthy one, full of mercy and truth and the healing power of love, and to begin to trust him is to be rightly aligned with the One who sent him. This trust is not an inherent, independent human capacity but a response to the gift of divine revelation. In Jesus and his circle we get a moving picture of what the rule and reign of God, *the new reality*, looks like when it shows up wherever you are. God's triune love showed up and made a difference.

On the initial call and commitment, Bock highlights five texts that present the basics:

1. 5:1–11   Peter the sinner's call
2. 5:27–32   Levi's call and subsequent banquet with sinners
3. 9:57–62   The reordering of all lesser loyalties

4. 12:49–53   Family division

5. 14:25–35   The total cost of discipleship

He then follows with a discussion of *the twelve* and its recasting of the twelve patriarchs as leaders of the nation and its tribes.

Bock's next section is titled "The All-Encompassing Character of Discipleship" and here he offers a list of five headings, some of which overlap with his earlier listing in *A Theology of Luke and Acts*.[29] The topics are his (*in italics*) and the comments mine:

1. *On Disciples*:
   The noun *mathetes* is used in the Gospels & Acts, but not outside them.
2. *Total Commitment*:
   While the disciples bumble, Jesus reorganizes life around himself.
3. *Suffering and Rejection*:
   Costly service for the sake of others is the norm of Jesus.
4. *The Disciples' Character: Love, Grace, Forgiveness, Mercy, and Service*.
   Disciples give away what they've been given by Jesus and do it freely.
5. *The Role of Parables*:
   The stories on the trip south are full of discipleship teaching.

His next section is "Community: Expansion to Gentiles, and Worship." That Jesus' mission was for his Jewish people, though with an eye beyond them to the Gentiles, is made clear. He is *Messiah* and *King of the Jews*, though he reserves the right to fill old titles with new understandings that postpone their this-worldly political implications.

But from early on it's clear that Jesus will not be limited to Jews as Gentiles come to him for teaching and healing (Luke 7:1–10, 8:26–39, 6:17). The mission through the Jews and to the world does not begin in Acts but is prefigured and grounded in the historical ministry of Jesus. It's not an add-on or an afterthought but intrinsic to the whole of who he is and what he does.

Jesus is from a pious home, and he is found in the synagogue, the temple, making pilgrimage, and keeping Passover. Though rejected at his home synagogue and temporarily halting temple operations since he is the new, indwelling presence, Jesus offers full obedience and glorifies the God of Israel.

Yet a third section on the breadth and depth of following Jesus is titled "The Character of the Disciple in Relationship to the World, and under it are found five headings: *Love and Mercy, Righteous Integrity, Possessions and the World, Suffering*, and *Service to the World*. Jesus loves God and neighbor full and in the right order. He is the template for the Good Samaritan who does not ignore pain and injury. He is merciful to sinners and speaks the truth in love. All he has is available to whomever needs it. He loves enemies, even the one's who slander and kill him. He wants outsiders and nobodies at the banquet (14:7–24). Women who have received the mercy of healing devote their lives to him (8:1–3).

---

29. 323–31.

The kind of integrity Jesus models and enables is laid out clearly in the discourse of 6:20–49 with its call for counter-cultural lives of radical generosity. It's a new life from the inside out, from the heart and out through the tongue in true speech, by the hands in serving, and with the feet in moving towards needs.

In his discipleship of those he calls, Jesus is creating a new kind of human person, one who lives with him, by him, and bears much good fruit. And this is nowhere more clearly demonstrated than in Jesus' warnings about how wealth and the options it brings can become an alternative center of loyalty, a rival God, an idol made of gold and silver. Use it, he says, but give it no place in your heart. Learn to live with what God supplies along the way, and never harden your heart to the poor and needy, the little and the last.

And because this new way is so counter to the way the world works, pressure and suffering will inevitably follow you as both the Evil One and his agents—both demonic and human—slander and lie about you and the One you follow. And since it is inevitable, prepare for it and take it as no surprise. You're in good company (6:23).

Remember that this is a public faith, meant to be heard and expressed in public, so mission is not just over there, it's under your nose, right where you are with the next person you meet. So if, on the basis of a second analysis from Bock, we offer another statement on discipleship fundamentals, it might be:

18. Discipleship is a totalizing commitment based on a compelling invitation to follow Jesus with others into a new life erected in the midst of the old. If you turn and take it, take it and trust it, it has the love and power, the wisdom and perseverance to fit you for divine service in the friendship of Jesus.

8. Dennis M. Sweetland. *Our Journey with Jesus: Discipleship according to Luke-Acts.* Collegeville, MN: Liturgical, 1990.

After an introduction (Chapter 1), this book-length treatment of discipleship in Luke and Acts falls into two parts:

1. A treatment of the genre of *Call and Commission Stories* of which there are eight in Luke (Chapter 2) and fourteen in Acts (Chapter 3). At this point a repetition of the seven standard components of the genre is in order:[30]

The Commissioning Form in Luke

Text	Introduction	Confrontation	Reaction	Commission	Protest	Reassurance	Conclusion
1:5–25	vv.5–10	v.11	v.12	vv.13b–17	v.18`	vv.13a, 19–20	vv.21–25
1:26–38	vv.26–27	v.28	v.29	vv.31–33, 35	v.34	vv.30, 36–37	v.38
2:8–20	v.8	v.9a-b, 13–24	v.9c	vv.11–12	x	v.10	vv.15–20

30. The basic articles on the genre are Hubbard, "The Role of Commissioning," 187–98; Mullins, "New Testament Commission Forms," 603–14. These stories are dealt with in some detail in Sweetland, *Our Journey with Jesus*, 44–84.

5:1–11	vv.1–2	v.3	vv.8–10a	vv.4, 10c	v.5	v.10b	v.11
9:1–11	v.1a	v.1b-c	v.6	vv.3–5	x	x	vv.6, 10–11
10:1–24	v.1a	vv.1b-2	implied in return	vv.3–15	v.3b im-plied	v.16	vv.17–24
24:1–9	vv.1–3	v.4	v.5a	vv.6–7	x	v.5b	vv.8–9
24:36–53	v.36a	v.36b	vv.37, 41	vv.44–48	x	v.49	vv.50–53

The Refusal of a Call in Luke

Text	Introduction	Request or Attraction	Difficult Task	Command to Follow	Departure: Negative Emotions	Further Teaching
18:18–30	v.18a	v.18b	vv.20–21	v.22	v.23	vv.24–30

2. A treatment of other relevant disciple materials under the following headings: "Christology and Discipleship" (Chapter 4), "The Way to Discipleship" (Chapter 5), "The Community and God's Plan" (Chapter 6), "The Community: Its Existence and Structure (Chapter 7), "Life Within the Community (Chapter 8), "The Importance of Luke-Acts For Us Today" (Chapter 9).

Sweetland is the first I've found who's taken the basic research of B.J. Hubbard and T.Y. Mullins and used it analyze all the call and commission stories in Luke-Acts. What Luke thinks important matters to Sweetland! Nothing is more basic than exposure to Jesus and the call that may come from it. At the end of his chapter on the Lukan call stories, Sweetland makes an important summary statement on discipleship:

> In the Gospel, Luke portrays the life of the Christian disciple as a journey. Those who would be followers of Jesus must leave their own way and join Jesus as he travels towards resurrection, ascension, and exaltation. The seeds of discipleship are sown as one sees the marvelous deeds of Jesus or his disciples and listens to his, or their words about salvation and the kingdom of God .... The life of the Christian disciple is characterized by prayer, radical renunciation of possessions, and cooperation with other members of the community to carry on the mission of Jesus by preaching the kingdom of God with its message of salvation.[31]

Nothing is more basic than Jesus' initiative to call men and women to himself. That the use of the genre is prominent in Luke and only more so in Acts is an issue of continuity: the risen Jesus continues to do what the earthly Jesus practiced; it's the same person!

Sweetland is also explicit in Chapter 4 that "Christology and Discipleship" are integrally linked as the person of Jesus—who he is and what he does—determines what

31. 43–44.

it means to be his apprentice. Also, the seven titles Jesus bears in Luke (Son of God, Messiah/Christ, Savior, Lord, Son of man, Servant, and Prophet) are each a window into the deep mystery of his identity as God the Son incarnate.

Chapter 5, "The Way to Discipleship," explores the multiple and complementary means of coming to trust in and follow Jesus. It is an outline of the components of conversion:

1. Listening/Hearing,

2. Seeing/Understanding,

3. Forgiveness/Reconciliation,

4. Repentance/Belief/Baptism.

What is missing in Sweetland is an appreciation of the role that miracles of healing, exorcism, resuscitations, and power over nature play in discipleship since Jesus seems to be doing this kind of thing every day. It's an integral part of the divine revelation he offers, and to it his followers have a nearly daily exposure (5:15–16, 17, 6:19, 9:1–11, 10:1–24). The *new reality* brings the healing power of love down to ground level with extraordinary results.

What is perhaps most salutary about Sweetland's book is that Chapters 6–8 are given to various aspects of the Community/Church Jesus creates, a people who pray, celebrate the Eucharist, live as families, deal with possessions, and practice-non-violence. As one British writer has put it, "The plural of disciple is church."[32]

Sweetland's catholic ecclesiology (his doctrine and experience of the church) sensitizes him that the fruit of Jesus is a new community, not just individual or small groups of followers. He recreates the ancient people of God around himself. Discipleship is *we and us* and only secondarily *I and me*. The communal aspect is often minimized in current Protestant treatments that often have an individualistic *Jesus and me* slant and fail to acknowledge how much the culture of expressive individualism has distorted our understanding of what it means to follow Jesus *in the company of others*.[33]

Sweetland's concluding chapter, "The Importance of Luke-Acts for Us Today" is a pithy summary of what it means to follow Jesus and to be his people across time. We participate in *the new reality* now, even as we pray for and expect its future culmination. If, after reading Sweetland, we summarize his insights in a single statement to add to the others, it might be:

19. The journey of discipleship begins with hearing and seeing Jesus through whatever avenues are accessible. This exposure to divine revelation is curated by the Holy Spirit who tugs us towards trust and surrender to Jesus, heartfelt repentance, and

32. Morgan, Alison, *Following Jesus.*

33. On the history of the transformation of the modern self, Trueman, *The Rise and Triumph of the Modern Self.*

a full participation in his people and mission. In his company we are changed in order to love God and neighbor with what God supplies.

9. Joseph A. Fitzmeyer. *The Gospel According to Luke, I-IX*. New York: Double-day, 1981. "Discipleship," 235–67.[34]

This thirty-two page essay on discipleship in Luke is part of Fitzmeyer's introduction to his two volume commentary as a topic under the heading "A Sketch of Lucan Theology."[35] Its headings are three, and I offer a summary and comment on each:

A.   The Response to the Christian Kerygma (early church preaching)

    1. Faith[36]

Having sketched out Luke's Christology in an earlier section,[37] Fitzmeyer organizes the responses to divine revelation under three headings, and the first is *Faith*, for which *belief* and *trust* are synonyms which fill out the fuller sense of the word. Faith is not a leap into the dark but into the light from the dark. It is trust based on evidence leading to a great reorientation of life (repentance).

The faith is the content, and *by faith* is the means of grace-enabled personal assent to Jesus. Trust is a common enough human capacity; everyone exercises it all the time, but for sinners to trust Jesus is not an innate capacity because of the damages of sin. To trust and thus surrender to God is a capacity that God heals, restores, and renders operative.[38] Jesus is found to be both true and trustworthy, and I entrust myself to him and his direction. It's a new beginning at the center of the self.

    2. Repentance and Conversion[39]

In Jesus I find myself addressed by God and called to a new life which is both a *turning from* and a *turning towards*. It is a turning from all that displeases God plus a turning away from a life organized around inherited loyalties. For the rest of life Jesus—and the Father who sent him and the Spirit who accompanies him—become the central loyalty, and faith is always a personal risk. Along the way I learn Jesus' ways of loving God and people, also to speak the truth and confront the lies in which we humans are all entangled.

I now live in a new world in the middle of the old. The name for this new relationship is *discipleship*; I become an understudy of Jesus who brings me back into a healed (forgiven) relationship with his Father and offers me a share in the Holy Spirit as an internal beacon and living link. Salvation as restoration is now and later, a glimpse now, the full vision later.[40] Only in the new age and with resurrection bodies will it be

---

34. See also his *Luke the Theologian*, Chapter 5, "Discipleship in the Lucan Writings," 117–145.

35. xii.

36. 235–37.

37. 192–226.

38. This usually goes under a heading much beloved of Wesleyans—*prevenient grace*.

39. 237–39.

40. For an excellent series of essays on salvation, see Talbert and Whitlock, *Getting Saved: The Whole Story of Salvation*.

completed. But between here and there is much struggle and confusion, much pain and suffering, deep joy and hope.

3. Baptism[41]

Baptism in its simplest sense is a water ritual associated with public incorporation into the community of Jesus' followers, his church.[42] It is borrowed from Judaism and refitted with Christian content and new meanings. So, strictly speaking, since this work is on discipleship in Luke, baptism is a later concern in Acts and is quickly adopted without explicit dominical command as in Matthew 28:16–20. It is simply taken for granted by the larger apostolic tradition from the very beginning (see Peter, Acts 2:38).

As long as Jesus-style discipleship was read as one more renewal movement within Judaism, there was no need for a marker ritual; the marker was that peoples lives were disrupted to begin following Jesus. But now that the church has been deposited with the Jesus revelation as sealed in the resurrection appearances and a formal commission to mission, a before-and-after maker of *the new reality* is employed: public water baptism and confession of Jesus as God the Son and Messiah. It was an identity marker and theological necessity.[43]

B.   The Demands of Christian Life

1. The Following of Jesus[44]

Fitzmeyer begins this heading with a definition, "To be a disciple of Christ one has to follow him along the road that he walks to his destiny in Jerusalem, his exodos, his transit to the Father." This is highlighted at the start of the travel narrative (9:51–19:27) with a thought unit devoted to the high cost of following (9:57–62) where the key word *follow* is repeated three times. Some have followed since the beginning of the ministry in Galilee, but now the costs are made even more plain and even more pointed and disrupting.

Discipleship is whole-life identification with Jesus, his words and works, his travels and conflicts. Following him is spatial and dynamic; you walk with and behind him where he sets the agenda and direction. You are not in control, except to stay or leave. Questions are fine, confusion normal, threats aplenty, but to stay with the process, as the disciples mainly do, and as Jesus recognized at their last meal, "Now you are those who have continued with me in my trials" (22:28) is to go through about as much change as can be processed in such a short time. Jesus is a very patient teacher of all

41. 239–41.

42. For recent treatments, see Witherington, *Troubled Waters*; McKnight, *It Takes a Church to Baptize*.

43. On Luke's presentation of the possible relations of the gift of the Holy Spirit to baptism (either before, during, or after), see Talbert, *Reading Acts*, 41–45.

44. 241–43.

who come to him. He knows, in ways we do not, what we are up against and how much there is to un-learn. He is the way; we walk in his way; we are sifted along the way.

Following means first observing (4:41–8:56), then participating in Jesus' mission (9:1–11, 10:1–24). This is the promise that Peter and the others will be "fishers of men and women" (5:11). It is announced, then demonstrated, then extended through them. They are caught up in his momentum.

2. Testimony[45]

The clearest basis for testimony/witness (*martyria*) is simply what they've seen and heard first hand, as Jesus notes in his final appearance and commissioning, "you are witnesses of these things" (24:47b). Together the twelve form a floating memory bank of Jesus' daily life, and this—when illumined by the resurrection appearance—becomes the content of the apostolic, foundational, self-correcting testimony and record concerning Jesus, his person and work.[46]

3. Prayer

To follow Jesus is to observe his prayer and to have your prayers molded by his model (11:1–13). This is signaled in his withdrawals for prayer (4:42, 5:16) and his prayer at key turning points in the story (his baptism [3:21–22, before choosing the twelve [6:12], before Peter's confession and the first passion prediction [9:18], at his transfiguration [9:28], at the disciples' return after mission [10:21–24 before he teaches the model prayer [11:1], at the Last Supper [22:19], in his agony in the garden [22:39–46], and on the cross [23:34, 46]).

Some of these are reports of prayer and others contain the words themselves. Jesus is clearly dependent on the Father and the Spirit, not a magician or conjurer who uses special knowledge and technique to manipulate spiritual powers.[47] He seeks the divine will in prayer and surrenders himself to each new challenge of filial obedience. He teaches on confidence and perseverance in prayer in several parables (18:1–8, 11:5–8) and bids his friend to join in praying for more workers (10:2). He lives by prayer to the Father who gives only good gifts to his children, and they must as well. Human energies are insufficient for divine work; it is the deepest, most dependent partnership.

4. The Disciples' Right Use of Material Possessions[48]

All the scholars note that money/mammon/riches is a major theme throughout Luke and Acts since how it's handled either builds up or tears down community. What it means to love God and neighbor is visible in what one does with wealth and possessions. It's such a powerful idol because of the status it confers and the things it quickly enables. So the question is: Do I have it, or does it have me?

---

45. 243.

46. On the role of eyewitness and self-correction in the tradition, see Bauckham, *Jesus and the Eyewitnesses*, 93–113.

47. For the debate on this issue, see Horsley, *Jesus and Magic*.

48. 247–51.

Faithful stewardship and letting God *squeeze me from time to time* is a check on sin and the vice of greed. For the disciples to leave their occupations and learn Jesus' provision for themselves and those they left behind was a major hurtle. That Judas betrayed Jesus "for a sum of money" (22:5) is an indicator of its potential for evil. The generous Jesus lived on resources from above and received his bread and shelter from supporters (8:1–3) and receptive people along the way. He was trust and love in motion. Having lived most of his life as a craftsman, he now survives on gifts and gratitude as he gives away what the Father gives him and what the Spirit curates and enables.

The stark contrast between the first of his blessing on the poor (6:20b) and the first of his curses on the rich (6:24) sets the frames for all his teaching on this loaded topic. Living for accumulation and hoarding demonstrates that one is totally out of touch with God, and that does not have a good end, as Jesus warns repeatedly (16:19–31).

What we speak of as stewardship, the fundamental insight of which is that all creation and all its possibilities belong to God, involves prudence, a wise use of property while practicing detachment, and to this Jesus speaks as well (3:11, 16:8a, 12:42, 8:3, 11:41, 16:9, 6:35, 12:33, 16:13). He is against money as a God and for it as a resource to love that all may flourish in a community of generosity.

C. Christian Life Together

It is characteristic, as I have again noticed in this chapter, that Catholic treatments of Luke place an emphasis on the communal and ecclesial dimensions of discipleship, as Fitzmeyer notes of Jesus that "he also envisions a certain organized and communal way of life for Christians—in effect, life in the Christian church."[49] That he began almost immediately forming a community of witnesses around himself is an indicator of things to come, i.e. the reformation of God's people around God's Son.

That there were 120 at the end of his life (Acts 2:15), including his family and the women disciples, means something permanent has been set in place, the vehicle through which the risen Lord will press from Jerusalem out into the world. The Spirit that was with him will soon be poured out upon them all; God is about to take up residence and rule in his church, and what is attributed to the church must square with the deposit of apostolic memory concerning Jesus. The risen Lord acts at ground level through the Spirit. What he was as a solo witness, they are now to be as a body, as previewed in the sendings of the twelve and the seventy(two). It's not too much to say that Luke has an ecclesiology (a doctrine or teaching on the church) grounded in what Jesus created and sustains. So if, after considering Fitzmeyer's contribution, we give him a voice, he might say:

20. Discipleship is Jesus' method of reproducing his vision and mission over time in a committed community of men and women who count him as worthy and trustworthy. They are his living memory, and—with the promised filling of the Spirit—his

49. 251.

extended presence in the world. All need what he supplies through them, which is a healed relationship with the Triune God of holy love.

10. K.N. Giles. "The Church in the Gospel of Luke." *Scottish Journal of Theology*, Vol. 34:2, April 1981, 121–146.

Giles' thesis is that—for Luke, "the church comes into existence during the ministry of Jesus"[50] and not, as others often claim, after his death and resurrection. And I agree, but then add a question: When is an oak an oak? From an acorn to its fullest height and girth, it's always an oak with continuity of identity and some discontinuity of form.

It is, perhaps a nod to Rome, to admit that Luke presents Mary as the first over whom the Trinity of Father, Son, and Spirit is named, a true disciple who questions and then surrenders in faith, thus a portrait or icon of the church. And also that with the call of Peter and three others (5:1–11) a non-familial body of followers begins to travel with Jesus. It is also true that not until the historical revelation in Jesus is completed as sealed by his resurrection and gift of the Spirit are all the pieces in place for the launching of a public body in mission. To artificially divide Luke into distinct epochs is an artificial schematization. What happens is not segments but an organic growth and movement with continuity of identity through a series of forms, all centered around the person of Jesus.

In terms of Luke's major source, Giles notes—as do others—that, in contrast to Mark's portrait, the disciples are a larger group than the twelve, the teaching of Jesus' is more public and less a special teaching for insiders (7:1, 8:9), and that the criticism of the twelve—while still present—is muted and spun in a positive direction.

Several notices in Luke expand our vision of who is a follower or disciple (6:12–16, 17, 10:1–24, 19:37). This insight broadens the frequent mention of *the disciples* as a larger pool (7:1, 11, 11:1, 12:1, 22, 16:1, 17:1, 22, 20:45, etc.) The classic Lukan disciple passages are offered to a larger audience (9:23, 14:25). The call is to all. The twelve are a symbolic core, but all disciples have relationship and mission with Jesus. Several of Mark's sharp critiques (Mark 7:18, 8:21, 9:20, 22) are omitted by Luke, and his general treatment is much more positive and merciful to their frailties and misunderstandings. Jesus' rebuke of them in Gethsemane is omitted.

In addition to these, Luke's treatment highlights several factors:

1. the disciples' confession of Jesus as *Lord* (5:8, 10:17, 12:4, 40) and *Christ* (9:20);

2. the cost of following (6:20–26, 9:57–62, 14:25–35);

3. the construal of following as a way—a journey (especially 9:51–19:27) of those who are "with" him (8:1, 38, 9:32, 22:14, 56, 22:44),

4. and the twelve disciples (8:1, 9:1, 10, 12, 18:31, 22:3, 47) as official emissaries or apostles (9:1–11, 24:36–53).

50. 121.

Giles' conclusion is that a good case can be made that the disciples in Luke are the church in its ideal form, frail but faithful:

> In the hearing and reading of the Gospel, Luke wished men to identify with the disciples: to confess Jesus as Lord, to accept his costly call to come with him and to continue the work he gave of preaching the kingdom of God.[51]

And if each is to make a contribution, so Giles:

21. Discipleship means that Jesus is fully committed to us, that we are growing in our capacity to follow him from the heart, and that together we will do for others what he has done for us, thus no superstars and all serve one another.

11. Charles H. Talbert. "Discipleship in Luke-Acts." In Fernando Segovia, *Discipleship in the New Testament*. Philadelphia: Fortress, 1985, 62–75.

Talbert begins with the assertion that to understand Luke is to take Acts as a commentary and in reading Acts to take Luke as a commentary. Since the actions of Jesus the founder in Luke are reproduced in the lives of key followers, first Peter and then Paul in Acts, it tells us that in discipleship the founder's life and values are to be translated into his followers. This is the goal of discipleship. Jesus is the model and example (6:40), and his followers are, over time, imprinted with his vision, values, and practices. We never exceed him as was possible with Jewish rabbis and their pupils, but we may become *like him* as a community of followers, each a tessera in his living mosaic.

Talbert discerns in Luke a developmental pattern used in the ancient world to describe philosophical and religious growth towards maturity from a beginner to one making progress to one perfected. Luke 2:40, 52 enclose a story about Jesus in the temple with growth reports using the Greek technical term *prokoptein/to increase*. Jesus later spoke of the end of his course, "Behold, I cast out demons and perform cures today and tomorrow, and on the third day I am being perfected" (13:32). It is in his voluntary suffering that Jesus is perfected in obedience to the divine will. This growth of Jesus that Luke chronicles and Talbert highlights is in five successive sections:

1. His dedication as an infant (2:22–24). He is God's unredeemed firstborn.

2. Youthful agreement with parents' commitments (2:41–52). He is in the Father's house, and defends his associations before returning home again.

3. Empowering for service by the Spirit (3:21–22). He is aimed at the world.

4. Acceptance of rejection, suffering, death (Chapters 9–23). He prophesies his own future in a series of passion predictions.

5. Resurrection, ascension, and exaltation (Chapter 24 + Acts). He is vindicated in a bodily resurrection from the dead.

The life of the disciples focuses on 3 and 5 above, as 1, 2, and 5 are told only of Jesus. In his complex argument Talbert demonstrates how the tradition about Jesus in

---

51. 145. For his fuller treatment of ecclesiology, see Giles, *What On Earth Is The Church?*

Luke shapes the portrayal of disciples in Acts. Talbert concludes with several observations which hold together what is so often divided in today's church:

1. Formation and mission go together. Both are necessary, and to set them over against one another is an error of reductionism.

2. Discipleship is communal and never merely personal or individualistic.

3. We live in the tension of the now and not yet of the kingdom. Mere enthusiasm—living only by supposed spiritual impulse and illumination—distortion, a form of naive fanaticism. We live in this world and by the traditions of Jesus and his followers even as we experience the gifts and powers of the Spirit in our mission. The experience of the numinous and of divine protection is expected, and suffering is also expected since the world has not yet changed.

As an aside, and in another article which incorporates much of the same material with an application to spirituality,[52] Talbert parallels Luke's model of Jesus' five stages with Evelyn Underhill's classic five stages of spiritual development:

1. Awakening,

2. Purification,

3. Illumination,

4. Purgation or the dark night of the soul, and

5. A Unitive life with God. [53]

The first two, *awakening and purification*, might be correlated with Jesus' temple experience at age twelve and his subsequent parental obedience and long immersion in the ordinary life of Nazareth; his *illumination* to his baptism, filling with the Spirit and public ministry of signs and wonders; *the dark night of the soul* to his embrace of the suffering that was ahead as signaled in his several passion predictions culminating in his torture and death; and *his unitive life with God* as his resurrection, ascension, and co-regency at the Father's right hand. Jesus passed through all the stages of human growth and spiritual development, and in the process perfectly fulfilled God's purposes, and this is maturity and perfection in love.

From Talbert we may draw yet another insight:

22. Discipleship is a progressive path of following Jesus. What he was historically continues among his people. The risen Jesus is still calling followers and forming them in his community for the sake of his mission. The empowerment of the Spirit is required for faithful obedience and obedient suffering because the world has not yet been changed.

---

52. Talbert, "The Way Of The Lucan Jesus," 237–49.

53. *Mysticism*, 445.

12. Craig S. Keener. The Historical Jesus of the Gospels. Grand Rapids: Eerdmans, 2012. Chapter 14, "Kingdom Discipleship," 196–213.

While Keener's treatment does not focus on Luke's Gospel alone, it is a valuable study of gospel discipleship, and so included.[54] Keener begins his examination of discipleship with a reminder that "Jesus summoned disciples to follow him, making his call more pressing than kinship or other social ties, than possessions, even their lives."[55] In contrast to other rabbis, the student did not choose the teacher but here the teacher choose the student. Keener comments, "Early Jewish and Greek tradition most frequently assumed that disciples are responsible for acquiring their own teachers of the law or philosophy."[56]

As "fishers of men (and women)" disciples were being trained by Jesus as the nucleus of his Jewish "kingdom of God" renewal movement. Jesus' call and their response dislocated them from their former lives and habits. And while it may have been the custom that no student stay away from home for over a month for Torah study,[57] still such absences were highly disruptive for those left behind. The tensions this created are heightened by Jesus' strong statements on the matter (Luke 14:26), especially when the loyalty he demands is personal, "Follow me," a claim many considered only God could make.

Even the command to honor father and mother is relativized in Jesus' radical statement on the call of the kingdom and the duty to bury a parent (9:59–60). Jesus claims supreme attention in the lives of his followers, which leaves us with a question: Just who is this strange man? He loosens ties to place and family, to kinship and possessions in order to introduce his followers into *the new reality* of God's rule and its fresh outworkings at ground level. What was primary is now secondary, and to enter the company of Jesus places you on a collision course with the powers-that-be, both Jewish religious leaders and Roman governmental leaders. And such rebels, as all knew, frequently ended up on crosses (14:27). People read Jesus' counter-kingdom as a genuine threat and responded accordingly.

Jesus' own detachment from possessions and the totalizing demands of family were one with his own teaching on the same. He lived in radical trust and dependence on the Father and the Spirit, and his followers must learn to do the same. In Jesus' company the disciples find themselves in new situations–say eating with tax collectors and other flagrant violators, visiting pagan demoniacs on their home turf–as Jesus offers new life to traditional outsiders. The holiness of Jesus is not defensive and fearful

54. For further general treatments on discipleship, see Wilkins, "Disciples" and "Discipleship," 176–89 and his more popular treatment in *Following the Master: A Biblical Theology of Discipleship*. For a history of discipleship, Katz, "Disciple, Discipleship," 888–920. An overview of making disciples is Hans Kvalbein, "Go therefore and make disciples, 48–53; L. Foster, "Discipleship in the New Testament."

55. 202.

56. Keener, *The Historical Jesus*, 202.

57. *M. Ket.* 5:6.

but life-giving and engaging. He is not stained or polluted by them; they are made clean by him. Jesus goes from village to village announcing and demonstrating *the new reality*; he actively seeks the healing and blessing of all people, not excluding the flagrant and notorious.

As before, so now. What might Keener add?

23. Discipleship means a laser focus on *the new reality* of God's rule that showed up in its chief personal agent, Jesus of Nazareth. Where we stand with him is a reflection of where we stand with the One who sent him. He is life's most important opportunity and worthy all he asks of you and more.

13. Peter Morden. *The Message of Discipleship*. London: IVP, 2018. "Introduction: Discipleship in the Bible and Today," 1–18.

So while our list of the Lukan qualities of discipleship is quite long enough, several quotes from Morden's introduction are worth preserving because of their bridge from Luke's world to our own:

1. "What we are faced with in contemporary Christianity is 'a discipleship deficiency.'"[58]

2. Giles quotes Richard Longnecker who counsels:

   What is needed for most of our theories about Christian discipleship is a firmer rootage in the biblical materials. And what is needed for our practice is a clearer grasp of the pattern of discipleship set out in the New Testament.[59]

3. "Discipleship is a particularly strong way of describing the Christian life, speaking as it does of a lifelong journey of following Jesus and of one hundred percent dedication to him."[60]

4. "In fact, disciples—as we see them in the New Testament—often exhibit great lack of faith and constancy. They struggle, make mistakes and slip up in all sorts of ways.... Rather than a record of exemplary discipleship, they misunderstand Jesus repeatedly, fail in ministry, squabble among themselves, refuse to wash one another's feet, fall asleep as Jesus agonizes in prayer and then completely desert him. In many ways it is an abject litany of failure. Although the disciples desert their Lord, the Lord never deserts them, never stops loving them, never stops calling them as his disciples."[61]

5. Giles quotes Archbishop of York John Sentamu:

   Discipleship was Jesus' big idea and and plan for the renewal of society; a catalyst and engine for building God's kingdom. Being a disciple is not about following a set of rules but about a relationship: a relationship with the living,

58. 1.

59. 3.

60. 7.

61. 9.

risen Jesus Christ. Jesus did not say, 'submit to these guidelines,' but 'follow me' and 'come and see.' A disciple lives in the way of Jesus. A disciple devotes the whole of their lives, and for their whole life-long, to imitating Jesus Christ. A disciple invites others to become disciples who, in turn invite others to be disciples.[62]

A Synthesis: What The Scholars Teach Us

Why make things so complicated? Why wade through all these complexities when all people want is a simple pathway to follow Jesus? I understand the frustration, but the plain fact is that with Luke and the rest of the New Testament we are dealing with religious documents from the ancient world that we need experts to help us navigate, even at the most basic level of manuscript evaluation and translation into English. Few of us are expert in ancient Greek, the worldview and customs of the ancient world, its literary forms and reading practices. But there are scholars who are experts and who take the time to ask good questions and give careful answers. They know not only the text but its history of interpretation through the ages and the current debates about what it meant then and what it might mean now. That God gave us such historical documents to carry the church's witness to divine revelation through time is an invitation to serious study, research, and writing. And that is what our scholars are called to do, the high-level scholarly work so that the rest of us can read wisely and faithfully.

What we have done in this exercise is to assemble thirteen Lukan scholars around a seminar table for a discussion of a speciality topic: What does the Gospel of Luke teach about Christian discipleship? They all know the original languages, the history of the interpretation, and the immense effects Luke has had on theology, liturgy, missions, and art. And when they pass a magnet labeled *discipleship* over the text of Luke, some things stick to it and others do not. They look for patterns and insights, themes and how Luke edited his sources and arranged them to present a persuasive narrative and commend Jesus to all.

Most of what they offer is not new at all because these texts have been carefully read for two thousand years by some of the finest minds of the church. There is a large overlap in their opinions and insights. All agree discipleship is a major topic in Luke, second only to the person of Jesus. All identify a handful of thought units that are classic discipleship texts. All agree that Luke has a less harsh view of the disciples and their foibles and failures than Mark's earlier portrait. All agree that women followers and complementary pairs of men and women are featured more in Luke than the other three gospels, and that he has a special interest in the poor, outsiders, Gentiles, and the person and gifts of the Spirit.

62. 15.

After sifting their arguments and conclusions, some technical questions remain unsettled, but what emerges is a consensus that Jesus was deliberate in his calling and training of followers, that they were with him on the road as observers and pupils because in the end he would entrust them as his personal ambassadors. That his leadership strategy of ministering to the masses but training a smaller group of zealots was effective is unquestioned because in three hundred years it essentially co-opted the Roman Empire and has been the source of more good than any other religious movement in history.[63]

Jesus still has many followers, many more admirers from a distance, and interest in him seems never to be exhausted as it bubbles up anew in every generation. He is the most important and consequential person ever to live, and for those who trust him as God the Son in the flesh and the final Judge of every person, every detail about him and his operations are treasured. His followers say he's more than fully alive and still doing what he's always done, which is to interrupt lives with a call to follow him, to learn his ways and means, and in the process to find oneself changing at the deepest level in a restored relationship with the Triune God of holy love. Initial trust unfolds into the risk of a lifelong following.

The witness of our scholars is that Luke has given us a faithful ancient biography of Jesus, one of four found in the New Testament, and that the stories of his followers indicate the deep and abiding imprint he made upon them.[64] Could it be true? I think so, and with very good evidences. He called and changed me, and for fifty years I've been trying to keep up with him, learn his ways, and follow his lead. There is no better friend or teacher than Jesus. He loves the world and each person, his church with all its flaws, and his plan is to bring the two together in a common loyalty to himself.

A Summary

Building on Longnecker's initial list of ten, here is a summary about discipleship from Luke's perspective as summarized by the scholars:

Longnecker

1. Discipleship is based on what Christ has effected for the redemption of humanity.

2. Discipleship must always be rooted in and shaped by the apostolic tradition.

3. Discipleship needs always to be dependent on God and submissive to his will, hence the importance of prayer.

4. Discipleship must always recognize the presence and power of the Holy Spirit

---

63. For a sample of this defense and apologetic, see Carroll and Schiflett, *Christianity on Trial*, 205–12.

64. For an introduction, see *The Gospel of the Lord*, 221–98.

5. Discipleship is to be involved in prophetic proclamation, with that proclamation focused on the work of Jesus.

6. Discipleship is to cherish, both in thought and action, the understanding of God's grace and the gospel as being universal.

7. Discipleship is to be committed to a lifestyle that allows no allegiance to take the place of allegiance to Jesus.

8. Discipleship is to be concerned for the poor, the imprisoned, the blind, and the oppressed.

9. Discipleship is to follow the example of Jesus and the apostles, particularly Paul, in matters of service, prayer, and cross-bearing.

10. Discipleship is to be a life of development in both one's faith and one's practice.

Green

11. Discipleship means we live together in an egalitarian community of men and women marked by joy, praise, and trusting prayer to the Father, even as we continue our mission with Jesus in a world of sin, death, and evil.

12. Discipleship means we live by God's abundance with an open heart and hand to the needs of others. Our gifts do not go with the obligation to reciprocate.

Martin

13. Discipleship is a costly walk with Jesus in which we die to old agendas and find a new center of loyalty and life in him. The signs of love and life he displays give us hope for the salvation of ourselves and the whole world.

Du Plessis

14. Discipleship means followers are not surprised when they meet hostility because of the One they represent. The Holy Spirit who enables supernatural mission also enables faithful witness under pressure, even martyrdom.

Wilkins

15. Discipleship to Jesus is relational, communal, and probing. Nothing in your lives will go unexamined as Jesus puts himself at the center of who you are. In the process you will be changed by divine love and bear his truth to others.

Hacking

16. Discipleship is a deep attachment to the person of Jesus, a risk of all you are for a chance to be his friend and student. The God who made it all and saved his people from Egypt has crossed my path in this most unusual man, and when I begin to obey him, I start to see as he sees and know that he is true.

Bock

17. Discipleship involves the highest rewards and most daunting demands, and many are tempted not to say an outright No but to dilute it into something more manageable. But a free and loving Jesus exposes all frauds, all substitutes, and re-issues his call, "Follow me, and I will make you . . . ."

18. Discipleship is a totalizing commitment based on a compelling invitation to follow Jesus with others into a new life erected in the midst of the old. If you turn and take it, take it and trust it, it alone has the love and power, the wisdom and perseverance to fit you for divine service in the friendship of Jesus.

Sweetland

19. The journey of discipleship begins with hearing and seeing Jesus through whatever avenues are accessible. This exposure to divine revelation is curated by the Holy Spirit who tugs us towards trust and surrender to Jesus, heartfelt repentance, and a full participation in his people and mission. In his company we are changed in order to love God and neighbor with what God supplies.

Fitzmeyer

20. Discipleship is Jesus' method of reproducing his vision and mission over time in a committed community of men and women who count him as worthy and trustworthy. They are his living memory, and—with the promised filling of the Spirit—his extended presence in the world. All need what he supplies through them, which is a healed relationship with the Triune God of holy love.

Giles

21. Discipleship means that Jesus is fully committed to us, that we are growing in our capacity to follow him from the heart, and that together we will do for others what he has done for us, thus no superstars and all serve one another.

Talbert

22. Discipleship is a progressive path of following Jesus. What he was historically continues among his people. The risen Jesus is still calling followers and forming them in his community for the sake of his mission. The empowerment of the Spirit is required for faithful obedience and obedient suffering because the world has not yet been changed.

Keener

23. Discipleship means a laser focus on *the new reality* of God's rule that showed up in its chief personal agent, Jesus of Nazareth. Where we stand with him is a reflection of where we stand with the One who sent him. He is life's most important opportunity and worthy of all he asks of you and more.

Thus far we have created two lists:

1. A list of fifty-one summaries from Luke's fifty-one thought units touching on Luke's story of discipleship as following Jesus.

2. A list of twenty-three statements either taken directly from scholars in their own words or as my summary of their insights.

Thus, Luke's complex narrative portrayal of Jesus and his followers is being clarified through attention to primary and secondary sources. And while there is overlap and repetition between the fifty-one and the twenty-three, rather than edit and reduce them to logical essentials, the choice is to let them stand as is, if for no other reason than to remind us what a messy process discipleship always is. The way is not an efficient, well-engineered straight line but a convoluted meandering, a walking with Jesus wherever the Father next directs him.

8

What Researchers Are Saying About Discipleship[1]

IN THE LAST TWO decades or so, beginning with the Eastbourne Consultation on Discipleship[2] in September 1999, there have been a series of major conferences on Christian discipleship as well as a growing number of increasingly sophisticated research projects on the same subject. Book and articles, videos and courses are multiplying around two basic questions:

1. What does it mean to be a follower of Jesus? and

2. What cultures, practices, and disciplines in the church foster faithful discipleship and the multiplication of Jesus followers over multiple generations?

The purpose of this chapter is to sample the consultations and research for insights into the current status of discipleship and the recommendations that follow.

Our format is the same as Chapter VII: What the Biblical Scholars are Saying. A full citation will be given, followed by a summary of insights with commentary interwoven. When completed, a synthesis and summary is offered. Along the way we will note any lists the authors offer for characteristics of mature disciples and disciple-making churches.

U.S.A. Studies

1a.   Ed Stetzer and Thomas Rainer, *Transforming Church: Creating a New Scorecard for Congregations.* Nashville: B & H, 2010.[3]

1. For a sampling of recent defintions of *disciple*, see Appendix 12.

2. For a summary, see Rabey and Rabey, *Side by Side: A Handbook.*

3. We are indebted to Lifeway Research, the research arm of the Southern Baptists, for the *Transformational Churches* project begin in 2008. The initial survey (2008) involved five thousand

The stated goal was to study healthy churches in order to create *a new scorecard* for churches, something more to do with vital discipleship than the institutional *three b's*: bucks, bricks, and bodies.

According to Stetzer and Rainer, healthy churches that are centered in the gospel and where people are being transformed by discipleship share seven inter-related qualities that work together in a *Transformational Loop* and are clustered under three headings: *Discern, Embrace, Engage*. They are not seven steps to success but an organic ecosystem under three headings, and a chapter of the book is given to exploring each factor. This is what church health looks like:

Discern: The church understands its community and context.

1. There is a missionary mentality where the story of God and the stories of people meet.

Embrace: Biblical values serve as ministry guideposts.

2. Vibrant leadership, shared vision, team leadership, pastoral accountability.

3. Relational intentionality, not just friendly but making friends of outsiders.

4. Prayerful dependence, perhaps the most important factor in the loop. "Where people pray, God works. Where God works, transformation happens."[4]

Engage: Focused activity leading to disciple-making.

5. Worship that is God-centered and sensitive to context.

6. Community, especially small groups that bridge to the community.

7. Mission, demonstrating Jesus words and deeds

Insight:
Though a truism, it takes healthy churches to create healthy disciples since it's a *we thing*, not just a *me thing*.

1b. Eric Geiger, Michael Kelly, Philip Nation. Transformational Discipleship: how people really grow. Nashville: B & H, 2012.

The premise of this book startled me: "not all discipleship is truly transformational."[5] I knew it, but winched to read it so bluntly stated. How often I

Protestants from a variety of denominations in the U.S. to discover qualitites from the top ten percent based on 3 criteria: 1) They agreed that the Bible was "the authoritative guide for faith and practice," 2) Exhibit a minimum ten percent growth in the previous give years (2003–2008), 3) Have an identified percentage of members in small group Bible study. In addition, surveys were complete by 15,000 church members. Three books have come from the project: 1) *Transformational Church* (2010), 2) *Transformational Discipleship* (2012), including an accompanying DVD, and 3) *Transformational Small Groups* (2014). Along with the research a church analysis tool and consultation process were also developed.

4. 144.

5. 7.

have delivered accurate biblical information without any means of accountability to translate it into action.

Another well-stated insight was that discipleship happens best when individuals are in a *vulnerable position,* which is best when circumstances expose the weakness of the individuals, the interdependence of the community, and the outward focus of the Christian life.[6] A third Wow! moment was to recognize what a high-leverage activity disciple-making is, "Christians are seven times more likely to disciple another person when they have first been discipled themselves." The authors remind us that to a knowledge of all that Jesus commanded there must be an obedience to the same. Transformation means holy affections, zeal for holy things, longings after God, longings after holiness, a desire for purity.

The research of Geiger and Kelly identifies eight Biblical factors that consistently show up in the lives of maturing believers. These *attributes of discipleship* are:

1. Bible engagement, likely in a small group or class

2. Obeying God and denying self

3. Serving God and others

4. Sharing Christ

5. Exercising faith

6. Seeking God

7. Building relationships

8. Unashamed (of Christ), transparency

Whereas the first volume, *Transformational Church,* uncovered the key factors indicating church health, this second volume creates a profile for growing disciples, and again there is an ecology of factors that work together. It's not by accident that anyone becomes a disciple of Jesus Christ or that a church make disciple-making a focus.

Insight:

While there is nothing surprising on this list, and we intuitively know from observation that maturing disciples touch all these bases since each of them are repeatedly highlighted in the New Testament, the research does strengthen the case that where mature disciples are being formed, these attributes are present.

1c. Ed Stetzer, Eric Geiger. Transformational Groups. Nashville: B & H, 2014.

The research base for this book—the third in a series— includes 2,300 churches from 15 denominations, less than half of which said they had a plan for discipling people, with just over half having someone responsible for the spiritual formation of children, students, and adults. Sounds pretty typical! In the earlier study, *Transformational Discipleship,* one of the items most predictive for maturity was participation in

6. 155–57, 173–74, 196–97.

a small class or group for Bible study. Geiger and Stetzer's work revealed five elements of vital small-groups that shape transformed disciples, and they are:

1. Mission orientation, following God's mission close at hand and around the world.

2. Word-driven mentality, firmly rooted in Scripture, more than a sharing group.

3. Multiplication mindset, grow and produce another group.

4. Stranger-welcoming, not closed but open groups with empty chairs.

5. Kingdom-focused, what God wants to accomplish in our midst, more that just the support of one another, valuable as that is.

In other words, as Stetzer summarizes:

> Transformational discipleship can happen when small groups are focused on God's mission, his kingdom, and his Word. And when they are welcoming strangers and intent on multiplying. All of this begins when people move out of the pew and into circles in order to be in community with one another and provoke one another to love and good deeds. This is essential.[7]

In a hyper-individualistic culture where loneliness and isolation are endemic, the church helps people learn to say *we* again, to form honest and respectful friendships, and to discover that Christians grow best in small groups. After all, didn't Jesus choose twelve, and inside that a small group of three? His kingdom laboratory was a small group of men and women disciples into whom he poured all they could hold until he increased their capacity.

In fact, the research reports that people "who attend a group at least four times a month show a significantly higher score in every area of discipleship compared with those who do not attend." In fact, "people in groups are more likely to share their faith, repent of sins regularly, give sacrificially, serve faithfully, and read their Bibles."[8] It's clear from the research that God is using groups to create people who look more and more like Christ.

Stetzer and Geiger affirm that it's really important that groups are gathering to do a few key things: practice spiritual disciplines, care for one another during life transitions, connect between meetings, have fun together, serve together, eat together, invite unchurched friends, and meet weekly.[9] The following quote gives both the rationale for and the reason why close community is critical to forming mature followers:

> Transformation is a communal experience, not an individual exercise. Jesus, God on earth, understood this fact. His model of disciple making must be ours. Jesus chose twelve, a small group. The synergy that occurred in that group of twelve aided greatly in the process of making these men mature disciples. The

7. Stetzer, "5 essential elements of transformational small groups."

8. www.smallgroups.com/articles/2014/resource-review-transformational-groups.

9. www.smallgroups.com/articles/2014/resource-review-transformational-groups.

conversations they engaged in, the time they served Rabbi Jesus together, the processing of Jesus' teachings around a campfire, even the missteps these men shared were all in Jesus' plan for making them into the mature disciples He needed them to be. Doing life together is an unquestionable essential in the disciple-making process.[10]

Insight:

While Jesus spoke and ministered to crowds, his focus was on a core group of zealots who left life as it was for life on the road with him and *the new reality*: God's present and future kingdom. Worship is corporate adoration, and preaching is corporate proclamation, but it is in small classes and face to face groups who blend love, mission, study, testimony, prayer, and gentle accountability that the gritty realities of living with and for Jesus and one another are worked out in community.

In an article, "5 Truths from 10 Years of Discipleship Research,"[11] Geiger gives us a succinct retrospective on his research:

1. Discipleship is intentional.

Those who are maturing desire to mature. They engage in discipleship opportunities and seek Christ in their daily lives. It's high leverage, and there's work to do here. For example, only 25% of pastors have a plan to develop Christ-formed leaders in their church.

2. Reading the Bible matters more than anything else.

Reading the Bible is the number one predictor for spiritual growth. Quite simply, those who read the Scripture grow.

3. The discipline of Bible engagement impacts every other discipline.

Some spiritual disciplines do not impact all the others. As an example, someone who serves may not be generous in giving. But engagement in the Word impacts every other discipline. Someone who lets the Word dwell in them simultaneously gives, serves, confesses sin, shares the gospel, etc.

4. Groups matter. A lot.

Those who are in some type of group (Sunday School, small group, etc.) are much more likely to display markers of spiritual growth than those not in a group.

5. There is a deep connection between discipleship and evangelism.

Disciples share the gospel. Those who are growing in Christ tell others about Him. Those who are not growing in their faith are much less likely to articulate the gospel."

2. Greg L. Hawkins and Cally Parkinson. *Move: What 1,000 Churches Reveal about Spiritual Growth*. Grand Rapids: Zondervan, 2011.[12]

---

10. www.smallgroups.com/articles/2014/resource-review-transformational-groups.

11. lifewayresearch.com/2018/05/31/five-truths-from-10-years-of-discipleship-research.

12. Also their two earlier publications from the same project, *Reveal: Where are You?* and *Follow Me: What's Next For You?*

This book is the culmination of the lengthy and sophisticated research project of Willow Creek Church (the *Reveal* study) from 2004 when their process began to the publication of this book seven years later.[13]

As most know, Willow Creek in South Barrington, Illinois was the model mega-church with its seeker-sensitive approach to the unchurched and the lightly-churched. It was an innovator in every area of church ministry and—along with Rick Warren and Saddleback Church in Lake Forest, California—set the agenda for many churches in America to move past the traditional model to a more culturally relevant and non-formal approach.

The cloud of sexual scandal that came over Willow Creek in 2018 has cast a shadow over all that went before it because of a culture that was light on pastoral—and sometimes staff— accountability. Still, there's much to learn from the research and the publications that followed.

One of the most important findings is a clustering of persons around four distinct stages on a spiritual continuum. They've often been observed but rarely so clearly named and warranted by research. The four clusters, each with a characteristic comment, are:

1. Exploring Christianity:
   "I believe in God but I'm not sure about Christ. My faith is not a significant part of my life"
2. Growing in Christ:
   "I believe in Jesus, and I'm working on what it means to get to know him."
3. Close to Christ:
   "I feel really close to Christ and depend on him daily for guidance."
4. Christ-Centered:.
   "God is all I need in my life. He is enough."

Other findings, some quite counter-intuitive to Protestant church culture, are:

1. Time spent in church does not predict spiritual growth.

2. Spiritual growth is all about increasing relational closeness to Christ, thus progress on the spiritual continuum does predict spiritual growth.

3. The church has the most influence on people in the early stages of the continuum. Weekend services are more critical for new believers but not so much for long-time attendees who now attend more for spiritual relationship and serving opportunities.

4. Personal spiritual practices predict Christ-centered living.

5. The church's most active evangelists, volunteers, and donors come from the higher steps of the continuum.

---

13. For an analytical article, see Sanou, "Toward a Biblical Model of Discipleship," 76–85.

6. One-quarter of the respondents were spiritually stalled or dissatisfied with the church's role in their spiritual growth.

In response to insight No. 6, Hybels admitted:

> We made a mistake. What we should have done when people crossed the line of faith and became Christians, we should have started telling people and teaching people that they have to take responsibility to become 'self feeders.' We should have gotten people, taught people, how to read their Bible between services, how to do the spiritual practices much more aggressively on their own." The church and its myriad programs have taken on too much responsibility for people's spiritual growth.[14]

In a lengthy review of *Move* and the research behind it,[15] Luke Simmons organizes his responses into three clusters and includes several key quotes from *Move*.

1. Confirmations:

- People want to be challenged. I've seen people respond to challenge time and again. "Nothing is more indicative of high-impact, discipling churches than a 'go-for-broke' challenge factor."

- The Bible is hugely important for spiritual growth. The authors write: "The most effective strategy for moving people forward in their journey of faith is biblical engagement."

- People need different things at different stages of their spiritual life. "What people need in order to grow closer to Christ depends on where they are now in their relationship with him."

- Christians must have personal time with God in order to grow:

> Nothing has a greater impact on spiritual growth than reflection on Scripture. If churches could do only one thing to help people at all levels of spiritual maturity grow in their relationship with Christ, their choice is clear. They would inspire, encourage, and equip their people to read the Bible—specifically, to reflect on Scripture for meaning in their lives.[16]

2. Surprises:

- Participation in church activities does not necessarily lead to increased spiritual maturity:

> All of our findings are derived from one essential fact: that spiritual growth—defined as an increase in love of God and for others—is not a product of

---

14. Bob Burney, "A Shocking Confession from Willow Creek Community Church."
15. faithfulandfruitful.com/2020/09/06/people-really-grow-spiritually-lessons-move.
16. www.faithfulandfruitful.com/2021/06/06/people-really-grow- spiritually- lessons- move.

growing participation in church activities or changes in lifestyle or the result of our natural aging process. Rather, spiritual growth advances in lockstep with a growing personal relationship with Christ.

- Organized small groups are more catalytic for people early on and less so later on.

  When we apply our context of human relationships to these findings, it makes perfect sense that organized activities become less important. The closer you are to someone, the more likely you are to depend on them to process your life issues, the less important organized settings tend to be. While you may have formed the relationship in a structured experience—in the workplace, perhaps, or at a neighborhood gathering—that setting is typically a springboard for the relationship, not something required to sustain it.

- Serving is the only organized church activity that moves people across all stages of their development.

  Interestingly, serving experiences appear to be even more significant to spiritual development than organized small groups. The implication for church leaders is that we must encourage people to serve—in any capacity, in whatever valid opportunity their gifts and interests lead them to.

- Churches need to promote and provide a high-expectation, non-negotiable, senior-pastor-owned pathway of first steps designed to jumpstart people's spiritual growth.

  The military uses boot camp to turn civilians into soldiers. Baseball uses spring training to test new players and try them out in different positions. Many colleges require freshmen to attend orientation week so they can become familiar with their new environment and a new set of expectations. These short-term launching pads into life experiences are analogous to the first best practice found among the most spiritually effective churches in the REVEAL database. They get people moving by providing a high-challenge, non-negotiable path of first steps to engage people in a process of spiritual growth—a process that will ultimately lead them to become followers of Jesus Christ.

  3. Challenges:

- The #1 priority of the senior leader(s) must be to make disciples.

  Five years of research findings point us to one singular conclusion— that the most essential decision a church leader makes is not what kind of worship service to offer or what kind of small-group system to build. It's the decision to lead his or her church with an unyielding and unequivocal commitment to a very easy-to-say, very hard-to-accomplish goal, which is, to do whatever is humanly possible to move people's hearts toward Christ.

- The senior leader(s) must have a white-hot relationship with Jesus.

    You cannot reproduce in others what you are not producing in yourself. The main thing you need to do—the one thing you must do— is fully within your reach. You must surrender all.

Insights:

Genuine discipleship to Jesus is never user-friendly. It cannot be made less that it is, which is a wholesale abandonment of the self to Jesus for his remaking. The path is progressive, and the goal is maturity, a truly Christ-centered life. Small groups and deep engagement with the Bible are predictive of growth. Passive program participation which demands little yields nothing.

Despite Willow's high level failures, their research is filled with insights. First of all that discipleship of not just for the new Christian but for the old one as well, with the challenges only continuing. Bible engagement, in private and in groups, is highly predictive for other indicators of serious discipleship. The religion of the expressive self is the new national faith that must be named and resisted.

3. *The State of Discipleship: A Barna Report Produced in Partnership with the Navigators*, 2015. Plus the companion book by Preston Sprinkle. *Go: Returning Discipleship to the Front Lines of Faith*. Colorado Spring: Navpress, 2016.

This is now the third full-on study we've considered. Published by Barna in 2015, *The State of Discipleship* is a partnership with The Navigators, a well-known military, college, and workplace para-church ministry focusing on evangelism and discipleship (think of them as the Green Berets of discipleship!).

While the study itself merits careful attention, a real bonus is the Preston Sprinkle book *Go* written as a dialog with the study and also with a second important book, Christian Smith's and Melinda Denton's *Soul Searching: The Religious and Spiritual Life of American Teenagers*.[17] I find myself returning again and again to the Sprinkle book, first because he's a New Testament scholar with cultural savvy, and because both his descriptions and prescriptions are so on target, a rare combination!

David Kinnamon opens *The State of Discipleship* with some personal observations titled *Discipleship In Future Tense* where he highlights three factors from the culture that touch us all, and they are:

1. *The Screen Age*, with its explosion of information and its challenge of traditional authorities. It's changing the rules of spiritual formation.

---

17. Oxford University Press, 2009.

2. *The Distracted Era*, with its explosion of possible choices for how to spend your time. Regular churchgoers are decreasing Sunday attendance and in the process loosening ties with their faith community and its rhythms.

3. *The Shift to Self*, and this is where Kinnamon bears down since over eighty percent of U.S. adults and only slightly less of practicing Christians agree with the following three statements which are part of the emerging *religion of Self* marked by three common affirmations:

- "the highest goal for life is to enjoy it as much as possible"

- "the best way to find yourself is to look inside yourself"

- "you have to be true to yourself"

He ends with this potent statement, "people must not only convert to become a disciple of Jesus, but also de-convert from the religion of Self."[18]

The report itself is thick with data from the interviews and surveys and illustrated with quality graphics for easy understanding. And, rather than expect readers to draw out the insights on their own, a helpful Executive Summary is found near the beginning and including the following summaries;

- That most Christian adults find the simple phrase *becoming more Christ-like* the one they most prefer for spiritual growth is not a surprise. *Discipleship* was fourth on the list, likely because it's already a sub-culture term for highly committed followers.

- A big insight was the enormous gap between Christian adults who gave their church a favorable 52 percent affirmation that my church "definitely does A good job helping people grow spiritually" whereas only 1 percent of church leaders agreed with this statement, with 60 percent feeling that churches are discipling "not too well." A confirming fact for the negative picture is that only 1 in 5 Christians adults are involved in a discipleship activity: Sunday school, fellowship group, book discussion, meeting with a mentor. And yet, 3 percent of Christian adults are "happy where they are in their spiritual life," and another 36 percent are "almost where they want to be." This is what I call *the great disconnect*. It sounds a bit rosy, and the report recommends the use of an inventory that helps people examine the reality of their spiritual growth, not just their perceptions.

- Another troublesome indicator is the individualist and isolationist preference by those who agree that spiritual growth is very or somewhat important (the most committed). Nearly two in five prefer to pursue spiritual growth on their own (the privatization of spirituality), whereas pastors from exemplar churches agree that the *we* dimension of groups and the accountability of one-on-one mentoring is critical. Leaders confess that most do not have much of a plan to promote

18. 12.

discipleship or a means to measure effectiveness. The greatest perceived barriers to serious discipleship are "the busyness of life" and "a lack of commitment to discipleship." Pace and apathy are prominent. A highlight was that over 90 percent of leaders were mentoring and coaching at least one other person, but that only about two thirds had someone working with them.

In summary, new models of discipleship are needed, ones that engage genuine spiritual hungers and longings, and provide a rich relational environment to learn from and make progress with others. Following Jesus is as much caught as taught. And while significant discipleship activities are ongoing with promising results, the pool of the distracted, the apathetic, the distracted, and the complacent is growing.

The onus is clearly on pastors, in conjunction with other church leaders—and perhaps specialists, to develop a flexible localized plan, not only to model and preach on discipleship, but to find a blending of groups and individual mentoring that sinks people deeper into the faith: its Book, its Lord, its truths and intellectual resources, its passions, habits and practices, joys and sorrows, and its mission "across the street and around the world."[19] There is no *one size fits all*, though there are models to consider and indigenize.

The spiritual formation Jesus offered was every day, all the time, on the road, and in the middle of the messes of life, every day a classroom and every meeting a laboratory in the ways and means of *the new reality.* Following Jesus as a pupil embraces the whole of life, including all the questions that bubble up along the way. You cannot follow him alone, and it will change you from the inside out. Jesus' goal is to stamp us with his way of seeing the world and of living in it in partnership with *the new reality*, the immediate presence of the kingdom of God.

Near the end of the Barna study is an Appendix titled "Educators: defining discipleship."[20] This sub-survey was sampled from those with formal positions in churches and para-church ministries who have discipleship as part of their job description, *the professionals.* The question posed them was "What are the most significant barriers to effective discipleship?" Their most common responses were:

- Educators most commonly cite church programs when asked to identify the most significant barriers to effective discipleship. Other barriers include:

- An overly formalized processes (rather than organic approaches that enable deeper, more meaningful, Spirit-led relationships);

- Hyper-focus on evangelism and conversion, to the detriment of ongoing nurture;

- Overemphasis on worship and experiential spirituality; a consumerist approach to church;

19. A favorite phrase of Dr. Al Vom Steeg, former President of The Mission Society for United Methodists.

20. 37–40.

- Church leaders not modeling and/or championing discipleship;

- Potential disciplers feeling under-equipped, not qualified or spiritually unready;

- Impatience, especially on the part of younger Christians;

- General busyness of life and an unwillingness to invest the considerable amount of time required for real spiritual growth;

- Distractions from media that prevent believers from learning how to really read and dig into the Bible (despite access through media to useful biblical tools);

- Individualistic nature of society, especially among Millennials. However, some point to a greater desire among young adults for meaningful relationships—a desire which the church can fulfill especially well through discipleship.

The making of disciples is not optional, and every age has its challenges. But to live in such a yeasty and experimental time as our own is a sign of the Holy Spirit's deep stirring of the church.

And, on the Preston Sprinkle book, I found it so full of good stuff that it's hard to summarize. So buy a copy, mark it up, and discuss it with a friend. Better yet, buy a copy for your pastors and invite them into the circle for a hard look at discipleship.

Insight:

I am grateful for all the exacting research groups like Barna and the Navigators carry out, but the information is often so intimidating to local pastors who need more than astute cultural analysis and lists of characteristics. If the local church is the primary venue for making disciples, where are the churches that seem to have found the sweet spot? What are the best examples? And what if the research reports contained a concluding section on the disciple-making practices of the most effective churches, both large and small? Most pastors need more than another research report; we need a place to visit, to see what it looks like, and to enter dialog with the local leaders on how messy the process remains.

4. *National Study On Disciple-Making In USA Churches*. Sponsored by Discipleship.org and Exponential and conducted by Grey Matter Research. www.exponential.org/resource-ebooks/disciple-making-study,ortheordinarymen.com/wp-content/uploads/2020/05/Discipleship-Making-in-the-US-Churches.pdf), March 2020.

With this report we have a cross section of U.S. Churches in terms of their disciple-making capacity. As the analysis of disciple-making deepens, five types of churches are identified in the U.S. (our own backyard). Warning! It is not a pretty picture.

Level 1   Subtracting from disciple-making efforts, a negative effect:

Level 1 churches are numerically declining, and 29 percent of the churches in the U.S. fit this category. Little passion for Jesus Christ. Little effect on the world around them.

Level 2   Plateaued, neither helping nor hurting disciple making:

Level 2 churches are numerically plateaued churches and 44 percent of U.S. churches are in this category. Stalled. Little effort to intentionally influence others for spiritual growth. Low expectations.

Level 3   Adding disciples by church programs:

Level 3 churches are numerically growing by addition and 27 percent of U.S. churches are in this category. They do not yet mobilize disciple-makers.

Level 4   Reproducing personal disciple-makers:

Level 4 churches are numerically growing and are also reproducing disciples and disciple-makers. Less than 5percent of U.S. churches fit this description. These churches have a disciple-making culture.

Level 5   Multiplying personal disciples makers:

Level 5 are churches where almost everyone makes disciples. The leaders live to make disciple-makers who then make others to the fourth generation. These churches are the fuel for disciple-making movements. Though present in other parts of the world, no examples can be currently identified in the U.S.

These movements are differentiated from Level 4 as "special movement(s) of the Holy Spirit as they rapidly multiply disciples and disciple-makers."[21] It is estimated that there are about a thousand such viral movements around the world.

Besides the not-so-encouraging profile are two additional findings:

1. That there is no common and compelling agreement on definitions. One telling statistic of that "just 15 percent of pastors said their church has both a simple, reproducible model to equip their members to make disciples and a framework or metric for measuring their success at doing so. Only 7 percent agreed strongly that they have both."[22]

2. Pastors are overly-optimistic and frequently overrate their effectiveness in this area by a wide margin.[23] The reports recommends clear definitions and common language, stronger leadership from Senior Pastors to making discipleship their core mission, a set of new metrics for Jesus-style disciple making, and a high-lighting of the strategies and models of churches with disciple-making cultures.

The definition of disciple-making the authors developed is as clear as it is demanding:

> People intentionally entering into relationships to help others follow Jesus,
> become more like Jesus,
> and join the mission of Jesus.
> Disciple making includes the whole process
> from conversion through maturation and multiplication,

21. 3.

22. A set of recommended definitions is found on pages 15–16 of the report.

23. 9.

which is making disciples who in turn make other disciples.[24]

An interesting part of the report is a listing of the traits of Level 4 and 5 churches. That there are some churches that substantially match this profile is a sign of hope, and for those of us in the Wesleyan movements, we find many parallels between this list and the kinds of expectations and disciple-making activities that characterized our early days. Level 4 is listed, and Level 5 (where 90% are disciple-makers) left your reading of the report.

Level 4: Reproducing Disciples[25]

(This happens when 24–50 percent of lay leaders become disciple-makers)

1. Jesus-style disciple-making is the core mission of the church. It is motivated by love for people lost without salvation in Jesus, and the church regularly *reproduces* disciples and disciple makers.

2. Disciple-making is the *emerging* cultural identity of the church—reflected in the *reproduction* of the church's values, actions, and words.

3. Every decision made and every dollar spent passes through the filter: "How does this help us make disciples in relational environments like Jesus?"

4. The church has a starting foundation of weekly fasting and prayer—asking for God to empower disciple-making.

5. The core leadership focus not just on making disciples, but on *making disciple-makers* (of lay leaders) with at least 20–39 percent of their time spent personally equipping people (outside weekend gatherings).

6. There is a joyful expectation that every disciple should "obey all of Jesus' teachings" and grow to become a disciple-maker.

7. 24–50 percent or more of adult lay leaders are personally engaged in leading roles of making and reproducing disciples.

8. Every leader uses the same simple, effective, and reproducible disciple-making model and a metric that tracks effectiveness. This is the disciplined application of the same model.

9. Core leaders hear stories on a weekly basis of formerly lost people now making disciples.

10. The disciple-making activities of the church result in planting new churches every year or two.

Insight:

If you were to design a cold slap in the face, this is it! We don't know what we're doing, don't know how to talk about it, and don't seem to care about the ineffectiveness

24. 10.

25. 13.

of our churches. And while the standards of these authors is high, they are much closer to the passion of the New Testament. We live with the sin of low expectations and find them perfectly fulfilled.

United Kingdom (U.K.) Studies

5.   "Time for discipleship: 21st Century Evangelicals, A Snapshot of the beliefs and habits of evangelical Christians in the U.K.— Spring 2014" Evangelical Alliance, eauk.org.

This is one of a series of research reports on various topics (work, church, education, money, family) published by the Evangelical Alliance beginning in 2011. This study surveyed a panel of 3,000 persons from eight partner organizations. The report opens with a "Top 10 key statistics" summary:

- 98% Strongly agree they can see God at work in their life in the long term.

- 31% Less than a third set aside substantial time for prayer each day.

- 26% Only a quarter feel well-equipped to witness and share their faith.

- 90% Strongly agree that attending church and small groups is helpful to their growth. and 60% say it is very helpful.

- 70% Find large Christian conferences/festivals help their walk with God.

- 90% Study the Bible every day or several times a week.

- 63% Get easily distracted when spending time with God.

- 40% Less than half agree their church does very well at discipling new Christians.

- 33% A third use Bible apps on their mobile device.

- 60% Have been inspired and influenced by a church leader/minister they knew.[26]

And, while there is nothing surprising here, the obvious calls for attention. Help with sustaining forms of daily prayer and Bible reading, strengthening small groups which blend Bible study with personal support, training in listening, simple apologetics, and making sure new Christians are loved and grounded all seem like straightforward responses to the "Top 10."

My hunch is that carving out mini-sabbaths to be disconnected from the digital world would be both a challenging and fruitful discipline to strengthen all the others. Never underestimate the influence of leaders, lay and clergy, who are faithful models and have stories to tell, as well as the impact of larger gatherings which assure us we are not alone but that God has his people everywhere. Busyness and distraction were noted and parallel the same theme in the U.S. research.

Sprinkled through the analysis are questions titled *Time to Consider*:

26. 2.

- Are you spending time with other Christians, talking about your faith and building each other up? Who might God be calling you to get alongside and support?

- Do you take time to get to know and learn from Christians of different ages from you?

- Do you feel equipped to share your faith? If not, how can you intentionally develop in this? If you do, how can you encourage others to be more confident in evangelizing?

- Would you say your church is intentionally discipling people, both new Christians and older ones? How can discipleship be developed in your church?

A bit later in the report came the confession by about a quarter (26 percent) that they ignore issues of global justice, with the same fraction admitting they are often self-centered. A full 68 percent indicated they'd come to faith before age 18, indicating the importance of faith practices in the family, youth, and children's ministries. Throughout the report was a refrain on how important Christian friends were, especially in the early years of the new life.

Near the end of the report was the heading *Challenges for the UK Church* and three items were highlighted:

1. Discipling new Christians: fresh attention must be given to mentoring and support.

2. Whole-life disciples: equal emphasis on using gifts and talents in the wider community and using them in the church.

3. Equipped to share: training and modeling to share faith in Christ with others.

Insights:

The value of this report is that Britain is now thoroughly post-Christian, but with great internal resources remaining. It could be they are a bell-weather for the U.S. Many feel embattled, and those who remain committed show great resilience and boldness in their witness. They seem to cooperate with others in ways we do not yet have to do in the States.

6. "Making Disciples," a joint research project of licc/Elim. 2020. licc.org.uk/ resources/ elim-research.

This is a smaller research report involving 16 Elim Pentecostal Churches, their pastors, 828 individuals in the churches and a focus group in each church, thus it reflects— by design—those who are most committed. It is an intra-church study (within one denomination) instead of inter-church study between a variety of denominations and was carried out in partnership with *licc*: London Institute for Contemporary Christianity. The key findings were five:

1. You don't have to be a 'super leader' to make whole-life disciples.

Even though we looked at churches that were identified as well-led, growing, and committed to making disciples, almost without exception every senior leader expressed their church's limitations in discipling people. Few felt they were able to present themselves confidently. In short—healthy disciplemaking churches are led by ordinary people just like you.

2. It's tough to grow as a disciple if you don't know your purpose.

When we compared people's self-reporting concerning their spiritual growth and their sense of purpose in life, the differences were remarkable. People who had a 'very clear' idea of God's purposes for them on their front lines were much more likely to describe themselves as 'growing' than those who did not. In other words, when people see their daily contexts through God's eyes, they're more likely to grow in their faith and confidence.

3. Intentional communication with the whole church is essential.

All the leaders were aware that what was needed in their church were practices that constantly reminded the congregation that the church's culture was about making disciples. Leaders of larger churches recognized they needed to spend time with the wider leadership teams to ensure discipling was part of the church's core DNA. In smaller churches, the ministers prioritized time in one-to-one discipling conversations with people.

4. Small groups matter—a lot!

It may sometimes be a struggle to connect people to them, but when people do engage with small groups, their discipleship benefits hugely. From being encouraged to discern your strengths and gifts to gaining accountability from a trusted group of peers, the impact of thriving small groups is huge.

5. As churches, we need to share wisdom about issues from every part of life.

To help people grow as disciples, it's important our ministry is focused on wider horizons than just gathered church activities. This needs to be explicitly stated, because people may have come to expect that guidance in church is more likely to be directed at personal or family issues—and less often at the things they face at work, in school, or with friends.

What struck me after reading this report was just how much it overlapped with No. 5 above, "Time for discipleship." But then, they're embedded in the same culture, aren't they? Several of the overlaps were:

1. An admission that the church does not value what I do beyond church activities (work); that the church does not encourage me to care about global issues (poverty, justice, creation-care); that the church does not help people see how to use spiritual gifts in everyday life;

Thus, both surveys highlight the large disconnect between church life and the rest of life. Discipleship is not yet holistic, and there are not enough bridges into the community;

2. Both highlight the critical nature of small groups for connection and growth, a place for face-to-face relationships, and accountability.

An insight not uncovered in the other studies is the more clarity that one has about *God's purposes where you are*, the more confidence their discipleship, a greater awareness of how their spiritual gifts connect with the larger world, and an increasing sense that the church cares about their life outside the church.

This appears to be some sort of tipping point, an issue that opens up into other good outcomes. Clarity about calling and vocation have multiple benefits, and those without it are less confident in their discipleship, less disciplined as Christians, less likely to know how to be a disciple in their context, and more likely to feel anxious and stuck as Christians.

This is an insight worth further development because of all the positives that flow from it. It's a big, important question: What is the purpose for your life as a Jesus follower? Could it be that a solid answer to this question is one of keys that unlocks so many other things in a person's life?

Insight:

Helping Christians find some clarity about their calling and purpose and challenging them to build bridges between their churches and all the others sectors of life is the challenge of this study. Since Pentecostals have felt like a minority witness for so long, you can feel their passion to claim the whole of life for a Jesus who fills them with the energies of love that their culture—and also other churches—so need.

7. "Talking Jesus: Perceptions of Jesus, Christians, and evangelism in England," Research conducted by the Barna Group on behalf of the Church of England, Evangelical Alliance, and Hope, 2015. talkingjesus.org/wp-content/uploads/2018/04/Perceptions-of-Jesus-Christians-and-Evangelism-Executive-Summary.pdf.

While this is not a study on discipleship in the same way as No. 1–6 above, it is valuable as a sophisticated study of British public opinion, and it tells the church what people are thinking about the issues that matter most to the church. It's as if Jesus again asked, "Who do men say that I am?" and the disciples came back with this report.

While Britain is surely deeper into the process of secularization than the U.S., I was still surprised to learn that 40 percent of the people in England do not realize that Jesus was a real person who actually lived and that 1 in 4 of 18–34 year olds think he was a mythical or fictional character. Of those interviewed, 57 percent self-identify as Christian, but only 9 percent are practicing, defined as those who report regular prayer, reading the Bible, and attending a church service at least monthly. Nominalism and cultural faith is a big challenge. But 43% percent have some belief in Jesus' resurrection in its stronger or weaker forms.

What was encouraging is that a full two-thirds of practicing Christians have spoken to a non-Christian about Jesus in the last month and that nearly three of four feel comfortable speaking about Jesus to non-Christians.

Insights:

Basic cultural literacy of the most basic information about the Christian faith is shrinking in the U.K., and this poses both challenges and opportunities for disciples. The state church, The Church of England, is shrinking in spite of genuine efforts and a few bright spots in some churches and cathedrals. The religion of the Self and its Appetites (hedonism) as well as an emboldened neo-paganism and polytheism puts us back in dialog with the alternatives we faced pre-Constantine. We've see this before!

Global Documents

8.   "Intentional Discipleship and Disciple-Making: An Anglican Guide for Christian Life and Formation." London: The Anglican Consultative Council, 2016. www.anglicancommunion.org/media/220191/intentional-discipleship-and-disciple-making.pdf.

Though informed by research of several types, this substantial document is more book than report. It's a full-blown, sophisticated theology of discipleship on an international scale, and the only one I'm currently aware of.

Part A: Theological Background has eight chapters. After a substantial introduction giving the history of the document, there follow two chapters on a biblical theology of disciple-making and a review of discipleship in the early church. The next three chapters cover the discipleship theologies of Roman Catholics, the Orthodox, and the Anglicans. Five marks of mission are featured in Chapter 6 with Chapter 7 on "Healing and Discipleship" insuring the inclusion of the charismatic reality.

Part B: Contemporary Anglican Praxis of Discipleship has nine chapters with the first four giving updates on Africa, Asia, Europe, and The Americas, so the intent is multi-cultural discipleship. The next four speak to Anglican discipleship with children and youth, the classic means of grace (Bible, Worship, Sacraments, Eucharistic Community), the issues of resources and support, and the cooperation of Church Mission and Development Agencies in the relief of poverty and other concerns. The concluding chapter is titled, "The Case for Intentional Discipleship in the Communion." What a thorough piece of work, and what a gift to the whole church.

Because of the depth and length of this report, my approach is not to summarize as with earlier treatments but rather to highlight the features that most apply to the topic at hand, "Discipleship in Luke and Beyond," with an emphasis on the *Beyond!* In the Forward Archbishop Ng Moon Hing speaks of the full range and implications of discipleship in the footsteps of Jesus:

> A narrow, pietistic attachment to Jesus, whether individualistic or ecclesial, was never what God intended and will not serve us well today. Following Jesus will and must change every aspect of our being. At the core will be our reconciliation with God, but this can never be complete until we are at peace with ourselves, in vital communion with the whole Body of Christ, in a renewed relationship with the whole human family, and discovering a new harmony with

creation as a whole. Wrestling with environmental issues, with peace-building and peace-keeping, with the complexities of human relationships, with truth, justice, and loving, and with the care of our family and ourselves—these are all key concerns for those who accept the invitation of Jesus to "follow.[27]

In Chapter 1, "A Biblical Theology of Disciple-Making," the authors make two basic statements about discipleship, then give eight marks of discipleship in the Gospel of Mark, to which I add the parallel passages in Luke. Jesus was doing two main things which would become perennially important for his followers in generations to come:

Assumptions:

1. He was giving us a model in his own actions of how to be a disciple-maker.

2. He was allowing his first disciples in their responses towards him to become, for us, a model of how we should respond to Jesus' call and follow him too, revealing the primary hallmark of Christian discipleship (that is, being a learner in Jesus' school, a follower of Jesus).

Jesus the Disciple-Maker:

1. His first calling of the disciples, which is clear and directional, vocational and radical (Mark 3.1–19, Luke 6:12–16).

2. His commitment to sharing his life with them (Mark 1:16–20, 2:13–17 // Luke 5:1–11, 27–32).

3. His intention to give time for de-briefing (6.6b–13, 30–32) and his use of recent events and teachings as an opportunity for further teaching and discussion, helping his followers to process externally what they had experienced (Mark 6:6b–13, 30–32 // Luke 9:1–11, 10:17–20).

4. His willingness to have an inner circle (Peter, James, and John) who would witness more intimately and directly three momentous events in his life: Rising from the dead, Transfiguration, and Agony (Mark 5.37–43; 9.2–8; 14.32–36 // Luke 8:40–56, 9:28–36, 22:40–46).

5. His willingness to chide and admonish, to expose and rebuke his followers, while being totally committed to their growth and restoration (Mark 8:17–21; 9.35–37 // omitted in Luke).

6. His ability to ask questions which would bring to the surface their wrong motivations or muddled ideas (Mark 9.33–34 // Luke 9:46–48).

7. His occasional giving of bizarre instructions which simply had to be obeyed 'because he said so,' but which would make sense later on (Mark 11.1–9, 14.12–16 // Luke 19:28–38, Luke 22:7–13).

27. ix.

8. His deliberate policy of letting them see him both in public and in private, both 'on the job' and more intimately 'as a friend.' (Read between the lines!

All of these will need to be borne in mind whenever we come to ask the contemporary question: How can we be disciple-makers in our own generation?

Later in the same chapter, the authors remind us that the one whose biography we read in four versions is the same risen Jesus we know and follow. They especially highlight Luke 24 with its six themes for future disciples:[28]

1. His Resurrection (vv.34, 46);

2. His Cross (vv.26, 46);

3. The Holy Spirit (v.49);

4. The Scriptures (vv.27, 44);

5. The Sacrament or breaking of bread (v.36);

6. The Mission (v.48).

The report is to be especially commended for its treatment of "Healing and Discipleship" in Chapter 7, including the ever-controversial work of deliverance and exorcism.[29] Discipleship which ignores evil or the gifts and powers of the Holy Spirit is less than Jesus intended and not adequate for the world we face.

In the section devoted to a review of Anglican discipleship in Africa, Asia, Europe, and the Americas, we hear from Malaysia of a form of disciple training (DT) adapted from SaRang Presbyterian Church in Seoul, South Korea which stresses a five-fold discipleship of life commitments:

1. Disciple of the Gospel of Christ: Each to learn to master and to articulate the whole Gospel.

2. Disciple of the Word of God: Each to learn to read the Bible and to feed himself spiritually.

3. Disciple of the Life of Prayer: Each to learn to pray and to listen to God through contemplation and spiritual disciplines.

4. Disciple of Service: Each to offer some months or years to serve God in a certain capacity within the Church or society.

5. Disciple of Mission: Each to make at least one mission trip per annum outside his comfort zone.[30]

Because Sunday eucharistic worship is so central to Anglican identity and practice, I was happy to be reminded how many of the elements of vital discipleship are

28. 22.

29. 51–57.

30. 88.

featured, celebrated, and imprinted in each Lord's Day service. Speaking of the common worship elements of the ancient church's liturgies, the authors write:

> To the sermon, baptism, Eucharist, ancient creeds, and the Lord's Prayer we could add other liturgical elements like the confession of sins, the announcement of forgiveness, the readings from Holy Scripture, the members' greeting each other with the kiss of peace. Weekly repetition played an important role in the formation of Christians in the ancient Church.

The liturgy was the early Church's most effective manner of Christian formation for all. After the formal period of instruction, followed by Baptism, the believers were weekly taught the Christian life through the liturgy of the Church—the verbal and visual re-enactment of all the basic aspects of the Christian faith they had learned about. Through its liturgy and all aspects of it, they were taught how to be true followers of Jesus Christ.

> This Christian formation or discipleship training was church-based, communal, and led by Church leadership. It was not something separate for those interested in classes, but something all believers were supposed to undergo, initially in formal training, and after their Baptism through participation in the communion of the saints in the normal life of the Church.[31]

Insight:

When, as a Methodist, I want clarity and comprehensiveness, as well as breadth and depth, I turn to the Anglicans. Too much of the discipleship literature being written today ignores the church, its liturgy and sacraments as the ornamentals of the faith rather than the substance of which are reminded every Lord's Day. Is this the legacy of the para-church ministries to which our churches out-sourced most of the heavy lifting for at least forty years? I love the pithy quote from Rev. Dr. Alison Morgan, "The plural of disciple is church."[32]

9. "The Arusha Call to Discipleship," The World Council of Churches Conference on World Mission and Evangelism, March 13–18, 2008. gs2019.anglican. ca/ wp-content/uploads/Appendix-3-Arusha.

As expected, a WCC statement on discipleship will highlight both Jesus' call to discipleship and the particularly contemporary locations where the following of Jesus engages the powers that make human life more difficult than it has to be, including economic arrangements. The courage of this statement is that most of the articles name a specific manifestation of sin for which courageous discipleship is a remedy, and I have italicized these statements. The Arusha document contains twelve statements of call for all disciples:

As disciples of Jesus Christ, both individually and collectively:

---

31. 30–31.

32. Note 35 above.

- We are called by our baptism to transforming discipleship: a Christ-connected way of life *in a world where many face despair, rejection, loneliness, and worthlessness.*

- We are called to worship the one Triune God—the God of justice, love, and grace—*at a time when many worship the false god of the market system* (Luke 16:13).

- We are called to proclaim the good news of Jesus Christ—the fullness of life, the repentance and forgiveness of sin, and the promise of eternal life—in word and deed, *in a violent world where many are sacrificed to the idols of death* (Jeremiah 32:35) *and where many have not yet heard the gospel.*

- We are called to joyfully engage in the ways of the Holy Spirit, *who empowers people from the margins with agency, in the search for justice and dignity* (Acts 1:8; 4:31).

- We are called to discern the word of God *in a world that communicates many contradictory, false, and confusing messages.*

- We are called to care for God's creation, *and to be in solidarity with nations severely affected by climate change in the face of a ruthless human-centered exploitation of the environment for consumerism and greed.*

- We are called as disciples to belong together in just and inclusive communities, in our quest for unity and on our ecumenical journey, *in a world that is based upon marginalization and exclusion.*

- We are called to be faithful witnesses of God's transforming love *in dialogue with people of other faiths in a world where the politicization of religious identities often causes conflict.*

- We are called to be formed as servant leaders who demonstrate the way of Christ *in a world that privileges power, wealth, and the culture of money* (Luke 22:25–27).

- We are called to break down walls and *seek justice with people who are dispossessed and displaced from their lands—including migrants, refugees and asylum seekers—and to resist new frontiers and borders that separate and kill* (Isaiah 58:6–8).

- We are called to follow the way of the cross, *which challenges elitism, privilege, personal and structural power* (Luke 9:23).[33]

- We are called to live in the light of the resurrection, which offers hope-filled possibilities for transformation.

Insight:

If you look back to reports No. 2 (Willow Creek's *Reveal* study), No. 5 ("Time for Discipleship"), and No. 6 ("Making Disciples") you will find a concern that current

---

33. The italics are part of the original document, intended to make the current challenges of discipleship clear.

models of discipleship often leave engagement with large social problems either unaddressed or minimized. This is not true of the Arusha document which pairs nearly every call to discipleship with a social pathology or problem to which it speaks. And while the issues are sometimes stated in trendy ways that reflect a shallow analysis, that they are stated is a sobering reminder that not only do many not know of Jesus, but that we do not know their suffering or show much interest in it.

A Synthesis: What the Researchers Teach Us[34]

Christian researchers and sociologists are like prospectors; they go digging in search of buried treasure, and sometimes find them and put them on display. So with each of these research projects and their summary reports. And while I can find no explicit collaboration among them, the common ground is considerable across cultures. As a summary I offer the following:

1. We have a very good idea of the characteristics that indicate church health and the practices that foster serious discipleship. But changing the deep ruts of our church culture to accommodate them is very difficult, and not always successful. Without pastors and other leaders who champion discipleship and restore it to the center of the church's life, little happens. Churches drift, and people looking for meaning and life stay away in droves.

2. The most vital discipleship moments are not in the U.S. or Britain but scattered around the globe where apostolic Christianity is growing in Disciple Making Movements (DMM) where to be a disciple is also to be a disciple-maker.

3. Where people gather face-to-face with one another with an open Bible to seek the Lord, hear from him and share his love, unusual things start to happen. And when such groups find a common calling in mission, watch out! They become magnetic and infectious, adding passion and vision to their churches. Such groups encourage their members to seek the Lord in Scripture and prayer, in trust and obedience between meetings and to share their testimonies at the next gathering. It's the way faith is built.

4. The old slogan, "If you fail to plan, then plan to fail," is nowhere more true than with discipleship. Without an understanding of the challenges that accompany each marker on the discipleship continuum, how can we aid our friends? A practical theology of the ways and means of starting and sustaining the journey of discipleship is needed. Pastors must lead, and with so many never having been trained in this kind of practical Christianity themselves, who will disciple them in the obedience and risk that goes beyond correct Christian information and

34. For a summary chart of the characteristics of mature disciples, see Appendix 15

institutional maintenance? Can careerists an shop-keepers become disciple-makers again?

5. Distractions and isolation are our veiled enemies. Shallow thinking and loneliness are their predictable outcomes. Discipleship is a team sport with Coach Jesus, to risk an overused sports metaphor, but it's true.

6. Disciple-making uses all sorts of resources, including curricula, but if doing the program becomes more important than building trusting friendships under the tutelage of the risen Jesus, it communicates all the wrong messages.

7. The Jesus we love and follow reclaims the whole of life. Becoming a holy huddle may be a short-term survival strategy, but hiding the treasures of the faith from a world in need is a crime. Jesus is the curriculum, and the four gospels are the manual for what he's still doing with followers, even us!

8. Start somewhere and start soon! Trust your prayerful intuitions and pray. Then gather several insiders and unlikelies in a circle and get going. Learn as you burn!

9

So What? What Now?

IF YOU'VE MANAGED TO read yourself this far, good for you! It's not easy, and not designed to be. This volume is written at the neglected interface between scholarship and the life of the church, and that's not a space many occupy. But it's where I've lived as a pastor for forty-five years now, and one of my personal projects has been to stop *dumbing the church down* to 6 keys and 10 secrets and 28 sure-fire methods. As I argued earlier, the essentials questions of Who? What? and Why? are prior to the three pragmatic ones we so love: When? Where? and How? So now I to take a brief swipe at So What? and What Now?

Remember that this is a limited study of discipleship in Luke, not even of Acts, or the other three Gospels, Paul's contributions in his letters, much less the General Epistles and Revelation which conclude the canon. Mine is not the whole picture, but it is a faithful slice and enough to keep us busy for a long time. Luke is a rope woven of two main cords, a gold one of Jesus and a deep blue one of his followers, with his enemies as a smaller red thread and his favorable multitudes as a smaller light blue thread. But enough of images and colors. Luke is very interested in who Jesus is and who his faithful—and not so faithful—followers are, and they are mutually dependent.

Think about it. With no followers there would have been no Jesus movement and ultimately no church, just a bright comet that crossed the night sky and flamed out. Face-to-face-exposure and life-to-life influence is where discipleship happens and lives are re-formed. It's never arms-length, anonymous, or private but always communal and costly. Think of a sculptor chiseling stone, a potter forming a lump into a pot, a wood-worker using a plane and then sanding a rough board. It's gracious pressure towards a beautiful end, but it is pressure nonetheless, the pressure of God's persistent Triune grace making demands and then enabling their performance. We who are mis-shapen are being re-shaped by a process someone else is supervising!

This was made clear to me only recently in a memorable encounter just outside Nashville in Murfreesboro, Tennessee. I felt sad, but it was a good sad because some good had been accomplished for one of my brothers who's a disabled veteran in chronic abdominal pain after multiple surgeries.

He'd been admitted to the psych unit of the VA Hospital for observation after a procedure at the Pain Clinic that did not reduce his pain . He was admitted because when they asked, "Do you ever think of harming yourself?" and his answer was, "Yes, I cannot live like this."

As I drove off I prayed, "Show them what to do, O Lord." It had been a while since I'd eaten, so I stopped at a restaurant and headed in. Then, as usual, went back to my SUV for the repentance of getting my Covid mask. I felt a set of keys in my jacket pocket, but the car would not unlock. Pulling them out, they were my brother's keys and mine were visible through the window in a cup holder.

But that wasn't supposed to happen. My doors are not supposed to lock with the key inside, but with my brother's *smart key* in my pocket apparently the system had been fooled, and I felt foolish. So I shot up an arrow, "Mercy and help is what I most need now, O Lord."

So what was I to do? Glad that I had AAA, I called for their fabled *road-side assistance* and in less than twenty minutes a young locksmith named Austin drove up in his oversized van. He comforted me with the words, "About half the calls I receive are when smart key technology doesn't work." And then, with his lock-pick, he opened the door in less than a minute. I was astounded and smiled, "Where can I buy one of those?" to which his reply was, "You can't. They are all registered to locksmiths."

Since he was a young man, around twenty I guessed, I asked, "Where did you learn to be a locksmith? Was it at a technical college?"

"No," he replied, "I rode with a locksmith for three months because you don't learn this stuff from books, only on the job. Later on you get certified." Even I can hear the Lord at such moments:

> My dear son Phil, this is how it is with discipleship. There are things to know and information to understand, but it's mainly show and tell, and show and try, and try and fail, and fail and learn, and learn it over and over in new situations. Someone who knows more than you do, a journeyman, teaches you the moves as a novice and then as an apprentice. And after a while you get it! And your ability to practice your craft keeps growing every day until you get the basics down.

We chatted for a minute more, and I thanked him profusely. When I saw the name on the truck I asked, "Does your dad own the company?" he smiled, "Yep! Sure does, and if I'm good enough, one day it'll be mine."

As he drove off, I glanced upwards, "Thank you, Lord, for that costly lesson in discipleship." Every day is a classroom for those enrolled in the Jesus school of costly following. Life is his raw material, and he will—if invited—turn it all into love and wisdom.

So go back and read the fifty-one discipleship statements I've drawn from Luke, then the twenty-three of the scholars, and finally the *Insight* section under each of the researchers. Then ask, "If this Jesus fellow is still alive and still doin' his stuff, what would it mean for me to be his student and apprentice and friend and follower with whoever else he calls into my circle of influence?" It's an essential question, life's most basic choice.

As I've read the contemporary literature on discipleship, I've been heartened by how many of the better-known authors, most all of whom are from other denominational backgrounds, draw their models of discipleship from John Wesley. What we Methodists have overlooked and ignored, our near friends have re-discovered and re-deployed to good effect. Several examples will serve to make the point:

1. Dr. Robby Gallaty in his book *Rediscovering Discipleship: Making Jesus' Final Words Our First Work*, devotes the whole of Chapter 6, "A Band-Aid for the Church," to Wesley's development of the three levels of discipleship formation (1. the society, 2. the class meeting, 3. the band meeting) and Chapter 9, "One for All, Not One at a Time" to a defense of the three levels of group discipleship. He also offers a chart to demonstrate how his pastoral plan at Brainerd Baptist Church in Chattanooga, TN draws from Jesus' pattern and Wesley's adaptation of accountable discipleship.

The Three-Strand Church Model[1]
The Master's Plan for Discipleship

Jesus' Model	Multitudes	The Twelve	The 3: Peter, James, John
Wesley's Model	Societies	Classes	Bands
3-Strand Model	Congregation	Community	Core
Group Size	50+	8–20	3–5
Focus	Celebration	Community/ Fellowship	Commitment
Population	Mixed gender	Mostly mixed gender	Gender specific
Message Content	General	Less general	Discipleship specific

2. Dr. Bill Hull, in his now classic *The Complete Book of Discipleship*, makes a clear appeal to Wesley in a section titled "Discipleship Done Right,"[2] and a second strong appeal to Wesley and this three-level plan of discipleship in his subsequent

---

1. 113.

2. 102–104.

volume *Conversion and Discipleship,* under the heading "John Wesley- Disciple Maker."[3]

3. Joel Comiskey in his book *2000 Years of Small Groups* devotes Chapter 11, "John Wesley, Founder of Methodism"[4] and Chapter 12, "The Methodist,"[5] to Wesley's contributions and legacy before jumping over 200 years to Chapter 13, "Modern House Churches." After Wesley, he implies, there's not much to be added for a long time.

This brings me to my first not-so-tentative recommendation, and that is for all who are serious about a recovery of accountable discipleship to consider the modern recovery of Wesley's Class Meetings. And while the history of the rise and fall of the Class Meeting in Methodism is widely available and much-debated,[6] our best current resource is Dr. Kevin M. Watson, *The Class Meeting: Recovering a Forgotten—and Essential—Small Group Experience,* with both the book and the DVD for training.[7]

His thesis is that too many small groups use curricula, and even the Bible, as the last place to hide from being truthful about their lived experience with God, and here I agree. We have, it seems, lost the ability to speak coherently in answer to the question: How is your life with God? The Class Meeting presumes attendance at Sunday worship, other preaching services, and the private searching of the Scriptures, but it has a distinctive purpose as Bishops Francis Asbury and Thomas Coke summarized:

> We have no doubt, but meetings of Christian brethren for the exposition of scripture-texts, may be attended with their advantages. But the most profitable exercise of any is a free inquiry into the state of the heart. Through the grace of God our classes form the pillars of our work, and, as we have before observed, are in considerable degree, our universities for the ministry.[8]

It is odd indeed the Methodists have, as one of our official Doctrinal Statements, a specific discipleship plan for accountable discipleship. It's known as *The General Rules* and it lays out not only a plan for groups and leaders but also several checklists for behavioral examination, including the sins most commonly practiced in that day. And at this point it's best just to lay it out for your reading:

3. 159–162.

4. 149–166.

5. 167–198.

6. The basic research remains Watson, *The Early Methodist Class Meeting.* For a popular treatment, see Henderson, *A Model For Making Disciples.* For an accounting of one attempt at retrieving the Class Meeting under the title of "Accountable Discipleship," how it rose and sputtered to a stop, see Campbell, Lawrence, Richey, editors, *Doctrines And Discipline,* "Class Leaders and Class Meetings," 245–66.

7. Dr. Kevin Watson's U-Tube videos are a good place to start understanding how such groups differ from other small group venues.

8. *1798 Doctrines and Disciplines,* 148.

THE GENERAL RULES OF THE METHODIST CHURCH[9]

[Bibliographical Note: The General Rules are printed here in the text of 1808 (when the fifth Restrictive Rule took effect), as subsequently amended by constitutional actions in 1848 and 1868.]

The Nature, Design, and General Rules of Our United Societies:

In the latter end of the year 1739 eight or ten persons came to Mr. Wesley, in London, who appeared to be deeply convinced of sin, and earnestly groaning for redemption. They desired, as did two or three more the next day, that he would spend some time with them in prayer, and advise them how to flee from the wrath to come, which they saw continually hanging over their heads. That he might have more time for this great work, he appointed a day when they might all come together, which from thence forward they did every week, namely, on Thursday in the evening. To these, and as many more as desired to join with them (for their number increased daily), he gave those advices from time to time which he judged most needful for them, and they always concluded their meeting with prayer suited to their several necessities.

This was the rise of the United Society, first in Europe, and then in America. Such a society is no other than "a company of men having the form and seeking the power of godliness, united in order to pray together, to receive the word of exhortation, and to watch over one another in love, that they may help each other to work out their salvation."

That it may the more easily be discerned whether they are indeed working out their own salvation, each society is divided into smaller companies, called classes, according to their respective places of abode. There are about twelve persons in a class, one of whom is styled the leader. It is his duty:

1. To see each person in his class once a week at least, in order:

    a. to inquire how their souls prosper;

    b. to advise, reprove, comfort or exhort, as occasion may require;

    c. to receive what they are willing to give toward the relief of the preachers, church, and the poor.

2. To meet the ministers and the stewards of the society once a week, in order:

    a. to inform the minister of any that are sick, or of any that walk disorderly and will not be reproved;

    b. to pay the stewards what they have received of their several classes in the week preceding.

There is only one condition previously required of those who desire admission into these societies: "a desire to flee from the wrath to come, and to be saved from their sins." But wherever this is really fixed in the soul it will be shown by its fruits.

9. *The Book of Discipline 2016*, 77–80. On the General Rules, see Watson, *A Blueprint for Discipleship*.

It is therefore expected of all who continue therein that they should continue to evidence their desire of salvation,

First: By doing no harm, by avoiding evil of every kind, especially that which is most generally practiced, such as:

The taking of the name of God in vain.

The profaning the day of the Lord, either by doing ordinary work therein or by buying or selling.

Drunkenness: buying or selling spirituous liquors, or drinking them, unless in cases of extreme necessity.

Slaveholding; buying or selling slaves.

Fighting, quarreling, brawling, brother going to law with brother; returning evil for evil, or railing for railing; the using many words in buying or selling.

The buying or selling goods that have not paid the duty.

The giving or taking things on usury—i.e., unlawful interest.

Uncharitable or unprofitable conversation; particularly speaking evil of magistrates or of ministers.

Doing to others as we would not they should do unto us.

Doing what we know is not for the glory of God, as:

The putting on of gold and costly apparel.

The taking such diversions as cannot be used in the name of the Lord Jesus.

The singing those songs, or reading those books, which do not tend to the knowledge or love of God.

Softness and needless self-indulgence.

Laying up treasure upon earth.

Borrowing without a probability of paying; or taking up goods without a probability of paying for them.

It is expected of all who continue in these societies that they should continue to evidence their desire of salvation,

Secondly: By doing good; by being in every kind merciful after their power; as they have opportunity, doing good of every possible sort, and, as far as possible, to all men:

To their bodies, of the ability which God giveth, by giving food to the hungry, by clothing the naked, by visiting or helping them that are sick or in prison.

To their souls, by instructing, reproving, or exhorting all we have any intercourse with; trampling under foot that enthusiastic doctrine that "we are not to do good unless our hearts be free to it."

By doing good, especially to them that are of the household of faith or groaning so to be; employing them preferably to others; buying one of another, helping each other in business, and so much the more because the world will love its own and them only.

By all possible diligence and frugality, that the gospel be not blamed.

By running with patience the race which is set before them, denying themselves, and taking up their cross daily; submitting to bear the reproach of Christ, to be as the filth and offscouring of the world; and looking that men should say all manner of evil of them falsely, for the Lord's sake.

It is expected of all who desire to continue in these societies that they should continue to evidence their desire of salvation,

Thirdly: By attending upon all the ordinances of God; such are:

The public worship of God.

The ministry of the Word, either read or expounded.

The Supper of the Lord.

Family and private prayer.

Searching the Scriptures.

Fasting or abstinence.

These are the General Rules of our societies; all of which we are taught of God to observe, even in his written Word, which is the only rule, and the sufficient rule, both of our faith and practice. And all these we know his Spirit writes on truly awakened hearts. If there be any among us who observe them not, who habitually break any of them, let it be known unto them who watch over that soul as they who must give an account. We will admonish him of the error of his ways. We will bear with him for a season. But then, if he repent not, he hath no more place among us. We have delivered our own souls."

The simple effectiveness of this plan was that it combined a weekly small group class meeting with a weekly mentoring session with the class leader who was, him or herself, subject to close supervision. Doing good of all kinds and avoiding evil of every kind were clearly defined, and a list of the primary means of grace is provided for all to participate in. Such a model might be updated and applied in almost any Christian church, and if participated in by the clergy and thereby modeled would do much good to restore the strength and sinew of our witness.

A second resource to consider is Peter Scazzero's book, *Emotionally Healthy Discipleship: Moving from Shallow Christianity to Deep Transformation,* which is his most recent iteration of his thesis that "It's impossible to be spiritually mature, while remaining emotionally immature."[10]

I remember my first exposure to Scazzero's book *Emotionally Healthy Spirituality* and how it made me cringe because of its accuracy. His wife Geri's book *I Quit: Stop Pretending Everything is Fine and Change Your Life* was a book I hid from my wife for years!

Their model to blend classic disciple practices with a long look inward into the factories that shaped us (our families!) proves to me that a wise borrowing from family systems theory is not incompatible with a rich biblical spirituality and the kind of mature people it produces.

10. www.faithgateway.com/spiritually-mature-emotionally-immature/#.YjnOQObMKyI.

Scazzero himself was immersed for years in all the practices of the Christian life, but something never went deep enough to change his programming. It was—as he confesses—a pious overlay with some benefits but no deep change. His insights are wrung out of his pain and embarrassment and of his embrace of the larger Christian tradition beyond his Pentecostal roots. While much of this vision seems culture-specific to the U.S., we will have to wait and see how much of it is portable to the global south.[11] The question Scazzero raises for me is this: How much of me is available to the Lord Jesus for him to reveal, heal, and restore? Just the parts for public consumption, or the gnarly, messy depths?

There is no lack of quality resources out there in *disciple world*. Before using any of them, I recommend that you read your way through all four gospels with a highlighter in hand. Use an old Bible you don't mind marking up, or a cheap new one just for this purpose. Mark anything and everything having to do with disciples. Ask the same question over and over. What did Jesus do? Why did he do it? How did he do it? And when you've done this and prayed over it, you might be reading to employ a curriculum without expecting more than it can deliver. Jesus is the focus, and we are the raw materials of disciple-making.

11. The website is emotionallyhealthy.org.

10

A Better Reading Of Matthew's Great Commission

THE MOST QUOTED TEXT on discipleship is no doubt Matthew's *Great Commission*, typically cited as 28:16–20.[1] It's been analyzed to death as the marching order of the Jesus' movement, much of which I agree with. But to make it the number one, central and consequential, above-all-else single purpose of the church is an error, but one that can be corrected with a bit of attention to literary issues, namely structure and genre.

To begin, Matthew never intended 28:16–20 to be read alone. How do I know this? Because in the world of ancient rhetoric you signaled the beginning and ending of a thought unit with a repetition of vocabulary or ideas to open and close the larger paragraph. And this we find in 28:9–10 being set in parallel to 28:16–20 in their common uses of the following:

	28:9–10	28:16–20
"And behold"	v.9a	v.20b
"came/approached"	v.9b	v.18a
"worshiped"	v.9b	v.17a
"go"	v.10	v.19a
"Galilee"	v.10	v.16

These are called *inclusions* or in more modern terms *verbal brackets*, and this is one of the common literary techniques used in the ancient world to indicate the breaks in a text that we—in our print culture—mark with indentions, paragraphing, and headings, but which Matthew, in his oral culture, indicated with repeated words and ideas for the ear of the hearer rather than the eye of the reader. How clever! So the proper unit to be read in worship and for a sermon in not just the last part (28:16–20)

---

1. For a history of the recent impact of the Great Commission, see Walls, "The Great Commission: 1910–2010," in Gunter and Robinson, *Considering the Great Commission*, 7–22.

but the entire paragraph or thought unit (28:9–20). This insight is reinforced with the observation that not only are there the inclusions of repeated vocabulary at the beginning and end but that the form of the two paragraphs is identical, consisting of two parts:

		28:9–10	28:16–20
1.	An Appearance and Worship Scene	v.9	vv.16–17
2.	A Mission Speech	v.10	vv.18–20
	Command	v.10a	v.19
	Promise	v.10b	v.20b

Yet a third insight is both 28:9–10 and 28:16–20 share the same literary type, most often designated as a *Commissioning Story*[2] and with nine possible components. Since all nine are found in the longer, final paragraph (vv.16–20) and a bit less in the shorter introductory paragraph (vv.9–10), we compare them in reverse order:

		Matthew 28:16–20	Matthew 28:9–10
1.	Introduction	v.16a	v.9a "And behold"
2.	Confrontation	v.17a	v.9a "Jesus met them"
3.	Reaction	v.17b	v.9c "fell and worshiped"
4.	Reassurance	v.18a	v.10a "Do not be afraid"
5.	Commission	vv.18b–20a	v.10b "go and tell"
6.	Objection	v.17b (doubt)	(absent until v.17b)
7.	Reassurance	v.20b	v.10c "will see me"
8.	Sign	v.20b	v.19c (double duty!)
9.	Conclusion	v.20c (close of age)	v.17–19 (delayed fulfillment)

These multiple lines of evidence (inclusions, form, genre) make the case that 28:9–10 and 28:16–20 are parallel scenes that open and close a larger thought unit (28:9–20) as Matthew has indicated in his ordering of the materials.

But what of the central of the three paragraphs, 28:11–15, the story of *The Easter-gate Coverup*? The simplest way to answer the question is to apply the same tools as before. The words of echo or inclusion are *a sum of money* (v.12b) parallel to *the money* (v.15a) and at the center a contrast between the lie told to the people (v.13) and the governor (v.14). And when these are visually plotted, we have four parts with a double center as follows:

1. vv.11–12 The Plan is Hatched: Soldiers and Money
    2. v.13 You Tell the People
    2' v.14 We Will Tell the Governor
1' v.15 The Plan is Dispatched: Soldiers and Money

What this means for 28:9–20 is that the conspiracy story at the center is bracketed by commissioning stories of the risen Jesus which make a lie of the central story! There is more here than just *The Great Commission* of vv.16–20 since it builds on *The*

2. For a genre chart, see Neyrey, *The Resurrection Stories,"* 27.

Lesser Commission of vv.9–20, both of which are testimonies against *The Eastergate Conspiracy* at the center. An appearance to the women (vv.9–10 based on vv.1–8) precedes a parallel appearance to "the eleven" (vv.16–20).

Reading just the end unit (vv.16–20) and not the whole of 28:9–20 distorts Matthew's witness to what the risen Jesus is up to! Women and men received appearances, worship, and are commissioned with commands and promises on an equal basis.

So this is why I object to discipleship being the central purpose of the church. It's not biblical, no matter how important it is because in both cases it is preceded by the presence of the risen Jesus *who is worshiped* as divine.

The worship of Jesus as God the Son, in concert with the Father and Spirit as in the triune formula of 28:19, is prior to and the ground of the disciple-making mission. So if you have to rank them, worship is first, and making disciples a close second.

The reason I've taken such pains to make this argument is that it is so ignored in the literature, much of which asserts without challenge that disciple-making is the number one or central purpose of the church.

Friends, we exist for the Triune God who comes to us in the flesh of Jesus the Jew, and only then for the world God loves. Worship and all that it implies is the grounds for the mission of making new followers. Matthew 28:9–10 is now offered in a structural format so that you may confirm my observations and repent!

28:9–20 APPEARANCES, FRAUD, AND THE GREAT COMMISSION.

A. vv.9–10 Women Encounter the Risen Lord, Worship, Mission Speech
1. v.9 First Encounter of the Women with the Risen Jesus and Worship
2. v.10 Mission Speech: Go and Tell the Brethren (Evangelize the church!)

B. vv.11–15 Guard Story: The Eastergate Coverup
1. vv.1–12 The Plan is Hatched: Soldiers and Money
2. v.13 You Tell the People: Less Embarrassing
2' v.14 We Will Tell the Governor
1' v.15 The Plan is Dispatched: Soldiers and Money

A' vv.16–20 Eleven Men Encounter the Risen Lord: Worship and Mission Speech
1. vv.16–17 Encounter with the Risen Lord and Worship Mixed with Doubt
2. vv.18–20 Mission Speech: Make Disciples Everywhere Among All Peoples

11

Discipleship and Doctrine

A Case Study in Official United Methodist Teaching

GETTING OUR BEARINGS

PROTESTANT BODIES TYPICALLY HAVE canonical doctrinal standards, meaning that the teachings put forth are voted on by the church in its official capacity as a representative body. So if you do not ask not, "What do *you* believe?" but, "What does *your* church believe and teach?" someone will likely hand you a book of church order, *The Book of Discipline 2016* in the case of United Methodists, *The Book of Common Prayer* in the case of Anglicans, *The Faith and Mission Statement* in the case of Southern Baptists, *The Book of Confessions* if Presbyterian, *The Book of Concord* if Lutheran, and *The Catechism of the Catholic Church* if Roman. Most independent churches also have some minimal form of doctrinal statement.

Such statements typically highlight a common core of apostolic faith in the Triune God, the Scriptures, the Apostles' and Nicene Creeds, and then go on to highlight their communion's special teachings and the practices and theologies that support them. Some are simpler, some more complex, but all such documents have a rich and controversial history. They were a necessary response to internal and external challenges. The people of God have a right to know what their church officially teaches, as does the surrounding world, both what we offer in common and where we differ from other Christian bodies.[1]

---

1. For a meaty volume by a doctrinal scholar, see Campbell, *Christian Confessions*. Also his volume

The Texts and History of United Methodist Teaching

The purpose of this essay is, in light of all the comes before from Luke, the Scholars, and the Researchers, to examine the official doctrinal deposit of my church, The United Methodist Church (UMC) in its present unified form, and to see how it addresses the issues of being a Jesus follower, a disciple with others in the church.

The five texts that comprise the Doctrinal Standards of the UMC are identified in *The Book of Discipline 2016* as:

1. The Articles of Religion (AR)

2. The Confession of Faith (CF)

3. The Standard Sermons of John Wesley (SS)

4. Wesley's Notes on the New Testament (NNT)

5. The General Rules[2] (GR)

Our Articles of Religion[3] are John's Wesley's abbreviation and editing of the Thirty-nine Articles of the Church of England[4] with a few additions for the American Methodists, and in number they are currently 25 with two legal additions. Our Confession of Faith[5] inherited from the Evangelical United Brethren in the 1968 merger, is a second editing of the same doctrinal tradition.

The Confession of Faith covers much the same ground in more modern language with a few exceptions, namely a fuller treatment of the person and work of Jesus in Article II, a fuller statement on the work of the Spirit in Article III, a clarification in Article IV that the Bible is "the true rule and guide for faith and practice," the addition of three purposes for the church in Article V: "The Church," that it "exists for 1) the maintenance of worship, 2) the edification of believers, and 3) the redemption of the world, and a strong teaching in Article XII, "The Judgment and Future State" on how the final judgment divides persons into two—and only two—categories.

Since the U.M. Articles of Religion are John Wesley's epitome of his church's Thirty-nine Articles of Religion,[6] their flow and outline is much the same, as are the

---

on our tribe of Wesleyans, *Wesleyan Beliefs*.

2. Since they are shorter, No. 1, 2, and 5 are printed in *The Book of Discipline*. There is, embarrassingly for doctrinal matters, a dispute over the exact number of Wesley's sermons that are canonical. A second irregularity is that some doctrinal statements ("Of Sanctification" and "On the Duty of Christians to the Civil Authority" are included for historical reasons and legislative enactment but are not part of the church's official Constitution. "The General Rules" are printed on pages 392-394. Not paying attention to the ordering of our doctrinal house is a failing.

3. *Discipline 2016*: 65–72.

4. *The Book of Common Prayer*.

5. *Discipline 2016*, 72–77.

6. For an analysis, see Oden, *Doctrinal Standards in the Wesleyan Tradition*.

EUB Confession of Faith which is a 1962 modern rewrite of the U.M Articles.[7] So if we grouped them by topic (not part of the official document), here is a comparison:

1. The Triune God

    AR1: Of Faith in the Holy Trinity | CF1: God

2. Jesus Christ

    AR2: Of the Word, or Son of God, Who Was Made Very Man | CF2: Jesus Christ

    AR3: Of the Resurrection of Christ

3. Holy Spirit

    AR4: Of the Holy Ghost | CF3: Holy Spirit

4. Scripture

    AR5: Of the Sufficiency of the Holy Scriptures for Salvation | CF4: Holy Bible

    AR6: Of the Old Testament

5. Theological Anthropology (The Human Condition and Its Healing)

    AR7 Of Original or Birth Sin | CF7: Sin and Free Will

    AR8 Of Free Will

    AR9: Of the Justification of Man | CF9: Justification and Regeneration.

    AR10: Of Good Works | CF10: Good Works

    AR11: Of Works of Supererogation

    AR12: Of Sin After Justification | CF9: Justification and Regeneration

6. The Church

    AR13: Of the Church | CF5: Church

7. Protestant Articles of Faith Versus Roman Catholic Practices

    a. On the Future Judgment

    AR14: Of Purgatory

    b. On Liturgical Language and Bible Translations

    AR15: Of Speaking in the Congregation in Such a Tongue as the People Understand

    c. On Sacraments

    AR16: Of the Sacraments | CF6: The Sacraments

    AR17: Of Baptism

    AR18: Of the Lord's Supper

    AR19: Of Both Kinds

    d. On the Finished Work of Jesus Christ

    AR20: Of the one Oblation of Christ, | CF8: Reconciliation Through Christ
    Finished upon the Cross

    e. The Marriage of Clergy (vs. Celibacy)

    AR21: "Of the Marriage of Ministers"

    f. On Liturgical Authority

    AR22: Of the Rites and Ceremonies | CF13: Public Worship of the Church

8. The Lord's Day | CF14: The Lord's Day

7. 467 On The Confession of Faith, see Frey, *The Making of an American Church*, 53–66; O'Malley and Vickers, Methodist And Pietist, 109–138.

9. On Government and Other Legal Issues

    AR23: Of the Rulers of the United States of America

    AR24: Of Christian Men's Goods | CF15: The Christian and Property

    AR25: Of a Christian Man's Oath

10. Legal Additions, Constitutional Additions

    Legal, Non-Constitutional | Constitutional

    Of Sanctification | CF11: Sanctification

    (Should come logically after AR12) and Christian Perfection

    Of the Duty of Christians | CF16: Civil Government

    to the Civil Authority

    Should come logically after AR23

11. Final Judgment | CF12: Judgment and the Future State

Note that while the general ordering is similar, the CF has combined articles in several instances, removed the anti-Roman-Catholic themes, expanded the articles on Jesus Christ, the Holy Spirit, the Church, the Sacraments, Justification and Regeneration, Sanctification and Christian Perfection, and added new articles on The Judgment, The Future State, and The Lord's Day. Thus in the Confession of Faith, the bitter Reformation debates are minimized, several themes from the New Testament made more explicit, and the distinctively Wesleyan elements enhanced. The Confession of Faith was a great gift to us all, and yet not fully received or appreciated for all that it highlights about our common faith.[8]

A Narrative Summary of the Articles of Religion and Confession of Faith

In the ordering of the Articles of Religion, the United Methodist Church confesses—with the ancient church—the Holy Trinity, one God in three persons: the Father, the Son, and the Holy Spirit, with Jesus as God the Son incarnate through a virginal conception for our forgiveness and salvation. He was truly and bodily raised, and the Holy Spirit is as fully God and worthy of honor and worship as the Father and the Son. The purpose of the Scriptures is to lead us to the knowledge of God, and extra teachings not grounded therein cannot be required as a test of salvation.[9]

Our scriptural canon is of two testaments in which salvation is offered to all, and though the ceremonies of the Old Covenant are not binding on the church, the moral law is. The situation of all human beings is the same as regards sin, by nature being corrupted in all their parts and capacities, with an inherent bent towards evil, and unable to save themselves. However, God's kindness and grace restores in us a measure of responsiveness that we may put our trust in Jesus Christ and begin a changed life of good works. It is the perfections of Jesus that count with God, his person and work, and we do not make a contribution to our restoration but only trust and utterly rely

8. For essays on this topic, see Frey, *The Making of An American Church.*

9. AR 1–5.

on what another does for us. It is expected that our healed relationship with God and the love that flows from it, will leads us into continual good works, all the while acknowledging that none of it is to our credit but instead a sign that we do indeed have new life within.[10]

We are forever frail and subject to lure and deceits of sin, but even if we fall—as we will, we may return to God through his kindness and mercy which leads us to repentance and enables our restoration. Our turning back is never done and is itself a sign of God's persevering grace.

We know the church is of God because here the Scriptures are faithfully read and preached and the two sacraments of baptism and communion celebrated to begin and sustain the life of a believer in the communion of the saints.[11]

As Protestant Christians, we reject the Roman Catholic doctrines of an intermediate state of purgatory after death as a place of atonement as well as the adoration of images and relics as not grounded in Scripture. We affirm that worship should be in the languages of the people and not in a single, holy tongue. The sacraments are only two, those with clear dominical support, and we baptize the children of Christian parents, as well as youth and adults on confession of faith, without apology.

We affirm that those who rightly received communion partake in the benefits of the body and blood of Christ, but reject all notions of transubstantiation as unnecessary and superstitious. We affirm that all who present themselves are to receive the sacrament in both its forms, bread and cup. Nothing may be added to the one perfect sacrifice of Christ, and it is not repeatable. That the clergy may marry is lawful and permitted as with laity.

And while the rites and ceremonies, liturgies and practices of a church are official and should be honored, customs may vary due to location and culture, so long as they are faithful and do not violate the Word of God.[12]

We recognize elected governmental leaders and our country as an independent nation not subject to foreign jurisdiction. We honor the rights of private property and its proper usage with an eye to God, the owner of all, ourselves as stewards, and the pressing needs of the poor to whom we are to give generously of our faith and our aid. In order to enable the courts in their pursuit of truth and justice, our people may take public oaths in court to verify truth telling.[13]

Having been saved from ours sins by Jesus Christ and given new life through the indwelling Holy Spirit, we expect to grow in our response to these great gifts as the Spirit deepens and broadens our grasp of this great love of God. We are not only forgiven of the penalties of sin, but washed from its defilements, delivered from its awful grip, and enabled by God to grow in the love of God and neighbor that leads

10. AR 6–11.

11. AR 12–13.

12. AR 14–22.

13. AR 23–25 and "Of the Duty of Christians to the Civil Authority."

to glad obedience to all God's commands from the heart. And as long as we live, we will live as faithful and lawful citizens of our land and encourage the same in others.[14]

The Perspective on Discipleship in the Articles and Confession

In terms of the individual twenty-five Articles of Religion plus the additional two of legislative enactment, the article "Of Sanctification,"[15] might equally be titled "Of Growth in Discipleship." It is presented here in phrases with indentations for easy comprehension and reads:

> Sanctification is that renewal of our fallen nature by the Holy Ghost,
>> received through faith in Jesus Christ,
>> whose blood of atonement cleanseth from all sin;
> whereby we are not only delivered from the guilt of sin,
>> but are washed from its pollution,
>> saved from its power,
> and are enabled, through grace,
>> to love God with all our hearts
>> and to walk in his holy commandments blameless.

Sanctification (being made holy in love by God) is a process beginning with initial faith in Jesus and continuing all our days, thus Justification and Sanctification are the beginning and growth of one process of God's grace. Having now been set into a right relationship with God, we find God at work in the whole of the created self. The full effects of sin—its guilt, pollution, and power—are dealt with through forgiveness, cleansing, and Christ's superior power to free us. Over time our desires are changed to love God with all we are, and to live within the good boundaries of his will and commands as an expression of love for neighbor as for the self. This process, the unfolding work of God bringing to expression a new kind of human being, is what discipleship/following is all about. As we follow the one who saved us, we are changed at every level. Note the repeated use of *our* and *we* in the Article. The is the faith of a community of Jesus followers!

Jumping ahead to the parallel statement in the Confession of Faith, Article XI: "Sanctification and Christian Perfection,"[16] we find a greatly expanded version of the same theme, only now with more explicit reference to John's Wesley's language and understanding of *Christian Perfection*: being made mature and complete in love.[17] As

14. AR "Of Sanctification."

15. *BOD 2016*, 72.

16. *BOD 2016*, 75.

17. The classic text is John Wesley, *A Plain Account of Christian Perfection*, plus his three sermons touching on the issue: "The Scripture Way of Salvation," "The Circumcision of the Heart," and "Christian Perfection." On the history of the doctrine, see Peters, *Christian Perfection*. For a post-mortem on a doctrine which has died and been buried among the Methodists, see Abraham, "Christian Perfection,"

you will note below, it falls into three paragraphs with the first being a restatement of the "Of Sanctification," only with a scriptural warning attached, "and to strive for holiness without which no one will see the Lord."[18] The first paragraph reads:

1. "We believe sanctification is the work of God's grace

   through the Word and the Spirit,

   by which those who have been born again

   are cleansed from sin in their thoughts, words and acts,

   and are enabled to live in accordance with God's will,

   and to strive for holiness without which no one will see the Lord."

   The next two paragraphs continue:

2. "Entire sanctification is a state of perfect love, righteousness and true holiness which every regenerate believer may obtain

   by being delivered from the power of sin,

   by loving God with all the heart, soul, mind and strength,

   and by loving one's neighbor as one's self.

   Through faith in Jesus Christ this gracious gift may be received in this life

   both gradually and instantaneously,

   and should be sought earnestly by every child of God."

3. "We believe this experience does not deliver us

   from the infirmities, ignorance, and mistakes common to man,

   nor from the possibilities of further sin.

   The Christian must continue on guard against spiritual pride

   and seek to gain victory over every temptation to sin.

   He must respond wholly to the will of God

   so that sin will lose its power over him;

   and the world, the flesh, and the devil[19] are put under his feet.

   Thus he rules over these enemies with watchfulness

   through the power of the Holy Spirit."

   The real issue, despite the oft-misunderstood word *Perfection*, is this: How much can the love and gracious power of the Triune God change us in this life? Only a little? Or a whole lot? Wesley answers the third question will a bold *Yes* and sets about plundering the Scriptures, the early church, and his own observations to explain what he

---

587–601. For a straightforward restatement of the teaching, see Watson, *The Class Meeting*, 35–52. See his new book *Perfect Love: Recovering Entire Sanctification* for an optimistic recasting of the doctrine.

18. Hebrews 12:14, "Strive for peace with all men, *and for the holiness without which no one will see the Lord.*"

19. One of the gifts of the E.U.B. merger that the word "devil" is now found in our Doctrinal Standards. A second gift is their Article XII: "The Judgment and the Future State" which affirms only two destinies and does not affirm universalism (that all are saved): "We believe all men (and women) stand under the righteous judgment of Jesus Christ, both now and in the last day. We believe in the resurrection of the dead; the righteous to life eternal and the wicked to endless condemnation."

saw: that some were so full of the love of God and neighbor that it dominated all their dealings. These people knew God in a greater degree than others, so why is that? And, being a good empiricist, Wesley went looking for an adequate explanation.

The second paragraph above is about the transforming power of divine love, whether in slow growth or sudden epiphanies and advances. It's ethical outworking is the love of neighbor. And because it is a possibility for all believers, it should be asked for and sought. Those who are more advanced in this divine love display something of what it means to be a new kind of human being, and the light shines through them with enough lumens to mark them out from others. And rather than name them as saints in a special category all their own and so safely ignored in the Hall of Fame, what if God puts them in our midst to raise a question: If them, why not me? Why am I not more changed by the love of the Father, the Son, and the Holy Spirit? What is it about their form of discipleship that has over time yielded such delightful results, a particular human personality imprinted with the light and love and joy and wisdom and wit of the Master himself?

Have you ever met someone who was soggy with love so that—when squeezed—it ran out over everyone? How is this phenomena to be explained? It is, I think, that they have been long marinated in the love of Christ, which when coupled at every level with a fresh surrender of the self, makes room for more love. They still, as paragraph three admits, wrestle with infirmities, ignorance, and all the common missteps of being human and mortal. And Yes, they must remain vigilant and not coast, must avoid being spiritually inflated as if they were un-temptable, and also actively seek God's will to obey it. And in this pathway of vigilant love, the hold of the world, the flesh, and the devil are greatly loosened. No longer victims or captives, their alertness to the ever-present resources of the Spirit keeps them free, holy, and happy in God.

These articles on Sanctification are what all our recent talk about discipleship is meant to yield, this kind of person, one fully convinced not only of the core truths of Christian teaching but one being changed into love at every level. And if discipleship does not do this, it's something other and less than Jesus came to provide.

Other articles in the Confession of Faith that bear more directly on discipleship are Article X: "Good Works"[20] which teaches that faith produces good works and that without such actions faith is deficient. To use a medical analogy, "If you're alive, let me check your vital signs!" Article XIII: "Public Worship"[21] assumes faithful membership in a local church and not a solo me-and-Jesus orientation. It states in its second sentence, "We believe divine worship is essential to the love of the Church, and that the assembling of the people of God for such worship is necessary to Christian fellowship and spiritual growth." Very clear.

The subsequent Articles in the CF on the "The Sacraments" (VI), "Sin and Free Will" (VII), "Reconciliation Through Christ" (VIII) are modern restatements of the

20. *BOD 2016*, 75.
21. *BOD 2016*, 76.

Articles of Religion,[22] but in Article X: "Justification and Regeneration"[23] there is an addition of real significance, and it reads:

> We believe regeneration is the renewal of man in righteousness through Jesus Christ, by the power of the Holy Spirit, whereby we are made partakers of the divine nature and experience newness of life. By this new birth the believer becomes reconciled to God and is enabled to serve him with the will and the affections.

The last two articles in the Confession of Faith, XV: "The Christian and Property," and XVI: "On Civil Government,"[24] restate and expand their parallels in The Articles of Religion with the last ("On Civil Government") adding a loaded statement about the cultural influence of disciples, "We believe that it is the duty of Christian citizens to give moral strength and purpose to their respective governments through sober, righteous, and godly living." Thus, the pious are their own political force with their own ways and means of leverage.

A reading of both the Articles of Religion and the Confession of Faith reveals that the terminology used to refer to Christians is diverse:

In The Confession of Faith
"the community of all true believers" (CF5),
"redemptive fellowship" (CF5),
"believers" (CF5),
"Christian's profession" (CF6),
"the household of faith" (CF6),
"one another" (CF6),
"children of Christian parents" (CF6),
"a mark of Christian discipleship" (CF6),
"penitent sinners" (CF9),
"partakers of the divine nature" (CF9),
"the believer" (CF9),
"those who have been born again" (CF11),
"every regenerate believer" (CF11),
"The Christian(s)" (CF11, 16),
"the righteous" (CF12),
"the people of God" (CF13),
"Christian citizens" (CF16).
In The Articles of Religion
"Unprofitable servants" (AR11),
"Faithful men/women" (AR13),

22. *BOD 2016*, 73–74.
23. *BOD 2016*, 74–5.
24. *BOD 2016*, 76–77.

"Christian men/women' (AR16, 25),

"Christians" (AR17, 18, 19, 24),

"lay people" (AR19).

"weak brethren" (AR22).

Note how rich and full the descriptors of The Confession of Faith are when compared with the limited and spare references of the Articles of Religion. This is a gift of the deep traditions of pietism of the EUBs when compared with the state Church of England and her true son John Wesley.[25]

And while the word *disciple* is not used in either set of Articles, the word *discipleship* is found once in CF6: "The Sacrament" in its statement on baptism:

> We believe baptism signifies entrance into the household of faith, and is a symbol of repentance and inner cleansing from sin, a representation of the new birth in Christ, and a mark of Christian discipleship.[26]

Disciple(s) is frequently found in the Gospels, but its use to speak of all Christians has increased markedly in recent decades, so that we may fairly speak of a *Discipleship Renaissance* in our day, perhaps due in part to the popularity of Dietrich Bonhoeffer's *The Cost of Discipleship*,[27] and also to its heavy use in the para-church discipling movements, especially Campus Crusade for Christ (now Cru) and The Navigators.

That the official U.M. mission statement now uses the phrase "to make disciples" and not "make believers" or "make Christians" is an indicator of how the concept, in its modern recovery, has gripped the imagination of many and driven us back to the Gospels and their program of who Jesus was and how he shaped his followers.

There are several legitimate perspectives from which the U.M. Articles of Religion and Confession of Faith can be read. One is as the minimal requirement for us claiming to be a church in the apostolic tradition. A second is as a Protestant accounting of the faith in a vigorous debate with Roman Catholics. A third is that of a renewal movement within a state church finding its own place as now independent offspring. And a new angle of vision, in light of this volume, is to read it as a call to the particulars of discipleship, and that I will attempt as part of my experiment.

A Narrative Recasting of the Articles and Confession

Our story falls into four great movements and is shaped, in its simplest form, like the downward and upward movements necessary to form a *Capital V*. Your pen starts from Creation, moved down in the Fall and all its consequences, then stops and moves upwards in a movement of Healing focused in Jesus Christ and leading to the New Creation.

---

25. On the recovery of Pietism as a living option, see Olson and Winn, *Reclaiming Pietism;* also Gehrz and Pattie, *The Pietist Option.*

26. *BOD 2016,* 74.

27. *Dietrich Bonhoeffer's Works,* Vol. 4.

Creation   New Creation

         V

Fall   Healing

The Triune God whose proper name is *The Father, The Son, and The Holy Spirit* created all this is and made it good. So deeply good in fact, that the beauty and joy of it could never be occluded by the disaster that followed when our first parents, naive as they were, broke trust with God, listened to an alien voice, believed a lie, practiced rebellion together, and did surely lose their innocence as they fell into the knowledge of good and evil, as was promised.[28] Life was now split; a great ripping tear was heard.

The effects were severe and long term: exiting a perfect world together, pain and toil, death and alienation, all of their children infected with a moral virus that in the end kills them, and in the near term corrupts their every capacity and makes them user-friendly to evil of all sorts, the chief of which is that the intuitive knowledge of God is now veiled. They live as they can and leave trails of pain and disaster behind.

A better world can be dreamed, but never attained. They are now trapped by alien powers they do not understand, and their names are *Sin* and *Death* and *Evil*. Their presence as squatters is everywhere and all the time and woven deeply into the fabric of life, so that they spoil everything. Whenever the purity and goodness, beauty and delight of the creation and its Creator shine through, they rush in to smear and overshadow it, malign and twist it, announcing it's only time plus chance with no meaning. So many lies are believed and so much damage is done. They all die.

But alongside the Disaster, and even before it, the One whose mutual love and cooperation made it all—the Father, Son, and Holy Spirit—shaped a Cure and a Healing, a Turn-around and a Do-over. The Triune God would, with great patience and perfect timing, rescue a tribe of nobodies and make them a divine experiment of what it takes to recreate a faithful people as a public alternative to the ways the peoples of the world were living and ruling and worshiping whatever their little gods were, their own false imaginations as inspired by the Great Competitor. And the story of that great ongoing project, its ups and downs is a collection of books we call *The Old Testament*, [29] because it is from the Jews that we receive so many gifts of God, and these never quit giving and must be preserved as the complex prequel for the sequel of Jesus and all that was new and old in him.

These first people were given a deep longing for a true and good king, one who would rule with love and justice so all would thrive and the nations comes to check them out. But no one met the standard, though one came closest and was remembered as a template. So the longing deepened through disappointments and exiles, but it was never forgotten no matter what happened. There had to be more, and when will our great God come and save us again? Prophets spoke, priests made sacrifices, kings bumbled along with powerful enemies, festivals were kept, the writings collected,

28. AR1, CF1, AR7, CF7.

29. AR6, CF4.

psalms sung, and prayers said in families and later in special gathering places call synagogues. Scribes studied, rabbis taught, children learned, Passover was for the yearly remembrance of the hope of freedom, and Yom Kippur for the renewed freedoms that come again with repentance and forgiveness.

And then it happened, secretly for the most part and off in a corner. God came down in person as the Father and the Spirit sent the Son on a mission behind enemy lines. Fresh revelation was given as the Lord God of Exodus and Israel opened the depths of the divine heart and we beheld—for the first time—the Holy Trinity: *the Father, Son, and Holy Spirit.*

Now hear how that unveiling came about. A young, inexperienced girl named Miriam agreed to partner with the divine, to welcome a son not conceived with a husband. And it was by the creativity of the Spirit's touch that Jesus came to be within her womb and to be assembled in the dark as any child.[30] One person with two natures, deity and humanity joined permanently and without confusion. Fully one of us as mortal, fully one with the One and Three who sent him.

Here is a new kind of human being, sinless, uncorrupted, delighting in the limits of obedience, the beginning of the Great Do-over, the great lifting of the ravaged world back to its Maker, the One who was so faithful and refused to surrender his handiwork to permanent despair and alien occupation. God invaded our world secretly, and nine months later went public on a limited scale in Nazareth and only thirty years later into the larger public eye.

Once begun by divine action, how ordinary it all was. A circumcised Jewish male baby with a name as common as our Tom or Sam, one who grew to become a boy and then a man in his village of Nazareth only several miles away from a sophisticated new city, Sepphoris and a major north-south roadway. It was Galilee, but it was not backwoods. He was schooled to read the Scriptures in Hebrew and to memorize Torah and make applications. We don't know the details of his schooling, but he was clearly bright and attentive, an observer of the natural world and the good and bad dealings of people.

So ordinary and unremarkable were his first three decades that all we have is a single story as he stood on the brink of Jewish manhood (Luke 2:40–52); and we know that, unlike most of the young men in his village, he never married. Some good things were put aside for the sake of things unique to him, the long conceived calling that would soon come to disrupt his life and put him on stage before kinsmen and kings. His long preparation was a self-offering of obedience long before he was called into the larger public to shake the world.

Now, as a footnote, because the Great Creeds and the Doctrinal Standards that follow mention only the beginning of his life as birth to a virgin and the end of his life as a cruel cross and a glorious bodily resurrection, these are not the only items that matter but are, in fact, a clever bracket for the whole of his life, as if to say:

30. AR2, CF2.

For what happens in the great middle between Mary who gave him life and Pilate who gave him death, go read the four stories of his life where he called followers, spoke of his Father, lived in the powers of the Spirit, healed and forgave and welcomed and confronted and then, near the end, took a long walk to Jerusalem to force his people and their rulers to come to terms with *the new reality* he offered in himself.

There, in the city of his people, and after a final meal together, there came a deadly collision as a friend sold him out and his little band was scattered with at least some of them regathered near his cross. The back and forth of the hearings was irregular, but finally the legal authority of Rome through its representative, one Pontius Pilate, caved into pressure and ordered him strung up on a cross between two other losers, a death reserved for slaves and political rebels. As a man he suffered as any man, but if he is more, say God's personal Agent sent among us—a Son to use a Jewish family metaphor, then this is deicide: the attempted execution of God. God has come too near, offers and demands too much, and must be humiliated and banished back upstairs so the powers can return to business as usual. Jesus was a threat to their world, a deeper threat than sword and chariot, and they all knew it!

Truth and love and hope rode into the city gates of Jerusalem in mock parade, and in only a few days Jesus was dead and buried, ground up in the cogs of expediency. All this Jesus voluntarily entered to expose just how deep and vicious was this world's resistance to its own Maker, the short name for which is *Sin*. He offered himself as an innocent sacrifice, as one on whom the world's deepest hatred would come to a single focus and be fully displayed in all its awful stupidity and senseless rage. The long history of sin from the start was exhausted in him, and in the surprise that followed two days later, the divine voice spoke in body language, "I will not allow the worst you can do to separate you from me. In Jesus you may be forgiven and called to a new life. You killed, and I raised him, so there!"

The movement that crumpled on Friday was relaunched on Sunday, and since that day his people, his followers and apprentices and pupils, have known his risen rule and the near presence of the Holy Spirit giving them light and power and endurance in the truths of who he is. Who is he? Our Savior. Our Lord. Our Rabbi. Our Friend. Our Hope. Our Champion. Our Pattern. He is the human face of the Living God, and to him the Holy Spirit delights to point.

His successors wash newcomers and welcome them to his table. Together they learn the rhythms of prayer and obedience, self-denial and delight in service, even to their mockers and enemies. They suffer and die like all men and women, but with a hope that comes from him alone. They risk it all on Jesus: Messiah, Lord, Friend, Teacher. And over time, in the midst of all life's hardships and disappointments, they grow in the love and service of God and the service and love of people near and far. They become God's enduring minority report that love really matters and possesses extraordinary powers. The are, in every age, his followers.

They gather on his day, retell his stories and the ones that came before him, sing him love songs, and know that they are held in the Triune arms of the Father, Son, and Holy Spirit. Their mission, near and far, is to tell his story and invite as many as will to enroll into their friendship and into his lifelong Academy of Discipleship, there to learn his ways and means in order to live them out together in every place they find themselves.

They are not naive about the way the world remains or the alien powers that still hold it in bondage. In fact, they are perhaps the least naive because they engage the opposing powers every day in their quest to remain loyal to Jesus Christ. They are warriors in a battle many do not acknowledge. But they are content to be his minority report, his annoying reminder that his love will one day rule unchallenged, and so to be aligned with him ahead of time is wisdom indeed. His is the only future, and so to know and love and follow him now is to be already aligned with the deepest grain of the universe, and that is a good place to live until you die and find yourself safe in his keeping.

To live all your days at cross purposes with your Creator and never to know your Savior or the sustaining powers of the Spirit is a lost life of frustration and of wandering and never finding. We believe that our beliefs and practices are true, can be verified in experience, and are deeply good for all people, which is why we are both evangelists and peace-makers when at our best. So ordinary. So magnificent. So true. So life-giving.

To be his pupil and become his agent together with others is the deepest meaning of being a human being. This is our claim, and this is our story in the Big Book as outlined in our official teachings. We are a serious people, because if this story is true, then nothing is more important. And so we live with the offensive claim that we know the truth about the Living and Triune God, not because we figured it out from below but because it was revealed to us from above in a long story whose final chapter is titled *Jesus the Messiah*.

His light came into our shadows, and we can now see what God is up to. It's a good way to live, and should you have questions or wish to enroll, we are here to help you along your way and to do for you what was done for us. It's taught; it's caught; it's fraught with abundant meanings, and can be sought but not bought.

Like you we own things, enjoy all good things—including marriage and family—and live under various governments in the countries we occupy, some of which are more just and generous than others. We speak against corruption and the abuse of power, uphold basic human rights because all bear God's image and imprint, and we do not ignore the poor at our doors but give for their relief as we share Christ and welcome them into our homes and fellowship. A day in seven is set aside for common worship and for the delights of rest and play, of building culture and friendships with God and people in our churches and where we live. It's the day we play at heaven and the coming kingdom as God's free, beloved children because we know that each and all of us have a future beyond imagining.

Because in a moment at the end of time, history as we have known it will be stopped in its tracks by the sudden arrival of *the new reality,* the kingdom of the Father and the Son and the Holy Spirit that shall change everything all at once. The judgment and separation, the great truth-telling, the extermination of sin and death and evil, the gift of resurrection bodies like that of Jesus to the faithful, and our entry into the delights of this world made new and fresh will be accomplished and done by divine action, as solemn as a tolling bell, as joyous as a wedding feast and the delights beyond it.

We have an appointment all will keep, and until then we intend to love and live and suffer and die as those who count this great and Triune God as our only hope in this life and in the age to come. This God of Jews and Jesus is utterly trustworthy, love beyond understanding, wisdom beyond knowing. And there is room for you in our story.

So will you consider the evidences of history and the testimony of his people concerning Jesus Christ and ask life's most important question: Will I follow him with the hopes of becoming more like him?

This narrative of our Doctrinal Standards should not surprises us since the Standards are later restatements—in light of later disputes—of the most basic narrative of Christian faith as offered in the grand drama of Holy Scripture and of its pithy summations in the Apostles' and Nicene Creeds. The chain of topics is the same.

So Yes, just as the Scriptures and the Creeds and the Articles of the various churches tell the same basic story, they are all discipleship documents with slightly different functions. The Scripture to tell the long version in full detail. The Creeds to make the Triune faith explicit and in the briefest form summarize the critical ideas from Creation and through Christ to his Church and the coming Consummation. The Articles secure the treasures in light of later developments and family disagreements. Thus we have considerable theological, intellectual, spiritual, and moral resources to deploy in our discipleship.

Remainders

This leaves us with a brief consideration of the remaining three of the five Doctrinal Standards: Wesley's Standard Sermons, his Notes on the New Testament, and the General Rules of the Societies.

The Church of England had its Book of Homilies to set the standard for Anglican preaching of the classic faith and its English Reformation update, and Wesley cast his Standard Sermons on the same model, which is a remarkable act of self-confidence to set his written collection alongside the approved canonical collection of its day, so never let us charge him with timidity!

He too aimed to uphold the classic faith of the church, its Reformation update, only now with a further developments in the doctrines of God's grace and the dynamic growth of the believer being perfected in love by the same divine energies. So to the question, "If we are indeed set right with God at the intersection of his enabling grace and our enabled trust, then what are the outcomes and challenges of such a new relationship?" Wesley had a clear answer, and that response is his collection of Sermons.

The Standard Sermons have an interesting textual history of their own, and the exact number that are to be counted as Constitutional is still debated among the purists (44? 53?). But what matters is not so much the precise boundaries as the clear purpose: to provide Biblical, Spiritual, and Moral direction for those who looked to Wesley as their spiritual father and for whom he felt a keen responsibility. They were read and adapted by Methodist preachers, read privately or with others for edification, and served as a compendium of Mr. Wesley's perspective on topics most vital to the emerging revival movement that he found himself guiding and directing. Except perhaps in the most flagrant and extreme cases, it is difficult to imagine their being used in charges against clergy for doctrinal defection.

While the Table of Contents of the oft-used Sudgen collection[31] lists the fifty-three sermons with no headings or groupings, and while there is some variance of order in the several editions, there is an evident clustering in the collection[32] that we may arrange under headings.

Sermons 1–15, beginning with "Salvation by Faith" and ending with "The Great Privilege of Those That Are Born of God" deal with the fresh appropriation of the Evangelical Faith, of repentance and and conversion, the various operations of the Holy Spirit across the entire breadth of salvation, and the necessity of the New Birth. Think of it as a collection on *Making a Good Beginning* and *What To Expect Soon Afterwards*. Here are several sermons on aspects of faith and trust, warnings to the slack, a definition of *Scriptural Christianity*, the necessity of a change of heart at the center of the self, the inward witness, and the use of the means of grace as places where we may meet God. They are full of abundant Scriptural references across the canon, carefully argued, and presented with some rhetorical flair. They present a case and aim to stir up all sorts of responses.

A second collection, Sermons 16–28, are an ordered exposition and application of a discipleship classic, Matthew's Sermon on the Mount. Here Wesley explores and applies Jesus' *Magna Carta* of what it means to be his follower. What this demonstrates is that Wesley not only dealt with a series of theological and spiritual topics as in Sermons 1–15 but that he shifted seamlessly to a *lectio continua* model of working through a large block of Jesus' teaching in order. He was on the one hand theological

---

31. *John Wesley's Fifty-Three Sermons.*

32. I was first made aware of these groupings in conversation with Dr. William J. Abraham and later in his *Methodism: A Very Short Introduction*, 44–45.

and topical and on the other expository with the text itself leading from one topic to another.

A third and shorter collection, Sermons 29–31, deal with the oft-disputed issue of God's law and its relationship to evangelical faith. We are not saved by keeping the law, but when we know God's heart, then we desire to keep it, and must. Wesley had no use for the freedoms of the gospel misused in lawlessness and in false understandings of Christian liberty as license. Preaching the truth and severity of God law is one of the primary means the Holy Spirit uses Scripture to awaken the lost from their slumbers.

The fourth and final collection, Sermons 32–53 are an assortment of messages on a host of relevant issues, a *grab-bag* if you please. Several are occasioned by attacks upon Wesley and his followers: "On Enthusiasm," "A Caution Against Bigotry." Several more, though not clustered together, deal with topics found in his church's Thirty-Nine Articles of Religion: "Original Sin," "On Sin in Believers," "The Repentance of Believers," "The Great Assize," and "The Lord of Righteousness." Several more lay out the meaning of distinctive Methodist emphases: "Christian Perfection," "The Scripture Way of Salvation," "The New Birth." At least two deal with money and its faithful use: "The Use of Money" and "The Good Steward," with two others with the social effects of faith, "The Cure of Evil Speaking," and "The Reformation of Manners." A distinct theme is the predictable struggles believers face with the Enemy of their souls and their own frailties: "Wandering Thoughts," "Satan's Devices," "The Wilderness State," "Heaviness Through Manifold Temptations." All in all, it's a quite wide-ranging set of sermons which demonstrate how astute was Wesley that the Scriptures and the faith address the gritty realities of life in Christ together.

Wesley's *Notes Upon the New Testament* are the least referenced of our Standards, and their purpose appears twofold: 1) To demonstrate that a scholarly approach to the New Testament is not incompatible with living faith, and 2) That the doctrines peculiar to Wesley and his followers are grounded in the plain sense of Holy Writ.

That *The General Rules* are an overt document of discipleship training model for real, apostolic and orthodox Christianity cannot be denied, and that such a peculiar document is placed among the five standards—as in no other branch of Protestantism—is a clear indicator that the serious formation of believers as disciples is near our core, though recently forgotten as we have been distracted by other concerns.

When the five documents that compose the Standards of my church are read through a disciple-making lens, several things are clarified. The two sets of formal doctrinal articles are abstractions from the Creedal tradition to address perennial challenges to the faith. With a bit of imagination they can be translated back into a narrative form covering the whole of the story of salvation from Creation to Consummation. The Standard Sermons are, in effect, a fifty-three lesson curriculum for teaching the discipleship basics with a Wesleyan spin and a focus on the whole of Jesus' Sermon on the Mount. The Notes are an invitation to an informed program of reading and meditation across the whole of both testaments, with the General Rules offered as a communal, small group program of accountable discipleship and encouragement with clear expectations and real teeth!

And while this clustering of standards is peculiar among the Protestant collections, a charitable reading is that all five form an *ecology of spiritual formation and discipleship* with each of the five having its own contribution to a more dynamic whole. Thus, the United Methodists, for all our recent neglect of meaningful discipleship and an abandonment of mutual discipline, are the custodians of a rich collection of official standards to hold us in the faith and to give the Holy Spirit combustible fuel to ignite us that we might again burn. The medicine for the disease that afflicts and debilitates us remains within our own medicine cabinet. So why we not dosing it out to one another and ordering fresh supplies?

12

On the Use of Discipleship Assessments

OUR MODERN OBSESSION WITH testing, measurement, evaluation, personal growth, and goal setting is now on full display in the proliferation of Discipleship Assessments available in the church and para-church marketplace, as the following list indicates. There are more on offer, but these are commonly used in the U.S. by all sorts of churches.

As part of this work on *Following Jesus: Discipleship in Luke and Beyond* I've taken the first six assessments and plan to soon work through the seventh. I have printed my evaluations, and begun to set some goals based upon them. They are:

1. Discipleship Pathway Assessment
    (www.lifeway.com/en/product/discipleship-pathway-assessment-P005216492)
    Cost: $5.00

2. Discipleship 360 Assessment
    Dana Allin, *simple discipleship* (Colorado Spring, CO: NavPress, 2018).
    $15.99 for the book, includes 1 free assessment, after that $15.00 each.
    Includes assessments by others.
    https://books.thedisciplemaker.org/simplediscipleship/#resources

3. The Real Discipleship Survey
    Dr. Phil Maynard of EMC3 Coaching
    $5.00
    www.discipleshipsurvey.com/1

4. The Discipleship Assessment
    Robert Logan, Church Smart Resources
    $17.99, discipleassessment.com
    Includes assessments by others. Group curriculum available.

5. Willow Creed *Reveal* Assessment

   No charge

   revealforchurch.com

   Many support resources, books, and video to support a church-wide process.

6. Emotionally Healthy Discipleship Assessment

   Peter Scazerro

   No charge

   www.emotionallyhealthy.org/mature/personal-assessment

   Book and curriculum to support Emotionally Healthy Discipleship

7. Core Discipleship Assessment, "Spiritual Life Journey Map"

   A 26 page self evaluation of 22 characteristics of spiritual maturity.

   No charge.

   www.corediscipleship.com/spiritual-life-assessment-tool.

My first learning is that I had no surprises. Places where good habits and practices were in place were confirmed, and areas where my maturity and practices were thinner were also confirmed. The six assessments overlapped in their findings and recommendations, but then they were all taken by the same person! I've been on this discipleship path for nearly fifty years now, and my forty years as a pastor made many of the marks of discipleship part of my job description for which I was paid!

I pray often, but not for long periods. I often miss a sabbath, even in retirement. I have some issues with boundaries (don't we all), and I need to spend more time with Scripture for personal enrichment rather than in its technical and scholarly analysis for research and writing. As a first son I'm eager to please those whom I admire and look up to (my beloved and now deceased father, revered professors, John Wesley, the Triune God) and often have trouble building sustaining friendships. All very human stuff.

The experience of the six assessments was largely confirmatory, meaning they clarified and brought to focus issues I was already— and in some case keenly—aware of. But for those who are new to discipleship or who have never taken such inventories, it could be a revelatory and fruitful process, parallel to the insights of taking the Myers-Briggs or DISK inventories for the first time, both of which were formative for me in the early years of ministry.

The best analogy for what should happen in churches is what happens to children in healthy families. An environment of love, provision, nurture and discipline keeps up with their physical and mental development, adding explicit teaching and habit formation where necessary. Most of the important stuff is modeled and observed rather then explicitly taught. What this means is that children have a chance to cross the choppy waters of adolescence and the forays of young adulthood with most of what they need to survive and thrive with bumps and bruises but perhaps not with major injuries to their bodies and souls. One of my rules of thumb is that if you get to age 18 with 70 percent of the basics in place, you are already a winner and way ahead of most of your peers.

Perhaps there was a time, 04 is it only the perpetual temptation of nostalgia, when churches were more like families and where the nudges towards maturing as a Jesus' follower came in the flow of life together? It was more organic and situational than a matter of inventories, feedback, goal setting, and accountability.

For the early Methodists, much of this kind of modeling and coaching came in the form of The Class Meeting where weekly the question was asked by those who knew the rest of your life, "How is your soul?" Or—in a more contemporary form, "How is your life with God?" The Class Leader checked in with you weekly outside the meeting for what we now call *personal mentoring*.

But anonymity, loneliness, and social isolation are the new order of the day. How often I observe people who simply do not have enough genuine social connections to stay healthy and alive with some sense of being cared for by others. And so what once may have occurred more naturally now has to be supplemented by artificial tools like discipleship assessments and spiritual gifts profiles, and in this sense I am grateful for them and offer the following encouragements and cautions:

1. That you have a desire to take one is a beginning indicator that the Holy Spirit is working to re-focus your life as a more aware follower of Jesus. Spiritual hunger and the question, "Is there more?" are signs of divine grace.

2. Don't do it alone. Find a partner or friend to join you in self-discovery. Better yet, find several others and meet to discuss your findings and how you can help each other grow in faithfulness.

3. Do not be discouraged if your scores are initially on the low end. It's not a competition but a cooperation with a Living Lord. We all have room to grow. As a wise woman once said to me with a smile, "Remember, Preacher Phil, every saint has a past, and every sinner a future."

So, based on my evaluation of the above assessments, here are my recommendations:

1. For most, the best starting point is the the book by Dana Allin, *Simple Discipleship*. It includes a code for a free assessment based on 8 Core Qualities and 20 Characteristics of discipleship. It's the most thorough of the inventories I sampled. The value is its simplicity, the validation of the inventory, and that it leads into a process of goal setting.

2. Several months after completing No. 1, read Peter Scazzero's *Emotionally Healthy Discipleship* and take the assessment. His most basic insight is that you cannot be a mature disciple of Jesus while remaining emotionally immature, and this means dealing with your heart, your habits, and your family of origin. This is not easy material, and I regularly find myself stung by Scazzero's insight and

personal stories. "That's me," I say, and "I don't like being labeled an emotional adolescent!" but in some cases, like conflict-avoidance and over-commitment, it's all too true.

3. Stay in a group that focuses on following Jesus together. Discipleship is not a solo but a team sport, and you cannot grow apart from others who are also followers. Discipleship is not Christian self-improvement but a surrender of the full self to Jesus in the company of his other friends. For what such group might look like, see Dr. Kevin M. Watson, The Class Meeting. Franklin: Seedbed, 2014, both the book and the DVD.

Afterword

To say that I've been consumed with this volume since September 2020 is an understatement. But as I take the long view, I find a series of people, places, practices, and providences that have brought this concern with of discipleship to a compelling focus. Jesus Christ has not changed, but we have, and our churches are the weaker for it. Yet everywhere I've been, I've always found lively, faithful disciples, some of whom are listed on the cover of this volume. So, in addition to these, here's my family tree of discipleship: My sturdy Methodist and Baptist forebears, particularly Lida, my paternal grandmother.

My parents Dr. Jim and Betty Thrailkill,

faithful to the church and a healer to all in their shared medical practice.

From them I learned the art of human diagnosis and the necessity of house calls.

To those who welcomed me into their fellowship and friendship as a fresh convert

in the heady days of *The Jesus Movement* at Wake Forest University,

especially Jan Fogleman, Jim Morgan, and Rich Montgomery.

To my professor and mentor Dr. Charles Talbert

whose lively faith and scholarly curiosity I have always sought to imitate.

My favorite quote of his is—as expected— framed as a chiasm,

"In other words, what is good for human beings glorifies God;

what glorifies God is good for human beings."

To my wife Lori, whose intuitive grasp of the faith

is a testimony to how early in life she found a friend in Jesus.

To Dr. William J. Abraham

with whom I shared an apartment in Kazakhstan for two weeks of seminary teaching.

I am a *canonical theist* because of his careful reasoning.

To Luke the physician and Gospel writer,

for the now thousands of hours of delight he has given me

in the exploration of his rhetoric and his faithful answers to two important questions:

Who is Jesus Christ? And what does it mean to be his follower?

I, like Peter, have been interrupted, addressed, and dislocated,

"Do not fear, henceforth you will be netting people."

Luke 5:10b

Appendix 1

Identifying Luke's Thought Units

THE TWO TESTS: 1) Inclusions As Boundaries, 2) Identified Internal Structures

This is my master list for the internal divisions of Luke's Gospel into Thought Units (1–94) and Major Internal Divisions (A-D). Most of the Inclusions for the Thought Units are verbal, meaning that the same or similar words are found at the beginning and ending of a unit. Where otherwise, they are noted. Under "Internal Structure" note that most of the units are Chiasms (concentric patterns) with the first number indicating the number of parts and the second whether there is a single or double center: 4:2, 5:1. And where otherwise, they are noted. It was on the basis of this research that the fifty-one units dealing with discipleship were identified.

A. The Preface, The Births, The Early Ministries of John and Jesus (1:1–4:30).

	Thought Unit	Inclusions	Internal Structure
1.	1:1–4	Verbal	2 // 3-Part Stanzas
2.	1:5– 25	Verbal	9:1 Chiasm
3.	1:26–38	Verbal	7:1 Chiasm
4.	1:39–56	Verbal	3:1 Chiasm
5.	1:57–80	Verbal	3:1 Chiasm
6.	2:1–21	Verbal	9:1 Chiasm
7.	2:22–39	Verbal	5:1 Chiasm
8.	2:40–52	Verbal	3:1 Chiasm
9.	3:1–22	Verbal	5:1 Chiasm
10.	3:23–38	Verbal	11 groups of 7 names
11.	4:1–15	Verbal	5:1 Chiasm
12.	4:16–30	Verbal	6:2 Chiasm

B. The Galilean Ministry (4:31–9:51)

13.	4:31–44	Verbal	6:2 Chiasm
14.	5:1–16	Verbal	4:2 Chiasm
15.	5:17, 18–26	Verbal	4:2 Chiasm
16.	5:27–28, 29–39	Verbal	4:2 Step
17.	6:1–5	Verbal	4:2 Chiasm
18.	6:6–11	Verbal	6:2 Chiasm
20.	6:12–16	Verbal	3:1 Chiasm
21.	6:17–19	Verbal	4:2 Chiasm
22.	6:20–23, 24–26	Verbal	2 Panels, Each a 4:2 Chiasm
23.	6:27–38	Verbal	3:1 Chiasm
24.	6:39–49	Verbal	3:1 Chiasm
25.	7:1–10	Verbal	4:2 Chiasm
26.	7:11–17	Verbal	4:2 Chiasm
27.	7:18–35	Verbal	4:2 Chiasm
28.	7:36–50	Verbal	5:1 Chiasm
29.	8:1–21	Verbal	5:1 Chiasm
30.	8:22–25	Command/Question	5:1 Chiasm
31.	8:26–33, 34–39	Verbal	5:1 Chiasm + 4:2 Chiasm
32.	8:40–56	Verbal	3:1 Chiasm
33.	9:1–11	Verbal	3:1 Chiasm
34.	9:12–17	Verbal	3:1 Chiasm
35.	9:18–22	Source/Outcome	3:1 Chiasm
36.	9:23–27	Verbal	5:1 Chiasm
37.	9:28–36	Verbal	7:1 Chiasm
38.	9:37–50, 51	Verbal	4:2 Chiasm

C. The Long Journey To Jerusalem and Climactic Events (9:51–24:53).

39.	9:51–56	Verbal	4:2 Chiasm
40.	9:57–62	Verbal	3:1 Chiasm
41.	10:1–24	Verbal	8:2 Chiasm
42.	10:25–28	Verbal	4:2 Chiasm
43.	10:29–37	Question + Answer	4:2 Chiasm
44.	10:38–42	Left Open Ended	6:2 Chiasm with 1' Open
45.	11:1–13	Verbal	3:1 Chiasm
46.	11:14–36	Verbal	Action + 4:2 Step
47.	11:37–54	Verbal	4:2 Chiasm
48.	12:1–12	Verbal	5:1 Chiasm
49.	12:13–34	Verbal	3:1 Chiasm
50.	12:35–40	Verbal (//Commands)	5:1 Chiasm
51.	12:41–48	Q + A (Verbal)	Q + 4:2 Chiasm

52.	12:49–59	Verbal	2 Oracles + 3:1 Chiasm
53.	13:1–5	Parallel Terms	4:2 Step
54.	13:6–9	Verbal	4:2 Step
55.	13:10–21	Verbal	6:2 Chiasm
56.	13:22–35	Verbal	Travel Report, 4:2 Step
57.	14:1–24	Verbal	4:2 Chiasm
58.	14:25–35	Theme: Hearing	4:2 Step
59.	15:1–3, 4–7, 8–10	Theme Joy of finding	Incident, 9:1 + 7:1 Chiasm
60.	15:11–24, 25–32	Theme:Joy of finding	12:2 + 8:2 Chiasm (open)
61.	16:1–8	Verbal	6:2 Chiasm
62.	16:9–13	Verbal	3:1 Chiasm (6:2 + 6:2 + 6:2)
63.	16:14–18	Thematic: 2 Vices	4:2 Chiasm
64.	16:19–31	Verbal	3:1 Chiasm
65.	17:1–10	Parallel Terms	1–2–3 Series
66.	17:11, 12–19	Verbal/Thematic	Two 4:2 Chiasms as a pair
67.	17:20–37	Parallel Questions	4:2 Chiasm
68.	18:1–8	Parallel Exhortations	4:2 Chiasm
69.	18:9–14	Verbal	6:2 Chiasm
70.	18:15–17	Verbal	4:2 Chiasm
71.	18:18–30	Verbal	7:1 Chiasm
72.	18:31–34	Verbal	Two, 3-Line Stanzas
73.	18:35–43	Verbal, Reversals	7:1 Chiasm
74.	19:1–10	Thematic: Jesus' arrival	8:2 Chiasm
75.	19:11–28	Verbal	4:2 Chiasm
76.	19:28–48	Verbal	4:2 Chiasm
77.	20:1–8	Verbal	4:2 Chiasm
78.	20:9–16a	Verbal	4:2 Chiasm
79.	20:16b–20	Opposing Reactions	4:2 Chiasm
80.	20:21–26	Verbal	4:2 Chiasm
81.	20:27–40	Verbal	6:2 Chiasm
82.	20:41–44	Verbal	4:2 Chiasm
83.	20:45–47	Warning + Reason	4:2 Chiasm
84.	21:1–4	Verbal	3:1 Chiasm
85.	21:5–38	Verbal	8:2 Chiasm
86.	22:1–38	Verbal	5:1 Chiasm
87.	22:39–46	Verbal	5:1 Chiasm
88.	22:47–53	Verbal + //Questions	4:2 Chiasm
89.	22:54–65	Verbal	5:1 Chiasm
90.	22:66–23:25	Verbal	4:2 Chiasm
91.	23:26–56	Verbal	6:2 Chiasm
92.	24:1–12	Verbal	4:2 Chiasm

93.	24:13–35	Verbal	9:1 Chiasm
94.	24:36–53	Verbal	3:1 Chiasm

Appendix 2

Synoptic Comparisons

The 51 Key Lukan Discipleship Units

A. Discipleship in the Preface and Birth Narratives (1:1–2:52)

Luke	L (Luke only)	Mark	Matthew
1. 1:1–4	✔		
2. 1:5–25	✔		
3. 1:26–38	✔		
4. 2:1–21	✔		

B. Discipleship in the Early Ministries of John and Jesus (3:1– 4:30)

Luke	L	Mark	Matthew
5. 3:1–22		1:1–6, 7–8, 9–11, 6:17–18	3:1–6, 7–10, 11–12, 13–17, 14:3–4

C. Discipleship in the Galilean Ministry (4:31–9:51)

Luke	L	Mark	Matthew
6. 4:31–44		1:21–28, 29–31, 32–34, 35–38, 39	7:28–29, 8:14–15, 16–17, 4:23–25
7a. 5:1–11	✔	x	x
7b. 5:12–16		1:40–45	8:1–4
8. 5:27–32		2:13–17	9:9–13
9a. 6:12–19		3:13–19, 7–12	10:1–4, 12:15

427

9b. 8:1–3	✔	x	x
10a. 6:20–23		x	5:3, 4, 6, 11, 12
10b. 6:24–26	✔	x	x
11. 6:27–38		x	5:39–42, 44–48, 7:12, 5:46, 45, 7:1–2
12. 6:39–49		x	15:14, 10:24–25, 7:3, 7:16–21//12:33–35, 5:24–27
13a. 8:1–3	✔	x	x
13b. 8:4–18		4:1–9, 10–12, 13–20, 21–25,	13:1–9, 10–15, 18–23, 13:12,
13c. 8:19–21	✔	x	x
14. 8:22–25		4:35–41	8:18, 23–27
15. 8:26–39		5:1–20	8:28–34
16. 8:40–56		5:1–43	9:18–26
17. 9:1–11		6:6b–13, 14–16, 30–33	9:35, 10:1, 9–11, 14:1–2
18. 9:12–17		6:35–44	14:15–21
19. 9:18–22		8:27–31	16:12–21
20. 9:23–27		8:34–9:1	16:24–28
21. 9:28–36		9:2–8	17:1–8
22. 9:37–50/51		9:24–29, 30–32, 33–37, 10:15, 9:37, 38–41	17:4–21, 22–23, 18:1–5,

D. Discipleship on the Journey to Jerusalem (9:51–19:28)

Luke	L	Mark	Matthew
23. 9:51–56	✔	x	x
24. 9:57–62	vv.61–62	x	8:19–22
25. 10:1–24	vv.17–20	x	9:37–38, 10:7–16, 11:22–23, 11:25–27, 13:16–17
26. 10:25–28		12:28–31	22:34–40
27a. 10:29–37	✔		
27b. 10:38–42	✔		
28. 11:1–13	vv.5–8	x	6:9–13, 7:7–11
29. 12:1–12		x	10:26–33, 12:32
30a. 12:13–21	✔		
30b. 12:22–31		x	6:25–33
30c. 12:32–34	v.32	x	6:19–21
31. 12:35–40, 41–48	vv.47–48	x	24:43–51
32. 14:25–35	vv.28–30, 31–33	x	10:37–38, 5:13
33a. 16:1–8	✔	x	x
33b. 16:9–13	✔	x	x
34. 17:1–10	✔	x	x

35. 17:20–37	V.20	x	24:26–28, 24:37–41, 10:39, 24:40, 24:28
36. 18:1–18	✔	x	x
37. 18:15–17		10:13–16	19:13–15
38. 18:18–30		10:17–31	19:16–30
39. 18:31–34		10:32–34	20:17–19
40. 19:11–28		11:1	25:14–30

E. Discipleship During Jesus' Final Days in Jerusalem (19:27–23:56)

Luke	L	Mark	Matthew
41 19:28–38		11:1–10	21:1–9
42a. 20:45–47		12:37b–40	23:1, 6–7
42b. 21:1–4		12:41–44	x
43. 21:5–38	vv.34–36, 37–38	13:1–4, 5–8, 9–13, 14–20, 24–27, 28–29, 30–32	24:1–3, 4–8, 9–14, 15–22, 29–31, 32–33, 34–36
44. 22:1–38	vv.21–23, 31–34, 35–38	14:1–2, 10–11, 12–16, 17–21, 22–25 42–45	26:1–5, 14–16, 17–19, 20–25, 26–29, 25–28
45. 22:39–46		14:26–31, 32–42,	26:30–35, 36–46
46. 22:47–53		14:43–52	26:47–56
47. 22:54–65		14:53–54, 66–72, 15:1	22:54–55, 69–75. 27:1
48. 23:26–56		15:21, 22–32, 33–41, 42–47	27:32, 33–44, 45–56, 57–61

F. Discipleship With The Risen Jesus (24:1–53)

Luke	L	Mark	Matthew
49. 24:1–12	VV.10–11	16:1–8	28:1–8
50. 24:13–35	✔	x	x
51. 24:36–53	✔	x	x

Analysis:

1. 19 of the 51 units are found only in Luke, thus L.

2. 1 of the 51 units has a parallel in Mark alone and not Matthew.

3. 28 of the 51 units have parallels in both Mark and Matthew.

4. 12 of the 51 units have parallels only in Matthew.

Appendix 3

The Raw Materials of the Holy Trinity

Tri-Personal Divine References in Luke's Gospel
(* = Most notable passages)

Text	God/Father/Lord	Son/Jesus	Holy Spirit
1:5–25	vv.6b, 8, 15a, 16, 17c	x	v.15c
1:26–38*	vv.26b, 28b, 30b	vv.31, 32b	v.35b
1:39–56	v.45b	vv.43, 4b	v.41b
2:1–21	v.9	v.11	x
2:22–39	v.29a	v.26b	vv.26, 27a
3:1–22*	vv.21–22	vv.21–22	vv.21–22
4:1–15*	vv.8, 12a	v.1, 3, 9b	vv.1, 14a
5:17–26	vv.21c, 25c, 26b	vv.18b, 24a	v.17 "power of Lord"
6:12–19	v.12d	v.12b ("he")	v.19b
9:1–11	vv.2, 11c	v.1a ("he")	v.1b ("power")
9:28–36*	vv.34–35	vv.34–35	x
10:1–24*	vv.2b, 21b, 22	v.1, v.22	v.21a
11:1–13*	vv.2b, 11a, 13d	v.1a	v.13e
12:1–12	v.5 (passive voice)	v.8	v.12
20:41–44	vv.41–44	vv.41–44	x
23:26–56	vv.34a, 46	vv.34a, 46	x
24:36–53*	vv.49a, 53	vv.36b, 51b	v.49

Appendix 4

Contrasting Biblical Discipleship and Modern Church (Club) Membership

Ancient Christian Discipleship	American Church (Club) Membership
Risky, High Cost	Safe, Low Cost
Contributor & Stakeholder	Consumer & Observer
In The World As A Clear Alternative Community	*Of The World* With A Few Moral Variations
Total Self Involvement	Segmented Self (Sunday Faith), "Come a little bit, do a little bit, give a little bit, and say a whole lot."
Obey In Behavior	Assent In Beliefs/ Doctrine
Active, Involved	Passive, Observers
Always Serious, High Adventure	Mostly Casual, Low Demand, Minimal Adventure
High Supernatural Exposure: Miracles Expected	Rare Exposure To Supernatural: Skepticism Is The Norm
Always On The Move	Rarely On The Move
At The Vital Center Of Life	Around The Edge Of Life As A Possible Option
High Challenge	High Comfort
Group Orientation: *We First*	Individual Orientation: *Me First*
Allegiance: Tight Bond, Severance Required	Affiliation: Loose Bond, Easily Abandoned
Home As Hospitality, Place Of Teaching	Home As Refuge, Hiding Place, Entertainment
Offer Life And Substance	Pay Club Dues
High Expectation For Transformation	Low Expectation For Transformation
Intense Training, Change Expected	Observing/ Critique Expected
Largely Outdoors	Largely Indoors
Organic Bond: Shared Life	Institutional Bond: Shared Space In Buildings

Follow Jesus, Learn His Ways, Share His Ministry	Admire Jesus, Worship Him, Pay Others To Do Work
Jesus As Leader, Model And Mentor	Jesus As Savior From Sins Worst Consequences
Confrontive And Blunt: Being True!	Convivial And Affable: Being Nice!
High Accountability	Low Accountability
Intense Fellowship: 24/7 + Conflict	Occasional Fellowship: Coffee/Cookies + Avoidance
Disciples Often Look Bad, Goofy, Incompetent	Members Focus On Image-Management, Looking Good
Location: Front Lines	Location: Behind the Lines
Ministry By Amateurs (for the love of it)	Ministry By Professionals (career clergy)
All Are Spiritually Gifted Ministers	Pay The Professionals (Clergy + Staff) To Do It For Us
Jesus And His Kingdom Mission Draw Resources	Institutional Maintenance Draws Large Resources
Holy Spirit As Creative, Disruptive Presence	Low Tolerance For The Unexpected

Appendix 5

What the United Methodist Church Teaches on the Incarnation

THE ARTICLES OF RELIGION II: OF THE WORD, OR SON OF GOD, WHO WAS MADE VERY MAN

A. His Person: Who He Is.   One Sentence, Every Line Is *A Yes* And *A No*, Affirmation And Negation

The Son,	Assumes God The Son: Second Person Of The Holy Trinity
1 who is the Word of the Father,	Perfect Agent Of Communication, Gk. *logos,* John 1:1-18
2 the very and eternal God,	No *Junior* God, Full And Equal Deity 1: *true and eternal*
3 *of one substance* with the Father,	Full And Equal Deity 2: Nicene Creed, Gk. *homoousious*
	Down Into Mary's Womb, *Down* Into Death, *Down* Into A Grave

B . His Work: What He Did, How He Came To Us.   Male Human Through A Female Human!

	One Incarnation + Three Outcomes + 3 Specification
took man's nature in the womb of the blessed Virgin;	Assumed A Male Human Nature, Luke 1:26-38
1a so that two whole and perfect natures,	Result 1: Two Whole Natures In One Person
b that is to say, the Godhead and Manhood,	Paraphrase, Echoed In *very God and very man*
2a were joined together in one person,	Mary's Womb, Result 2: Joined In One Person
b never to be divided;	Incarnation Never Ends, Permanent In Jesus' Resurrection Body
3a whereof is one Christ,	Jesus Is Not Two Persons, Result 3: One Messiah In Two Natures
b very God and very Man,	Echoes Earlier *Godhead* and *Manhood*
c who truly suffered: 1) *was crucified,* 2) *dead,* 3) *and buried*,	3 Creedal Phrases
	Pilate not Named, No Rescue For Jesus

C. The Why: What We Needed: Gift Of A Healed Relationship Through Costly Forgiveness.

	2 Grand Purposes: Reconciliation, Atonement
1 to reconcile his Father to us,	Our Primary Need = Restored Relationship With God
	To Show The Fullness Of The Father's Love
2 and to be a sacrifice,	Means = Jesus' Voluntary Self-Offering As God The Son
not only for original guilt,	Problem 1: The Nature And Weight We Inherited
3 but also for actual sins of men.	Problem 2: The Weight Of Sin We Added
	A Rhetoric Of 3 Throughout: 3 Assertions In 3 Parts

Appendix 6

Bishops Coke and Asbury Notes in the 1798 Book of Discipline (KJV).[1]

1. The Incarnation of the Son in the flesh of Jesus

- John 1:14   And *the Word* [who was God, v.1] was made *flesh*.

- Phil. 2:7, 8 Christ Jesus [who though it was not robbery to be made equal with God, vv.5–6] was made *in the likeness of men*; and being found in fashion *as a man*, he humbled himself unto death, even the death of the cross.

- 1 Tim. 3:16 Without controversy, great is the mystery of godliness, *God* was manifested in the *flesh*

2. Benefits of the Incarnation: Christ as redemption, sacrifice, peace, reconciliation

- Col. 1:14: In whom [God's dear Son] we have *redemption* through his blood, even *the forgiveness of our sins.*

- Eph. 2:13, 16: Now, *in Christ Jesus*, ye who sometimes were far off, are *made nigh* by *the blood of Christ.* For he is *our peace*,- that he might *reconcile* both [Jews and Gentiles] *unto God* in one body by *the cross*, having slain the enmity thereby.

- 1 Tim. 2:6: Who [Christ Jesus] gave himself a *ransom for all.*

Pastor Phil's *Unofficial* Summary:

God the eternal Son assumed permanent full humanity as Jesus in Mary's virginal womb. As the Messiah of the Jews he comes to heal the ancient breach of rebellion and sin between us and his Father. The full sacrifice of his daily life comes to

---

1. Transcribed with headings added from Oden, *Doctrinal Standards,* 214.

a focus in his voluntary suffering and death. In Jesus alone are we invited to come home to the Triune God and then live into and out of that new relationship in the church and world.

Appendix 7

Luke and Roman Imperial Theology and Propaganda.

(Underlining indicate Imperial language)

1. The Prience Inscription, Augustus Caesar as World Savior, 9 B.C., Birthday Inscription: "*Providence*. . . has brought into the world *Augustus* and filled him with a hero's soul for *the benefit of mankind*. A *Savior* for us and our descendants, he will *make wars cease and order all things well*. The *epiphany of Caesar* has brought to *fulfillment past hopes and dreams*."[1]

2. The Myra Inscription: to the "*divine Augustus* Caesar, *son of a god*, imperator of land and sea, the benefactor and *savior* of *the whole world*.[2]

Thus, there is proclaimed on the birthday of Caesar (in these and other inscriptions) the he fulfills ancient hopes, is the focus of divine Providence, is son of God, as *Augustus* is worthy of worship, is titled *Savior*, has an epiphany or manifestation, and brings peace to all the world as the benefactor of all. His birthday (Sept. 23) was later made the beginning of the new year.

Luke believes that such claims about Augustus are idolatrous, but in Jesus they are true. Each claims to bring a "gospel about the creation of a peaceful world." Their means of doing it are not the same. One is through violence and victory, the other through justice and the inbreaking power of God's kingdom. Jesus gave non-violent resistance. They are rival political and religious claims, then and now. Hitler is not Feuher (leader); Jesus is!

1. Talbert, *Luke*, 34.
2. Talbert, *Luke*, 34.

Appendix 8

A Checklist of Possible Spiritual Openings For Evil

(See Ephesians 4:27, 6:10–18; 1 Peter 5:8–9.)

As you read the Bible passages and list of questions, ask the Holy Spirit to recall to your mind every involvement you may have had. Keep in mind that many of these activities are clearly of the occult; others may not be as apparent. Please mark any and all activities, even if there is a question in your mind as to their occult nature, so that you are confident that you renounce all *possible* influences of evil in your life. Take the time to read the biblical texts under each heading, not just rush through the questions. Those who take time to read the recommended texts rarely have a protest or misunderstanding about the questions under each heading. You are initiating a *truth encounter* that may lead to a *power encounter.*

Place a check beside each item in which you have participated, whether *just for fun,* out of curiosity, or in earnest. If there are issues that go beyond simple confession of sin and forgiveness, you may wish to make an appointment with a pastor for counsel and prayer to break any bondages associated with these activities which are forbidden in Scripture.[1]

Keep your house clean! Forgiveness and freedom go together as God sifts our lives over time. This document presumes you are a follower of Jesus and that you are prepared to be honest with yourself and at least one other person about your history. Having Christ at the center of your life makes dealing with these realities so much easier. The basic idea is that seeking supernatural aid apart from God and the appointed means of grace in the church is a form of spiritual treason that is dangerous and deceitful. It will harm you.

---

1. For a fuller treatment of these issues, see Cindy Jacobs. *Deliver Us From Evil.* Ventura: Regal, 2001.

This is a representative list for common occult practices in Western culture. It is not exhaustive but typical and must be indigenized into other cultures with their world views and practices. Dealing with this stuff eliminates dual loyalties.

A. *Soothsayers/Fortune-tellers*:

See Deuteronomy 18:9–16; Isaiah 2:6; Daniel 2:26–28; Acts 16:16.

1. Have you ever had your fortune told by tea leaves, palm reading, a crystal ball, a fortune-teller, or any other means?

2. Have you ever read or followed horoscopes, or had a chart made for yourself to predict your future? Have you every read any other type(s) of birth signs?

B. *Necromancy, Spiritualism*:

See Leviticus 19:31, 20:6; 1 Samuel 28:7–11; 2 Kings 21:6; Isaiah 8:19–22.

3. Have you ever attended a seance or spiritualist meeting?

4. Do you believe in reincarnation? Have you ever had a reincarnation reading?

5. Have you every played with a Ouija board, crystal ball, Dungeons & Dragons or other occult games?

6. Are you—or any family across generations— involved in any secret societies that require loyalty oaths and practice ritual initiations? Have you compared their views and practices with the Christian faith and scriptures?

7. Have you ever had a tarot card reading or practiced cartomancy (using playing cards for fortune-telling or other magical purposes)?

8. Have you ever played games of an occult nature, using ESP, telepathy, some forms of hypnotism, etc?

9. Have you every consulted a medium, spiritualist or numerologist? Have you every acted as a medium? Have you every practiced channeling?

10. Have you every sought healing through magic spells or charms or through a spiritualist? Have you ever used a charm or amulet of any kind for protection or "good luck?" Are you superstitious?

11. Have you every practiced table lifting, levitation of objects, pendulum swinging, lifting of bodies, automatic writing, astral or soul travel?

C. *Occult Books, "Contact" Objects and Other Media*:

See Exodus 19:25–20:6; Deuteronomy 5:8–10, 7:25–26; 2 Kings 23:1–25; Psalm 97:7; Isaiah 42:17; 2 Corinthians 10:3–5.

12. Do you have anything in your home that was given to you by someone in the occult? Do you have anything in your home of an occult nature?

13. Have you followed the writings of Edgar Cayce, Jean Dixon or a New Age author? Do you own or like to view demonic types of books or movies?

D. *Sorcery or Magic*:

See 2 Kings 17:17, 21:6; Malachi 3:5; Acts 8:11, 13:4–12, 19:19–20.

14. Have you every practiced sorcery or magic?

15. Have you every practiced mind control over any person or animal, cast a magic spell or sought a psychic in person or through a psychic hotline?

E. *Sins of the Flesh, Sins of the Eyes*:

See Matthew 5:28; Romans 6:12–14, 8:13–14; 1 Corinthians 6:13, 18–20; Galatians 5:16–21; 1 Thessalonians 4:3–8; James 1:14–15; 1 Peter 2:11; 1 John 2:16.

16. Have you ever used LSD, marijuana, cocaine, crack-cocaine or any mind-expanding or mind-altering illegal drugs? Have you ever abused prescription drugs? Have you ever had a problem with alcohol?

17. Have you repeatedly exposed yourself to pornography in magazines, the internet, TV or stage shows, books, movies? Is porn taking up more and more time in your mind and heart?

18. Have you ever been involved in sexual deviation?

19. Have you ever had sexual relations with a person who was not your legal spouse?

20. Have you had an abortion? Have you fathered a child who was aborted? Have you been involved in abortion in any way (viewed/witnessed one, assisted in one, performed one, encouraged a friend to have one?

F. *Devil Worship*:

See 2 Chronicles 11:15; Psalm 106:37; 1 Corinthians 10:20–22; Revelation 9:20–21, 13:4.

21. Have you ever made a pact with Satan or been involved in or witnessed Satan worship or black magic?

G. *Witchcraft*:

See 1 Samuel 15:23, 28:7; 2 Kings 9:22, 23:24; Isaiah 8:19, 19:3, 29:4; Micah 5:12.

22. Have you ever attended witchcraft or voodoo activities?

H. *Death*:

See Exodus 20:13, Job 3:20–23; 1 Corinthians 6:19–20.

23. Have you every planned or attempted to take your own life?

24. Have you ever planned or attempted to take someone else's life?

Appendix 9

The Women in Luke's Gospel[1]

(L = Luke Only)

Woman/Women	Luke	Source
Elizabeth, wife of Zechariah the priest	1:5–25, 36–37, 40–45, 57–61	L
Mary, mother of Jesus, be-trothed of Joseph	1:27–56; 2:5–7, 16–19, 22–24, 33–35, 39–51; 8:19–21, 11:27–28	L
Anna, the prophetess	2:36–38	L
Herodias, adulterous wife of King Herod	3:19	Mark
The widow of Zarephath / Gentile	4:25–26	L
Mother-In-Law of Simon-Peter	4:38–39	Mark
The widow at Nain	7:11–17	L
Jesus praises John, "Among those born of woman, no one is greater than John. . . .:	7:28	Matt
Jesus' saying, "Yet wisdom is vindicated by all her children'	7:35	L
Woman who anoints Jesus' feet with ointment and washes them with tears	7:36–50	L
Mary, called Magdalene from whom 7 demons had gone out.	8:2	Mark
Joanna, wife of Chuza (Herod's Household Manager	8:3	L
Susana—A woman who accompanied Jesus and the twelve.	8:3	L

1. Adapted from Burchard, "The Women in Luke's Gospel, Part 3"; Felix Just, "Women in the Synoptic Gospels."

Many (un-named) Women with Jesus and the twelve—helping out of their means	8:3	L
Jesus' mother and brother come. Those who hear and do God's word are his mother/brothers	8:19–21	Mark
The Daughter of Jairus	8:42–49, 56	Mark
The woman with an issue of blood	8:43–48	Mark
Jesus send seventy (72) disciples on mission, likely women	10:1–20	L
Martha & Mary—Sisters	10:38–42	L
Woman shouts a blessing, "Blessed is the womb that bore you. . . breasts that nursed you"	11:27–28	L
The queen of the South as a positive example	11:31	Matt
In parable men and women slaves are beaten by wicked manager	12:45	L
Families divided: father/son, mother/daughter, mother-in-law/daughter-in-law	12:53	Matt
The woman bent over by a disabling spirit	13:10–16	L
Kingdom parable of a woman who hid leaven in flour	13:21	Matt
Jesus wants to gather Jerusalem's children like mother hen who protects her brood	13:34	Matt
Disciples must hate father, mother, wife, children, brothers, sisters	14:26	Matt
Parable of the woman who finds a lost coin	15:8–9	L
Brief saying against men divorcing their wives or marrying divorced women	16:18	Mark
In the days of Noah, people were marrying and giving in marriage	17:26–27	Matt
Lot's wife	17:32	L
Two women will be grinding grain, one taken, one left	17:35	Matt
Parable of the widow and the unjust judge	18:1–8	L
Honor your father and mother	18:20	Mark.

Disciples who have left wives, brothers, parents, children. . . will be rewarded	18:28–30	Mark
The (Sadducees scenario of a) wife with 7 dead husbands	20:27–33	Mark
The widow who gave all she had	21:2–4	Mark
The Women who are pregnant in the last days—"Alas for them. . . great distress!!"	21:23–24	Mark
A servant girl in the courtyard who tells Peter "You were with him."	22:56–57	Mark
The women who mourned on the road to the cross	23:27–31	L
The women who had followed him from Galilee (including Mary Magdalene, Joanna, and Mary the mother of James—and other women)	23:49, 55, 56; 24:1–10, 22–23	Mark, L
Two disciples on road to Emmaus. Men. Couple (Cleopas, 24:18) tell how some women went to the tomb and saw a vision of angels	24:22–24	L

Appendix 10

A Few Thoughts on Biblical Power Encounters

(John Wimber)

"PROCLAMATION OF A FAULTY gospel will produce faulty or, at best, weak Christians. Such is the case all to often today. Instead of a call to the lordship of Christ and membership in his kingdom, people are hearing a gospel that emphasizes self: come to Jesus and get this or that personal need met, be personally fulfilled, reach your potential. This, however, is not the costly kingdom gospel that Christ proclaims, 'Whoever wants to save his life will lose it, but whoever loses his life for me and for the gospel will save it' (Mark 8:35).

Often the kingdom is likened to a Caribbean cruise on a luxury liner. People change into their leisure clothes, grab their suntan lotion, and saunter down to the docks. What a shock it is when they find that entering the kingdom is really more like enlisting in the navy and doing battle with the enemy. The enemy follows no rules of war. Satan considers nothing unfair; he is not a gentleman. The sooner Christians understand this, the more serious they will become about being equipped and properly trained for the kingdom. . . there are no demilitarized zone's. There is never a lull in the fighting. We are born into the fight, and -unless the Day of the Lord comes—we will die in the fight. We should never expect the battle to cease . . . . Jesus is about the Father's business, which is releasing those held captive by Satan.

Any system or force that must be overcome for the gospel to be believed is cause for a power encounter, which Dr. Peter Wagner defines as 'a visible, practical demonstration that Jesus Christ is more powerful than the false gods or spirits worshiped or feared by a group of people.' When warm and cold fronts collide, violence ensues: thunder and lighting, rain or snow, even tornadoes or hurricanes. There is a conflict and a resulting release of energy. It is disorderly, messy and difficult to control. Power encounters are like that. When the kingdom of God comes into direct contact with the kingdom of the world (when Jesus meets Satan), there is conflict. And usually it too is disorderly, messy, and difficult for us to control . . . . Often witnessing the presence of the Spirit in a Christian will open non-Christians to the gospel of the kingdom of God"[1]

1. Wimber, *Power Evangelism*, 8–23.

Appendix 11

A Psychiatrist And The Demonic

IN 2016 THE WASHINGTON Post ran a controversial op-ed piece titled, "As a psychiatrist, I diagnose mental illness. Also, I help spot demonic possession." The subtitle read, "How a scientist learned to work with exorcists." The author, Richard Gallagher, is a board-certified psychiatrist and a professor of clinical psychiatry at New York Medical College. Dr. Gallagher wrote:

> For the past two-and-a-half decades and over several hundred consultations, I've helped clergy from multiple denominations and faiths to filter episodes of mental illness—which represent the overwhelming majority of cases—from, literally, the devil's work. It's an unlikely role for an academic physician, but I don't see these two aspects of my career in conflict. The same habits that shape what I do as a professor and psychiatrist—open-mindedness, respect for evidence and compassion for suffering people—led me to aid in the work of discerning attacks by what I believe are evil spirits and, just as critically, differentiating these extremely rare events from medical conditions.
>
> Is it possible to be a sophisticated psychiatrist and believe that evil spirits are, however seldom, assailing humans? Most of my scientific colleagues and friends say no, because of their frequent contact with patients who are deluded about demons, their general skepticism of the supernatural, and their commitment to employ only standard, peer-reviewed treatments that do not potentially mislead (a definite risk) or harm vulnerable patients. But careful observation of the evidence presented to me in my career has led me to believe that certain extremely uncommon cases can be explained no other way.
>
> So far the article has generated nearly 3,000 comments, mostly from people whose worldview does not permit the reality of demon possession or even the existence of demons.[1]

1. Gallagher, "As a psychiatrist, I diagnose mental illness."

Appendix 12

Scriptural Echoes in Luke 19:28–48

(*Italics* indicate deliberate echoes)

1.   Luke 19:28 // Zech. 14:1–9, 16

        (Messiah appears on Mount of Olives, rules, worshiped.

        "Behold, a day of the LORD is coming, when the spoil taken from you will be divided in the midst of you. [2] For I will gather all the nations against Jerusalem to battle, and the city shall be taken and the houses plundered and the women ravished; half of the city shall go into exile, but the rest of the people shall not be cut off from the city. [3] Then the LORD will go forth and fight against those nations as when he fights on a day of battle. [4] *On that day his feet shall stand on the Mount of Olives which lies before Jerusalem on the east;* and the Mount of Olives shall be split in two from east to west by a very wide valley; so that one half of the Mount shall withdraw northward, and the other half southward. [5] And the valley of my mountains shall be stopped up, for the valley of the mountains shall touch the side of it; and you shall flee as you fled from the earthquake in the days of Uzzi'ah king of Judah. Then the LORD your God will come, and all the holy one's with him. . . . [9] *And the LORD will become king over all the earth;* on that day the LORD will be one and his name one. [16] Then every one that survives of all the nations that have come against Jerusalem shall go up year after year *to worship the King, the LORD of hosts,* and to keep the feast of booths."

2.   Luke 19:28–36 // Zechariah 9:9–10

        (King comes riding a symbol of peace, not war)

        [9] *"Rejoice greatly, O daughter of Zion!*
Shout aloud, O daughter of Jerusalem!
Lo, your king comes to you; triumphant and victorious is he,
humble and riding on an ass, on a colt the foal of an ass.
[10] I will cut off the chariot from E'phraim
and the war horse from Jerusalem; and the battle bow shall be cut off,

and he shall command peace to the nations;
his dominion shall be from sea to sea, and from the River to the ends of the earth."

3.   Luke 19:30 // Number 19:2
       (an animal never used for work)
       [2] "This is the statute of the law which the LORD has commanded: Tell the people of Israel to bring you a red heifer without defect, in which there is no blemish, and upon which a yoke has never come.

4.   Luke 19:30 // 1 Sam. 16:7
       (An unridden animal is fitted for a king.)
       [7] "Now then, take and prepare a new cart and two milch cows *upon which there has never come a yoke*, and yoke the cows to the cart, but take their calves home, away from them. "

5.   Luke 19:36 // 2 Kgs. 9:13
       (Coronation procession of Jehu)
       [13] Then in haste every man of them *took his garment, and put it under him on the bare steps*, and they blew the trumpet, and proclaimed, *"Jehu is king."*

6.   Luke 19:38 // Ps. 118:26
       (Royal psalm used in yearly enthronement liturgy)
       [26] *"Blessed be he who enters in the name of the LORD!*
We bless you from the house of the LORD."

7.   Luke 19: 45 // Malachi 3:1
       (Messenger suddenly appears in the temple)
       "Behold, I send my messenger to prepare the way before me, *and the Lord whom you seek will suddenly come to his temple; the messenger of the covenant in whom you delight, behold, he is coming, says the LORD of hosts.*"

8.   Luke 19:46 // Isaiah 56:7
       (temple described as house of prayer)
       "These I will bring to my holy mountain, and make them joyful *in my house of prayer*; their burnt offerings and their sacrifices will be accepted on my altar;
for my house shall be called *a house of prayer for all peoples.*"

9.   Luke 19:46c // Jeremiah 7:9–11, 15
(Jesus recasts a quote for a new audience.)
       [9] Will you steal, murder, commit adultery, swear falsely, burn incense to Ba'al, and go after other gods that you have not known, [10] and then come and stand before me in this house, which is called by my name, and say, `We are delivered!'— only to go on doing all these abominations? [11] *Has this house, which is called by my name, become a den of robbers in your eyes?* Behold, I myself have seen it, says the LORD. . .. [15] *And I will cast you out of my sight*, as I cast out all your kinsmen, all the offspring of E'phraim."

10.   Luke 19:46 // Zech. 14:21
(Since all is sacred, no traders needed in temple)

[21] "and every pot in Jerusalem and Judah shall be sacred to the LORD of hosts, so that all who sacrifice may come and take of them and boil the flesh of the sacrifice in them. *And there shall no longer be a trader in the house of the LORD of hosts on that*

Appendix 13

What is a Disciple? A Sampling of Definitions

1a. "The life of a disciple may be summed up as a person
who has given his or her allegiance to Jesus as Savior,
who has been ushered into the way of walking with Jesus as Master,
and who is being transformed into the likeness of the Master
through obedience to his Word."[1]

1b. "A disciple is one who has come to Jesus for eternal life,
has claimed Jesus as Savior and God,
and has embarked on a life of following Jesus."[2]

1c. "Discipleship means living a fully human life in this world
in union with Jesus Christ,
growing in conformity to his image
as the Spirit transforms us from the inside-out,
being nurtured within a community of disciples
who are engaged in that lifelong process,
and helping others to know and become like Jesus."[3]

2. "A disciple is a student or follower of Jesus.
A disciple has decided to submit to at least one other person
as that person follows Jesus Christ.
Because character develops in community,
the disciples intention is to go deeper with God
and to be shaped into the image of Christ."[4]

1. Wilkins, *Following the Master*, 220.

2. Wilkins, www.cslewisinstitute.org/webfm_send/3212.

3. Wilkins, old-v1.metamorpha.com/blog/2011/10/02/michael-Wilkins-disciple-making-for-changing
-times-and-changing-churches.

4. Hull, *The Complete Book of Discipleship*, 68.

3. "A disciple is someone who is following Jesus,
    being changed by Jesus,
    and is committed to the mission of Jesus."[5]

4. "A disciple is a learner, a student, an apprentice—*a practitioner*, even if only a
    beginner. . .. disciples of Jesus are people who do not just profess certain views as
    their own but apply their growing understanding of life in the Kingdom of the
    heavens to every aspect of their life on earth."[6]

5. "God intends for the followers of Jesus to be:
    a. his cooperative friends,
    b. seeking to live in creative goodness
    c. for the sake of others
    d. through the power of the Holy Spirit,"[7]

6. "A disciple is one
    who adheres to Jesus as he proclaims and embodies God's kingdom,
    responding to his call to be with him and share in his work,
    listening to and learning from him."[8]

7. "A disciple of Christ is one
    who believes his doctrine,
    rests on his sacrifice,
    imbibes his spirit,
    imitates his example (Mat 10:24; Luke 14:26, 27, 33; John 6:69).[9]

8. A disciple of Jesus is a person
    who has heard the call of Jesus
    and has responded by repenting,
    believing the gospel,
    and following."[10]

9. "And as a disciple of Jesus I am with him, by choice and by grace, learning from
    him how to live in the kingdom of God. This is the crucial idea. That means, we
    recall, how I live within the range of God's effective will, his life flowing through
    mine. Another important way of putting this is to say that I am learning from
    Jesus to live my life as he would live my life if he were I. I am not necessarily
    learning to do everything he did, but I am learning how to do everything I do in
    the manner that he did all that he did."[11]

5. Harrington and Patrick, *The Disciple Maker's Handbook*, 35.

6. Willard, *The Great Omission*, xi.

7. Hunter, *Christianity Beyond Belief*, 76.

8. Adapted from blog.lexhampress.com/2019/06/25/what-makes-a-disciple-a-biblical-definition-of-discipleship.

9. Farrar, christianlifetodayministries.com/2021/02/17/christian-word-definition-disciple.

10. www.byfaithonline.com/discipleship,

11. Willard, mwerickson.com/2021/05/05/dallas-willard-on-what-a-disciple-is.

10. "A disciple is one who seeks to fulfill the will of the Father
    by actively following Jesus the Son
    while continually depending on the Holy Spirit for guidance and strength."[12]

11. "Christian discipleship is a relational journey
    whereby learners obey the command of Jesus,
    such that their world view is transformed."

12. Biblical discipleship is "Becoming and being a flourishing follower of Jesus
    who embodies the character of Christ
    by engaging in a lifelong, personal pursuit of holistic transformation
    and doing so within a like-minded community of faith
    that's corporately committed to being and making other disciples."[13]

13. "Christian discipling is an intentional, largely informal learning activity. It involves two or a small group of individuals who typically function within a larger nurturing community and hold to the same religious beliefs. Each makes a voluntary commitment to the other/s to form close, personal relationships for an extended period of time in order that those who at a particular time are perceived as having superior knowledge and/or skills will attempt to cause learning to take place in the lives of those others who seek their help. Christian discipling is intended to result in each becoming an active follower of Jesus."[14]

14. "In Christianity, disciple primarily refers to a dedicated follower of Jesus . . . In the ancient world, a disciple is a follower or adherent of a teacher. It is not the same as being a student in the modern sense. (1) A disciple in the ancient biblical world actively imitated both the life and teaching of the master. (2) It was a deliberate apprenticeship which made the fully formed disciple a living copy of the master."[15]

15. "Someone devoted to learning Jesus."[16]

12. Martyn, www.biblicaltraining.org/call-to-discipleship/spiritual-life-leader.

13. www.learnreligions.com/discipleship-definition-4132340.

14. Collinson, "Making Disciples and the Christian Faith," 242. Collinson, when analyzing Jesus-style discipling in comparison with the schooling mode of classrooms, curricula, and grading, highlights the following characteristics. It is: 1) Relational, 2) Intentional, 3) Mainly Informal, 4) Typically Communal, 5) Reciprocal, 6) Centrifugal Focus (outward in shared mission). The discipling model matches the core teaching of the Christian faith better than the schooling model (241, 248–250).

15. en.wikipedia.org/wiki/Disciple_(Christianity).

16. Marshall and Payne, The Vine Project.

Appendix 14

Jesus' Method and Other Rabbis of His Day.[1]

Issue	Jesus	Other Rabbis
Call/Initiative	Whom he chooses to invite	Rabbi waits to be chosen by students (e.g. Matt 8:19)
Place Of Teaching	Itineracy: Synagogues, workplace, homes, market temple	Home, Synagogue, Stable Location
Content	Free Formation Of New Tradition	Static Tradition
Followers	Men, women, tax collectors, sinners	Adult males only
Tenure	Permanent Commitment, Lifelong	Limited Period of Commitment To A Teacher (Acts 22:3)
Authority	Underived (from above, i.e, God)	Scholarly Precedent, Tradition
Potential	Never exceed master (Matt 23:8–11)	May exceed master
Phrase "follow after"	Jesus' call	Never used to describe becoming a student of the law (Hengel: 51)
Allegiance/ focus	To Jesus: his person and work Image: Leader/follower	To Torah: written and oral traditions Image: Teacher/student
Title: Fit Cultural Understanding	Called "Rabbi" Followers: Mark 4:30, 38, 10:35, 13:1 Pharisees: 12:14 Saducees: 12:18 Scribe: 12:32	Called "Rabbi"
Effects On Family And Vocation	Severe Dislocation, Takes Precedence	Included In The Relationship

1. Contrasts compiled Anderson, *The Gospel of Mark*, 87–88; Edwards, *The Gospel According To Mark*, 49; Hengel, *The Charismatic Leader*; Thiessen and Merz, *The Historical Jesus*, 214; Donaldson, "Call To Follow," 67–77; Fredrichsen, "*Disciple(s)* in the New Testament," 717–739.

Explicit Symbolic Function	*Twelve* As New Patriarchs/ New Israel	No Evidence
Support	Abandon work (Luke 9:61)	Must have a trade
Crisis	Yes, Kingdom is near (1:14–15), kairos	No, kingdom still future: chronos
Healing and Exorcism	Disciples imitate their Master	Not offered or expected

The most basic insight from this comparison is us that inherited a cultural institution and adapted it to his training purposes.

As a summary of the differences between Jesus' understanding and demands of being his follower as compared with the contemporary Greco-Roman and Jewish models, Timothy A. Fredrichsen writes:

> The possible background as well as the use of (*mathetes*) and related vocabulary in the Gospels and Acts and in later Christian writings pose more complexity than one might first expect. Although the Greek philosophical understanding of disciples and the Old Testament models of Elijah and Elisha provide possible background, they do not fully prepare the way for the distinctive usage of *disciple(s)* during the ministry of Jesus and in the Gospels.
>
> Rather than the would-be disciple seeking out a master, discipleship begins with Jesus initiating call. Discipleship is not a passing phase of life, but is a life-long relationship with Jesus and other disciples, in which one finds his/her new and true family. In a related matter, to be a disciple of Jesus is a radical commitment that relativizes all other relationships to family, village and livelihood to the point of facing persecution and even death. In addition, once one is a disciple of Jesus, one is always a disciple, rather than being one who aspires to become a master with his/her own disciples.
>
> Finally, seemingly unlike the Greek and Jewish notions of the ideal disciple, there are no ideal disciples in the Gospels, but only fallible ones, who nevertheless can also be rehabilitated by their master and Lord.[2]

2. Fredrichsen, "Disciple(s)," 738–789.

Appendix 15

What Researchers Identify as the Primary Characteristics of Maturing Disciples

(* = Inventory Available for Assessment)

*Transforming Discipleship[1]	*Simple Discipleship[2]	Navigators[3]	Bill Hull[4]	*Robert Logan[5]
Bible Engagement	Gospel Saturated Life	Identified with Christ	In conversation with God through Word and Prayer	Experiencing God
Obeying God and Denying Self	Connected to God	Obedient to the Word	Responds to God daily in obedience	Spiritual Responsiveness
Serving God and Others	Exhibiting the fruits of the Spirit	Fruitful for Christ	Has join and is contented in spirit	Sacrificial Service
Sharing Christ	Understanding the Bible and Christian Theology		Reveals Christ daily by bearing fruit	Generous Living
Exercising Faith	Missional Living		Loves others as Christ loved others	Disciplemaking
Seeking God	Engaging Others Towards Discipleship			Personal Transformation
Building Relationships	Community			Authentic Relationships
Unashamed of Christ (transparency)	Fulfilling God's Call on Their Life			Community Transformation

1. Geiger, Kelly, Nation, *Transformational Discipleship*, 59.

2. Allin, *simple discipleship* (Colorado Springs, CO: NavPress, 2018), 168.

3. www.navigators.org/the-marks-of-a-disciple.

4. *Conversion and Discipleship*. Grand Rapids: Zondervan, 2016, 215.

5. http://discipleassessment.com.

Off My Shelf: For Further Reading on Discipleship

Barna Group. *Growing Together*. Barna Group, 2022.

Bird, Michael F. *What Christians Ought to Believe: An Introduction to Doctrine Through The Apostles' Creed*. Grand Rapids: Zondervan, 2016).

Christianity: Fundamental Teachings. Istanbul, Turkey: The Turkish Bible Society, 2017).

Deere. Jack. *Why I Am Still Surprised by the Power of the Spirit*. Grand Rapids: Zondervan, 2020.

Dickerson, John S. *The Jesus Skeptic: A Journalist Explores the Credibility and Impact of Christianity*. Grand Rapids: Baker, 2019.

Dickson, John. *A Doubter's Guide to Jesus*. Grand Rapids: Zondervan, 2018.

Foster, Richard. *A Celebration of Discipline*. San Francisco: Harper and Row, 1998.

———. *Prayer: Finding the Heart's True Home*. San Francisco: Harper and Row, 1992.

Hull, Bill. *The Complete Book of Discipleship*. Colorado Springs: NavPress, 2006.

———. *Conversion and Discipleship: You Can't Have One without the Other*. Colorado Springs: NavPress, 2016.

———. *The Discipleship Gospel: What Jesus Preached We Must Follow*. HIM Publications, 2018.

McLaughlin, Rebecca. *The Secular Creed*. Austin: The Gospel Coalition, 2021.

McKnight, Scott, and Ondrey. *Finding Faith, Losing Faith*. Waco: Baylor University Press, 2008.

———. *The Jesus Creed: On Loving God And Others*. Brewster: Paraclete, 2014.

———. *The King Jesus Gospel*. Grand Rapids: Zondervan, 2011.

———. *One Life: Jesus Calls, We Follow*. Grand Rapids: Zondervan, 2010.

Morgan, Alison. *The Word on the Wind*. Oxford: Monarch, 2011.

Ogden, Greg. *Transforming Discipleship*. Downer's Grove: IVP, 2016.

———. *Discipleship Essentials: A Guide to Building Your Life in Christ*. Downer's Grove: IVP, 2007.

Olson, Roger E. *Counterfeit Christianity: The Persistence of Errors in the Church*. Nashville: Abington, 2015.

Rogers, Kevin. *A Simple Model of Discipleship*. N.p.: Rogers, 2020.

Sanders, Fred. *The Triune God*. Grand Rapids: Zondervan, 2016.

Scazerro, Peter. *Emotionally Health Discipleship: Moving from Shallow Christianity to Deep Formation*. Grand Rapids: Zondervan, 2021.

Stott, John. *The Radical Disciple: Some Neglected Aspects of Our Calling*. Downer's Grove: IVP, 2010 .

To Be a Christian: An Anglican Catechism. Wheaton: Crossway and The Anglican Church in North America, 2020.

Trueman, Carl. *The Creedal Imperative*. Wheaton: Crossway, 2012.

Wright. N.T. *Simply Good News*. San Francisco: HarperOne, 2015.

Young, David. *King Jesus And The Beauty of Obedience-Based Discipleship*. Grand Rapids: Zondervan, 2020.

Willard, Dallas. "Discipleship." old.dwillard.org/articles/artview.asp?artID=134/

———. *The Divine Conspiracy: Rediscovering our Hidden Life in God*. San Francisco: HarperSanFrancisco, 1998.

———. *The Great Omission: Reclaiming Jesus's Essential Teachings on Discipleship*. San Francisco: HarperOne, 2006.

———. "How to be a disciple." www.religion-online.org/article/how-to-be- a-disciple.

———. "The New Testament Picture of Discipleship." renovare.org/articles/ the-new-testament-picture-of- discipleship.

———. *Renewing the Christian Mind: Essays, Articles Interviews*. San Francisco: HarperOne, 2016.

———. *Renovation of the Heart*. Colorado Springs: NavPress, 2002.

———. *The Spirit of the Disciplines*. San Francisco: HarperOne, 1991.

Bibliography

Abraham, William J. *Canonical Theism: A Proposal for Theology & the Church*. Grand Rapids: Eerdmans, 2008.

———. "Christian Perfection." In James E. Kirby and William J. Abraham, editors. *The Oxford Handbook of Methodist Studies*. Oxford: Oxford University Press, 2011.

———. *Methodism: A Very Short Introduction*. Oxford: Oxford University Press, 2019.

———. *Wesley for Armchair Theologians*. Louisville: WJK, 2005.

Akenson, Donald H. *Exporting the Rapture: John Nelson Darby and the Victorian Conquest of North-American Evangelicalism*. Oxford: Oxford University Press, 2018.

Allen, Amy Lindeman. *For Theirs Is the Kingdom: Inclusion and Participation of Children in the Gospel according to Luke*. Minneapolis: Fortress, 2019.

Allin, Dana. *Simple Discipleship*. Colorado Springs: NavPress, 2018.

Anderson, H. *The Gospel of Mark*. Grand Rapids: Eerdmans, 1976.

Arias, Mortimer. *The Great Commission: Biblical Model for Evangelism*. Nashville: Abington, 1992.

Arnold, Clinton. "The Kingdom, Miracles, Satan and Demons." In Christopher Moran and Robert Peterson, editors, *The Kingdom of God*. Wheaton: Crossways, 2012.

"The Arusha Call to Discipleship." The World Council of Churches Conference on World Mission and Evangelism, March 13–18, 2008. www.gs2019.anglican. ca/wp-content/uploads/Appendix-3-Arusha.

Ayo, Nicholas. *The Lord's Prayer*. New York: Rowan and Littlefield, 2002,

Bailey, James and Lyle Vander Broek. *Literary Forms in the New Testament*. Louisville: WJK, 1992.

Bailey, Kenneth. "The Manger and the Inn." www.biblearchaeology.org/research/new-testament-era/2803-the-manger-and-the-inn.

———. *Poet and Peasant*. Grand Rapids: Eerdmans, 1976.

———. *Through Peasant Eyes: More Lucan Parables*. Grand Rapids: Eerdmans, 1980.

Bannister, Doug. *The Word & Power Church: What Happens When A Church Experiences All God Has To Offer*. Grand Rapids: Zondervan, 1999.

Bates, Matthew. *Salvation by Allegiance Alone: Rethinking Faith, Works, and the Gospel of Jesus the King*. Grand Rapids: Baker, 2017.

Bauckham, Richard. *Jesus: A Very Short Introduction*. Oxford: Oxford University Press, 2011.

———. *Jesus and the Eyewitnesses: The Gospels as Eyewitness Testimony*. Grand Rapids: Eerdmans, 2006.

Bazanna, Giovanni Battista. "Early Christian Missionaries as Physicians: Healing and its Cultural Value in the Greco-Roman Context," *Novum Testamentum* 51 (2009) 232–51.

Beck, Brian. "*Imitatio Christi* and the Lucan Passion Narrative." In William Hornbury and

Braaten, Carl E., and Robert W. Jenson. *Either/Or: The Gospel or Neopaganism*. Grand Rapids: Eerdmans, 1995.

Bielby, James K., and Paul Rhodes Eddy, *Understanding Spiritual Warfare: Four Views*. Grand Rapids: Baker, 2012.

Bird, Michael. *Evangelical Theology*. Grand Rapids: Zondervan, 2013.

———. *The Gospel of the Lord: How the Early Church Wrote the Story of Jesus*. Grand Rapids: Eerdmans, 2014.

———. *What Christians Ought To Believe*. Grand Rapids: Zondervan, 2016.

"The Blessed Virgin Mary in Christian Faith And Life: A Statement Of Evangelicals And Catholics Together." *First Things*, November 2009. www.firstthings.com/article/ 2009/11/ do-whatever-he-tells-you-the-blessed-virgin-mary-in-christian-faith-and-life.

Bock, Darrell. *Jesus in Context*. Grand Rapids: Baker, 2005.

———. *Jesus the God-Man*. Grand Rapids: Baker, 2016.

———. "A Note on the Women as Witnesses and the Empty Tomb Resurrection Account." In W. David Beck and Michael R. Licona, editors, *Raised on the Third Day: Defending the Historicity of the Resurrection of Jesus*. Bellingham: Lexham, 2020.

———. *A Theology of Luke and Acts*. Grand Rapids: Zondervan, 2012.

———. *Who is Jesus? Linking the Historical Jesus With The Christ of Faith*. New York: Howard, 2012.

The Book of Common Prayer. New York: Church Hymnal, 1979.

The Book of Discipline 2016. Nashville: The United Methodist Publishing House, 2016.

Dietrich Bonhoeffer's Works. Vol. 4. Minneapolis: Fortress Press, 1996.

Borg, Marcus J., and John Dominic Crossan, *The First Christmas*. San Francisco: HarperOne, 2007.

Bosch, David J. "The Meaning of Being a 'Disciple.'" *Missio Apostolica* 3, (May 1995) 51–54.

Bray, Gerald, *The Faith We Confess: An Exposition Of The Thirty-Nine Articles*. London: Latimer Trust, 2009.

Breck, John. *The Shape of Biblical Language*. Crestwood: SVS, 1994.

Breen, Mike. *Building a Discipling Culture*. 3dm International, 2017.

Brower, Wayne. "Understanding Chiasm and Assessing Macro-Chiasm as a Tool of Biblical Interpretation," Concordia Theological Journal 53:1 (2018) 99–127.

Brown, Andrew, and Linda Woodward. *That Was The Church That Was: How the Church of England Lost the English People*. London: Bloomsbury, 2016.

Brown, Michael L., and Craig S. Keener. *Not Afraid of the Antichrist*. Grand Rapids: Chosen, 2019.

Bruce, F.F. *Peter, Stephen, James & John: Studies in Non-Pauline Christianity*. Grand Rapids: Eerdmans, 1979.

Burchard, Kenny. "The Women in Luke's Gospel, Part 3." http://thinktheology.org/2013/2/12/ women-lukes-gospel-pt-3.

Burney, Bob. "A Shocking Confession from Willow Creek Community Church." www.town hall.com/columnists/bobburney/2007/10/30/a-shocking-%E2%80%9Cconfession%E2% 80%9D-from-willow-creek-community-church-n1381140.

Burridge, Richard. *Four Gospels, One Jesus: A Symbolic Reading*. Grand Rapids: Eerdmans, 2005.

Burroughs, Presian. "The Christian and Property." www.unorthodoxy.wordpress.com/ 2015/ 06/28/the-christian-and-property.

Campbell, Dennis. *Christian Confessions: A Historical Introduction*. Oxford: Oxford University Press, 1996.

———. *Doctrines And Discipline, Vol. 3 of United Methodism and American Culture*. Nashville: Abington, 1999.

———. *Wesleyan Beliefs: Formal and Popular Expressions of the Core Beliefs of Wesleyan Communities*. Nashville: Abington: 2010.

Carol, Vincent, and David Shiflett. *Christianity on Trial: Argument Against Anti-Religious Bigotry*. San Francisco: Encounter Books, 2002.

Carroll, John T. *Luke*. Louisville: WJK, 2012.

———. "What Then Will This Child Become? Perspectives on Children in the Gospel of Luke," In Martha Bunge, editor, *The Child in the Bible*. Grand Rapids: Eerdmans, 2008.

Chadwick, Dennis W. *Both Here And There: Studies in Concentric Parallelism in Luke*. Eugene: Wipf & Stock, 2018.

Clark, David J. "Criteria for Identifying Chiasm." *Linguistica Biblica* 5 (1975) 63–72.

Coleman, Robert E. *The Master Plan of Discipleship*. Grand Rapids: Revell, 1998.

Collins, Kenneth J., and Jerry Walls. *Roman but Not Catholic*. Grand Rapids: Baker, 2017.

Collins, Kenneth J., and Jason E. Vickers. *The Sermons of John Wesley: A Collection for the Christian Journey*. Nashville: Abington, 2013.

Collinson, Sylvia Wilkey. "Making Disciples and the Christian Faith." *Evangelical Review of Theology* 29:3 (2005) 242.

Comiskey, Joel. *Making Disciples in the Twenty-First Century*. Moreno Valley: CCS Publishing, 2013.

Cooper, Terry D. *Making Judgments Without Being Judgmental*. Downer's Grove: IVP, 2006.

Copan, Victor A. Copan. "*Mathetes* and *Mimetes*: Exploring a Tangled Relationship," *Bulletin for Biblical Research*. 17.2 (2007) 313–23.

Coppedge, Allan. *The God Who is Triune*. Downer's Grove: IVP, 2007.

Culpepper, R. Alan. *Luke: The New Interpreter's Bible, Vol. IX*. Nashville: Abington, 1995.

———. "The Pivot Of John's Prologue." *New Testament Studies* 27, 9–10.

Dahood, Michael. *Psalms*. Garden City: Doubleday, 1966.

Dawson, Gerrit Scott. *Jesus Ascended: The Meaning of Christ's Continuing Incarnation*. Phillipsburg: P & R, 2004.

Deere, Jack. *Why I Am Still Surprised by the Power of the Spirit*. Grand Rapids: Zondervan, 2020.

DeSilva, David A. "X Marks the Spot? A Critique of the Use of Chiasmus in Macro-Structural Analyses of Revelation." *Journal for the Study of the New Testament* 30.3 (2008) 343–371.

Dickerson, John S. *Jesus Skeptic*. Grand Rapids: Baker, 2019.

di Marco, Angelico. "Der Chiasm in der Bibel." *Linguistica Biblica* 44 (1979).

Dinkler, Michal Beth. "Building Character on the Road to Emmaus: Lukan Characterization in Contemporary Literary Perspective." *JBL* 136:3 (2017).

Donaldson, James. "Call To Follow: The Twofold Experience Of Discipleship In Mark." *Biblical Theology Bulletin* (1975).

Dorsey, David A. *The Literary Structure of the Old Testament: A Commentary on Genesis - Malachi*. Grand Rapids: Baker, 1999.

Down, Sharyn. *Mark*. Macon: Smyth & Helwys, 2000.

Dunn, James D.G. *Jesus' Call to Discipleship*. Cambridge, Cambridge University Press, 1992.

du Plessis, Isak. "Discipleship according to Luke's Gospel." *Religion & Theology* 2 (1995) 58–71.

Edwards, James. *The Gospel According To Mark*. Grand Rapids: Eerdmanns, 2002.

———. *Luke*. Grand Rapids: Eerdmans, 2015.

———. "Parallels and Patterns Between Luke and Acts." *Bulletin for Biblical Research*, 27:4 (2017) 485–501.

Eberstadt, Mary. *How the West Really Lost God: A New Theory of Secularization*. West Conshohoken: Templeton Press, 2013.

Edwards, Taylor Burton. *Living into the Mystery: A United Methodist Guide for Celebrating Holy Communion*. www.bookstore.upperroom.org/Products/DRPDF9/living-into-the-mystery.aspx.

Efird, James M. *End-Times: Rapture, AntiChrist, Millennium*. Nashville: Abington, 1986.

Ellis, Peter. *The Genius of John*. Collegeville: Liturgical, 1984.

English, J.T. *Deep Discipleship*. Nashville: B & H, 2020.

Evans, Craig A., and N.T. Wright. *Jesus: The Final Days*. Louisville: WJK, 2009.

Farrow, Douglas B. *Ascension Theology*. London: T & T Clark, 2011.

Felton, Gayle Carlton. *This Holy Mystery: A United Methodist Understanding of Holy Communion*. Nashville: Discipleship Resources, 2005.

Fitzmeyer, J.A. "Discipleship in the Lucan Writing." In *Luke the Theologian: Aspects of his Teaching*. New York: Paulist, 1989.

———. *The Gospel According to Luke*. New York: Doubleday, 1985.

Foster, Richard. *Freedom of Simplicity: Finding Harmony in a Complex World*. San Francisco: HarperSanFrancisco, 1981.

Foster, Robert L. "Discipleship in the New Testament." In *Society of Biblical Literature Teaching the Bible*. www.sbl-site.org/assets/pdfs/tbv2i7_fosterdiscipleship.pdf.

Francis, James. "Children and Childhood in the New Testament." In S. Barton, editor, *The Family in Theological Perspective*. Edinburgh: T & T Clark, 1996.

Fredrichsen, Timothy A. "*Disciple(s)* in the New Testament: Background usage, characteristics and historicity." *Salesianum* 65 (2003) 717–39.

Frey, Robert L., ed. *The Making of an American Church: Essays Commemorating The Jubilee Year of the Evangelical United Brethren Church*. Landham: Scarecrow, 2007.

Fuller, Reginald H. "The Decalogue in the New Testament." *Interpretation*, 1989.

Gallagher, Richard, M.D. *Demonic Foes: My Twenty-Five Years as a Psychiatrist Investigating Possessions, Diabolic Attacks, and the Paranormal*. San Francisco: HarperOne, 2020.

Gallaty, Robert F. *Rediscovering Discipleship: Making Jesus' Final Words Our First Work*. Grand Rapids: Zondervan, 2015.

Garland, David. *Luke*. Grand Rapids: Zondervan, 2011.

———. *A Theology of Mark's Gospel*. Grand Rapids; Zondervan, 2015.

Garrett, Susan R. *The Demise of the Devil: Magic and the Demonic in Luke's Writings*. Minneapolis: Fortress, 1989.

Gavrilyuk, Paul. "Scripture and the *Regula Fidei*: Two Interlocking Components of the Canonical Heritage." In William J. Abraham, et. al, *Canonical Theism: A Proposal for Theology & the Church*. Grand Rapids: Eerdmans, 2008.

Gehrz, Christopher, and Mark Pattie III. *The Pietist Option*. Downer's Grove: IVP, 2017.

Geiger, Eric, et.al. *Transformational Discipleship: how people really grow*. Nashville: B & H, 2012.

Giles, Kevin. *What On Earth Is The Church? An Exploration in New Testament Theology*. Downer's Grove: IVP, 1995.

Green, Joel. *Dictionary of Jesus and the Gospels*. Downer's Grove: IVP, 1992.

———. *Luke*. Grand Rapids: Eerdmans, 1997.

———. *New Testament Theology: The Theology of the Gospel of Luke*. Cambridge, Cambridge University Press, 1995.

Go, Byung Chan. "Understanding the Chiastic Structure of the New Testament." www.dx.doi. org/10.17156/BT.77.11., 317–44.

Gonzalez, Justo. *Luke*. Louisville: WJK, 2010.

Green, Michael, and R. Paul Stevens. *New Testament Spirituality: True Discipleship and Spiritual Maturity*. Guildford: Eagle, 1994.

Hacking, Keith J. Signs and Wonders: Then and Now: Miracle-working, commissioning and discipleship . Nottingham: Apollos, 2006.

Harrington, Bobby, and Josh Patrick, *The Disciple Maker's Handbook*. Grand Rapids: Zondervan, 2017.

Harrington, Daniel J. *Jesus and Prayer: What the New Testament Teaches Us*. Frederick: The Word Among Us, 2009.

Harvey, John D. *Listen to the Text: Oral Patterning in Paul's Letters*. Grand Rapids: Baker, 1998.

"Healing Services And Prayers, Introduction," *The United Methodist Book of Worship*. Nashville: U.M. Publishing House, 1989.

Heidinger, James V. *The Rise of Theological Liberalism And The Decline of American Methodism*. Franklin: Seedbed, 2017.

Hellerman, Joseph H. "Wealth and Sacrifice in Early Christianity: Revisiting Mark's Presentation of Jesus' Encounter with the Rich Young Ruler." *Trinity Journal*, 21/2 (2000).

———. *When the Church Was a Family: Recapturing Jesus' Vision for Authentic Christian Community*. Nashville: B & H, 2009.

Henderson, Michael. *A Model For Making Disciples: John Wesley's Class Meeting*. Nappanee: Francis Asbury, 1997.

Hendrickx, Herman. *The Third Gospel for the Third World, Volume Three-B, 13:22–17:10*. Collegeville: Liturgical, 2000.

Hengel, M. *The Charismatic Leader and His Followers*. New York: Crossroads, 1981.

Hill, Craig. *In God's Time: The Bible and the Future*. Grand Rapids: Eerdmans, 2002.

Hill, Wesley. *The Lord's Prayer: A Guide to Praying to our Father*. Bellingham: Lexham, 2019.

Hing, The Most Reverend Ng Moon. *Intentional Discipleship and Disciple-Making: An Anglican Guide for Christian Life and Formation*. London: Anglican Witness and The Anglican Consultative Council, 2016.

Hirsh, Alan, and Debra Hirsch, *Untamed: Reactivating a Missional Form of Discipleship*. Grand Rapids: Baker, 2010.

Holland, Tom. *Dominion: How the Christian Revolution Remade the World*. New York: Basic Books, 2019.

Hopping, Joshua. *The Here And Not Yet*. Ladysmith: Vineyard International, 2017.

Horbury, William, and Brian McNeill, eds. *Suffering and Martyrdom in the New Testament: Studies Presented to G.M. Styler*. Cambridge: Cambridge University Press, 1980.

Horsley, Richard A. *Jesus and Magic*. Eugene: Cascade Books, 2014.

House, Christie. "United Methodist mission statement revised." http:www.umnews.org/ en/ news/ united-methodist-mission-statement-revised.

Howard-Brook, Wes, and Anthony Gwyther, *Unveiling Empire: Reading Revelation Then and Now*. Maryknoll: Orbis, 2000.

Hubbard, Benjamin J. "The Role of Commissioning Accounts in Acts." In Charles H. Talbert, *Perspectives on Luke-Acts*. Danville: ABPR, 1978, 187–91.

Hull, Bill. *The Complete Book of Discipleship* . Colorado Springs: NavPress, 2006.

———. *Conversion & Discipleship: You Can't Have One Without the Other*. Grand Rapids: Zondervan, 2016.

———. *The Cost of Cheap Grace: Reclaiming the Value of Discipleship*. Colorado Springs: NavPress, 2019.

———. *The Discipleship Gospel*. HIM Publications, 2018.

———. *Straight Talk on Spiritual Power: Experiencing the Fullness of God in the Church*. Grand Rapids: Baker, 2002.

Hultgren, Arland. *The Parables of Jesus*. Grand Rapids: Eerdmans, 2000.

Hunter, George C. *The Apostolic Congregation: Church Growth Reconceived For A New Generation*. Nashville: Abington, 2009.

Hunter, Todd. *Christianity Beyond Belief*. Downer's Grove: IVP, 76.

———. *Our Favorite Sins: The Sins We Commit & How You Can Quit*. Nashville: Nelson, 2012.

Issler, Klaus. "Jesus' Example: Prototype of the Dependent, Spirit-filled Life." In Fred Jeffrey, David Lyle. *Luke: Brazos Theological Commentary on the Bible*. Grand Rapids: Brazos, 2012.

Jennings, David R. *The Supernatural Occurrences Of John Wesley*. Sean Media, 2012.

Johnson, Luke T. *The Creed: What Christians Believe And Why It Matters*. New York: Doubleday, 2003.

———. "The New Testament's Anti-Jewish Slander and the Conventions Of Ancient Polemics." *Journal of Biblical Literature* 108/3 (1989) 419–41.

Just, Felix. "The Gospel of Luke and the Acts of the Apostles." www.catholic-resources. org/ CBI-Orange/2013-11-02-Handouts-LukeActs.pdf.

———. "Women in the Synoptic Gospels." www.catholic-resources.org/Bible/ Synoptics_ Women.

Kay, William, and Robin Parry, eds. *Exorcism and Deliverance: Multi-Disciplinary Studies*. Milton Keynes: Paternoster, 2011.

Karris, Robert J. "Luke 23:47 and the Lucan View of the Death of Jesus." *Journal of Biblical Literature* 105 (1986) 68–70.

———. "Women and Discipleship in Luke," *Catholic Biblical Quarterly* 56/1 (1994) 1–20.

Katz, Maya Balakirsky. "Disciple, Discipleship." In *De Gruyter Encyclopedia of the Bible and its Reception*, 888–920. www.academia.edu/ 6021902/Discipleship_Disciple.

Keener, Craig. "Assumptions in Historical-Jesus Research: Using Ancient Biographies and Disciples' Traditioning as a Control." *Journal for the Study of the Historical Jesus* 9 (2011) 26–58.

———. *Christobiography: Memory, History, and the Reliability of the Gospels*. Grand Rapids: Eerdmans, 2019.

———. *The Historical Jesus of the Gospels*. Grand Rapids: Eerdmans, 2012.

———. "The Historicity of the Nature Miracles." In Graham Twelftree, *The Nature Miracles of Jesus*. Eugene: Wipf & Stock, 2017.

———. *Miracles: The Credibility Of The New Testament Accounts, Volume 1*. Grand Rapids: Baker, 2011.

Kelber, Werner. "Western Culture as Communications History," www.rice.edu/ presentat/ kelberpres.

Kinman, Brent. "Jesus' Royal Entry into Jerusalem." *Bulletin for Biblical Research* 15:2 (2005) 414–21.

Kodell, Jerome. *The Eucharist in the New Testament*. Collegeville: Liturgical, 1988.

Koenig, John. *Recovering New Testament Prayer*. Eugene: Wipf & Stock, 2004.

Koester, Craig R. *Revelation and the End of All Things*. Grand Rapids: Eerdmans, 2001.

Konyndyk, Rebecca. *Glittering Vices: A New Look At The Seven Deadly Sins And Their Remedies*. Grand Rapids: Brazos, 2009.

Kreeft, Peter. *Back to Virtue*. San Francisco: Ignatius Press, 1986.

Kuhn, Karl Allen. "The Emmaus story: resurrection as a transformative transition." *Proceedings* 16 (1996) 17–39.

———. *The Kingdom according to Luke and Acts*. Grand Rapids: Baker, 2015.

Kurz, William S. "Luke 22:14–38 and Greco-Roman and Biblical Farewell Addresses." In

Charles Talbert, ed. *Luke-Acts: New Perspectives from the Society of Biblical Literature Seminar*. New York: Crossroad, 1987.

Kvalbelin, Hans. "Go therefore and make disciples: The concept of discipleship in the New Testament." *Themelios* 13 (1988) 48–53.

Lee, Dorothy. *Ministry of Women in the New Testament*. Grand Rapids: Baker, 2021.

Leon-Dufour, Xavier. *Sharing the Eucharistic Bread*. Mahwah: Paulist, 1987.

Levine, Amy-Jill, and Ben Witherington III. *The Gospel of Luke*. Cambridge: Cambridge University Press, 2018.

Lewis, C.S. *Mere Christianity*. New York: Harper Collins, 2001.

Liddell, Henry G. and Robert Scott. *A Greek-English Lexicon*. Oxford: Clarendon, 1952.

Longenecker, Bruce W. *Rhetoric at the Boundaries: The Art and Theology of New Testament Chain-Link Transitions*. Waco: Baylor, 2005.

Longnecker, Richard N. "Taking Up the Cross Daily: Discipleship in Luke-Acts." In Richard Longnecker, ed., *Patterns of Discipleship in the New Testament*. Grand Rapids: Eerdmans, 1996, 50–76.

Luter, A. Boyd, and Michelle V. Lee, "Philippians As Chiasmus: Key to the Structure, Unity and Theme Questions," *NTS* 41 (1995) 89–101.

Mack, B.L. *Rhetoric and the New Testament*. Minneapolis: Fortress, 1990.

"Making Disciples," a joint research project of licc/Elim. 2020. licc.org.uk/resources/ elim-research.

Mann, Ronald E. *Chiasm in the New Testament*. Dallas: Dallas Theological Seminary, 1984.

Marshall, Colin, and Tony Payne. *The Vine Project: Shaping Your Ministry Culture Around Disciple-Making*. Sydney: Matthias Media, 2016.

Marshall, I. Howard. "Jesus: Example and Teacher of Prayer in the Synoptic Gospels." In Richard N. Longnecker, editor, *Into God's Presence: Prayer in the New Testament*. Grand Rapids: Eerdmans, 2001.

Martin, R.P. "Salvation and Discipleship in Luke's Gospel" *Interpretation*, 30 (1976) 366–80.

Maxey. James. "The road to Emmaus: changing expectations: a narrative-critical study." *Currents in Theology and Mission* 32:2 (April 2005) 112–23.

McComiskey, Douglas. *Lukan Theology in the Light of the Gospel's Literary Structure*. Eugene: Wipf & Stock, 2006.

McCoy, Brad. "Chiasmus: An Important Structural Device Commonly Found In Biblical Literature." www.onthewing.org/user/BS_Chiasmus%20-%20McCoy.pdf,

McGrath, Alister. *The Passionate Intellect: Christian Faith and the Discipleship of the Mind*. Downer's Grove: IVP, 2014.

McKnight, Scot. *Embracing Grace: A Gospel for All of Us.* Brewster: Paraclete, 2005.

———. *Following King Jesus.* Grand Rapids: Zondervan, 2019.

———. *It Takes a Church to Baptize.* Grand Rapids: Brazos, 2018.

———. *The Jesus Creed: On Loving God And Others.* Brewster: Paraclete Press, 2014.

———. *The King Jesus Gospel: The Original Good News Revisited.* Grand Rapids: Zondervan, 2011.

———. *The Real Mary: Why Evangelical Christians Can Embrace the Mother of Jesus.* Brewster: Paraclete, 2007.

———. *Turning to Jesus: The Sociology of Conversion in the Gospels.* Louisville: WJK, 2002.

Mealand, David A. "'The Seams and Summaries' of Luke and of Acts." *Journal for the Study of the New Testament* 38/4, 382–502.

Moreland, J.P. *Love Your God with All Your Mind: The Role of Reason in the Life of the Soul.* Colorado Springs: Navpress, 2012.

Morgan, Alison. *Following Jesus: The Plural of Disciple is Church.* Somerset: ReSource, 2015.

Morrou, H.I. *History of Education in Antiquity.* New York: Sheed and Ward, 1956.

Mullins, T.Y. "New Testament Commission Forms, Especially in Luke-Acts," *JBL* 95 (1976) 603–14.

Murchison, William. *Mortal Follies: Episcopalians And The Crisis of Mainline Christianity.* New York: Encounter Books, 2009.

Naselli, Andrew D. Naselli. *How To Understand And Apply The New Testament.* Phillipsburg: P & R, 2017.

Nathan, Rich, and Insoo Kim. *Both-And: Living The Christ-Centered Life In An Either-Or-World.* Downer's Grove: IVP, 2014.

Neale, David. *Luke.* Kansas City: Beacon Hill, 2011.

Neyrey, Jerome. *The Resurrection Stories.* Collegeville: Liturgical, 1988.

Norman, Robert. *Samuel Butler and the Meaning of Chiasmus.* London: St. Martin's, 1986.

O'Collins, Gerald. *The Lord's Prayer.* New York: Paulist, 2007.

———. *The Tri-Personal God: Understanding and Interpreting the Trinity.* New York: Paulist, 1999.

Oden, Thomas C. *Becoming A Minister.* New York: Crossroad, 1987.

———. *Classic Christianity.* San Francisco: HarperOne, 1992.

———. *Doctrinal Standards in the Wesleyan Tradition.* Nashville: Abington, 2008.

———. *Pastoral Theology: Essentials of Ministry.* New York: Harper & Row, 1983.

———. *The Word of Life.* New York: Harper & Row, 1989.

Odgen, Greg. *Discipleship Essentials: A Guide to Building Your Life in Christ.* Downer's Grove: IVP, 2007.

Olson, Roger E., and Christian T. Collins Winn. *Reclaiming Pietism: Retrieving an Evangelical Tradition.* Grand Rapids: Eerdmans, 2015.

O'Malley, Stephen, and Jason E. Vickers. *Methodist And Pietist: Retrieving The Evangelical United Brethren Tradition.* Nashville: Abington, 2011.

Orr, Peter C. *Exalted Above the Heavens: The Risen and Ascended Christ.* Downer's Grove: IVP/Apollos, 2018.

Ortberg, John. *Love Beyond Reason: Moving God's Love from Your Head to Your Heart.* Grand Rapids: Zondervan, 1998.

O'Toole, Robert F. "Parallels between Jesus and his disciples in Luke-Acts: a further study." *Biblische Zeitschrift* 27/2 (1983) 195–212.

Oyemoni, Emmanuel Oyemoni. "The Challenges Of The Concept Of Medicine And Healings In The Gospel Of Luke For The Church In Africa." *Ogbomosa Journal of Theology* 15.3 (2013) 113–27.

Parsons, Mikeal L. and Michael Wade Martin. *Ancient Rhetoric and the New Testament.* Waco: Baylor, 2018.

———. *Luke.* Grand Rapids: Baker, 2015.

———. *Luke: Storyteller, Interpreter, Evangelist.* Peabody: Hendrickson, 2007.

———. *Rethinking the Socio-Rhetorical Character of the New Testament.* Waco: Baylor University Press, 2009.

Pelican, Jaroslav. *Whose Bible Is It: The History of the Scriptures Through the Ages.* New York: Viking, 2005.

Pennington, Jonathan. *The Sermon on the Mount and Human Flourishing.* Grand Rapids: Baker, 2017.

Perrin, Nicholas. *The Kingdom of God: A Biblical Theology.* Grand Rapids: Zondervan, 2019.

Peters, John L., *Christian Perfection and American Methodism.* Nashville: Abington, 1956.

Pinter, Dean. "The Gospel of Luke and the Roman Empire." In Scot McKnight and Joseph B. Modica, editors, *Jesus Is Lord, Caesar Is Not: Evaluating Empire In New Testament Studies.* Downer's Grove: IVP, 2013.

Plevnik, Joseph. "The Eyewitnesses of the Risen Jesus in Luke 24." *CBQ* 49 (1987) 90–103.

Porter, Stanley. "Philippians As A Macro-Chiasm And Its Exegetical Significance," *New Testament Studies* 44 (1998) 213–21.

Porter, Stanley E. and Bryan Dyer, eds. *The Synoptic Problem: Four Views.* Grand Rapids, 2016.

Powell, Mark Alan. *Fortress Introduction To The Gospels*, Second edition. Minneapolis: Fortress, Press, 2019.

———. "Salvation in Luke-Acts." *Word & World* 12/1 (1992).

———. *What Is Narrative Criticism? Guides to Biblical Scholarship New Testament Series.* Philadelphia: Fortress, 1991.

Rabey, Steve and Lois, eds. *Side by Side: A Handbook, Disciple-Making For A New Century.* Colorado Springs: Cook Communication and NavPress, 2000.

Reid, Robert S. *Preaching Mark.* St. Louis: Chalice, 1999.

Resseguie, James. *Narrative Criticism of the New Testament: An Introduction.* Grand Rapids: Baker, 2005.

Roberts, Mark D. *Can We Trust the Gospels.* Wheaton: Crossway, 2007.

Robbins, Jim. "Ecopsychology: How Immersion in Nature Benefits Your Health." www.e360.yale.edu/features/ecopsychology-how-immersion-in-nature-benefits-your-health.

Rogers, John H. *Essential Truths For Christians: A Commentary on the Thirty-Nine Articles and an Introduction to Systematic Theology.* Blue Bell: Classical Anglican Press, 2011.

Roschke, Ronald W. "Healing in Luke, Madagascar, and Elsewhere." *Currents in Theology and Mission* 33:6 (2006) 460–71.

Rossing, Barbara. *The Rapture Exposed: The Message of Hope in the Book of Revelation.* New York: Chosen Books, 2004.

Rowe, C. Cavin Rowe. *Early Narrative Christology: The Lord in the Gospel of Luke.* Grand Rapids: Baker Academic, 2009.

Ruthven, Jon Mark. *What's Wrong With Protestant Theology: Tradition or Biblical Emphasis.* Tulsa: Word & Spirit Press, 2014.

Samples, Kenneth Richards. *7 Truths That Changed the World.* Grand Rapids: Baker, 2012.

Samra, James G. "A Biblical View of Discipleship," *Bibliotheca Sacra* 160 (2003) 219–34.

Sanders, Fred. *The Triune God*. Grand Rapids: Zondervan, 2016.

———. *Wesley on the Christian Life: The Heart Renewed in Love*. Wheaton: Crossway, 2013.

———. *Jesus in Trinitarian Perspective*. Nashville: B & H Academic, 2007.

Sanou, Boubakar. "Toward a Biblical Model of Discipleship: A Case Study of the Willow Creek Community Church." *Journal of Adventist Mission Studies,* Vol. 12:2 (2016) 76–85.

Scott, Bernard. *Hear Then the Parable*. Minneapolis: Fortress, 1989.

Scazerro, Peter. *Emotionally Healthy Discipleship*. Grand Rapids: Zondervan, 2021.

Seneca. *Epistles 1–65*. Translated by Richard M. Gummere. Loeb Classical Library, 75.

Senior, Donald Senior. *The Passion of Jesus in the Gospel of Luke*. Collegeville: Liturgical, 1990.

Smith, Christian, and Melinda Denton. *Soul Searching: The Religious and Spiritual Life of American Teenagers*. Oxford: Oxford University Press, 209.

Smith, Dennis E. *From Symposium to Eucharist: The Banquet in the Early Christian World*. Minneapolis: Fortress, 2003.

Smith, James Bryan. *The Good and Beautiful God: Falling in Love with the God Jesus Knows*. Downer's Grove: IVP, 2009.

Snodgrass, Klyne. *Stories with Intent*. Grand Rapids, 2008.

Springer, Craig. *How to Follow Jesus*. Grand Rapids: Zondervan, 2020.

———. *How To Revive Evangelism: 7 Vital Shifts in How We Share Our Faith*. Grand Rapids: Zondervan/Alpha, 2021.

Staley, Jeffrey Lloyd. "The Structure of John's Prologue." *CBQ* 48 (1986) 241–64.

Stegman, Thomas D. "Reading Luke 12:13–34 as an Elaboration of a Chreia: How Hermogenes of Tarsus Sheds Light on Luke's Gospel." *Novum Testamentum* 49 (2007) 328–52.

Stetzer, Ed. "5 essential elements of transformational small group." www.biblical leadership. com/blogs/5-essential-elements-of-transformational-small-group,

Stevenson, Kenneth W. *The Lord's Prayer: A Text in Tradition*. Minneapolis: Fortress, 2004.

Stock, Augustine. *Call to Discipleship: A Literary Study of Mark's Gospel*. Wilmington: Michael Glazier, 1982.

———. "Chiastic Awareness and Education in Antiquity." *Biblical Theology Bulletin* 14 (1984) 23–27.

Storms, Sam. *Understanding Spiritual Gifts: A Comprehensive Guide*. Grand Rapids: Zondervan, 2020.

———. *Understanding Spiritual Warfare*. Grand Rapids: Zondervan, 2021.

Strauss, Mark L. *Introducing Jesus: a short guide to the gospel's history and message*. Grand Rapids: Zondervan, 2018.

Sudgen, Edward, ed. *John Wesley's Fifty-Three Sermons*. Nashville: Abington, 1983.

Sweetland, Dennis M. "Discipleship and Persecution: Luke 12:1–12." *Biblica* 65:1 (1984) 61–80.

———. "Following Jesus: Discipleship in Luke-Acts." In E. Richards, editor, *New Views on Luke and Acts*. Collegeville: Liturgical, 1990, 109–231.

———. *Our Journey with Jesus: Discipleship according to Luke-Acts*. Collegeville: Liturgical, 1990.

Talbert, Charles H. "Artistry and Theology: An Analysis of the Architecture of John 1:19–5:47." *Catholic Biblical Quarterly* 31 (1970) 341–366.

———. "The Bible as Spiritual Friend." *Perspectives in Religious Studies* 13:1 (1986) 5–64.

———. "Discipleship in Luke-Acts." In F.F. Segovia, editor, *Discipleship in the New Testament*. Philadelphia; Fortress, 1985, 283–310.

———. *"Getting Saved": The Whole Story of Salvation in the New Testament*. Grand Rapids: Eerdmans, 2011.

———. *Literary Patterns, Theological Themes, and the Genre of Luke-Acts*. Missoula: Scholars Press, 1974.

———. *Reading John: A Literary and Theological Commentary on the Fourth Gospel*. New York: Crossroads, 1992.

———. *Reading Luke: A Literary and Theological Commentary on the Third Gospel*. Macon: Smyth & Helwys, 2002.

———. "Redaction Criticism: On the Nature and Exposition of the Gospels." *Perspectives in Religious Studies* 6 (1979) 4–16.

———. "The Way of the Lukan Jesus: Dimensions of Lukan Spirituality." *Perspective in Religious Studies* 9/3 (1982) 237–49.

Tennent, Timothy C. Invitation to World Missions. Grand Rapids: Kregel, 2010.

Theissen, Gerd. *The Miracle Stories of the Early Christian Tradition*. Philadelphia: Fortress Press, 1983.

Theissen, Gerd, and Annette Merz. *The Historical Jesus: A Comprehensive Guide*. Translated by John Bowden. Minneapolis: Fortress Press, 1996.

Thompson, Ian H. *Chiasmus in the Pauline Letters*. Sheffield: Sheffield, 1995.

Thrailkill, Phil. *Mary: Lessons in Discipleship from Jesus' Earthly Family*. Fort Valley: Bristol, 2007.

———. *Resurrection: A Pastor's Reading of the Major New Testament Resurrection Passages*. Fort Valley: Bristol, 2013.

"Time for discipleship: 21st Century Evangelicals, A Snapshot of the beliefs and habits of evangelical Christians in the U.K.— Spring 2014." Evangelical Alliance, eauk.org.

Toon, Peter. *The Ascension of our Lord*. Nashville: Nelson, 1984.

Topel, John. *Children of a Compassionate God: A Theological Exegesis of Luke 6:20-49*. Collegeville: Liturgical, 2001.

Trueman, Carl. *The Rise and Triumph of the Modern Self: Cultural Amnesia, Expressive Individualism, and the Road to Sexual Revolution*. Wheaton: Crossway, 2020.

Tyra, Gary. *The Dark Side of Discipleship: Why and How the New Testament Encourages Christians to Deal with the Devil*. Eugene: Cascade Books, 2020.

Twelftree, Graham H. *In the Name of Jesus: Exorcism among Early Christians*. Grand Rapids: Baker, 2007.

———. *The Nature Miracles of Jesus: Problems, Perspectives, and Prospects*. Gresham: Cascade, 2017.

———. *Jesus the Miracle Worker*. Downer's Grove; IVP, 1999.

Underhill, Evelyn. *Mysticism*. New York: Meridian Books, 1974.

The United Methodist Hymnal. Nashville: U.M. Publishing House, 1989.

Vanhoozer, Kevin J. *Hearers and Doers: A Pastor's Guide to Making Disciples Through Scripture and Doctrine*. Eugene: Lexham, 2019.

Venter, Alexander. *Doing Healing*. Cape Town: Vineyard International: 2009.

Vickers, Jason E. *Wesley: A Guide for the Perplexed*. New York: T & T Clark, 2009.

———. *A Wesleyan Theology of the Eucharist: The Presence of God for Christian Life and Ministry*. Nashville: General Board of Higher Education, 2016.

Vinson, Richard B. *Luke*. Macon: Smyth & Helwys, 2008.

Virtue, David W. *The Seduction of the Episcopal Church*. Pomfret: J2B, 2019.

Walls, Andrew. "The Great Commission; 1910–2010." In W. Stephen Gunter and Elaine Robinson, editors. *Considering the Great Commission: Evangelism and Mission in the Wesleyan Spirit*. Nashville: Abington, 2005.

Ward, Keith. *What the Bible Really Teaches*. New York: Chosen, 2005.

Watson, David L. "Class Leaders and Class Meetings: Recovering a Methodist Tradition for a Changing Church." In Dennis Campbell, et. al., *Doctrines and Discipline*. Nashville: Abington, 245–266.

———. *Contagious Disciple Making*. Nashville: Nelson, 2014.

———. *The Early Methodist Class Meeting*. Nashville: Discipleship Resources, 1985.

Watson, Kevin M. *A Blueprint for Discipleship: Wesley's General Rule as a Guideline for Christian Living*. Nashville: Discipleship Resources, 2009.

———. *The Class Meeting: Reclaiming a Forgotten (and Essential) Small Group Experience*. Franklin: Seedbed, 2013.

———. *Perfect Love: Recovering Entire Sanctification*. Franklin: Seedbed, 2021.

Welch, J.W, ed. *Chiasmus in Antiquity: Structures, Analysis, Exegesis*. Hildesheim: Gerstenberg, 1981.

Wesley, John. *A Plain Account of Christian Perfection*. Kansas City: Beacon Hill , 1966.

Wesley, John. *Sermon 139: On Love*. www.umcmission.org/Find-Resources/John- Wesley-Sermons/Sermon-139-On-Love.

Whetsel, Bob. *Spiritual Waypoints: helping others navigate the journey*. Indianapolis: Wesleyan, 2010.

———. *Waypoint: Navigating Your Spiritual Journey*. Indianapolis: Wesleyan, 2010.

Wilkins, Michael. *The Concept of "Disciple" in Matthew's Gospel: As Reflected in his use of the Term "Methetes,"* Leiden: E.J. Brill, *Novum Testamentum Supplements* 59, 1988.

———. "Disciples" and "Discipleship." In Joel B. Green, et. al, editors, *Dictionary of Jesus and the Gospels*. Downer's Grove: IVP, 1992.

———. *Following the Master: A Biblical Theology of Discipleship*. Grand Rapids: Zondervan, 1992.

Willard, Dallas. "The New Testament Picture of Discipleship." www.renovare. org/articles/the-new-testament-picture-of-discipleship.

———. *Renewing the Christian Mind*. San Francisco: HarperOne, 2016.

Wilson, Jared C. *The Imperfect Disciple: Grace for People Who Can't Get Their Act Together*. Grand Rapids: Baker, 2017.

Wilson, Victor M. *Divine Symmetries*. New York: University, 1997.

Willard, Dallas. "Discipleship." www.old.dwillard.org/articles/artview.asp?artID=134.

———. *The Great Omission*. San Francisco: HarperOne, 2006.

———. *Renewing the Christian Mind*. SanFrancisco: HarperOne, 2016.

Williams, Don. *Start Here: Kingdom Essentials for Christians*. Ventura: Regal, 2006.

Williams, Peter J. *Can We Trust the Gospels?* Wheaton: Crossway, 2018.

Willimon, William H. *Pastor: The Theology and Practice of Ordained Ministry*. Nashville: Abington, 2002.

Wimber, Carol. *John Wimber: The Way It Was*. London: Hodder & Stoughton, 1999.

Wimber, John. *Everyone Gets To Play*. Boise: Ampelon, 2008.

———. *Power Evangelism*. Grand Rapids: Chosen Book, 2009.

Witherington, Ben. *The Gospel: A True Story Of Jesus*. Franklin: Seedbed, 2014.

———. *Jesus and Money: A Guide for Time of Financial Crisis*. Grand Rapids: Brazos, 2010.

———. *John's Wisdom*. Louisville: WJK, 1995.

———. *Making a Meal of It: Rethinking the Theology of the Lord's Supper*. Waco: Baylor 2007.

———. *New Testament History: A Narrative Approach*. Downer's Grove: IVP.

———. *New Testament Rhetoric*. Eugene: Wipf & Stock, 2009.

———. "Sacred Texts in an Oral Culture: How Did They Function?" www.ben witherington. logspot.com/2007/10/sacred-texts-in-oral-culture.

———. *Revelation and The End Times*. Nashville: Abington, 2010.

———. *The Shadow of the Almighty: Father, Son, and Spirit in Biblical Perspective*. Grand Rapids: Eerdmans, 2002.

———. *Troubled Waters: Rethinking the Theology of Baptism*. Waco: Baylor, 2007.

———. "Where Did Rapture Theology Come From," www.youtube.com/watch?v=d_c VXdr8mVs.

Witte, John. "A Manifold Resurrection: Why the Risen Jesus Met People in Five Different Ways—And Still Does." *Christianity Today*, April 2007, 62–65.

Wright, Brian J. *Communal Reading in the Time of Jesus: A Window Into Early Christian Reading Practices*. Minneapolis: Fortress, 2017.

———. "Don't Just Read Alone." www.thegospelcoalition.org/article/dont-just-read-alone.

Wright, Christopher J.H. *Here Are Your Gods: Faithful Discipleship In Idolatrous Times*. Downer's Grove: IVP, 2020.

Wright, N.T. *Jesus and the Victory of God*. Minneapolis: Fortress, 1996.

———. "The Lord's Prayer as a Paradigm of Christian Prayer." In Richard Longnecker, *Into God's Presence: Prayer in the New Testament*. Grand Rapids: Eerdmans, 2001

———. *Surprised by Scripture*. San Francisco: HarperOne, 2014.

———. *The Resurrection of the Son of God*. Minneapolis: Fortress, 2003.

Wilkins, Michael. "Following Jesus: discipleship in Luke-Acts." In E. Richards, ed., *New Views on Luke and Acts*, 109–123. Collegeville, Liturgical, 1990.

———. *Following the Master*. Grand Rapids: Zondervan, 1992.

Wilson, Ken. *Jesus Brand Spirituality: He Wants His Religion Back*. Nashville: Nelson, 2008.

Wuellner, W. "The Rhetorical Structure of Luke 12 in Its Wider Context." NEOTESTAMEN-TICA 22 (1988) 280–310.

Made in United States
Orlando, FL
20 June 2023

34353214R00265